# IRISH

## SWORDSMANSHIP:

## FENCING *and* DUELING

*in*

## EIGHTEENTH CENTURY IRELAND.

WRITTEN BY

BEN MILLER

To which is also added,

*A FEW MATHEMATICAL and CRITICAL REMARKS*
*on the SWORD.*

NEW-YORK,
HUDSON SOCIETY PRESS.

*Anno* MM. XVII.

Hudson Society Press
159 Southside Avenue, #3
Hastings on Hudson, New York 10706

Front cover image of Captain David "Tyger" Roche copyright and courtesy of the National Library of Ireland. Call number: EP ROCH-JH (1) I .
Back cover image of *Henry Munro, chief of the Irish rebels* courtesy of the Anne S.K. Brown Military Collection, Brown University Library.
Cover art and book design by Bronwyn Frazier-Miller.

Printed in the United States of America

DISCLAIMER: The author, publisher, creators, and distributors of this book are not responsible, in any way whatsoever, for any loss, damage,  injury, or any other adverse consequences that may result from the study, practice, or improper use made by anyone of the information or techniques contained in this book. All use of the information contained in this book must be made in accordance with what is permitted by law, and any damage liable to be caused as a result thereof will be the exclusive responsibility of the user. Many of the techniques described herein could lead to serious injury if not practiced under the guidance and training of a qualified instructor using appropriate safety equipment. This book is not a substitute for formal training. It is the sole responsibility of every person planning to train in the techniques described in this book to consult with a licensed physician before beginning.

*Publisher's Cataloging-in-Publication data*

Miller, Ben.
  Irish Swordsmanship: Fencing and Dueling in Eighteenth Century Ireland / Ben Miller.
    pages cm.
  *Paperback:* ISBN 978-0-9990567-0-7
  *Hardcover:* ISBN 978-0-9990567-1-4
  1. Fencing. 2. Dueling. 3. Swordplay. 4. Martial arts—History—18th century. 5. Ireland—History. I. Miller, Ben. II. Title.

Library of Congress Control Number:  2017908240

FIRST EDITION

10 9 8 7 6 5 4 3 2 1

Dedicated to my father, David Paul Miller,
and my brother, Brian Michael Miller

# CONTENTS

Preface                                                           vii


PART I: History

I    Dueling *in* Eighteenth Century Ireland              1

II   Noted Irish Duelists                                        73
     i    Captain Peter Drake                            75
     ii   Richard Buidhe Kirwan                          91
     iii  David "Tyger" Roche                            99
     iv   George Robert Fitzgerald                       109
     v    Alexander "Buck" English                       125
     vi   Richard Brinsley Sheridan                      130

III  Irish Amazons *and* Stage Gladiators              145

IV   Eighteenth Century Dublin: Europe's Wild West    195

V    Fencing Schools *and* Masters *in* Eighteenth Century    219
     Ireland

VI   The Knights *of* Tara   269

VII   Anthony Gordon, *the* Last Knight *of* Tara   289

PART II: The Treatise

    Essay *on* Authorship   341

    Topical Guide *to* Contents   351

    Note *to the* Reader   355

    *A Few Mathematical and Critical Remarks on the Sword*   357

    Glossary *of* Technical Terms   415

APPENDICES

   I   The Irish Dueling Code *of* 1777   429

   II   Works *on* Fencing *and* Dueling *by* Irish Authors   433

   III   First Resolutions *of the* Knights *of* Tara   437

   IV   Second Resolutions *of the* Knights *of* Tara   439

   V   List *of the* Knights *of* Tara   443

   VI   Rules *of the* Cherokee Club   445

   VII   The Irish Pike Exercise   447

    Bibliography   465

    Index   483

    About the Author   484

# PREFACE

This is a book about the Irish swordsmen and swordswomen who lived, fought, fenced, dueled, and died during the eighteenth century. It is the product of more than ten years of research, and the process of how it came to be is a story in and of itself. That said, discussing the origins of any book can be a tricky business. The author and philologist J.R.R. Tolkien once decried any attempt to investigate the supposed "influences" on a literary work, stating,

> I object to the contemporary trend in criticism, with its excessive interest in the details of the lives of authors and artists...only one's guardian Angel, or indeed God Himself, could unravel the real relationship between personal facts and an author's works. Not the author himself (though he knows more than any investigator), and certainly not so-called 'psychologists.'[*]

While I largely agree with Professor Tolkien, the truth is that the roots of this book are deep—and it would not have come to fruition were it not for the encouragement, guidance, and support of numerous individuals throughout the last several decades. It is within my acknowledgments to them that the story of this book's origins can be told.

The initial genesis of this book can be traced to my father, David Paul Miller. It was he who, when I was a child, regaled me with tales of his Irish Catholic grandmother, Agnes Kelly —who, though having settled in the redwood forests of Northern California, would still leave a dish of milk outside every night "for the fairies." Agnes's parents, Patrick and Mary Kelly, hailed from County Galway (from the towns of Gort, Inchamore, and Loughrea). My father's stories about his maternal grandparents, and his numerous Irish relatives, captured my imagination at an early age, and fostered my initial interest in Irish history. Later, my father would also assist in researching our family's Irish Protestant heritage, tracing his paternal ancestry back to the American Revolutionary War hero, Captain John Baldridge, and his forbears from

---

[*] Humphrey Carpenter, ed., *The Letters of J.R.R. Tolkien* (London: Harper Collins, 1995), 213.

Belfast, Tyrone, Derry, and Down. In addition to furthering my interest in Irish history, this collaboration with my father helped me to hone the detective skills which would later become invaluable in researching the history of fencing. It was also Dad who organized and led our first family trip to Ireland, an experience which I will never forget.

Later, while attending New York University, my interest in Irish culture—first fostered by my father—led me to study under Professor Pádraig Ó Cearúill, at that time the only native Irish speaker running an American college program for the Irish language. Under Professor Ó Cearúill's tutelage I continued my studies abroad as part of New York University's "Summer in Dublin" program, held at Trinity College, Dublin, which led to additional time spent in Belfast and the Gaeltacht in Donegal. It was from Pádraig that I learned that true insight into Irish culture, and its history, was not to be gleaned from the classroom study of Joyce or Beckett—but from Ireland's rustic, oral, linguistic, artistic, and cultural traditions, which were (and are) still very much alive in the hearts, minds, and spirits of its people.

The actual conception of this book came about later, in 2005, when I commenced my study of traditional fencing at the Martinez Academy of Arms. I had already received training in several martial arts disciplines, including Western boxing and Krav Maga in New York City, and Filipino Arnis while living in the Philippines—all under notable instructors whom I greatly respected and admired. And yet, I could not help feeling somehow unfulfilled in these martial arts. Upon my return to New York, I began researching and visiting additional schools and training halls. I had heard that a special, different kind of fencing was being taught at the Martinez Academy—that is, an older style with a martial mindset. It seemed incumbent upon me to at least witness what was being practiced there. What awaited me was something far more extraordinary and significant: the Academy was one of the last schools in the world still offering instruction in authentic surviving traditions of the older, martial styles of European swordsmanship. The various fencing systems taught at the Academy included a vast, almost countless number of techniques that had entirely vanished from the modern Olympic sport, as well as from other fencing lineages. Additionally, the usage of ancient European weapons such as the rapier, sword and dagger, single dagger, cloak, staff, cane, military saber, and others were being taught. The Academy was run by Maestro Ramón Martínez and Maestro Jeannette Acosta-Martínez, the former having been taught these systems and techniques by his own master, Maître d'Armes Frederick Rohdes. A German born in 1897, and a veteran of at least one actual combat encounter with sharp broadswords, Rohdes had learned a variety of historical systems from his master, Marcel Cabijos, and others in Europe. Cabijos, a Frenchman and veteran of the First World War, had, in a high-profile contest held on December 10ᵗʰ, 1926, notably defeated the épée and saber champion of the United States, Leo Nunes, with only a twelve-inch dagger pitted against Nunes's considerably longer dueling sword.*

---

*   For a fuller account, see "Man with Dagger Beats Epee Expert" in the *New York Times*, December 11, 1926.

Here, in an age when Asian fighting systems had become synonymous with the term "martial arts," I had encountered a rare, surviving vestige of our own Western heritage, a culturally fundamental art that had roots stretching back nearly a thousand years, and which I saw being executed with great control, finesse, speed, and precision. From the very beginning, I was hooked—and the study of traditional fencing has since become a lifelong pursuit.

After commencing study at the academy, my interest in both fencing history and Ireland naturally overlapped. At that time, very few resources on Irish fencing history were publicly available, aside from the excellent but long out-of-print memoirs of Sir Jonah Barrington. The more I read period accounts of Irish fencers and duelists, however, the more it became clear to me that—at least during the eighteenth century—these individuals comprised some of the most formidable swordsmen in all of Europe. If this was the case, I wondered, then why hadn't more been written about them?

In retrospect, I believe that several factors are responsible. The most obvious one pertains to the primitive state of the Irish publishing industry during the eighteenth century. In a 1732 letter to Sir Charles Wogan, Dublin author Jonathan Swift observed that books "cannot be printed here with the least profit to the author's friend in distress. Dublin booksellers have not the least notion of paying for a copy. Sometimes things are printed here by subscription; but they go on so heavily that few or none make it turn to account."[*] Given such conditions, few Irish treatises on fencing ever made it to print, and few others were likely ever attempted. Those that were printed existed in extremely limited quantities, becoming rarer and more obscure as the centuries progressed; thus, the only known original Irish treatment of swordsmanship published in Ireland during the eighteenth century (*A Few Mathematical and Critical Remarks on the Sword*) has been almost completely overlooked by scholars, as has the only surviving eighteenth century Irish treatise on bayonet fencing (Anthony Gordon's *Letter on the Bayonet Exercise,* written in 1783). Several other treatises—including one allegedly written by Gordon—do not seem to have survived the ravages of time, and are now, unfortunately, presumed to be lost. Although, in recent decades, a couple of notable works on dueling in Ireland have been published[†], the history of Irish swordsmanship—at least from the early modern period onward—has been almost completely ignored or glossed over.

It seemed that a void was in need of filling, and this book was conceived.

For their help in preparing the current work for publication, I would like to thank the following people:

My wife, Bronwyn Frazier-Miller, for her consummate and time-consuming work in expertly restoring numerous antique images for inclusion in this book, for her assistance with book design, and for her ever-steadfast love and support.

---

[*]  *The Works of Dr. Jonathan Swift* (London: C. Bathurst, 1766), 205.

[†]  See Michael Barry's *An Affair of Honour* (1981), and James Kelly's *That Damn'd Thing Called Honour* (1995).

Maestro Ramón Martínez and Maestro Jeannette Acosta-Martínez, for their ever-invaluable guidance, insight, and encouragement, for their continued mentorship on and off the *salle* floor, for their feedback on the manuscript of this book, and for their assistance with the glossary. After all these years, I am still continually astonished by the Maestros' profound depth and breadth of knowledge of fencing. I am especially thankful to Maestro Acosta-Martínez, considered to be the foremost expert in the world on the French small-sword, for patiently answering my numerous questions relating to this project.

My parents, David and Pam Miller, as well as Jack and Pam Frazier, for their love and support throughout the years.

Maestro Jared Kirby, for his immense assistance and expertise in tracking down and acquiring many of the rare sources and treatises quoted and discussed throughout this book.

Professor Pádraig Ó Cearúill of New York University, for providing feedback and suggestions regarding the many Irish language terms and passages quoted and discussed in this text.

Martin H. Weissman, author and Professor of Mathematics at the University of California, Santa Cruz, for his insight into Anthony Gordon's application of mathematics to fencing.

Maestro Cecil Longino of Salle Saint-George, for his assistance with research.

Elani Koogle, for translating German-language passages from Alexander Doyle's fencing treatise, *Neu Alamodische Ritterliche Fecht- und Schirm-Kunst*.

Carl Massaro and David Mastro, for their feedback on portions of the manuscript.

And now, a special word must be said with regard to research.

As anyone who has tried it can readily attest, researching eighteenth century Irish history can be a daunting task. This is due to the sad fact that many of the official records from the period no longer exist. In 1922, during the height of the Irish Civil War, the Public Record Office of Ireland (then located in the Four Courts) was seized by Anti-treaty forces. Following shelling by the Free State army, explosions burned and destroyed the vast majority of records there pertaining to eighteenth century Irish history, including civil, court, legislative, military, will, and land records. Consequently, it has often been impossible to obtain genealogical information pertaining to the individuals featured in this book. My inquiries to some of Ireland's most renowned libraries and archives often resulted in responses such as the following:

Dear Mr Miller,

Thank you for your email...I have checked the indexes, also known as calendars, to wills sent to the prerogative courts and there is mention of a Cornelius Kelly around the time you believe he died. The original will was destroyed during the Civil War in 1922, however.

Likewise, the sole surviving issues of many of Ireland's eighteenth century newspapers remain in private hands, or are currently inaccessible.

Despite these obstacles, a number of librarians and archivists have been extremely helpful in referring me to some of the more obscure extant sources available. In doing so, many of them kindly donated their time and labor. In particular, for their assistance, guidance, and insight, I am indebted to the following individuals: Niamh McDonnell, Archivist, National Archives of Ireland; Francis Carroll, Senior Library Assistant, National Library of Ireland; Robert Gallagher, Library Administrator, Church of Ireland RCB Library; Dr. Mary Clark, City Archivist, Dublin City Archives; Eithne Massey, Dublin and Irish Local Studies Collections, Dublin City Library and Archive; Leanne Harrington, Assistant Librarian, Manuscripts & Archives Research Library, Trinity College Dublin; Judith Hoben, Library Assistant at Belfast's Linen Hall Library; and Steve Dolan, of the South East Galway Archaeological & Historical Society. I must also give a special thanks to Glenn Dunne of the National Library of Ireland, for granting me permission to include in this book several historic images from the Library's renowned collection.

Beyond the scope of archival research, other individuals in Ireland whom I would like to thank include: Patrick Sutton, Director of the historic Smock Alley Theatre in Dublin, for supplying a photograph of his theater (former home of the Knights of Tara) and for granting me permission to use it in this book; Ed Hannon, of *VisionsOfThePastBlog.com*, for generously supplying two of his excellent photos of the dueling ground at Roscam Round Tower and Chuch in Galway, and for granting permission to include them here; Charles Stanley Smith and Deirdré-Ann Lally of *An Taisce*, for supplying and granting permission to use a photograph of Dublin's historic Tailor's Hall; Owen J. Dunbar of Wexford, for informing me of the existence of William Lamport, the reputed "Irish Zorro," and for his assistance in researching Lawrence Oliver Byrne, and the latter's connection to the 1798 United Irishmen rebellion.

Across the water, in England, several other individuals are greatly deserving of mention. These include David Bretherton, of the Thame Museum in Oxfordshire, for generously sharing his eighteenth century broadsides and articles on stage-fights involving Irish gladiators; Jane Muskett, Archivist at Chetham's Library in Manchester, for her assistance with research; and Sarah Hobbs, Archives Officer at Manchester Central Library, for locating Thomas Barret's rare engraving of the gladiator known as "Old Chopping-block."

One of the great sagas in the writing of this book was the search for the elusive manuscript, *An Idea of Defence* (1804), of which only one copy exists. I had first come across this title in a 1908 catalogue for the Royal United Service Institute's library. Aware that the manuscript's author was almost certainly Anthony Gordon—a prominent Irish fencer and member of the Knights of Tara—I immediately contacted the Institute, but was shocked to find that they had no record for any such text, and that much of their collection had been sold, auctioned off, or lost after the closing of their doors during the 1960s. After a year of searching, and countless inquiries, I gave up all hope of ever finding this text. Then, on the very eve that the proof of this book was to be submitted to the printers, I stumbled across an entry for Gordon's manuscript (under a slightly modified title) in the catalogue of the National Army Museum in Chelsea, London. It is in moments like these, the happiest and most timely of "coincidences," when one cannot help but be aware of a Divine Providence at work, to which I am most extremely grateful. For their assistance in facilitating the scanning of this text, and the granting of permission to use it herein, I would like to express my great thanks to Ian Maine, Assistant Director of Collections, Sarah Hume, Reader Services, Dr Alastair Massie, Head of Research and Academic Access, and Dawn Watkins, all of the National Army Museum.

Here, in the United States, I owe a special thanks to Gerald "Jay" Gaidmore, Director of Special Collections at the SWEM Library, College of William and Mary, Williamsburg, Virginia, for granting me access to the Libary's exceedingly rare copy of Anthony Gordon's first treatise, *A Letter on the Bayonet Exercise*. Additionally, I would like to thank Peter Harrington, Curator of the Anne S.K. Brown Military Collection at Brown University Library, for granting permission to use several images from the Collection in this book.

In closing, I would like to note that one of the great challenges in researching the subject of this book has been to separate actual history from mere apocrypha. In my attempt to do so, I was surprised at just how many of the extraordinary aspects of Irish duels turned out to be true—for instance, the frequency of their occurrence, the skill of their practitioners, and their observance by groups of hundreds and even thousands of spectators. Additionally, some incredible discoveries—such as the fact that the famous swordsman, the Chevalier de Saint-Georges, had been spectacularly defeated by the Irish fencing master James Kelly in front of hundreds of members of the French, English, and Irish nobility—are not only true, but are being presented here in print for the first time in more than two hundred years. On the other hand, many of the cherished nineteenth and twentieth century stories about personalities such as David "Tyger" Roche and George Robert "Fighting" Fitzgerald turned out to be false—interpolated from the lives of other individuals, or concocted out of thin air by unscrupulous authors and editors. It is my hope that this book will set the record straight—as far as the surviving historical evidence allows—and that the words and wisdom of Ireland's venerable fencers can now reach a wider audience, as they no doubt originally intended; or, in the words of the great Irish author Lord Dunsany, that this book's contents will

mark a dead man's thoughts for the wonder of later years, and tell of happenings that are gone clean away, and be a voice for us out of the dark of time, and save many a fragile thing from the pounding of heavy ages; or carry to us over the rolling centuries, even a song from lips long dead on forgotten hills.

Ben Miller
New York, July 2017

# PART ONE

"The Duel." Engraved for *Walker's Hibernian Magazine*.

# I

## DUELING *in* EIGHTEENTH CENTURY IRELAND

*"The sword by the side, in those times, when in the street, was as much an appendage as the hat on the head..."*[1]

Throughout past centuries, the Irish were frequently renowned for their skill with the sword. Since the age of antiquity, the history of Ireland has abounded with tales and accounts of warriors, travelers, noblemen, and adventurers engaging in heroic feats of swordsmanship.[2] This love of, and reliance on, the use of the sword by the Irish, continued throughout the medieval and the Renaissance eras, during which time the people of Ireland utilized various types of blades as personal sidearms, for use in both war and civilian self-defense. Likewise, the custom of settling disputes through the mode of single combat is recorded in the earliest of Irish annals,[3] and the notion of a "fair" and equitable combat, fought between two adversaries (or between equal numbers of adversaries) became central to Irish culture—even observable in accounts of battlefield incidents.[4] On a smaller scale, the custom of single combat also manifested itself in judicial duels. The last known instance of a trial by combat in Ireland, recorded in *Holinshed's Chronicle*, occurred in 1583, and was "valiantly" fought with sword and target between Connor Mac Cormack O'Connor and Teig Mac Gilpatrick O'Connor at Dublin Castle.[5] After this time, single combat in Ireland became relegated to the duel.[6]

During the seventeenth century, the ideal of the Irish swordsman-adventurer was exemplified by real-life individuals such Maolmordha "the Slasher" O'Reilly[7] and William Lamport, the latter of whom was certainly one of the most extraordinary characters of his age. Born in Wexford, Ireland, between 1611 and 1615, Lamport was educated by Jesuits in both Dublin and London, and became fluent in fourteen languages. During the span of his short life, he fought in various battles and sieges throughout Europe, engaged in court intrigue as well as piracy, and sailed to the New World, where he became known by the Hispanicized *nom de guerre* Don Guillén de Lombardo y Guzmán. In Mexico, Lamport fought against injustice and attempted to lead a popular rebellion of natives, black slaves, and oppressed *mestizos*. He was arrested by the Inquisition, enacted a daring prison escape, and then publicly defied and ridiculed his former captors by tacking broadsides to church doors under cover of night. Lamport was eventually recaptured and sentenced to be burned at the stake, but, on the appointed day—in 1659—he cheated the executioner by strangling himself while the flames were still being lit. In subsequent years, Lamport would become a celebrated figure in Mexican history—and, according to some, would serve as one of the inspirations for the fictional character Diego de la Vega, known to the entire world as Zorro.[8]

It was not until the eighteenth century, however, that the fame of the Irish swordsman truly reached its peak. This was due, in no small part, to the massive prevalence of dueling in Ireland during the same period. One author declared that prior to 1800, "Ireland was the garden of duellists," and that the island supplied "a stock of missionaries to the rest of the world."[9] The Dublin duelist Joseph Hamilton referred to Ireland as the *Land of Duel*," and claimed that the custom "was formerly practised [here], to a most extravagant extent," adding that "there is not, we are convinced, a respectable family throughout that portion of the empire, which cannot tell of numerous wounds acquired in single combat."[10] The English historian Andrew Steinmetz wrote that in Ireland, "we find an impulsive race of beings, who flung themselves into the practice [of dueling] with a boisterous abandon or gaiety..."[11] Although Steinmetz was writing with unrestrained cultural prejudice, his designation of Ireland as one of the prime dueling hotbeds in Europe is borne out by numerous period accounts. One Dublin gentleman, for instance, writing from the city in 1769, testified that

> Duels are more frequent here, I believe, than in any part of the king's dominions...I have heard, at a coffee-house, a couple of journeymen, or shopmen, talk as coolly and familiarly of the convenience of a room in a certain tavern, for the exercise of a brace of points or pistols, as of an alley for a match of nine-pins...[12]

Another author, writing during the same period, declared that "duels were every day fought"

William Lamport of Wexford, later known as *Don Guillén de Lombardo y Guzmán.*

in Dublin during the early part of eighteenth century.[13] And in 1770, the following letter appeared in a prominent Dublin newspaper:

SIR,

I read a paper of yours with much pleasure before I left Dublin, wherein you truly ridicule the great impropriety of improper persons wearing swords. Was you to be in the county of Galway with me, you would find such excellent themes, that I do not know whether these Quixotes of Ireland would not stand more corrected by your pen, than by any other chastisement whatsoever. Every fellow in this county fences, and if you look awry at your barber while he is shaving you, he will let your windpipe alone, to have the pleasure of running you thro' the body with his sword...The officers of the army have too frequently found themselves in many disagreeable circumstances from these upstarts; for no honour could flatter their vanity like that of a duel with a King's officer. They are in general good swordsmen, the skill of which instrument leads them into these frays. Passing through this *pushing** country, I had occasion for a pair of breeches, and upon the taylor's bringing them home, I objected to their wideness between the legs; "O! My dear creature (says he) you'll not find them so at all, when you've occasion to make a lunge." At which he instantly lunged out with his shears in his hand, and was near cutting off my nose to throw himself into his favourite attitude.[14]

This local trend was still in full force in 1790, when Charles Topham Bowden traveled to Galway and noted that the inhabitants were "greatly addicted to fashionable vices, of which duelling is not the least." After spending time in Dublin, Bowden similarly remarked that "duelling is much more prevalent here than in any other city I have ever visited...scarce a week passes in which one or two are not recorded by the newspapers."[15] One Irish duelist, reflecting on his life in Ireland during the same period, recounted:

> No person who felt a penchant for chivalry need wait a single hour for a thrust. Every gentleman then wore his sword or *couteau de chasse*, which there could be no trouble in drawing.[16]

In further surveying the history of the era, it is clear that the reputation earned by Ireland for harboring great swordsmen was merited, as numerous firsthand accounts attest to Irish prowess with the sword. We find, for instance, that the famous British fencing and boxing champion James Figg—who reportedly maintained a record of two-hundred and seventy-one wins and only one loss—was stymied, in a rare occurrence, by an old Irish fencer who, though "stiff and slow" with age, nevertheless threw Figg into a "confusion," thus "disappointing" him in all his designs.[17] Such skill also extended to duels. Donald McBane, a Scottish swordsman regarded as one of the most prolific duelists of all time (having fought close to one hundred personal combats), by his own account, only admitted to having met his match once later in life—when he fought, to a draw, a fencing-master from the west of Ireland.[18] Another example of Irish prowess in duels can be found in the case of Captain Peter Drake, an Irish swordsman who fought the renowned English sword-champion James Miller (later a distinguished author of a treatise on fencing). During the course of their combat, Drake so dominated Miller that the latter "got behind one of the Trees, and begged [Drake] would let him breath." Unwilling to take advantage of his adversary in such a manner, Drake granted Miller's request, and the combat came to an end (the two men eventually became friends).[19] When two Irish adversaries

---

* *Pushing*: In eighteenth century fencing terminology, a *push* is a thrusting attack executed on a lunge or a pass.

—equally matched in skill—deigned to face each other, the resulting combat could be long and bloody. In 1773, the *Hibernian Magazine* reported that:

> A few days ago a duel was fought in a field near Clonmell, between two private men of the second regiment of horse, named McCormick and Creagh; they fired a case of pistols each, and then took to their broadswords, with which they fought about forty minutes, when Creagh, jaded by the loss of blood, declined the combat: He received twelve cuts in different parts of his head and body, and McCormick eight; they were masters of the broad sword, looked on to be as able men as any in the regiment to which they belong, and in much esteem with their officers and the inhabitants of the town. Their seconds (two others of the private men) are censured for their encountering with swords, and it is said their colonel has summoned a court-martial to enquire into their conduct.[20]

## HISTORICAL BACKGROUND

To understand the dueling fervor which prevailed in Ireland during the eighteenth century, one must look back to a pivotal moment in the island's history—that is, to the end of the Williamite–Jacobite War, or "War of the Two Kings," which would determine Ireland's fate for centuries to come. After the Battle of the Boyne in 1690, and with the final capitulation of Jacobite forces at Limerick in 1691, the power of the old Catholic aristocratic order in Ireland effectively came to an end. According to the nineteenth century historian John Edward Walsh, this event would directly give rise to the culture of single combat that was to come:

> Duelling in Ireland is now happily a thing of the past. The mania seems to have commenced after the battle of the Boyne, and terminated with the Union [of 1800]. The effect of the first was to disband a number of military men by the dissolution of the Irish army, who wandered about the country without employment or means of living, yet adhering with tenacity to the rank and feelings of gentlemen. They were naturally susceptible of slight or insult, and ready, on all occasions, to resent them by an appeal to their familiar weapons—the sword or pistol. Their opponents, the Williamites, had been soldiers likewise, and were not likely to treat with due respect ruined and defeated men. These causes...brought on constant collisions, which were not confined to the parties, but soon extended through all classes.[21]

As a result of the treaty concluded at Limerick, the Jacobite army was allowed to withdraw to the continent—and with it, approximately fourteen thousand Irish Catholic soldiers, who passed directly into the service of France. In subsequent decades, these soldiers would be followed by tens of thousands of additional Irish recruits, who continued to serve the cause of

*Irish Carabineer*

1791 watercolor of an "Irish carabineer." *Courtesy of the Anne S.K. Brown Military Collection, Brown University Library.*

King James and his successors. This immense army-in-exile, though mostly centered in France, would disperse additional Irish soldiers to the Austrian, Spanish, Venetian, Neapolitan, and Sicilian militaries. In accordance with the agreed-upon articles of the Treaty of Limerick, such emigration was initially allowed by the British government. During the first decade of the eighteenth century, however, laws were enacted declaring it high treason to correspond or liaise in any way with "the Pretender" (King James) or his agents, or to recruit money for his cause, and the record shows that scores—if not hundreds—of men were hanged, drawn, and quartered in Ireland for attempting to enlist in the forces of the one they claimed to be "the rightfull King" (*an rí ceart*)—or "dear Jemmy," as he was sometimes colloquially referred to.[22]

The Irishmen who joined the continental foreign service would become known, famously, as the "Wild Geese,"—both celebrated and lamented in Irish poetry and song:

> I'll sell my rock, I'll sell my reel,
> I'll sell my only spinning wheel,
> To buy for my love a sword of steel,
> *Is go de tu mo mhurnin slàn...*
>
> But now my love has gone to France,
> To try his fortune to advance,
> If he e'er come back 'tis but a chance,
> *Is go de tu mo mhurnin slàn.*[23]

Another specimen of poetry, entitled "The Wild Goose.—The Irish Cavalier, 1690," provides further socio-cultural context, and illustrates the importance with which the sword was held by Irish soldiers-in-exile—those "unhappy gentlemen, who, by the loss of plentiful fortunes at home, had nothing left them but their swords."[24] It reads, in part:

> My trusty sword, sole heritage of acres fair and wide,
> Lands stretching from the sea beat cape to broad Blackwater's tide;
> Lands forfeited to Saxon churls because I owned my king,
> Worshipped my God as I was taught—Faith such returns will bring.
>
> Faith cannot brook the lying tongue, Faith will not seek the slave;
> I threw my hazard on one cast—I lost—and all I gave—
> All that I had, love, home and friends—to set my country free;
> I freely staked, I freely lost, my sword is all to me.
>
> Lords of the lands that once were mine, my titles now ye hold—
> Titles ye won not sword in hand, but bought with ill-got gold;
> I scorn your purchased honours, though they once to me were dear,
> I boast a prouder title far—an Irish Cavalier.[25]

It is worth noting that Patrick Sarsfield, the celebrated Irish Jacobite military leader responsible for leading the initial "flight" of the Wild Geese into exile, was himself an ardent duelist.

In 1681, Sarsfield challenged the English peer Lord Grey of Warke to a duel in response to disparaging remarks the latter had made about Irishmen; in another affair, Sarsfield was "run through the body near the shoulder, very dangerously"; in yet another, his lung was pierced, along with his adversary's. Nevertheless, Sarsfield still managed to survive these wounds to pursue a military career, before finally being killed at the Battle of Landen in 1693.[26]

During their time abroad, the Wild Geese became renowned for their skills with arms, and participated in nearly every major European war of the century, distinguishing themselves in the famous battles of Blenheim, Oudenarde, Steenkerque, Malplaquet, and Fontenoy. A French narrative relates that, at the Battle of Marsaglia, the Irish regiments "fought with an extreme valour," having "in the space of half a league...dispatched more than 1000 of the enemy with sword-thrusts, and clubbed muskets." Another contemporary recounted that "the Duke of Savoy, having perceiv'd great numbers of Irish to be in the line, ordered his men, to attack them, with sword in hand. In this attempt, his Royal Highness committed an important errour. For, by that method of fighting, the Irish generally prevayl. The attack being given, the Confederates were soon forc'd to...take their flight..." According to one historian, the French victory at the famous Battle of Fontenoy was "chiefly attributable to the Irish." This same battle, notably, was the setting of a memorable single combat with swords between an Irish and British officer:

> As the Irish approached the British, an officer of the Brigade, Anthony Mac Donough, younger brother of Nicholas Mac Donough, Esq. of Birchfield, in the County of Clare, (an offshoot from the old sept of the Mac Donoughs of Sligo,) being in advance of his men, was singled out, and attacked, by a British officer. But the spirit of the gallant Briton was above his strength. Mac Donough, as the fresher man, soon disabled his adversary in the sword-arm, and making him prisoner, sent him to the rear; fortunately for him, as he was so fatigued, that, in all human probability, he must have fallen in the charge or retreat; and, it is pleasing to add, that these gentlemen afterwards became great friends. This rencontre, in the presence of both forces, occasioned a momentary pause, followed by a tremendous shout from the Brigade at the success of their own officer, the effect of which could only be felt by a spectator; and, at such a critical juncture, that startling shout, and the event of ill omen to the British with which it was connected, were remarked to have had a proportionable influence upon them.

This same Anthony Mac Donough eventually returned to county Clare, where he continued to recruit for the Irish Brigade. Though urged to return to France, Mac Donough—having since married—declined going back. According to a history of the brigades, he "lived to be some years above 80, and was the maternal grandfather of the late Anthony Hogan, Esq., Solicitor, of No. 18, Kildare Street, Dublin."[27]

The Irish duelist and celebrated Jacobite military leader, Patrick Sarsfield (ca. 1660–1693).

Such men could not help but be influenced by the cultures of the foreign nations into which they ventured. A vivid example was provided by Michael Kelly, who, while walking through Cork during the 1790s, encountered a "very fine-looking elderly gentleman" named Captain O'Reilly, a duelist and former officer who "had served many years in the Irish Brigade" throughout Europe. Now reckoned "one of the most eccentric men in the world," O'Reilly had become a polyglot fluent in German, French, Italian, English, and Irish, which he frequently mixed in conversation:

> No sooner had the noble Captain [O'Reilly] shaken me heartily by the hand, than he exclaimed, "*Bon jour, mon cher Mic, je suis bien aisc de vous voir*, as we say in France. *An bfhuil tu go maith?*[*] *J'etois fache* that I missed meeting you when you was last in Dublin; but I was obliged to go to the County Galway to see a brother officer, who formerly served with me in Germany, as *herlich ein kerl*, as we say in German, as ever smelt gunpowder. *Dair mo laimh*[†]—*il est brave comme son epée*, as fearless as his sword..." The Captain told me, furthermore, that he had been cheated some years before out of a small property which his father left him in the County Meath, by a man whom he thought his best friend. "However," said the Captain, "I had my satisfaction by calling him out, and putting a bullet through his hat; but, nevertheless, all the little property that was left me is gone. But, *grace au ciel*, I have never sullied my reputation, nor injured mortal...In all my misfortunes, cousin, I have never parted with the family sword, which was never drawn in a dirty cause; and there it hangs now in a little cabin which I have got in the County Meath. Should ever Freddy Jones discard me, I will end my days in *risposo e pace* with the whole universal world."[28]

It is to some of these worldly "Wild Geese" that history owes the existence of fencing texts detailing the use of the small-sword, including those published by Daniel O'Sullivan (in France) and Alexander Doyle (in Germany). Likewise, it was on the continent, in places such as Paris, where many swordsmen of the Irish brigades continued to hone their fencing skills. Some of these individuals, like Daniel O'Sullivan, chose to remain in France, where their descendants became absorbed into the culture of their adopted nations. Other fencing masters, such as William O'Brien and James Pardon, returned to Ireland, where they continued to spread the fencing knowledge that they had gained abroad. Still others, such as Peter Drake, Thomas Macnamara, and Richard Buidhe Kirwan, participated in a vast number of duels before finally returning to Ireland.[29]

Many Catholic soldiers, however—as Walsh states—never left Ireland in the first place. Those who chose to remain after 1691 faced a new challenge—life under the infamous "penal laws," designed to disempower Catholics, Presbyterians, and other non-Anglican Protestant

---

\* *Irish:* "Are you well?"

† *Irish:* "By my hand [I swear]."

dissenters. According to historian William Lecky, author of the most comprehensive eighteenth century history of Ireland,

> The Irish Catholics, after the revolution, had been disarmed. With the semi-feudal habits which survived in Ireland far into the last century, it was the custom of Irish gentlemen to ride abroad themselves armed and attended by large numbers of servants with sword and pistols. In the absence of police, and amidst the still widely prevailing lawlessness, each house-holder was obliged to undertake the defence of his own home and family. An armoury and a supply of muskets and pikes formed part of the ordinary furniture of a country house. If no restrictions had been placed upon the Catholics, their numbers would have enabled them to extemporize a force which might rekindle the civil war. As a pledge for the security of the public peace, the right to possess arms in these large quantities was limited to those who were in fact its guardians, and Catholics were restricted to their fowling-pieces.[30]

The penal laws, according to numerous statutes, aimed in part to "disarm the papists" and prohibited Catholics from bearing swords or firearms, or even serving as apprentice sword-cutlers.[31] As one resident Catholic complained in 1724,

> By laws since made, all and every *Roman Catholick* of the kingdom (except a few lords and three or four colonels of the troop that were actually in *Limerick* and *Galway* at the time they surrendered) are disabled under severe penalties, to carry arms offensive or defensive of their own, or the defence of their houses and goods, other than pitch forks, or such instruments as the peasants till the earth with; Nay many gentlemen, who formerly made a considerable figure in the kingdom are now a days, when they walk with canes or sticks only in their hands, insulted by men armed with swords and pistols, who of late rose from the very dregs of the people. *Servi Dominati Sunt nobis!* [Slaves rule over us!][32]

With such laws in force, one might wonder how so many Catholics came to be famed as duelists and fencing masters in eighteenth century Ireland. The simple answer to this is that the prohibition to bear arms was not effectively enforced for more than a few decades. As the severity of the penal laws increased, so did popular resistance to them. In 1729, Lord Fitzmaurice wrote from Killarney, County Kerry, of the numerous Catholics that had "skenes [daggers] and pocket pistols always about them," complaining, "yet I could not find a man that would help me to bring these lawless people to justice, they being all papists that carry these weapons of offence, as well as those whose assistance I asked. All these persons are protected by different clans here."[33] By 1730, the laws prohibiting arms existed in theory only, and were no longer practically implemented, as can be seen in the following anecdote:

In the summer of 1730, a Catholic gentleman was indicted at Galway for carrying arms in the streets. His religion was avowed; the fact was not disputed. The defence was that the Disarming Act applied only to persons who were alive at the time that it was passed, and on this ground he was acquitted. The Dublin Catholics at once put on their swords, at once carried pistols in their holsters; and, when they rode into the country, had their half-score or score of armed servants behind them. Two years later, as if deliberately to assert the re-establishment of their right, Lord Gormanston and one of the Barnwells, both Catholics, appeared with swords at the assizes at Trim.

They were both popular men, and against them individually there was no ill-feeling; but the grand jury, 'men of fortune, and several of them members of Parliament,' feeling that acquiescence would be a public sanction to the Galway interpretation of the law, met the challenge as boldly as it was made. Gormanston and Barnwell were indicted under the old Disarming Act, and the question was referred to the Dublin judges for decision...The Catholics had been heard to boast that they could ensure the failure of all future attempts to take their weapons from them...Gormanston and his companion were found guilty, apologized, and received a pardon, at the unanimous petition of the grand jury. But the assertion of the law was deprived of its force by the imbecility of the Viceroy and his masters. [34]

Thus, "in a country of pathless mountains and bogs, which a long line of coast threw open to privateers from the Continent, disarming was impossible; and, in spite of the laws, it was well known that Connaught was full of weapons."[35] Counties Galway and Mayo, both part of Connacht, would reportedly become home to Ireland's best swordsmen and the "ablest schools of the dueling science."[36] By 1760, all pretenses regarding the bearing of arms were thrown aside:

Galled by a distinction which was a badge of distrust and inferiority, and encouraged by the obvious determination of the English Government to paralyze the penal laws as far as Ireland would allow them, the Catholic gentry, at the beginning of the reign of George II, openly resumed their swords, and were believed to have collected stores of arms, like the Protestants, in their houses. The magistrates had a power by law to issue search warrants; but if they used such a power, they were likely to be murdered, burnt in their beds. If they escaped Irish vengeance, they fell under the displeasure of the English Government. [37]

Towards the end of the century, Ireland's Protestant government gradually relaxed the penal laws, in the hopes of drawing more Catholics into the British service and the Irish volunteers, or local militias. In the 1790s, the laws prohibiting Catholics bearing arms were largely abolished.

Just like members of the ancient Catholic order, the relatively newer Anglo-Irish Protestant Ascendancy—which governed Ireland throughout the eighteenth century—would also become part and parcel of the island's dueling culture. A complex picture of Ireland's Protestants—as a group—emerges when factoring in the complexities of the island's cultural and genealogical history. The so-called "Old English" or *Seanghaill*, descended from twelfth-century English, Welsh, and Norman settlers, had long intermixed with, and been absorbed into, the native Irish Catholic population. Likewise, some Anglo-Irish Protestants—in addition to those of Welsh and Scottish descent—were themselves partly descended from the old Gaelic Irish who had adopted Protestantism in order to keep their lands, and to reap the legal and societal bene-fits that being a Protestant afforded. Thus, Ireland's Protestant culture had long been inter-meshed with the island's history, and, considering this socio-cultural complexity, it is difficult to know what influence Welsh, Scottish, and English dueling traditions may have had on Irish ones, or vice versa. As early as 1690, dueling was in full force among Ireland's Protestants, prompting the Lord Justices of Ireland to publicly decry the "Quarrels and Duels [that] have frequently happen'd between the Officers and Soldiers of the Army in this Kingdom," and to issue a Dublin proclamation warning those "who shall send, receive, or deliver any Challenge, or give any real Affront to any other."[38] By the eighteenth century, Anglo-Irish Protestant dueling culture had diverged markedly from that of England, where pistols had, since the mid-1600s, been the primary dueling weapon of choice.[39] By contrast, Irish Protestants—just like their Catholic brethren—as a group preferred the sword for use in duels up until at least the year 1750.[40] One prejudiced author, writing in the *Dublin University Magazine*, theorized that the Irish propensity for dueling was innately embedded in the native character, and infected any person—or group—who lingered long within the confines of its shores. To this, Ireland's Protestants were not considered exempt.[41] During the last quarter of the eighteenth century—as shall be seen—Irish Protestants largely became, in many respects, the arbiters of Ireland's dueling culture, and the ones most responsible for guiding its precepts.

Thus, the practice of dueling in Ireland extended to nearly all levels of society—to both Catholics and Protestants, to nationalists and unionists, to rich and poor, to gentlemen and mechanics.[42] For, although the duel was ostensibly a custom afforded only to gentlemen, all ranks of Irish society were "in a kind of emulation" of the upper class method of living; according to one journal of the period, "Our country gentlemen appear in the equipage of the first quality. Our farmers and graziers are turned to gentlemen...and our tradesmen live in as much splendour."[43] John Walsh recounted that dueling in Ireland "extended through all classes," and, in 1775, a visitor to the country's south remarked that "the contagion of [dueling here] infects all ranks."[44] Indeed, in surveying the many period accounts of Irish duels, one

Charles O'Brien (1699-1761), 6th Viscount Clare, commander of Clare's Regiment of "Wild Geese."
The O'Briens of Clare were "enthusiastic duellists" and would produce two noted fencing masters.

finds occasional examples of participation by members of the poorest of classes, as can be seen in the following notice, from 1769:

ENNIS, Aug. 7. This town and neighbourhood was this morning shockingly alarmed at a report of an impending duel, to be fought by two journeymen brogue [shoe] makers with swords and pistols, but the unfortunate consequences which were apprehended from this affair, were happily prevented by the timely interposition of a magistrate, who put them both in stocks.[45]

Two years later, another such instance was reported by the Dublin press:

14

To such an amazing Pitch has Duelling come to in this Kingdom, that the lower Order of Hiber-
nians have dropt Boxing and taken to Sword and Pistol, for Instance, Tuesday last, one Jack Cack,
an old Cobler, and Kelly, a Barber, discharged a Case of Pistols at each other...This Affair
happened in Corn-market.[46]

The practice of dueling was especially universal in Galway, where the lower and middle classes
were ever ready to resort to the use of the sword.[47] When a visiting young duelist named
George Robert Fitzgerald made unwanted advances towards a woman in a Galway millinery
shop, the following scene ensued:

The young lady's exclamations brought a Mr. Lynch into the shop. He was an eyewitness of Mr.
Fitzgerald's indecent attempt upon her, he reprimanded him in severe, yet manly terms, but far
from succeeding in his wish of freeing the young lady from the persecution she suffered, Mr.
Fitzgerald used every means he could think of to intimidate him; first, by producing his *Andrew-
ferrara*, so he called his sword: but Mr. Lynch answered him, that he could easily procure such
another, and was not ignorant in the use of it.[48]

When Fitzgerald, who was a member of the upper-class landed gentry, declined this challenge
due to the lower-class "birth of Mr. Lynch," the latter immediately procured a wealthy friend
to fight in his stead. Fitzgerald was then forced to fight.[49]

Although they largely condemned the practice, even members of the clergy—both Catholic
and Protestant—occasionally participated in duels.[50] In the end, the only groups truly exempt
were those too impoverished to afford a sword, and women. For, although there is at least one
record of an Irish female sending a challenge to a duel, the ensuing meeting ended in an affair
of a different nature:

Here goes a comicall relation of a strange match between Lady Kingston, a widdow to the Lord
Kingston, an Irish lord, & a leiftenant of the King's foot; that she, having a mynd to marry him,
sent him a challenge to meet at a tyme & place to fight, not naming the challenger, & hee coming
there, tho' she was unknowne to him; & looking about for the challenger, at last saw a lady in a
mask, who told him she was the person hee looked for, & then told him the occasion, & after
some discourse carried him off in her ca[rriage], & in a very few howers marryed him; & its sayd,
hath 1500 li. per annum estate, & worth 10,000 li. in money.[51]

By the late eighteenth century, Ireland had fully cemented its fame throughout Europe as a
nation of ardent duelists. As one former combatant summarized,

Within my recollection, this national propensity for fighting and slaughtering was nearly
universal, originating in the spirit and habits of former times. When men had a glowing ambition

to excel in all manner of feats and exercises, they naturally conceived that manslaughter in an honest way (that is, not knowing which would be slaughtered,) was the most chivalrous and gentlemanly of all their accomplishments; and this idea gave rise to an assiduous cultivation of the arts of combat...[52]

# THE IRISH DUELIST IN POPULAR CULTURE: IMAGE AND REALITY

During the second half of the eighteenth century, reports of Ireland's extraordinary dueling culture traveled abroad, where various British authors and essayists wrote of the Irish fondness for single combat—often mingling such accounts with their own prejudices regarding what they believed to be the inherently flippant nature of the Irish. These views would manifest themselves in the popular culture of the era, and in Ireland itself—in plays such as *Modern Honour* and *The Duellist*, the latter of which included exchanges such as the following:

> GAN. When I commanded in Ireland, my doublet was pinked like the flounces of a fine lady's silk petticoat; and all in the cause of my friends. The man who would not be run through the body for his friend, ought to be kicked out of the world for a scoundrel...Would you insinuate that a gentleman has not a right to do himself justice by putting to death a scoundrel?
>
> WIT. By the laws, General?
>
> GAN. By the laws of honour, sir.[53]

One of the most famous fictional examples of the over-eager duelist can be found in Richard Brinsley Sheridan's *The Rivals*, whose character Sir Lucius O'Trigger spouted lines such as,

> Remember now, when you meet your antagonist, do every thing in a mild and agreeable manner. —Let your courage be as keen, but at the same time as polished, as your sword.[54]

Later, the popular image of the Irish duelist was further immortalized by William Makepiece Thackeray in his famous novel, *The Luck of Barry Lyndon*, in which the protagonist learns "the use of the sword, both small and broad" and engages in a series of duels, casually relating such incidents in the following manner:

> The next day I rode thirty-five miles into the territory of the Elector of B, and met Monsieur de Schmetterling, and passed my sword twice through his body; and rode back with my second, the Chevalier de Magny, and presented myself at the duchess's whist that evening.[55]

In examining the actual period accounts of Irish duelists, it is clear that portrayals such as the above contained a grain of truth—and yet, were by no means a fair or complete depiction. There is no doubt that dueling was a deeply embedded aspect of Irish culture during the eighteenth century—and that the stereotype of the hot-blooded Irish duelist, eager to fight upon the slightest whim or provocation, was embodied by at least a small number of real-life duelists, such as George Robert "Fighting" Fitzgerald and Alexander "Buck" English. However, as shall be seen, other lesser-known Irish duelists such as Peter Drake and David Roche are recorded in certain cases as doing everything they could to avoid a quarrel or combat, until the only alternative was suffering public disgrace. Moreover, in the nine separate eighteenth century accounts that we have been able to find of duels fought fairly with the small-sword or pistol in England, between Irish and English combatants (or between Irishmen and foreigners residing in England), the Irish duelist is described as the victor in seven out of nine cases.[56] It was likely this trend which caused one London newspaper, in a column about dueling, to warn its readers that "in contentions with any of that body of gentlemen [Irishmen], one is liable to be wounded in *mind*, *body*, and *estate*."[57] Considering the aforementioned statistics, it is perhaps unsurprising that, in a nation frequently charged by nationalist sentiment, English authors would resent and publicly disparage Irish duelists.

A much more sympathetic view of Ireland's dueling culture, however, was offered by Abraham Bosquett, a native of Sandymount, County Dublin,[58] who had "been four times a Principal, and twenty-five times a Second" in various duels. In his treatise on dueling, Bosquett observed,

> I have always found, that, in the provinces, districts, and cities, where the decision of differences, by single combat, had most prevailed, (for instance, the province of Connaught, in Ireland, the city of Dublin, the city of Galway, and some others,) the gentry were the most polite and friendly, and the middle classes the most civilized and respectful, of any other people, perhaps, in any other country; and even the lower classes, tractable and good-natured to excess. Such qualities constitute the true basis of genuine politeness. The lower orders are prone to ape their superiors, whether it be in virtue or in vice...Where men dare be rude and insulting, free from the dread of castigation, or being called to account for their conduct in a spirited way, politeness, good breeding, nay, common good manners, are dispensed with, and the lie given and taken as words of course. Men of fine feelings are always the least prone to give offence; though generally the most apt to take it, if insolence, insult, or rudeness, be a concomitant.[59]

Bosquett's claim is not unique, and the notion that the duel provided for greater enforcement of courtesy and politeness can be found in other dueling treatises and texts of the era.[60] It is also born out by the firsthand account of at least one other Irish duelist, who described the social climate in Dublin during the late eighteenth century:

> To such lengths did respect for the [female] sex extend, and so strong was the impression that men were bound to protect it even from accidental offence, that I remember if any gentleman presumed to pass between a lady and the wall in walking the streets of Dublin, he was considered as offering a personal affront to her escort; and if the parties wore swords, as was then customary, it is probable the first salutation to the offender would be "Draw, sir!" However, such affairs usually ended in an apology to the lady for inadvertence. But if a man ventured to intrude into the boxes of the theatre in his surtout or boots, or with his hat on, it was regarded as a general insult to every lady present, and he had little chance of escaping without a shot or a thrust before the following night.[61]

Likewise, as late as 1796, a fatal duel involving Edward Swetnam, a prominent revolutionary member of the United Irishmen, resulted from his "bumping" a lady at the opera.[62]

The county of Galway—an area where dueling was extremely prevalent—was frequently remarked upon for the politeness of its residents. A 1786 tract claimed that "the inhabitants of this town [of Galway] have been evermore remarkable, for the most spirited opposition to the impertinencies of the officers of the army, and for affability and hospitable demeanor to such of them, as conducted themselves with politeness and propriety."[63] One account of an old Galway duelist, related in later years by his own daughter, described the particular standard of courtesy adhered to by prospective combatants:

> My father on one occasion challenged, or was challenged by, a Mr. French of Port Carron, who lived some miles from us, to fight...My father summoned a friend from a distance to act as his second, and they were walking up and down outside our gate, earnestly discussing the details of the meeting which was to take place next morning, when a gentleman in a gig came driving along the road. My father stopped the gig, and politely invited its occupant to come up to the house and dine. The offer was equally courteously declined, and the gig drove on.
>
> "Who's your friend?" asked the second.
>
> "That's French of Port Carron," said my father calmly.
>
> "And what do you mean, sir," roared the second in angry amazement, "by bringing me here on such a fool's errand? Pretending you're going to fight this man, and then inviting him to dinner!"
>
> "And do you think, sir," retorted my father, equally hotly, "that I'd allow Mr. French or any other gentleman to drive past my gate without asking him in to dine? But I'll fight him tomorrow all the same, as sure as my name is Martin, whether he'd dined with me or not."
>
> In the end, however, when the parties met on the field, the seconds succeeded in patching up a reconciliation, and no encounter took place.[64]

Duel between Lords Townshend and Bellamont, fought over an Irish political dispute. *Hibernian Magazine,* 1773.

No doubt taking such "Irish" politeness into consideration, Jonathan Swift, perhaps eighteenth century Ireland's most renowned English-language author, defended the duel in his short work, *A treatise on good manners and good breeding.* Swift wrote,

> I should be exceedingly sorry to find the legislature make any new laws against the practice of duelling; because the methods are easy and many for a wise man to avoid a quarrel with honour, or engage in it with innocence.[65]

## THE IRISH DUELIST AS FOLK HERO

It is important to note that, in a society in which many lower and middle-class individuals considered themselves disenfranchised and oppressed by unfair laws, the duel was a potential mode of obtaining justice that was generally deemed both legally and morally acceptable. Though possibly romanticized, the following account of a combat—alleged to have taken place in County Cork—demonstrates a more positive sentiment towards dueling than was generally seen in the press of the period:

In 1798, a fateful year, a party of British soldiers were stationed at Millstreet and went through exercises at "The Yeos field" at Drishane [Castle].

It happened that a poor country woman was grossly insulted by an English officer and, having no redress from the so-called government, carried her tale to a Mr. McCarthy, a descendant of the great native family who in ancient days ruled over wide districts.

He saw the justice of her case, but was, of course, powerless to give her redress; as a gentleman, however, it was open to him according to the duelling custom of the time to challenge her assailant. This he did, and the British officer was compelled by his own comrades—many of whom no doubt, as honourable men, despised him—to accept the challenge.

The venue was fixed at Glashatrocha Bridge—the Englishman, who was a noted swordsman, stipulating that they should fight with that weapon. Many thousand spectators lined the Glens on both sides of the Bridge. Needless to say, they were whole-heartedly with Mr. McCarthy, and many feared his overthrow by the more expert officer.

Their fears were, however, groundless, for as the old Shanachy* who delighted in re-telling the tale exclaimed, "With one mighty sweep of his broadsword McCarthy whipped the foreigner's head off." His victory was celebrated for long by the glens men who looked upon it as a great victory for the common people fought by one of their old chieftains.[66]

Despite the association between dueling and the aristocracy, numerous accounts show that Irish duelists were often regarded as local heroes, beloved by members of the lower-class populace. When the Kirwan estate—owned by one of Galway's most celebrated dueling families—was approached by a huge company of Ribbonmen (an eighteenth century secret society formed to exact vigilante justice from oppressive landlords), the Kirwans were, despite their aristocratic status, left alone:

[The Ribbonmens'] purpose in visiting the Kirwans...was not to terrorise, but to reassure them. As they rode up to the house, a hundred men or more, they were heard to call out to the occupants not to take fright...They told [Martin Kirwan] that he had nothing to 'feare' from them, adding that they would set a guard every night to 'pratict his House.' Martin replied, 'Boys, go home.' He thanked them for their courtesy and expressed his sympathies with their cause, but advised them against pursuing their present illegal activities. The Ribbonmen then gave three 'chers [cheers]' each for the Master, the Mistress, Master Edmund and the rest of the family before riding off in the direction of Dunmore.[67]

Likewise, the Kirwan family's most accomplished duelist, Richard *Buidhe* ("Yellow Richard"), was "celebrated in song and story as 'the poor man's friend, [and] the protector of the oppressed.'"[68] The portrayal of the Irish duelist as an avenger of wrongs, and as a defender of

---

*   *Shanachy*: From the Irish *seanchaí*. A custodian of tradition, a historian, an antiquary, a reciter of ancient lore.

the common people, can be seen in the following account of a Limerick duelist, passed down through local oral tradition:

> Captain Baily was a renowned duellist in his day, and had many associations in both Lough Gur and Castleconnell, Co. Limerick...Captain Bailey was beloved by the tenants of Lough Gur and neighbourhood. He often took the part of the tenants and often saved them from the "Rack Rents." He was a sub-agent to the De Fanes.
>
> Once when coming from Castleconnel to Lough Gur he saw some tenants being evicted for "Rack Rents" by a party of military under Captain Barrett from Bruff. The Captain [Barrett] was very cruel and committed a cruel deed. Captain Bailey came on the scene and pursued him and overtook him at Ballingirlough, where the two Captains fought a duel and in which Bailey was the victor. Captain Barrett was killed.
>
> Captain Bailey was a well known drinker and duellist...The sword was the weapon generally used by Captain Bailey in all his duels...his dead body [was] brought to Teampall Nuai, where it now lies interred, within the ruins of the old family vault at the South Eastern corner of the cemetery.[69]

The duel was also a recourse for those Irish intent on maintaining their ancestral pride. The English barrister Sir John Carr, reflecting on the period, wrote that "it was not from a sanguinary disposition, but solely from the chivalrous desire of preserving the far-famed bravery of his country from the stain of a doubt, that often induced an Irishman to mingle in a fray where he could have no interest or provocation."[70] One account of a combat in County Tipperary, which almost certainly took place during the eighteenth century, relates how a member of the old Irish aristocracy became insulted when a local British officer addressed him as a "collier" (coal miner), rather than as a person of rank. A challenge immediately followed:

> Years ago, a family named Gahan lived in Coolquill Castle and they were noted duelists. They had over 300 men working a coal and culm mine. They used to supply all the soldiers' barracks of the County Tipperary—Templemore, Fethard, and Clonmel. A new regiment came to Fethard one time and, seeing Gahan's name on the books for supplying coal, wrote a letter to *Collier* Gahan Coolquill. When Mr. Gahan got the letter, he ordered his horse to be got ready. He rode into the Barracks in Fethard and asked for the officer. When the officer appeared, [Gahan] had the letter on the point of his sword. He asked the officer, was it he that wrote the letter? And he said it was. Gahan challenged him to a duel, which they fought on the Green. After half-an-hour, Gahan ran him through with the sword.[71]

Despite the obvious sympathy for duelists among many of Ireland's classes, however, the press largely continued to rail against the practice—labeling it as savage, "gothic," and unsophisticated. During the next century, one Irish author—rankled by what he viewed to be hypocritical attacks by the British press on the motives and integrity of Irish duelists—would offer the following rebuttal:

> The unsettled state of mind...among English and Scotch editors of newspapers (we are more consistent in Ireland) is remarkably unsatisfactory. If a gentleman happens to be killed "entirely" in a duel, however fairly, the fact is regarded almost in the light of murder; and, in any case of serious wounds, is denounced in the lurid leading columns. But, let us observe, if neither party is wounded at all, then both parties are treated as fools, and the whole affair is covered with ridicule! Well,—some people are shocked at a single event; and other people are shocked at a multitude of similar things. One man being killed in a fair and honourable duel causes the pen of your English and Scotch editors to vibrate with emotion and moral denunciation; but these moral gentlemen are not at all shocked—indeed very few people really are—at a telegram recording the carnage in battle of thousands of the "enemy"—our fellow creatures—rendered none the less dreadful by the horrible technical coolness with which a batch of butcheries is designated, on our own side, as "casualties!" The victims of legitimate butcheries are not classed as men, but as casualties! Their blood was water—their mutilated bodies have been thrown and jumbled together in a casual-ward pit—their souls are neither here—nor there! So much for the popular morality of civilized nations, as Mr. John Bright might say. Of course, it is a different question—viz., that of an individual quarrel, and of a national quarrel (i.e., of a collected number of individuals)—but the broad and bleeding fact remains the same.[72]

Probably the most balanced description of Irish duelists as a group comes from the pen of Sir Jonah Barrington, an Irish Protestant who lived in Ireland throughout the late eighteenth century, and who was himself a participant in several duels as both principal and second. In his voluminous memoirs, Barrington chronicled the many duels of his time, and left detailed portraits of numerous Irish duelists. So definitive is Barrington's account, that nearly all subsequent nineteenth century histories which treat of dueling in Ireland rely on it exclusively. Barrington explained,

> It was the fashion of those days to cast upon the Irish gentry an imputation which though they by no means generally deserved, yet it would be uncandid not to admit that there was some partial ground for the observation that they showed a disposition to decide petty differences by the sword, and too fastidious a construction of what they termed the "point of honor." This practice certainly continued to prevail in many parts of Ireland, where time and general intercourse had not yet succeeded in extinguishing altogether the romantic but honorable spirit of Milesian chivalry: and...it is not surprising that hasty and unnecessary encounters should occasionally occur among a people perpetually actuated by the pride of ancestry and the theories of honor. But, even in these contests, the Irish gentleman forgave his adversary with as much readiness as he fought

him: he respected the courage which aimed at his own life; and the strongest friendships were sometimes formed, and frequently regenerated, on the field of battle. It is natural to suppose that this practice should have been noticed, and perhaps exaggerated, by the English people, whose long enjoyment of police and of industry had endowed them with less punctilious and much more discreet propensities.[73]

As shall be seen, an examination of numerous period accounts of Irish duels proves at least the second half of Barrington's description to be more or less accurate.

## CHARACTERISTICS OF IRISH DUELS AND DUELISTS

During the eighteenth century, the practice, procedure, and etiquette of dueling in Ireland strongly resembled that which was practiced in continental Europe. However, a few unusual characteristics sometimes set the "Irish duel" apart from mainland traditions. Of these, one of the most striking features was its openness. Elsewhere in Europe and America, duels were private affairs, typically held in secret, far away from the prying eyes of the law or the press. In Ireland, by contrast, such precautions were rarely taken—a possible consequence of the authorities' decidedly tolerant view towards dueling. In the absence of the need for secrecy, duels were sometimes attended by hundreds or even thousands of spectators. At a combat held in County Laois in 1759, recounted by Jonah Barrington,

> The entire country for miles round attended to see the combat, which had been six months settled and publicly announced, and the county trumpeter who attended the judges at the assizes was on the ground.[74]

Lord Clanricarde recounted that, at a duel fought near the Galway-Tipperary border, "there were at least two thousand persons present, all Tipperary men, as the Galway peasants did not dare to cross the bridge...A regular lane was made, lined by spectators on each side." Such an arrangement could be extremely hazardous; when, during this combat, the signal was given to fire, one of the principals "not only shot his antagonist dead, but also one of the peasantry who, in his eagerness to see the sport, had pushed forward and received the ball in his head."[75] In 1783, at another duel fought on Maryborough green, "hundreds of the towns-people went to see the fight...the ground was regularly measured; and the friends of each party pitched a ragged tent on the green, where whiskey and salt beef were consumed in abundance."[76] More than a decade later, in 1798, a planned duel near Baggot Street, Dublin, was attended by "four or five hundred" people.[77] And, at the very end of the century, when a combat was arranged between Henry Grattan and Isaac Corry,

> All Dublin knowing [of the impending duel], there was at least a thousand people assembled to see the fun. A person, whom we should now call a policeman, came up and forbade the proceeding. [Corry's second], who was a powerful man, took the intruder in his arms, and deposited him in a little ditch, out of which he might have stepped with the greatest ease; but his conscience being quieted, and his Irish curiosity awakened, he remained with the most amiable abnegation in the ditch till all was over. Mr. Corry was wounded.[78]

At Lucas's Coffee-House, a Dublin meeting-place whose back-yard was frequently the setting for deadly duels, entire companies of men "flocked to the windows to see that the laws of honor were fully observed, and to bet upon the probable survivor."[79] Spectators at duels were common enough that the Catholic archbishop of Cashel—as well as the bishops of Waterford —felt compelled to write statutes warning: "Spectators [at duels] are severely punished by the church because by their presence they countenance that horrid crime and thereby excite the passions of the unhappy duellists and encourage them..."[80] Vast audience attendance at duels would long be remembered in Irish oral tradition. An account of a duel fought in Cork during the eighteenth century (but not set down in writing until 1905) included the detail that "when the appointed day arrived, great crowds gathered on the plain below Kanturk Castle to see...a sanguinary combat"[81]; another account, finally written down in 1938, of a duel in Ballydonagh, Galway, mentioned that "a great crowd gathered at the New Gate to see this great fight."[82]

Such publicity, it seems clear, was often sought by the duelists themselves. In 1730, when two Irishmen fought a duel in Philadelphia, a bemused Benjamin Franklin noted the uncommon presence of crowds:

> Saturday last, about nine o'Clock in the Morning two young Hibernian Gentlemen met on Society Hill, and fought a gallant Duel before a Number of Spectators not very usual on such Occasions. The Cause of their Quarrel is it seems unknown; and as they were parted without much Difficulty, and neither of them received any considerable Hurt, it is generally looked upon to be only a Piece of Theatrical Representation.[83]

While Franklin may have dismissed the seriousness of this encounter, the same could not be said for the vast majority of duels in Ireland. Author James Kelly, in his statistical analysis of one hundred and forty-four duels which took place in Ireland between 1716 and 1770, has found that at least seventy—roughly half—resulted in a fatality for one of the combatants.[84] There is no doubt that dueling in Ireland was a very dangerous business.

In contrast to such highly-publicized affairs, it is clear that some of the combats termed "duels" in Ireland during this time were not duels at all, but *rencontres*. As defined in Dublin's *Hibernian Magazine*:

> A rencontre is no more than an accidental meeting, on which spot the parties are supposed to have given each other an immediate affront, such as the lie, calling one another coward, scoundrel, &c. which are terms of indignity one cannot give with impunity, nor the other receive tamely and maintain the character of a gentleman.[85]

During the first half of the eighteenth century, numerous instances of prearranged single combat recorded in Ireland fall somewhere in between the definition of a *rencontre* and an actual duel. In these cases, disputes proceeded from an injury to verbal or written challenges, followed by the appointment of a time and place for combat. However—in contrast to what was required for genuine duels—such affairs often took place without the involvement of seconds or witnesses, and neglected proper etiquette and procedure. An early example of such a combat occurred in County Carlow in 1718, and was described extensively in a broadside:

> Lieutenant *Berkley*, Mr *Culling* and one *Owins*, meeting at a Publick House at the aforesaid *Talla*, it appear'd that Mr. *Owins* and Lieutenant *Berkley*, having some Discourse, of which neither could agree in their opinions; their Language pass'd to that Highth, that a Quarrel ensued, and a Challenge was made between the Lieut. and *Owins* to decide it the next Morning.
>
> But Mr. Culling having taken part with the aforesaid Owens, against the *Lieut.* and the said Owens, not coming to answer his Promise that Morning, the Lieut. sent a Challeng to the aforesaid Mr. Culling.
>
> *Mr. Cullen had no sooner received the Challenge, but he immediately dressed and went to the Place mention'd in the Challenge, which was Talla-green, where, as soon as he came, he found Mr. Berkely there ready to receive him, upon which the said Mr. Culling, without asking any Questions, immediately drew and made the first Pass; which the Lieut. put by, and being a nimble Man, threw his Sword from his right Hand to his left, and at the first Thrust, run him thro' under the right Breast, of which Wound he fell down, and liv'd but 4 Ours after.*
>
> He had as much Sense, as to declare to his Friends, That Lieutenant Berkley had done nothing but Justice to him, having been affronted by him, but said nothing concerning the aforesaid Owens...
>
> *Afterwards, the Lieutenant Mr. Barkley went immediately and took a Horse and rode off, but 'tis thought he will come to no Damage.*[86]

Regarding the procedural aspects of the duel, a peculiar Irish custom was said to have been practiced by the "Bucks"—a loose confederation of cosmopolitan young men prone to engaging in small-sword duels. According to John Warburton,

> It was their practice to walk up and down through Lucas's Coffeehouse, with a train to their morning gown, sweeping the floor, and challenge any man to fight who by accident trod upon it.[87]

During the nineteenth century, the custom of "trailing a coat" for the purpose of inviting a challenge was also used by Irish shillelagh fighters hailing from poor, rural districts. In 1813, Thomas Crofton Croker observed such a tradition, which he described as a remnant of "feudal practices":

> A man will sometimes, from a mere love of combat, and without any malice, take off his coat, and holding it by the collar, trail it through the assembly, challenging or beguiling any one to step on it; which insult he no sooner succeeds in obtaining, than he feels justified in knocking down the offender, and the sport begins. The pleasure derived from this sort of occupation may doubtless be felt by men who will tell you, they carry a cudgel 'just to keep the cold out of their hands.'[88]

Jonah Barrington, who also witnessed this custom among Irish stick fighters, claimed that it stemmed from the medieval tradition of "throwing down a glove or gauntlet," being "a relic of that practice."[89] However, Barrington's assertion is currently unsubstantiated by earlier historical evidence in Ireland, and the act of inviting a challenge from a random adversary is, in all respects, contrary to the ethos of dueling. Such a custom—if it indeed existed among duelists—was likely only practiced by the Bucks, or confined to the most extreme belligerents.

## MINDSET OF THE IRISH DUELIST

As to the distinguishing characteristics of the duelists themselves, it is clear that, in surveying the available evidence, what set Irish combatants apart from those in much of the rest of Europe was their remarkable pyschological-emotional approach to combat—that is, their cool-headedness (termed *sang-froid* by the French), their indifference to personal danger, and their unshakable, devil-may-care attitude. At least two accounts of Irish *sang-froid* can be found in the memoirs of Henry Angelo, one of Britain's most celebrated fencing masters. Henry, whose mother was Irish,[90] recounted how his father, the great fencing master Domenico Angelo, had attended a duel during one of his extended sojourns in Ireland:

> In the year 1753 my father was in Ireland, where he was hospitably received by the father of the late member for Galway, Mr. R. Martin. There he was present at a duel which took place between

Mr. Martin and a gentleman of the name of Jack Gardiner. Mr. Martin received the first fire, and the bullet grazed and tore the gold lace off his hat. He, however, did not express the least alarm, but with the most perfect *sang froid*, taking off his hat and making his bow, he exclaimed, "By God! Gardiner, you are a d—d good shot!"[91]

Under the heading, *"Shamrock vs. Fleur de Lis,"* Angelo described another duel he had personally witnessed, this one between an Irish swordsman—a "counsellor in Dublin" who had previously studied under the renowned French fencing master La Boëssière—and a rival French Chevalier. According to Angelo, this incident occurred around 1790:

Monsieur Chevalier, at that time first dancer at the Opera-house here, and who was considered one of the best fencers at Paris, was a constant visitor, not only assisting in improving my scholars, but gratifying me, for I ever preferred to be opposed to a scientific antagonist. Mr. McD——t and Chevalier were usually opponents, and one day, the former being displeased at receiving the other's thrust, after having given the first hit, some words arose between them, which I did

Fencing master Domenico Angelo (1717-1802), who witnessed duels
during his stay in Ireland, and who married the Irish Elizabeth Johnson.

not hear, when they left off. They dressed themselves and quitted the room together; finding that on the stairs they had some angry conversation (this was in June, about three o'clock), and had both gone, I suspected some appointment had been made...I was then some way off, running; however, I was in time to see them get over a gate, when, hastening to the place, in a field, I saw them with their coats off, sword in hand, just going to engage; I called out, and ran towards them, but not in time to prevent them from beginning. Here was a *commencement*, far different to those methods they had previously practised before me in the Haymarket, as caution and skill are necessary when opposed to the point of a sword. It was not now a button covered with leather—a lesson to the many I have seen violently rushing on, who, after repeated efforts, have succeeded in giving a hit. This is not fencing. It is not scientific in the school, and is dangerous in the field...

Fortunately the delay, caused by the hesitation who should attack first, enabled me to be in time to part them. When I inquired what could be their motive for going out with swords, or whether any thing had been said to give offence, or any apology expected, they both seemed not to know what brought them at that distance together. All that I could elicit was, Chevalier was called out, and he said, *"de tout mon coeur."* To give you an idea of the short time I beheld the grand combat, the Frenchman, endeavouring to intimidate his [Irish] adversary, kept making a noise; though he made the first lunge, he took good care to be out of distance at the time, whilst the other, whom I had often seen not so cool and collected with a foil, now, with all that *sang froid*, laughed, and cried, *"poh!"* on his first receiving the attack, and at Chevalier's not coming nearer. This *faire semblant* of the one to appear courageous to frighten, or the other's *fierté*, could not have continued long; the result might have been dangerous, or fatal.

Now peace having been proclaimed, and the swords sheathed, we all adjourned to a teagarden, near Hogmore-lane, where the glass passed round pretty freely. Chevalier, who at Paris had often drawn his sword, shewed us sufficient proofs of the different rencontres he had experienced there, his right side and breast exhibiting many places where he had been wounded...After this last bout, unlike the classical opponents, they always met with good humour, and found my room preferable to the field.[92]

Such *sang-froid* may have been a product of the Irish duelist's upbringing, which often began at an early age. In a 1786 letter, the Marquis of Lothian stated his conviction that "a great part of the flippancy of the Irish is owing to an early knowledge of that science [of fencing]."[93] A few years later, in 1794, the training of one young Irish duelist was summarized in the pages of the *Anthologia Hibernica*:

Galgas was the son of a gentleman of considerable landed property in the west of Ireland. Whilst at school he was always considered a lad of spirit...As he grew up, and having acquired a considerable knowledge of the art of fencing, he exchanged the weapons of a pugilist for the sword, and before he had attained the age of twenty, had fought six or seven duels, and had several more on his hands, in all of which he behaved gallantly, and either disarmed or wounded his antagonists.[94]

Similarly, George Robert Fitzgerald, Ireland's most notorious duelist, was introduced to dueling while still a teenager.[95] It is also related that Thomas Macnamara, of County Clare, being "a good swordsman fought no less than thirty duels" and was never wounded, "and yet he had not then reached his twenty-first year of age."[96]

Although it is difficult to speak in generalities about Irish duelists as a group, a curious mix of ferocity, tenderness, charity, and philanthropy was often observed by their friends and associates. As one journal summarized it, "the characters of the men of this period were composed of [a] strange and inconsistent a mixture of good and evil qualities." Captain David "Tyger" Roche, one of Ireland's most prolific duelists, was known to burst into tears upon the act of being struck or insulted, and to long endure the insults of abusive persons before finally resorting to the sword. George Robert Fitzgerald, one of the most notorious duelists that ever trod the soil of Europe, was often remarked upon for his gentleness and deference towards women—though he was, judging by the historical evidence, a monster in nearly all other respects. Another example was Jack Gallaspy of Galway, whose character was, reputedly, "one of the strangest compounds that ever existed." According to a portrait drawn in 1756,

By his vast strength and activity, his riches and eloquence, few things could withstand [Gallaspy]. He was the most prophane swearer I have known:—fought everything, debauched everything, and drank seven in a hand...He was in the first place far from being quarrelsome, and if he fought a gentleman at the small sword, or boxed with a porter or coachman, it was because he had in some degree been ill used, or fancied that the laws of honour required him to call an equal to an account, for a transaction. His temper was naturally sweet. In the next place, he was the most generous of mankind. His purse of gold was ever at his friend's service: he was kind and good to his tenants: to the poor a very great benefactor. He would give more money away to the sick and distressed in one year, than I believe many rich pious people do in seven. He had the blessings of thousands, for his charities, and, perhaps, this procured him the protection of heaven...he never was sick, nor did he ever receive any hurt or mischief. In health, joy, and plenty, he passed life away, and died about a year ago at his house in the county of Galway, without a pang or any kind of pain.[97]

These same contradictions were sometimes acknowledged by the duelists themselves. In his memoir, the Jacobite duelist Peter Drake, a native of County Meath, described his own character as follows:

Humane and benevolent, generously affected with the Misfortunes of others, though so hardened and insensible to my own, that when under Sentence of Death, I cannot recollect it to have given me the least Concern.—In short, I had not one good Quality that was not in a great Degree allayed with something like its Reverse, and to a Constitution of Mind, formed of such discordant Principles, can I alone attribute that incorrigible Madness, and Inconsistence of Conduct, to be found almost every where in my Story.[98]

Another "singular character" was Beauchamp "King" Bagenal, a native of County Carlow who had reportedly fought "more than half a score of duels." In later years, after becoming lame due to an accident, Bagenal reportedly continued to fight his duels in a churchyard "by resting against one of the tombstones."[99] Jonah Barrington described him thus:

> His person was fine—his manners open and generous—his spirit high, and his liberality profuse. During his tour [in Europe], he had performed a variety of feats which were emblazoned in Ireland, and endeared him to his countrymen. He had fought a prince—jilted a princess*—intoxicated the Doge of Venice—carried off a Duchess from Madrid—scaled the walls of a convent in Italy—narrowly escaped the Inquisition at Lisbon—concluded his exploits by a celebrated fencing match at Paris; and he returned to Ireland with a sovereign contempt for all continental men and manners, and an inveterate antipathy to all despotic kings and arbitrary governments...Prodigally hospitable, irregular, extravagant, uncertain, vivacious; the chase, the turf, the sod, and the bottle, divided a great portion of his intellects between them...However, in supporting the independence and prosperity of Ireland, he always stood in the foremost ranks.[100]

After serving in Irish House of Commons and in Parliament, Beauchamp Bagenal died in 1802.

## THE PHILOSOPHY OF DUELING

In order to better understand the mentality of Ireland's duelists, it is necessary to look beyond the accounts and the critics, and examine the concepts of honor which guided the combatants themselves. For, despite the almost continuous stream of condemnations directed at the custom by the eighteenth century British and Irish press, the duel was regarded by those who practiced it to be a highly civilized and sophisticated method of settling quarrels in an age when honor was held in higher regard than life, body, and property. In the prevailing mentality of the era, when reputations were so highly valued, insults and defamation of character were themselves considered forms of assault, which, sometimes, could only be legitimately rectified by resorting to a ritual armed combat. As one author explained in 1704,

> You must not invade your Neighbours Honour, nor make any Attempt upon his Reputation: A good Name is no contemptible Treasure; the Wise Man prizes it above an Estate; it sets off Birth, and gives an Air even to Poverty; it shines brighter than Wealth, and sparkles more than all the

---

\* Charlotte of Mecklenburg-Strelitz (1744-1818).

Tinsel Gawdry of Fortune; it supports Grandure, and sweetens Misfortune. A Bankrupt that has lost his Coin, if he has not forfeited his Honour, has Resource at Command. Though his Fortune be fallen, he has a Fund to rebuild it on: But a Man without Honour is dead to all the Offices of Society and Commerce; now when his moral Capacity lies in the Grave, his Physical one alone creates Misery and Contempt to himself, Sport for Some, and Pity for Others.[101]

If a man's good name was called into question, his very identity was considered under attack. Thus, the duel itself was regarded as a form of self-defense. Since the legal system could not be relied upon to protect a person's reputation, dueling was viewed as "the only means…by which a man who has been injured by someone who possesses no rights over him, can wash away the stain left by the injury he has received."[102] Or, as Samuel Johnson concisely stated in 1783, "A man may shoot the man who invades his character, as he may shoot him who attempts to break into his house."[103]

Irish society's complex relationship with dueling is illustrated in the following article—published in 1775 by *Walker's Hibernian Magazine*—which extols the necessity of dueling while at the same time condemning its excesses:

THE man who is so tenacious of his honour as to fight with every person who thinks proper to asperse his character, and the Idiot who is callous to accusation and dead to unjust reproof, are cowards of the rankest class. He that fights with every body, and he that won't fight at all, proceed upon the same principle, and are dastards in their natures; but wide is the difference between the man of honour and the poltroon, the Idiot and the man of sensibility.

The author of the article follows this with an elaborate condemnation of the duel, lambasting the practice as a cultural artifact hailing from "days of ignorance and barbarism." However, this argument is then qualified:

Though every sensible person must condemn a spirit of duelling, yet I will be bold enough to assert that there are particulars, who cannot with any degree of manhood refuse a challenge when given, or even avoid giving one upon particular occasions; and no society of men in the world can so justly lay a claim to it as the gentlemen of the military.

The idea of cowardice is a contamination to the essence of a soldier, it is his peculiar province neither to give or take an affront; in either case he is disregarded by his employers, he is despised by his brother officers, and treated with contempt even by the common soldiery. His life, his being, his very soul exists but in the maintenance of his honour; that once forfeited, adieu to the character of the gentleman, the man, and the soldier; a character too nice to be the sport of laziness, and too honourable to be the jest of the upstart. It is well for that officer whose line of conduct is not to offend, but at any rate his life is not to be coveted; he is every moment on a precipice, and the least false step is sure to shatter his fame and fortune, and often his life. Only one thing can save him from absolute shame, and that is for an offence committed, an honourable concession...[104]

Thus was dueling proper countenanced—while dueling in excess, heat, and frivolity was condemned. In the context of the period, this was a markedly balanced, rather than contradictory, attitude towards the custom.

Irish law was considerably more tolerant in its attitude towards dueling than was the press. After a tour of Ireland during the late 1770s, Arthur Young remarked that "I believe it is a fact, at least I have been assured so, that no man was ever hanged in Ireland for killing another in a duel..."[105] Although duelists were, in fact, occasionally apprehended, in all instances wherein such combats were deemed to have been conducted fairly and according to the "laws of honour," the arrested combatant was acquitted—or, if a principal had been killed, the survivor was "found guilty of manslaughter in his own defence and set free." In less straightforward cases, offenders were frequently found guilty but then pardoned.[106] Oftentimes, such court cases ended up commending or even glorifying the surviving duelists. In 1769, for instance, *Freeman's Journal* reported,

> We hear from Ennis Assizes, that Massy Stackpoole, Esq., was tried for killing Mr. Hoops in a Duel, and acquitted with great honour to his character and conduct, by a most respectable Jury of the County of Clare.[107]

The sympathy shown by the courts to duelists was likely due, in part, to the fact that so many members of the bench were themselves former combatants. According to Jonah Barrington,

> The number of grave personages who appear to have adopted the national taste, though in most instances it was undoubtedly before their elevation to the bench that they signalised themselves in single combat, removes from me all imputation of pitching upon and exposing any unusual frailty; and I think I may challenge any country in Europe to shew such an assemblage of gallant judicial and official antagonists at fire and sword...in my time, the number of killed and wounded amongst the bar was very considerable.[108]

Barrington followed this observation with an extensive list of chief justices, judges, and attorneys who had all taken part in duels. A perfect example of one such "personage" was John Scott, who had fought at least four duels.[109] While serving as Ireland's Attorney-General from 1777 to 1782, Scott's stance on the custom and practice of dueling was decidedly moderate—no doubt informed by his own past experience. Scott explained,

There are cases where it may be, and when it is, prudent for a man to fight a duel—cases in which the law does not afford him redress—cases of persevering malignity, cases of injured honour, cases of a wounded spirit; and a wounded spirit who can bear? In cases of this complexion the Court will never interfere with its discretionary authority against a man.[110]

Scott would later, in 1793, be created 1st Earl of Clonmel, County Tipperary, and would greatly influence the development of bayonet fencing in Ireland.[111]

To further explicate and refine the procedure, etiquette, philosophy of the duel, a number of duelists (or defenders of dueling) published short essays on the code in various journals and magazines. The following article, which first appeared in 1769, gives one a more intimate sense of the notions of honor which informed the spirit and mindset of the duelist:

> *Thoughts on the Unwritten Laws of Honour.*
>
> S I R,
>
> BY the general consent of all the civilized nations in Europe, every gentleman, properly so called, is by the laws and rules of honour, either to act up to those laws and rules, on every important occasion throughout life, or to forfeit the name and character of a gentleman and man of honour irretrievably. These laws are unwritten, and therefore it is always pre-supposed, by every person calling himself a gentleman, that the code or pandect of these unwritten laws of honour have been inculcated into his heart, mind, and even into his very blood, from his earliest infancy. It is this inculcation, which, properly speaking, is termed a good or a refined education.
>
> By the laws of honour above-mentioned, every gentleman is strictly bound and enjoined not to receive a *lye* or a *blow* from any person whatever, that is to say, from the Sovereign under whom he is a subject, down to the meanest and most despicable man breathing, without resenting such indignity in the manner such indignity ought to be resented, under the pains and penalty of not being ever afterwards admitted into the company of gentlemen. By this doctrine, it should seem, that a gentleman who has not the spirit to resent so gross an insult, stands *ipso facto* as much and as effectually excommunicated out of the society of real gentlemen, as a leper stands excommunicated from the society of all his neighbours in general by the old Levitical law.[112]

Although the above code was likely written by an English author, the vast majority of duels recorded in Ireland echo its precepts—as can be observed in the following account of an Irish duel, fought in Dublin in 1719:

> Mr. Lee coming lately from the Country, went and paid a Visit to Mr. Smith, being well acquainted, and having something to inform him, concerning some Affairs of his in the Country, they went to a Tavern, and after a considerable Time, spent in Dispute they seem'd Friends, and went to the Four-Courts, after which, they went again and took a Bottle at a Tavern in Christ-

Church-Lane; where some People say, they fell out upon their former Story; and add, that it was about some Law Business, others affirm, their Quarrel was concerning the Character of a young Gentlewoman.

Mr. *Lee* us'd very scurrilous Language to Mr. *Smith*, who, rather than breed a Quarrel, told him, That he could not think a Gentleman of his Education, would be guilty of such ill Manners; but since he found him a Man so willing to give way to Passion, he would take his Leave of him, and wish'd him better Company.

Mr. *Lee*, finding Mr. *Smith* so desirous of Peace, imputed his Behaviour to Cowardice, and with great Scorn and Derision, drank to his Honour.

Mr. *Smith* finding, himself under a Necessity of Resentment, told him, That his Opinion was, that a Gentleman of Manners, was a Gentleman of Courage, and desir'd him to appoint the Place, where he expected Satisfaction; upon which, they agreed to go to the *Tholsel**, it being past Change Time: They immediately went, and as soon as they enter'd, they drew, and the second Pass, Mr. *Smith* ran Mr. *Lee* thro' under his right Breast, who immediately fell, and lies now in the *Tholsel*.

Mr. Smith made his escape, and is not as yet taken.[113]

It should be noted that, despite the frequently violent outcomes of such encounters, the ultimate object of the duelist was not necessarily to kill or even injure his adversary. A short code on the duel, published in 1779, gives further insight into this concept:

> In fighting with the *sword*, a *blow*, or the *lie direct*, can scarcely be expiated but by a thrust through the body; but any lesser affront may be wiped off by a wound in the *sword arm*; or, if the injury be very slight, any wound will be sufficient. In all this, it is to be noted, that the receiving of such wound by either party constitutes reparation for the affront; as it is a rule of justice peculiar to the *Code of duelling*, that the blood of the injured atones for the offence he has received, as well as that of the injurer for the offence he has given.[114]

The European custom was, in a great sense, about showing up, and exposing one's own life to the hazard of a potentially lethal combat, or to the possibility of such a combat—thus proving that the participant considered his honor to be more important than his life. This aspect of dueling also explains why so many adversaries became close friends after surviving potentially deadly combats with each other. Jonah Barrington explained that the Irish duelist "respected the courage which aimed at his own life," and further noted,

---

\* *Tholsel*: derived from the Middle English *tolsell*. A public building, originally erected for the purposes of collecting taxes.

It is, in fact, incredible what a singular passion the Irish gentlemen (though in general excellent-tempered fellows) formerly had for fighting each other and immediately making friends again. A duel was indeed considered...by no means a ground for future animosity with his opponent.[115]

At the heart of the duel also lay the concept of fairness, or equitability, wherein the conditions ensured that both principals had an equal opportunity for victory or defeat.[116] In such a combat, it was forbidden to take any "mean" advantage over an adversary. To do otherwise would be to admit one's own dishonorable nature, and to suffer public and personal disgrace. Several Irish anecdotes illustrate this concept with particular vividness. The first, concerning a disabled (but most determined) duelist, was reported in 1783:

Mr. D'Arcy of Galway is a very singular character: he unites a fund of humour and sound sense, to true Hibernian dialect and courage. In the last Galway election he had a dispute with a young gentleman, whom he challenged. As a duel is not to be avoided in that field of Mars, the gentleman alleged they should meet on very unequal terms, as Mr. D'Arcy, who has not the use of his limbs, is carried about from place to place in the arms of chair-men, and hoped he would desire any of his friends to meet him in this place. D'Arcy swore it never was his mode of fighting, nor that of his country, to do it by proxy, and insisted that he must meet himself. His adversary finding no alternative, went to the ground at the appointed hour, where he found Mr. D'Arcy seated in his arm-chair, anxious for the combat. His adversary again struck with the disparity, and determined not to be out-done in spirit, dispatched his second for another arm-chair, and in that sedantary posture they fought, till after some shots the matter was happily adjusted.[117]

A second anecdote which demonstrates the concept of fairness took place one year later, in 1784, and concerns the duelists' comparative skill with the chosen weapons:

On Sunday morning a duel was fought between a student at law from Ireland, and a Scotch physician. An argument on the propositions was the cause of the quarrel. They measured no ground. The Scotchman fired first, and wounded his antagonist in the hip. The Irishman then fired and wounded his adversary in the neck, over the collar-bone; the Scotchman, with his second shot, wounded the Irishman in the breast. The Irishman now observed, that though he had a right to break ground and advance, he would not avail himself of that advantage; and throwing his pistol on the ground, drew his sword. The Scotchman refused to draw. You have had, said he, my life in your power, and I cannot use the advantage I have now over you. I know you cannot fence, whereas I am a master of the science. The seconds interposed—the combatants shook hands, and the principle of generosity displayed by them had such an effect, that the whole party burst into tears. We are happy to find the wounds were so slight, there is no apprehension of bad consequences.[118]

Another anecdote was recounted by Joseph Hamilton during the early nineteenth century, and probably refers to an eighteenth century incident:

At a small town in Ireland, a young fellow had reduced his pistol to so great a certainty, that he boasted he could snuff his candle at ten yards. This, however, did not (on a proper occasion,) prevent a very bulky man from calling him out. They were placed by the Seconds at the distance of ten yards, and were ordered to fire by signal when, after the discharge of two shots each, the affair was settled without any accident. On their return, the friend of the candle-snuffer could not help asking him, "How he that hit a candle at the same distance, could miss so great a mark?" The answer was truly candid:—"My dear Jack, I knew the candle could not fire at me."[119]

The mention of an overweight duelist recalls a particular paragraph of the 1779 code, which reads as follows:

In affairs decided with pistols, the distance is, in like manner, to be regulated by the nature of the injury. For those of an atrocious sort, a distance of only twenty feet, and pistols of nine, nine and a half, or ten inch barrels, are requisite; for slighter ones, the distance may be doubled, and a six, or even five inch barrel will serve. Regard, moreover, is to be had to the size of the persons engaged; for every stone above eleven the party of such weight may, with perfect honour, retire three feet.[120]

So important was the dueling ethos in Ireland, that it was there that the most notable English-language dueling code of the eighteenth century would be authored—one that would influence the custom, as well as its chroniclers, in Great Britain and America for more than a century to come.

## WEAPONS OF THE IRISH DUEL

During the eighteenth century, duels in Ireland were fought primarily with the small-sword, rapier, broadsword, and pistol. Sometimes the sword and pistol were used in combination, and, occasionally, combats were fought on horseback. Irish dueling weapons were often treated with reverence by their owners, and were passed down within families from generation to generation. Jonah Barrington recounted:

Every family then had a case of hereditary pistols, which descended as an heirloom, together with a long, silver-hilted sword, for the use of their posterity...The family rapier was called "skiver the pullet" by my grand-uncle, Captain Wheeler Barrington, who had fought with it repeatedly, and run through different parts of their persons several Scots officers, who had challenged him all at once for some national reflection. It was a very long, narrow-bladed, straight cut-and-thrust, as sharp as a razor, with a silver hilt and a guard of buff leather inside it. I kept this rapier as a curiosity for some time; but it was stolen during my absence at Temple.[121]

Likewise, according to oral tradition in County Clare,

It was usual for every respectable family to have, as its most cherished possessions, pistols and swords that were used in [dueling]. They were always kept clean and oiled. The handles were often notched, telling the number of encounters they were in.[122]

During the nineteenth century, Samuel Carter Hall, of Waterford, similarly remarked, "At Castlebar [in County Mayo] I was shown a pistol marked with seven notches—each notch indicated that it had sent a bullet into an adversary."[123]

Prior to 1750, the sword was the most popular weapon of choice in Irish duels; afterwards, the pistol came to predominate, although sword-duels still remained fairly common.[124] In 1782, a poet published a series of stanzas criticizing a prominent Dublin producer of dueling pistols, lauding the sword as a more humane weapon:

*Some room is left to shew the fencer's art;*
*Honour more often than revenge is sought;*
*The pistol aims directly at the heart;*
*No pow'r of saving when the battle's fought.*[125]

One of the most unusual combination of weapons to be used in a duel occurred in 1759, and is also related by Barrington. In this brutal combat—said to be fought in the old Irish tradition—the participants were armed with swords, daggers, and pistols, and began their fight on horseback. Later, when one of the duelists was unhorsed, the combat continued on foot. Barrington's account begins thus:

The ancient mode of duelling in Ireland was generally on horseback. The combatants were to gallop past each other at a distance marked out by posts, which prevented a nearer approach: they were at liberty to fire at any time from the commencement to the end of their course; but it must be at a hand-gallop: their pistols were previously charged alike with a certain number of balls, slugs, or whatever was most convenient, as agreed upon...

My grandfather, Colonel Jonah Barrington of Cullenaghmore, had a great passion for hearing and telling stories as to old events, and particularly as to duels and battles fought in his own neighbourhood or by his relatives; and as these were just adapted to make impression on a very young curious mind like mine, at the moment nearly a carte blanche (the Arabian Nights for instance, read by a child are never forgotten by him), I remember, as if they were told yesterday, many of his recitals and traditionary tales, particularly those he could himself attest; and his face bore, to the day of his death, ample proof that he had not been idle amongst the combatants of his own era.

The battle I remember best, because I heard it oftenest and through a variety of channels, was one of my grandfather's about the year 1759. He and a Mr. Gilbert had an irreconcilable grudge; I forget the cause, but I believe it was a very silly one. It increased, however, every day, and the relatives of both parties found it must inevitably end in a combat, which, were it postponed till the sons of each grew up, might be enlarged perhaps from an individual into a regular family engagement. It was therefore thought better that the business should be ended at once, and it was decided that they should fight on horseback on the green of Maryborough; that the ground should be 100 yards of race and eight of distance; the weapons of each, two holster pistols, a broad-bladed but not very long sword—I have often seen my grandfather's, with basket handle, and a skeen* or long broad-bladed dagger; the pistols to be charged with one ball and swan-drops.

The entire country for miles round attended to see the combat, which had been six months settled and publicly announced, and the county trumpeter who attended the judges at the assizes was on the ground. My grandfather's second was a Mr. Lewis Moore, of Cremorgan, whom I well recollect; Gilbert's was one of his own name and family—a captain of cavalry.

All due preliminaries being arranged, the country collected and placed as at a horse-race, and the ground kept free by the gamekeepers and huntsmen mounted, the combatants started and galloped towards each other. Both fired before they reached the nearest spot, and missed. The second course was not so lucky. My grandfather received many of Gilbert's shot full in his face; the swan-drops penetrated no deeper than his temple and cheek-bones, the large bullet fortunately passed him. The wounds, not being dangerous, only enraged old Jonah Barrington, and the other being equally willing to continue the conflict, a fierce battle hand to hand ensued; but I should think they did not close too nearly, or how could they have escaped with life?

My grandfather got three cuts, which he used to exhibit with great glee—one on the thick of the right arm, a second on his bridle-arm, and the third on the inside of the left hand. His hat, which he kept to the day of his death, was also sliced in several places; but both had iron skull-caps under their hats, which probably saved their brains from remaining upon the green of Maryborough.

Gilbert had received two pokes from my grandfather on his thigh and his side, but neither dangerous. I fancy he had the best of the battle, being as strong as and less irritable than my grandfather, who, I suspect, grew towards the last a little ticklish on the subject; for he rushed headlong at Gilbert, and instead of striking at his person, thrust his broadsword into the horse's body as often as he could, until the beast dropped with his rider underneath him; my grandfather then leaped off his horse, threw away his sword, and putting his skeen or broad dagger to the throat of

---

\*   *Skeen*: An anglicization of *scian* (pl. *sceana*), Irish for "knife."

Illustration of the duel between Colonel Jonah Barrington and Gilbert, from the title page of Sir Jonah Barrington's *Personal Sketches of His Own Times*.

Gilbert, told him to ask his life or die, as he must do either one or the other in half a minute. Gilbert said he would ask his life only upon the terms that, without apology or conversation, they should shake hands heartily and be future friends and companions, and not leave the youths of two old families to revenge their quarrel by slaughtering each other. These terms being quite agreeable to my grandfather, as they breathed good sense, intrepidity, and good heart, he acquiesced, and from that time they were the most intimately attached and joyous friends and companions of the county they resided in.[126]

## DUELING GROUNDS IN IRELAND

In the year 1788, the following extraordinary account appeared in the pages of a London periodical:

A gentleman, whom business of consequence compelled to visit Ireland, was tired with a long walk through the streets of Dublin, when a Coffee-house opportunely presented itself to his view, into which as he entered a man, of a martial appearance, who was talking to a waiter, immediately attracted his attention, in the course of whose conversation he overheard him enquire if there had been any sport there, and the waiter's reply to this effect:

"O, no, Captain, no *fun at all,* since the death of Fitzgerald, (it is a pity he was not suffered to escape, to keep up the breed of Duellists) to be sure we have had a little *popping,* but only two men killed for this last six months."

It is natural to suppose, that the Englishman, who had not much relish for *fun* of this sort, was not altogether free from apprehensions of this terrifick votary of Mars, which he soon terminated, by abruptly leaving the room. Upon a description of the place when he returned to his lodgings, he was informed it was called *Lucas's Coffee House,* where gentlemen, who had more hot blood in their veins, than brains in their heads, might be accommodated with an opportunity of trying their courage *gratis,* with an elegant assortment of various weapons, and the strictest secrecy to be depended upon, where men of *honor* resorted every morning, equally prompt to attend as seconds, or be engaged as principals; or should the combatants selfishly choose to have all the *fun* to themselves, they would still, with the strictest *honor,* guard them from interruption. The Englishman was astonished to hear a meaning appropriated to *fun,* which he, although coming from its favourite residence, had hitherto been unacquainted with...[127]

Although the story is a colorful one, it is either embellished to the point of inaccuracy, or fabricated. George Robert Fitzgerald had died in 1786, nearly twenty years after the closing of Lucas's Coffee-House, and so the waiter's comment about his death could not have occurred in that time and place. The tale is, however, illustrative of the immense legend and reputation that had already grown around this very real dueling ground—one of Dublin's most popular. Since the very beginning of the eighteenth century, Lucas's had been "one of the most fashionable places of public resort in Dublin," where, over coffee and glasses of cherry brandy, Dublin duelists, dressed in splendid ruffled finery, met to gamble, converse, and engage in single combat. In 1706 it was described:

At noon Lucas's was usually crowded by the city beaux; dressed in all that was fine and gay, with prim queues or martial Eugene wigs, bugled waistcoats, Steinkirk breast ruffles, and gold clocks in their silk stockings, they strutted about the coffee-house, read the newspapers, sipped coffee, rolled to the park or playhouse in a chair or coach and six, and passed a part of their evenings either in the galleries of the houses of parliament or in the theatres, where the stage was thronged with them on benefit nights; and the sober citizens complained that even at divine service they were distracted by those extravagant *petit maitres*.

It was in the yard behind Lucas's to which "fiery disputants" retired to "settle their differences in a hostile manner." During these combats, according to one early history of Dublin,

> The company flocked to the windows to see that the laws of honor were fully observed, and to bet upon the probable survivor of the infatuated men who were crossing their swords beneath in deadly combat; and when death terminated the encounter, the thoughtless spectators retired to discuss the relative qualities of their Margaux, Graves or Haut-brian claret, the then favorite wines.[128]

The press of the era is full of reports of duels at Lucas's. Following is but a sampling of contemporary notices, the first of which was published in 1725:

> They write from Dublin, That on the 12th instant, between seven and eight at Night, Captain Jones, on a Furlow from Port Mahon, and Mr. Nugent, a young Gentleman lately from the Temple, had some words as Lucas's Coffee-House, upon which they went into the Yard and drew, and the latter received a mortal Wound in his left Breast (he using his left Hand) and died instantly: They fought five Minutes: Captain Jones absconds, but tis believed would soon surrender.[129]

Another, from 1727, recounts:

> Last Night a Rencounter happen'd at Lucas's Coffee-House between Cornet Ayres and Quarter-Master Wills, both belonging to Colonel Stanhope's Regiment of Dragoons, now in our Barracks; in which the latter was wounded.[130]

Only one month later, another duel was fought at Lucas's.[131] In 1730, the *Intelligencer* railed against

> *Lucas's Coffee-House*, where the only Virtuosos of the gaming Science are daily and nightly to be seen. If *Blasphemy, Cursing, Swearing, Duelling, Running of Heads against the Wall, Throwing Hats and Wigs in the Fire, Distortions of the Countenance, Biting of Nails, Burning of Cards, Breaking of Dice-Boxes,* can be called a *Loss* of Temper, they are found in the aforesaid Places, in the highest Degree of Perfection. And to make out the last and greatest Loss, which is, *The Loss of Life.*[132]

Yet another news account, from 1748, reads:

Last Friday a Duel was fought between Mr. Mervyn and Mr. Hamilton, at Lucas's Coffee-House, in which Mr. Hamilton was mortally wounded.[133]

Additional duels at Lucas's were reported throughout the next twenty years.[134] Finally, in 1768, Lucas's was demolished to make way for Dublin's Royal Exchange. Its legend, however, would continue to endure. Five years later, in 1773, Horace Walpole yet wrote that "Persian princes love single combat as well as if they had been bred in Lucas's Coffeehouse."[135]

After the demise of Lucas's, a new resort was soon established for Dublin's duelists: Daly's Chocolate House, opened by Patrick Daly on Dame-street "early in the reign of George III." According to one Dublin journal,

it soon became the most famous establishment of its kind in Ireland, and was the usual resort of the nobility and members of parliament...strange anecdotes have been told of the various extraordinary scenes which were enacted at Daly's; the windows of some of the apartments are said to have been occasionally closed at noon, and deep gambling carried on by candlelight. As in Bath, it was not uncommon to see a gambler, suspected of cheating, flung out of one of the upper windows; and sanguinary duels were frequently fought in the precincts of the club-house.[136]

News of the combats at Daly's reached as far as London, where, in 1775, the *General Evening Post* reported:

*Dublin, Dec. 27.* On Friday night two gentlemen, Lieutenant F—— and Ensign C——, went to Daly's chocolate-house to play at hazard, when the Lieutenant having lost all his money, called to the Ensign to lend him part of what he had, which not being complied with, words arose, when they retired to the coffee-room, drew their swords, and Mr. F—— was run through the body, just under the breast, and expired immediately.[137]

In addition to serving as the setting for numerous *rencontres*, Daly's was the place where would-be duelists exchanged challenges and negotiated the terms of combat. Such duels were then often fought in nearby Phoenix Park or on St Stephen's Green. At least one such recorded incident at Daly's involved George Robert Fitzgerald.[138] Before its eventual disappearance, Daly's Chocolate-house was the last of Dublin's major interior dueling grounds.

Out in the sun, however, Ireland's most noted ground was undoubtedly Phoenix Park—a vast expanse to the west of the town, and to the north of the River Liffey. As described in the *Dublin Penny Journal,*

Who that has ever set foot on Irish soil, has but heard of the "*Phœnix Park*," with its *fifteen* acres of *fighting* ground, level as a bowling-green, and skirted on ever side with groves of hawthorn, beneath whose sheltering shadows so many *honourable men* have, from time to time, drawn the trigger, and, in the twinkling of an eye, sent into eternity, unblessed and unforgiven, so many of their fellow-creatures...The Phoenix Park derives its name and origin from a manor-house, on whose site the present Powder Magazine was erected in 1738. The manor was called in the Irish vernacular tongue *Fionn-uisge*, pronounced *Finniské*, which signifies clear or fair water, and which, articulated in the brief English manner, exactly resembled the word *Phœnix*...[139]

The newspapers of the eighteenth century are filled with reports of duels in Phoenix Park—the majority of which involved firearms, and oftentimes a combination of sword and pistol:

We are informed, that a duel was lately fought in Phoenix Park, between a gentleman of great fortune in the county of Carlow, and an officer of dragoons; the parties fired two pistols each, one of which wounded the officer in the breast, the seconds then interposed, and would have accommodated matters, but the principals being refractory, continued the engagement with their swords, till the officer ran his antagonist through the side, who was carried home without hopes of recovery.[140]

In addition to Phoenix Park, nearby Oxmantown Green, "an area of rough commonage to the northwest of the city, extending from today's Church Street as far as the Phoenix Park," was also the setting for occasional combats.[141] To the immediate south of the city, the field of Donnybrook fair was also used.[142] Within the heart of Dublin itself, St Stephen's Green Park was the most popular exterior dueling ground.[143] As early as 1734, we are told that

On Monday Morning last, a Duel was fought in Stephen's Green, between one Mr. Brown, of the County of Kilkenny, and one Mr. Doyle, both Attorneys: The former, I am informed, received a slight Wound under his Left-Breast, and in grappling at his Adversary's Sword, received a Cut in one of his Hands.[144]

Of the numerous combats which took place on St Stephen's Green, perhaps the most infamous was that which was fought in 1779 by George Robert Fitzgerald and Alexander "Buck" English, before a large crowd.[145]

Numerous dueling grounds also existed in Ireland's other counties. As early as 1698, a visitor named John Dunton wrote of a dueling ground located in County Fingal:

Most of our way to Malahide we kept near the sea, and on the left we were diverted with the agreeable prospect of several good houses and a fine grove called Clontarf Wood, a place where men of heat go to bleed one another in duels and those possessed with the gentler fire of love carry their mistresses to take the country air and find their names growing on the trees.

Galway's picturesque dueling ground: the field of *Gleann Gort an Airgid*, situated next to the medieval ruins of the Abbey of Roscam overlooking Oranmore Bay. *Photos courtesy of Ed Hannon, www.visionsofthepast.ie*

Clonmel, in County Tipperary, also contained a "favoured duelling ground" located on the "downstream side of the town" beside the river Suir, where "a boat was kept moored for the use of participants in case of a hasty withdrawal."[146] And in County Mayo, according to Samuel Carter Hall, a frequently-used ground was located near the city of Castlebar:

> It was, as any one familiar with the social history of that time is well aware, in Ireland, and among Irishmen, that the practice of duelling chiefly flourished. A mile or so out of Castlebar I stood in a field where it was stated to me that sixty fatal duels had taken place, the last being that of an uncle who had shot his nephew—or a nephew who had shot his uncle.

Hall, unfortunately, provided no further details regarding this ground's precise location.[147]

In County Galway, the most popular dueling ground was, reportedly, the field of *Gleann Gort an Airgid*, situated next to the picturesque medieval ruins of the Abbey of Roscam, overlooking Oranmore Bay.[148] Another frequented ground, known as the "Field of Mars," was located on the east side of Galway City, adjacent to Merlin Park.[149] This site was well-remembered by local residents as late as 1841, and was described by William Gregory (the husband of Lady Gregory) in his memoirs:

> The first year (1841) that I came to live at Coole, I rode one day into Galway. When I got to Merlin Park, I asked a countryman the name of the place, and found him, as one always finds Irish peasants, most agreeable and communicative.
>
> "I suppose you know all about that field?" he said, pointing to one opposite the wall of Merlin Park.
>
> "No," said I; "I am quite a stranger."
>
> "Well, sir," he said, "that's the place where the gentlemen of Galway used to fight their duels. Many's the duel I saw there when I was young, for I live quite convenient."
>
> "Did you ever see a real good duel?" I asked.
>
> "To be sure I did; and lots of them."

According to Gregory, another dueling ground was located at Portumna, in a "field on the other side of the Shannon, about half a mile from the bridge which connects Galway with Tipperary."[150]

Jonah Barrington mentions two traditional rural dueling grounds, both located in County Laois (at that time known as Queens County). The first was on the Down of Clopook, near the village of Luggacurren. The Down was surmounted by an ancient structure known as the Dun of *Cloch-an-Phúca*, a megalithic Hill Fort whose name roughly translates as "the fort of the Pooka's stone".[*] Barrington described it thus:

> There had been from time immemorial a spot marked out on level ground near the Down of Clapook, Queen's County, on the estate of my granduncle, Sir John Byrne, which I have often visited as classic ground. It was beautifully situated near Stradbally, and here, according to tradition and legendary tales, the old captains and chieftains used to meet and decide their differences. Often did I walk it over, measuring its dimensions step by step. The bounds of it are still palpable, about 60 or 70 steps long, and about thirty or forty wide large stones remain on the spot where, I suppose, the posts originally stood to divide the combatants, which posts were about eight or nine yards asunder, being the nearest point from which they were to fire. The time of firing was voluntary, so as it occurred during their course, and, as before stated, in a hand-gallop.

The second dueling ground mentioned by Barrington was contained within the Rock of Dunamase, a set of ruins situated quite close to Clapook atop a nearby hill:

Engraving of the *"Castle of Dunamase in the Queen's County."* According to Jonah Barrington, these "most beautiful...inland ruins" contained a traditional dueling ground.

---

[*] *Pooka*: From the Irish *púca*. A fairy creature from Irish folklore.

If the quarrel was not terminated in one course, the combatants proceeded to a second; and if it was decided to go on after their pistols had been discharged, they then either finished with short broadswords on horseback or with small swords on foot; but the tradition ran that when they fought with small swords, they always adjourned to the rock of Donamese, the ancient fortress of the O'Moors and the Princes of Offely. This is the most beautiful of the inland ruins I have seen in Ireland. There, in the centre of the old fort, on a flat green sod, are still visible the deep indentures of the feet both of principals who have fought with small rapiers and their seconds; every modern visitor naturally stepping into the same marks, the indentures are consequently kept up, and it is probable that they will be deeper one hundred years hence than they were a year ago.

Long after Barrington recorded these words, and newspaper reports of duels had been destroyed or locked away in library archives, the legends and lore surrounding Irish duelists and their combats continued to survive in oral tradition. Even as late as the twentieth century, references to minor dueling grounds can be found in scraps of local folklore, such as the following, recorded in Donegal:

There is a field on the road between Ballyshannon and Belleek. In this field there are two trees which are situated opposite each other and are equal distances from the center of it. This place was the field where there was a duel fought...Both men are buried in the graveyard of St Ann's church. The particulars are inscribed on the tombstone.[151]

Undoubtedly, many other dueling grounds existed in Ireland, whose names have now been lost to history.

## DOUBLE AND TRIPLE DUELS

A rare occurrence in Ireland, but one nonetheless worthy of mention, was the duel involving more than two principals. In continental Europe, during wartime, duels between rival regiments sometimes involved vast numbers of combatants, and the memoir of the Irish duelist Peter Drake includes an account of a duel concerning no less than fourteen principals, drawn up "in two Ranks, seven against seven," and in which Drake participated.[152] Although Drake's combat took place in France, duels involving more than two principals are recorded in Ireland as early as the seventeenth century—as are similar combats between Irish Catholic royalists stationed abroad.[153] Of the former, one particularly notable combat was a "triple duel" fought with swords near Phoenix Park, Dublin, in 1670:

To-day has produced news of a triple duel near the Phoenix Park—the Lord [William] Brabazon and Captain Savage (brother, I think, to the Earl of Rivers) who are captains of horse; [Colonel Fitzgerald] (the young Earl of Kildare's uncle), and Lieutenant Bridges, of the Royal Regiment, both of whom were dangerously wounded; Lieutenant Trevor Lloyd and Captain Slaughter, and Lloyd hath slain Slaughter. They all fell out at play last night at the Castle Tavern. I do not know what the result will be, but those that were not hurt are fled.

Regarding this duel's bloody outcome, another contemporary account relates that "Lord Brabazon, Mr. Fitzgerald and Mr. Slaughter were worsted...Fitzgerald is run through the body...Brabazon and Fitzgerald were wounded and Slaughter killed. Lloyd and Bridges were also wounded."[154]

During the next century, another incident of a duel involving four combatants took place in Dublin, and involved one Thomas Mathew—a native of of Tipperary, and a personal friend of Jonathan Swift. According to the author who originally related the story, the combat occurred "towards the latter end of Queen Anne's reign"— likely placing the date of this event between 1710 and 1714:

It was towards the latter end of Queen Anne's reign when Mr. Mathew returned to Dublin, after his long residence abroad. At that time party ran very high, but raged no where with such violence as in that city; insomuch, that duels were every day fought there on that score. There happened to be, at that time, two gentlemen in London who valued themselves highly on their skill in fencing; the name of one of them was Pack, the other Creed; the former a major, the latter a captain, in the army. Hearing of these daily exploits in Dublin, they resolved, like two knight-errants, to go over in quest of adventures. Upon enquiry, they learned, that Mr. Mathew, lately arrived from France, had the character of being one of the first swordsmen in Europe. Pack, rejoiced to find an antagonist worthy of him, resolved, the first opportunity, to pick a quarrel with him; and meeting him as he was carried along the streets in his chair, jostled the fore-chairman. Of this Mathew took no notice, as supposing it to be accidental. But Pack afterwards boasted of it in the public coffee-house, saying, that he had purposely offered this insult to the gentleman, who had not the spirit to resent it. There happened to be present a particular friend of Mr. Mathew's, of the name of Macnamara, a man of tried courage, and reputed the best fencer in Ireland. He immediately took up the quarrel, and said, he was sure Mr. Mathew did not suppose the affront intended, otherwise he would have chastised him on the spot; but if the major would let him know where he was to be found, he should be waited on immediately on his friend's return, who was to dine that day a little way out of town. The major said, he should be at the tavern over the way, where he and his companion would wait their commands. Immediately on his arrival, Mathew, being made acquainted with what had passed, went from the coffee-house to the tavern, accompanied by Macnamara. Being shewn into the room where the two gentlemen were, after having secured the door, without any expostulation, Mathew and Pack drew their swords; but Macnamara stopped them, saying, he had something to propose before they proceeded to action. He said, in cases of this nature, he could never bear to be a cool spectator: 'So, Sir,' addressing himself to Creed, 'if you please, I shall have the honour of entertaining you in the same manner.' Creed, who desired no better sport, made no other reply than that of instantly drawing his sword; and to work the four champions fell, with the same composure, as if it were only a fencing match with foils. The conflict was of some duration, and maintained with great obstinacy by the two officers, notwithstanding the great effusion of blood from the many wounds they had received. At length, quite exhausted, they both fell, and yielded the victory to the superior skill of their antagonists.— Upon this occasion, Mathew gave a remarkable proof of the perfect composure of his mind during the action. Creed had fallen the first: upon which Pack exclaimed, 'Ah, poor Creed! are you gone?' 'Yes,' said Mathew, very composedly, 'and you shall instantly *pack* after him,' at the same time making a home thrust quite through his body, which threw him to the ground. This was the more remarkable, as he was never in his life, either before or after, known to have aimed at a pun.

The number of wounds received by the vanquished parties was very great; and what seems almost miraculous, their opponents were untouched. The surgeons, seeing the desperate state of their patients, would not suffer them to be removed out of the room where they fought, but had beds immediately conveyed into it, on which they lay many hours in a state of insensibility. When they came to themselves and saw where they were, Pack, in a feeble voice, said to his companion, 'Creed, I think we are conquerors, for we have kept the field of battle.' For a long time their lives were despaired of, but, to the astonishment of every one, they both recovered. When they were able to see company, Mathew and his friend attended them daily, and a close intimacy afterwards ensued, as they found them men of probity, and of the best dispositions, except in the Quixotish idea of duelling, whereof they were now perfectly cured.[155]

Pistol duels involving more than two combatants also took place. The following example involved four combatants, including "old John Bourke, of Glinsk" and Amby Bodkin:

They fought near Glinsk, and the old family steward and other servants brought out the present Sir John, then a child, and held him upon a man's shoulder, to see papa fight. On that occasion, both principals and seconds engaged: they stood at right angles, ten paces distant, and all began firing together on the signal of a pistol discharged by an umpire. At the first volley, the two principals were touched, though very slightly. The second volley told better;—both the seconds, and Amby Bodkin, Esq. staggered out of their places: they were well hit, but no lives lost. It was, according to custom, an election squabble.[156]

Notably, Bodkin—as shall be seen—would further impact the history of Irish dueling by assisting in the creation of Ireland's first official dueling code.

## IRISH DUELS RUN AMOK

Ideally, all duels were supposed to be conducted in a manner which faithfully adhered to the strict set of rules and procedure contained in the unwritten laws of honor. However, in actual practice, for a variety of reasons, such adherence did not always occur—occasionally resulting in unnecessary brutality and disastrous accidents. The most frequent causes of such calamities were the selection of incompetent seconds, the complete absence of seconds (thus relegating the combat to a *rencontre*), and an insufficient knowledge of rules and procedure. An early account of one such incident was set down in 1725, and reads as follows:

DUBLIN, August 21.

Last Week a Duel was fought at Birr in the King's County [Offaly], between —— Eyres, Esq; of the Family of Eyres-Court, and —— Moore, Esq; of the County of Gallway: The Quarrel begun about some Reflections made by the former to the Disadvantage of Mr. Moore, the Words were spoken to Mr. Armstrong, a Gentleman of that Country, who resented the Affront in Favour of Mr. Moore, and told him thereof; upon which, a Challenge was sent to Mr. Eyres, who met his Antagonist accordingly with a Gentleman along with him, and Mr. Moore brought the above-mentioned Mr. Armstrong as a Second. After several Thrusts were exchang'd, and desperate Wounds given on each Side; Mr. Moore had the Misfortune to fall on his Back, and Mr. Armstrong endeavouring to help him up, was ran through the Body (it is said) by Mr. Eyres, and died immediately.[157]

In the above case, it appears that one of the seconds was killed because proper dueling procedure had not been followed. During the next decade, an example of a similar outcome is recorded as having taken place at a castle in northern Cork:

1733, April 13, Castle Lyons. This day sevenight, a bloody action happened in the neighbourhood of Mitchelstown between one Newell, gamekeeper to Lord Kingston, & a son of the late Ned Raymond's, wherein the latter was slain. The cause of quarrel was about a greyhound, & so trivial as not worth naming. They entered the lists on horseback with sword & petronel, the former having discharged at & missed the latter, the other rid up to his breast but missed fire, whereupon he immediately dismounted & drew, as Newell did the like, & having made some *sasas** at each

---

\* *Sasas*: A likely reference to the fencing vocalization, "sa-sa," made on a feint or attack, sometimes mentioned in eighteenth century literature: *"Nimblewrist:* That was a home thrust!—Good sir, I hope you're for a breathing this morning? - [*Takes down a foil.*] I'll assure you, Mr. Mockmode, you will make an excellent swordsman; you're as well shaped for fencing as any man in Europe. The duke of Burgundy is just of your make; he pushes the finest of any man in France.—Sa! sa!—like lightning." *The Dramatic Works of Wycherley, Congreve, Vanbrugh, and Farquhar* (London: George Routledge and Sons, 1871), 493. For more details on fencing vocaliza-

other, both received some slight wounds, but still the combat lasted, till at length one of Raymond's spurs got hold of his stockings, whereby he fell on his face to the ground, at which the other stabbed him through the back, & not long after expired.[158]

Such an outcome could have been prevented by the involvement of competent and attentive seconds, whose duty it was to vigilantly ensure fair play and the protection of their respective principals. Such *rencontres*—fought without the presence of seconds—were especially dangerous, as the participating principals essentially placed all trust in their adversaries to behave honorably, and engaged in potentially deadly combat without any possible safeguards. Not all who entered into *rencontres* had honorable intentions, and, as a result, disaster sometimes ensued. A vivid example can be found in a duel involving John "Jack the Buck" Geoghegan of Westmeath and an unscrupulous Frenchman. According to one account,

These two...quarreled about their lady-love in the saloon of Covent Garden Theatre one night. The Frenchman challenged Geoghegan, who had used some violence towards him. The challenge was accepted; and both being armed, as was the fashion at that period, they agreed to meet at the portico of St. Paul's Church, Covent Garden, immediately after the play. They then separated; Geoghegan re-entered the house, and the Frenchman went home.

At the appointed time the adversaries met, drew their swords, and engaged. Geoghegan parried a thrust, and made sure of his man; but instead of entering it, his sword broke on the breast of his antagonist, who ran him through the body. In falling, Geoghegan grappled with, but was unable to hold him. With the stump of his sword, however, he scored him down the back.

On leaving the theatre, the Frenchman had gone home and put on a "prudence," something like a quire of paper in the shape of a cuirass. Geoghegan recovered from the wound, but it was the remote cause of his death.[159]

Perhaps the most brutal Irish *rencontre* with swords, however, took place in 1781 in Cork. According to a local historical journal:

Here follow the facts. Captain Robert Hickson, of a line regiment, a Kerryman, and a fine fellow of six feet in height, and altogether of a very commanding and soldierly appearance, was on a visit at that time with his uncle, George Hickson, then a resident in Cork city. He had a great reputation as an expert swordsman, and at that period there was in Cork a gentleman called Brereton, also a noted swordsman and duellist. Brereton, confident of his own skill with his weapon, it appears, was in the habit of picking quarrels with men, in order to provoke them into duelling with him. Hearing, therefore, of Captain Hickson's reputation, he sought him out with the same

---

tions, see Remarks 33 and 66 of *A Few Mathematical and Critical Remarks on the Sword*, presented in Part II of this book.

purpose in view. They met in a coffee house in Brown Street, and were, unfortunately, unaccompanied by any friends at the time. Brereton at once accosted Hickson thus, "I presume you are Hickson, of whom I have heard so much," and Hickson having replied in the affirmative, Brereton at once challenged him there and then to combat. The duel was fought under very terrible, even savage, circumstances, for, Captain Hickson having accepted the challenge, they locked the door of the room in which they were, charging the waiter to admit no one. Both were armed with swords, as was then the custom with gentlemen, and in this case there were no seconds. Captain Hickson, at the beginning of the duel, was pressed very hard by the consummate sword-play of his adversary, Brereton, and was obliged for a considerable time to remain on the defensive. At last, however, while still retiring before his adversary, he made a pass which proved fatal, as he ran Brereton right through the body, who, falling on the floor, called out, "Hickson, you have killed me." Hickson supported him in his arms, saying, "Brereton, Brereton, are you dead?" but there was no voice, nor any that answered. The one thrust had proved fatal.[160]

A contemporary news report, published immediately following the duel, gave a much different account of the combat:

The Duel was in a publick Room of that City [Cork], and they fought till Hickson, by a back-handed Stroke, had almost severed Brereton's Head from his Body.[161]

Two weeks later, an anonymous writer called this account a "gross absurdity" and asserted that the alleged "stroke" could not have occurred, as small-swords were not capable of delivering such cuts:

A correspondent, to this paper, wishes to know, from the impartial narrator of Mr. G. Brereton's *duel*, in what kind of form that *small sword* was made which could carry an *edge*, so as to fracture a skull.[162]

However, no account of the duel actually specified the use of small-swords, and, according to the *Journal of the Cork Historical and Archaeological Society*, "the sword which [Hickson] used in this fatal encounter with Brereton was 'a cut and thrust,' and was bequeathed by him to his cousin, Robert Hickson, of Tralee." According to this source, Hickson escaped to Kerry, rejoined his regiment, later settled in Tralee, and was not "afterwards troubled by any legal procedure or prosecution because of the duel." However, all legal issues aside, the combat's lack of proper etiquette and procedure continued to haunt the Hickson family in other ways:

Ever after the duel [Hickson] was known as Brereton-Hickson, and for a long time great enmity existed between the people of Cork and Kerry because of it; so much so, that many of the latter were afraid to go to Cork city on business. It seems that nothing could persuade the Corkmen that Brereton had not been unfairly killed; but, apparently, he had brought his death upon himself. He was on his own ground; he was the aggressor; and was a party to, if not even the proposer, of the dreadful conditions of fighting without seconds.

According to the journal's account, this accusation of "foul play" was so often repeated, "that at length Captain Hickson's brother, George, and his cousin, Robert, offered to fight any two Corkmen who maintained it, on the bounds of the two counties, a challenge which was not accepted."[163]

Duels with pistols were subject to similar outcomes. Of these, several accounts are provided by Abraham Bosquett—who, after the turn of the century, published his own dueling code, *The Young Man of Honour's Vade-Mecum*.[164] Bosquett hailed from the Dublin area, where he lived throughout the 1780s, eventually relocating to England some time prior to 1798.[165] In his treatise on dueling, Bosquett recounted the disastrous mistakes that resulted from inattention to proper dueling procedure:

I was present on an occasion when the Principal shot his own Second through the cheek, knocking in one of his double teeth, not by the ball, but by a part of the pistol barrel, that was blown out near the muzzle. I was also on the ground when a Principal shot himself through his foot, at the instep, which nearly cost him his life, but put an end to farther proceedings at the moment; his Second had given him his pistol at full cock, with a hair trigger, which he held dangling at his side, before the word was given, and in that position it went off. On another occasion the Second had charged his friend's pistol so carelessly, that the ball and powder had fallen out before he presented; when, but not till after receiving the opposite fire, snapping, and burning prime, (the matter being then accommodated) he discovered, on making several attempts to discharge his pistol in the air, that it was unloaded.

It frequently occurs also that the flints are so badly adjusted, and so bad in themselves, through the ignorance or inattention of the Seconds, and the pistols so much out of order, that the Principal, who is subject to such remissness in his friend, often stands in a very awkward and precarious state. I have known a pistol snapped a dozen times before it went off, though the flint was often chipped; this was putting a man in serious apprehensions of his life, eleven times oftener than he expected. It is no unusual case that a pistol hangs fire, due to the dampness of the powder, or foulness of the touch-hole, by which you always lose your aim, and of course, your fire, and it may be your life.

Throughout much of his book, Bosquett also warned of the dangers inherent in selecting seconds who were not fully versed in—or faithful to—the dueling code. He related the following anecdote:

Two learned doctors, who had had a long paper war, met one evening in the pit of one of the Dublin Theatres, where their resentments burst out, with reciprocal violence, between each act. Both were men of abilities, and extremely eloquent, and afforded, by these interludes, much entertainment to the audience, who clapped the victors of the moment in proportion to the impression they had made. My friend, who sat near me, had rather the advantage; but, on the curtain dropping, was called upon by his adversary to meet him at an early hour next morning, at the four-mile stone on the north road, and immediately withdrew. This seemed to stun my friend a little, who had not before been concerned in an affair of honour of this nature. However, he determined to fight, finding it could not be avoided; the other having publicly declared, he would post him if he did not. In consequence of this, he requested me to be his Second, to which I consented, in the hope of being able to reconcile the parties; and if not, at least to protect him from any undue advantage that might be taken of him, he being an Englishman, a stranger, and quite a novice in the duelling art...I therefore took my friend into training during the night, prepared the pistols, aired the powder, and gave him the necessary cautions and instructions, which should be accurately understood, both offensively and defensively, and which generally afford to the experienced duellist a decided advantage.

We got to the ground at six, the hour appointed, and shortly after the others arrived; the Second was the same I expected. After a distant salute I took him aside, and observed, that it was rather unfortunate that we had not had an opportunity of talking the affair over before we came there; but that, as it was not of a desperate nature, a mere war of words, I conceived it might be as much to their honour to make a mutual apology as to fight; when he immediately vociferated, that he would not consent that his friend should either give or take any apology; that they came there to fight, and that whilst a ball remained (pulling out a handful of bullets) or until one or the other fell, they would not quit the field. In this, however, his Principal did not second him. Whilst charging the pistols, our opponent's Second addressed himself to my friend in these words:—"Sir, I am glad to meet you here; I have an affair to settle with you the moment this is over, if you survive my friend;"— whom I immediately called forward, and told him the unmanly and infamous declarations his Second had made, whom, as it seemed, he had brought there with a view either to intimidate or assassinate my friend; but that, as I came there to protect him at all points, he must instantly take the ground with me, or immediately withdraw his declaration and apologize; the latter, by the advice of his Principal, who disapproved his conduct, he preferred.

We then proceeded to measure the ground, which he proposed to be seven yards, (vulgarly but incorrectly called paces.) In this, however, I over-ruled him, after much resistance, and placed them at twelve yards asunder. By agreement, they fired at the same moment, my friend's ball passing through the hat of his opponent, and his grazing the left jaw of my friend, and would certainly have broken both jaws, had he not given a full front face. After the first fire, I interfered again, and having made an impression, reconciled them, much to the visible dissatisfaction of my opponent, who had put the second pistol into the hands of his friend, exclaiming, that the town would call it a shabby business if they did not proceed. They made, notwithstanding, mutual apologies, shook hands, and ever after lived on a friendly and intimate footing.

These experiences made enough of an impression on Bosquett for him to declare that "in the variety of instances [in duels] which have occurred, where life has been lost, several shots exchanged, and the most dangerous wounds received, four fifths at least, of these duels might have been prevented, by a timely and judicious interference by qualified and well-disposed Seconds."[166]

Because of incidents such as the foregoing, it eventually became clear to Ireland's leading duelists that the unwritten laws of honor were no longer sufficient, and that, for the benefit of all prospective combatants, it was necessary to set down a code in writing.

## THE IRISH DUELING CODE OF 1777

Ireland's first official dueling code was originally written and compiled at Clonmel, County Tipperary, during the summer assizes of 1777, and was signed by Crow Ryan, Amby Bodkin, and James Keogh. Initially, the Clonmel code existed solely in the form of manuscript copies, which were privately distributed and circulated. Fifty years later, in 1827, the majority of the code was published in print for the first time when Jonah Barrington included it among his memoirs. In the pages of his work, Barrington introduced the code in the following manner:

A comprehensive code of the laws and points of honour was issued by the southern fire-eaters, with directions that it should be strictly observed by gentlemen throughout the kingdom, and kept in their pistol-cases, that ignorance might never be pleaded...These rules brought the whole business of duelling into a focus, and have been much acted upon down to the present day.

According to Barrington, the original code contained a total of thirty-six rules, which, consequently, became known in Galway as "the thirty-six commandments." Barrington, however, included only twenty-seven of these rules in his memoirs. No other copy or version of the 1777 code has ever been found, and the nine missing rules may now be presumed to be lost. Barrington explained the disparity between his own transcription and the original code as follows:

This code was not circulated in print, but very numerous written copies were sent to the different county clubs, etc. My father got one for his sons, and I transcribed most (I believe not all) of it into some blank leaves.

Sir Jonah Barrington (1757-1834), pictured in *The Rise and Fall of the Irish Nation*.

As transcribed by Barrington, the Clonmel code is succinct but comprehensive. It contains the rules and procedure governing the behavior of both principals and seconds, the sending and receiving of challenges, the selection of weapons, the choosing of ground, the positioning of combatants, the loading of firearms, the conditions pertaining to duels and *rencontres* with both swords and pistols, possible grounds for reconciliation, the resolution of disputes between seconds, and numerous other statutes.

Notably, the code also includes provisions forbidding techniques that had been utilized and abused by Ireland's most notorious duelist, George Robert Fitzgerald. During his pistol duels, Fitzgerald had often evaded his antagonists' shots by lunging and "shortening his person, as low as possible." Fitzgerald also had, in several known cases, taken an extra shot at his adversary, and afterwards claimed such shots to be accidental.[167] Thus, the creators of the code almost certainly had Fitzgerald in mind when they wrote the following rules:

> In all cases a miss-fire is equivalent to a shot, and a snap or a non-cock is to be considered as a miss-fire...
>
> No party can be allowed to bend his knee or cover his side with his left hand; but may present at any level from the hip to the eye.

Regarding the specific use of swords, the code noted that such combats were to be fought "side by side with five paces interval." The following directions were also included in Article five:

> If swords are used, the parties engage till one is well blooded, disabled, or disarmed; or until, after receiving a wound, and blood being drawn, the aggressor begs pardon.
>
> N. B.—A *disarm* is considered the same as a *disable*: the disarmer may strictly break his adversary's sword; but if it be the challenger who is disarmed, it is considered as ungenerous to do so.
>
> In case the challenged be disarmed and refuses to ask pardon or atone, he must not be *killed* as formerly; but the challenger may lay his own sword on the aggressor's shoulder, then break the aggressor's sword, and say, "I spare your life!" The challenged can never revive that quarrel—the challenger may.

Article twenty-five also made the following provision:

> In simple unpremeditated *rencontres* with the small sword, or *couteau-de-chasse*, the rule is—first draw, first sheathe; unless blood be drawn, then both sheathe, and proceed to investigation.

The code ended with the proviso that "all matters and doubts not herein mentioned will be explained and cleared up by application to the committee, who meet alternately at Clonmel and Galway, at the quarter sessions, for that purpose."

In his memoirs, Barrington also included several anecdotes of duels which illustrate the influence exerted by the code. The first concerned an affair of honor involving a friend of Barrington's; of especial interest in this account is the combatants' use of measure, as well as "feints" executed with pistols rather than swords:

> The Galway rule No 2. was well exemplified in a duel between a friend of mine, the present first counsel to the Commissioners of Ireland, and a Counsellor O'Maher. O'Maher was the challenger: no ground was measured; they fired *ad libitum*. G—y, never at a loss upon such occasions,

took his ground at once, and kept it steadily; O'Maher began his career at a hundred paces distance, advancing obliquely and gradually contracting his circle round his opponent, who continued changing his front by corresponding movements; both parties now and then aiming, as feints, then taking down their pistols. This *pas de deux* lasted more than half an hour, as I have been informed; at length, when the assailant had contracted his circle to firing distance, G—y cried out, suddenly and loudly, O'Maher obeyed the signal, and instantly fired, G—y returned the shot, and the challenger reeled back *hors de combat.*

One of Barrington's most detailed firsthand accounts of a duel illustrates the zealousness with which Irish duelists sometimes adhered to the code. The story concerns his own potentially deadly duel with Richard Daly, a well-known theater owner, whom Barrington described as "a young gentleman of Galway...[who] had the greatest predilection for single combat of any person, not a society fire-eater, I ever recollect: he had fought 16 duels in the space of two years—three with swords and 13 with pistols—yet with so little skill or so much good fortune that not a wound worth mentioning occurred in the course of the whole." To serve as his second in this duel, Barrington selected his friend Richard Crosbie, a "curious character" who was also the leader of a notorious Dublin gang known as the Pinking Dindies.[168] Barrington recounted:

I was surprised one winter's evening at college by receiving a written challenge in the nature of an invitation from Mr. Daly to fight him early the ensuing morning. I never had spoken a word to him in my life, and scarcely of him, and no possible cause of quarrel that I could guess existed between us. However, it being then a decided opinion that a first overture of that nature could never be declined, I accepted the *invitation* without any inquiry—writing in reply that as to place, I chose the field of Donnybrook fair as the fittest spot for *all* sorts of *encounters.* I had then to look out for a second, and resorted to a person with whom I was very intimate, and who, as he was a curious character, may be worth noticing. He was brother to the unfortunate Sir Edward Crosby, Bart., who was murdered by a court-martial at Carlow, May, 1798. My friend was afterwards called "Balloon Crosby," being the first aeronaut who constructed an Hibernian balloon, and ventured to take a journey into the sky from Ireland...

It was before seven o'clock on the 20th of March, with a cold wind and a sleety atmosphere, that we set out on foot for the field of Donnybrook fair, after having taken some good chocolate and a plentiful draught of cherry brandy, to keep the cold wind out. On arriving, we saw my antagonist and his friend, Jack Patterson, nephew to the chief justice, already on the ground. I shall never forget Daly's figure. He was a very fine looking young fellow, but with such a squint that it was totally impossible to say what he looked at, except his nose, of which he never lost sight. His dress—they had come in a coach—made me ashamed of my own: he wore a pea-green coat, a large tucker with a diamond brooch stuck in it, a three-cocked hat with a gold button-loop and tassels, and silk stockings, and a *couteau-de-chasse* hung gracefully dangling from his thigh. In fact, he looked as if already standing in a state of triumph, after having vanquished and trampled on his antagonist. I did not half-like his steady position, showy surface, and mysterious squint; and I certainly would rather have exchanged two shots with his slovenly friend, Jack Patterson, than one with so magnificent and overbearing an adversary.

My friend Crosby, without any sort of salutation or prologue, immediately cried out, "Ground, gentlemen ground, ground, ground! damn measurement!" and placing me on his selected spot, whispered into my ear, "*Medio tutissimus ibis*: never look at the head or the heels: *hip* the macca-roni! the hip for ever, my boy! hip, hip!"—when my antagonist's second, advancing and accosting mine, said, Mr. Daly could not think of going any further with the business; that he found it was totally a mistake on his part, originating through misrepresentation, and that he begged to say he was extremely sorry for having given Mr. Barrington and his friend the trouble of coming out, hoping they would excuse it and shake hands with him. To this arrangement, I certainly had no sort of objection; but Crosby, without hesitation, said, "We cannot do that *yet*, sir: I'll *show* you we *can't*," taking a little manuscript book out of his breeches pocket, "there's the *rules!* look at that, sir," continued he, "see No. 7: 'no apology can be received *after* the parties meet, *without a fire*.' You see, there's the rule," pursued Crosby, with infinite self-satisfaction; "and a young man on his *first blood* cannot break rule, particularly with a gentleman so used to the sport as Mr. Daly. Come, gentlemen, proceed! proceed!"

Daly appeared much displeased, but took his ground, without speaking a word, about nine paces from me. He presented his pistol instantly, but gave me most gallantly a full front.

It being, as Crosby said, my first blood, I lost no time, but let fly without a single second of delay, and without taking aim: Daly staggered back two or three steps, put his hand to his breast, cried, "I'm hit, sir!" and did not fire. Crosby gave me a slap on the back which staggered me, and a squeeze of the hand which nearly crushed my fingers. We got round him: his waistcoat was opened, and a black spot about the size of a crown-piece, with a little blood appeared directly on his breast-bone. I was greatly shocked: fortunately, however, the ball had not penetrated; but his brooch had been broken, and a piece of the setting was sticking fast in the bone. Crosby stamped, cursed the damp powder or under-loading, and calmly pulled out the brooch.

Daly said not a word, put his cambric handkerchief doubled to his breast, and bowed. I returned the salute, extremely glad to get out of the scrape, and so we parted without conversation or ceremony, save that when I expressed my wish to know the cause of his challenging me, Daly replied that he would *now* give no such explanation; and *his* friend then produced his book of rules, quoting No. 8: "If a party challenged accepts the challenge without asking the reason of it, the challenger is never bound to divulge it afterwards."[169]

So influential was Clonmel code, that, for the next one hundred years, it was widely quoted in both Irish and American dueling codes, as well as in virtually every nineteenth century English-language history of dueling.[170]

## THE NINETEENTH CENTURY TRANSITION

During the year 1798, all of Ireland was shaken by the outbreak of a massive rebellion led by the Society of United Irishmen, a nationalist revolutionary group seeking independence from Great Britain. Although primarily Protestant-led, the United Irishmen embraced a membership comprising Roman Catholics, and included Presbyterians, Methodists, Protestant dissenters, and even politically radical elements of the Anglo-Irish Ascendancy. Despite receiving external support from France, the 1798 rebellion was ultimately defeated, resulting in bloodshed and the deaths of its most prominent leaders. In its aftermath, the British government initiated the Acts of Union (1800), which united the Kingdoms of Great Britain and Ireland to create the United Kingdom. In effect from January 1st, 1801, the Acts introduced direct rule from London, and severely curtailed the political autonomy of the Anglican Protestant Ascendancy which had come to largely define Irish dueling culture towards the end of the eighteenth century. According to one historian, this "deprived the code of honour of one of its most important public stages," and the custom of single combat in Ireland thus arrived "past its zenith."[171] Although duels would still continue to be fought throughout the next century, by 1806, Sir John Carr could write that "the practice of duelling [here in Ireland]...is subsiding...military duels in Ireland are rare."[172] Three years later, author Richard Lovell Edgeworth similarly observed,

> Hibernian promptitude to duelling has so much diminished, that it has ceased to be a characteristic reproach or ridicule. Even in the county of Galway, which was formerly famous for such fighting gentlemen as *Blue-Blaze-Devil-Bob, Nineteen-Duel-Dick, Hair-Trigger-Pat,* and *Featherspring-Ned,* these formerly honourable agnomens would no longer be cited with triumph by ancient families; they are sinking fast into oblivion. There is no longer a class of men, who make a profession of duelling, though every now and then instances among fashionable loungers, or redhot politicians, of men, who, unable to keep their tempers, or to acquire notoriety by any better means, signalize themselves by firing shots at one another, in hopes of filling a paragraph in the newspapers of the day.[173]

In 1829, however, another Dublin author contrarily declared, "there is scarcely a single hour elapses without a hostile meeting in some part of the island," explaining that "comparatively few of the cases are recorded in the public journals."[174]

During the early nineteenth century, the sword became virtually unknown as a dueling weapon in Ireland, and was supplanted by the near-universal use of the pistol.[175] During the first decades of the century, Dublin author Joseph Hamilton, claiming thirty years of experi-

Frontispiece of Joseph Hamilton's *Some Short and Useful Reflections Upon Duelling* (1823).

ence "in the direction of both principals and seconds," published no less than five different versions of his treatise on dueling—in which he largely condemned the practice, and treated almost exclusively of pistol duels.[176] Likewise, in 1817, Abraham Bosquett—who had previously left Dublin for England—published his *Young Man of Honour's Vade-Mecum*, a text containing advice on dueling etiquette, safety, and procedure, as well as anecdotes of the author's duels in Ireland.[177] In 1820, while on his deathbed, Henry Grattan—one of Ireland's most famous politicians—reportedly uttered the following final advice to his son: "Always be ready with your pistol."[178]

At the same time, Irish renown for swordsmanship went into severe decline, and its once illustrious fencing academies all but disappeared.[179] Though Irish swordsmen would still continue to attain renown on the battlefields of Europe[180], the influence of Ireland's past greatness concerning the art of the sword would now be felt more through the activities of its emigrants and descendants, rather than through its residents. The former included the half-Irish Henry Angelo, as well as Sir Richard Francis Burton—whose father, the duelist Joseph Netterville Burton, hailed from Tuam, County Galway. While in England, the younger Burton would challenge a man to a duel for having disparaged his mustache[181], and would go on to author a number of important texts on the sword.[182] Throughout the first half of the nineteenth century, Major R. I. Dunn, a duelist and former Irish citizen, would open numerous fencing schools in America—in cities such as New Orleans, Virginia, Massachusetts, and Kentucky—where he offered instruction in weapons as diverse as the small-sword, broadsword, "cut-and-thrust", quarterstaff, and walking cane, and where he would publish two treatises on the use of the sword.[183] But it was, perhaps, another particularly celebrated soldier, duelist, and Dublin native who would, in 1817, offer the greatest final testimony to the Irish passion for dueling, swordsmanship, and for the small-sword in particular:

I conceive that nothing can be more desirable than to teach officers and soldiers the use of the sword. The want of the knowledge of the use of the sword has, to my certain knowledge, more than once made our officers appear to disadvantage in the broils which are not unfrequent with the French and other officers on the Continent. They are obliged to defer the settlement of the dispute till a pistol can be got; and the acknowledgment of the ignorance of the use of the weapon which every officer carries, besides being in itself degrading, is generally considered and taken as proof that our officer wishes to avoid the contest by him who is probably himself the most desirous of avoiding it. I therefore think the knowledge of the use of the sword, or the science of fencing, is essentially necessary to every officer who is to wear one…The knowledge gives suppleness and address to the body and limbs, and applies to the use of the broadsword; but everybody who knows what a sword is, is aware that a man with a broadsword has no chance with one who has a small sword. The very act of lifting up his arm to use the former, would give the opportunity to him who should know the use of the latter to run him through the body.

The author was Arthur Wellesley, better known to the world as the Duke of Wellington.[184]

---

1    John O'Keeffe, *Recollections of the life of John O'Keeffe*, *Volume 2* (New York: B. Blom, 1826), 137-138.

2    David Willis McCullough, *Wars of the Irish Kings* (New York: Three Rivers Press, 2002).

3    According to the medieval *Metrical Dindshenchas*, the custom of single combat was first brought to Ireland by Brea, son of Senboth: "The duel (not good the custom) was instituted by [Brea] the noble gracious son of Senboth." *The Metrical Dindshenchas* (Dublin: Dublin Institute for Advanced Studies, 1991). Numerous accounts of single combat in ancient and medieval Ireland can be found in the *Táin Bó Cúalnge*, *The Annals of the Four Masters*, *The Annals of Tigernach*, and Geoffrey Keating's *The History of Ireland*. Regarding Irish sword-use, see also comments by the Roman author Solinus, quoted in Patrick Weston Joyce, *A Social History of Ancient Ireland, Volume 1* (New York: Longmans, Green, and Co., 1903), 115.

4    In 1599, when Robert Devereux, 2nd Earl of Essex, encamped with his army on a hill in the province of Leinster, he was approached by rebel leader Ony mac Rury O'More, who "shewed himselfe with 500 foote and about 40 horse two myles from our campe." Rather than immediately engaging in the English in battle, O'More issued "a challeng which he had made a few daies before, to fight 50 of his with 50 of ours with sworde and target, which was consented unto by the lorde lieutenant." Richard Butler, *A Treatice of Ireland, by John Dymmok. Now first published from a MS. preserved in the British Museum, with Notes, by the Rev. Richard Butler, A. B., M. R. I. A. in Tracts relating to Ireland. Volume 2.* (Dublin, University Press, Graisberry and Gill, 1843), 32.

5    "A certeine combat was fought and tried before [the lord justices] in the castell of Dublin, beweene two Oconhours, verie neere coosens & kinsmen: the one was named Teig mac Guill Patrike Oconhour appellant; the

other was named Con mac Cormake Oconhour defendant. One of thest appealed and charged the other for sundrie treasons in the late rebellion, and which could have no other triall but by combat, which was granted unto them. Whereupon, according to the lawes and orders of England for a combat to be tried, all things were prepared, the daie, time, and place appointed; and according to the same, the lord iustices, the iudges, and the councellors came and sat in the place appointed for the same, ev erie man in his degree and calling. And then the court was called, and the appellant or plaintife was brought in before the face of the court, being stripped into his shirt, having onlie his sword and target (which were the weapons appointed) and when he had doone his reverence and dutie to the lord justices and to the court, he was brought to a stoole set in the one of the ends within the lists, and there sat. After him was the defendant brought in, in the like maner and order, and with the like weapons: and when he had doone his dutie and reverence to the lord justices and to the court, he was brought to his chaire placed in the other end of the lists. Then were their actions and pleadings openlie read, and then the appellant was demanded whether he would averre his demand or not? who when he had affirmed that he would, the partie defendant was likewise asked whether he would confesse the action, or stand to the triall of the same? who did answer as did the other, that he would averre it by the swoord.

"Upon this their severall answers, they were severallie called the one after the other, everie of them taking a corporall oth that their quarell was true, and that they would justi[...]e the same both with swoord & blood. Thus they being sworne are brought backe againe everie of them to their severall places as before. And then when by the sound of a trumpet a signe was given unto them when they should enter into the fight; they arose out of their seats, and met ech one the other in the middle within the lists, and there with the weapons assigned unto them, they fought: in which fight the appellant did prevaile, and he not onlie did disarme the defendant, but also with the sword of the said defendant did cut off his head, and upon the point of the same sword did present it to the lord justices, and so with the victorie of his enimie he was acquitted. Thus much I thought good to saie somwhat of much, of the maner of a combat, which together with manie circumstances thereunto belonging is now for want of use almost cleane forgotten, and yet verie necessarie to be knowne. And as for this combat it was so valiantlie doone, that a great manie did wish that it had rather fallen upon the whole sex of the Oconhours, than upon these two gentlemen." *Holinshed's Chronicles of England, Scotland and Ireland. In Six Volumes. Vol. VI. Ireland* (London: Printed for J. Johnson, F. C. and J. Rivington, 1808), 454-455.

6   For accounts of Irish duels which took place during the sixteenth and seventeenth centuries, see James Kelly, *That Damn'd Thing Called Honour* (Cork: Cork University Press, 1995), 24-35.

7   "Maolmordha O'Reilly (who married Catherine, daughter of Charles O'Reilly), was a very able captain and a celebrated partisan during the civil wars of 1643 in Ireland, and acquired the surname of 'Myles the Slasher.' In the year 1644, Lord Castlehaven, then commander of the Confederate Army of the North, encamped at Granard, in the county of Longford, having ordered Maolmordha, with a chosen detachment of horse, to defend the bridge of Fineaugh (Finia) against the attacks of the Scots, then bearing down on the main army with a very superior force. Maolmordha was slain, fighting bravely at the head of his troops, as a second Horatius Codes, in the middle of the pass.

"His body being found the next day among the slain was brought by his friends to Cavan, and interred with his ancestors in the monastery originally founded by them in that town...I was religiously brought up. Indeed, the slightest tendency towards scepticism or disrespect to the Sacred Writings would have afflicted my family, and would have been summarily reproved. I am not quite sure, nevertheless, that a lesser degree of punishment would have followed any doubt on my part of the achievements of 'Myles the Slasher.' Shall I confess, however, that it cost me an effort to believe the relation of his placing himself in the centre of the pass, and calmly waiting the approaching host, with the determination of Fitzjames...and of his standing erect within the gorge, and he with his single hand slaying in succession four and twenty of the assailants; and of the twenty-fifth—"A wary, cool, old sworder took, The blows upon his cutlass, and then His own put in—"and, raising himself in his stirrups, lunged at the neck of Myles. The Slasher, missing parry, dipped his head and caught within his teeth his adversary's sabre, and there held it as in a vice; then, raising his own powerful arm, he severed that of his antagonist which held the sword—the body of the maimed man falling over the bridge from a convulsive move-ment when struck.

"Myles, however, who would not evade the Hyrcan tiger's spring, was not proof against the shameless strat-agem to which the enemy resorted. Finding him unapproachable on level ground, they embarked a company of halberdiers in a boat at hand, and passing under the bridge compelled him with their pikes to quit his post, and he ultimately fell. The bridge was instantly traversed, and the battle gained." Andrew O'Reilly, *The Irish Abroad and at Home; at the Court and in the Camp. With Souvenirs of "The Brigade." Reminiscences of an Emigrant Mile-sian. Volume I* (London: Richard Bentley, 1853), 66-70. The source given by O'Reilly for this account is *The Genealogy of the very ancient and illustrious House of O'Reilly*, an eighteenth century manuscript, once in German hands, that has just recently been republished by Belfast's Linen Hall Library. A similar account of Myles "the Slasher," passed down through oral tradition, was recorded in 1938 by Gerard Reynolds, a resident of Balli-namore, County Leitrim. The Schools' Collection, Volume 225, Page 311. http://www.duchas.ie/en/cbes/4658448/4656848/4662046

8   The case identifying Lamport as the inspiration for of Zorro was first put forth by Professor Fabio Troncarelli of Tuscia University. This thesis is disputed by some scholars. Danilo H. Figueredo has listed many striking similarities between Lamport and Zorro in his *Revolvers and Pistolas, Vaqueros and Caballeros: Debunking the Old West* (Santa Barbara: Praeger, 2015). Historical figures such as Joaquin Murrieta, Salomon Pico, and Tiburcio Vasquez are also cited as inspirations for Zorro. According to author Gerard Ronan, who has written the most extensive biography of Lamport to date, "The most one can say about William Lamport is that his story may have played a part in the creation of Zorro." Gerard Ronan, *The Irish Zorro: The Extraordinary Adventures of William Lamport* (Dingle: Brandon, 2004), 289.

9   *All the Year Round*, May 10, 1862.

10   Joseph Hamilton, *The Only Approved Guide through all the Stages of a Quarrel* (London: Hatchard & Sons; Bentham & Co. Liverpool; and Millikin, Dublin, 1829), iv, 220.

11   Andrew Steinmetz, *The Romance of Duelling, Volume I* (England: Richmond Pub. Co, 1971), 48.

12   *Hibernia curiosa. A letter from a gentleman in Dublin, to his friend at Dover in Kent. Giving a general view of the manners, customs, dispositions, &c. of the inhabitants of Ireland. With occasional observations on the state of trade and agriculture in that kingdom. Collected in a tour through the kingdom in the year 1764.* (London: Printed for W. Flexney, 1769), 129-131.

13   "The Remarkable Anecdotes of Mr. Thomas Mathew" in *The Scots Magazine, Volume 47* (Edinburgh: Murray and Cochrane, 1785), 36-39.

14   This letter is dated October 1, and was written from Galway. *Hoey's Dublin Mercury*, November 8, 1770.

15   Charles Topham Bowden, *A Tour Through Ireland* (Dublin: W. Corbet, 1791), 25, 213.

16   Jonah Barrington, *Personal Sketches of His Own Times, Volume III* (London: Colburn and Bentley, 1832), 134-135.

17   For a full account of this individual (Christopher Perkins) and his battles with Figg, see Chapter III.

18   Donald McBane, *The Expert Sword-Man's Companion: Or the True Art of Self-Defence. With an Account of the Authors Life, and his Transactions during the Wars with France. To which is Annexed, the Art of Gunnerie* (Glasgow: J. Duncan, 1728), 128-129.

19   For a firsthand account of this episode, and for more information on Peter Drake, see Chapter II.

20   *The Hibernian Magazine, or, Compendium of Entertaining Knowledge*, December, 1773, 671.

21   John Edward Walsh, *Sketches of Ireland Sixty Years Ago* (Dublin: James McGlashan, 1847), 31.

22   Breandán Ó Buachalla, "Irish Jacobitism in Official Documents", in *Iris an dá chultúr*, Vol. 8 (1993), 128-138.

23   From the bilingual song *Siúil a Rún* (anglicized: "Shule Aroon") published in Charles Gavan Duffy, *The ballad*

*poetry of Ireland* (Dublin: J. Duffy, 1845), 130-131.

24  John Cornelius O'Callaghan, *History of the Irish Brigades in the Service of France, from the Revolution in Great Britain and Ireland Under James II, to the Revolution in France Under Louis XVI* (Glasgow: Cameron and Ferguson, 1883), 31.

25  *Journal of the Cork Historical and Archaeological Society, Vol. II, 2nd series* (Cork: Guy & Co., 1896), 278-279.

26  John Todhunter, *Life of Patrick Sarsfield, Earl of Lucan: With a Short Narrative of the Principal Events of the Jacobite War in Ireland* (London: T. F. Unwin, 1895), 8. Kelly, 31.

27  O'Callaghan, 177-178, 357-358, 366.

28  Colonel James E. McGee, *Sketches of Irish Soldiers in Every Land* (New York: J. A. McGee, 1873), 261-265.

29  See Chapter II for the details of the lives of Drake and Kirwan. For Macnamara, see Nottidge Charles Macnamara, *The story of an Irish sept: their character & struggle to maintain their lands in Clare* (London: J.M. Dent, 1896), 259. This last text quotes from a little volume, purportedly published about 1710 and entitled, *A Full Account of the Life of Thomas Macnamara*, which unfortunately not been met with.

30  William Edward Hartpole Lecky, *History of Ireland in the Eighteenth Century, Volume I* (London: Longmans, Green, 1913), 578-581.

31  Denys Scully, *A statement of the penal laws which aggrieve the Catholics of Ireland: with commentaries; in two parts* (Dublin: H. Fitzpatrick, 1812), 172-175.

32  Cornelius Nary, *The Case of the Roman Catholicks of Ireland humbly represented to both houses of Parliament* (Dublin: 1724), 124-25.

33  Lecky, *Volume I,* 470

34  Lecky, *Volume I,* 578-581.

35  Lecky, *Volume I,* 365.

36  Jonah Barrington, *Personal Sketches of his own Times, Vol. II* (Philadephia: Carey, Lea, & Carey, 1827), 7.

37  Lecky, *Volume I,* 578-581.

38  *By the Lords-Justices of Ireland: A Proclamation against Duelling. Charles Porter, Tho: Coningesby. His Majesty Being Informed That Heretofore Quarrels and Duels Have Frequently Happen'd between the Officers and Soldiers of the Army in This Kingdom* (Dublin: Printed by Andrew Crook assignee of Benjamin Took, printer to the King and Queens most excellent Majesties on Ormonde-Key, 1691).

39  Alexander Hay, "News of the Duels: Restoration Duelling Culture and the Early Modern Press", *Martial Arts Studies 3*, Cardiff University Press, Winter 2016, 89-102.

40  Kelly, 73-74, 81.

41  "It so happened that every new comer, friend or invader, adapted himself to the fashion of the natives, assuming the same love of battle, bloodshed, and rapine; he came not to teach, but to learn for the worse,—and so the foreigner was ever 'Ipsis Hibernis Hibernior.' It might be almost supposed that there was in the climate some predisposing cause for a propensity to pugnacity; for, let the immigrant be of what race he might—Belgic, Milesian, Danish, Norman, or English—he soon fell into the national vice, and became adapted to the land of Ire." *Dublin University Magazine*, v. 16, July 1840, 5-6.

42  Walsh states that Irish duels "extended through all classes." Walsh, *Sketches of Ireland Sixty Years Ago*, 31. James Kelly, in his wide-ranging modern study of Irish duels, states: "Observance of the code of honour in early eighteenth-century Ireland was not confined to the Protestant landed elite which provided the bulk of the country's aristocracy. This was a testimony to the relative openness of the Protestant ruling elite that dominated Irish life in the eighteenth century, as well as to the less than rigid attitude of that elite to the practice of duelling." Kelly, 51.

43  Lecky, *Volume I*, 294.

44  Walsh, 31. Thomas Campbell, *A Philosophical Survey of the South of Ireland, in a series of letters to John Watkinson* (Dublin: Printed for W. Whitestone, 1778), 117.

45  *Dublin Mercury*, August 19, 1769.

46  *Public Register or The Freeman's Journal*, August 8, 1771.

47  *Hoey's Dublin Mercury*, November 8, 1770.

48  *Lives of the Late George Robert Fitzgerald, and P.R. McDonnel, Esqrs.* ([1786]), 8-9.

49  For an account of Fitzgerald's ensuing duel, fought with Michael French of Galway, see Chapter II.

50  The *Dublin Mercury* of February 1, 1770, reported: "They write from Dublin, that in consequence of a political dispute, a duel was fought near Timolin, between Capt. L—— and a young clergyman, in which the latter was so dangerously wounded that his life is despaired of." For an extensive account of the Irish Catholic Abbot Ferris's challenge to a "mortal combat with swords," see Andrew O'Reilly, *The Irish Abroad and at Home; at the Court and in the Camp. With Souvenirs of "The Brigade." Reminiscences of an Emigrant Milesian* (New York: P. M. Haverty, 1857), 239-258.

51  Thomas Longueville, *Pryings among private papers, chiefly of the seventeenth and eighteenth centuries* (London: Longmans, Green, 1905) 152.

52  Barrington, *Personal Sketches, Vol. II*, 6.

53  William Kenrick, *The Duellist, a comedy in five acts and in prose* (Dublin: Printed for Messrs. Williams, Wilson, Husband, Colles, Walker, and Jenkins, 1774), 4-5. A Gentleman of that city [Dublin], *Modern honour: or, the barber duellist: a comic opera in two acts; as it is now performing at the Theatre-Royal in Smock-Alley* (Dublin: Printed for the author by R. Stewart, Abbey-Street, 1775).

54  Richard Brinsley Sheridan, *The Rivals, a comedy. As it is acted at the Theatre-Royal in Covent-Garden* (London: Printed for John Wilkie, 1775), 58.

55  William Makepeace Thackeray, *The Luck of Barry Lyndon: A Romance of the Last Century, Volume 1* (New York: D. Appleton & Co., 1853), 250.

56  Following is one specimen of such an account: "On Wednesday Morning last Mr. Grace, a Gentleman of Ireland, and a Lieutenant of a Man of War, fought a Duel in the Fields behind Montague-House, in which the latter was severely wounded, and disarm'd.—The Cause we are inform'd, was owing to some National Reflections, which the Lieutenant made Use of at a Tavern near Temple-Bar the Evening before, when in Company with Mr. Grace." *Derby Mercury*, November 4, 1742. See also *Ipswich Journal*, May 11, 1734. *Ipswich Journal*, May 15, 1736. *Derby Mercury*, August 22, 1746. *Derby Mercury*, March 31, 1749. *Dublin Mercury*, April 11, 1769. *Hoey's Dublin Mercury*, June 20, 1771. *Saunders's News-Letter*, November 5, 1785. See also the account of the duel between Peter Drake and James Miller, printed in Chapter II.

57  *Argus*, December 21, 1789.

58  "Abraham Bosquet, of Stangate, in the Parish of Lambeth, in the County of Surry, Esquire, formerly of Sandy-mount, in the County of Dublin, and late one of his Majesty's Commissaries of the Musters..." *The Repertory of Arts and Manufactures, Volume IX* (London: G. & T. Wilkie., 1798), 381.

59  Abraham Bosquett, *The Young Man of Honour's Vade-Mecum, Being a Salutary Treatise on Duelling. Together with the Annals of Chivalry, the Ordeal Trial, and Judicial Combat, from the Earliest Times* (London: C. Chapple, 1817), 21-22.

60  "For my own part indeed I hope no act of legislation will be devised, capable of putting a stop to duelling; for I consider it one of the greatest safeguards of polished society, and the surest pledge of courtesy and decorum." An English Gentleman, *The United States and Canada During the Years 1822-1823* (London: Baldwin, Cradock, and Joy, 1824), 352. "The practice [of duelling] is severely censured by all religious and thinking people; yet it

has very justly been remarked, that 'the great gentleness and complacency of modern manners, and those respectful attentions of one man to another, that at present render the social discourses of life far more agreeable and decent, than among the most civilized nations of antiquity; must be ascribed, in some degree to this absurd custom.' It is certainly both awful and distressing to see a young person cut off suddenly in a duel, particularly if he be the father of a family; but the loss of a few lives is a mere trifle, when compared with the benefits resulting to Society at large." A Traveller, *The Art of Duelling* (London: Joseph Thomas, 1836), 1.

61 Jonah Barrington, *Historic memoirs of Ireland; comprising secret records of the national convention, the rebellion, and the union; with delineations of the principal characters connected with these transactions, Vol. I* (London: Published for H. Colburn by R. Bentley, 1835), 80.

62 Kelly, 207.

63 *Lives of the Late George Robert Fitzgerald*, 6.

64 "Old Galway Life," in *The Living Age, Seventh Series, Volume XXII*, (Boston: Living Age Company, Incorporated, 1904), 611.

65 Jonathan Swift, *The works of Jonathan Swift D. D., Dean of St. Patrick's, Dublin. Carefully selected: with a biography of the author, by D. Laing Purves; and original and authentic notes* (Edinburgh: William P. Nimmo & Co., 1880), 488.

66 Recorded in 1938, this story was told by Jeremiah Cronin, of Church Street, Millstreet, age 48 years. The writer comments: "Local tradition tells the tale and history confirms its accuracy...Like all things of this world, its memory faded until recent times when the people are again beginning to take an interest in the brave deeds of their ancestors. It is commonly supposed that the sword [used in the duel] is still in the possession of some farmer of the above district who probably is not interested in local history." The Schools' Collection, Volume 323, Page 262-264. http://www.duchas.ie/en/cbes/4921690/4890288

67 Anne Partlon, "The Life and Times of Sir John Waters Kirwan (1866-1949)" (PhD diss., Murdoch University, 2011), 22.

68 Ibid., 19-21.

69 From the account of Mr. John Clancy, Carpenter, Grange, Kilmallock, Co. Limerick. The Schools' Collection, Volume 516, Page 234, 249.

70 Sir John Carr, *Stranger in Ireland; or, A tour in the southern and western parts of that country in the year 1805* (Philadelphia: F. Bradford, 1806), 151.

71 Although this story comes from oral tradition, many of the details found in it can be verified: "In 1666 Daniel Gahan and his wife Susanna, widow of Thomas Ashe, were granted of about 1,000 Irish acres in the barony of Slievardagh, county Tipperary, including Coolequill. O'Hart records three sons of this marriage, Sir Daniel, George and John. Sir Daniel had no children and was succeeded by George. George's grandson, Daniel of Coolquill Castle, parish of Crohane, barony of Slievardagh, married Hannah Bunbury of Kilfeakle, co heiress of her uncle, Matthew Bunbury. In 1793 their daughter Marianne married William Tighe of Woodstock, county Kilkenny. Daniel Gahan was a Member of the Irish House of Commons in 1797. He had no sons and O'Hart writes that his property was inherited by his daughters Marianne Tighe and Penelope Gledstones [Gledstanes]." A Civil Survey found that "a coal mine is also recorded on the townland." From the National University of Ireland Galway's Connacht and Munster Landed Estates Database. The story of the duel was told in 1938 by by Thomas Rochford of Killenaule, Co. Tipperary, age 56. The Schools' Collection, Volume 564, Page 197. http://www.duchas.ie/en/cbes/5162116/5155568

72 *History of Duelling in all Countries; Translated from the French of M. Coustard de Massi, with Introduction and Concluding Chapter by Sir Lucius O'Trigger* (London: Newman & Co., 1880), 114-115.

73 Barrington, *Historic memoirs of Ireland*, 82-83.

74 Barrington, *Personal Sketches, Vol. II*, 31.

75 Lady Gregory, *Sir William Gregory, K. C. M. G., Formerly Member of Parliament and Sometime Governor of Ceylon: An Autobiography* (London: J. Murray, 1894), 15.

76 Barrington, *Personal Sketches, Vol. II*, 19.

77 Kelly, 208.

78 *The London Quarterly Review*, No. CCIX, January, 1859, 16.

79 *Selections from The Irish quarterly review, First series. Vol II* (Dublin: William B. Kelly, 8 Grafton Street, 1857), 322-333.

80 Statutes of Archbishop Bray, quoted in William P. Burke, *History of Clonmel* (Waterford: Printed by N. Harvey & co. for the Clonmel Library Committee, 1907), 157.

81 *Journal of the Cork Historical and Archaeological Society, Vol. XII, 2nd series* (Cork: Guy & Co., 1906), 92.

82 Account by Lawrence Kilkenny of Ballytunck, in The Schools' Collection, Volume 56, Page 359. http://www.duchas.ie/en/cbes/4583337/4580778

83 *Pennsylvania Gazette*, February 10, 1729/30.

84 Kelly, 82.

85 *Walker's Hibernian Magazine*, December, 1775.

86 *An Account of a Desperate Duel, Fought at Talla-Green, in the County of Catharlow, between Lieutenant Barkley, a Lt. of Horse, and Mr. Edvv. Culling, Steward to the Late Lord Chief Justice Doyn's Eldest Son, Viz.* (Dublin: Printed by Thomas Toulmin, 1719).

87 John Warburton, *History of the City of Dublin: From the Earliest Accounts to the Present Time; Containing Its Annals, Antiquities, Ecclesiastical History, and Charters; Its Present Extent, Public Buildings, Schools, Institutions, &c., to which are Added, Biographical Notices of Eminent Men, and Copious Appendices of Its Population, Revenue, Commerce and Literature, Volume 2* (Dublin: T. Cadell and W. Davies, 1818), 1115.

88 Thomas Crofton Croker, *Researches in the South of Ireland* (London: Murray, 1824), 231.

89 Barrington, *Personal Sketches, Vol. III*, 257. For more information on the history of Irish stick fighting, see John W. Hurley, *Shillelagh: The Irish Fighting Stick* (Pipersville, PA: Caravat Press, 2007).

90 Henry recounted, "My mother was a native of that dear little island." See *The Ancestor*, Volume 8, January, 1904, 8.

91 Henry Angelo, *Reminiscences with Memoirs of His Late Father and Friends, Including Numerous Original Anecdotes and Curious Traits of the Most Celebrated Characters that Have Flourished During the Last Eighty Years, Volume II* (London: Henry Colburn and Richard Bentley, 1830), 348.

92 Ibid., 298-305.

93 Carl Thimm, *A Complete Bibliography of Fencing & Duelling: As Practised by All European Nations from the Middle Ages to the Present Day* (London and New York: John Lane, 1896), 74.

94 *Anthologia Hibernica: or, Monthly Collections*, September, 1794.

95 Kelly, 152.

96 Nottidge Charles Macnamara, *The story of an Irish sept: their character & struggle to maintain their lands in Clare* (London: J.M. Dent, 1896), 259.

97 *The Monthly Review, Volume 35* (London: R. Griffiths, 1766), 40-42.

98 Peter Drake, *The Memoirs of Capt. Peter Drake: Containing an Account of Many Strange and Surpising Events, Which Happened to Him Through a Series of Sixty Years, and Upwards; and Several Material Anecdotes, Regarding King William and Queen Anne's Wars with Lewis Xiv. of France.* (Dublin: Printed and sold by S. Powell in Crane-Lane, for the author, 1755), vi-vii.

99  John Ryan, *The History and Antiquities of the County of Carlow* (Dublin: Richard Moore, 1833), 358-359.

100 Jonah Barrington, *Rise and Fall of the Irish Nation* (New York: D. & J. Sadlier, 1848), 191-192.

101 William Darrell, *The gentleman instructed, in the conduct of a virtuous and happy life. Written for the Instruction of a Young Nobleman* (London: Printed for E. Evets at the Green Dragon in St. Paul's Church-Yard, 1704), 113.

102 Giacomo Casanova, *The Duel* (London: Hesperus Press Ltd., 2003), 20. The original edition of Casanova's book, entitled *Il duello,* was first published in Italian in 1780.

103 James Boswell, *The Life of Samuel Johnson, LL.D., Volume II* (London: Henry Baldwin, 1791), 450.

104 *Walker's Hibernian Magazine*, December, 1775.

105 Arthur Young, *A Tour in Ireland. 1776–1779* (London, Paris, New York, Melbourne: Cassell & Co. Ltd., 1887), 189.

106 Kelly, 50.

107 *Freeman's Journal*, March 21 to 25, 1769.

108 Barrington, *Personal Sketches, Vol. II,* 4, 6.

109 Kelly, 149

110 Michael MacDonagh, *Irish Life and Character* (London: Hodder & Stoughton,1898), 33-34.

111 See Chapter VII.

112 *The Gentleman's Magazine, and Historical Chronicle.* May, 1769, 240-241.

113 *An Account of a battle fought between Mr. Smith, an attorney in Smithfield, and Mr. Lee, son to Captain Lee in the county of Westmeath viz* ([Dublin]: Printed in the year MDCCXIX).

114 *The Mirror. A periodical paper, published at Edinburgh in the years 1779 and 1780. Volume I.* (London: A. Strahan, 1786), 78.

115 Barrington, *Historic memoirs of Ireland,* 82-83; *Personal Sketches, Vol. II,* 6.

116 See the definition published by the Association for Historical Fencing: http://www.ahfi.org/the-duel/

117 *Independent Ledger*, April 26, 1784.

118 *Saunders's News-Letter*, November 5, 1785.

119 Joseph Hamilton, *Some Short and Useful Reflections Upon Duelling, which Should be in the Hands of Every Person who is Liable to Receive a Challenge, Or an Offence. By a Christian Patriot.* (Dublin: Printed by the Author, by C. Bentham, 1823), 84.

120 *The Mirror. A periodical paper, published at Edinburgh in the years 1779 and 1780. Volume I.* (London: A. Strahan, 1786), 78-79.

121 Barrington, *Personal Sketches, Vol. II,* 7.

122 Recorded in Clooney, Co. Clare, by Mícheál Mac Clúmháin. The Schools' Collection, Volume 593, Page 348. http://www.duchas.ie/en/cbes/5177635/5174755

123 Samuel Carter Hall, *Retrospect of a Long Life: From 1815 to 1883, Volume 1* (London: Richard Bentley & Son, 1883), 47.

124 Kelly, 73-74, 81.

125 *Stanzas on duelling: inscribed to Wogdon, the celebrated pistol-maker. By an Irish volunteer.* (London: Printed for J. Kerby, 1782), 9.

126 Barrington, *Personal Sketches, Vol. II,* 51-57.

127 *The Trifler: a new periodical miscellany. By Timothy Touchstone,* Number XXX. Saturday, December 20, 1788 (London: Printed for the Authors and Sold by Messieurs Robinsons, Pater-Noster Row, 1788), 389-390.

128 *The Irish quarterly review, First series. Vol II* (Dublin: William B. Kelly, 8 Grafton Street, 1857), 322-333.

129 *Newcastle Courant*, December 4, 1725.

130 *Daily Journal*, January 12, 1727.

131 *Weekly Journal or British Gazetteer*, February 25, 1727.

132 *Intelligencer, no. 1-20* (London: Francis Cogan, 1730), 42.

133 *General Advertiser*, January 21, 1748.

134 *Pue's Occurrences*, July 18, 1758. *London Evening Post*, December 2, 1755. *Lloyd's Evening Post and British Chronicle*, February 1, 1758. A past duel at Lucas's is recounted in the *Independent Chronicle*, December 27, 1769.

135 *The Correspondence of Horace Walpole, Volume 32* (New Haven: Yale University Press, 1965), 107.

136 *The Irish quarterly review. No. VII*, September, 1852, 524.

137 *General Evening Post*, January 3, 1775.

138 *Whitehall Evening Post*, November 6, 1781. *Walker's Hibernian Magazine, 1786* (Dublin: Thomas Walker, 1786), 614.

139 *Dublin Penny Journal*, June 6, 1835.

140 *Dublin Mercury*, January 31, 1769. For other examples, see *Read's Weekly Journal*, October 3, 1730, *Middlesex Journal and Evening Advertiser*, August 26, 1775, *St. James's Chronicle or the British Evening Post*, October 12, 1776, *Morning Chronicle and London Advertiser*, August 30, 1779, *London Star*, April 23, 1791, and *Lloyd's Evening Post*, February 22, 1797.

141 Franc Myles, *Early development of Smithfield & Stoneybatter*, 2015. For more information, see http://www.smithfieldstoneybatter.com/history.html For an account of Donald McBane's duel on Oxmantown Green, see Chapter V: Fencing Schools and Masters in Eighteenth Century Ireland.

142 Barrington, *Personal Sketches, Vol. II*, 23.

143 *Evening Post*, April 5, 1718. *Dublin Journal*, October 16, 1725. *Daily Courant*, June 6, 1734. *St. James's Chronicle or the British Evening Post*, October 16, 1779.

144 *Daily Courant*, June 6, 1734.

145 *Dublin Evening Post*, April 29, 1779.

146 Michael Barry, *An Affair of Honour* (Fermoy, Ireland: Éigse Books, 1981), 2.

147 Hall, 46-47.

148 Barry, 2.

149 "Old Galway Life," in *The Living Age, Seventh Series, Volume XXII*, (Boston: Living Age Company, Incorporated, 1904), 611. See also Peadar O'Dowd, *Old and new Galway* (Galway: Archaeological, Historical & Folklore Society, 1985), 111.

150 Gregory, 16-17.

151 Account taken from Mr. McGettigan, College Street, Ballyshannon, Co. Donegal, in 1938. *The Schools' Collection*, Volume 1028, Page 22. http://www.duchas.ie/en/cbes/4428253/4388710

152 See Chapter II.

153 Kelly, 32.

154 Robert Pentland Mahaffy, *Calendar of the state papers relating to Ireland preserved in the Public Record Office. September 1669—December 1670.* (London: Printed for H. M. Stationery Off., by Eyre and Spottiswoode, 1910), xxviii, 322, 326.

155 See "The Remarkable Anecdotes of Mr. Thomas Mathew" in *The Scots Magazine, Volume 47* (Edinburgh: Murray and Cochrane, 1785), 36-39.

156 Barrington, *Personal Sketches, Vol. II,* 34.

157 *Dublin Journal,* August 21, 1725.

158 Thomas Longueville, *Pryings among private papers, chiefly of the seventeenth and eighteenth centuries* (London: Longmans, Green, 1905) 155-156.

159 Andrew O'Reilly, *The Irish Abroad and at Home; at the Court and in the Camp. With Souvenirs of "The Brigade." Reminiscences of an Emigrant Milesian* (New York: D. Appleton and Co., 1856), 42-43.

160 *Journal of the Cork Historical and Archaeological Society, Vol. IX, 2nd series, No. 57* (Cork: Guy & Co., 1903), 25.

161 *St. James's Chronicle, or the British Evening Post,* October 11, 1781.

162 *Morning Herald and Daily Advertiser,* October 25, 1781.

163 *Journal of the Cork Historical and Archaeological Society,* 25-26.

164 Bosquett, *The Young Man of Honour's Vade-Mecum.*

165 See *The Repertory of Arts and Manufactures, Volume IX.* Abraham was probably connected to the same Bosquett family whose members had studied at Trinity earlier in the century; all hailed from Lisburn, County Antrim. *Alumni dublinenses: a register of the students, graduates, professors and provosts of Trinity college in the University of Dublin,1593-1860* (Dublin: A. Thom & co., ltd., 1935), 82. In 1786 Abraham presented a medical manuscript, written in 1690 by Francis Bosquet, to Trinity College. *Catalogue of the Manuscripts in the Library of Trinity College, Dublin, to which is Added a List of the Fagel Collection of Maps in the Same Library* (Dublin: Hodges, Figgis, & Company, Limited, 1900), 396. In 1787, Bosquett published an elaborate, romantic poem, which he dedicated to the Duchess of Rutland. *Howth, a Descriptive Poem: By Abraham Bosquet, Esq. Late Commissary of Musters* (Dublin: Printed by P. Byrne, No. 108, Grafton-Street, 1787).

166 Bosquett, *The Young Man of Honour's Vade-Mecum,* 2-8, 17.

167 For full accounts of these incidents, and of Fitzgerald's many duels, see Chapter II.

168 For more information on Crosbie and the Pinking Dindies, see Chapter IV.

169 Barrington, *Personal Sketches, Vol. II,* 23-28.

170 Subsequent dueling treatises which quote from the Clonmel code include John Lyde Wilson's *The Code of Honor: Or, Rules for the Government of Principals and Seconds in Duelling* (Charleston, S.C.: J. Phinney, 1858) and Joseph Hamilton's *The Only Approved Guide through all the Stages of a Quarrel* (London: Hatchard & Sons; Bentham & Co. Liverpool; and Millikin, Dublin, 1829).

171 Kelly, 222-223.

172 Carr, 150-152.

173 Richard Lovell Edgeworth, *Essays on professional education* (London: Printed for J. Johnson, 1809), 189.

174 Hamilton, *The Only Approved Guide through all the Stages of a Quarrel,* 220.

175 Kelly, 214.

176 Hamilton, *The Only Approved Guide through all the Stages of a Quarrel,* iv.

177 See Appendix II.

178 *The Living Age, Third Series, Volume XXIX* (Boston: Littell, Son & Co., 1865), 27.

179 See Chapter V: Fencing Schools and Masters in Eighteenth Century Ireland.

180 Andrew O'Reilly recounted the following incident, which took place during the Napoleonic Wars: "The first soldier retired, and was succeeded by a burly, comical-looking young [Irish] fellow of some five-and-twenty years. The Colonel regarded him earnestly...When he was out of hearing, [Colonel] Ponsonby said: 'That is one of the bravest and one of the oddest fellows I ever saw. While lying on my back wounded, our regiment charged the lancers a second time, as you will recollect. This Mr. Murphy, cut off from his troop, was attacked close to

the spot where I lay by two lancers. He used his sword, as I suppose he would have done a shillelah in a row at a fair, knocking the lancers alternately aside, and with a rapidity which made their thrusts harmless. His enemies kept poking at him for some time, and compelled on his part only defensive measures. At length his classic recollections came to his aid (I would swear the fellow had read Virgil), and he feigned a retreat. He was pursued; when wheeling round at the proper moment, and parrying the lance of the foremost of his pursuers, he cut him down. The second pressed on, and met a similar fate, receiving from the brawny arm of Murphy a cut which told somewhere near his collar bone, and must have divided him. His body fell to the earth without groan or motion, and Murphy scarcely glancing at his handiwork, trotted off...'" O'Reilly, Volume 2, 217-218.

"At the battle of Castalla, in Spain, in April, 1813, between the Allies under Sir John Murray, and the French under Marshal Suchet, a like encounter occurred between an Irish officer of the 27th Enniskillen Foot, and one of the enemy's officers, though with a more fatal result to the officer defeated there, than at Fontenoy. While the French, says Napier, 'were unfolding their masses, a grenadier officer, advancing alone, challenged the Captain of the 27th grenadiers to single combat. Waldron, an agile, vigorous Irishman, and of boiling, courage, instantly sprung forward, the hostile lines looked on without firing a shot, the swords of the champions glittered in the sun, the Frenchman's head was cleft in twain, and, the next instant, the 27th, jumping up with a deafening shout, fired a deadly volley, at half pistol-shot distance, and then charged, with such a shock, that, maugre their bravery and numbers, the enemy's soldiers were overthrown, and the side of the Sierra was covered with the killed and wounded." O'Callaghan, 358.

181 Burton recounted, "In the autumn term of 1840, at nineteen and a half, I began residence in Trinity College...My reception at College was not pleasant. I had grown a splendid moustache, which was the envy of all the boys abroad, and which all the advice of Drs. Ogle and Greenhill failed to make me remove. I declined to be shaved until formal orders were issued to the authorities of the college...As I passed through the entrance of the College, a couple of brother collegians met me, and the taller one laughed in my face. Accustomed to continental decorum, I handed him my card and called him out. But the college lad, termed by courtesy an Oxford man, had possibly read of duels, had probably never touched a weapon, sword or pistol, and his astonishment at the invitation exceeded all bounds. Explanations succeeded, and I went my way sadly, and felt as if I had fallen amongst *epiciers*." Lady Isabel Burton, *The Life of Captain Sir Richard F. Burton, Volume I* (London: Chapman & Hall, 1893), 70. Regarding his views on dueling, Burton wrote in 1885, "The sword is *the* weapon for affairs of honour. The pistol is only a *pis aller* when the curriculum has been neglected and gentlemen have not learned to use their weapons; and as for the shot-gun and cowboy revolver—faugh! The knife, however fairly used, has assassin-like proclivities... although it is the bravest of weapons which most wants a man behind it." *The Academy*, August 1, 1885.

182 See Richard F. Burton, *A New System of Sword Exercise for Infantry* (London: W. Clowes and Sons, 1876); *The Book of the Sword* (London: Chatto and Windus,1884); *The Sentiment of the Sword: A Country-House Dialogue* (London: Horace Cox, 1911); *A Complete System of Bayonet Exercise* (London: William Clowes & Sons, 1853); Review of Ben Truman's "Field of Honor," in *The Academy*, August 1, 1885. Burton never lost interest in Ireland, as evinced by his numerous articles on Ogham writing, written for the *Athenæum* and the *Transactions of the Royal Society of Literature*. Much of this material was published in Burton's book *Ogham-Runes and El-Mushajjar: a Study* (London: Harrison & Sons, 1882).

183 "A History of Cane Self-Defense in America: 1798-1930," Ben Miller, last modified August 16, 2016, https://martialartsnewyork.org/2016/08/16/a-history-of-cane-self-defense-in-america-1798-1930/. See also Appendix III.

184 *Dispatches, Correspondence and Memoranda of Field Marshal Arthur Duke of Wellington, K.G.: May 1827 to August 1828, Volume 12* (London: John Murray, 1865), 141-142.

# II

NOTED IRISH DUELISTS

RÉGIMENTS IRLANDAIS

CLARE, DILLON, LALLY, ROTH.

(1750)

Irish Jacobite soldiers. From Eugène Fieffé's *Histoire des troupes étrangères au service de France.*

# i.

## CAPTAIN PETER DRAKE

*"I scorned to gain the Prize in so ungenerous a Manner, and returned
him his Sword, desiring him to defend himself..."*

In the year 1755, a curious tome appeared on the shelves of Dublin's booksellers, purporting to contain the real-life memoirs of a swordsman, gambler, adventurer, rake, occasional pirate, and former Jacobite soldier-in-exile named Peter Drake. Any notion that the book was a work of fiction was swept away when, after its publication, the book was swiftly and "rigidly" suppressed by the author's extended family—who, embarrassed by the revelations of Peter's martial and amorous escapades, bought out every copy they could get their hands on. The author, however—though nearly broke—had, for several years, been hosted and supported by many noted members of Dublin's aristocracy, who were evidently fond of the old soldier, and entertained by his many vivid tales. Fortunately for posterity, a few copies of Drake's book survived, and it is in this autobiography that is to be found the most detailed firsthand account of an eighteenth century Irish duelist.

Drake's tale is vivid, graphic, and extraordinary—so much so that one nineteenth century writer believed Drake to be the inspiration for a character in Sir Walter Scott's novel *The Legend of Montrose*.[1] Drake was, however, a real person. He and his family are referenced in John Burke's *A Genealogical and Heraldic Dictionary of the Landed Gentry of Great Britain & Ireland*. According to the first volume of this series, Peter Drake belonged to the noted family of Drakes-of-Drakerath, in the Barony of Kells, County Meath. He is described as "a cadet of the family...a soldier of fortune, who followed the wars through all the fields of Europe in the beginning of the last century..." The volume further tells us that Peter's father, George Drake, was the son of William of Drakerath, and that his mother was Elizabeth Stanley of County Louth.[2] According to author Paul Jordan-Smith, Drake, for all his vices, must have been a thoroughly entertaining and personable fellow to have inspired so bountiful a welcome for so many years. He must have been more than a mere spinner of tall tales...his stories of life behind the lines in France, Belgium, Holland, and elsewhere are most illuminating. Few books known...give such detailed accounts of manners and morals in the European military camps during the first half of the eighteenth century.[3]

During Drake's extensive military career, he was wounded numerous times, receiving a bayonet-thrust at the battle of Cassano, and seven sword-cuts and bullet wounds at Malplaquet—including one which required surgeons to remove a piece of his skull. In addition to his battlefield combats, Drake engaged in numerous duels and *rencontres*. No other eighteenth century autobiography compares to Drake's in terms of vividness and ingenuousness—excepting only, perhaps, the memoir of the celebrated Scottish swordsman, Donald McBane.[*]

Drake tells his own story better than any other author ever could, so we will largely let him do the telling. In the opening of his memoir, Drake provides the following description of himself:

To begin then with my Person; my Height is exactly Five Feet Ten Inches and Three Quarters, my Limbs neither athletically clumsy, nor finically delicate, but rather that due Composition of both, which constitutes the Appearance of a strong, well-proportioned Man; extremely active, and so indefatigable in point of bodily Labour, that I never knew, or scarcely ever heard of any who was capable of undergoing more...The Regularity of my Features were were such as induced the World to call a me handsome Man, and indeed, in my Youth, the Testimony of my Glass, joined to many successful Amours, has made me vain enough to think, that it did not altogether flatter me.[4]

Drake had been born on October 12, 1671. After the capitulation of Catholic forces at Limerick in 1691, Drake, along with thousands of other Irish Catholic soldiers, traveled to France with the forces of Jacobite leader Patrick Sarsfield to continue fighting in the cause of King James. Of the time immediately following this event, Drake relates,

...having heard from some Acquaintances, of a Brother of mine, who was a Cadet in Colonel *Arthur Dillon's* Regiment of Foot[†], quartered at a Town called *Lierce*, seven Leagues from

---

[*] Donald McBane, *The Expert Sword-Man's Companion: Or the True Art of Self-Defence. With An Account of the Authors Life, and his Transactions during the Wars with France.: To which is Annexed, The Art of Gunnerie* (New York: Jared Kirby Rare Books, 2017).

[†] Colonel Arthur Dillon (1670-1733) of Roscommon. Dillon's Regiment of "Wild Geese" served as a part of the French army during the Nine Years' War (1688-97) and the War of the Spanish Succession (1701-14); was later promoted to Lieutenant-Général and created Count, Viscount, and lastly Earl of Dillon by Louis XIV in 1721.

*Perpignan*, I escaped thither, and was introduced by my Brother to his Colonel, who immediately entered me as a Cadet in his own Company. Here we spent our Winter, and early in the Spring marched to *Barcelona*, in order to lay Siege to that City, before which we sat down in the Year 1697, and took it, after a Siege of two Months, with the Loss of Eight Thousand Men; and the Garrison, on capitulating, were suffered to march out with all the Honours of War, The Town being taken, Ten Thousand *French* Troops were ordered to garrison it, and our Regiment was of the Number.

It was at this time that Drake fought his first duel:

Here I remained till the Peace of *Ryswick*, and in this Town had the Misfortune to quarrel with one *Allen*, a Cadet of the Company in which I served: The Cause of our Difference was his frequently calling me *Boy* and *Stripling*, with other Terms which seemed to reflect on my Courage; which Usage so provoked me, that one Night in the Guard-house, where he spoke of me with Contempt, I called him out, challenged him, fought, and disarmed him.[5]

Following this episode, Drake continued to serve in France and Spain during the War of the Grand Alliance. In 1699 he left the Jacobite service and returned to Ireland. After being arrested, Drake escaped from prison and journeyed to his home in County Meath. From thence he traveled to Dublin, where, in 1700, he frequented the fencing school of Captain Butler, from whom he learned "to handle the small Sword."[6] Desperate for money, as well as any means to leave Ireland, Drake joined a British regiment destined for Holland, under the command of Colonel Pierre de Belcastel. After taking part in a shipboard sword-fight, and engaging in further adventures, Drake embarked for the Netherlands. There, after a dispute in a fencing school, Drake fought another single combat with swords:

*Gertrudenberg* is a small, but strong Town within three Leagues of *Breda*. Here I spent the Winter as Gentlemen of that Profession generally do, with slender Diet, and hard Duty, learning among the Girls to speak *Dutch*, in which I made a pretty good Progress. There was likewise a Fencing school I often frequented, where I became acquainted with one *Butler*, who was a Quartermaster in a Regiment of *Dutch* Horse. One Day we had a Dispute about a Thrust I made, the Button of my Foil tearing his Coat a little: He seemed to resent it, asking me if I thought I could push so well with the Point? I told him I could not tell unless I tried: He replied sharply, that he would try me the first Opportunity. I observed to him, that he seemed to be angry at what was not intended to injure him; but if that did not give him Satisfaction, he must please himself; that I would neither seek nor avoid him.

The next Day we met accidentally in the Street, and he asked me, if I would take a Walk on the Rampart? I answered in the affirmative. In short, we went, fought and wounded each other; I ran him in the Sword Arm, and he ran me through the left Breast, and so we parted, to take care of ourselves. This happened about the latter End of *February*...[7]

In early 1706, after having rejoined the Jacobite service under the French, Drake took part in the "bloody" and famous battle of Ramillies. He then marched with his regiment to Brussels, Ghent, Oudenard, and Tournay, "where the Army was dispersed in the strong Towns." Here, Drake quarreled with a rival German officer over the affections of a lady, resulting in another *rencontre*. Drake humorously relates:

I took up my Quarters at a House of Entertainment where was a good Ordinary. The Landlord had three Daughters reputed handsome: I addressed the eldest, as being of most consequence in the House. My Flame affected at first an Indifference, but I had some Reasons to think it but a Copy of her Countenance, either to try my Sincerity, or see how I could bear a Rival; she, in consequence of this, encouraged a *German* Lieutenant. One Day returning home, I found him sitting in Company with the three Sisters, and, as I thought, too close to my Mistress. It would have passed for Coolness in me, if I had not resented such Familiarity, and he might attribute it to my Want of Courage, both which I was resolved to prevent, it being a military Maxim not to suffer a Rival, though the Love be not real; I therefore seated myself down, and appeared more uneasy then I really was, which caused some Mirth, and a few dry Jokes at my Expence: Upon which I told this Man of War, that I had some Pretensions to the Lady, and was resolved to assert them, advising him civilly to spare himself the Trouble of any future Visit. He asked (with a loud Laugh) if I knew whom I talked to? I answered, Yes, and would let him know who talked to him, at the same Time striking him over the Face. He put his Hand to his Sword; I proposed taking a Walk without the Gates, as quarrelling in Garrison was forbid: He readily accepted it, and out we went. After having gone about a Quarter of a League, he proposed, that at the first drawing of Blood, the Person wounded should, at our Return, resign all Pretensions to the Lady. I agreed, and immediately we drew, and in a trice disarmed him. I asked him, if he thought that equal to the first Blood? He answered me in the negative, though I had it in my Power to draw it without Danger, as he had no Sword; but I observed to him, I scorned to gain the Prize in so ungenerous a Manner, and returned him his Sword, desiring him to defend himself, which he really did pretty smartly, and we exchanged several Thrusts, till at last I had the good Fortune to wound him slightly in the Sword Arm. Then I demanded of him, if he was satisfied to stand to the Terms, or if he would proceed farther. To which he replied, that he would contend no longer with so generous an Enemy, but relinquish according to Agreement; and so we came back lovingly together to our Company, who were in no small Concern for us. There was a Surgeon sent for to dress his Wound, in whose Presence my Antagonist took the Fair One by the Hand, and delivered her to me. She seemed in some Degree concerned, though, in reality, she valued herself highly, for being thought an Object worth contending for. Thus ended this Love quarrel, and I had no more Rivals (at least to my Knowledge) whilst I staid here.[8]

Later, in 1706—shortly after the siege of Menin—Drake participated in an unusual regimental "mass" duel involving no less than fourteen combatants. The star of this episode, however, was not Drake himself, but a gallant and memorable Frenchman named Monsieur de la Salle:

There happened a strange and unlucky Adventure in the Town, which I cannot omit relating, as I was in some Measure concerned in it. Here were thirteen of us, all Friends, and Bottle Companions, merry-making together, two of the most intimate (both Officers in the same Regiment) fell out, as is often the Case, about a Trifle next to nothing, nor could either be appeased without fighting; this Humour unhappily drew in the rest, some declaring for one Side, some the other. It was at last agreed, that at the Opening of the Gates we should walk out to decide the Matter at the Points of our Swords; and soon after hearing the Drums beat the *Revallie*, all began to rouse their Spirits, and thought less of the dismal Consequence that followed; we went towards the Gate to the Number of thirteen.

Here something odd, as humorous, happened, for going to the appointed Place, we met one Monsieur *de la Salle*, a Lieutenant of Grenadiers, who was well acquainted with us all. He insisted on knowing our Destination, and what we were about, which being told, and observing there were but thirteen, said, the Party was unequal, that there must be seven to six, or somebody go home, which he swore he would prevent, by making one to produce an Equality; that he could not, nor would, see so many of his Friends ingaged in a Cause of Honour, and be an idle Spectator. Thus this whimsical Gentleman, instead of endeavouring to soften Matters, added Fewel to Fire. As we were approaching the Place of Action, some proposed to the two Principals to put an End to the Dispute; and I was at the same time speaking to *la Salle* (the last Comer) on the same Subject, who laughed heartily, and with a loud Voice, cried out, (*puisque le vinn est tire il fault le boire*) that is *Since the Wine is drawn, it must be drank*; to which I answered, if it must be so, he and I must touch Glasses together; to which he chearfully agreed, at the same Time embracing me: By this time we reached the fatal Place, where an Accommodation was proposed again, but in vain. Upon which we drew up in two Ranks, seven against seven; and, it was agreed, that *la Salle* should give the Word to draw, which he did chearfully and audibly. The Fight began, every Man tilting at his Opponent, and the two Principals engaged; and in a short time killed each other: There was another lost on the Part for which I fought, and some wounded on both Sides; and I had the good Fortune to wound and disarm Monsieur *de la Salle*. Thus ended this unchristian and bloody Skirmish, to the Shame, Scandal and Confusion of all those who were unthinkingly concerned.

When the Conflict was at an End, three more and myself went off for *Lisle*, and remained there for some Time, till we were certainly informed that the Thing was connived at, having been considered only as the Result of Drunkenness. Convinced of the Truth of this, we returned to *Tournay*, and heard little more of the matter; I went directly to see Monsieur de la Salle, who was now almost recovered of his Wound, being but slight: He expressed his Joy at seeing me, but was under the greatest Concern that he had not joined me in my Endeavours to make up that unhappy Quarrel.[9]

At end of 1706, Drake obtained a discharge from the army. He traveled to Dunkirk to "try his Fortune at Sea,"—that is, to join a privateer. At the beginning of 1707 he found a captain desiring "fifty resolute men" to outfit a such a ship. Drake was appointed lieutenant, due to the fact that the captain "thought me capable of heading a Parcel of brave Fellows in boarding a Ship, which wanted little, beside Activity and Resolution; neither of which he believed I wanted." Just before a planned expedition to the West Indies, Drake quarreled with a particularly unscrupulous officer, resulting in yet another combat with swords:

Two Days after, there happened an unlucky Accident that had well nigh put a Stop to my Expedition. I went into a Tavern kept by a Man, who had three Years before been a Sergeant in the same Regiment with me, to take a Glass, and a Farewel before I embarked. Here I unfortunately met by chance a Woman, who had more Beauty than Virtue, with whom I began to frolick. In the midst of our Dalliance, there entered a smart young Officer, who seemed much out of humour at our Freedoms, and at once bid me to unhand the Lady, or he would oblige me: I civilly asked him, if she was his Wife or Sister? He answered me neither, hitting me a sharp Slap on the Cheek: Upon which I tripped up his Heels, which struck his Head against the Stones: The Landlord, and the rest of the Company hearing the Noise, came in and prevented farther Mischief for the present; however, we had sufficient Opportunity of speaking, and appointed to meet next Morning at eight o'Clock on the Parade, to decide this Difference. He had not Patience to wait the Time; for at seven he came to my Lodging, knocked at my Chamber-door, and asked if I was asleep? I answered that I was up and dressed, and expressed my Concern that he gave himself the Trouble of coming, for I intended a most punctual Observance of Time and Place; but that the Hour was not as yet come. That is true, said he, but that inasmuch as Men often forget what they promise over Night, he came to rub up my Memory. I thanked, and told him, mine was very good. So we walked out, in order to wait the Opening of the Gates; when he asked, which we should go out at, I said it was indifferent to me; but however I named one. He objected, from a Possibility of my having some ill Design in it, which gave me a very bad Opinion of him; then he nominated one in his Turn, and I refused for the Reason before alledged. At last, the Point being settled, to the Satisfaction of both, we pitched upon a convenient Place, where having made several Passes at each other, he retired a little, and in his Retreat fell against a small Sand Hill. I put my Sword under my Arm, and bid him rise; we engaged a second Time, and I soon disarmed him, promising however notwithstanding his Behaviour to restore his Sword in Town, where the Dispute began, if he thought proper to meet me there. He earnestly entreated that I would not expose him, offering to ask Pardon publickly, if I required it, or give me any other Satisfaction I should desire.

As he was an Officer, I was unwilling to expose him, so returned him his Weapon, and we walked in seeming Friendship together, until we came within Sight of the Centinels; when all on a sudden, whilst I turned my Head, he drew, which I fortunately perceived, and flew back, before he had time to make his Thrust: I drew also, and made at him, resolving to have his Life, as a

Punishment for his Perfidy, or die in the Attempt; so attacked him with uncommon Fury, and in a short time ran him through the Body. This done, I made all imaginable Haste to Town, went to my Captain, and told him what had happened, who advised me to take Boat, and go directly on board.[10]

Drake eventually re-entered the French service yet again. In 1709, after being cordially introduced to the great "Pretender" himself, James Francis Edward Stuart—better known as King James—Drake traveled to Valenciennes and joined the *Gens d'Arms*. A fortnight later, he took part in the fateful battle of Malpaquet, one of the grandest and bloodiest events of the War of the Spanish Succession. The opposing forces, led by Britain's famed Duke of Marlborough, notably included a Scottish Highland soldier and duelist named Donald McBane, who would later publish his own memoirs. During the French retreat, Drake—already thrice wounded—became separated from his squadron, and found himself surrounded by five enemy Germans:

[They] resolved to finish me, which they certainly would have done, had I not been very well mounted, and pretty strong: I made the best I could of a bad Market: I exchanged some Cuts, and fired both my Pistols, but what Execution they did, if any, I cannot tell; in this Encounter, I received three Wounds.

Despite this narrow escape, Drake was surrounded by the enemy again—this time more numerous than before, and many of whom had no intention of showing any mercy. Drake's immense cleverness and presence of mind under pressure is illustrated by his account of what happened next:

Having lost much Blood, I resolved to surrender myself Prisoner. In order to this, I took my Carrabine, cocked it, having my Sword hanging at my Wrist, and took the Reins of my Bridle in my Mouth, and thus marched up to a fresh Squadron, just marched within the Entrenchment: I rode up to the commanding Officer, and begged Quarters: He had a Pistol cocked in his Hand; told me in the *German* Language, which I understood, calling me a *French Hounds-foot*; that he would give me Quarters with a Brace of Balls, lodging the Muzzle of his Pistol on my right Shoulder, and firing at the same time; I was resolved not to be behind hand with him, and to sell my Life as dear as I could: As soon as I heard the Word, I fired my Carrabyne; so that his Shot and mine went off instantaneously. I shot the upper Part of his Head, and he tumbled forward: I saw his Brains come down; his Ball only grazed on my Shoulder, and tore the Flesh a little; but the Powder blew off, and burnt the Breadth of an Oyster-shell off my Coat; and the Wadding, which was Toe, lodged between my Waistcoat and Shirt, setting them both on Fire. Most of the Front Rank of the Squadron, if not all, fired a Volley at the same Time; so that I had eleven Shot fairly marked on my Cuirass, or Breast-plate, and two through the Skirts of my Coat. Though the relating of this Catastrophe takes some time, yet it was all done in an Instant: I immediately turned about, clapped Spurs to my Horse, and gallopped towards another Squadron of the same Regiment that was marching in: As I went along, I cocked my Carrabine again, though there was nothing in it, and went up to the commanding Officer of this Squadron, in the same Posture as before, and demanded Quarters, who, in a Gentleman-like civil Manner, assured me I should have good Quarters, and I immediately dropped my Carrabine which was hung to the Swivel of my Belt. There was a Dragoon, called by his Name, to whom I was given in Charge: There came up to me a young Officer of the Squadron; he was a Cornet, and spoke to me in the *French* Language, telling me, that I was very much wounded: I told him, it was the Fortune of War: He asked me, if I would drink a Glass of Wine: I told him, it would be a valuable Present in my present Condition. He took out a flat Flask from his Bosom, desiring me to take a hearty hearty Pull; but when I took it, I could not lift it to my Head, my Wounds growing stiff, and being disabled of both Arms; however, he held it up to me himself, and I took three or four go-downs, and he kindly made me a Present of the rest...

Though bleeding from seven wounds, Drake was well-treated by his Hanoverian captors. The next morning, he had the good fortune to encounter the Duke of Marlborough, who generously granted Drake passage back to French lines where he could have his wounds treated. In the town of Bavay, after undergoing extensive and painful surgery, Drake came to the personal notice of King James, who ordered that Drake be given the tidy sum of "Twenty *French* Louis d'Ors."[11]

By 1711, Drake had left the Jacobite service for that of the British—mainly for monetary reasons—and enlisted under the Duke of Ormonde. During this time, he fought another duel which resulted from his attempt to arbitrate a dispute among friends:

There was one *Farrell*, who was a particular Friend and Acquaintance of mine, a Sergeant in Brigadier *Newton*'s Regiment; his Wife kept a great Sutler's Tent, where a good Number of the head Officers dined every Day, for she kept an exceeding good Ordinary: This *Farrell* came and asked me to go walk, which I did, and dined with him, and others. After Dinner, a Dispute arose between *Farrell* and somebody in Company about a Point of Practice in military Affairs. I was appointed the Arbitrator of this Difference, which, after due Consideration, I determined against *Farrell*, for which Judgment *Farrell* forced me to fight him, in my own Defence I gave him a slight Wound in the Belly, and brought him home to his Wife. I mention this, to shew my Reader how inconsiderately Men often expose their Lives for Trifles...[12]

In 1712, Drake came to be stationed in Oakley "two or three Miles of *Harwich*", Essex, where he stayed for several weeks. Here, Drake became embroiled in another quarrel, when one of his fellow boarders began to spread "scandalous rumors" declaring that Drake and the landlord's wife were having an affair. After getting wind of the rumors, Drake determined to personally confront the man responsible:

Next Day turning out fine, after Breakfast, I asked *Jessop* if he would take a Walk; with all my heart, said he. We walked into the Fields, along the Side of a Wood, talking of the Time drawing near for our going to Flanders. I asked him, if he knew by what Means this scandalous Report was spread about Mrs. Palmer and me; that it was a base Action to villify an honest Woman's Reputation in so gross a Manner; adding, that I would give any thing in my Power to know from whence it sprung, and would leave no Stone unturned to find it out. He said, I was much in the right of it, but he could not satisfy me: I told him, he might inform me as well as Mrs. Palmer. I then asked him, if ever I had boasted to him, or any other Person, to his Knowledge, of a criminal Correspondence held between her and me, or ever bragged of any such Favours conferred upon me by her he said he never knew, nor ever heard of any such thing: I asked him, how he came to tell Mrs. Palmer so; he swore he never did. We had each a good Oak Sapling in our Hands, and Swords by our Sides. I told him, that I was positive Mrs. Palmer would not belye him; I then hit him a small Stroak, to provoke him to draw; but it had not the desired Effect, for he still swore he never said any such thing. I struck him again, swearing, if he would not draw, I would give him a good Beating; but, Coward like, he chose a severe Drubbing, rather than be Man enough to draw his Sword. I then insisted on his clearing himself publickly of having uttered any such Thing to Mrs. Palmer, as he had denied it to me; to which he agreed: We then parted, but he did not return home till Dinner-time. Unluckily for him, and as lucky for me, there happened to be some Labourers of the Town in the Wood, unseen by us, binding of Faggots, they saw and heard all that passed, and did not fail giving a full Account of the whole Affair, which was soon spread over the whole Town. Mrs. Palmer, who it most concerned, heard of it long before Dinner, though I did not know she had had so early Intelligence. Mr. Hogges, in a merry Mood, told me, that he heard of my Exploit, and that *Jessop* deserved what he had got...so this Affair ended little to *Jessop's* Credit, and I continued as much in Favour with my Landlord and Landlady as ever, and her Reputation not in the least violated.[13]

After leaving and then returning again to Harwich, Drake was provided with yet another antagonist to try his mettle:

There joined with us a Gentleman that had been a Lieutenant of Foot in the Queen's Service in *Spain*, but had been broke there for some Misdemeanor. He inlisted himself for a Trooper, and was a Man of Courage, but quarrelsome, and full of himself, which caused frequent Broils and Disputes with most of the Troopers, and with some of the Town's People.

He often threw Reflections upon my Country, to provoke me to a Quarrel, which I avoided as long as we staid here, though (by the bye) it made me suspected by some to be a Coward. He would often say, that I had not *Jessop* to deal with, which gave me no manner of Concern, knowing myself, and judging if ever we should fall out, which I expected, and any Misfortune should happen, the Blame would mostly be laid on him. I never would converse with him when I could avoid it, which strengthened him, and others in the Opinion that I was afraid of him...

A dispute with the soldier (whose name was Collister) at the gaming table would finally provoke a combat between he and Drake, resulting in an unintentionally gruesome wound:

One Day there was a Dispute arose about a Bet, which is generally decided by the Company; every body but myself being asked from the Caster, the Question at last was put to me, I gave my Opinion as I really thought it was, and as was judged by the Company to be so, Mr. *Collister*, to shew his Manhood and Breeding together, told me I lyed like an *Irish* Scoundrel: I replied, that I knew no Scoundrel in the Regiment, except he was one, and that this was Language I neither gave, nor would take; so without further Ceremony broke his Head with an Oak Sapling; the Company interfered, and prevented further Mischief for that Day. We played on, and he was often told by most of the Company, how much he was in the wrong, but it had little Effect on him, for he assured them he had not done with me yet. He left no Stone unturned to meet me in a convenient Place, neither did I go a Yard out of my Way to shun him.

Two Days after, as I was taking a Walk at one End of the Town, near the Fields, he stepped out of a Publick-house, unseen by me, and clapped me on the Shoulder, swearing a great Oath, that he had caught me at last, and that he would, before we parted, try what Mettle I was made of. In short, we did not walk above forty Yards before we drew, and decided this Matter. We had several Thrusts at each other; at last, thinking I had a good Opportunity, I made a full Thrust at him, when he, at the same Instant, altered his Position, making making a Thrust in Secoon, as the Masters call it, and received the Thrust I intended at his Body, under his Eye, through the Cheek, which came out under the Tip of his Ear: He swore he had it, I told him not where I intended it, but much good might do him with it; he said he was satisfied; I answered, so was I; then bid him deliver his Sword, which he did; I went to him, and tied his Handkerchief to mine, to stop the Blood, then I went with him to a Surgeon, had him dressed, and parted good Friends, never quarrelling with him after. This made Noise enough, and was the chief Subject talked of among the military Gentlemen for some Days. Mr. Seagrove endeavoured, as much as in him lay, to fix the Blame upon me, and threatened to confine me on board; but Mr. *Hogges*, and others, assured him, that *Collister* was intirely in the wrong, and that if I should be any ways punished, the Marquis, who he knew to have a great Regard for me, would take it very ill; so I escaped that Danger.[14]

In 1714, Drake took up residence in London, where he came into social contact with James Miller, a noted prize-fighting champion and stage-gladiator who had crossed swords with the likes of James Figg, Timothy Buck, and Donald McBane. According to a contemporary account, Miller "was a most beautiful Picture on the Stage, taking in all his Attitudes, and vastly engaging in his Demeanor. There was such an easy Action in him, unconcerned Behaviour and agreeable Smile in the midst of Fighting, that one could not help being prejudiced in his Favour."[15] In subsequent decades, Miller would go on to author a notable treatise on fencing with various weapons, entitled, *A Treatise on backsword, sword, buckler, sword and dagger, sword and great gauntlet, falchon, quarterstaff*.[16] Drake's contact with Miller, though amiably commenced, would soon result in a *rencontre* between the two:

This Summer I had an odd Adventure, odd I must call it, from its Circumstance, and the Manner it happened, to shew how rashly and inconsiderately some People contrive Diversions to amuse and divert themselves and others, which may endanger their Lives. This was the Case here, and happened thus: There was at this time in *London*, among many famous Prize-Fighters, one *James Miller*, mightily esteemed by the Quality and General Officers, who were Lovers of that Sport, on account of his smiling Countenance, even when warmly engaged on the Stage; I also liked him very well, and was often in Company with him. One Day I took a Walk to *Lambeth* Wells, a Place for Dancing, and other Diversions; as I was paying at the Gate, one of the Drawers came, and told me, there was a Gentleman wanted to speak with me; he shewed me to Mr. Miller, who was taking a Glass with some Company: He said, he saw me come in, which made him send for me to take a Glass, which I accepted of. In about half an Hour the Musick was ordered to the Gallery; the Company moving to re-assume the Dancing, I called for a Flask of Wine; Mr. Miller said, when the Dancing was over, the Company would join, and accept of my Flask; but by the Time the Diversion was ended, it began to rain Mr. Miller then bespoke a large Parlour, and brought the Company thither, about Eleven in Number, only one Lady, whose Name was Hopkins; she kept a Tavern in Earl's Court, and seemed to have some Knowledge of me. I am so particular in this, it being necessary to my Story. Mr. Miller was at this Time in the Horse Grenadiers. I knew none of the Company but him; we drank pretty briskly about, and began to be merry; Toasts went about, mine was called for; I toasted Mrs. Jolly; Mrs. Hopkins immediately got up, and uttering some indecent Expressions, bid me be the Messenger of them, and that her Name was Bess Hopkins; I told her, I never interfered in Ladies Quarrels. A Gentleman, in a laced Hat and Waistcoat, who sat near her, gave himself the Trouble to come round to me, with a seeming angry Countenance, to inform me, I must not take amiss any thing the Lady said, for if I did, he should be very angry: I assured him, I was naturally inclined to be civil to the Fair Sex, and the Lady was at Liberty to say what she pleased; he swore by his Maker, shaking his Head, it was my best Way; I desired he would not ingross any Merit to himself from my Meekness, for if he had said half so much, it was fifty to one, he would not come off so cheap; he then returned to his Seat. I sat near a French Gentleman, who was Mr. Miller's Sergeant; we discoursed in French; Mr. Miller sat on one Side of Mrs. Hopkins, the Gentleman above spoke of on the other; I observed they were all three whispering and laughing, but did not imagine they were plotting against me. The Rain continuing very heavy, there was no Thoughts of going. We being all in a merry Mood, Mr. Miller obliged us with a Song, to which all the Company bore a Chorus, performed in this Manner; at the End of each Verse, the Company (no one to be excused) were to hum through the

Nose, striking gently on it with his Finger all the Time; when any was out of Tune, Mr. Miller was to give it a light Squeeze with his Fingers to put it to rights; this was done, or repeated to every one three times. He had smeared the Inside of two of his Fingers with some Snuff and Candle Grease; with these he tuned my poor Nose; this caused a general Laugh in the Company, I joined with the rest, though I did not know the Cause, nor think that I was the Object of their Mirth. The Company being thus diverted at my Expence for some time, the French Gentleman, who sat near me, whispered me to go clean my Nose, which was all black; I was very much surprised, and went out of the Room to look in a Glass, and found both Sides of my Nose, from the Eyes to the Tip, as black as a Coal. I took no Notice, but returned to the Company in the same Pickle, and sat in my Place, as if I had known nothing of the Matter, which increased their Mirth the more; some talked of Faces, others were describing Features, but I fell to singing, though I knew all this was levelled at me. At length, I got up, and said, I had all those Features they spoke of, rough as they were; among the rest I had a Nose, that he who blacked it, if he did it with Intent to affront me, was a Rascal and Scoundrel; Mr. Miller, to shew the Cap fitted him, made a Stroke with his Cane across the Table at me; then the Company interfered to prevent further Mischief. He was struggling with some Gentlemen to get to me, swearing I should go out of the Room; I desired him to sit down, saying, he had done enough in blacking my Nose, and confirming his Intent of affronting me by a Blow; that if I bore all this he might be easy, and let the Company be so too. All would not do, I must quit the Room; I told him, though he was the Man who brought me in, and I knew no one in Company but himself, yet he, nor no single Man should, or was able to put me out; that I appealed to the Company, or the major Part of them, if I had given Offence to any; if I had, I would willingly withdraw; they all declared to the contrary, that no Man could behave civiller, and that Mr. Miller was in the wrong.

To shew my Disposition for the Peace of the Company, I proposed, that any Person who spoke one Word more of the Dispute, should forfeit a Flask of Wine; this was agreed on by all; Mr. Miller, in less than an Hour, forfeited three, for which he paid as they were brought in: I desired that he and I might go out to speak a few Words together; this was opposed by the Company, unless we left our Swords, and promised not to go to handy Grips (a Sport I am sure neither of us liked) this we promised. He and I went into another Room, and agreed to take an Opportunity to slip the Company, on a Signal to be made, and meet in the Walk as soon as the Rain was over; then we returned to the Company.

About Break of Day it held up, the Company were mostly dispersed about the Room, some snoring in Corners, others sleeping on Chairs, &c. and our Dispute forgot; in short, finding this favourable Opportunity, I walked close by Mr. Miller, then trod on his Foot (the Signal agreed on) and went to the Walk. I had no sooner got to the upper End, and sat down in an Alcove, than he appeared at the other; when he saw me, (tho' the whole Length of the Walk was between us) he clapped his Hand to his Sword, and came in that Posture within ten or twelve Yards of me. I immediately drew, and we both attacked smartly; he gave Ground almost as fast as he came up. In this Retreat he received two slight Wounds, or rather Scratches, in his Sword Arm, he got behind one of the Trees, and begged I would let him breath. I said, though you deserve no Favour, I would scorn to take the Advantage. I put my Sword under my Arm, bidding him to draw Breath. About this Time being missed, four of the Gentlemen came, and found us in this Posture, which prevented our going to it again, so we parted for that Time, and all went to their respective Homes. This Duel was talked of for some Time, especially among the military Gentlemen; it also gained me some Reputation for having engaged one of the principal Heroes of the Stage.

After this, I slept in a whole Skin for twelve Years, no Person challenging, or engaging me, in the many Disputes and Broils I had during that Time. Mr. Miller and I sought each other, but to no Purpose, for some Days. At length we met by the Persuasion of some Friends, but neither for that Time would own himself in the wrong, especially my Antagonist, who warmly insisted upon the Grossness of the Affront, from the Appellation of Rascal and Scoundrel before a whole Company; and I, on the other Hand, on the Baseness he was guilty of in causing me to be a Laughing-stock, especially as he knew he was the only Acquaintance I had there, and that it was by his Invitation I entered into their Company. The Blow he gave me with his Cane was sufficient to demand a Gentleman-like Satisfaction, which I requested of him the first Opportunity; he assured me I might depend upon it. As our Friends could not at this Meeting make the Breach up, we parted.

Some Days after, our Friends hit on this Method to satisfy us both, and make a friendly Conclusion of the Affair; viz, that the Company who were at Lambeth Wells that Night, or as many of them as could be got (Mrs. Hopkins excepted) should be invited to a Dinner at a Time and Place which should be appointed, there to state, and fairly lay the Matter in Debate before them, and whoever it was given against, should beg the others Pardon, and pay the Expence, not exceeding a Guinea, what might be more, to be equally clubbed by the Company: This was communicated, and agreed to, by Mr. Miller and me. The Company was invited on a certain Day, and my House, the Queens Arms, was proposed for the Meeting: This I rejected. Then the Fountain Tavern in Catherine-street was named, where the Company met, and dined: As soon as the Cloth was taken away, Wine and Glasses brought, and the Servants gone, the Cause was opened, debated, and given against Mr. *Miller* by all the Company, even his own Officers, there being two present. He chearfully submitted to the Verdict, paid his Guinea, and begged my Pardon; we embraced, and continued intimate Friends ever after.[17]

Early in the spring of 1715, while still in Lambeth, Drake attempted to provoke a duel with an Englishman notorious for his hatred of the Irish. It was yet another example of a quarrel explicitly arising due to feelings of nationalism:

There was then in *London* one Captain *Hardyman*, of whom I had heard a great deal, but never had the Honour to see him, though I often wished it. This Gentleman was reputed brave, but quarrelsome, which are rarely to be met with in one and the same Person. Those two Talents he chiefly put in Practice against the *Irish*, publickly professing a mortal Hatred to that Nation, having or pretending to have, so good a Nose, that he could smell an *Irishman* from the rest of the human Specie: I had not been long in the [Ale] House, but I saw six or seven Gentlemen drinking their Pints; whom I knew. I called for a Pint, but before I had finished it, in came a portly Gentleman, and called for a Pint of *Derby*; some of the Gentlemen got up, wishing him a good Morning, by the Title and Name of Captain *Hardyman*. I was really glad to see him, though I neither intended nor expected any Dispute with him, but soon found to the contrary. He was not ten Minutes in the Room, before he began to suck his Breath through his Nostrils, as if taking Snuff, swearing, damn him, he smelt an *Irishman*. I heard one of those who sat at the next Table, say, Now the Game begins. In a very little Time, the Captain repeated his Words again; I looked very earnestly at all the Company, and was sure there was no *Irishman* in the Room but myself; I resolved, if he should repeat it again, to shew my Resentment; he did not keep me long in Suspense, when, with an audible Voice, he swore, d—n his Bl—d, he smelt a rank Smell of an *Irishman*; I called for a fresh Pint of Ale, got up, and walked very gravely towards him, and addressing him in this Manner;

"Sir, as I am the only *Irishman* in this Room, whose rank Smell could be so offensive to you"—
Without hearing any more, he asked me in a lofty Manner, "What then, Sir ?"

"Why, Sir, I think I am obliged in Honour to prevent (as much as in me lies) its having a worse Effect on you, by washing it away, which I shall do in this Manner," flinging the Pint of Ale in his Face, which blinded him for a while. I went to my Seat, called for another Pint, sat above half an Hour, till he had, with the Help of the Landlady and some of the Company, dried himself, and got his Sight restored. At last, finding he did not offer to resent it, I paid for my Ale, and went away, though I declare I never in my Life was in a better Disposition to take a Breathing, or measure the Length of my Sword than at this Time, but kind Providence was more favourable to me than my own Wishes, by softning this reputed terrible Man's Heart to a peaceable Disposition, to the Wonder of all who knew him, or heard this Affair.[18]

Drake's last known combat occurred in March 1726, while he was still in London. Ending unfavorably for Drake, it illustrates the extremely dangerous nature of *rencontres* engaged in without the participation and oversight of seconds:

In the Beginning of April, my Partner and I went to *Bath*; he diverted himself during the Season at Hazard, of which he was very fond, and I at my Offices as usual, of which I kept him in the Dark. Thus we past the Time between London and *Bath* until *March* 1726; when an Accident happened, that had like to put an End to my Sport and Life. It was thus: One of the three above spoke of, whose Name was *Kerford*, whether by Bribe or Carelesness of the Door-keeper I know not; but on the first of this Month he slipt in, when the House was full of Company; I was going down to the Parlour, and met him on the Stairs; I ask'd him where he was going; he said to the Hazard Room; I told him the Table was full (which was true) he answered, he would go up nevertheless; I assured him he should not, upon which a Struggle ensued: I had the Advantage, being a Step or two above him, I push'd him down to the Bottom, followed him close, and collar'd him: He drew his Sword, but the Door-keeper coming at that Instant, we disarmed him, to prevent farther Mischief, which he was very fond of, I desired him civilly to go about his Business, and he should have his Sword; this he refused unless he had it first, and I would go to take a Bottle with him at the Tavern. I knew what this meant, and said I had no Business there, for I had good Wine at Home if I was disposed to drink; if he had any Thing to say to me, I was going to my House at *Lambeth*, and would give him a Cast in my Boat (for I really had a Mind to try his Mettle) which proved to be base. A Boat being come, I ordered the Servant to give him his Sword, I took mine, and desired him to walk to the Boat; we cross'd the Water, and landed at Stone-gate; he drew in the Presence of a great Number of Watermen, desiring me to do the same; I told him, with an audible Voice, the better to be heard, that I had no Quarrel with him; asking him what he meant. This I did, in case any Misfortune should happen, that the Standersby might prove I was forced against my Will to this rash Action, nor was I mistaken. I walked on through a narrow Lane, between some pleasant Gardens; he past by me with his Sword still drawn; I desir'd him softly to put up his Sword, and walk to the *Pott-house*, where he knew there was a convenient Green, there we might adjust the Matter without so many Witnesses, but he would not hear nor put up his Sword. The Watermen followed to see the Event: By the Time we got to the Green the Mob encreased greatly, here I flung off my Coat, drew, and to it we went. He was but an indifferent Sword's-man, and Was Left-handed, which a little puzzled me at first, but I soon got over it. I gave him a slight Wound in the left Shoulder, and may say (without Vanity) I might easily have dispatched him, had I been as bloody-minded as he proved. However, I gave him another Touch in the left Wrist, then ask'd him, if he was satisfied; he swore he was not, nor would be, until he had my Life, or lose his in the Attempt. He was a clever, active Man, which did him some Service on this Occasion, for on hearing these Words, I made a full Thrust at his Body. I thought I had done his Business, but he fortunately escaped the Danger, by a sudden and seasonable Spring back-ward. Nevertheless, the Point penetrated his Clothes and Shirt to his Skin. This instant, two Gentlemen of the Company I had left engaged at Hazard, being informed, that Mr. *Carford* and I were gone to *Lambeth* together in a Boat, having had a Dispute, they feared some Mischief mignt follow. They took Boat, and joined us at the Instant above mentioned, drew their Swords to part us, and fell a battering on ours with such Fury, that mine flew out of my Hand, which *Carford* observing, jump'd forward on it, making a full Thrust at me, which I escaped in my Turn, by a Spring backward; he pursued close; I retired ten or twelve Paces, till I got to a Rail, where the Watermen, *&c.* gathered about me. All this Time neither the Gentlemen, nor any of the People had the Presence of Mind to secure this Man, who was close to me, nor take up my Sword to give it me to defend myself: He watching an Opportunity, shortened his Sword, and, over a Man's Shoulder, stabbed me in the Throat. Finding myself wounded in this barbarous Manner, I desired he might be secured, which was done by the Watermen, who declared he had murdered me, for my Stock being taken off, the Blood spouted as far and free, as if a Horse had been bled. There was a Gentleman drest in Black, who was a Surgeon, or pretended to be one; he drest the Wound, without so much as probing it. The Minute my Stock was taken off, I felt a Pain come from the Wound, running over my Shoulder to the Small of my Back, as if cut with a Knife; the Surgeon bled me but to no Purpose; the Pain continued, so that I could not stand. I was carried to my House, in an Arm-chair, by the Watermen.

Carford was immediately arrested and "committed to the County Gaol," while Drake was conveyed to a surgeon, who "probed the Wound" near his collar-bone and found that "if it had gone a Quarter of an Inch deeper, [Drake] must have been killed on the Spot." It took the Irishman more than a year to recover from this injury. When he finally did, his would-be assassin was put on trial. Surprisingly, Drake decided to intervene on his behalf:

When I was before the Grand Jury, I told them, that with God's Blessing, I was cured of my Wound, and was willing to drop the Prosecution and that my Antagonist might be discharged. One of the Gentlemen was pleased to tell me, that I must be very good-natured to Forgive a Man who basely attempted to murder me...[19]

Following this episode, in September, 1738, Drake traveled to Ireland to visit his family, then returned again to England, where he embarked upon a career as a gamester. He ran a gambling business which was particularly reliant upon the games of Pharaoh and Hazard. When these games were banned by the British government in 1739, Drake switched to the games of Rowly Powly and Passage. These, too, were eventually banned by a law which was to take effect on March 25, 1745. Drake recounted,

The 25th of *March* drawing near, when an End was to be put to our Business, I resolved never more to concern myself with Gaming, but return to *Ireland*, there to spend the Remainder of my Days among my Friends as invited.[20]

Back in Ireland, Drake settled into retirement, relying upon the generosity and support of the local nobility, whom he frequently entertained with his humorous personality and exciting tales of his life. He ended his memoir with the following paragraph:

I shall conclude with observing, that through the almost numberless Vicissitudes of an ill-spent and loose Life, of between sixty and seventy Years, I have, through this Channel, an Opportunity of exposing the Follies of inconsiderate Youth which were all centered in myself, wishing, at the same Time, that there may be some Passages so interesting, it may not only be pleasing, but serviceable to the Publick. Then my greatest Happiness and Satisfaction that I can desire from it, in this advanced Age, is, that if it succeeds, I shall flatter myself it will do some Good.
    FINIS.[21]

# ii.

# RICHARD BUIDHE KIRWAN

*"No mortal man is his equal..."*

In surveying the many stories and legends connected with dueling in eighteenth century Ireland, the most romantic figure to be found among them all is undoubtedly Richard Moy Kirwan of Galway. According to one Galway journal,

> The history of Yellow Richard Kirwan, of Woodfield, commonly called Yellow Richard Kirwan of the Sword, the great grandfather of Major Kirwan...is blended with romance, and would fill a thrilling chapter of one of our modern novels. An incident in his eventful career is worth relating.[22]

Kirwan, who earned the sobriquets "Dick of the Sword" and "Nineteen Duel Dick" for his many duels and skill at swordsmanship, was reportedly regarded as "the great duellist of his age." He became known by the moniker "Yellow Richard" (or *Risteárd Buidhe* in the Irish of the period) due to his supposedly sallow complexion.[23] Described as "a man of fierce aspect and collossal build," Richard was reportedly "lithe, muscular, and wiry," and "six feet three inches in height," with "the limbs of a Hercules, of a dark yellow complexion, and with black grizzly locks like the head of a gorgon."[24]

Richard was descended from one of the fourteen "Tribes of Galway," a "predominantly Catholic oligarchy, consisting of the principal families of the region, of which only two—the Kirwans and the D'Arcys—were of native Gaelic Irish stock" (the other tribes being chiefly of Norman or Welsh ancestry).[25] A nineteenth century source informs us that

> His ancient family [was] one of the chief tribes of Galway, and are descended from Heremon, second son of Milesius, the Spanish prince, and founder the Milesian dynasty. The Kirwans origi-

nally settled in Galway in 1442, and possessed large territorial estates throughout the county. The barony of Dunmore was nearly all Kirwan property, besides very large domains throughout Galway, and the adjoining county of Mayo.[26]

Another source adds,

Clement Kirwan, in 1648, built the castle of Cregg, in the county of Galway, which was the latest edifice of that description erected for the purpose of defence in that part of Ireland. He was succeeded in the family estates by his son, Captain Patrick Kirwan [father of "Yellow" Richard]...[27]

An old family history related that "The Kirwans of Woodfield...were Disparate [Desperate] Duellists."[28] In Galway, this was not particularly unusual. The earlier inhabitants of the county had been described as "possessing an inordinate quantity of pride,"—or, as described by Lord Clanricarde in 1641, they "were not without a large potion of pride, and particularly piqued themselves on entertaining high notions of honour."[29] The inhabitants of Galway became regarded as "remarkable" for the practice of dueling, leading Jonah Barrington to observe that of all of Ireland's counties, "Galway was most scientific at the sword" and one of the "ablest schools of the dueling science."[30]

Anne Partlon, who has probably performed more extensive research on the Kirwans than anyone else to date, relates the following about Richard and his family:

The Kirwans had remained Catholic until the time of James II, whereupon several representatives converted to preserve their estates. Patrick, the founder of the Cregg line, had been in 1646 a member of the Supreme Council of the Catholic Confederation which led the Galway resistance against the Parliamentarians in the Civil War. He was later commended by General Ireton, Cromwell's son-in-law, for the protection he had extended to Protestants during the nine-month siege of the city...

If the family archivist is to be believed, the Kirwans were good landlords. Yellow Richard is celebrated in song and story as 'the poor man's friend, the protector of the oppresed and the Father of the Orphant':

> *His house was the house of the poor reduced Gentleman he fed*
> *the poor and cloothed the Naked his memory will for ever Live*
> *in the minds of [the] Hole Country where he lived...*

According to [an] unknown chronicler, he was 'so adored in the County of Galway that all his turf was always cut for him.' He gave an acre of land rent free to each of twelve old tenants who had lived on the estate for generations, and was said to be more considerate to reduced gentlemen than to men of property. Several of these 'reduced gentlemen' lived in the Kirwan household. He never charged a widow rent and his house 'was a hame for the Distressid.'[31]

During the early eighteenth century, Richard left Ireland to serve as one of the "Wild Geese"— a soldier in the famed Irish Brigade. During his time abroad, he became a "Captain in the Austrian service." Due to his "irresistible propensity for duelling," however, Richard was expelled by the Austrians, and "went into the French army under Marshal Saxe," wherein he "greatly distinguished himself at [the battle of] Fontenoy."[32]

It was at this time that an incident occurred in Richard's life which would greatly affect his own faith, and determine the religious and political alliance of his family for generations to come. According to Partlon,

> It was Yellow Richard's brother, Martin of Cregg, who converted the main branch of the family to Protestantism—and Yellow Richard himself who ensured that his own descendants would be Catholic. Before going to France, Richard had become engaged to Christina Maria Bermingham, daughter of Nicholas of Barbesford, Tuam, and a descendant of that Lord Athenry with whom William O'Kirovane quarrelled. Christina, a local beauty, was a devout Catholic and, when taking leave of her beloved, gave him a single decade of the rosary, fashioned in amber and silver, and blessed by the Pope. Christina implored Yellow Richard to keep it with him at all times. He promised to do so, adding laughingly that if he received any proof of its protective powers, he would become a Catholic. Legend has it that, during the battle of Fontenoy, Yellow Richard was struck in the breast by a bullet which spent itself harmlessly on the beads he had concealed in an inner pocket.
>
> When at length he returned to Ireland, he might have reflected that his safety had been purchased at a terrible price for, in his absence, Christina had been afflicted with smallpox. Although she survived, she had been so ravaged by the disfiguring disease that she felt compelled to release her sweetheart from their engagement. Yellow Richard remained true, however. He married his Christina, whom he declared he loved as much as ever, and converted to Catholicism. A folksong commemorating their romance was popular in the West of Ireland for many years afterwards.[33]

Upon his return to Ireland, Richard reportedly became embroiled in a series of duels which would cement his place in Galway lore as one of the country's most famed swordsmen. Following is a lengthy account of two such episodes, culled from an 1870 issue of Galway's *Tuam Herald*, which appears to be largely drawn from family tradition:

After the stirring incidents of his stormy career, [Richard] resolved to settle down in private life and retire to Cregg Castle, the family seat of the Kirwans. While residing there he one day received a letter from his eldest brother, Martin Kirwan, acquainting him of a challenge from an English officer in London. The day was appointed for the duel to take place, and Martin Kirwan urgently requested his brother to come to London and be present on the occasion. Yellow Richard set out with one servant, who had formerly shared his fortunes on the Continent, and was noted for his fidelity to his master. With this faithful attendant he travelled day and night without stopping to take rest or sleep during the journey, so that he might be in time for the duel and if possible save his brother's life. Already he had lost an uncle and three brothers in duels, and he was anxious to preserve the life of his remaining brother. With a generous devotion worthy of a noble spirit he exclaimed, on receiving the letter acquainting him of his brother's predicament, "Am I not to be left even one brother?" and so he resolved to assume his brother's quarrel and fight the duel himself.

He arrived at the place appointed just in time, and managed the affair so adroitly that he became the principal in the quarrel, and challenged his brother's antagonist, who was killed in about five thrusts. The fame of the duel spread like wildfire all over London, as Yellow Richard was well known throughout Europe as the great duellist of the age. No man could stand before him five minutes, as was indicated by the fate of the English officer, who had fallen dead at his feet in the first encounter, pierced through his heart by his rapier.

Shortly after this event, Thomas Lynch of Lobery Castle, the uncle-in-law of Yellow Richard, arrived in London with a view to assist his redoubtable nephew, in case he might be hard pressed. Lynch was known to be a proud and fiery man, as brave as he was proud, and he travelled all the way from Ireland, resolved to avert the fate of his nephew. After the duel Martin Kirwan and his brother retired to their hotel, intending to return home as soon as their affairs were settled. In the meantime the friends of the officer who was killed, and in fact all the Englishmen who heard of the affray were eager to see this wild Irishman who had caused such commotion. Yellow Richard was a man of fierce aspect and collossal build, being six feet three inches in height, with the limbs of a Hercules, of a dark yellow complexion, and with black grizzly locks like the head of a gorgon. Few could look upon his lion port and awe-commanding mein, without a feeling of inward dread. Lithe, muscular, and wiry, he was more than a match for any man who had dared to incur his resentment.

A plot was laid by the confederates of the slain man, to take the life of the Irish rebel, as Yellow Richard was called. But it happened, while they were making up their plan, that the servant in the house, being an Irish girl, overheard the conspirators as they detailed the particulars of their intended attack. The plan devised was somewhat novel in idea, and rather formidable in reality. The best duellist in England was selected to fight the Irish rebel. But previous to the encounter, his new antagonist encased himself in steel armour beneath his clothes, which he wore as if they were his ordinary habiliments. The only vulnerable part of his person left exposed was his neck, the Englishman in his hurry having forgotten the possibility of danger in that particular place.

Thus armed he came forward to throw down the gauntlet of defiance, and dare the Irish rebel to the fight. Yellow Dick was as yet ignorant of the conspiracy formed against his life. His enemies had previously taken apartments opposite the hotel where he was lodged, with a view of watching an opportunity to assassinate him. But the Irish rebel was a dangerous customer to deal with, as he always carried his rapier, and was fully prepared for any sudden attack.

While he was one day walking out of his hotel, the duellist alluded to in steel armour walked up to him, and insulted him on the spot, and commanded him to draw and defend himself. Yellow Richard was not long in accepting the peremptory order, and drawing his trusty rapier advanced to measure its length against his antagonist's. They attacked each other with great fury in the public streets of London, and fought with desperation. The people gathered round the combatants in crowds to witness the dreadful passage of arms between the English officer and the wild Irish rebel, who, though decidedly superior as a swordsman, was driven back from place to place as he in vain made fierce thrusts of his rapier at the body of his antagonist. Every thrust was repelled by the steel armour which was impenetrable. As often as our hero aimed his weapon, with practised eye and deadly arm, his rapier bent against the hidden armour, and he was forced to despair, while bleeding with numerous wounds which he was thus unable to return. As he was on the point of giving up the unequal combat through sheer exhaustion and chagrin, the Irish servant saw the fearful spectacle from the windows of the hotel, where numbers of ladies were crowded in order to witness the dreadful melee.

At that juncture, just as the man in armour was about to give the *coup-de-grace* to his weakened antagonist, the Irish girl called out, as if by sudden inspiration, in her native tongue, and at the peril of her life, "*Earing, O Earing, keagh a muring Sheth na Cerry in Erin?*"* which in English is, "Irishman, O Irishman, how do they kill the sheep in Ireland?"

Yellow Richard rallied at the sound of his countrywoman's voice, and remembered the mode of killing sheep in his country, which was by sticking them in the neck, sprang forward like a lion, and aiming his rapier at the throat of his enemy ran it up to the hilt, and he fell dead at his feet. As Yellow Richard drew his weapon out of its gory orifice, the blood ran down his arm in such quantities that it gathered in a pool where he stood.

After the terrible conflict his brother Martin and uncle Thomas Lynch bore their heroic relative to the hotel. After being admitted the Irish servant girl closed the door against the crowd, who followed her countryman to take his life. It is related that as he entered the room he asked for a pinch of snuff from his uncle, and holding out his right hand dripping with blood he was so struck with the sickening sight that he ever afterwards refused to take snuff with the fingers of the right hand, and from that day to the close used his left hand for the purpose. The blood on his rapier was never wiped off being allowed to congeal on the blade in its sheath. He preserved the trusty weapon which had never failed him in his sore need with religious care, and it has been

---

* A more accurate rendition in the Galway dialect of Irish is: "*A Éireannaigh, a Éireannaigh, cén chaoi a mharaíonn siad na caoirigh in Éirinn?*"

handed down from sire to son from that time to the present, being now in the possession of his grandson, Yellow Edmond Kirwan, father to Major Kirwan. The rapier can now be seen at 79 Eccles-street, Dublin.[34]

It is possible that this story has been embellished and romanticized. Its climax (involving a hidden suit of armor) bears close resemblance to that of several other tales relating to Irish duelists, and may be nothing more than pure folklore.[35] However, the account of Kirwan's duel appears to be the most detailed of these tales, giving rise to the possibility that it was the original model. The story's claim that Richard had "already...lost an uncle and three brothers in duels" is largely verified by Burke's *Genealogical and Heraldic History of the Landed Gentry of Ireland*, which describes the following fates for three of Richard's brothers: "2. George, killed in a duel in France...4. Anthony, killed in Galway. 5. Edmund, killed in a duel in India."[36] The following news report, published in a 1755 issue of the *Derby Mercury*, also notes:

> *Dublin, Nov.* 25. Saturday a Duel was fought in Lucas's Coffee-House, between Edward Brereton, jun. Deputy Serjeant at Arms, and Patrick Kirwan, of Cregg in the County of Galway, Esq; on a Challenge given by the latter; when, after some Passes on both Sides, Mr. Kirwan receiv'd a Wound in his right Breast, of which he died in a few Hours. His Antagonist was likewise wounded, but we hear he is in a fair Way of Recovery. The Coroner's Inquest brought in their Verdict, Manslaughter by Mr. Brereton in his own Defence.[37]

This Patrick Kirwan, who had been "an accomplished swordsman," was actually Richard's nephew—the son of Martin Kirwan, the surviving brother for whom Richard had allegedly fought his duels.[38]

Whether or not the tale printed in the *Tuam Herald* is true, Richard's reputation as one of Ireland's most formidable duelists seems confirmed by nearly all extant period sources. One relates that a local "squireen" named French, while on his death-bed, urged his sons to seek satisfaction from any man who insulted them, but to avoid challenging Richard Kirwan of Woodfield, "for no mortal man is his eaqual [sic]."[39]

Richard and his wife Christina settled outside Dunmore, in the barony of Ballymoe, on a vast, nearly twelve-thousand acre estate. Their marriage was reportedly a happy one, though marred by the death of their fourteen year old daughter. A manuscript in the F.S. Bourke Collection, entitled *Galway the City of the Tribes*, claims that

> The death of this child, her father's favourite, devastated Yellow Richard, who was never seen to smile afterwards. For ten days, as she lay dying, he refused to leave her bedside. Shortly before she died, she told him that she was going away and asked him to come with her, to which Yellow

Richard replied that he would 'as the World is now no comfort to me'. It was another promise kept. A year later, in 1779, he followed her to the grave.[40]

Richard was evidently beloved by the local populace. Of his death, the following tale is related:

There is a grisly story about his disinterment during the construction of a new tomb. As the body was unearthed, it was greeted by a spontaneous outpouring of sorrow from the mourners, led by his widow, Christina, who promptly fainted. When she recovered, she insisted on nursing her late husband's head in her lap. Her son, Martin, added to the spectacle by kissing the relic several times during the day 'and never staped crying untill it was intered.'

As news of the event spread, it was said that "the hole Country young and old min and wimin came to See his Head and all cryed as if he was there Father."[41]

David "Tyger" Roche, from a print originally appearing in *Walker's Hibernian Magazine*, December, 1775. Image copyright and courtesy of the National Library of Ireland, EP ROCH-JH (1) I .

# ··· iii.

## DAVID "TYGER" ROCHE

*"One whose name attained so much celebrity as to become a proverb."*

David "Tyger" Roche had reportedly "fought many duels, but to his great honour, never without the utmost force and reluctance, and always in the cause of truth and justice."[42] He was the nephew of the Dublin-based Irish peer, Viscount de Rupe and Fermoy, and a member of "one of the oldest and most distinguished of the Anglo-Norman families [that] settled in Ireland." The early Roches had presided at Castle Widenham, County Cork, and—despite their Anglo-Norman heritage—had often allied themselves with the Gaelic aristocracy. In 1580, during the Second Desmond rebellion, Lord Roche was suspected of aiding rebel forces, and was temporarily "seized" by Sir Walter Raleigh. More than half a century later, the Roches overtly took part in the failed Irish rebellion of 1641. As a result, the family lost their lands and had their titles "laid under an outlawry" by Oliver Cromwell.[43] Local folklore contains the following anecdote, said to have occurred at this time:

> During Cromwell's stay in Ireland, there lived in Ballylegan, Glanworth, Co. Cork, a very strong man named Roche whose skill in swordsmanship was noised over all Munster. There chanced to be a body of Cromwell's soldiers passing north of Glanworth. Roche, hearing of their coming, gathered together a body of strong men from Glanworth and arranged to attack the soldiers at Hawe's *bohreen*.* Roche's men were inside both ditches to attack the soldiers. When the attackers saw the soldiers coming and, seeing they were outnumbered, they fled, leaving Roche alone.
>
> Roche stepped out on the *bohreen* with a sword in his hand and said, "I defy any two men single handed, and no person will dare pass."

---

\* *Bohreen*: From the Irish *bóithrín*. Literally, a "little road," or narrow country lane, often lined by hedges or ditches.

Two men stepped forward, but Roche's skill bested them. This continued for some time. The soldiers soon became aware of Roche's slaughter. They surrounded Roche and brought him to the ground. A gallows was put up at the end of the *bohreen*, and Roche was hanged there.[44]

Although their lands were never returned, the Roches managed to keep their peerage during subsequent centuries.

David Roche the duelist was born in 1729, the son of James Roche of Abbeystrewry, Cork.[45] Roche's early years are best described in a piece written in 1774 for *The Universal Magazine*:

> GENUINE MEMOIRS *of Captain* DAVID ROCHE, *commonly called the* TYGER.
>
> This unfortunate Gentleman...was born in Dublin, in the year 1729, and was instructed in the elements of polite education in that metropolis. His turn for a military life was so apparent, that the late Earl of Chesterfield, while he was Lord Lieutenant of that kingdom, offered to give him a commission; but his friends, having different views with respect to his settlement in life, declined that Nobleman's favour...[46]

After reportedly taking part in a riot by "Collegians" during which a night watchman was killed, Roche was compelled to flee Dublin. He made for his ancestral Cork, where, boarding a ship, he "went over to North America." Upon the outbreak of the French and Indian War, Roche enlisted as a volunteer in a provincial regiment, and "gave proofs of his courage in several skirmishes with the Indians in the French interest." It was around this time, after being wrongly accused of theft, and convicted on false testimony, that Roche participated in a fracas which would earn him his famous moniker of "Tyger":

> [Roche] was brought to a Court Martial; and tho' many circumstances appeared in his favour, he was ordered to quit the service, with every mark of disgrace. Distracted at this sentence, Roche challenged his prosecutor, who refused to meet meet him, as he had been degraded from the rank of a Gentleman; on which, he insulted the Officer in the grossest terms, and flew to the Piquet Guard, where he attacked the Corporal sword in hand. The man defended himself, till his companions came to his assistance; and, on their disarming the assailant, in a paroxysm of despair, he jumped at Burke's throat, and almost strangled him before they were disengaged. From his behaviour on this occasion, he obtained the name of the TYGER.

Roche would later be exonerated of any role in the alleged theft. In the meantime, while the rest of his army marched north to participate in the famous battle of Ticonderoga, Roche was "left totally abandoned by his friends, and penniless, at Albany, a town many miles from that fortress." Still determined to take part in the fighting, he

> with singular resolution, joined a party of Indians allied with the English, and, by forced marches, arrived time enough to attack with the troops under General [James] Abercrombie, when he received four wounds, and gave various proofs of uncommon courage in the transactions of that unfortunate day.

After spending years in New York, where he endured "a variety of distresses," Roche obtained passage on board a vessel bound for England.[47] There, in March, 1763, Roche took part in his first legitimate duel:

> Thursday 7-night a Duel was fought near Lea-Bridge, England, between Capt. Smith and the celebrated Captain Roche, wherein one of them was wounded in the Arm. The Weapons they used on this Occasion were pistols.[48]

Roche soon engaged in another duel, when he attempted to purchase an officer's commission, but found that

> the disgraceful treatment he had met with in America was mentioned as an objection to his being received in the regiment: He traced the origin of this report, with great industry, to a Captain Campbell, whom he insulted in the British coffee-house at Charing-cross; the Captain resented his behaviour with great spirit, and a duel immediately ensued, in which both parties were dangerously wounded.[49]

This combat between Roche and Campbell was described in greater detail in a British journal:

> *Capt. Roche's account of the affair.*
>
> In the British Coffee-house Capt. Roche called the other to an account before all his countrymen, in the manner he deserved, with his sword to his breast, which Capt. Campbell declined, but afterwards challenged Capt. Roche to fight him with pistols, which was agreed. They proposed meeting in Hyde-park, but were prevented by the multitude who knew of the affair. Then they retired with their seconds, captains Rutter and Paterson, to the fields leading to Chelsea, where they fought never at a greater distance than six yards, with liberty to advance and fire when they please; when Capt. Roche advancing within three yards upon Capt. Campbell, and firing, his pistol's ball took off a piece of Capt. Campbell's elbow sleeve, who returned with the utmost resolution the fire, and shot Capt. Roche through his left hand and arm.

*Capt. Campbell's account.*

The rise of this dispute was owing to a court martial held on Capt. Roche, in the year 1757, at Halifax in Nova Scotia, by which he was broke. This circumstance being mentioned by Capt. Campbell some months ago, with intention to serve a friend, was soon carried to Capt. Roche who thought proper to resent what he looked upon as an injury to his character; he met Capt. Campbell in coffee-houses, at Ranelagh, and in the Park, and on every occasion provoked him by abusive language; but an incident happened which brought the affair to a final issue. Capt. Roche went to the British coffee-house on purpose to find Capt. Campbell, and having some words retorted upon him, he drew his sword, which Capt. Campbell parried with his in his left hand, while he made use of his cane in the other. They were soon parted, and a challenge ensued. They met next morning accompanied with seconds. They agreed to fire at pleasure. Capt. Roche fired his first pistol at about six yards distance, Capt. Campbell advanced to within three or four yards, and fired his first pistol at the very instant, almost, that Capt. Roche fired his second and last. Capt. Roche was wounded in the left hand, which ended the affair, as Capt. Campbell disdained taking away a life he had then in his power: he was solicitous, only, of avoiding any reflections his character might suffer from what had passed; and having gained his point, his resentment gave way to humanity.[50]

The duel would not be his last. Roche now reportedly "declared in all public places, and caused it to be every where known, that, as he could not obtain justice on the miscreant who had traduced his character in America, he would personally chastise every man in England who presumed to propagate the report." Roche proceeded to take part in several affrays, before finally being publicly exonerated of his alleged crime due to a deathbed confession. The declaration of the guilty culprit was "properly attested, and universally received, and restored the injured Roche at once to character and countenance."

After this vindication, Roche received a lieutenancy in a newly-raised regiment. He soon returned to Dublin "with considerable eclat," and the

reputation of the injuries he had sustained, the gallant part he had acted, and the romantic adventures he had encountered among the Indians, in the woods of America, were the subject of every conversation. Convivial parties were every where made for him. Wherever he appeared, he was the lion of the night. A handsome person, made still more attractive by the wounds he had received, a graceful form in the dance, in which he excelled, and the narrative of his hair-breadth escapes, with which he was never too diffident to indulge the company, made him at this time the observed of all observers in the metropolis of Ireland.[51]

Roche attained further celebrity during the 1760s, when he led the fight against a violent local gang referred to as "Sweaters," who were probably the forerunners of the infamous Pinking

Dindies.[52] One night, while strolling the streets of Dublin, Roche reportedly "heard the shrieks of a woman crying for assistance." He rushed to the aid of "an old Gentleman, his son and daughter," and, drawing his sword, met in combat the "whole party" of assailants:

> [Roche] ran to [the daughter's] assistance, and rescued her, after desperately wounding the ring-leader and two others of that abominable gang.
>
> The credit he got by this exploit was increased by his collecting together a number of Officers, who entered into an agreement to rid the public of those despicable disturbers of the city; which they spiritedly executed, and in a few weeks their depredations were no longer complained of.[53]

After this time, Roche engaged "in a career of extravagance" and soon accumulated great debt. He was arrested, cast into the prison of the King's Bench, and sentenced to confinement. While incarcerated, Roche reportedly suffered a nervous breakdown, and "submitted to insults and indignities with patience, and seemed deprived not only of the capability to resent, but of the sensibility to feel them." It was related:

> On one occasion he had a trifling dispute with a fellow-prisoner, who kicked him, and struck him a blow in the face. There was a time when his fiery spirit would not have been satisfied but with the blood of the offender. He now only turned aside and cried like a child. It happened that his countryman. Buck English, a personage of some notoriety, was confined at the same time in the Bench; with him also he had some dispute, and English, seizing a stick, flogged him in a savage manner. Roche made no attempt to retaliate or resist, but crouched under the punishment.[54]

Alexander "Buck" English, the man who had abused Roche, was one of Dublin's most notorious duelists. When Roche was finally liberated from prison, he challenged English to a duel, and a combat was appointed to take place in Hyde Park, London:

> Wednesday, about one o'clock, a duel was fought with pistols between Captain Roache and a Mr. English, of the kingdom of Ireland.—The seconds marked out the ground at twelve yards asunder, when Captain R. fired his first shot, and received that of Mr. E. without any effect, upon which the former advanced five or six paces, and fired his other pistol, as did Mr. E. his second, without any execution; upon which Captain Roche addressed his adversary and said, that firing a pistol was not a sufficient satisfaction for the insult he had received, and therefore insisted upon their both loading again. Mr. E. upon this replied that he should have made him an apology for the offence before matters had been driven to that extremity, had he not apprehended it might have been attributed to fear: therefore now like a gentleman making the apology, and the seconds interfering, the affair was adjusted to the honour and satisfaction of both parties. Capt. Cummings was second to Capt. Roache, and Capt. Sandiford to Mr. English.[55]

In 1769, Roche began a foray into politics, and fought another duel with a "Captain Flood, who had offended him in a coffee-house."[56] According to the *Universal Magazine*, Flood had "grossly insulted [Roche] at the Colcannon Club." In this affair, Roche "gave a fresh proof of his spirit and generosity." During the same period, returning one night to his apartments at Chelsea, Roche was

> attacked at midnight by two ruffians, near the water-works, who presented their pistols to his breast; on which he jumped backwards, and drew his sword, declaring he would not be robbed. Proctor, one of the villains, immediately fired, and the ball grazed the Captain's head; he then briskly attacked them, and, pinning (to use his own expression) one of them to the wall, the other fled. Roche secured his prisoner, and his companion was taken the next morning. For this offence they were tried in the January sessions 1773, at the Old Bailey, and Proctor capitally convicted; but by the intercession of Roche, who shewed great humanity upon the tryal, afterwards received his Majesty's mercy, and was transported.[57]

A contemporary report of the same assault provided additional details regarding Roche's bravado:

> *Proceedings Yesterday at the Public Office in Bow-street.*
> Captain David Roche charged John Proctor and William Godlington with assaulting him in the road to Chelsea with an intent to rob him. It appeared that Proctor fired a pistol, the ball of which grazed the Captain's ear, and was so close to him that the paper of the charge fell on his shoulder. Hereupon the Captain cried out, "Fire again, my lad," and instantly drew his sword, and pinned one of them against some rails, while the other ran away; but Mr. Roche calling aloud to the guard, they were both taken, and are to be tried jointly at the present Old Bailey sessions for an attempt to rob...[58]

In 1773, Roche took part in a *rencontre* which was to become the most highly-publicized combat of the decade. Roche, who had recently married, was appointed captain of a company of foot in the East India service, which embarked for India in May, 1773. During their time at sea, Roche and his wife were repeatedly insulted and abused by a Lieutenant Ferguson, who—citing apparent rumor—declared that Roche had been guilty of cowardice during his service in America. A Sergeant Brown later stated in court:

> It was publicly known that Capt. Roche had endeavoured to accommodate matters, and had made concessions, and that Mrs. Roche had exerted herself to no purpose, [but Ferguson] still persisted in his refusal to accommodate and make up the differences then subsisting between them.[59]

Ferguson's abusive behavior included, among many things, repeatedly insulting Roche's wife in public, and bursting unannounced into Roche's bedroom while he and his wife were in bed. Finally, after Ferguson declared his intention to make a public "presentation" of Roche's cowardice to the governor and council of Bombay, Roche declared that "the affair must be terminated by the point of the sword."

For many days prior to their appointed combat, Ferguson and an associate could be heard "fencing in their cabin" with foils, and "practicing in order to prepare himself for a duel with Capt. Roche." Ferguson also attempted to intimidate Mrs. Roche in the absence of her husband, as described in the following account:

> At seven o'clock the next morning, Mrs. Roche going on deck to take a view of Cape Town, she observ'd Lieut. Ferguson and his brother Adam looking into a chest that stood upon deck, from which he took out three swords, weighed and *poised* each in his hand, and after fixing one, turned round towards Mrs. Roche, and making a lunge, as at fencing, said to her, "This shall do the *rascal*'s business before night."[60]

When both men finally embarked on shore of the Cape of Good Hope for their *rencontre*, Roche was instead met with attempted assassination. Ferguson ambushed Roche and attacked from behind, beating him over the head and arm repeatedly with a loaded cane—and bending Roche's sword in the process. With one arm broken, his blade bent, and blood dripping across his face, Roche was severely handicapped. Nevertheless, he recovered his presence of mind and engaged his adversary:

> Thus assaulted, and in danger of his life, the world, we hope, will think Captain Roche justified in drawing his sword, and calling upon Ferguson to do the same, which he did, and fought with both sword and cane, attempting to beat down Captain Roche's sword, and at the same time lunging with his, both of which Captain Roche repulsed, and defended himself...

At that moment, a friend of Ferguson's named Grant approached to witness the scene, but did not interfere:

> In this situation were Captain Roche and Lieutenant Ferguson...were now coming hastily to the extreme. Captain Roche's sword had been bent by a blow from Ferguson's cane; and therefore now Captain Roche fought under every disadvantage, the one with sword and cane, the other with a bent sword; notwithstanding which, in order to make Ferguson desist, Captain Roche pricked him several times in the sword hand; and as Ferguson pushed on violently, Captain Roche pricked him again on the thigh above knee; and still kept retreating, Ferguson pursuing with the utmost acrimony, lunging with his sword, and striking with the cane alternately. The acrimony

that discovered itself in the mind of Mr. Ferguson, made him still push on, and Captain Roche, to convince Ferguson of his inferiority in the art of fencing, gave him a slight wound in the tender part of the belly, even on the left side, at the same time calling out to Mr. Grant to take him away. To this very humane and merciful request, Grant thought proper to make no answer; and as Ferguson's malice encreased, and Captain Roche saw himself at last in the utmost danger of his life, he made a lunge at Ferguson, which, owing to the sword being bent, entered between the ribs, and proved mortal to a man, who drew all his misfortunes upon himself; a man who fell, but at the last, when it was in the power of Captain Roche to have taken his life at the first onset.[61]

Ferguson succumbed to his wounds within hours. Word of the affray's fatal outcome quickly reached London, where it was reported,

The last letters from the Cape of Good Hope declare, that capt. David Roche, formerly one of the candidates at the Middlesex election, having quarrelled, during his continuance at that port, with Farquharson, Esq; a duel ensued, in which the latter was run through the breast, and died in a few hours after.[62]

Having tried and examined Roche, a local Dutch Court of Judicature "declared that Capt. Roche behaved like a *man of honour*, that he stood in his *own defence*, and *honourably acquitted him*."[63] Conversely, in March of 1774, the *Universal Magazine* published an unflattering biography of Roche, ending with a false statement that he had been executed—or, more specifically, "broke on the wheel at the Cape of Good Hope...and thus terminated, in a shameful manner, a life which, if it had been regulated by the dictates of reason, might have been eminently serviceable to the community."[64] Only one month later, Roche was resurrected when Edward Gibbon wrote, "Tyger Roch is certainly got off from the Cape to Mauritius in a French ship."[65]

At about this time, it appears that Roche began to publicly embrace his moniker. He signed a political broadside, printed in February 1774, as "TYGER ROCHE," and included the following note:

If any reports should be propagated that I met with a small disgrace at the Cape of Good Hope, and suffered without a legal trial by jury, I beg you will look upon it as a scandalous aspersion upon my fame and character. I am upon my return in the first ship, loaded with the spoils of the East, and propose soon to have the high honour of being more personally known to you all.[66]

One month later, the *London Evening Post* referred to "the celebrated Capt. Tyger Roche, who fought and killed Capt. Ferguson."[67] Roche was once again arrested and imprisoned for taking part in the duel. An appeal of murder was brought against him, and a commission issued to try it. A lengthy, highly-publicized trial was held at the Old Bailey, in London, on December 11, 1775. The jury, believing Ferguson's killing to have been neither "malicious [or] deliberate," brought in a verdict of acquittal. Back in Dublin, a comprehensive account of the trial was published in *Walker's Hibernian Magazine*, which included a full-page engraving of Roche. The journal lauded the Dubliner, insisting,

> Only one thing can save [the duelist] from absolute shame, and that is for an offence committed, an honourable concession; and we trust in God the candid reader, in the course of this narrative, will perceive such a consistency of conduct, such an irreproachable behaviour in Captain Roche, as will convince him that that unfortunate gentleman has acted a most worthy part. He was not the aggressor, he made a concession without committing an offence, and at last, in his own defence, fairly and honourably took the life of a rash man, who had long concerted and pre-determined the death of Captain Roche.[68]

As far as press and society was concerned, Roche appears to have been vindicated once again.

After this episode, as far as is currently known, Roche disappeared into obscurity. In 1777, upon inheriting his uncle's peerage, Roche was encouraged to take his family's seat in the Irish House of Lords, but does not appear to have done so.[69] He was still living as late as 1800, when he is recorded as having authorized a land grant under the title "David, viscount Roche and Fermoy."[70] A short biography of David, based on the 1774 article in *The Universal Magazine*, and printed many decades later in *The Dublin University Magazine*, is decidedly unflattering and contradictory. It portrays Roche as both cowardly and bloodthirsty—and, at times, almost seems as though it could have been written by one of his detractors. The article ends with the following assessment:

> A writer of the last century, in speaking of the Irish character, concludes with the remark:—"In short, if they are good, you will scarcely meet a better: if bad, you will seldom find a worse." These extremes were frequently mixed in the same person. Roche, at different periods, displayed them. At one time, an admirable spirit, great humanity, and unbounded generosity; at another, abject cowardice, ferocity, treachery, and brutal selfishness. The vicissitudes of his fortune were as variable as his character: at times he was exposed to the foulest charges, and narrowly escaped ignominious punishment; at others, he was the object of universal esteem and admiration.[71]

*Harper's Magazine* similarly judged Roche to be "among the characters distinguished for unbridled indulgence and fierce passions, who were, unfortunately, too frequently to be met with in Ireland in the last century," concluding that he was "one whose name attained so much celebrity as to become a proverb."[72]

David Roche, undoubtedly, would have disagreed—and, thus, it seems fair to close this chapter on his life with some of his own words. During his 1775 trial for killing Lieutenant Ferguson, Roche made the following statement in his own defense:

My LORDS,

Your Lordships have heard the evidence against me, which is incompetent in law: I submit it to your Lordships, whether, in the character of an officer, or a man, I could submit to the treatment of Lieut. Ferguson without drawing my sword. Your Lordships are convinced I was knocked down and assaulted previous to my drawing; and that Mr. Ferguson fought with both sword and cane. That after having been knock'd down, I called out to my assailer to draw, that I even called to his friend to take him away. What could I do more to establish my character as an officer, or as a man of humanity? After this, my Lords, Self-defence will justify me in the eyes of God and Man, that as a private gentleman, much more an officer, I could do no less than I have done. Your Lordships will see the neccessity of defending myself when an inevitable attack, premeditated and consulted, was made upon my life, and the variety of affidavits transmitted to the Court of Directors, in conformation of it, and of the whole proceedings will prove this matter to your Lordships fuller satisfaction.[73]

# iv.

## GEORGE ROBERT FITZGERALD

*"The man who had fought more duels than any other of his time…"*

According to various works of history, George Robert Fitzgerald was either Ireland's best duelist, or its worst. No Irish swordsman ever generated more controversy or notoriety than Fitzgerald, and such was his fame that his cognomen, "Fighting Fitzgerald," has survived into modern folklore as a popular motto.[74] Even during his own lifetime, legends arose about the immense number of duels in which he had taken part. In an 1829 dueling code, Dublin author Joseph Hamilton wrote that

> The English ambassador, when introducing George Robert Fitzgerald at the Court of France, represented that conspicuous Irishman as having fought no less than thirty duels, which induced the king to say, that his life would make an excellent appendix to that of Monsieur Jack, the Giant Killer. Having wronged the memory of Mr. Barrington in the introduction to this work, by saying twenty six, instead of thirty, we lose as little time as possible in making the *amende honorable*. We believe that out of the thirty duels, only six and twenty were fatal.[75]

Despite this and other accounts augmenting Fitzgerald's reputation as eighteenth century Ireland's "most prolific and ruthless duellist"[76], Fitzgerald's record as a combatant is surprisingly unflattering. He does not appear to ever have won a duel with swords—fought fairly, that is—and instead, frequently resorted to cheating, trickery, and even fleeing the scene outright at opportune moments. How then, are we to reconcile such a record with Fitzgerald's reputation as the most feared duelist in eighteenth century Ireland? Aside from sheer luck, the evidence suggests that Fitzgerald's willingness to do whatever it took to survive—no matter how dishonest, underhanded, or unflattering—was the factor most responsible. As one observer of the period wrote, Fitzgerald certainly possessed a portion of courage, but with all the cunning imaginable; no man was more forward to fight, and yet he rarely fought a duel, either with sword or pistol, in which he did not contrive to have some advantage over his opponent; against the former weapon his body was usually cased, his waistcoat being lined with an elastic substance, as was the case when he fought with Mr. *French*, and in fighting with pistols, it was usual for him to drop on one knee, as his antagonist was about to fire.[77]

As has been previously explicated, the purpose of the duel was to place two principals on equal footing, under the care and observation of seconds, and, if necessary, to resolve their dispute through a combat fought under strict rules and fair conditions. In stark contrast to these precepts, Fitzgerald sought to use the custom of the duel to his own advantage by subverting it.

George Robert Fitzgerald was born during the 1740s in County Mayo to a wealthy Protestant family. Posthumously published biographies of Fitzgerald almost unanimously describe his personality as fiery and ferocious—or as one put it, "unreasonable...restless and turbulent in his temper; captious and irascible; vindictive and sanguinary in his resentments." He was, it was claimed,

easily provoked; he would quarrel upon the most trifling occasion; and having once conceived an enmity towards another, was of that implacable, revengeful and sanguinary nature as to suffer nothing but the blood of the person from whom he supposed he had received an injury, to appease his wrath, or satiate his spirit of resentment.[78]

Such descriptions have largely defined the literary portrayals of Fitzgerald in recent centuries, and throughout modern times. Period accounts suggest that they are, however, somewhat inaccurate. There is no doubt that Fitzgerald was a man of great cruelty, and his violent abuse of servants, friends, animals, and even close family members is well documented. But, despite these monstrous proclivities, Fitzgerald's appearance and outward persona were described by those who knew him as remarkably genteel—almost effete. According to his mortal adversary Richard Martin, "the elegant and gentlemanly appearance of [Fitzgerald], as contrasted with the savage treachery of his actions, was extremely curious, and without any parallel of which I am aware."[79] Likewise, *The Dublin University Magazine,* drawing upon a wealth of earlier accounts, described Fitzgerald in the following detail:

He was rather low in stature, but elegantly made, and of very prepossessing countenance; his eyes were keen, penetrating, and towards men, of a haughty, indignant expression; but all his looks and manners towards women were affable and fraught with softness; polished, to a fault, in his address, and very agreeable and sparkling in conversation. Indeed, we have heard one who was

GEORGE ROBERT FITZGERALD Esq.ʳ

George Robert Fitzgerald, from a print originally appearing in *Walker's Hibernian Magazine*, November, 1781. Image copyright and courtesy of the National Library of Ireland, PD FITZ-GE (1) I.

frequently in his company, say that when he first saw him, on his return from France, dressed out in all the expensive elegance of the Court of Versailles, the button and loop of his hat, his sword knot, and buckles all brilliant with diamonds; his coat and vest, as rich as the brocades and velvets of the French loom could make them; a muff on his left arm, and two enamelled watch chains, with a multitude of seals dangling from either fob—his tout ensemble so light, foppish, and yet distinguished, he could not believe that that was the man who had fought more duels than any other of his time; and had shown on these and other occasions, a ferocity and blood-thirstiness very much out of character indeed with his appearance in a ball-room.[80]

Jonah Barrington, who was well-acquainted with several individuals who knew Fitzgerald personally, remarked:

I have read, in biographical books, George Robert Fitzgerald described as a great, coarse, violent Irishman, of ferocious appearance and savage manners. His person and manners were totally the reverse of this—a more polished and elegant gentleman was not to be met with. His person was very slight and juvenile, his countenance extremely mild and insinuating; and, knowing that he had a *turn* for single combat, I always fancied him too *genteel* to kill any man except with the *small*-sword.[81]

As the eldest son and heir to his father's fortune, Fitzgerald was, during his youth, sent to be educated at Eton, where he acquired the reputation of being "deeply read and passionately fond of the classical authors."[82] Leaving school at an early age, Fitzgerald entered the army, and took up quarters in the town of Galway. Here, at the age of sixteen, Fitzgerald fought his first duel, over unwanted advances he had made towards a girl working in a milliner's shop. After being challenged by Michael French, the friend of a man who had witnessed the incident,

Mr. French and he consenting, they retired to a convenient room, locked the door, and took their places. FitzGerald fired first and missed, his ball entering the wainscot. French's pistol missed fire, for the best reason—he had forgotten to prime it. George Robert, observing this, stepped forward, and offered his antagonist his powder-horn. This placed Mr. French in a very embarrassing position, from which he was relieved by persons bursting into his room on hearing the report of the pistol.

In a day or two afterwards, FitzGerald fought a duel with a Lieutenant Thompson in Galway, was hit in the temple, and fell in a pool of blood. The surgeon, on examining the wound, asserted he must be trepanned. After a long time he recovered, but his brain, it is said, was affected; and many years after he was laid in his dishonoured grave this fracture was pointed to in his whitened skull by those who would fain excuse his acts of wild daring and revenge.[83]

After his recovery, Fitzgerald married and traveled to the Continent, spending time in Paris, and ingratiating himself at the court of Louis XVI. Subsequently he returned to Ireland, residing at his house, at 28 Upper Merrion Street, Dublin, and at Rockfield, near Turlough, County Mayo.

In Dublin, Fitzgerald fought another duel with John Toler, afterwards Lord Norbury.[84] In 1783 he returned to Mayo, where he insulted the leader of the Connaught Circuit, Sergeant Browne, and challenged his nephew, Denis Browne, to a duel. According to a contemporary account,

> Browne, very properly declined meeting him at those weapons [pistols]: neither could he consider himself on an equal footing with him at the small sword, as continual practice, and amazing agility gave him a superiority over a heavy man, little accustomed to active exercise, and, therefore, exposed to inevitable destruction. The only weapon, that he could consider as best calculated for putting them both on such a footing as to give neither a certain advantage over the other, was the broad-sword; with the use of which Collector Browne was somewhat better acquainted, than with that of the others. Fitzgerald seems content to meet him even at this, but wanted only to assure him from the security of his own house; and Mr. Browne, taking his sword under his arm, unsuspicious of surprize or foul dealing, was walking along the avenue, to call on a neighbouring gentleman to attend him as his friend, when, on a sudden, Fitzgerald, turning short upon him, renewed his charge of cowardice, and, at the distance of ten yards, fired a loaded pistol at his head. Happily for Mr. Browne the attempt visibly made upon his life, in so treacherous a manner, did not succeed; he, therefore, immediately returned, with all possible haste to his house...[85]

Browne properly insisted that he would have nothing further to do with Fitzgerald, who had acted as an assassin.

Despite Fitzgerald's reputed prowess at swordsmanship, he frequently avoided using swords in actual duels, as can be seen in the anecdote involving Browne. During his time in London, Fitzgerald attempted to increase his skill in fencing by frequenting the school of Monsieur Claude Reda, located at the Opera House. Henry Angelo, who often fenced with Fitzgerald there, later stated that the Irishman actually "knew very little of the art." Angelo recounted:

> Fitzgerald, well known in the Vauxhall affray* with Parson Bate (late Sir Dudley), had the reputation of not only being a good shot, but a capital fencer, though, in fact, he knew very little of the art, and was only desperate when opposed to the button of a foil, rushing on when there was no danger to apprehend. I can speak to this fact, as I have often been his antagonist; and know that if

---

* The "Vauxhall affray" involved Fitzgerald's substitution of his own footman (an expert boxer) in a challenge at fisticuffs, and is recounted at length in the *Authentic Memoirs of George Robert Fitzgerald, Esq.* (London: Printed for the Editor; sold by E. Dodd, 1786).

the point of a sword had been opposed to him it would have very much altered his ardour. At that time Monsieur Redas, a famous fencing-master, taught at the Opera House, previous to my teaching there, and had an assistant, who was the *plastron de salle* (a mark for every one to push at). Among the many he had to contend with, Fitzgerald preferred him to all the other fencers, making him subservient to his pretended skill. The fact was, that the Frenchman (Monsieur Charriot) who was the prevot, now and then got some little *douceur* from him, and was too *politique* to hit his lucrative adversary too often. It was far different with all the others who fenced with Fitzgerald: not suffering themselves to be beat, they took care never to spare him.

Angelo also related the following account of Fitzgerald's reprehensible behavior on the fencing floor:

One day I was present when Charriot was not pleased with the number of hits he had quietly and voluntarily received; and Fitzgerald having boasted that he had been beating him, so roused Monsieur's pride, that the next time, forgetting the presents his forbearance had procured him, he retaliated on his vaunting antagonist, determined no longer to be his tool. Charriot made the first attack, and so enraged Fitzgerald, that he stretched out his arm and poked his eye out.[86]

Despite this unflattering assessment by Angelo, Fitzgerald publicly boasted of his skill at arms. He spoke of himself as an "adept" who understood the "*science* of arms as SCIENCE," and claimed that he was "accustomed to study arms not superficially, but *scientifically*," thus giving him "a thousand other *fair* advantages...over a novice."[87] Fitzgerald seems to have actively cultivated an aura of invincibility—probably to scare away potential challengers, and instill nervousness in those who actually deigned to fight him. For a while, at least, this tactic seems to have worked.

Privately, Fitzgerald was most likely aware of his actual lack of skill—for, when fighting duels with the sword, he typically took surreptitious, devious precautions. One example—in which Fitzgerald armored himself with a hidden breastplate—can be found in the recollections of John Marsh:

He once provoked a gentleman, (Major Cunningham, an old friend of the writer's,) to fight him. The weapon agreed on was the small sword; and both parties, for some time, appeared to be well-matched: at length, a judiciously aimed thrust at Fitzgerald's breast would have laid him upon the turf, had not the Major's sword bent round and snapped in two, near the middle, owing to the point striking forcibly against a polished hard surface. Enraged at such a dishonourable and cowardly resource, Cunningham pulled off his hat, and flinging it with all his might in Fitzgerald's face, exclaimed, "You infernal rascal!—so, this is the way in which you have been enabled to overcome so many brave men: but I shall take care that you fight no more duels! Cowardly dog!"

As he uttered the last words, he rushed towards him, in order to dispatch him with the remaining part of the sword which he still held in his hand; but Fitzgerald turning round, took to his heels with all his might, and, running across several fields, took shelter in a farm house. His opponent eagerly pursued him, followed by the amazed seconds, who could by no means comprehend the cause of this mysterious chase.

When they arrived at the cottage, the gentleman mounted the stairs, and searched all around for several minutes, but the redoubted hero was no where to be found: he had escaped by jumping out of a back window, at the very instant his antagonist had entered the house.[88]

Fitzgerald was known to secretly armor himself for pistol duels as well. The following account was related by Richard Martin of Connemara, who had faced Fitzgerald in one such combat:

I stood against a projecting part of the barrack-wall, and desired Mr. Fitzgerald to come as close as he pleased. He said a cannon would not carry so far. I answered, "I will soon cure that, for I will now march up until I lay my pistol to your face." I accordingly advanced, until our pistols touched.

We both fired: he missed me, but I hit him full in the breast, and he fell back, supporting himself by a projection of rock, and exclaiming, "Honour, Martin, honour!"

I said,—"If you are not disabled, I will wait as long as you choose!"

At this moment, he couched treacherously like a cat, presented, fired, and hit me. I returned the fire, and hit him; he again recovered, came up, begged my pardon, asked to shake hands...

Despite being hit twice, Fitzgerald was evidently unharmed. Martin later reminisced,

My surprise at Fitzgerald's being alive and well, after having received two shots from horse-pistols full upon him, was soon cleared up—he had plated his body, so as to make it completely bullet-proof. On receiving my fire he fell from the force of the balls striking him direct, and touching his concealed armour. My wound was in the body.[89]

There is yet a third account of Fitzgerald fighting a duel while wearing hidden armor. It pertains to an incident that occurred in the streets of Castlebar, County Mayo, wherein Fitzgerald quarreled with his father's friend, a man named Caesar Ffrench:

On George Robert becoming more and more unsatisfactory and arrogant, Ffrench lost his temper, ran off to his inn for his sword, and returning, found Fitzgerald haranguing the mob and detailing his injuries. Ffrench at once desires him to draw, which, with great coolness he did; first, however, appealing to the people, to bear witness to his own good conduct, and to the impropriety of his antagonist. Both were excellent swordsmen and they fought for a length of time up and down the street, making passes and feints, to the delight and admiration of the bystanders. At length Ffrench got a smart wound in the hip, which roused him to double exertion; and being the heavier and stronger man, he pressed George Robert so hard, that be felt that his only way to save his life was to throw himself on the ground as if he had fallen by chance. Of course, Ffrench was too honourable a man to take advantage of his fallen foe; and his wound now being very trouble-some, he was conveyed to his inn; whereupon Fitzgerald, with his usual arrogance, asserted that he had conquered his antagonist, inasmuch as he had wounded him, and had also possession of the field. It was said on this occasion, that Fitzgerald had on a sword-proof buff waistcoat, and there were those present who asserted that they saw Ffrench's sword bend on his body.[90]

During yet another duel which had resulted from a dispute in Flanders, Fitzgerald was again suspected of wearing armor, or—as his antagonist's second put it—of being *plastroné*. Fitzger-ald's second, Archibald Hamilton Rowan (a leader of the revolutionary group, the United Irishmen), later recounted the scene in his autobiography:

We agreed to precede the carriages on horseback in the morning, and that as soon as we perceived a spot in the Austrian territory adapted to the purpose, we should mark off eight paces, at which distance we should place them; and they agreed to our decision, instead of that formerly insisted on. A short delay was occasioned by Mr. O'Toole having mislaid the ramrod of the Major's pistols. I offered him the use of Mr. Fitzgerald's; but he declined it, saying that he had already lost a part of his skull in a similar affair with an officer of his regiment, by lending his pistols. The ramrod was soon found, and the gentlemen had taken their ground, when Major Baggs beckoned and spoke to Captain O'Toole, who came up to me, and apologizing for the suspicion, said he thought Mr. Fitzgerald might be *plastroné*.

Fitzgerald, hearing what was said, threw off his coat and waistcoat, when, to the great surprise of us all, he exhibited himself with his shirt tied close round his body, by a broad riband *couleur de rose*, while narrower ones closed his shirt-sleeves round the lower and upper joints of the arms. This, he explained to us afterwards, was a precaution necessary, from the terms first agreed upon for their meeting, by Messrs. Hodges and O'Toole. It now became my duty to examine the Major's body. On my advancing towards him, he unbuttoned all his coats, and throwing them open, said to me, "Sir, you may feel me." I replied, that the suspicion having originated with him, I must insist on his following Mr. Fitzgerald's example, and stripping, as he had done. He did so immediately. It was a strong frost, and the Major asked me might he put on his clothes again. To which Mr. Fitzgerald immediately answered: "Oh, let the Major be covered."

They were now standing on the ground we had marked. Major Baggs sunk on his quarters, something like the Scottish lion; Fitzgerald stood as one who had made a lounge in fencing. They fired together, and were in the act of levelling their second pistols, when Major Baggs sunk on his side, saying, "Sir, I am wounded."

"But you are not dead," replied Fitzgerald; and at the same moment discharged his second pistol at his fallen enemy. Baggs immediately started on his legs, and advanced on Fitzgerald, who throwing his pistol at him, quitted his station, and kept a zig-zag course across the field, Baggs following him. I saw the flash of the Major's second pistol, and at the same moment Fitzgerald lay stretched on the ground. I was just time enough to catch Baggs as he was falling after having fired his second shot. He swooned from intense pain, the small bone of his leg being broken. Mr. Fitzgerald came up to us, saying, "We are both wounded; let us go back to the ground." But Baggs was taken to his carriage. As I was assisting Fitzgerald, whose wound was in the fleshy part of his thigh, I could not avoid asking him how he came to discharge his second pistol. His answer was: "I should not have done so to any man but Baggs."[91]

This last statement by Fitzgerald was, of course, untrue; he had also done the same to other individuals.

Fitzgerald's habit of "accidentally" taking a second shot at his adversary is documented in several accounts. One such duel took place in 1773, and was fought with a Captain Scawen, who had previously fought eleven duels.[92] The combat was arranged after Fitzgerald and Scawen had engaged in a violent public scuffle, the particulars of which were recounted in a journal of the period:

Mr. Fitzgerrald, having heard that Capt. Scawen had given his opinion freely on the late Vauxhall affray, and that entirely against him, asked him at the Cocoa-tree, whether he had made use of such expressions; to which the other answered in the affirmative, adding, "That as he had appealed to the public, any man had a right to give his opinion." Whereupon the former insisted upon his going out with him immediately with swords. This was, however, prevented, by Capt. Scawen being put under an arrest. Mr. Fitzgerrald having reported it afterwards, that Capt. Scawen would not meet him, and called him a poltroon, the latter went into the St. James's whole Coffee-house, where he saw Mr. Fitzgerrald, and told him, that notwithstanding the arrest he was under, he was ready to go out with him, and was prepared accordingly, pulling out a cafe of pistols, desiring him to take one, which he refused, insisting on fighting only with swords; on this Capt. Scawen struck him a blow on the head with a stick, which knocked him down. Recovering himself, Mr. Fitzgerrald drew, and made a pass at the Captain, which the latter parried with his stick, and then presented a pistol, declaring, if he attempted to make another pass he would blow his brains out. At this instant the Colonel of the guard arrived, and again put Capt. Scawen under an arrest.

Scawen immediately sent Fitzgerald a challenge, and a time and place were appointed to "determine the affair in an honourable manner." Although Fitzgerald had insisted on using swords for their initial *rencontre*, he now selected pistols as dueling weapons. The ensuing meeting was later related by Scawen's second, Captain Nicholas Nugent:

The seconds having measured the distance, which, by mutual agreement, was ten paces, each gentleman took his post. Mr. Scawen, in going to his ground, asked Mr. Fitzgerald if he chose to fire first? Who replied, it was a matter of indifference to him; but altering his opinion, said he would take the first shot; to which Mr. Scawen readily assented. Mr. Fitzgerald then presented his pistol and fired; the shot seemed to pass very near Mr. Scawen. After Mr. Fitzgerald had fired his first pistol, he took hold of the other, and stood with it in the attitude of presenting, to receive Mr. Scawen's fire. Mr. Scawen then presented his pistol, but before he could pull the trigger, was surprized at the report of Mr. Fitzgerald's second pistol. On this Mr. Scawen immediately recovered his, telling Mr. Fitzgerald at the same time, that as both his pistols were discharged, he could not think of firing at him, and instantly discharged his in the air. Mr. Fitzgerald replied, I assure you I did not mean it—my pistol went off by accident; but I'll load again.

The seconds and surgeons here interposed, in order to accommodate the affair; and Mr. Scawen coming up, addressed himself to Mr. Fitzgerald, and said, he hoped his behaviour had now sufficiently convinced him that he was not deficient in point of courage; and as a further reparation for the blow he had given, he was not ashamed to present him with a cane (which at that instant he took from the French surgeon) desiring him to use it as he thought proper. Mr. Fitzgerald, after raising the cane (which did not appear to me to have touched Mr. Scawen) politely returned it, saying, "I retract all the aspersions I ever cast upon your honour, am now convinced you never deserved them, and wish there may be no retrospect of past transactions."

A reconciliation being thus happily effected, the parties returned on their way to Lisle, where Mr. Fitzgerald likewise made a handsome apology for having fired his second pistol, declaring it was accidental. The whole company afterwards passed the evening together, and separated the next morning perfectly satisfied.[93]

As a result of this much-publicized duel, Fitzgerald's celebrity continued to grow. He became the subject of a satirical poem published the same year, entitled *The Triumph of Brittania*. This book, which was "humbly inscribed to George Robert Fitzgerald, Esq.," contained stanzas such as:

> Then, my FITZGERALD, shall thy genius shine,
> Then shall the trophies of the war be thine;
> Each harmless Waiter shall thy courage prove;
> Each feeble Watchman thy resentment move...

As well as:

> Ye pasteboard heroes of the *tragic* field,
> Contempt your doom, and Cowardice your shield!
> View this example, great FITZGERALD see!
> Old Honour's son begot on Probity.[94]

Although contemporary reports overwhelmingly portrayed Fitzgerald as an unmitigated scoundrel, in all justice to the duelist, a series of unpublished letters between he and his wife, Jane Conolly, reveals a much different side of George Robert's character—that of a doting husband who deeply loved his family. While traveling abroad in France, Fitzgerald diligently wrote his family twice per week, referring to his wife as his "dearest Angel":

I shall send you a faithful account of every adventure that happens during my absence from my Dearest Life & soul Jane. I shall transmit it by post twice a week. I beg you wife in return do the same. I hope to have every thing done in a month, & then I am determined never to go on a journey without my two Dears. Kiss her [daughter Mary Anne] for me, & assure her I will not forget her things...Adieu my sweetest Life & soul, be assured no one thing can take you, & the sweetest Bambina one moment out of my head when absent from you, once more adieu my sweetest Jane believe me ever your Most Doting Husband. G R Fitz:Gerrald

Likewise, a letter from Jane to George Robert, entitled "for my angel George while away from me," is brimming with care and concern. Among her many pleas for his safety, she urged him "to take care not to get into any quarrelsome company, to give me your word of Honour not to get into any scrapes, & to return to your Doting fond Jane as soon as you can..."[95]

In 1775, Fitzgerald quarreled with a soldier and fellow gambler named Thomas Walker. Fitzgerald had bought out Walker's debt from another creditor, and immediately demanded the full amount from Walker directly. When Walker refused, Fitzgerald physically struck him with his cane, and was promptly challenged to a duel with pistols. In the combat's aftermath, both principals published pamphlets in an effort to manage society's perception of the duel. Fitzgerald, in his initial tract, called Walker a "*papier-maché* poltron" and "little rascal" that was "bankrupt of honour," and justified his caning of Walker in the following terms:

I do not therefore presume to exculpate myself for the error I rashly committed in striking Mr. Walker with my cane, BEFORE I knew him to be a coward, and I should hold myself utterly inexcusable, had he not himself, in some measure, invited the affront, by his previously declaring he should not shelter himself under the wing of the law. The provocation he gave me certainly was very great. [96]

Walker himself then offered his own versions of events, denouncing the "formidable Mr. FitzGerald" as full of "bufoonery" and "malignant zeal," and as a man who had been unfairly "aided by his dexterity in arms, blood and violence."[97]

Fitzgerald's voluminous counter-reply to Walker, which is full of sarcasm and unabashed bravado, offers a fascinating glimpse into the mind of Ireland's most notorious duelist. Rebutting Walker's pamphlet point-by-point, Fitzgerald made extraordinary claims such as the following:

> You say, I turned my horse about *on a sudden*, and swung my stick, WHICH struck you in the face...Now, as it is not the blow itself, but the sense and intention of the striker that gives the affront, and as the stick had neither any sense, sensibility, or sensation of the blow given, it necessarily follows there was no offence worth mentioning, committed either *ex parte* Baculi, or *ex parte* Geraldini...As to the offence in question, we have already mutually agreed that it was not given by ME, but by my CANE, which like a swinging gate upon full swing, chanced to meet your face in its rapid progress, and unfortunately gave you a blow, *slam-bang*, just in the midway of your chin and nasal protuberance.

Responding to Walker's accusation that he had unfairly evaded his adversary's bullet by "shortening his person, as low as possible," Fitzgerald explained:

> Before you sent me the challenge, you should have considered as well your own consummate ignorance, as my supposed knowledge in the science of arms. All our other gymnastic exercises are only calculated *for the graceful:* a few lessons are sufficient to make us fit free and easy on horseback, or dance a minuet without aukwardness and stiffness; but the science of arms is admitted into our education, not merely for the *graceful*, which always is of a *personal* nature, but upon the more enlarged principle of *public* as well as *private* utility. An excellent marksman, or an accomplished swordsman, does not seem to be born for himself only, but for his friends, his parents, and his country; and by all political writings is universally allowed to be, so far as his own individuality extends, the *Decus* & *Tutamen* of that state of which he is a member.
>
> Ignorant as you are in this branch of polite education, it does not seem at all extraordinary to me that you would be surprized to see me throw myself into the most advantageous position I possibly could, to receive your fire. Of what benefit is theoretic knowledge, if it is not to be carried into practice at the only time it can be of essential service to us? Accustomed to study arms not superficially, but *scientifically*; the moment you levelled your pistol at me, and at the very instant that you fired, at that very instant I made as outstretched an *elonge* as it was possible for me to make, and by thus throwing myself into a *side-way* position, I not only presented as little surface of body as could be, but also lost full sixteen inches of my natural height. Besides, by throwing myself into this attitude, and by keeping my eye in a direct level with the muzzle of your pistol, I was enabled to cover both my head and heart from your fire; for the bullet must first have penetrated the palm of my hand, *before* it could have reached the lobes of my brain; and it must have perforated the whole horizontal length of my right arm, which is almost impossible, before it could have made its passage to my heart. This, Sir, is properly understanding the *science* of arms as a Science; and even when you shall have advanced thus far, there are a thousand other *fair* advantages an ADEPT hath over a novice, which no mercenary artist either will or can teach

you, and which are only to be acquired by intense study and private practice, which like a masked battery, should never be made known to our adversary, but by its sudden, unexpected effect...

It is very true, Sir, from the time you presented your pistol, I never stirred an inch from my ground; for when I made the elonge I have mentioned, I still kept my left foot close on the marked-out ground, and only altered my attitude by advancing my right foot about *sixty inches*.

Fitzgerald also insinuated that Walker had secretly armored himself. This was an extraordinary claim, considering the fact that Fitzgerald himself was guilty of using the trick on multiple occasions:

So, then, you had one SURTOUT on: are you certain you had not half a dozen? If no more than one surtout, pray how many coats and waistcoats? You give us no account of your under-garments. I ask these questions, Sir, because after reading your pamphlet, I took the same pistol, charged it with the same quantity of powder, used a bullet cast in the same mould, measured out twelve good paces with a yard-wand, and then fired at a thick stick, which I had previously covered over with two waistcoats lined, one coat lined, and one double-milled drab surtout. What think you, Sir, was the result? Why, Sir, the ball penetrated through the surtout, the coat, two waistcoats, and lodged itself an inch deep in the stick. There is nothing like experimental philosophy for a fair proof, it beats your *ipse-dixits* all-halloo. You see, Sir, how ingeniously I pass away my private hours—I am always hard at study.

Following his long rebuttal, Fitzgerald flippantly heaped additional insults on Walker, referring to the "enormous depravity and deformity" of the latter's "corrupted heart." He also threatened Walker with further violence:

My dear Daisey, you need not be under any such perpetual horrors, for you may be assured, that I *myself* shall not cane you again: Yet I think it proper to acquaint you, that I generally carry that maudite stick in my hand; and I must tell you, over and above, it has acquired a wonderful alacrity in swinging about from one side to another; so that if you should accidentally be passing by, within the sphere of its activity, and *it* should unluckily give you a second time another swinging stroke just across your eyes, your nose, or your shoulders, you cannot well blame me, after the caution I have thus given you to keep out of its way...

Fitzgerald concluded his tract with the following self-portrait—which is, curiously, both narcissistic and self-deprecating:

Now, Sir, prepare your *camera obscura*, and draw from it, if you please, the principal lights and shades of my character. That I have many—many faults and foibles (and where is the living man that has not?) I readily allow.— Nay, I will go hand in hand a step farther with you, and allow that all my faults and foibles, collectively TAKEN, will overshade the very bed of my good qualities, singly taken. But what Painter, no not even Rembrandt himself, throws his whole mass of shades into one point of view? ...As to good qualities, some I have perhaps, though few in number. This however I can say for myself, no man can impeach my courage in the Field, my honour on the Turf, or my credit on the Royal Exchange.[98]

Whether or not Fitzgerald's tracts succeeded in reinforcing his aura of invincibility in the mind of the public, the charade was not to last. Fitzgerald's career as a duelist came crashing down four years later, in 1779, when he made the mistake of engaging in a public combat with another of Ireland's most feared swordsmen, Alexander "Buck" English. Unlike Fitzgerald, English's skill was genuine. Their combat was fought before a large crowd on St Stephen's Green. During several "passes," English wounded Fitzgerald in several places, and the latter was overthrown by the "superior force" of the former. Fitzgerald's life was saved when members of the crowd intervened to separate the two.[99]

Following the tragic death of his wife, Jane, in 1780, Fitzgerald began to engage in highly eccentric behavior—keeping a pet bear, which he used to frighten those he disliked, and embarking on midnight hunts accompanied by a pack of baying hounds and "a number of servants well mounted carrying flambeaux."[100] He engaged in a severe quarrel over the family estate, and came into violent conflict with his own father and brother. Fitzgerald also claimed that, in the aftermath of his combat with Alexander "Buck" English, the elder Fitzgerald had attempted to enlist the help of English for the purpose of having both of his sons killed:

Old Mr. Fitzgerald (for in these paroxisms of insanity, I can no longer call him my father,) hearing there had been a slight rencounter between myself and Mr. English, member in the present parliament, openly declared in [Daly's] Coffee-House, that he would give the gentleman the reversion of one moiety of his estate, on condition he would contrive to make a German quarrel* with his two sons, and send them both out of the world.—Mr. English happening soon after to come into the Coffee-House, was accosted by old Mr. Fitzgerald to the like purport and effect, which, as it was a most infamous proposition, Mr. English treated him as a madman, though not without some marks of contempt, indignation, and resentment.[101]

Fitzgerald later imprisoned his father—whom he reportedly kept in a cave and violently abused—and was challenged to a pistol duel by his brother, Charles Lionel Fitzgerald.[102] George Robert consequently "employed a man to shoot his own brother, who actually

---

* *A German quarrel:* "A bad, unjust quarrel, started over a trifle, for nothing, begun brutally, without rhyme or reason." Philibert-Joseph Le Roux, *Dictionnaire comique, satyrique, critique, burlesque, libre et proverbial* (Lyon: Chez le Héritiers de Beringos fratres, 1735), 13.

waylaid and discharged a piece at him, but happily it missed aim."[103] This massive family quarrel led to violent incidents which put Fitzgerald in flagrant violation of the law; he was accused of murder, while others declared that he had attempted "to disturb the public peace and security of the kingdom." Fitzgerald was arrested and imprisoned, but soon broke out of jail. He became an outlaw, and—with the assistance of a paid militia—fortified his Mayo estate with "works which were impregnable," including a number of cannons retrieved from a ship-wreck. A military expedition consisting of one hundred and fifty infantry, fifty cavalry, and thirty-five artillery was dispatched from Dublin to capture Fitzgerald—but the latter, "from his scouts, having learned the strength of the army, and well knowing the personal bravery and conduct of its commander, thought proper to make a precipitate retreat in the night..." Fitzgerald escaped to Dublin, in the hopes of effecting "an escape by sea," but was "betrayed or Discovered at a Hotel for the Reward of £300," apprehended, and lodged in the New Gaol.[104]

During his time in prison, Fitzgerald penned a lengthy poem entitled *The Riddle*, written in doggerel measure. It was inscribed to John Scott, the Attorney-General of Ireland, whom, in various stanzas, Fitzgerald openly mocked and accused of unjust persecution. Full of classical and biblical allusions, as well as bawdy references, Fitzgerald's *Riddle* has never been solved, and remains an enigma to this day.[105] *The Gentleman's Magazine* was impressed enough by the poem to declare that it "shews Mr. Fitzgerald to have been, what the world scarcely knew before, a man of some erudition."[106]

Following his release, in addition to *The Riddle,* Fitzgerald published a lengthy, four hundred and sixty-three page book, entitled *An Appeal to the Public.* In it, Fitzgerald accused his father and brother of horrendous, violent behavior. He defended his own actions in Mayo, portraying himself as the victim of his vengeful family, and claimed to have been targeted by enemies within the government.[107]

Then, in 1784, Fitzgerald did something that, to an outsider, seemed unthinkable—he joined the Knights of Tara, a celebrated Irish fencing society whose goal was to restrict and regulate dueling. Fitzgerald is mentioned in the group's official resolutions of 1784.[108] Given the expressed mission of the Knights—which came into clear conflict with his own proclivities —it may be that Fitzgerald merely wished to fraternize with the group's more experienced swordsmen, and attend their lavish fencing tournaments and fancy masquerade balls.

Fate finally caught up with Fitzgerald in 1786, when he took a violent dislike to Patrick Randal McDonnell, a local attorney, magistrate, and Colonel of the Mayo Volunteers.[109] A series of property disputes and legal conflicts between the two finally led to armed skirmishes. Fitzgerald's men captured McDonnell; when an attempt was made to rescue the latter, one of Fitzgerald's crew shot and killed McDonnell in cold blood. Fitzgerald was seized by an angry mob, jailed, and tried for murder. Fitzgerald and two of his accomplices, Timothy Brecknock and John Fulton, were found guilty and sentenced to be hanged.

The day of execution arrived on June 12, 1786. Only one week later, Fitzgerald's unusual physique would be described in the pages of Belfast's *Evening Post* as follows:

> Every part of Fitzgerald's body was scarred with wounds, which he had received in the various rencounters and duels he had been engaged in. There was a large hole where a ball had lodged in one of his hips, another in the small of one of his legs, his head had been trepanned, and his right side was so perforated with pricks of the small sword, that it had an appearance not easy to describe.[110]

In subsequent centuries, many sensational, conflicting accounts of Fitzgerald's execution would be published—alternately claiming that he had become intoxicated, sobbed uncontrollably, shrieked out like a "wild" animal, or, with fearless bravado, joked with both the hangman and the spectators. Such tales, however, appear to be without foundation. The most reliable firsthand account of the event—written from Castlebar at the time of Fitzgerald's execution, and printed in the weeks following—is more subdued, and even dignified:

> Fitzgerald seemed at first but a little affected—there was a settled solemnity in his countenance, which appeared to be the result of absolute resignation. At intervals it was easy to discover, although he did not express it by word or action, that the certain approach of his dissolution made a very deep impression on him—some people assert that he shed a few tears, but that I did not observe. He every now and then looked round him—and seemed to take a "longing, lingering look."—He spoke very little, and prior to his execution, appeared as if engaged in prayer...
>
> Fitzgerald next mounted the ladder, and here all that desperate courage and temerity, for which his whole life had been distinguished, seemed to return—he no longer betrayed the smallest symptom of fear, but plunged himself off the ladder—the rope broke with the sudden check, and he got a severe shock. He now appeared impatient for the moment of his annihilation; he rose upon his feet without any assistance, and called to the Sheriff to procure a stronger rope instantly —a rope was at hand; it was immediately fastened round his neck; he again mounted the ladder— he leaped a second time—and plunged into eternity. It was thought from the lightness of Mr. Fitzgerald's body, that it would be a considerable time before breath would leave him—but he expired in a very few minutes, in a much shorter space than either of his fellow sufferers.

After "hanging the usual time," Fitzgerald and his two accomplices were "cut down, dismembered, quartered, and their heads severed from their bodies."[111] After decades of surviving numerous potentially deadly duels, and instilling fear and awe into the hearts of his fellow countrymen, George Robert Fitzgerald was finally dead.

# V.

# ALEXANDER "BUCK" ENGLISH

*"Quite simply the most dangerous opponent anybody could meet on the duelling field..."*

William Alexander English was born in Springfield, County Tipperary.[112] Few solid facts about his early life and background are actually known. The *Memoirs of George the Fourth* relates the following fanciful tale about how English's family first obtained their fortune:

> [Alexander English] acquired his property in a very singular manner, for his father, who was a day-labourer, being at work on the lands of Shoonhill, county Tipperary, then the property of the ancestors of the late Lady Caroline Damer, he found a large earthen vase filled with gold, that was supposed to have been hidden there upon the arrival of Oliver Cromwell at the siege of Clonmell. With this money, old William English purchased lands and houses, which at his death became the property of his son, William Alexander English...[113]

Regarding Alexander's religious upbringing, it was related that "the Buck was reared a good Roman Catholic."[114] His obituary, published in 1794, states that,

> Born to a large estate, the earlier part of his life was spent in scenes of the most unbounded dissipation; but these were curtailed when he got into the hands of a litigious attorney, who, for years, kept him out of his property.[115]

English was, reputedly, "one of the most extraordinary characters of the day."[116] During his years in Dublin, he became known as one of the famous "Bucks" due to his predilection for taking part in duels and *rencontres*. Later, English earned the distinction of having faced two of

Ireland's best-known duelists, David "Tyger" Roche and George Robert Fitzgerald—and of having defeated the latter.

English's first known duel took place in Cork in April, 1774, and was with a grocer named Samuel Powell. The historian James Kelly relates the details of this encounter as follows:

> Powell was the aggressor. He knocked English down with an undrawn sword, but it was not long before both men, swords drawn, were locked in combat. English's superior swordsmanship soon made itself felt. He broke through Powell's defences and killed him with a single thrust. Having acquired the taste for combat, English soon found it difficult to overlook insult.[117]

According to another account, "Mr. English was tried for his life, for the murder of Mr. Powell, and was with difficulty acquitted, and escaped narrowly from being torn to pieces by the mob in Cork."[118]

The next year, in May, 1775, English fought a pistol duel "in a field near Spring-house" with Robert Bradshaw of Alleen, County Tipperary. Although a total of four shots were fired, there were no injuries except for a "slight graze which English received from a passing bullet."[119] A contemporary report noted,

> Each fired a case of pistols, and a ball from one of Mr. Bradshaw's shots grazed the right thigh of Mr. English, without doing any injury; each gentleman behaved with becoming valour. The second to Mr. English, James Thornhill of Tipperary, Esq; To Mr. Bradshaw, Edward Croker, of Bruff, in the county of Limerick, Esq.[120]

Later, English was arrested and incarcerated. While in the prison of the King's Bench, he came into contact with the duelist David "Tyger" Roche. The two reportedly "had some dispute," and English, "seizing a stick, flogged him in a savage manner."[121] When Roche was finally liberated from prison, he challenged English, and a combat was arranged to take place in Hyde Park, London. Afterwards, Scotland's *Caledonian Mercury* published a lengthy account of the duel:

> Mr. English came to the ring at one o'clock, according to appointment, and seeing Mr. Roche's carriage at some little distance, sent his friend to inform him he attended there, agreeable to Mr. R—'s desire, and begged to be made acquainted with his commands. Mr. R— sent him backward, his pistols were charged with a single ball each, and that he did not chuse to measure ground; on which Mr. E— charged his pistols in the same manner, took his ground, and desired Mr. R— to come as near him as he thought proper; Mr. Roche accordingly advanced within a small distance of Mr. English, and fired, which Mr. E— returned. The friends then interfered in order to bring about a reconciliation; but Mr. R— requiring an apology from Mr. English, Mr. E— refused to

make any, and begged the gentlemen would retire; on which Mr. E— discharged his second pistol, which was returned by Mr. R—, Mr. R— then told Mr. E—, that if he did not make him an apology, he must charge his pistols again, as he did not look upon what passed as a sufficient atonement for the injury he had received. To the latter proposal, Mr. E— immediately agreed, he alledging that he did not think any apology due from his conduct, considering the provocation given him. Here the friends again interfered, and an explanation being entered into, Mr. R. declared he had meant no offence to Mr. E. by the words he addressed to him at Spa, on which Mr. English assured him, he was very sorry for having mistaken his intention, and for the part he acted in consequence of that error. Thus the affair terminated, to the satisfaction of both parties, without any other ill effect, than Mr. Roche having his cloaths shot through in two places.[122]

By this time, English had already been elected as a member of "Irish Parliament," wherein he represented Taghmore, County Wexford.[123] Two years later, in December of 1778, English took part in yet another duel after having a dispute with a Tipperary landowner named McDowell. According to Kelly:

Both men fulfilled the requirement of the code of honour by receiving one shot, but whereas English was prepared to press the matter to a bloody resolution, his opponent had had enough and 'precipately quit the field in spite of every remonstrance and severity of expression that could be made use of to prevent him.' This was a most unusual turn of events; but it reflected what many felt about Alexander English—that he was quite simply the most dangerous opponent anybody could meet on the duelling field.[124]

The climax of English's dueling career came one year later, in 1779, when he fought a very public sword combat with Ireland's most famous duelist, George Robert Fitzgerald, before a large crowd on St Stephen's Green. As reported in the *Dublin Journal*,

Late on Monday evening last, a duel was fought with swords, at Stephen's-green, between Wm. Alexander English, Esq; member for Taghmore, and Geo. Robert Fitzgerald, Esq. Their passes and advances were so rapid that they very soon closed, when Mr. English's superior force over-throwing Mr. Fitzgerald, several gentlemen who were present interposed, and with difficulty disarmed and separated them.[125]

During this so-called "clash of champions," English wounded Fitzgerald in several places before "delivering the *coup de grace*"; the men were then parted by members of the crowd.[126] A second-hand account related by Charles Marsh indicates that English may have executed a disarm towards the combat's *finale*, for Fitzgerald was...saved from death by a particular friend of the writer, who wrested the sword from the hand of his powerful antagonist, (the famous Buck English,) as he was about to plunge it in his back, after a hard chase, and at a most unfair advantage,—for Fitzgerald was unarmed.[127]

It may also be that Marsh's account refers to a different combat entirely, or to the incident which precipitated the actual duel. Whatever the case, Fitzgerald had finally been deprived of his aura of invincibility.

After this time, English is not recorded as having dueled again. In October, 1783, he was re-elected to Parliament as a representative for Enniscorthy, County Wexford.[128] When English finally passed away in 1794, an obituary in the *Sporting Magazine* offered the following details regarding his life:

> The celebrated Buck English, who lately died in Ireland, spent the latter part of his life in litigious turmoil, and was a man who experienced infinite vicissitudes of fortune...he threw a waiter out of a window, and desired him to be "charged in the bill!" In his career, he fought two duels with swords, in the streets of Dublin—was a member of parliament, and, and excellent speaker; was thrown into a loathsome prison for debt, where his constitution was totally destroyed, and died immediately on his enlargement, and just as he recovered his fortune.[129]

A brief, and far-less glorious obituary, printed in his native Ireland, merely stated:

> DEATHS...On Ranelagh-road, William Alexander English, esq. many years a representative in parliament for the borough of Enniscorthy.[130]

The legends about English and the duels he had fought continued to grow long after his passing. More than fifty years later, in 1851, he was the subject of Dr. Shelton McKenzie's story, *Buck English*, set in Cork in the year 1770. In this fictional tale, English is depicted as a gallant, romantic figure, who—much like Shakespeare's Romeo—ascends an ivy-covered wall to visit his forbidden paramour, Lucy. When a rival for Lucy's affections publicly insults English, the latter responds with an elegant challenge:

> English remained so quiet under this intentionally offensive allusion, that some who did not know him well began to think him deficient in courage. The insult was repeated, in other and harsher words, until English's forbearance was ended. He leant across the table, and said in a low voice, "Mr. Penrose, those words must be withdrawn or atoned for."
>
> "Take them as you please," said Penrose; "I stand by them."
>
> "Then," answered the other, "let me name Captain Cooper as my friend; whom shall he meet on your part?" ...A distant bow denoted his acquiescence, and thus, almost without its being

known to more than three or four persons besides the parties themselves, was arranged a meeting for life or death. The outward show of civility was maintained on both sides, though hostile feelings rankled beneath.[131]

History, of course, differs from this fiction. Period accounts of English's actual character vary widely. Margaret Leeson, a Dublin brothel manager who claimed to have repelled English's romantic advances, remembered the duelist as a "murderous... infamous assassin," describing him as "lascivious, passionate, vindictive, aspiring, cruel, determined, and quarrelsome."[132] By contrast, Sir James Campbell, who spent an evening with English at a local inn, described him as "civil" and "very agreeable," while the *Irish Quarterly Review* claimed that English "was long remembered for the humane disposition which he evinced on one occasion, by throwing a quantity of hot half-crowns to a number of importunate mendicants."[133]

# vi.

## RICHARD BRINSLEY SHERIDAN

*"I struck Mr. Mathews's point so much out of the line, that I stepped up and caught hold of his wrist, or the hilt of his sword, while the point of mine was at his breast..."*

Richard Brinsley Sheridan was born in Dublin in 1751. His father, Thomas Sheridan, was an actor and manager at the Smock Alley Theatre, where he attained considerable renown. The Sheridan family would eventually move to England, where Richard would become one of Britain's best known playwrights, penning such classics as *The Rivals* and *The School for Scandal*. The *Rivals* would become especially infamous for its over-the-top, comic portrayal of the Irish duelist—as embodied by its character, Sir Lucius O'Trigger.[134] On a more serious note, Sheridan himself would take part in his own series of potentially lethal duels during the 1770s, which would be highly publicized in the London press, and which he would later recount in intimate detail.

Sheridan's introduction to swordsmanship began while he was still living in Ireland. There, the Sheridan family had met and become close friends with Henry Angelo and his father, the famous fencing master Domenico Angelo. Henry recounted in his memoirs,

My father and his *chère amie* had made a visit to Ireland, and it was during his short sojourn there that his friendship commenced with the Sheridan family, which lasted, with mutual and uninterrupted intimacy, through life. The happiest days of my youth, indeed, were amongst those which I experienced under the roof of Mr. Thomas Sheridan, of whom and his son, Richard Brinsley, the kind and indulgent friend of my boyhood, I shall have much to say in these frail recollections of my chequered career.[135]

Richard Brinsley Sheridan (1751-1816), after a portrait by Sir Joshua Reynolds.

After Sheridan's move to England, the friendship between he and Henry only deepened, and Henry recalled that his friend was "a constant visitor at my father's, both at his town and country house."[136] During Sheridan's visits to the Angelo home, he often encountered another of Europe's most famed swordsmen, the Chevalier d'Eon, with whom they all "frequently sat for hours over the bottle."[137] Sheridan began studying fencing directly under Domenico; Henry stated that Sheridan "had been a scholar of my father while at Harrow school," and added that "my father, in return for the elder Sheridan's kindness, as an occasional preceptor to me, instructed his son, Richard Brinsley, in the use of the small sword..."[138] Henry also recalled that he and Richard would engage in "fencing matches" at family parties and gatherings.[139]

Sheridan's skill at swordsmanship would be put to the ultimate test in 1772, when a dispute arose over his romantic involvement with Elizabeth Anne Linley, a soprano singer known as "the Maid of Bath" who was greatly admired for her beauty. The Sheridan family had moved to Bath four years earlier. Alfred Hutton provides the following colorful account of how Richard and Elizabeth first became acquainted:

The arts practised by the two families were sufficiently similar to promote mutual sympathy, but not sufficiently identical to engender professional jealousy, so they shortly became extremely intimate. Miss Sheridan was the bosom friend of the Maid of Bath, and the elder brother, Charles, speedily enrolled himself among the number of her courtiers. But a Caesar suddenly arose in the shape of a junior member of the Sheridan family, Richard Brinsley by name, a young fellow of twenty, who had just finished his education; a most attractive young gentleman. He was something of a poet, he was remarkably handsome, with a keen wit and a spice of romance about him; moreover, he rode well, danced to perfection, and understood the handling of the small sword to a remarkable degree, an accomplishment highly desirable in those days. He possessed a chivalrous soul, and was, in fact, a sort of youthful Don Quixote, only minus the age, the wrinkles, and the absurd extravagance. He was liked and admired by everyone, the only person in the whole of Bath with whom he could not get on being his own father, the old professor of speech-making, whose pedantic rules of the art of elocution his son could in no way put up with. Small wonder, then, that, like Caesar, he came, he saw, and he conquered.

The crowd of Miss Linley's admirers gradually melted away, the faithful Charles being the last of them, and much tittle-tattle thereon arose among the scandalmongers of the city, who were promptly taken to task by the chivalrous Richard, who espoused the cause of the young lady from a feeling of friendship, which soon developed into one of a more romantic kind.

Hutton then relates the circumstances leading to Sheridan's duel:

At this juncture a Mephisto appeared on the scene in the person of a Captain [Thomas] Matthews[*], a married man who had left his wife behind him in the country, and who turned out to be an unmitigated scoundrel. This fellow got himself introduced to old Linley under colour of being able to assist him largely with his influence in the matter of placing concert tickets and getting up musical performances, and although the real reason of his attentions was a vastly different one, neither the father nor the mother of the young lady was aware of it, or they must have been so greedy of gain as to ignore it altogether. Matthews carried on the siege for a long time, but without the success he had anticipated, and he at last so far transgressed the rules of decency as to threaten to carry the fair one off by force. The poor girl was so terrified that she decided to take refuge, at least for a time, in a convent in France, whither Richard Sheridan escorted her; but during the journey he declared his unalterable affection for her, and they were privately married by the parish priest of a little village near Calais.

---

[*] A portrait of Captain Thomas Matthews (1741-1820), painted about 1772 by Thomas Gainsborough, currently resides in the Museum of Fine Arts, Boston.

Matthews, balked of his prey, was beside himself with rage and wounded vanity, and in revenge inserted letters and other, matter in the Bath papers attacking the character of the lady as well as that of his successful rival. Charles Sheridan, the brother, took the matter up, contradicted the slanders, and was on the point of requiring satisfaction at the sword's point, when the cowardly Captain, hearing that hostilities were in the air, bolted from Bath and took refuge in London. But "out of the frying-pan into the fire": the refugee found himself face to face with a more implacable enemy, Richard Brinsley, who immediately sent his friend Mr. Ewart to him to demand reparation after the fashion of the day. He was referred by Matthews to a Captain Knight, whom he chose as his second. It was decided that the meeting should take place in Hyde Park, and that the instruments used in it should be swords, Matthews having a strong objection to the pistol.[140]

Elizabeth Anne Linley, after the portrait by Gainsborough.

According to Henry Angelo, Matthews had a special reason to prefer the sword as a dueling weapon—he "had learnt fencing in France, and was considered very skilful in the science..."[141]

Following is Sheridan's personal account of his first combat with Matthews, in a letter addressed to Captain Knight, Matthews's second:

Mr. Ewart accompanied me to Hyde Park, Chap. about six in the evening, where we met you and Mr. Mathews, and we walked together to the ring. — Mr. Mathews refusing to make any other acknowledgement than he had done, I observed that we were come to the ground: Mr. Mathews objected to the spot, and appealed to you. — We proceeded to the back of a building on the other side of the ring, the ground was there perfectly level. I called on him, and drew my sword (he having previously declined pistols). Mr. Ewart observed a sentinel on the other side of the building; we advanced to another part of the Park. I stopped again at a seemingly convenient place: Mr. Mathews objected to the observation of some people at a great distance, and proposed to retire to the Hercules' Pillars till the Park should be clear: we did so. In a little time we returned. — I again drew my sword; Mr. Mathews again objected to the observation of a person who seemed to watch us. Mr. Ewart observed that the chance was equal, and engaged that no one should stop him, should it be necessary for him to retire to the gate, where we had a chaise and four, which was equally at his service. Mr. Mathews declared that he would not engage while any one was within sight, and proposed to defer it till next morning. I turned to you and said that 'this was trifling work,' that I could not admit of any delay, and engaged to remove the gentleman (who proved to be an officer, and who, on my going up to him, and assuring him that any interposition would be ill timed, politely retired). Mr. Mathews, in the mean time, had returned towards the gate; Mr. Ewart and I called to you, and followed. We returned to the Hercules' Pillars, and went from thence, by agreement, to the Bedford Coffee House, where, the master being alarmed, you came and conducted us to Mr. Mathews at the Castle Tavern, Henrietta Street. Mr. Ewart took lights up in his hand, and almost immediately on our entering the room we engaged. I struck Mr. Mathews's point so much out of the line, that I stepped up and caught hold of his wrist, or the hilt of his sword, while the point of mine was at his breast. You ran in and caught hold of my arm, exclaiming, 'Don't kill him.' I struggled to disengage my arm, and said his sword was in my power. Mr. Mathews called out twice or thrice, 'I beg my life.' — We were parted. You immediately said, 'There he has begged his life, and now there is an end of it;' and, on Mr. Ewart's saying that, when his sword was in my power, as I attempted no more you should not have interfered, you replied that you were wrong, but that you had done it hastily and to prevent mischief — or words to that effect. Mr. Mathews then hinted that I was rather obliged to your interposition for the advantage; you declared that 'before you did so, both the swords were in Mr. Sheridan's power.' Mr. Mathews still seemed resolved to give it another turn, and observed that he had never quitted his sword. — Provoked at this, I then swore (with too much heat perhaps) that he should either give up his sword and I would break it, or go to his guard again. He refused—but, on my persisting, either gave it into my hand, or flung it on the table, or the ground (which, I will not absolutely affirm). I broke it, and flung the hilt to the other end of the room.[*] He exclaimed at this. I took a mourning sword from Mr. Ewart, and presenting him with mine, gave my honour that what had passed should never be mentioned by me, and he might now right himself again. He replied that he 'would never draw a sword against the man who had given him his life:' —but, on his still exclaiming against the indignity of breaking his sword (which he had brought upon himself) Mr. Ewart offered him the pistols, and some altercation passed between them. Mr. Mathews said, that he could never show his face if it were known how his sword was broke — that such a thing had never been done — that it cancelled all obligations, &c. &c. You seemed to think it was wrong, and we both proposed, that if he never misrepresented the affair, it should not be mentioned by us. This was settled. I then asked Mr. Mathews, whether (as he had expressed himself sensible of, and shocked at the injustice and indignity he had done me in his advertisement) it did not occur to

---

[*]  According to the Clonmel dueling code of 1777, "The disarmer may strictly break his adversary's sword; but if it be the challenger who is disarmed, it is considered as ungenerous to do so." Sheridan, being the challenger, was thus acting in accordance with this precept.

him that he owed me another satisfaction; and that, as it was now in his power to do it without discredit, I supposed he would not hesitate. This he absolutely refused, unless conditionally; I insisted on it, and said I would not leave the room till it was settled. After much altercation, and with much ill-grace, he gave the apology, which afterwards appeared. We parted, and I returned immediately to Bath.

Following the combat, Matthews published the following apology:

Being convinced that the expressions I made use of to Mr. Sheridan's disadvantage were the effects of passion and misrepresentation, I retract what I have said to that gentleman's disadvantage, and particularly beg his pardon for my advertisement in *The Bath Chronicle*.

THOMAS MATHEWS.[142]

At this point, it seemed as though the quarrel was at an end. However, as a result of the duel, Matthews found himself, according to Hutton, "irretrievably disgraced, both as a man of honour and a man of courage." He retired to his estate in Wales, but there found himself "shunned by everyone." Infuriated by this reception, Matthews traveled again to Bath in the hopes of arranging a second encounter with Sheridan. The latter recounted,

I, there [in Bath], to Colonel Gould, Captain Wade, Mr. Creaser, and others, mentioned the [first] affair to Mr. Mathews's credit — said that chance had given me the advantage, Mr. Mathews had consented to that apology, and mentioned nothing of the sword. Mr. Mathews came down, and in two days I found the whole affair had been stated in a different light, and insinuations given out to the same purpose as in the paper, which has occasioned this trouble. I had *undoubted authority* that these accounts proceeded from Mr. Mathews, and likewise that Mr. Knight had never had any share in them. I then thought I no longer owed Mr. Mathews the compliment to conceal any circumstance, and I related the affair to several gentlemen exactly as above.

Matthews thus challenged Sheridan again. Although the Irishman's friends were "most averse to his descending to meet one so utterly disgraced" as Matthews, Sheridan nevertheless accepted. A second duel was then arranged. It would be considerably bloodier than the first.[143]

On July 4, *The St. James's Chronicle* printed the following "Extract of a letter from Bath":

Young Sheridan and Captain Mathews of this town, who lately had a rencontre in a tavern in London, upon account of the maid of Bath, Miss Linley, have had another this morning upon Kingsdown, about four miles hence. Sheridan is much wounded, but whether mortally or not is yet uncertain. Both their swords breaking upon the first lunge, they threw each other down and with the broken pieces hacked at each other rolling upon the ground, the seconds standing by, quiet spectators. Mathews is but slightly wounded, and is since gone off.[144]

A lengthier account of this combat was later drawn up by Matthews's second, William Barnett. It portrays Sheridan in an unflattering light—and, in fact, included several details which would be directly contradicted by Sheridan's own account:

On quitting our chaises at the top of Kingsdown, I entered into a conversation with Captain Paumier, relative to some preliminaries I thought ought to be settled in an affair, which was likely to end very seriously;— particularly the method of using their pistols, which Mr. Mathews had repeatedly signified his desire to use prior to swords, from a conviction that Mr. Sheridan would run in on him, and an ungentlemanlike scuffle probably be the consequence. This, however, was refused by Mr. Sheridan, declaring he had no pistols: Captain Paumier replied he had a brace (which I know were loaded). — By my advice, Mr. Mathews's were not loaded, as I imagined it was always customary to load on the field, which I mentioned to Captain Paumier at the White Hart, before we went out, and desired he would draw his pistols. He replied, as they were already loaded, and they going on a public road at that time of the morning, he might as well let them remain so till we got to the place appointed, when he would on his honour draw them, which I am convinced he would have done had there been time; but Mr. Sheridan immediately drew his sword, and, in a vaunting manner, desired Mr. Mathews to draw (their ground was very uneven, and near the post-chaises). — Mr. Mathews drew; Mr. Sheridan advanced on him at first; Mr. Mathews in turn advanced fast on Mr. Sheridan; upon which he retreated, till he very suddenly ran in upon Mr. Mathews, laying himself exceedingly open, and endeavouring to get hold of Mr. Mathews's sword; Mr. Mathews received him on his point, and, I believe, disengaged his sword from Mr. Sheridan's body, and gave him another wound; which I suppose, must have been either against one of his ribs, or his breast-bone, as his sword broke, which I imagine happened from the resistance it met with from one of those parts; but whether it was broke by that, or on the closing, I cannot aver.

Mr. Mathews, I think, on finding his sword broke, laid hold of Mr. Sheridan's sword-arm, and tripped up his heels: they both fell; Mr. Mathews was uppermost, with the hilt of his sword in his hand, having about six or seven inches of the blade to it, with which I saw him give Mr. Sheridan, as I imagined, a skin-wound or two in the neck; for it could be no more,— the remaining part of the sword being broad and blunt; he also beat him in the face either with his fist or the hilt of his sword. Upon this I turned from them, and asked Captain Paumier if we should not take them up; but I cannot say whether he heard me or not, as there was a good deal of noise; however, he made no reply. I again turned to the combatants, who were much in the same situation: I found Mr. Sheridan's sword was bent, and he slipped his hand up the small part of it, and gave Mr. Mathews a slight wound in the left part of his belly: I that instant turned again to Captain Paumier, and proposed again our taking them up. He in the same moment called out, 'Oh! he is killed, he is killed!' — I as quick as possible turned again, and found Mr. Mathews had recovered the point of his sword, that was before on the ground, with which he had wounded Mr. Sheridan in the belly: I saw him drawing the point out of the wound. By this time Mr. Sheridan's sword was broke, which he told us. — Captain Paumier called out to him, 'My dear Sheridan, beg your life, and I will be yours for ever.' I also desired him to ask his life: he replied, 'No, by God, I won't.' I then told Captain Paumier it would not do to wait for those punctilios (or words to that effect,) and desired he would assist me in taking them up. Mr. Mathews most readily acquiesced first, desiring me to see Mr. Sheridan was disarmed. I desired him to give me the tuck[*], which he readily did, as did Mr. Sheridan the broken part of his sword to Captain Paumier. Mr. Sheridan and Mr. Mathews both got up, the former was helped into one of the chaises, and drove off for Bath, and Mr. Mathews made the best of his way to London.[145]

In his own account, Sheridan vigorously disputed several of the details related by Barnett. In particular, he insisted that he had not rushed onto Matthews's point—but rather, after closing with Matthews, the latter had attempted to wound him with the "jagged" or blunt part of the sword. Sheridan explained:

The first point in Mr. Barnett's narrative that is of the least consequence to take notice of, is, where Mr. M. is represented as having repeatedly signified his desire to use pistols prior to swords, from a conviction that Mr. Sheridan — would run in upon him, and an ungentlemanlike scuffle probably be the consequence. This is one of those articles which evidently must be given to Mr. Mathews: for, as Mr. B.'s part is simply to relate a matter of fact, of which he was an eye-witness, he is by no means to answer for Mr. Mathews's *private convictions*. As this insinuation bears an obscure allusion to a past transaction of Mr. M.'s, I doubt not but he will be surprized at my indifference in not taking the trouble even to explain it. However, I cannot forbear to observe here that had I, at the period which this passage alludes to, known what was the theory which Mr. M. held of *gentlemanly scuffle*, I might, possibly, have been so unhappy as to have put it out of his power ever to have brought it into practice.

Mr. B. now charges me with having cut short a number of pretty preliminaries, concerning which he was treating with Captain Paumier, by drawing my sword, and, in a vaunting manner, desiring Mr. M. to draw. Though I acknowledge (with deference to these gentlemen) the full right of interference which seconds have on such occasions, yet I may remind Mr. B. that he was acquainted with my determination with regard to pistols before we went on the Down, nor could I have expected it to have been proposed...

But Mr. B. here represents me as drawing my sword in a *vaunting* manner. This I take to be a reflection; and can only say, that a person's demeanour is generally regulated by their idea of their antagonist, and, for what I know, I may now be writing in a vaunting style...

Mr. B.'s account proceeds, that I 'advanced first on Mr. M.,' &c. &c.; 'which, (says Mr. B.) I imagine, happened from the resistance it met with from one of those parts; but whether it was broke by that, or on the closing, I cannot aver.' How strange is the confusion here! — First, it

---

[*]   *Tuck:* from the French *estoc*. A sword.

certainly broke; —whether it broke against rib or no, doubtful; — then, indeed, whether it broke at all, uncertain. But of all times Mr. B. could not have chosen a worse than this for Mr. M.'s sword to break; for the relating of the action unfortunately carries a contradiction with it;— since if, on closing, Mr. M. received me on his point, it is not possible for him to have made a lunge of such a nature as to break his sword against a rib-bone. But as the time chosen is unfortunate, so is the place on which it is said to have broke, —as Mr. B. might have been informed, by enquiring of the surgeons, that I had no wounds on my breast or rib with the point of a sword, they being the marks of the jagged and blunted part.[146]

Immediately following the combat, Sheridan was driven from the ground to the White Hart Inn, where his wounds were attended to by eminent surgeons from Bath. The next day, Sheridan was conveyed to his father's house, where he was confined for several weeks, eventually recovering.[147] On April 13, 1773, their parents finally having consented to the match, Richard Brinsley Sheridan and Elizabeth Anne Linley were married by license.

Of the duel's aftermath, Henry Angelo wrote in his memoirs, "I recollect Dick Sheridan (his appellation then) shewing me a wound in his neck, then in a sore state, which he told me he had received from his antagonist on the ground..."[148] Despite the outcome of the second combat, Angelo offered the following praise for Sherdian and his own father's teachings:

> It was in consequence of the skill which [Sheridan] acquired under [Domenico's] tution, that he acquitted himself with so much address, when opposed to the captain, whose reputation was well known in the circles of fashion, as an experienced swordsman.[149]

In later years, Sheridan was often remarked upon for his calmness of mind and cool composure, which had no doubt served him well in the duels. His unique character and sense of humor can perhaps be best observed in his reported reaction to the sight of his own theater burning down, an incident which occurred on February 24, 1809:

> It is said that, as he sat at the Piazza Coffeehouse, during the fire [of the Drury Lane Theatre], taking some refreshment, a friend of his having remarked on the philosophic calmness with which he bore his misfortune, Sheridan answered, "A man may surely be allowed to take a glass of wine by his own fire-side."[150]

---

1   Paul Jordan-Smith, foreword to *Amiable Renegade: The Memoirs of Captain Peter Drake, 1671-1753* (Stanford University Press, 1960), xi-xvii.

2   John Burke, *Burke's genealogical and heraldic history of the landed gentry, Volume I* (London: H. Colburn, 1847), 349.

3   Paul Jordan-Smith, xvi-xvii.

4   Peter Drake, *The Memoirs of Capt. Peter Drake: Containing, an Account of Many Strange and Surprising Events, which Happened to Him Through a Series of Sixty Years, and Upwards; and Several Material Anecdotes, Regarding King William and Queen Anne's Wars with Lewis XIV of France, Volume I* (Dublin: S. Powell, 1755), vi-vii.

5   Drake, *Memoirs, Volume I*, 6.

6   For a fuller account of Drake's training under Butler, see Chapter V.

7   Ibid., 48-49.

8   Ibid., 84-86.

9   Ibid., 86-88.

10  Ibid., 94-96.

11  Ibid., 182-192.

12  Drake, *Memoirs, Volume II*, 67-66.

13  Ibid., 130-131.

14  Ibid., 136-139.

15  Capt. John Godfrey, *A Treatise Upon the Useful Science of Defence* (London: T. Gardner, 1747), 40.

16  Captain James Miller, *A Treatise on backsword, sword, buckler, sword and dagger, sword and great gauntlet, falchon, quarterstaff* (London: [1738]).

17  Drake, *Memoirs, Volume II*, 186-190.

18  Ibid.,194-195.

19  Ibid., 236-241.

20  Ibid., 265.

21  Ibid., 281.

22  *Tuam Herald*, November 26, 1870.

23  Anne Partlon, "The Life and Times of Sir John Waters Kirwan (1866-1949)" (PhD diss., Murdoch University, 2011), 17-18.

24  *Tuam Herald*.

25  Partlon, 16.

26  *Tuam Herald*.

27  Michael Donovan, "Biographical Account of the Late Richard Kirwan, Esq.", *Proceedings of the Royal Irish Academy (1836-1869)*, Vol. 4 (1847-1850), lxxxii.

28  Partlon, 17.

29  James Hardiman, *The history of the town and country of the town of Galway: from the earliest period to the present time* (Dublin: Printed by W. Folds, 1820), 314.

30  Jonah Barrington, *Personal Sketches of his own Times, Vol. II* (Philadephia: Carey, Lea, & Carey, 1827), 7.

31  Partlon, 19-21.

32  *Tuam Herald*.

33  Partlon, 19-20.

34  *Tuam Herald*.

35  See, for instance, the account of John McKenna, from Gortaneden, Co. Kerry (ca. 1934-1938). The Schools' Collection, Volume 432, Page 316. http://www.duchas.ie/en/cbes/4707621/4685919/4707880

36  Sir Bernard Burke, *A genealogical and heraldic history of the landed gentry of Ireland* (London: Harrison & Sons, 1912), 372.

37  *Derby Mercury*, December 5, 1755.

38  Donovan, lxxxv.

39  Partlon, 18.

40  Ibid., 20.

41  Ibid., 21.

42  *Walker's Hibernian Magazine*, December, 1775.

43  *Morning Chronicle and London Advertiser*, January 14, 1777. Charles Smith, *The ancient and present state of the county and city of Cork: Containing a natural, civil, ecclesiastical, historical and topographical description thereof* (Cork: Printed by J. Connor, 1815), 337. John-Bernard Burke, *A Genealogical and Heraldic Dictionary of the Peerages of England, Ireland* (London: Henry Colburn, 1846), 692-693. Bernard Burke, A Visitation of the Seats and Arms of the Noblemen and Gentlemen of Great Britain and Ireland (London: Hurst and Blackett, 1855), 197-199. *The Gentleman's Magazine*, July, 1855.

44  Told by Mr. D. Fitzgibbons, age 70, from Ballylegan, Glanworth, Co. Cork. The Schools' Collection, Volume 373, Page 36.

45  *Gentleman's Magazine*, July, 1855.

46  *The Universal Magazine*, March, 1774.

47  Ibid.

48  *Dublin Courier*, March 9, 1763.

49  *Universal Magazine.*

50  *The Fortnight's Register, or, a Chronicle of Interesting and Remarkable Events, Foreign and Domestic*, June 4, 1763.

51  *Harper's New Monthly Magazine, Vol. IV, December 1851 – May 1852* (New York: Harper & Brothers, 1852), 762-763.

52  For more information on the Pinking Dindies, see Chapter IV.

53  *Universal Magazine.*

54  *Harper's*, 763-764.

55  *Kentish Gazette*, December 21, 1776.

56  *Harper's*, 763-764.

57  Universal Magazine, March, 1774.

58  *London Chronicle*, January 14, 1773.

59  David Roche, *A plain and circumstantial account of the transactions between Capt. Roche and Lieut. Ferguson, from their first meeting to the death of Lieut. Ferguson. To which is added, the trial and depositions at the Cape of Good Hope, where Capt. Roche was acquitted: also his second apprehension ; and the judicial proceedings of the governor and Council of Bombay* (London: Sold by G. Allen, 1775), 76.

60  *Walker's Hibernian Magazine*, December, 1775.

61  Ibid.

62  *The Town and country magazine, or, Universal repository of knowledge, instruction, and entertainment, Vol. 6* (London: Printed for A. Hamilton, 1774), 54.

63  *Walker's Hibernian Magazine*, December, 1775.

64  *Universal Magazine.*

65 Edward Gibbon, *The miscellaneous works of Edward Gibbon, Esq.: with memoirs of his life and writings. Composed by himself: illustrated from his letters, with occasional notes and narrative, by the right honourable John, Lord Sheffield* (London : Printed for John Murray, 1814) 120.

66 *Middlesex Journal and Evening Advertiser*, August 27, 1774.

67 *London Evening Post*, March 14, 1775.

68 *Walker's Hibernian Magazine*, December, 1775.

69 *London Gazetteer and New Daily Advertiser*, January 13, 1777.

70 *Calendar of the Patent Rolls of the Chancery of Ireland* (Dublin: 1800), 313-314.

71 *The Dublin University Magazine*, December, 1843.

72 *Harper's*, 760.

73 Roche, 91-92.

74 "There were few men who flourished in my early days that excited more general or stronger interest than Mr. George Robert Fitzgerald of Turlow..." Barrington, *Personal Sketches, Vol. II*, 274.

75 Joseph Hamilton, *The Only Approved Guide through all the Stages of a Quarrel: Containing the Royal Code of Honor* (London: Hatchard & Sons; Bentham & Co. Liverpool; and Millikin, Dublin, 1829).

76 Kelly, 151.

77 *Authentic Memoirs of George Robert Fitzgerald, Esq; with a Full Account of His Trial and Execution, for the Murder of Patrick Randell Mcdonnell, Esq* (London: Printed for the Editor; sold by E. Dodd, 1786), 98.

78 *The Life of George Robert Fitzgerald, Esq. Containing Every Interesting Circumstance Which Happened to That Unfortunate Man: Including Several Anecdotes of His Family; to Which Is Added a Number of Facts, Relative to His Trial and Execution* (London: J. Ridgway, 1786), 5, 10.

79 Barrington, *Personal Sketches, Vol. II*, 273.

80 *Dublin University Magazine*, September, 1840.

81 Barrington, *Personal Sketches, Vol. II*, 274.

82 Oliver J. Burke, *Anecdotes of the Connaught Circuit: From Its Foundation in 1604 to Close Upon the Present Time* (Dublin: Hodges, Figgis, 1885), 114.

83 Burke, 116.

84 *Dublin University Magazine*, September, 1840.

85 *Lives of the Late George Robert Fitzgerald, and P.R. McDonnel, Esqrs.* ([Place of publication unknown, 1786]), 40.

86 Angelo, *Reminiscences, Vol. II*, 119-121.

87 George Robert Fitzgerald, *The Reply to Thomas Walker, Esq. Ci-devant Cornet in Burgoyne's Light Dragoons* (London: Parker; J. Ridley; and T. Evans, 1775), 29-31.

88 Charles Marsh, *The clubs of London; with anecdotes of their members, sketches of character, and conversations, Volume 1* (London: H. Colburn, 1828), 43.

89 Barrington, *Personal Sketches, Vol. III*, 145-147.

90 *Dublin University Magazine*, August, 1840.

91 Archibald Hamilton Rowan, *Autobiography of Archibald Hamilton Rowan, Esq: With Additions and Illustrations* (Dublin: T. Tegg and Company, 1840), 64-66.

92 *Authentic Memoirs*, 16.

93 *The Covent Garden Magazine Or the Amorous Repository*, September, 1773.

94 *The Triumphs of Brittania. A Poem.* (London: Printed by the author, 1773).

95 Correspondence between George Robert Fitzgerald and Mrs Jane FitzGerald, mostly dated 1776, National Archives, D239/M/E/5021-5029. Notably, many nineteenth century biographies of Fitzgerald erroneously claim that by the time these letters were written, Fitzgerald was estranged from his wife and daughter.

96 George Robert Fitzgerald, *An appeal to the Jockey Club, or, A true narrative of the late affair, between Mr. FitzGerald and Mr. Walker* (London: Parker; J. Ridley; and T. Evans, 1775).

97 Thomas Walker, *An answer to Mr. Fitzgerald's Appeal to the gentlemen of the Jockey Club* (London: G. Kearsly, 1775).

98 Fitzgerald, *The Reply to Thomas Walker, Esq.*

99 *Dublin Evening Post,* April 29, 1779. Kelly, 151.

100 *Memoirs of the Life of the Late George R. Fitzgerald and P. R. McDonnel, Esqrs.* (Dublin: James Moore, 1786), 34.

101 George Robert Fitzgerald, *An Appeal to the Public* (Dublin: 1782), 67.

102 Ibid., 276.

103 *London Chronicle*, June 20, 1786.

104 *Walker's Hibernian Magazine*, November, 1781. Copy of a letter sent to William FitzHerbert about George Robert FitzGerald, dated 22 December 1781, National Archives, D239 M/E 5078.

105 George Robert Fitzgerald, *The Riddle. By G----- R----- F--------, Esq.* (Dublin: 1782). See also *The Riddle. By the Late Unhappy George-Robert Fitzgerald, Esq. With Notes, by W. Bingley* (London: Printed for the editor, and sold by R. Jameson, 1787).

106 *The Gentleman's Magazine*, August, 1787.

107 Fitzgerald, *An Appeal to the Public.*

108 *Hibernian Journal; or, Chronicle of Liberty*, April 23, 1784.

109 *Walker's Hibernian Magazine*, July, 1786.

110 *Belfast Evening Post*, June 19, 1786.

111 *London Gazetteer and New Daily Advertiser*, June 21, 1786. This same account was unscrupulously altered by the editors of *Walker's Hibernian Magazine* in their June 1786 issue to include the creative detail that Fitzgerald had let out a "wild shriek."

112 James Kelly, 150.

113 Robert Huish, *Memoirs of George the Fourth, descriptive of the most interesting scenes of his private and public life, and the important events of his memorable reign; with characteristic sketches of all the celebrated men who were his friends and companions as a prince, and his ministers and counsellors as a monarch. Compiled from authentic sources, and documents in the king's library in the British museum, Vol. 1* (London: Printed for T. Kelly, 1830), 405.

114 Margaret Leeson, *Memoirs of Mrs. Margaret Leeson, written by herself; in which are given anecdotes, sketches of the lives and bon mots of some of the most celebrated characters in Great-Britain and Ireland. Vol 3* (Dublin: Printed and sold by the principal booksellers, 1797),

115 *Sporting Magazine*, May, 1794.

116 Huish, 405.

117 Kelly, 150.

118 *Sporting Magazine*, May, 1794.

119 Kelly, 150-151.

120 *Hibernian Magazine*, July, 1775.

121 *Harper's New Monthly Magazine, Vol. IV, December 1851 – May 1852* (New York: Harper & Brothers, 1852), 762-764.

122 *Caledonian Mercury*, December 25, 1776.

123 Ibid.

124 Kelly, 151.

125 *Dublin Evening Post*, April 29, 1779.

126 Kelly, 151.

127 Charles Marsh, *The Clubs of London: with anecdotes of their members, sketches of character, and conversations.*, Vol. 1 (Philadelphia: Carey, Lea & Carey, 1828), 137-138.

128 *Walker's Hibernian Magazine*, October, 1783.

129 *Sporting Magazine*, May, 1794.

130 *Walker's Hibernian Magazine*, June, 1794.

131 *The Keepsake* (London: Hurst, Chance and Co, 1851), 175-187.

132 Leeson, 74, 87.

133 James Campbell, *Memoirs of Sir James Campbell, of Ardkinglas, written by himself*, Vol. 2 (London: H. Colburn and R. Bentley, 1832), 264-265. *The Irish quarterly review. Vol. 2, Part 2* (Dublin: W. B. Kelly, 1852), 535.

134 Richard Brinsley Sheridan, *The Rivals, a comedy. As it is acted at the Theatre-Royal in Covent-Garden* (London: Printed for John Wilkie, 1775), 58.

135 Henry Angelo, *Reminiscences with Memoirs of His Late Father and Friends, Including Numerous Original Anecdotes and Curious Traits of the Most Celebrated Characters that Have Flourished During the Last Eighty Years, Volume I* (London: Henry Colburn and Richard Bentley, 1830), 5.

136 Ibid., 85.

137 Ibid., 55.

138 Ibid.; see also Henry Angelo, *Reminiscences with Memoirs of His Late Father and Friends, Including Numerous Original Anecdotes and Curious Traits of the Most Celebrated Characters that Have Flourished During the Last Eighty Years, Volume II* (London: Henry Colburn and Richard Bentley, 1830), 417.

139 Angelo, *Reminiscences, Vol. I*, 54.

140 Alfred Hutton, *The Sword Through the Centuries* (Mineola, N.Y.: Dover Publications, 2002), 237-239.

141 Angelo, *Reminiscences, Vol. II*, 417.

142 Thomas Moore, *Memoirs of the life of the Right Honourable Richard Brinsley Sheridan, Volume I* (London: Longman, 1826), 78-85.

143 Hutton, 239-240.

144 Moore, 92.

145 Ibid., 88-91.

146 Ibid., 95-98.

147 Ibid., 98.

148 Angelo, *Reminiscences, Vol. II*, 417.

149 Angelo, *Reminiscences, Vol. I*, 85.

150 *The London Literary Gazette and Journal of Belles Lettres, Arts, Sciences, Etc.*, October 8, 1825.

Trade card depicting Figg's Ampitheatre. The authorship of this etching has been attributed to both William Hogarth and Joseph Sympson. From Samuel Ireland's *Graphic Illustrations of Hogarth* (1794).

# III

## IRISH AMAZONS *and* STAGE GLADIATORS

*"The two first and most profound Swordsmen in the Kingdom of
Ireland, whom in combat the Universe never yet could parallel…"*

During the early eighteenth century, a large number of Irish fencers, including at least four women, took part in another form of ritualistic combat practiced outside of the conventions of the duel. This was the dangerous gladiatorial stage-fight, fought with sharp weapons, that was made famous by English champion James Figg at the infamous "Bear Garden" in Hockley-in-the-Hole, London. The fencing scholar and antiquarian Egerton Castle described this form of combat as follows:

> The stage-fight of the eighteenth century, although the outcome of those "prizes" played in public by the old "Maisters of Defence," or their scholars, was a prize-fight in another sense. Its object was to win, not merely glory, but likewise the stakes deposited on the wager, as well as the gate-money, which became the property of the gladiator who "kept the stage to the last."

In 1672, a Frenchman named Josevin de Rocheford visited the Bear Garden, and observed the dramatic pomp and ritual preceding such combats:

> We went to the 'Bergiardin', where combats are fought by all sorts of animals, and sometimes men, as we once saw. Commonly, when any fencing-masters are desirous of showing their

courage and great skill, they issue mutual challenges, and before they engage parade the town with drums and trumpets sounding, to inform the public there is a challenge between two brave masters of the science of defence, and that the battle will be fought on such a day.

What followed these processions was violent and often gruesome. On the appointed day, to the sound of trumpets and beating drums, the two combatants would ascend the stage, strip to their chests, and, on a signal from the drum, draw their weapons and commence fighting. The combat would continue until one participant conceded the match, or was unable to continue. In de Rocheford's account, the combatants continue fighting while enduring horrific wounds, including severed ears, cut scalps, and half-severed wrists.[1] Sometimes both combatants' legs were purposely strapped to the floor of the stage, forcing the fencers to hold their ground no matter what the cost. During these particular contests, combatants were often wounded so that they were, to use their own term, "*made a devil of*; that is, cloven in the foot."[2] Bouts occurred with different types of weapons, including the two-handed sword, back-sword, small-sword, single rapier, rapier and dagger, sword and buckler, sword and targe, sword and gauntlet, falchion, and quarterstaff.[3] Although such fights were not intended to end in death, the wounds received were often serious enough to incur it.[4] In 1729, it was reported that "the *Irishman* who had a piece taken out of his Skull at Mr. *Fig*'s Ampitheatre last Week, in a Battle with a Gladiator, was thought last Thursday to be at the Point of Death."[5]

Although the majority of these stage-fights took place in England, the custom also made its way to a variety of far-flung British colonies—to places as remote as Jamaica, Barbados, New England, Maryland, Scotland, and Ireland. During the 1720s and 1730s, a large percentage of stage-fighters were Irish, hailing from cities such as Dublin, Drogheda, Derry, Limerick, Kilkenny, Cork, and Waterford, and sporting colorful appellations such as, "Tall Boy," the "Strong Irishman," the "Invincible Irish Championess," the "Terrible Butcher from the Kingdom of Ireland," and "the Black King." In many cases, such fighters were publicly proclaimed to be "champions" of Ireland. As we have been able to find only a handful of specific references to stage fights with sharp weapons taking place in Ireland, it may be that these titles were merely self-assumed. A number of references in English sources indicate that large numbers of combats did take place in Ireland; however, accounts of these were either not recorded by the somewhat scant Irish press of the period, or have not survived. Nevertheless, the fact of their occurrence seems indisputable, and is attested to by the records of many English, Irish, and Welsh combatants who listed participation in Irish stage-fights among their martial achievements. For instance, in 1719, William Broadmead, a Serjeant of Dragoons from Devonshire, claimed that he had fought "many good Masters in England and Ireland."[6] In 1727, a Welsh gladiator named John Crumpton declared that "about 6 Years past, [I] fought

Three Battles in London, with good Success, and since, the best Masters in the Kingdom of Ireland."[7] And again in 1729, Joseph Johnston, a cordwainer and "Master of the Noble Science of Defence" noted that he had "fought the best Masters in Ireland, and likewise in most Parts of England."[8] An acceptance to a 1728 challenge issued in Oxford, by an "undaunted Irish Champion" named James Hughes who had "already conquer'd all the masters in [his] own Country,"[9] also indicates that gladiatorial combats were taking place in Ireland in great numbers:

> I, James Hughes, from the North of Ireland, Master of the said Science, known by the Name of the Terrible Champion in those Parts, having fought 114 Battles with Success, excepting two in London, which was with the famous Mr. Sutton, and then came off with great Credit, and Equal, will not fail meeting Mr. Gill at the Place above-mentioned, where I hope to give the same Satisfaction, in order to let the Spectators see, that the Kingdom of Ireland can produce as good a Swordsman as any in England...[10]

In another similar challenge, the English champion Edward Sutton indicated that he had previously fought the Irish champion Francis Sherlock in a contest set in Dublin, and provided details pertaining to the conditions of their fight:

> ...if he dare fight in the same manner as Mr. Sherlock did Mr. Sutton, in Dublin, viz. without a Shirt, in a thin Linnen Waistcoat laced close to the Skin, with white Drawers and Stockings, where no Cut can be hid, and for the Sum of Fifty Guineas, at the following Weapons, viz. single Sword, Sword and Dagger, Sword and Buckler, single Falchion, and Case of Falchions, of each three Bouts, no Wounds to be dress'd till the Battle is over...[11]

Likewise, John Bernard, "Champion of Londonderry" and "Master both at Sword and Staff," declared that he had "fought the famous Mr. Parks several times in Dublin."[12] Additionally, when confronted by a challenger claiming to be the student of a "famous" English master, James Figg himself quipped that he had never known or heard of "above two or three [masters] in Ireland, that were Famous"—Figg's point being that, aside from himself, the only other masters in all of the British isles meriting the description of "famous" were in Ireland.[13]

The only actual firsthand account of an early eighteenth century prize-fight in Ireland that we have been able to find was recorded by the duelist Peter Drake, who merely noted that the combat took place in the hold of a ship moored off of Dublin, that "several strokes" were exchanged before the match was broken up, and that the combatants were later pursued by the authorities.[14] Thus, for more information on the lives, times, and exploits of Irish gladiators, it is necessary to look to English accounts from the same period.

Following is a list of fifty-one Irish gladiators, mentioned and described in the literature of the era, who were known to have been active between 1700 and 1750:

Robert Langdon, Felt-Maker, from Dublin (1700-1701)

John Padwin, born in Ireland (1709)

Thomas Aylmer, from Dublin (1714-15)

James Sherlock, from Dublin, "Head Master of the Science of Defence in the Kingdom of Ireland" (1716)

Richard Stevenson, from Dublin (1721)

Robert Blake, "late from Ireland" (1721)

William Finn, of Ireland (1723-1732)

James Collins, Cook, from Ireland (1723)

Christopher Perkins, Taylor, from Dublin (1724-1728)

Bonduca O'Brian, "the bold Female Hibernian Heroine" (1725)

Robert Clayton, from Drogheda (1725)

Joseph Hamlin, from Ireland (1725)

Matthew Shelton, from Dublin (1726)

William Grinsill, from Dublin (1726)

Andrew O'Bryan, of the Kingdom of Ireland (1726)

Metcalf Sheldon, from Dublin (1726-1727)

Mary Welsh, "the Invincible Irish Championess" from "the famous City of Dublin" (1726-1729)

Thomas Elmore, "the famous Master from Dublin" (1726-31)

Barnet Hughes, from Ireland, "Kinsman to the terrible Champion of the North in that Kingdom" (1727)

Brian Le Bunn, from Dublin (1727)

Hugh MacDonald, from Dublin (1727)

Bryan Mac Kenny, from Ireland (1727)

Bryan Burn, from Ireland (1727)

Robert Barker, "the Terrible Butcher from the Kingdom of Ireland" (1727-1733)

Felix Mac Guire, from Dublin, "First Master and Swordsman in Vogue in the Kingdom of Ireland" (1727-35)

Clerk "the Irish Gladiator" (1728)

James Hughes, from the North of Ireland, "known by the name of the *Terrible Champion* in that Kingdom" (1728)

John Dunn, Farmer, from Ireland (1728)

Michael Butler, of Kilkenny (1728-31)

Charles Wright, of Dublin, "commonly known by the name of Tall Boy" (1728-32)

Mary Waller, the "Hibernian" (1729)

Nicholas Hussey, Printer, from Ireland (1729)

Andrew Mac-Colley, of Sligo, "vulgarly call'd the Strong Irishman" (1729-31)

William Sherlock, "Head Master of the Science of Defence in the Kingdom of Ireland" (1729-34)

Philip MacDonald, Carpenter, from Dublin (1730)

Thomas Farrell, from the Kingdom of Ireland (1730)

John Savage, from Ireland, "commonly known by the name of the Bold Sailor" (1730)

William Holmes, of Waterford (1730)

Mathew Masterson, Irish Serjeant, lately come from Gibraltar (1730)

James Roach, from the City of Dublin (1730)

Anthony English, from Cork (1730-45)

Rowland Bennet, from Dublin (1721-45)

William Hanna, from Ireland (1732)

John Homes, from the City of Cork (1732)

Robert Thomas, from Dublin (1732)

John Bernard, "commonly called the Champion of Londonderry" (1732)

William King, Tobacconist, from Dublin, "commonly known by the name of the Black King of Morocco, lately arrived from the Kingdom of Spain" (1732)

Lætitia Mac-Guire, "well-known by the name of the bold Quaker" (1733)

Francis Sherlock, from Dublin (1736-52)

James Fitzgerald, from Ireland (1743)

William Johnston, Woolcomber, from Limerick (1745)

# IRISH CHAMPIONS

Between 1700 and 1720, only four Irish combatants are known to have been recorded as taking part in stage-fights in England. Then, in the early 1720s, an explosion in the number of Irish participants occurred. One of the first in the new wave of Irish gladiators—at least that we know of—was one James Collins, whose challenge was published in May of 1723:

At the boarded House in Marybone-Fields, this present Wednesday, being the 29th of May, will be performed a Trial of Skill between ROBERT WALDRON, Plummer, and JAMES COLLINS from Ireland, Cook, at the usual Weapons fought on the Stage. Note, Mr. Collins having given Mr. Waldron an unfortunate Cut over the Eye and Nose, (when they fought to divert the

Company some Time since) occasions this Invitation; and it's expected to be the sharpest Battle fought a great while; which must give intire Satisfaction to the Quality, Gentry, &c. The Doors will be open at Four, and the Masters mount at Six precisely.[15]

During the 1720s, stage-fights including Irish participants also took place at the "Great House" in Marylebone Fields, at Figg's Ampitheatre in Southwark, London, and at Stokes's Ampitheatre in Saddler's Wells. The opponents of the celebrated Figg included numerous Irishmen, such as Philip McDonald ("the Dublin carpenter"), William Finn of Ireland, William Holmes of Waterford, Rowland Bennet of Dublin, and Nicholas Hussey, "a Printer of Ireland," who, we are assured, conducted himself "with great Honour."[16] One particular challenge, issued by McDonald on September 4, 1723, gives the reader an idea of how the fame of "Mr. James Figg," having spread to Ireland, inspired would-be Irish champions to cross the sea for the lure of glory and prize-money:

> Whereas I, PHILIP MCDONALD, Carpenter from Dublin, Master of the Noble Science of Defence, after having attack'd the most celebrated Masters of that Place with Universal Success and Applause, as also an Eminent Master of England, the Particulars of all which I forbear to Instance, because, that as I speak it of myself, it may be censured as Partial: But hearing that Mr. James Figg excels so much all other Masters, that no one is able to put themselves in Competition with him, the great Report of which is spreading itself all over the aforesaid Parts, excited me to come over, to dispute with him that Character, in order for which, I hereby invite him to meet me as above...

Figg accepted McDonald's challenge, and only a week later, on September 11th, 1723, McDonald issued another:

> Whereas I PHILIP MCDONALD, Carpenter from Dublin, Master of the Noble Science of Defence, who Fought Mr. Figg last Wednesday, but under what Disadvantages (as being altogether a Stranger, and my late Arrival, which I confess was on purpose) I leave to the candid Censure of the Spectators: But for a further Specimen of my Skill (which hitherto has equall'd all I ever met with) that no Cut may be obscur'd, I do once more invite the said Mr. Figg to meet me as above, and exercise the usual Weapons fought on the Stage, in plain Buff, and he that gives the Majority of Cuts to have the whole House.[17]

A survey of several hundred stage fights that took place in England during the 1720s and 1730s reveals that roughly half of contesting gladiators were Irish. By comparison, only a few Scottish, Welsh, and foreign combatants are recorded, while the remaining portion (approximately half) of all gladiators are recorded as being English.[18] During the same period, a

"The Bear Garden." From Dr. Doran's *Their Majesties Servants, or Annals of the English Stage* (1865).

Frenchman named Antoine François Prévost d'Exiles attended a stage-fight at Figg's amphitheatre, and noted the prevalence of Irish combatants:

> The same Day we went to see a Diversion very extraordinary and no where known but in *England*, I mean Combats of Gladiators which they call Prize-fighting, a *Roman* Custom kept up in this Island for near two thousand Years. We found assembled in the Place of Combat a Crowd of Persons of all Ranks. The Theatre where the Combatants fight is in the Middle of a large Hall, and surrounded on all Sides by the Spectators, seated upon Benches raised one above the other to the very Roof....The last Combat is with the Sword, which is commonly undertaken by *Irishmen*, who, by a publick Challenge, by Way of Advertisement in the News Papers, with a Rodomontade* that makes People laugh, engage themselves to fight with all who dare expose themselves to the cruel Edge of their terrible Sword; and then they give you a List of the rash Fools that have lost their Lives or been wounded by them; so that, take their own Word for it, they are so many *Cæsars* and *Alexanders*, and yet they are almost constantly beat by the *English*, particularly by a certain Prize fighter called *Figg*, who handles a broad Sword with the greatest Dexterity of any Man alive. I have been assured that he has fought publickly more than a hundred Times, without having received any considerable Wound...[19]

---

\* Boastful or inflated talk or behavior.

Although Prévost claimed that Irish combatants were "almost constantly beat by the English," a survey of numerous accounts of British stage fights indicates that, during the 1720s, this was not the case, and there were, in fact, only two Englishmen who consistently beat Irish swordsmen. One was, of course, the aforementioned champion James Figg, who reportedly achieved a lifetime record of two-hundred and seventy-one wins and only one loss (although, as shall be seen, this figure seems open to dispute). The other was Edward Sutton, the only individual officially recorded as having decisively defeated Figg. Nor were Irish combatants always boastful—although such braggadocio seems to have been a common feature of British stage-fights, utilized by both English and Irish fighters to help inflame partisan sentiment and enhance publicity. When, in April, 1723, William Finn challenged Figg to a stage-fight, the English champion commended Finn's graciousness:

Encouraged by the Fame that he will acquire, that encounters with Success the famous Mr. James Figg, I WILLIAM FINN, of Ireland, do invite him to meet me at the Place and Time above appointed, and to Exercise with the usual Weapons of the Stage. I desire no favour, and hope to give a general Satisfaction.

I JAMES FIGG, from Thame in Oxfordshire, am ready to meet Mr. William Finn at the Time and Place appointed. I esteem well of him from the Modesty of his Invitation, and hope to behave as becomes me.[20]

William Finn (sometimes "Fenn"), was an "upholder" who, in 1714, appeared on the lists of the Ancient Freemen of Dublin.[21] Although the outcome of the combat between Finn and Figg was not recorded, nine years later, the former was in the news again, challenging Edward Sutton to a fight at Stokes's Amphitheatre:

Wm. Fenn, from the Kingdom of Ireland, Master of the noble and laudable Science of Defence, being willing to engage that Heroick Master now in Esteem Mr. Edward Sutton, if he accepts of my Invitation at the Place above-mention'd, the best Man take the whole Box, and the Money therein, and with a Resolution am resolv'd to let his Countrymen know he is not the Man they take him to be, and to give him and the Spectators to understand I am not the Pretender of that noble Art called Defence, but a profound Master in all its Branches Offensive and Defensive. I hope all my Countrymen, called Masters, for the future will take Pattern by me to behave them-selves like Men of Valour, and not to have a Stain in their Character, for the Honour of Hiber-nian Glory.

William Fenn.

N.B. Whereas Mr. Sibblis has inserted in his Advertisements of fighting me after a Fellow called Ofoot, from Canterbury, a Drummer of the Foot Guards, who does not know the Fort of the

Sword from the Feeble, if he will come to the Place above-mention'd I will fight him my Left Leg ty'd up, if he does not I shall post him as a Coward.

Sutton accepted Finn's challenge, stating that their combat would be a "decisive Battle between these two Kingdoms, which is the best Master," and added that "Ofoot is not a Master, nor any Man in Kent, only myself, as the World can testify."[22] Another report published the same year described the outcome of a match between Finn and Sutton:

We have an Account from Lynn-Regis in the County of Norfolk that a great Tryal of Skill was perform'd there on the 16th Instant, between William Finn of Ireland and Edward Sutton of Gravesend, who went thro' all the Weapons with great Courage, and much to the Satisfaction of the People; the Mayor and Aldermen order'd them to go off Hand and Hand, and the Populace carry'd Finn round the Town upon their Shoulders.[23]

Months later, when Sutton was challenged by one William Hanna of Dublin[24], the result was again favorable to the Irish combatant:

WILLIAM HANNA from Dublin in the Kingdom of Ireland, Master of the Noble Science of Defence, having on Wednesday last engag'd that renowned Champion Mr. Sutton, the Kentish Hero, to the entire Satisfaction of the Spectators then present...he receiving cuts from me and not returning any again, which he is pleas'd to say was by Accident, I do hereby give him the second Invitation to fight me six Bouts at single Sword, and six Bouts at the double Weapons...

Responding to this challenge, Sutton acknowledged his "receiving a small Cut." He explained, "had the Edge of my Sword taken Place this Hibernian must have gone to the lower Regions, but Fortune is a Gamester..."[25] Such reports make clear that, contrary to Prévost's account, many Irish gladiators of the period were extremely formidable.

## CHRISTOPHER PERKINS

One of the earliest Irish gladiators to contest during the eighteenth century was also one of the most renowned. His name was Christopher Perkins, and his first extant printed challenge —published in 1724—indicates that he was already a "celebrated" master, and veteran of numerous stage-fights in Ireland:

AT the usual Place, at Hockley in the Hole, to Morrow the 22d of April, will be perform'd a Tryal of Skill by two of the most celebrated Masters of the Science of Defence that are now, or have been known in Europe, the famous Mr. PERKINS, Taylor, from Dublin in Ireland, and Mr. JAMES FIGG of Oxfordshire. The former of which having flourish'd in those Parts with equal Honour and Applause, as Mr. James Figg has in these; so that there is likely to be another strange Phenomenon, or Eclipse, which was not prognosticated by our Astrologers, but it is not yet known whether it will be Total.[26]

Although the outcome of their combat was not recorded, a recollection by Captain John Godfrey, written decades later in 1747, paints an impressive picture of Perkins—of a swordsman who, though stiff and slow with age, had evidently stymied his fabled adversary:

> I will anticipate my Characters of the MASTERS, by bringing in one Perkins an Irishman. The Man certainly was a true Swords-Man, but his Age made him so stiff and slow in his Action, that he could not execute all that his Judgement put him upon; yet, by Dint of that, he made up for his Inactivity, he always, at first setting out, pitched to this Posture, lying, as I said before, low to the Inside, so wide as to hide all the Outside, with his Wrist so ready raised, that nobody knew what to do with him. I have seen FIG, in Battles with him, stand in a kind of Confusion, not knowing which way to move: For as FIG offered to move, the old Man would also move so warily upon his Catch, that he would disappoint him in most of his Designs.[27]

Another challenge by Perkins, published one year later, indicated that the English champion Edward Sutton had already evaded the opportunity to face him on multiple occasions:

> Whereas I, Christopher Perkins, from Ireland, Master of the noble Science of Defence, have lately receiv'd three several Challenges from the triumphant Mr. Sutton, the Pipemaker of Gravesend; but when the Day of Trial has Come, he has refus'd to fight me, to the Disappointment of many worthy Gentlemen, who came, expecting to see him convinc'd; that he is not so good a Master, or so brave a man he pretends himself to be; from which refusals, I hope others will be of Opinion with me, that he is not that great Man he would be thought: Therefore, that Gentlemen may not be disappointed again of seeing a good Battle, I the said Christopher Perkins, and Thomas Elmore, both Masters of the noble Science of Defence, do invite the famous Hero Mr. James Figg, and his Companion John Wells, to meet as above, and exercise the usual Weapons practis'd on the Stage.[28]

By October of 1725, Figg himself had partnered with Perkins, for the purpose of fighting Sutton and another gladiator named Robert Carter, pitting two against two:

> We Edward Sutton and Robert Carter, Masters of the Noble Science of Defence, having been much insulted by Mr. Figg and Mr. Perkins; therefore, that such Things shall not be in Force, and to do our selves Justice, we do Invite them at the usual Weapons practised on the Stage... We James Figg and Christopher Perkins, Masters of the said Science, are not a little pleas'd, that the

Engraved portrait of James Figg by John Faber, after John Ellys, ca. 1727-1729.

abovesaid Combatants have at last work'd themselves into Courage enough to give us this publick Invitation; not doubting but to confute the many extravagant Bravadoes they have been guilty of, in a Manner, that they will shew, they are as great Strangers to Modesty, as to the true Judgment of the Sword...And Mr. Perkins questions not but to satisfy all Spectators, that there will be no occasion for Mr. Sutton to put himself to the Expence of erecting a Stage in the Field to decide their Superiority in the Science. Note, No Cut to be ty'd up; and to fight with their own Swords.[29]

Although no account of this fight could be found, one month later, Perkins was ready to fight again, and this time alongside a new and particularly unusual combatant named "Bonduca."

## BONDUCA O'BRIAN

On November 20, 1725, *Guests Journal* reported,

We hear that the gentlemen of Ireland have been long picking out an Hibernian heroine to match Mrs. Stokes, the bold and famous city championess. There is now one arrived in London, who by her make and stature seems likely enough to eat her up. However, Mrs. Stokes being true English blood (and remembering some of the late reflections that were cast upon her husband by some of the country folk) is resolved to see out *vi et armis.* This being likely to prove a notable and diverting entertainment, it is not at all doubted but that there will be abundance of gentlemen crowding to Mr. Figg's ampitheatre to see this uncommon performance.[30]

Years earlier, Stokes (under her maiden name Elizabeth Wilkinson) had bested a basket-woman named Hannah Hyfield in a bare-knuckles boxing match, and had later fought a fish-woman named Martha Jones—also with fisticuffs. Now, however, Mrs. Stokes proposed to take part in a more dangerous manner of combat—one with sharp weapons. Only three days following the announcement in *Guest's Journal*, the following appeared in the *Daily Post*:

AT Mr. Figg's New Amphitheatre, joyning to his House, the Sign of the City of Oxford, in Oxford Road, Marybone Fields, To-morrow, being the 24th of this Instant November, will be perform'd a Tryal of Skill by the following Combatants.

We Christopher Perkins, Taylor, from Dublin, Master of the Noble Science of Defence, and Champion of Ireland (who have lately fought the best English Masters with a general Applause) together with Bonduca O'Brian, the bold Female Hibernian Heroine, having heard of the Valour of the famous Mr. Stokes, and his much admired Consort the brave City Championess, do invite them at the following Weapons, viz. Back Sword, Sword and Dagger, Sword and Buckler, and Quarter-staff; and we don't doubt of giving convincing Proofs of the Hibernian Bravery, to the entire Satisfaction of all Spectators.

We James Stokes, Citizen of London, and his Wife the celebrated City Championess, having heard an extraordinary Character of Mr. Perkins, and his Heroical Countreywoman, do accept their Challenge with a hearty Good Will; and are resolved to make them know, that there is a

---

* *Vi et armis:* Latin, "with force and arms." A legal term for the remedy brought by the plaintiff for an immediate injury committed with force.

great deal of Difference between the Irish Dear Joys[†], and a courageous Couple, who belong to the chief City of the most Warlike Nation in the World.[31]

The female gladiator who would fight on the side of Perkins had no doubt been named for the lead character of *Bonduca,* a historical romance and tragi-comic play dramatizing the story of Boudica, the Celtic queen who had led a revolt against the Romans in 60 AD.[32] No more definitive information, unfortunately, has been found regarding Bonduca O'Brian, or her combat with Elizabeth Stokes. However, on February 23, 1728, a Swiss traveler named César-François de Saussure wrote a letter from London, in which he vividly described a combat involving a female Irish gladiator. Although it is impossible to say with certainty, given what is known about the other few female gladiators of the period—as well as the timing of Saussure's letter (in which he described British customs he had witnessed since 1725)—it seems possible that O'Brian and Stokes are the combatants described therein. If so, then the outcome of this contest explains O'Brian's subsequent disappearance from the British stage. Saussure related,

> The day I went to see the gladiators fight I witnessed an extraordinary combat, two women being the champions. As soon as they appeared on the stage they made the spectators a profound reverence; they then saluted each other and engaged in a lively and amusing conversation. They boasted that they had a great amount of courage, strength, and intrepidity. One of them regretted she was not born a man, else she would have made her fortune by her powers; the other declared she beat her husband every morning to keep her hand in, etc. Both these women were very scantily clothed, and wore little bodices and very short petticoats of white linen. One of these amazons was a stout Irishwoman, strong and lithe to look at, the other was a small Englishwoman, full of fire and very agile. The first was decked with blue ribbons on the head, waist, and right arm; the second wore red ribbons. Their weapons were a sort of two-handed sword, three or three and a half feet in length; the guard was covered, and the blade was about three inches wide and not sharp—only about half a foot of it was, but then that part cut like a razor. The spectators made numerous bets, and some peers who were there some very large wagers. On either side of the two amazons a man stood by, holding a long staff, ready to separate them should blood flow. After a time the combat became very animated, and was conducted with force and vigour with the broad side of the weapons, for points there were none. The Irishwoman presently received a great cut across her forehead, and that put a stop to the first part of the combat. The Englishwoman's backers threw her shillings and half-crowns and applauded her. During this time the wounded woman's forehead was sewn up, this being done on the stage; a plaster was applied to it, and she drank a good big glass of spirits to revive her courage, and the fight began again, each combatant holding a dagger in her left hand to ward off the blows. The Irishwoman was wounded a second time, and her adversary again received coins and plaudits from her admirers. The wound was sewn

---

† *Dear Joy*: A term for an Irish person, often derogatory, popularized in the 1680s.

up, and for the third time the battle recommenced, the women holding wicker shields as defensive weapons. This third combat was fought for some time without result, but the poor Irishwoman was destined to be the loser, for she received a long and deep wound all across her neck and throat. The surgeon sewed it up, but she was too badly hurt to fight any more, and it was time, for the combatants were dripping with perspiration, and the Irishwoman also with blood. A few coins were thrown to her to console her, but the victor made a good day's work out of the combat. Fortunately it is very rarely one hears of women gladiators.

Two male champions next appeared. They wore short white jackets and breeches and hose of the same colour; their heads were bare and freshly-shaven; one of them wore green ribbons, the other yellow. They were hideous to look at, their faces being all seamed and scarred. They also commenced by paying each other grotesque and amusing compliments, and then fell on each other with the same sort of weapons the women had used...The two combatants received several wounds, one of them having his ear nearly severed from his head, and a few moments later his opponent got a cut across the face, commencing at the left eye and ending on the right cheek. This last wound ended the fight and entertainment, and I went away regretting my half-crown and determined never to assist at one of these combats again.[33]

As for Christopher Perkins, his challenge to Edward Sutton was eventually accepted in 1726. The outcome of this "extraordinary" event was described—somewhat ambiguously—in the pages of the *Ipswich Journal*:

Yesterday was performed an extraordinary Trial of Skill, at Mr. Stokes's Ampitheatre, in Islington Road, between the Irish Champion Mr. Perkins, and Mr. Sutton, the Kentish Hero, when the latter by his undaunted Courage gave his Antagonist such Proofs of his Invincibility, that 'tis thought he will never more engage with the renowned Men of Kent.[34]

Notably, while the above account offers a glowing account of Sutton, it neglects to explicitly state whether or not Sutton actually defeated Perkins—a somewhat glaring omission. Local newspapers seemed to delight in pitting Irish and English combatants against each other, and almost universally relished in English victories. Wins by Irish combatants, on the other hand, rarely appeared in contemporary English press accounts—and can instead be found in subsequent memoirs, as well as in the challenges issued by the Irish swordsmen themselves. For example, the following challenge, published in 1728, explained:

Whereas I John Dunn, Farmer from Ireland, Professor of the noble Science of Defence, having in my several Engagements with the most celebrated Masters in the said Science of Defence given such signal Proofs of my Abilities therein, as has obliged them to confer me their Superior, and for Memorandum when I fought Mr. Gill three Bouts at Sword I cut him nine Inches in the Belly, which he insists was not fair; therefore to let him know I can cut him fair, and to give him Proof thereof do invite him to meet me and fight at all the Weapons now us'd on the Stage, and with the best Skill he is Master of...[35]

The "Mr. Gill" mentioned above by Dunn was none other than William Gill, who, according to John Godfrey, was a true prodigy, and "a Swords-Man formed by FIG's own Hand."[36]

The next year, it was arranged for Christopher Perkins to fight Gill, after Figg himself was forced to withdraw from the match, reportedly due to an injured arm. Perkins's ensuing challenge was particularly belligerent, suggesting that Gill was a mere proxy put forth to shield his master, as well as making light of Figg's reputation for invincibility:

> I WILLIAM GILL, from Gloucester, Professor of the Noble Science of Defence, and Scholar to the celebrated Mr. Figg, in Behalf of my said Master (who was to have fought the noted Mr. Perkins on the above Day, but by Reason of an Impediment in his Right Arm is render'd as yet incapable of performing in that Way) do invite the said Mr. Perkins to meet me as above, and exercise the usual Weapons practised on the Stage.
>
> I CHRISTOPHER PERKINS, from Dublin, Professor of the said Science, who have fought the best Masters in the Three Kingdoms with a general Applause, and never yet refused any, particularly the invincible Mr. Figg, as his Countrymen style him, am willing to accept of this Invitation, to cut off this Limb of Defence (for I can style him no otherwise) in order to come at the Head.[37]

The last public mention of Christopher Perkins occurred in July of 1728, when, in a final challenge to Figg, the Irishman announced his intention to permanently leave England:

> Whereas I CHRISTOPHER PERKINS...who have often fought Mr. Figg, and have always came off with great Applause; so now taking my last Farewell of him, do once more invite him to meet me and exercise the usual Weapons practised on the Stage, it being the last Time of my fighting in England, wherein I hope to give Mr. Figg, and all Gentlemen entire Satisfaction at my taking my Leave of England.
>
> I JAMES FIGG...will not fail to meet this bold Inviter, at his Time and Place appointed, where I doubt not but to give him something to remember me, at Parting, he designing to leave England, wherein I hope to give all Gentlemen entire Satisfaction, as I have hitherto done.

Following this last challenge, Christopher Perkins disappears into the mists of history. It would not be until the mid-1730s that another Irish swordsman would come to completely dominate the world of British stage-fighting.

## MARY WELSH and ROBERT BARKER

Although Bonduca O'Brian failed to re-emerge on the British stage-fighting scene, on October 1, 1726, Mrs. Stokes, it was reported, had found another able and willing Irish female antagonist in the person of Mary Welsh (or Welch):

> *At the Request of several English and Irish Gentlemen.*
>
> At Mr. STOKES's Amphitheatre, in Islington Road, near Sadler's Wells, on Monday next, being the 3d of October, will be perform'd a trial of skill by the following Championesses.
>
> Whereas I Mary Welch, from the Kingdom of Ireland, being taught, and knowing the noble science of defence, and thought to be the only female of this kind in Europe, understanding there is one in this Kingdom, who has exercised on the publick stage several times, which is Mrs. Stokes, who is stiled the famous Championess of England; I do hereby invite her to meet me, and exercise the usual weapons practis'd on the stage, at her own amphitheatre, doubting not, but to let her and the worthy spectators see, that my judgment and courage is beyond hers.
>
> I Elizabeth Stokes, of the famous City of London, being well known by the name of the Invincible City Championess for my abilities and judgment in the abovesaid science; having never engaged with any of my own sex but I always came off with victory and applause, shall make no apology for accepting the challenge of this Irish Heroine, not doubting but to maintain the reputation I have hitherto establish'd, and shew my country, that the contest of it's honour, is not ill entrusted in the present battle with their Championess, Elizabeth Stokes.
>
> Note, The doors will be open'd at two, and the Championesses mount at four.
>
> N.B. They fight in close jackets, short petticoats, coming just below the knee, Holland drawers, white stockings, and pumps.[38]

Of the fight's outcome, Welsh proclaimed that she had "given Proofs of my Skill being equal, or rather superior, to hers, in the Noble Science of Defence," however, following the match, "several Disputes...arose concerning our last Engagement, and that it is reported the Cut which Mrs. Stokes receiv'd then, was not given by the Judgment of the Sword..." Therefore, another match between Welsh and Stokes was arranged for the twenty-fourth of October.[39]

The result of this fight was not recorded. Three months later, however, it was arranged for Welsh to fight again, this time against Elizabeth Bedford of Wakefield. In her public challenge, Welsh vowed to "give entire Satisfaction, as I did when I fought Mrs. Stokes, and also maintain the Character I have assum'd, and shew my Country that the Contest of it's Honour is not ill entrusted in the present Battle with their Championess."[40]

That summer, another fight between Stokes and Welsh was scheduled. This time, it was announced that Mrs. Stokes's husband, James—a rival of Figg's—would also participate, as would an additional Irish male antagonist, to fight on the side of Ms. Welsh:

In Islington road, on Monday, being the 17th of July, 1727, will be performed a trial of skill by the following combatants.

We Robert Barker and Mary Welsh, from Ireland, having often contaminated our swords in the abdominous corporations of such antagonists as have had the insolence to dispute our skill, do find ourselves once more necessitated to challenge, defy, and invite Mr. Stokes and his bold Amazonian virago to meet us on the stage, where we hope to give a satisfaction to the honourable Lord of our nation who has laid a wager of twenty guineas on our heads. They that give the most cuts to have the whole money, and the benefit of the house; and if swords, daggers, quarter-staff, fury, rage, and resolution, will prevail, our friends shall not meet with a disappointment.

We James and Elizabeth Stokes, of the City of London, having already gained an universal approbation by our agility of body, dextrous hands, and courageous hearts, need not preambulate on this occasion, but rather choose to exercise the sword to their sorrow, and corroborate the general opinion of the town than to follow the custom of our repartee antagonists. This will be the last time of Mrs. Stokes' performing on the stage.[41]

In another challenge to the two, Welsh and Barker insisted they would give "indelible Testimonies of our Superiority, and manifest to all the worthy Spectators, that as we are allied by our Nation, we are likewise Concomitants in Renown."[42]

Eight months later, however, Welsh returned to the stage again in Figg's Great Room, "having receiv'd so many Affronts from Elizabeth Hughes, she being taught by several Masters of the Sword, extols herself to a high Degree; but I believe the World is sensible I am the only Championess in Europe..." At the same event, Barker was also to face Gill separately.[43] Welsh and Barker appeared to have married, for in August the former appeared under the name of "MARY BARKER, Wife of the abovesaid Robert Barker," declaring that "I believe the World is sensible I am the only Championess in Europe."[44] In another challenge, she stated,

Whereas I Mary Barker, from Ireland, (of which Kingdom I am always proud to own myself a Native) having in my former encounters with Mrs. Stokes, the English Championess, been thought to have experienc'd the Superiority of her Skill in the Sword, to my Disadvantage, am prompted, as well in Regard to my own Character, as in Honour to my Country, to give her a new Invitation to exercise with me all the usual Weapons practis'd on the Stage; and having since my past Controversies with her, been assisted with the Instruction of the ablest Masters in the Science, doubt not but in this Battle to behave myself so, as to make her ample Retaliation for her past Insolence...

The same challenge also noted that Welsh (now Barker) was a native of County Tipperary.[45] Her last known fight took place in 1729, when the *Daily Journal* announced that "on Monday next, there is to be a Boxing Match at the Green Dragon on St. Michael's Hill for 7 Guineas, by one Mary Buck of this City, and Mary Barker from London."[46]

Although Welsh would leave the stage-fighting scene, her new husband—now a "celebrated *Hibernian* Hero"—would re-emerge to fight several additional contests. In 1727, Barker had challenged James Figg, claiming that he had "on Wednesday the Eighth Instant, engage[d] the terrifying Mr. James Figg, when, tho' I had not the Superiority, yet I found him neither Inimitable, nor Invincible; Now...I do hereby invite him to a Second Performance..."[47] The same year, he also twice fought John Needs, of Somersetshire.[48] His next combat, held at Figg's Great-Room in Oxford, in October of 1728, was instigated by the following challenge:

> Whereas I Robert Barker, the terrible Butcher from the Kingdom of Ireland, who have fought all the best Masters of that Kingdom, and gain'd a general Applause, am still ambitious of maintaining the Character I have established in the Noble Science of Defence, do therefore invite William Gill to meet me and exercise the usual Weapons practised on the Stage; and he that gives the most Cuts at Sword, and Blows at Staff to have the whole House, wherein should he fail, I will post him for a Coward in all Manner of Company for the future.[49]

Although Gill accepted the challenge, the outcome of the combat is unknown. Five years later, Barker appeared again to challenge John Seale to a combat at Stokes's amphitheatre:

> At Mr. Stokes's amphitheatre, Islington Road, on Monday, 24th June, 1733, I, John Seale, *Citizen of London*, give this invitation to the celebrated *Hibernian* Hero, Mr. Robert Barker, to exert his utmost abilities with me: And I, Robert Barker, accept this invitation; and if my antagonist's courage equal his menaces, glorious will be my conquest! Attendance at two; the Masters mount at five. *Vivant Rex et Regina.*[50]

This was Barker's last known combat; after 1733, his name is absent from the extant records.

Elizabeth Stokes, however, was to fight one last "Hibernian" heroine. In 1729, Charles "Tall Boy" Wright, from Dublin, incited by an "insatiable thirst for Glory," challenged James and Elizabeth Stokes to a "Tryal of Skill" for fifty pounds. Wright announced that this time, his "scholar," Mary Waller would fight alongside him. James and Elizabeth heartily accepted the challenge, insisting that they were not "intimidated by the haughty Rhodomontades of such Hibernian Boasters."[51]

## ROWLAND BENNET

Along with James Collins and Christopher Perkins, one of the earliest Irish stage gladiators to engage in a "Tryal of Skill" at Maryebone Fields was Rowland Bennet, a smith from Dublin. His first known challenge was issued in 1721 to John Parkes of Coventry.[52] Bennet must have done well in his first fight, for his next challenge—published in 1723—took aim at James Figg, and, interestingly, posited the use of a newer style of fencing versus the "Old Stile":

At the Boarded-House in Marybone-Fields, this present Wednesday, being the 19th Day of June, will be perform'd a Tryal of Skill by the following Masters.

Whereas I ROWLAND BENNET, from Ireland, Master of the Noble Science of Defence, having since my last Arrival in England, had the Opportunity to see Mr. James Figg exercise the usual Weapons on the Stage, the particulars of which I forbear to Instance but by what I was then an Eye-witness of, am fully perswaded, that if the proper Method be executed against him, he (like Sampson with his Hair off) is like other Men. For a Tryal of which, I do now invite him to meet me, and Exercise, the usual Weapons fought on the Stage.

I JAMES FIGG...Master of the said Science, to give the said Rowland Bennet an Opportunity of putting this proper Method in Execution, will not fail to meet at the Place and Time appointed, hoping the Spectators may from thence receive entire Satisfaction, assuring him before hand, that what Method I shall make use of will be by the way of Old Stile.[53]

Bennet seems to have lost this combat with Figg, although apparently without incurring any serious injury. On August 21, 1723, he again announced,

Whereas I, ROWLAND BENNET from Ireland, Master of the Noble Science of Defence, who in those Parts, as also in these, have had the Opportunity both of seeing and experiencing the best Masters, must confess, upon Mr. Figg's declining the Stage, that he has not left his Equal; but upon his recommending his Scholar Mr. William Flanders, as the only Person capable of succeeding him in Judgment and Execution of the Sword, and without Vanity, believing my self to be his Equal, if not Superior; I, for a Decision of the same, do hereby invite the said Mr. Flanders to meet me as above, and Exercise the usual Weapons fought on the Stage.[54]

In 1727, Bennet, now a "Hibernian Professor of the Noble Science of Defence," having already fought Figg "many" times, challenged the English champion yet again, aiming to "shew that the true Roman Spirit is no where to be found more than in Hibernian Blood (which delighteth to encounter all Difficulties)."[55] That same year, Bennet also faced Edward Sutton in combat. He later recounted:

[I] gave him a Cut on the Forehead, and [I] only receiving a small Cut on the Leg, which was by Accident, [and] was to have fought him the second Battle, but he declining...left the Kingdom, and went to North Britain, and made an Excuse he was sent for, I believe more for fear of my Sword than any thing else...[56]

The year 1729 was a momentous one for Bennet. Having now fought Figg a total of twenty-one times, it was arranged for Bennet to face Figg's own mentor and fencing master, Timothy Buck.[57] According to John Godfrey,

TIMOTHY BUCK was a most solid Master, it was apparent in his Performances, even when grown decrepit, and his old Age could not hide his uncommon Judgement. He was the Pillar of the Art, and all his Followers, who excelled built upon him.[58]

During their fight together, Bennet delivered a devastating blow which permanently removed Buck from the stage-fighting world. That year it was noted that Bennet had merely "disabled [Figg's] Master Mr. Buck." The wound appears to have been fatal, however, as the next year, Bennet was described as the one "by whose unfortunate Hand fell that ever memorable Gladiator, Mr. Timothy Buck." At the same time, Figg publicly paid "the greatest Deference and Respect to the Name of my deceased Master, and in Compliance with his surviving Victor, will not fail being as punctual in every Article, as he is in nominating the Hand which gave that fatal Blow; which shall not be forgot..."[59] That June, Bennet was described as "the Demolisher of the renown'd Mr. Buck."[60]

During the same period, Bennet teamed up with Sligo native Andrew Mac-Colley, "vulgarly call'd the strong Irishman," to face both Figg and Sutton together.[61] Mac-Colley claimed to have already had "many Victories in most Parts of that Kingdom [Ireland]," and had come "over on Purpose to attack the reputed famous English Champions." He first appeared in England in 1729, and was described as a "Hibernian Hector," who had "fought one hundred and six Battles, and never was defeated."[62] In 1730, it was reported that "Mr. Figg's Head was threatened to be cut off by Mr. Mac-Colley," while Bennet quipped in print:

Brittania has not a Son to whom we ought to pay Obeyance, in respect of Valour, having more than once engag'd her Darling Figg, whose Fame, together with that of Mr. Edward Sutton's, seems to stagnate the Blood of Swordsmen, and fill the World, with Wonders of their Performances; tho' in the End, like Æsop's teeming Mountain, a Mouse is the Product of the mighty Ball. If the said Gentlemen can Act, as they lately took Occasion, to Dictate, we do hereby desire them not to be sparing at the Time and Place above appointed, when, the last Drop of Blood, we may command, shall be spent, with Pleasure, in Hibernia's Cause, or her Honour be for ever lost, by our unexpected and meritorious Fall.[63]

Within two years Mac-Colley would retire from the English stage. His last prize was fought in August, 1731, when, backed by the Earl of Kildare, and teamed up with fellow Irishman Thomas Farrell, he took to the stage to show "the Beauty of the Sword in the Science of Defence."[64]

Bennet continued to fight with other partners. In 1730, the following announcement appeared in the pages of the local press:

At Mr. Figg's great room to-morrow, the 20th of this instant May, by the command of several noblemen and others, will be shewn in full proof the judgment of the sword in all its noble branches, offensive and defensive.

We, Mathew Masterson, Serjeant from Gibraltar, and Rowland Bennet, from the city of Dublin in the kingdom of Ireland, masters of the said science, both having lately tasted our error by unwarily receiving wounds from Mr. Figg, and resolving if possible to return the keen rebuke by our chastizing swords, make this challenge the hostility of our confederate arms, inviting them to the brightest of their performances, Mr. Figg taking Mr. Gill to his assistance, and fighting us at the time and place above for the benefit of the whole house, which Mr. Masterson and the said Gill are solely to have to themselves; the victor of them two defraying all charges, and taking the surplus to himself as free plunder. It is that makes a soldier a Caesar or a Marius, without the help of Lilly, who was most unmercifully whipped last Wednesday in quarto by a Yorkshire Jockey with Roman epithets, in order to extort rules for declining a good house in favour of the present tense singular; but the grammatical tit being too highmettled to be verb-ridden, left his Elorian corrector in an infinitive ill-mood, confounded in particles in search of the great negative—nothing.

MATHEW MASTERSON, ROWLAND BENNET.[65]

An account of the particulars of the combat between Figg and Masterson can be found in the memoirs of Antoine François Prévost d'Exiles. It reads as follows:

[Figg's] Antagonist was an Irish Serjeant, lately come from *Gibraltar*. They both appeared upon the Stage in their Shirts, and their Heads bare, and had a red Ribbon tied about their Arm to hold up the Sleeve of their Shirt. Boldness and Courage, with a Mixture of Calmness appeared in their Looks. *Figg* offered the Serjeant the Choice of Swords, of several that were brought upon the Stage, about two Inches in breadth, and the Points ground off. I had the Curiosity to take one of them in my Hand, and found that it was sharp edged enough to cut off an Arm or a Leg. The Combatants, after shaking Hands, as a Mark of Friendship and Esteem, put themselves in a Posture of Defence, crossed their Weapons, and began a furious Attack. We must not imagine that there was any foul Play in the Case, or that they were not serious, they let fly at one another so heartily, and with such Vigour and Rapidity, that the Spectacle became terrible, and the whole

Assembly was in a profound Silence. The Serjeant made a Blow at *Figg*, which cut a pretty large Piece of his Stocking, without touching the Leg. Figg, whose Coolness and Judgment were surprizing, felt the Stroke; ho, ho! *said he*, I see thou hast a Mind to my Leg, but take Care of thy own, and with the same Breath whipped off a large Piece of the Calf of his Adversary's Leg, which fell upon the Stage; the general Applause was given to this clean Slash by clapping of Hands, and crying *bravo, bravo, encora, encora*, which is a sort of Approbation that they have learned from the *Italians*. The Serjeant, not able to support himself, sat down and looked at his Blood, which ran in Streams. I was told that they had Powders whose Effect operates a speedy Cure.

The scheduled combat between Bennet and Gill, unfortunately, was not described. Instead, D'Exiles merely noted:

We saw several others fight afterwards, who gave and received several Wounds. This Diversion gave us an Opportunity to make several Reflections; it is certain that it has it's Utility, being a sort of School where Youth are formed to Intrepidity, and to the Contempt of Death and Wounds; but, on the other Hand, we agreed, that there was something cruel and barbarous in it. If the Effusion of human Blood is so looked upon as an Evil, even when it is just and necessary, it would seem contradictory to the Laws of Humanity and Nature to make a Diversion of spilling it. Nevertheless this Custom is authorised in *England*, and probably not without strong Reasons in so wise a Government, where every Thing is calculated for the publick Good.[66]

Combats matching multiple Irishmen against multiple Englishmen must have been a success with audiences, for a similar contest was soon announced, pitting three Englishmen against three Irishmen. It was held at Stokes's Ampitheatre, for a purse of one hundred guineas, and was attended by members of the nobility:

On Wednesday, the 21st of this Instant July, by the Command and under the Direction of several British and and Irish Peers, as well as Gentlemen of both Countries, the following Combat will be fought by three of the principal Swordsmen on each side, for the Honour of Great Britain against that of the Hibernian, *Terra Firma*, the like of which has never been attempted but once in these Realms. The Combatants for Ireland are *Felix Mac Guire*, *Andrew Mac Colley* and *Nicholas Hussey*, reputed the best Product of that Country; and for Great Britain, the inimitable couragious *Sutton*, of Great Britian, *Joseph Johnson*, of Stapleton in Yorkshire, a Person of solid Judgment and intrepid Valour; and lastly, the all-conquering sincere *Gill*, of Gloucester; Men the nearest upon Ballance of any in Christendom, who are to fight on these Conditions, viz. Each man to change Swords every Bout, and when the Weapons are gone through, if the Company be dissatisfy'd they shall appoint two of the best or any two to fight for the Box, which will be set on the Stage for the purpose.[67]

As for Bennet, he continued to take part in prize-fights throughout 1731, when he left a wound, or so-called "Legacy," upon the wrist of Edward Sutton. He further noted, "I have not that Vanity to stile myself Head Master of my native Country, nor Inadvertency enough to harangue on too many Abilities; tho' it is obvious to the Gentlemen of these Parts, that I have as great a right to the Title of Master, as any of my Predeccessors, or Fellow Countrymen in Being can pretend to..." Departing London for Chester, Bennet would be remembered by Edward Sutton as the one who had never "sufficiently aton'd" for the slaying of "immortal Buck, whom jilting Fortune caused to fall by his untimely Steel."[68]

Nearly fifteen years later, Bennet would briefly return to the stage at Broughton's Ampitheatre, where he fought with "the usual Weapons" against Joseph Johnson.[69] By this time, he had been fighting on the stage for twenty-four years. Bennet's stage-fighting career was, thus, the longest known of any Irish gladiator.

## FELIX MACGUIRE

Felix MacGuire, another of Ireland's most noted prize-fighters, first appeared at Figg's Ampitheatre in August of 1727, having heard "of the Fame and wondrous Character of the much-admired Oxonian Champion..." His earliest known announcement claimed that he was formerly a "Serjeant in Sir J. Whitwrong's Regiment of Foot,"* and that he had "fought the best and most noted Masters in [Ireland] and several other Kingdoms with a general Applause."[70] Later that year, it was reported that MacGuire had:

fought Mr. Parkes several Times in that Kingdom [of Ireland], and came off with Honour; and since my Arrival here have fought Mr. Figg and Mr. Sutton with the same Applause; Mr. Parkes being a Spectator at the Battle on Wednesday, last, and he talking much of his Judgment of the Sword, I do invite him to meet and exercise me at the usual Weapons practised on the Stage...[71]

That fall, MacGuire fought Sutton and came off as "Victor." Sutton dismissed the outcome of the contest by stating, "I know not any [match] I have lost, by having met once with an Accident: However, I shall not make any Excuse for myself..."[72] MacGuire also contested with Parkes, as well as Figg, whom he "wounded...in the Belly, and gave him other convincing Proofs of my Judgment therein..."[73]

---

* Sir John Whitwrong's Regiment of Foot was stationed in various places in Ireland during the early eighteenth century. See *The Political State of Great Britain*, July, 1712.

During the next several years, MacGuire seems to have settled into retirement, claiming the title of "First Master and Swordsman in Vogue in the Kingdom of Ireland." Also taking his place on the stage was MacGuire's apprentice, William Holmes, a native of Waterford to whom the former had served as "Tutor."[74] MacGuire made up his mind to return to the stage when a controversy ensued over the fencing technique exhibited by his student. MacGuire explained that,

> contrary to all Expectation, Mrs. Elizabeth Stokes, styl'd the invincible, matchless, unconquerable City Championess, took upon her to condemn the Method of Mr. Holmes's displaying of raising his Guard, &c. before a Grand Appearance then assembled, which with regret I was oblig'd to hear; and in regard the said Gentleman was my Pupil, I so far resent it, that I hereby invite the said Mr. James Stokes, together with the said Elizabeth his Wife, at their own Seat of Valour, and at the Time appointed, to face and fight me and a Woman I have train'd up to the Science from her Infancy, one of my own Country, who, I doubt not, will as far exceed Mrs. Stokes as she is said to have done those she has hitherto been concern'd with.

Regarding MacGuire's tantalizing reference to a new female gladiator which he had "train'd up...from her Infancy," Stokes responded as follows:

> I James Stokes, Citizen and Shagreen Case-maker of London, in conjunction with Elizabeth my Wife, will not fail gratifying the Request of our formidable Invitors, on the Account of Mr. MacGuire, who we know to be a Person of as good Conduct and Character as ever visited these Realms in his Capacity, being proud he has taken the indefatigable Pains to train up a Woman worthy my Wife's engaging, and who is likely to afford so much Satisfaction to the Publick; it is what we have often wish'd, as her Bravery will shine with greater Lustre in Conquest over so fine a Female...

A fight was thus arranged for November 23, loftily billed as "the compleatest Trial of Skill in the Science of Defence that has been seen in the Memory of Man."[75] Although the outcome of this contest—if recorded—is no longer extant, as shall be seen, another woman would emerge to fight next to MacGuire in the years to come.

In the meantime, MacGuire's male protege, William Holmes, challenged James Figg to a contest of arms. The disastrous results of this bloody combat were reported in the pages of the *Derby Mercury*:

> Yesterday, the invincible Mr. James Figg fought at his Amphitheatre, Mr. Holmes, an Irishman, who keeps an Inn at Yaul near Waterford in Ireland, and came into England on purpose to fight this Champion, when Mr. Figg (fighting with his usual Bravery and Judgment) at the second Bout

cut him over the left Wrist to the Bone, in so desperate a manner that he was disabled and went off the Stage; this being the Two Hundred and seventy-first Prize Mr. Fig has Fought, and was never conquer'd.

In celebration of Figg's victory, the following poem, written "in Honour of this British Heroe," was published:

F I G G's Triumphant: Or, Hibernia's Defeat.

Inspir'd with generous Thrift of Martial Fame,
Figg's early Years presag'd his future Name;
As Hannibal, e're grown to Manhood's Bloom,
Swore in his Blood fell Emnity with Rome,
Like Ardor did our Infant Hero grace,
Like dire Aversion to th' Hibernian Race:
Long in successful Fights both Champions view'd,
Their Oath accomplish'd, and their Foes subdu'd;
But here th'illustrious Parrallel must end,
And Africk's Warrior to Britania's bend,
Events unequal their last Fights attend;
The former loses what he earn'd before,
The latter closes all his past with one grand Triumph more.

On the same day that Holmes was disabled, "another Gladiator of the Irish Establishment, seeing his Countryman Defeated" made a "Speech upon the Stage." It was none other than MacGuire:

I Felix Maguire from the City of Dublin, finding the Rising Sun of my Native Country's Glory setting on Britannia's Orb, am fully determin'd to dissipate the melancholly Cloud hanging over Hibernia's drooping Head, by inviting Edward Sutton the Kentish Hero to meet me upon this Stage on the 21st of this Instant to fight, otherwise forfeit the Box. And calls to Remembrance the Song of an old Author, who sings,

Not Man, nor Sword I dread; but Winter's Frost,
Unless I fight, more than I'm worth will cost.

Sutton immediately accepted this challenge, and responded with his own lines of poetry:

Wer't thou Great Holmes, or the revived Ghost

Of famous B - - - k<sup>*</sup>, my Courage is not lost;

For know, base Slave, that I am one of those,

Can fight a Man as well in Verse as Prose:

And when thou'rt dead, write this upon thy Hearse.

Here lies a Swordsman that was slain in Verse.

Regarding the proposed combat, local journals noted that "great wagers have been laid on both sides."[76] A month later, it was announced that Holmes, evidently having recovered from the "accidental blow...received on his metacarpus," would join MacGuire in his fight against Figg and Sutton:

At Mr. Figg's Great Room, at his house, the sign of the City of Oxford, in Oxford Road, to morrow, Wednesday Nov. 11, the Nobility and Gentry will be entertained (for the last time this season) in a most extraordinary manner with a select trial of skill in the Science of Defence, by the four following Masters; viz.

We, William Holmes and Felix Mac Guire, the two first and most profound Swordsmen in the Kingdom of Ireland, whom in combat the Universe never yet could parallel, being requested to return to our native country, are determined to make our departure ever memorable to Great Britain, by taking our solemn public leave of the renowned Mr. Figg and Mr. Sutton, at the time and place appointed; to which we hereby invite them, in order to prove we can maintain our titles, and claim a preference in the list of Worthies.

Tis not the accidental blow Mr. Holmes received on his metacarpus the last time he fought Mr. Figg, has shocked his courage, or given room to Mr. Mac Guire to decline his interest; no, it has been the fate of the best Generals to retreat, and yet to conquer; and the loss of a leg or an arm has augmented the glory of a commander, because blind fortune, and not the want of conduct, forfeited a limb which force nor envy e'er could take away.

We James Figg, from Thame in Oxfordshire, and Edward Sutton of renowned Kent, by the lofty language and pointed similies of the above bravo's, guess at their aspiring minds, and sincerely promise, since they covet to be great men, that, if at the time and place appointed they obtain a victory, by the sword, we will present them with our truncheons, being four feet longer than that with which Alexander was honoured at the head of his army, and far more serviceable in case of a rupture: on the other hand, if it be our fortune to deprive them of their intended glory in one sense, we will endeavour to be grateful in another, by sending them home, like Admirals Bembo or Carter, whose names the loss of a leg and an arm made ever memorable, and may serve for the copy of their departure, if blind Fortune (as they call it) act according to custom, &c.

---

<sup>*</sup>   Probably a reference to Timothy Buck.

Note, Mr. Holmes and Mr. Figg are to fight the first bout; Mr. Mac Guire and Mr. Sutton the second: Mr. Holmes alternately with Mr. Figg, Mr. Mac Guire and Mr. Sutton in like manner, and so successively during the battle; and, if one be disabled, his associate to go through the weapons with his two antagonists. A full house being expected, gentlemen are desired to meet sooner than usual, the masters being commanded to mount at three precisely, by reason of the shortness of the days, and the length of a double battle, &c.[77]

Although the outcome of this combat is not recorded, several months later, MacGuire fought another match with Sutton, wherein he reportedly suffered a horrifying injury:

Mr. Macguire, the Prize-Fighter, had his Nose cut clear from his Face by Mr. Sutton, at Figg's Ampitheatre last Wednesday.[78]

Following this incident, Sutton openly mocked MacGuire's wound, admonishing "Foreign Bravos" to "guard against that Arm, which so lately deny'd the great Mac Guire the Liberty of blowing his Nose easily..."[79] Accounts of MacGuire's injury were evidently exaggerated, for only one month later, the Irishman was back in the public eye, explaining,

I received a small Cut on the Nose by Mr. Sutton in a late Engagement with him, which he has taken Care to represent all he could to his own Advantage, by magnifying his Merits on that Score, and lessening mine to a degree of Insolence; tho' it happen'd he soon after met with the same Mischance, which at one Time or other attends Mankind in general; therefore as nothing but Blood can palliate the gross Offence, I hereby intreat him again to face and fight me at the Time and Place above, when and where every Artery in my Body shall be drained, or my invincible Arm shall procure the desired Satisfaction, my Sword ever yet going the full Length of my Wishes, when push'd on with brave Revenge, which e'er to Mischief pav'd the bloody Way...[80]

A crude illustration of MacGuire, published several years after this time, appears to show him with a slightly misshapen, but largely intact, nose.[81]

MacGuire continued to face numerous adversaries on the stage throughout 1732 and 1733, including Edward Sutton, Thomas Sibblis—whom MacGuire defeated "by a Cut in his Belly,"—and "five of the greatest Heroes to Great Britain." Of these last five, MacGuire claimed he had "defeated them all."[82] In 1733, MacGuire repeatedly challenged Figg's protégé, William Gill, to a combat—but the latter, after initially accepting, neglected to show up on the appointed day:

This Battle shall be superior to the Non-performance of Mr. Gill, who for his own Safety declin'd the Stage last Wednesday, though often call'd for by his impatient Adversary, F. Mac-Guire...[83]

# At his MAJESTY's Bear-Garden.

*In* Hockly-in-the-Hole, *this present* Wednefday, *being the* 14th *of* May, 1735. *Will be performed a Tryal of Skill by the following Great Mafters in that Noble Art,* call'd DEFENCE.

WHEREAS I *Felix Mac Guire,* from the Kingdom of *Ireland,* Mafter of the Noble and renown'd Science of Defence, who was challenged by Mr. *Elfegood,* at his Battle laft *Wednefday* ; and he having. fince thought better on it, has declined the fame; but rather than fo Noble a Science fhould lie Dormant, I do challenge the celebrated Mr. *Banks* to face me, if he has Spirit to attempt it, and not triumph at the late Succefs of his Countrymen over *Hibernia* ; for I'll fhew them the Odds of that, and give them a Receipt in full for the Debts owing from my Country, and plainly fhew that 'tis not by their Judgment, for that Misfortunes often attend the Great, the Generous and Wife. I have been indeed ill ufed by feveral *Englifhmen,* and am now refolved to make all even by rectifying all Deficiencies. All this fhall be perform'd by my Keen Sword, and the infulted Arm of your Humble Servant,

FELIX MAC GUIRE.

I *Richard Banks,* Mafter of the abovefaid Science of Defence, will not fail meeting this Defperado (being not in the leaft intimidated by his Threats) and difpute his Judgment in all Points ; and as to his Chat concerning the Succefs lately obtained by my Fellow Countrymen, he fhall

Detail of an extremely rare surviving broadside, announcing the combat between Felix Mac Guire and Richard Banks to be held on May 14, 1735. *Image copyright and courtesy of the National Library of Ireland,* LO Folder 4/1735/2.

In 1733, MacGuire began appearing alongside a female fighting partner—his wife, Lætitia (sometimes spelled "Leticce"), also known as "the bold Quaker." The two contested as a team for the first time during the summer season, and were soon challenged by a rival English couple, Thomas and Sarah Barrett. Claiming to have been "judg'd equal" in their first contest, the Barretts issued another challenge, to which the MacGuires responded as follows:

> I Felix Mac-Guire, and Lettice my Wife, well known by the name of the bold Quaker, will not fail meeting these daring Inviters at the Times and Place appointed, not doubting but to give Intire Satisfaction to the Spectators and them some Marks with our keen Weapons.
> FELIX and LETTICE MAC-GUIRE.[84]

A few weeks later, yet another "Trial of Skill" was arranged between "the following Champions and Championesses, viz. *Felix Mac-Guire,* Fencing-Master from Dublin, and *Lætitia* his Wife; with *Richard Banks,* and the *Unconquer'd City Championess*"—this last being a likely reference to Elizabeth Stokes. It was further noted that "Mrs. Sutton and Mrs. Barrett not being able to give the Gentlemen any Satisfaction, the European Championess, if she be not disabled by the abovesaid Lætitia Mac-Guire, will give them both five Guineas to fight her the same Day."[85]

On May 14, 1735, MacGuire issued his last known challenge. Notably, it was printed on a large broadside which included an engraving of MacGuire and his adversary, Richard Banks, crossing swords on stage (see opposite image). The two are surrounded by various weapons, and attended by seconds holding quarterstaves. It is the last we ever hear of Felix Macguire.

# MICHAEL BUTLER

According to extant records, Michael Butler of Kilkenny, "Master of the noble Science of Defence," first appeared in England in September of 1728. He had come, it was claimed, after "hearing of the great Fame Mr. Figg has established in disabling so many of my Countrymen." This circumstance, according to Butler, "oblig'd me in Justice to my Country to come over to have a Trial of Skill with [Figg] at the Weapons practis'd in the Stage, thinking myself in no ways inferior to that terrible Champion, or any of his Countrymen that profess the Science..."[86] As was typical, the outcome of Butler's first combat with Figg was not reported by the press. However, less than one month later, Butler challenged Edward Sutton to a similar combat, in which he incurred a wound. Butler's second challenge to Sutton, delivered soon afterwards, offered more details about his own background:

Whereas I Michael Butler, from Kilkenny, in the Kingdom of Ireland, Master of the Noble Science of Defence, and in my own Country a Terror to all the Swordsmen there, and conquer'd all the Masters that I ever engaged with, which are Forty-seven, but having had a Battle with the famous Mr. Sutton, the Kentish Champion, in which, by an accident, he gave me a large Cut, tho' I think it not done by his Judgment; therefore I dare him to meet me once more at the Place above-mention'd, where I shall make him and his Votaries know that I shall retrieve my Character from that Misfortune, and remain Champion of Europe; and if the Gentlemen are not satisfy'd, I will fight the Weapons thro' till they are pleased, to shew that the Irish Blood is as good as the English.

In his own response, Sutton admitted that he "did not by Judgment give him the last Cut," but promised to give him "double this time, which shall be by Judgment and Agility of Body."[87]

Two years later, a public challenge issued in Ipswich by Butler claimed that in the interim, he "had the Honour to perform at Windsor before his present Majesty twice." His elaborate challenge explained:

At the Sign of the George in St. Mathew's, on Thursday next being the 14th of this Instant January, will be the most smartest Trial of Skill known in the Memory of Man, by the Champion of England, and the Champion of Ireland, viz.

I MICHAEL BUTLER from Kilkenny in the Kingdom of Ireland, Master of my Sword in all its Branches, Offensive of Defensive, having had the Honour to perform at Windsor before his present Majesty twice, and likewise most Persons of Quality in the three Kingdoms with a general Applause with the invincible Kentish Hero, called the Champion of Europe, I do hereby invite him once more to a third Trial, and doubt not in the least but to Eclipse him of his Laurells which he has hitherto gain'd by the Sword, and to make him understand the Kingdom of Ireland can produce as good a Master as any in Europe.
MICHAEL BUTLER.

I EDWARD SUTTON of Gravesend in Unconquer'd Kent, Master of the said Science, which never yet knew the Scandal of a Defeat, or ever refused any Man in Christendom, viz. French, Dutch, or any other Nation whatsoever, will not fail Meeting this Hibernian Hector at the Place above mention'd; those Gentlemen that will honour me with their Company, may be sure to see as good Performance as was ever yet known in the Memory of Man; and do intend to let the World know I wear the Flag of Defiance at my Main-top-mast-head; making no farther Appology, but I intend to make the Town amends for my last Battle I fought in this Place, which shall be the utmost Care of your humble Servant,
EDWARD SUTTON.[88]

Only a few weeks later, another fight between Butler and Sutton was announced, to take place at the White Horse Tavern, and in which each combatant's "Left Foot" would be "strapt down to the Stage":

At the White Horse Tavern in Ipswich, on Thursday next, being the 28th of this Instant January, will be an extraordinary Tryal of Skill by the following Champions:

I MICHAEL BUTLER of the Kingdom of Ireland, Master of the Noble Art of Defence, having lately ingaged with Mr. Sutton, having been his Equal and Superior in all other Battles that I have Fought with him, except the last in this Town, (which was by the Force of his Arm and not by the Judgment of his Sword) was oblig'd by Persons of no skill in that Science to give way. This is to let him know, that I do give him a second Invitation and will Fight him at Length, at Sword and Dagger, and Sword and Buckler, with the Left Foot strapt down to the Stage, and the Single Sword and Quarter Staff not strapt. The Reason is to let the Gentlemen that will honour me with their Company, know that I do not but doubt to get the Victory over this Kentish Hero, and give him a Rowland for his Oliver. The best Man taking the whole Box, paying Charges.
MICHAEL BUTLER.

I EDWARD SUTTON of Gravesend in the County of Kent, Commander of my Sword, and the Scourge of my Enemies, knowing the abovesaid Champion rather to exceed in Words than Actions, will not fail meeting him; and the Conquest will be render'd more Glorious if it falls on my Side, as thro' Providence it hath hitherto done, by declaring Men of Merit, and disdaining iinterest for Balance with true Honour, which some of our Protection may or ought to contemplate and reflect on; and according to his desire I will answer him, and use him as a Stranger, in giving him his way, which is not common in this Art, or ever was done only twice, since the sword was in Request.     EDWARD SUTTON.[89]

Butler evidently defeated Sutton during this match, for, several months later—in May—a challenge published by John Wells, one of Figg's students, referred to Butler as "an all-conquering Hibernian Hero, who has lately fought and defeated most of the renowned Swordsmen in the British Isles, and torn the Bays from the Temples of the invincible Mr. Sutton, whose Kentish Courage never till now met with a Repulse..." Butler acceded to Wells's request, stating:

I Michael Buttler, from Kilkenny in Ireland, by whose invincible Arm, not only the above Kentish Hero, but his Superiors, have been reduc'd to the Title of Common Men, will not fail in like Manner, to oblige the above Gentleman with my Performance, at the Time and Place appointed, the Experiment of which may cost him dear, if that good Fortune still attend me, which has hitherto crown'd all my Undertakings with a never-failing Glory...[90]

Following the combat with Wells, Butler engaged in another contest with Figg's main protégé, William Gill. This fight would, unfortunately, be Butler's last. John Godfrey recounted how, during this event, Butler came to his tragic end:

From the narrow Way [Gill] had of going down (which was mostly without receiving) he oftener hit the Leg than anyone; and from the drawing Stroke, caused by that sweeping Turn of the Wrist, and his proper way of holding his Sword, his Cuts were remarkably more severe and deep. I never was an Eye-Witness to such a Cut in the Leg, as he gave one BUTLER, an Irishman, a bold resolute Man, but an awkward Swords-Man. His Leg was laid quite open, his Calf falling down to his Ankle. It was soon stitched up; but from the Ignorance of a Surgeon adapted to his mean Circumstances, it mortified; Mr. Cheselden was applied to for Amputation, but too late for his true Judgement to interfere in. He immediately perceived the Mortification to forbid his Skill; and refused to be concerned in what he knew to be beyond his Power. But another noted one was applied to, who, through less Judgement, or Value for his Character, cut off his Leg above the Knee, but the Mortification had got the Start of his Instruments, and BUTLER soon expired.[91]

## THE SHERLOCK FAMILY

The Sherlocks were a dynasty of Dublin gladiators, all of whom fought on the English stage. The final scion of the family, Francis, would notably become the last Irish champion to take part in English gladiatorial fights—a world which he would come to completely dominate. Francis was probably a descendant or younger relative of James Sherlock, a "Master of the Noble Science of Defence" from Dublin, who had briefly appeared on the English stage-fighting scene in 1716. Later notices would refer to James as the "famous...Head Master of the Science of Defence in the Kingdom of Ireland." In 1716, James fought Figg's own master, Timothy Buck, before disappearing from recorded history.[92]

By 1729, however, another representative of the Sherlock family would appear on the stage in the person of William Sherlock, the son of James. His earliest known challenge declared,

I, William Sherlock, of the City of Dublin, Son of James Sherlock, Head Master of the Science of Defence in the Kingdom of Ireland who have fought some of the best Masters in that Kingdom, and acquitted myself with Honour; hearing the Fame of the English Champions in general, and of the famous Mr. Sutton in particular, am come over on Purpose to fight any of the said Champions in general, but more especially Mr. Sutton, whom I hereby invite to meet me at the Time and Place above-named, where I doubt not but to convince him that my Courage and Judgment render me a Match for him, or the most Able and Skilful Master in this Kingdom.
*William Sherlock.*[93]

Sherlock must have already been a formidable gladiator, for, if his various statements are to believed, he proceeded to engage in a series of combats with Sutton. In most of these he came off victorious. In May, he claimed to have "lately put the Skill of the Celebrated Mr. Sutton to the Test, in the Presence of several Persons of Distinction, and competent Judges of the Science, when I prov'd myself his Equal, if not his Superior."[94] Two weeks later he further added that he

> put the Skill of the celebrated Mr. Sutton twice to the Test, and, in both Encounters, came off with Honour superior to that of any of his former Antagonists, especially in the last, which was on the 2d of May, when he received a Cut on the Head from me, which he was not able to return, I having a very visible Advantage over him, till we came to Quarter-Staff. I therefore invite him to another Engagement at the Time and Place...at the following Weapons only. Six bouts at Single Sword, Three Bouts at Sword and Dagger, Three Bouts at Sword and Buckler.[95]

At the end of the month, William Gill referred to the "as of yet unconquered Mr. William Sherlock," with Sherlock noting that he had fought "the celebrated Mr. Sutton 3 times, and came off with as much Honour as any of my Countrymen have before me..."[96] None of these various statements were disputed by Sutton, who merely reiterated his desire "to meet such dexterous Heroes as this boasting Challenger..."[97] William Gill was evidently keen to fight Sherlock, for at the beginning of June, Sherlock noted that Gill "hath been pleased to cast Aspersions on me and all others of the Kingdom of Ireland, who profess themselves Masters of the Science of Defence, and did send me a scandalous Letter full of scurrilous and opprobrious Language." Sherlock thus assured the public that "I will not fail to meet him at the Time and Place appointed, and convince him that Demonstration is the Ground of Argument; which shall be the earnest Endeavour of their humble Servant, *William Sherlock.*"[98]

In 1731, Sherlock noted that he had challenged James Figg to a combat, but that the latter had "declined the stage," forcing Sherlock to challenge Sutton yet again.[99] Three years later— on December 7, 1734—James Figg, England's most renowned gladiator, passed away.[100] Exactly three weeks later, on December 28, William Sherlock joined him, having evidently suffered a mortal wound in combat:

> *Dublin, December* 30... On Saturday last died, William Sherlock the famous Gladiator who received a Cut in his right Arm about ten Days ago, from one Sutton an English Prize-fighter. Sherlock's Arm was cut off two Days before he died.[101]

## FRANCIS SHERLOCK

Although William was now gone, within two years, another gladiator named Francis Sherlock—also from Dublin—would replace him on the English gladiatorial stage. Given that William was already in England, Francis is probably the same individual mentioned in the *Dublin Intelligencer* of July 28, 1731, which reported that "Young Sherlock, the prize-fighter, was almost murdered by a grenadier at St. James' Fair."[102] The writer John O'Keeffe, who had become acquainted with Sherlock's sister, also related the following story about Sherlock, in which he was said to have defeated Figg before the latter's death in 1734. As this account inaccurately suggests that Figg was a Dutch foreigner, it is difficult to know whether the story is apocryphal, or was based on an actual incident which was later embellished:

Sherlock, who many years before had been victor in every broad-sword contest of consequence, at a time when the skilful management of that weapon was considered of importance in London. A highly distinguished military commander, and patron of the art, or, as it was then called, the science of defence, not much liking the idea of Sherlock being winner of all the stage-fought laurels, imported into London from the Continent a grand broad-sword player, of the name of Figg, and the word now was "a Figg for the Liffey boy."* Emulation arose to animosity, and on the day of trial the place of action was thronged by both civil and military. Expectation and bets ran high, but mostly in favour of the foreign champion.

The two combatants on the stage, their swords drawn: Sherlock shook hands with his opponent, and said, "Mynheer Figg—guard it as well as you can, I'll cut off the third button of your coat." To it they went, the foreigner parried, yet Sherlock, with the admirable sleight of his art, had the third button on the point of his sword. "Now," said he, "I have been told, and I believe it, that, under this show of a mere contest for superior skill at our weapon, you intend to put a finish to me at once. I have proved to you that I could take your third button, and now, if I choose, I'll take your upper button; so guard your head." While his antagonist was endeavouring to guard his head, Sherlock's sword took a little slice off the calf of his leg, and thus, by the terms of the encounter, Sherlock having drawn the first blood, was declared conqueror. Thousands of guineas were sported upon this broad-sword match.[103]

No journalistic account has yet been found to verify this story.

Francis's earliest known challenge to have survived in print was published in the *Daily Advertiser* of August 4, 1736, and reads as follows:

---

* This witticism was no doubt a response to the pun *"A fig for the Irish,"* popularized by Ben Johnson, and which "arose from the reputation Figg had acquired in defeating the sturdiest Hibernian heroes of his time." See Samuel Ireland's *Graphic Illustrations of Hogarth* (London: R. Faulder and J. Egerton, 1794), 90.

At his Majesty's Bear-Garden in Hockley-Hole.

On Friday next, the 6th instant, will be a trial of skill between the following masters, viz.

Whereas I, Francis Sherlock, from the kingdom of Ireland, well known for my courage and judgment of the sword, did, in the Daily Advertiser of the 27th of July last, invite Mr. Sutton to fight me in a field, or behind a hedge; and whereas he, the said Mr. Sutton, in his answer in the Daily Advertiser of the 30th of the said month, accepted my invitation, but thought it more proper to engage at the above said place, where it is usually done; this is therefore to desire the said Mr. Sutton not to fail meeting me according to his promise, at the time and place appointed, making no farther apology. Your's, &c.

FRANCIS SHERLOCK.

I, Edward Sutton, from Gravesend, in *unconquered* Kent, well known for my courage and bravery, (when I fought the last battle with Mr. Holmes, at the abovesaid place, I fought a bout with him after I had fought the weapons through, without the loss of one drop of blood on the following occasion.— Mr. Holmes having received several cuts, being in a great passion pulled off his stocking in a bravading way, and by chance cut me a small cut on my head) will not fail meeting this Hibernian bravado with the same resolution as I always had for the honour of thy country; and as there have been several battles fought between the English and Irish, I desire this may be a decisive battle, and doubt not but to end it to the honour of Old England, and of your humble servant,

EDWARD SUTTON.[104]

Later it was noted that, Sutton had, at some point, traveled to Dublin, where he fought a combat with Sherlock at "single Sword, Sword and Dagger, Sword and Buckler, single Falchion, and Case of Falchions, of each three Bouts, no Wounds to be dress'd till the Battle is over..."[105] Little more than a year after their 1736 contest, however, Sutton passed away.[106] With two of Britain's greatest gladiators—Figg and Sutton—now gone, a void arose. It would be filled by Francis Sherlock, who would soon become the isle's undisputed champion.

Francis Sherlock was described as a "celebrated prize fighter, who opposed *Faddi*, the stout *Hungarian*, at *Broughton's* Amphitheatre, in Tottenham-court-road, before the *Duke of Cumberland*, and many of the nobility who were amateurs of the science of defence."[107] Another account of a devastating combat between Sherlock and a "German" gladiator noted:

In the memory of many, *Sherlock*, an *Irishman*, fought a *German* brought over by the late *Duke of Cumberland* for the special purpose of *prize-fighting*. The combat was on the stage of the Theatre in the *Haymarket*, and the fight was bloody. The *German* laid open the *Irishman's* cheek, from his ear to his mouth the wound was sewed and bound up and the second act terminated with the

*German's* life; his antagonist with a backhand blow, cutting him from hip to hip, and so deep as to divide his bowels so that his exit from the stage and from the *world* were on the same instant.[108]

In 1745, Sherlock fought another combat inside the lavish Hay-Market Theatre, this time against Joseph Johnson of Yorkshire:

AT THE NEW THEATRE
IN THE HAY-MARKET, ON WEDNESDAY THE
29th Of This Instant April.

The beauty of the Science of defence will be shown in a Trial of Skill, between the following masters, viz:—

Whereas, there was a battle fought on the 18th of March last, between MR. JOHNSON, from Yorkshire, and MR. SHERLOCK, from Ireland, in which engagement they came so near as to throw each other down. Since that rough battle, the said SHERLOCK has challenged JOHNSON to fight him, strapt down to the stage, for twenty pounds; to which the said JOHNSON has agreed; and they are to meet at the time and place above mentioned, and fight in the following manner, viz., to have their left feet strapt down to the stage, within the reach of each other's right leg; and the most bleeding wounds to decide the wager.[109]

Johnson's skill, and manner of fighting, was recounted in detail by John Godfrey:

Mr. JOHNSON is a staunch Swords-Man. I do not know anyone now who has so great a Share of Skill and undaunted Resolution, mixed together. He is a thorough MASTER of the true Principles of the Back-Sword...JOHNSON fights most from the Hanging, and executes more from it, than any I ever saw from that unready Guard...he differs from all the rest in using that Guard.[110]

Later that year, in July, another combat between Sherlock and Johnson was arranged, to take place at Broughton's Ampitheatre. It was noted that Sherlock's "Prowess is greatest in the noble (and too much neglected) Science of Defence," and that "there are several great Bets depending thereon..."[111] During the contest, things became so heated that Johnson's second, Richard Banks, was attacked by a man named Thomas Hodgkins who, as Banks recounted, "came on the Stage, drew a Sword, and made several Cuts at me, which I defended with my Staff."[112] Sherlock ultimately won this battle, after which he issued a public declaration challenging "any Man in Europe."[113]

In September, another Irish gladiator named William Johnston, hearing of Sherlock's fame, traveled from Limerick to London with the intent to challenge the latter. However, "finding [Sherlock] an Irishman," Johnston desisted, and proceeded to challenge all English fighters instead.[114]

Like Figg and Sutton before him, Sherlock had now become the top gladiator whom all others sought to displace. During the same year that he received Johnston's challenge, Sherlock fielded a threat from Anthony English, of Cork, who took to the newspapers to publicly disparage Sherlock for being skilled with the small-sword:

> To Mr. F R A N C I S  S H E R L O C K.
>
> S I R,
>
> Remember you declin'd my Challenge at Bristol six Years ago; and as I burn with the same Thirst of Glory, I am still the more provok'd at your now trifling and Excuses since my Arrival at London, I would have you to understand, all your Judgment and Delicacy at the Line and Posture of the Small Sword, only serve to enflame the Spirit and Courage of a true Englishman; therefore, Mr. Sherlock, if you are not for letting the World judge of our Success, chuse the most obscure Corner, Hedge, or Ditch, where we shall decide in real Flesh and deep Wounds of the best Master; or if you deserve the Character the Town affords you, and be any ways, thro' Excess of Valour, prodigal of Blood, I shall be ready to divert the Spectators, with three Bouts at the Broad Sword, at Broughton's Ampitheatre, gratis.
>
> Anthony English.[115]

Sherlock immediately accepted English's challenge, and the two—both said to be "good masters of the Small and Back Sword"—fought a combat at Broughton's Ampitheatre.[116] The result of this match is not recorded; however, its likely outcome can be discerned from the fact that Anthony English was never heard from again, while Sherlock continued to attain even greater celebrity.

The following years brought a series of continued victories to Francis Sherlock. In 1746, he fought a combat using the sword and targe against a rival Highlander. According to the *Stamford Mercury*,

> Wednesday Noon there was a severe Trial of Skill between Mr. Sherlock from Dublin, and Mr. McDonald from the Highlands of Scotland, at Broughton's Amphitheatre in Oxford Road, when the Highlander was entirely discomfited at his own Weapons in a few Minutes.[117]

A few weeks later, Joseph Johnson invited the same McDonald to fight, wondering if "the pretended Highlander thinks he has made any Improvement in the Sword and Target since he has fought Mr. Sherlock."[118]

During the next year, Sherlock faced a "Hollander" in a combat which resulted in yet another victory for the Irishman:

Yesterday was the Trial of Skill at Broughton's Amphitheatre in Oxford road, between Mr. Sherlock and the Hollander, at the usual Weapons fought on the Stage, when Mr. Sherlock beat his Antagonist. It was a smart Battle.[119]

That November, it was also reported that "Sherlock beat Lill at Mr. Broughton's Amphitheatre; he gave him several cuts."[120]

Sherlock's celebrity was now at its height. It no doubt increased when, that same year, the English Captain John Godfrey published his *Treatise Upon the Useful Science of Defence*. In its pages, Godfrey alternately praised and criticized Sherlock's manner of fencing, stating:

Mr. SHERLOCK must be pronounced an elegant Swords-Man, with uncommon merit. His Designs are true and just, encouraged by an active Wrist and great Agility of Body. He pitches to the Small-Sword Posture, the Recommendation of which I here repeat. I know there are great Demures against it, but I will venture to justify him in it. He is certainly right to use that Guard, most properly called a Guard, which best stops the too near Approach of his Adversary, and at the same Time supplies him with more readiness to Action. But though I am willing to give every Man his due Merit, I cannot step into the Filth of Flattery; therefore must confess, Mr. SHERLOCK is not faultless. I will point out one Defect, and leave it to Judges whether I am right in my Observation. It is his Subjection and Proneness to starting, by which he may evidently put himself in the Power of a Man of much inferior Judgement. I have often see Mr. SHERLOCK engaged with a Man of far less Abilities of himself, when upon a bare Stamp with the other's Foot, and Movement of his Sword, he has hurried back with Precipitation. Sure Mr. SHERLOCK must own he hereby gives his Opposer great Advantage; however, I leave him with this Acknowledgement, that if he had Mr. JOHNSON's firm stable Resolution, he would rival any I have mentioned.[121]

Two years later, in 1749, it was arranged for Sherlock to fight a Frenchman named Beaugrand. The *General Advertiser* enthused that, "We are assured, and to the great Joy of the Gentlemen skilled in the Sword, that Mr. Sherlock has once more condescended to appear on the Stage, which nothing could have induced him to do, but to prevent Mr. Beaugrand the Frenchman's Progress."[122] This combat took place on February 13; its outcome was described as follows:

Yesterday was fought at Broughton's Amphitheatre in Oxford Road, the great Battle between Sherlock and Beaugrand the Frenchman; they fought nine Bouts, when Beaugrand received three Cuts; two small ones, one on the Leg, and a deep one under the Eye, and Sherlock none. They both behaved in a very genteel Manner, and fought with great Courage.[123]

Despite this overwhelming victory, financial troubles now caught up with Francis Sherlock. Several years prior, he had been declared a fugitive for debt, and in 1749, he filed for bankruptcy.[124] The next year, he was incarcerated in debtor's prison. During this time, local newspapers printed a story claiming that,

> Last Friday Mr. Sherlock, the famous Prize-fighter, was killed in a Duel in the King's-Bench Prison, Southwark.[125]

This report, however, was false. Within a week, Sherlock—evidently in good health—was billed to fight a contest with a "Mr. Flanders":

> We can now assure the Publick, that on Wednesday next the Battle between Mr. Sherlock and Mr. Flanders, is to be decided; as this is the last time of those two great Swordsmen appearing on the Stage, great Betts are depending. They have agreed between them if the Cuts given on each side be equal, in the Nine Bouts of the Sword, they are to begin again and fight, in order to determine by a Majority of Cuts only, who the winning Man shall be; and in order to prevent Disputes on the Stage, three Gentlemen are to be appointed as Umpires, to determine each Bout of Fighting.[126]

It was also noted that these "two famous Swordsmen" were to wield the "the Back-sword," and had been "match'd for a considerable Sum of Money."[127] Although the outcome of this particular contest is not extant, Sherlock fought another combat only a week later—yet again with "Beaugrand, the Frenchman," which resulted in yet another victory:

> Yesterday was fought at Broughton's Amphitheatre in Oxford road, the great Battle between Sherlock and Beaugrand, the Frenchman; they fought nine Bouts, when Beaugrand receiv'd five Cuts, and Sherlock none.[128]

At the same time, it was announced that "Mr. Sherlock Teaches [fencing] at Charing-Cross Coffee-house."[129]

The last known contest involving Sherlock was proposed on April 1, 1752. The announcement for it contains few details, and merely mentions that "Mr. Sherlock and another Fencing-Master, are once in a Month to fence for one hundred Pounds with an half Inch Gauntlet."[130] That year, the *Covent-Garden Journal* extolled the Irishman's skill, declaring that "Mr. Sherlock is, I believe, justly allowed to be superior to all Europe in the Skill of the Broad Sword."[131]

Although he may have ceased fighting for prizes, a decade later, in 1763, Francis Sherlock was still listed in the London directory as a fencing-master teaching on Queen-street, Westminster.[132] Fencing and combat would not be his only legacies. His son, William (probably named for his father's predecessor), had been born in Dublin around 1738, and would become a noted portrait artist, illustrating the figures in Smollett's famous *History of England*, and serving as the Director of the Society of Artists.[133] Likewise, William's own son, William P. Sherlock, would become a noted landscape and architectural "artist of remarkable merit." Today, the artworks of both Sherlocks still reside in the collections of the British Museum and the Victoria and Albert Museum.[134] A text published in 1796 noted that the elder artist "was the son of Sherlock, the celebrated prize fighter," who still "flourished" as of 1762.[135] The life of Ireland's last and most renowned gladiator came to an end in 1764, when the *London Evening Post* announced:

> A short time since died, in Little Queen-street, Westminster, Mr. Francis Sherlock, the celebrated Master of Defence, and formerly a most distinguished Prize-fighter on the stage, who was the only man that ever beat the famous Figg, which broke his heart.[136]

## THE LAST DUBLIN PRIZE FIGHT

At the midpoint of the eighteenth century, the tradition of British stage-fighting went into rapid decline. At Broughton's Amphitheatre, Francis Sherlock ceased making appearances, and boxing contests replaced sword contests as the dominant form of gladiatorial entertainment.

The last known incident of a prize-fight fought with sharp weapons in Ireland occurred about 1753, and involved a British gladiator named Thomas Barrett. Decades before, in 1730, Barrett had managed his own "Great Booth" in Bird-Cage Alley, Southwark, where he had repeatedly faced Irish opponents:

> Whereas...I Thomas Barrett, Master of the Science of Defence, who ever fac'd the most imminent Dangers, and have reduc'd the greatest Masters of the Sword by a Power superior to those who have been dignify'd with Imperial Titles, fought the famous Mr. Michael Butler [of Kilkenny], in which Battle an equality of Blood was lost on both Sides, where by the Glory of an intended Conquest was dawn'd, and the Victor held doubtful; In order to know the Man, I hereby invite him once more to try his Fortune at the Time and Place first above mention'd, being determin'd to maintain that Character the Publick have been pleas'd to honour me with, and of which Time itself can only deprive me, &c.
>
> Thomas Barrett.[137]

Soon afterwards, Barrett, along with his wife Sarah, contested against Felix and Lætitia MacGuire.[138] Twenty years later, Barrett fought his last battle in Dublin—one which would, unfortunately, be fatal to the itinerant Englishman. A story of his demise was recorded by

Thomas Barrett, "Master of the Science of Defence," killed in Dublin ca. 1753. After an original engraving by Thomas Barrit, courtesy of Manchester Libraries, Information and Archives, Manchester City Council, reference number BR MS f 399 B13.

Thomas Barrit, an old Manchester antiquary who evidently well-remembered the gladiator possessing a name nearly identical to his own. Barrit recounted,

When I was a boy about eight years old, a noted prize fighter came to Manchester, by name Thomas Barret, an old man, with his face cut and scarred all over, so that for the most part he went by the name of "Old Chopping-block." He taught the science of defence (or what I should think was sometimes offence), in a large room at the Old Boar's Head, Hyde's Cross. While in town he articled with a stranger to show their feats of arms in public, in a yard near Salford Chapel; at which place I attended to see the exhibition, which was performed upon a stage in manner following: First, the champions entered the lists in their shirts, and bare-headed, with each a quarter-staff, about two yards long and as thick as the handle of a pike. These they brandished and whirled about with surprising dexterity; not forgetting every now and then to reach each other a lusty souse upon the sides, shoulders, or head, which was no ways displeasing to the spectators. This exercise being ended, and a little time spent in refreshing, the combatants approached each other with basket-hilted broadswords, and each a target (*i.e.* a large shield or buckler) upon their left arm; seconds likewise being appointed and upon the stage with poles, to prevent them going to extremities. In a little while both targets, not being covered with leather, were slit in pieces; and Old Chopping-block after this received a cut upon the cheek, near the nose. He immediately returned the compliment, cutting his antagonist directly upon the brow; by which their faces were almost covered with blood. After some few flourishes with their weapons, old Barret received another wound on his face, near the former, which he did not seem to approve; and, spying an opening in his adversary, gave him such a slice on the forehead, and with such earnestness, that the seconds, thinking it not prudent that the business should be continued any longer, parted them. This affair, however, not subsiding, a second challenge was given and place appointed, which was the Old Boar's Head yard, where I again attended a few days later. The fellows again mounted the stage with swords; but old Barret taking the advantage, cut his antagonist in the side, which was declared unfair play. Thus this combat ended, and was the last swordplay I ever heard of in England. In some while after Thomas Barret went to Ireland, and there followed the same business, and in a combat received a cut in his belly, which let his bowels out and ended his days.[139]

This last Irish combat, it was said, took place in Dublin. At the end of one of his many scrapbooks, Barrit—who was also a noted engraver—included an image of the old gladiator. Beneath it, Barrit scrawled a few additional biographical details:

Thomas Barrett. From the many cuts in his face called Old Chopping Block, a noted Prize Fighter; lost his life in single combat in Dublin about the year 1753, supposed to have been the last man in these kingdoms who made prize fighting his profession, his weapons were the broad sword & quarter staff, & at times used the target, he taught the use of the broad sword for the army, and the quarter staff for Park Keepers, Woodmen, and others.[140]

## LATER CONTESTS IN IRELAND

Although the ritualistic, gladiatorial combats fought with sharp weapons appear to have vastly declined—or ceased entirely—in Ireland during the 1750s, less fatal contests involving cudgels and single-sticks long continued to endure among the lower-classes. In 1781, *Walker's Hibernian Magazine* announced that a contest at Back-Sword was "to be play'd" for a purse of five guineas in the village of Rathcoole, southwest of Dublin. It was noted that the "man who breaks two heads, and saves his own, to quit the stage, and be allowed a tier; no head to be allowed, unless the blood runs one inch..."[141] Later, in 1787, an editorial in the *Dublin Evening Post* complained that

In parts of the town, where great numbers of the nobility resort, it is impossible but there must be many idle domestics and followers; and these people will naturally seek some amusement, to fill their vacant hours. The neighborhood of Merrion-square is precisely of this description. In the fields opposite the houses, it was usual for groups to assemble on Sunday evenings, to entertain themselves with cudgel-playing, wrestling, and other gymnastic exercises. These groups were generally composed of over-grown chairman, pampered footmen, stable-boys, helpers from the adjacent gentlemens' houses; and what is not a little strange, their masters suffered this profanation of the Sabbath, almost under their very noses, much to their dishonour. A party of Police, however, on Sunday last went out, under Ald. Exshaw, to disperse a tumultuous meeting of this description that had assembled there.[142]

The agents of the law, however, were not successful in completely extirpating the custom. Only two years later, the following bold announcement appeared in the pages of the *Evening Post*:

LAMMAS DAY, August 12, 1789.
*DUNLEARY.*
IRISH FESTIVITY...

CUDGEL-PLAYING—in love and amity:

Each and every stout Combatant must shake hands and kiss before they are suffered to play.—Proper Judges on the boards, to preserve good temper and fair play.

To the best Player a silver laced hat; Dunleary, Dalkey, and Bullock Boys, and their adjacent allies, on the contiguous coasts—against—ALL Ireland.[143]

During the 1770s and 1780s, members of the Irish Volunteers, or home militias, rigorously trained in the use of the sword, and frequently engaged in contests of swordsmanship. Numerous specimens of Volunteer medals, given out as prizes to members of the Cork, Kerry, Roscommon, Tipperary, and Limerick militias, still remain extant, and were reproduced in the pages of the nineteenth century *Journal of the Cork Historical and Archaeological Society* (see above image).[144] Such skill would be put to the ultimate test in 1798, when numerous units of the Irish Volunteers fought on opposing sides during the United Irishmen Rebellion.

1  Egerton Castle, *Schools and Masters of Fence* (London: George Bell and Sons, 1885), 189-190, 201-204. Walter Thornbury, *Old and New London, a Narrative of Its History, Its People, and Its Places* (London: Cassell, Petter, Galpin & Co.,1881), 308.

2  *Ipswich Journal*, June 10, 1727.

3  Josias Maynard and William Swinnow. *A Tryall [of] Skill, Betwen Josias Maynard Citizen, and Cutler of London, and Master of the Noble Science of Defence ... of the House of White Friers, and William Swinow, Alias Scot, Citizen and Cooke of London, and Master of the Noble Science of Defence, of the House of Tower Royall.* 1652.

4  Examples of notable prize-fighters who died as a result of wounds incurred while contesting include "Norfolk Champion" William Emmerson, Timothy Buck of Clare-Market, Michael Butler of Kilkenny, and the celebrated "famous gladiator" William Sherlock (killed by Edward "Ned" Sutton in 1735). *Ipswich Journal*, April 15, 1721. *Derby Mercury*, January 15, 1735.

5  *Universal Spectator and Weekly Journal*, July 26, 1729.

6  *Weekly Journal or Saturday Post*, June 20, 1719.

7  *Weekly Journal or Saturday Post*, March 11, 1727.

8  *Daily Post*, April 30, 1729.

9  *Daily Post*, March 25, 1728.

10  From a copy in possession of the Westminster City Archives.

11  *Daily Advertiser,* October 10, 1743.

12  *Daily Journal,* June 13, 1732.

13  *Daily Post,* October 1, 1723.

14  Drake, *Volume I,* 34-35.

15  From a copy in possession of the Westminster City Archives.

16  *Caledonian Mercury,* August 21, 1729. Also, see copies of various challenges in possession of the Westminster City Archives.

17  From a copy in possession of the Westminster City Archives.

18  The author conducted a survey of more than 300 gladiatorial contests occurring between 1700 and 1750. The handful of gladiators who were neither Anglo nor Irish include the "celebrated Highland prize-fighter" Donald McBane; one "Mr. McDonald from the Highlands of Scotland"; an unnamed "German brought over by the late Duke of Cumberland"; "Faddi, the stout Hungarian"; John Crumpton (of Wales); "Mr. Jones" (of Wales); Thomas Soon (of Wales); Thomas Philips (from Jamaica, of African ancestry), George Nervil Turner, "a Black"; William Tompson, "a Black"; Abraham Meilck Mordecai (Jewish), and Paterishy Comer (from Seville, Spain).

19  Antoine François Prévost d'Exiles, *The Memoirs and Adventures of the Marquis de Bretagne and Duc d'Harcourt: The wonderful Vicissitudes of Fortune, exemplified in the Lives of those Noblemen, To which is added The history of the chevalier de Grieu and Moll Lescaut. Translated from the Original French by Mr. Erskine, Volume II* (London: T. Cooper, 1743), 228-231.

20  From a copy in possession of the Westminster City Archives.

21  Dublin City Library & Archives. This online listing of early Dublin freemen is a Dublin City Council project, under the overall direction of Dublin City Librarian, Margaret Hayes, and Dublin City Archivist, Dr. Mary Clark. The project was researched and developed by genealogist John Grenham.

22  *Daily Journal,* May 3, 1732.

23 *London Evening Post*, March 18, 1732.

24 *Daily Post*, July 4, 1732.

25 *Daily Post*, July 12, 1732.

26 *Daily Post*, April 21, 1724.

27 Capt. John Godfrey, *A Treatise Upon the Useful Science of Defence, Connecting the Small and Back-Sword, And showing the Affinity between them* (London: T. Gardner, 1747), 29-30.

28 From a copy in possession of the Westminster City Archives.

29 *Daily Post*, October 21, 1725.

30 *Guests Journal*, November 20, 1725.

31 *Daily Post*, November 23, 1725.

32 Francis Beaumont and John Fletcher, *Bonduca, a tragedy* (London: Printed for J.T., 1718).

33 Cesar de Saussure, *A foreign view of England in the reigns of George I and George II: The letters of Monsieur Cesar de Saussure to his family* (London: John Murray, 1902), 277-279.

34 *Ipswich Journal*, September 24, 1726.

35 From a copy in possession of the Westminster City Archives.

36 Godfrey, 41.

37 *Daily Post*, August 1, 1727.

38 *Weekly Journal, or The British Gazetteer*, October 1, 1726.

39 *Weekly Journal, or The British Gazetteer*, October 22, 1726.

40 *Weekly Journal, or The British Gazetteer*, January 27, 1727.

41 Castle. Thornbury. W. R. Chambers, *W. R. Chambers's journal of popular literature, science and arts, Volume 59* (London: W. R. Chambers, 1882). Samuel Palmer, *St. Pancras: being antiquarian, topographical, and biographical memoranda, relating to the extensive metropolitan parish of St. Pancras, Middlesex; with some account of the parish from its foundation* (London: S. Palmer, 1870).

42 *Weekly Journal, or The British Gazetteer*, July 3, 1727.

43 *Daily Post*, April 20, 1728.

44 *Daily Post*, April 22, 1728.

45 *Weekly Journal, or The British Gazetteer*, August 24, 1728.

46 *Daily Journal*, June 3, 1729.

47 *Daily Post*, March 21, 1727.

48 *Weekly Journal, or The British Gazetteer*, September 9, 1727.

49 From a copy in possession of the Westminster City Archives.

50 *Bentley's Miscellany*, Volume VIII (New York: Jemima M. Mason, 1841), 175.

51 *Weekly Journal, or The British Gazetteer*, May 24, 1729.

52 *Daily Courant*, April 11, 1721.

53 From a copy in possession of the Westminster City Archives.

54 Ibid.

55 *Daily Post*, April 18, 1727.

56 *Daily Journal*, May 31, 1729.

57  *Weekly Journal,* April 25, 1730.

58  Godfrey, 40.

59  *Weekly Journal,* April 25, 1730.

60  *Daily Post,* June 30, 1730.

61  *Daily Post,* March 17, 1731.

62  *Daily Post,* April 2, 1729. *Daily Post,* March 11, 1730.

63  *Daily Post,* June 15, 1730.

64  *Daily Advertiser,* August 10, 1731.

65  James Peller Malcolm, *Anecdotes of the Manners and Customs of London during the eighteenth century* (London: Longman, Hurst, Rees, and Orme, Paternoster Row, 1808), 345-346.

66  Antoine François Prévost d'Exiles, *The Memoirs and Adventures of the Marquis de Bretagne and Duc d'Harcourt: The wonderful Vicissitudes of Fortune, exemplified in the Lives of those Noblemen, To which is added The history of the chevalier de Grieu and Moll Lescaut. Translated from the Original French by Mr. Erskine, Volume II* (London: T. Cooper, 1743), 228-231.

67  *Daily Advertiser,* July 19, 1731.

68  *Daily Journal,* April 20, 1731.

69  *Daily Advertiser,* July 1, 1745.

70  *Daily Post,* August 8, 1727.

71  From a copy in possession of the Westminster City Archives.

72  *Daily Post,* September 26, 1727.

73  *Daily Post,* September 6, 1727.

74  *Daily Post,* November 23, 1730.

75  Ibid.

76  *Derby Mercury,* October 22, 1730.

77  John Nichols and the late George Steevens, *The genuine works of William Hogarth; illustrated with biographical anecdotes, a chronological catalogue, and commentary* (London: Longman, Hurst, Rees, and Orme, 1808-17) 108-109.

78  *Caledonian Mercury,* April 22, 1731

79  *Daily Journal,* April 20, 1731.

80  *Daily Post,* May 17,1731.

81  *At his Majesty's Bear-Garden. In Hockly-in-the-Hole, this present Wednesday, being the 14th of May, 1735. Will be performed a tryal of skill by the following great masters in that noble art, call'd defence* (London: Printed by G. Buckeridge in Baldwin's-Garden, 1735).

82  *Daily Post,* June 5, 1732. *Daily Post,* June 28, 1732. *Daily Post,* July 18, 1733. William John Pinks, *The History of Clerkenwell* (London: Charles Herbert, Goswell Road, 1881), 485-486.

83  *Daily Post,* July 18, 1733.

84  *Daily Post,* August 8, 1733.

85  *Daily Post,* August 20, 1733.

86  *Daily Post,* September 11, 1728.

87  *Daily Journal,* Oct 9, 1728.

88  *Ipswich Journal,* January 2, 1731.

89 *Ipswich Journal*, January 16, 1731.

90 *Daily Journal*, May 17, 1731.

91 Godfrey, 41-42.

92 *Daily Courant*, August 16, 1716.

93 *Daily Journal*, April 16, 1729.

94 *Daily Journal*, May 2, 1729.

95 *Daily Journal*, May 14, 1729.

96 *Daily Journal*, May 28, 1729.

97 *Daily Journal*, May 14, 1729.

98 *Daily Journal*, June 4, 1729.

99 *Daily Post*, March 23, 1731

100 *Daily Post*, December 9, 1734.

101 *Derby Mercury*, January 15, 1735.

102 *Dublin Intelligencer*, July 28, 1731.

103 John O'Keeffe, *Recollections of the life of John O'Keeffe, Volume 2* (New York: B. Blom, 1826), 136-138. It may also be that O'Keeffe was not remembering a contest between Figg and William Sherlock at all, but was confusing it with one of Francis Sherlock's later contests with "Faddi, the stout Hungarian," or with the German gladiator that he fought before the Duke of Cumberland. Figg had, of course, died by this time.

104 *The Sporting Magazine*, January, 1799.

105 *Daily Advertiser*, October 10, 1743.

106 "On Tuesday last died at his House at Gravesend, Edward Sutton, the famous Prize-Fighter." *Daily Post*, October 22, 1737.

107 Anthony Pasquin, *An authentic History of the Professors of Painting, Sculpture and Architecture who have practised in Ireland, involving original letters from Sir J. Reynolds which prove him to have been illiterate, to which are added Memoirs of the Royal Academicians* (London: H. D. Symonds, 1796), 19.

108 Reprinted in *The Graphic: A Weekly Illustrated Newspaper*, Volume 40, July to December, 1889.

109 Charles Mackay, *An Antiquarian Ramble in the Streets of London: With Anecdotes of Their More Celebrated Residents, Volume I* (London: Bentley, 1846), 35.

110 Godfrey, 43-44.

111 *Penny London Post or Morning Advertiser*, July 31, 1745.

112 *Daily Advertiser*, August 19, 1745.

113 *Daily Advertiser*, September 11, 1745.

114 *Daily Advertiser*, September 13, 1745.

115 *Daily Advertiser*, August 31, 1745. See also challenge from "Anthony Inglish, from Cork, in the Kingdom of Ireland," in the *Weekly Journal*, March 14, 1730.

116 *Daily Advertiser*, September 4, 1745.

117 *Stamford Mercury*, May 22, 1746.

118 *Penny London Post or Morning Advertiser*, June 2, 1746.

119 *Derby Mercury*, October 9, 1747.

120 *Derby Mercury*, November 20, 1747.

121 Godfrey, 44-45.

122 *General Advertiser*, February 7, 1749.

123 *Derby Mercury*, February 9, 1749.

124 *London Gazette*, May 31, 1743. *London Magazine*, October, 1749.

125 *Ipswich Journal*, February 3, 1750.

126 *General Advertiser*, February 8, 1750.

127 *General Advertiser*, January 1, 1750; February 12, 1750.

128 *Ipswich Journal*, February 17, 1750.

129 *General Advertiser*, February 8, 1750.

130 *General Advertiser*, April 1, 1752.

131 *Covent-Garden Journal*, January 18, 1752.

132 Thomas Mortimer, *The universal director; or, the nobleman and gentleman's true guide to the masters and professors of the liberal and polite arts and sciences* (London: Printed for J. Coote, in Pater-noster-row, MDCCLXIII), 25.

133 Pasquin, 19. Victoria and Albert Museum, *A catalogue of the miniatures* (London: Printed for H.M. Stationery Off., by Wyman and Sons, 1908) 31-33.

134 Sidney Lee, ed., *Dictionary of National Biography, Volume LII* (London: Smith, Elder, & Co., 1897), 97.

135 John Warburton, *History of the City of Dublin, Volume 2* (Dublin: T. Cadell and W. Davies, 1818), 1186.

136 *London Evening Post*, May 29, 1764.

137 *Weekly Journal or British Gazetteer*, July 25, 1730.

138 *Daily Post*, August 8, 1733.

139 John Harland, *Collectanea Relating to Manchester and Its Neighborhood, at Various Periods*, Vol. II (Printed for the Chetham Society, 1847), 91-92

140 Thomas Barritt, *Ancient Armour and Weapons in the possession of Thomas Barritt* [1793-1811], MS.

141 *Walker's Hibernian Magazine*, September, 1781.

142 *Dublin Evening Post*, May 15, 1787.

143 *Dublin Evening Post*, August 1, 1789.

144 "On Some Medals and Mottoes of the Irish Volunteers" in *Journal of the Cork Historical and Archaeological Society, Vol. IV, 2nd series* (Cork: Guy & Co., 1898), 33-48, 186-197. *Journal of the Cork Historical and Archaeological Society, Vol. VI, 2nd series* (Cork: Guy & Co., 1900), 214-222; *Journal of the Cork Historical and Archaeological Society, Vol. V, 2nd series* (Cork: Guy & Co., 1900), 35-38, 183-192. *Journal of the Cork Historical and Archaeological Society, Vol. IX, 2nd series* (Cork: Guy & Co., 1903), 159. *Journal of the Cork Historical and Archaeological Society, Vol. III, 1st series* (Cork: Guy & Co., 1894), 320.

An IRISH CHEROKEE.

*Walker's Hibernian Magazine*, April, 1792.

# IV

## EIGHTEENTH CENTURY DUBLIN:
## EUROPE'S WILD WEST

In 1775, an Englishman named Richard Twiss wrote the following advice to those considering travel to Ireland:

> There are many qualifications which, however trifling they may appear, will be found of great service to travellers. A moderate skill in the use of the sword, guns, and pistols, may happen to be necessary; and it would not be amiss frequently to practise fencing, and shooting at a mark.

Lest anyone doubt the truth of this statement, Twiss provided the following footnote for clarification:

> * I am aware that this may appear ludicrous, but it is meant seriously.[1]

Judging from the historical evidence, Twiss's advice seems to have been well-founded. The disempowerment of the old Catholic aristocratic order, the outlawry of many of its members, and the implementation of the penal laws by Ireland's new ruling class had left vast swaths of the common populace resentful and mistrustful of the government and its agents. In such an environment, lawlessness thrived. During the eighteenth century, Ireland became renowned for the presence of rural highwaymen, *rapparees* (ex-guerrilla fighters turned bandits), and celebrity criminals such as Naoise O'Haughan (of Antrim), "Captain Power" (of Cork), James Carrick (of Dublin), James Butler (of Kilkenny), John Mulhoni (of Connaught), Charles Dempsey, alias "Cahier na Cappul" (of Wicklow), "Captain Gallagher" (of Mayo), William "Willy" Brennan (of Cork), James Mac-Faul (of Carrickfergus), Donchadh Dubh (of Cork), "Strong" John Macpherson, Thomas "Squire Becket" Butler, Richard Balf, and "Captain" James MacLaine (of Monaghan), the last of whom was infamously known to hide his face behind a Venetian mask while accosting his victims. Although such highwaymen were often affectionately referred to as "gentlemen robbers" due to their humorous wit and superficially genteel demeanor, their crimes and depredations were numerous and often violent.[2]

The widespread existence of such threats made the carrying personal sidearms in eighteenth century Ireland a necessity, especially when also considering the fact that there was no reliable presence of law enforcement in the sense that we think of it today.

In no place was this more true than in Dublin, where the streets were overrun with notoriously violent gangs such as the Bucks, Mohawks, Cherokees, Cutting Weavers, Ormonde Boys, Liberty Boys, and Pinking Dindies. Although a form of police did exist in Dublin during the era, their forces were low in number and thinly spread. At the beginning of the eighteenth century, there were no police on duty by day in the city, while at night, the streets were patrolled by the Watch system. It was the job of this handful of night watchmen— stationed alone with lanterns and pole-arms—to single-handedly enforce the law, and call out the military in the event that they found themselves outnumbered or out-armed. In 1715, a statute recited that these watches were very weak, and that it was necessary to strengthen them. However, even subsequent to this, the Watch system did not improve much. In 1723, the civil patrolmen, nicknamed the "Charlies," were formed as armed constables to patrol Dublin City, and were reformed as an unarmed force in 1786 as the Dublin Police.[3] In 1763, the arms and accoutrements of the "Watchmen of the several Parishes of this City in St. Stephen's-Green" included "Light Infantry Caps, Halberts, and Back-Swords, and...Lanthorns flung on belts."[4] In 1795, the arms of the "new Dublin Watch" were described as follows:

> An ash pole, armed with a bayonet, or with a hook and spear, adopted by each watchman is to be provided with an alarm rattle, and is to proclaim the hours.[5]

The above descriptions are notable for the complete absence of any mention of firearms. By 1798, there were forty-eight peace officers, six office constables, and from 450 to 600 watchmen. This, for a city with a population of approximately 180,000 people, was barely adequate.[6]

Engraving, made circa 1750, of "Captain" James MacLaine of County Monaghan, shown armed with a small-sword; at his feet lies his trademark disguise—a Venetian mask.

An example of the procedure and response time of law enforcement in eighteenth century Dublin can be found in the following anecdote—culled from Margaret Leeson's 1797 memoirs —which illustrates the stunning speed at which armed altercations with sharp weapons could unfold in the streets Dublin:

Sally Hayes and I were invited to dine with a friend of hers in French-street, and we took [Mr.] Cunynghame with us. We passed the day very cheerfully, but there happened a great fall of snow, and when it was time to come home, there was no carriage to be got. However, as we felt no cold, being tolerably warmed with good wine, we resolved to walk home. It was pretty late, and we came on, kicking the snow before us, as if we cared for nobody. We had come down about half the length of the street, when we were met by Counsellor B—y and another; who said to Cunyng-hame, you have two ladies, and one is sufficient for you, you may therefore give me the other. On this a dispute arose, and they knocked each other down. The officer had neither sword nor cane, but the counsellor had a sword, which he drew, and made a push at Cunynghame, which passed a-slant through his cloth waistcoat, and slightly grazed his breast, but did no other damage. The captain being enraged, wrenched the sword out of the counsellor's hand, and broke it in two; and then, with the assistance of me and Sally Hayes, gave them both a very sufficient beating. The counsellor called the watch, and Mr. Cunynghame set off for home, and leave us, as by that time we knew each other. The watch came, and they charged us, and we them. We all stood above half an hour in the snow, scolding and abusing each other; till being heartily tired, and growing very cold, we let each off, and shook hands. Indeed, to give the little counsellor his due, he behaved in a spirited manner, and called upon me several times to obtain the captain's address, which I declined giving, as I knew a duel must have ensued.[7]

By the time the watch or constables arrived at the scene of an altercation, the fracas was typically long over, and the perpetrators often nowhere to be found. Thieves and footpads, roving in bands of five or even ten persons, and armed with swords, frequently attacked, beat, and robbed pedestrians. Irish newspapers of the period are full of such accounts, the following of which is typical:

On Monday Night the 29th Inst. a young Gentleman was attacked in Thomas street by Five Foot-pads armed with Swords and Pistols, who robbed him of the following articles...[8]

As is the following:

About three o'Clock on Sunday Morning, a Gentleman was stopped in Abbey-street, near Capel-street, by a Footpad armed with a drawn Sword, who robbed him of four Guineas and his Watch. Though repeatedly called to, and within twenty Yards of two different Stands, not a Watchman would come to his Assistance.[9]

So unreliable was the Watch, in fact, that the only citizens who typically survived these encounters with both life, body, and property intact, were those that were well-armed and martially proficient:

> About twelve o'Clock at Night, a Gentleman was attacked on Ormond-quay by three Footpads, but defending himself with a Small Sword and calling the Watch, the Villains desisted; but no Watchman appearing, they made a second Attack, in which he wounded one of them; they then escaped into the Market.[10]

It may be that, in many cases, such crimes had been coordinated with the assistance or collusion of the Watchmen themselves, who tended towards corruption. In his memoirs, Jonah Barrington recounted personally taking part in group crimes in which members of the Watch were complicit—and from which they profited—during his youth:

> We were in the habit of going about the latter on dark nights, in coaches, flinging out halfpence, and breaking the windows of all the houses we rapidly drove by, to the astonishment and terror of the proprietors. At other times we used to convey gunpowder squibs into all the lamps in several streets at once, and by longer or shorter fusees contrive to have them all burst about the same time, breaking every lamp to shivers and leaving whole streets in utter darkness. Occasionally we threw large crackers into the china and glass-shops, and delighted to see the terrified shop-keepers trampling on their own porcelain and cut-glass, for fear of an explosion. By way of a treat we used sometimes to pay the watchmen to lend us their cloaks and rattles, by virtue whereof we broke into the low prohibited gambling-houses, knocked out the lights, drove the gamblers down stairs, and then gave all their stakes to the watchmen. The whole body of watchmen belonging to one parish (that of the Round Church) were our sworn friends, and would take our part against any other watchmen in Dublin. We made a permanent subscription, and paid each of these regularly seven shillings a-week for his patronage.[11]

Likewise, a 1784 article, after describing in detail the immense number of weekly violent crimes that had been committed in Dublin, lamented that

> The Inactivity of the Watchmen is very reprehensible in this Neighbourhood; nor do the Lamps afford a Ray of Light to the endangered Passengers, though the Public are so heavily encumbered with Lamp Money... Robberies are become so frequent, and are attended with such Circumstances of Boldness and Inhumanity, that they demand peculiar Attention and Interference. The Peace has let loose Thousands upon the Public, several of whom have come hither to reap a depredatory Harvest... Prevention should be as much as possible be effected. Constant nightly Patroles seem at present to be necessary... As mere Punishments have been found ineffectual, other Methods should be tried. Want, Profligacy, and Desperation will require several Restraints. To be obliged

in a civilized Kingdom, under the Eye of Government, to live in a State of Defence, is both disreputable and disagreeable. It brings our Wisdom and Police into Question.[12]

When, in the unusual case that the watch, or constables, did arrive on time to interfere with the perpetrators, the former were frequently out-manned and out-armed—and a shocking number of firsthand reports show law enforcement actually losing their battles with criminals. Obviously, in such an environment, civilian knowledge of the use of arms was paramount in the interests of self-defense.

## THE GANGS OF DUBLIN

The widespread use of the sword in Ireland, made famous by its duelists, also extended to the criminal classes. In Dublin, the most famous of these gangs, or "clubs," included the Mohawks, Cherokees, Bucks, Cutting Weavers, Ormonde and Liberty Boys—as well as the most infamous of all, the Pinking Dindies. As little has been written about these groups during the modern era—and as an understanding of them tends toward a more comprehensive view of Ireland's sword culture, as well as the need for civilian self-defense instruction in eighteenth century Dublin—a description of them is merited.

The Liberty and Ormonde Boys were perhaps Dublin's most sectarian gangs, and certainly the greatest in number. Both groups were well-remembered for their use of falchions and shillelaghs in riotous urban combat. In his recollections of eighteenth century Dublin street culture, J. D. Herbert included "a hasty sketch of their actions," recalling that,

A set of fellows of the lowest description, frequenting Ormond Market, assistants and carriers from slaughter-houses, joined by cattle-drivers from Smithfield, stable-boys, helpers, porters, and idle drunken vagabonds in the neighbourhood of Ormond Quay, formed a body of fighting men, armed with falchions, as they called them,—oakstaves of casks hardened by smoking in chimneys, sharpened on one side, and a hole cut in one end to admit a hand to answer for a handle—some preferred shilelahs,—but all armed for combat, were prepared to meet the Liberty Boys, a set of lawless desperadoes, residing in the opposite side of the town, called the Liberty. Those were of a different breed, being chiefly unfortunate weavers without employment: some were habitual and wilful idlers, slow to labour, but quick at riot and uproar.

No two armies in ancient days could have felt more glowing spirit, inveterate hatred, or obstinate resolution, to die or conquer, than those two parties of brutal combatants; and they could give no reason for their abominable destructive aversion to each other, but that the Ormond should not subdue the Liberty, and vice versa with the other party. Unfortunately for the citizens of Dublin, the sabbath-day was fixed upon always for the awful conflict, and until this fight was over no person dare venture into the streets. There were several patches of waste ground near the environs, but at some distance from each other; and it was an inviolable secret on what ground they were to meet until the action had nearly begun. As soon as the discovery was made, notice was given to the chief magistrates, the Lord Mayor, sheriffs, or aldermen, which were nearest the field of battle; then a body of soldiers were, under the direction of one of those civil officers, led to disperse them, and often obliged to fire on them before they could put them to flight, as it was found the best plan, there was so much trouble and expense in imprisoning and bringing them to trial. This monstrous evil, I well remember, lasted for years, and could not be, or was not put down until the police were established. Then the Liberty and Ormond surrendered their liberties, and Dublin got rid of those plagues, the Pinking Dindies and the Liberty and Ormond Boys.

In the forementioned conflicts many lives were lost, and innumerable fractures and mutilations. An eminent surgeon, Mr. Deare, had so many of those wretched patients, that the practice enabled him to cure fractures of the skull, which might have failed under the usual treatment, he called them Ormond fractures.

A desciption of the massive, wide-scale battles waged by the gangs can also be found in an 1847 issue of the *Dublin University Magazine*—in an account supposedly drawn from the remembrances of elderly Dublin residents:

Among the lower orders a feud and deadly hostility had grown up between the Liberty boys, or tailors and weavers of the Coombe, and the Ormond boys, or butchers who lived in Ormond-market on Ormond-quay, which caused frequent conflicts; and it is in the memory of many now living that the streets, and particularly the quays and bridges, were impassable in consequence of the battles of these parties. The weavers descending from the upper regions beyond Thomas-street poured down on their opponents below; they were opposed by the butchers, and a contest commenced on the quays which extended from Essex to Island bridge. The shops were closed; all business suspended; the sober and peaceable compelled to keep their houses, and those whose oceasions led them through the streets where the belligerents were engaged, were stopped, while the war of stones and other missiles was carried on across the river, and the bridges were taken and retaken by the hostile parties. It will hardly be believed in the present efficient state of our police, that for whole days the intercourse of the city was interrupted by the feuds of these parties. The few miserable watchmen, inefficient for any purpose of protection, looked on in terror, and thought themselves well acquited of their duty if they escaped from stick or stone. A friend of ours has told us that he has gone down to Essex-bridge, when he has been informed that one of those battles was raging, and stood quietly on the battlements for a whole day looking at the combat, in which above a thousand men were engaged. At one time the Ormond boys drove those of the Liberty up to Thomas-street, where rallying, they repulsed their assailants and drove them back as far as the Broad-stone, while the bridges and quays were strewed with the maimed and wounded...

These feuds terminated sometimes in frightful excesses. The butchers used their knives not to stab their opponents, but for a purpose then common in the barbarous state of Irish society, to *hough*\* or cut the tendon of the leg, thereby rendering the person incurably lame for life. On one occasion of the defeat of the Ormond boys, those of the Liberty retaliated in a manner still more barbarous and revolting. They dragged the persons they seized to their market, and dislodging the meat they found there, hooked the men by the jaws, and retired, leaving the butchers hanging on their own stalls.

The spirit of the times led men of the highest grade and respectability to join with the dregs of the market in these outrages, entirely forgetful of the feelings of their order, then immeasurably more exclusive in their ideas of a gentleman than now... The students of Trinity College were particularly prone to join in the affrays between the belligerents, and generally united their forces to those of the Liberty boys against the butchers. On one occasion, several of them were seized by the latter, and to the great terror of their friends, it was reported they were hanged up in their stalls, in retaliation for the cruelty of the weavers. A party of watchmen sufficiently strong was at length collected by the authorities, and they proceeded to Ormondmarket: there they saw a frightful spectacle, a number of college lads in their gowns and caps hanging to the hooks. On examination, however, it was found that the butchers, pitying their youth and respecting their rank, had only hung them by the waistbands of their breeches, where they remained as helpless, indeed, as if they were suspended by the neck.[13]

In his memoirs, Herbert also included a description of a gang known as the "Cutting Weavers," who were most feared for their use of the knife:

Another party of lawless myrmidons were allowed frequently to commit the greatest enormities, with no further punishment than dispersion by a magistrate and soldiers; after perhaps an outrageous attack on the passengers in the public streets, who became obnoxious victims to their anger from the dress they wore, and were subjected to their vengeance in the most summary, violent, and brutal assaults. These delinquents were weavers out of work, and they considered their want of employment proceeded from the fashion of wearing India nankeens, muslins, &c, and French silks. For the purpose of deterring persons from the wear of these articles of dress, they assembled in numerous bodies, and, with knives made for the occasion, cut every foreign dress worn by man or woman, no matter of what rank, if they were walking, and, in some cases, have stopped carriages, and destroyed ladies' dresses, putting every one to the knife, and in terror and fear of their life; for they were so infuriate, that description fails in giving an adequate idea of the horror

---

\* One history recounts that in 1784, "Several [soldiers] were brutally houghed by butchers in the streets, and the crime assumed such dimensions that a special Act was passed to make it capital, and to throw the support of the wounded soldiers on the district if the culprit was not detected." William Edward Hartpole Lecky, *A history of Ireland in the eighteenth century, volume II* (London: Longmans, Green & Col, 1913), 392.

and alarm many suffered under this wild and savage-like operation. It was a fine field for the doctors: nervous fevers produced to them an abundant harvest. Another mode of revenge taken by those lads of the loom was seizing on some mercer, haberdasher, or tailor, who might have been the vender or maker of those objectionable dresses; and when they got such a well-known character in their possession, they hurried him along, to the utter dismay or hope of escape of him or friends, until they had done with him. After dragging him through miry channels—for this practice was followed in muddy weather generally—they brought him, perhaps to the Weavers' Square, a situation in the Liberties of Dublin, something like the Grass Market, Edinburgh. There they stripped him naked; then, with a brush, not camel's hair, they daubed him over with warm tar; then a bag of feathers was got, and every one who could get at the victim stuck the feathers over him: then they led him in mock triumph through the Liberties, and, when satiated, let him get home, if he was able. They dispersed, as, probably, by this time the soldiers were approaching.

In these conflicts, or rather riotous acts, many were wounded, several killed,—particularly when the party resisted the magistrate, after the Riot Act had been read. Alderman James, in one instance, after repeated efforts to quell their rage, and cause them to disperse, finding advice, remonstrance, all arguments fail, and their determination fixed to obstinacy, and a disposition to retaliate on him, was obliged to order the soldiers to fire on them. The soldiers fired at first powder only, but stones being returned for their lenity, an order to load with ball was given: even here the military acted with great moderation; they levelled their muskets so as to discharge above the heads of the unfortunate infatuated multitude. This was noticed by them, and they became more bold and violent; then Alderman James laid his cane across the barrels and lowered them, when a number were taken down; if I remember right, fourteen were killed by that discharge. Alderman James was honoured by the weavers with the title of Alderman Level Low, which he bore with patience the rest of his life.

Alderman Sir Anthony King directed a military party against the Cutting Weavers at another of their outrages, when some lives were forfeited, and he was christened Sir Anthony Tinker. He was a brazier by trade.[14]

Although it neglects to mention the specific use of knives, the following news report, published in 1773 in the *Hibernian Magazine*, probably depicts the Cutting Weavers:

DUBLIN.

A number of people, armed with swords, sticks, &c. paraded the streets of this city, and made several persons whom they met with nankeen waistcoats and breeches on, take them off, which they cut to pieces; they likewise cut several ladies muslin coats.[15]

Later, in 1784, Lord Rutland, the newly appointed Lord Lieutenant of Ireland, wrote that the Weavers were fomenting "internal disorder" in Dublin, further noting that "there is no doubt of their design to commit private assassination...Every discovery we make tends to confirm it, and the *glorious* idea is kept alive by the encouragements of the newspapers and the pulpits...It is a damnable scene, and I most cordially detest it."[16]

## THE BUCKS

Another group rightly feared by Dublin's populace were the so-called "Bucks." Although often referred to as a "gang" in nineteenth century histories, the Bucks appear to have exhibited no real organization, and the term—as it was originally used during the period—seems to have denoted a class of high-spirited young men who delighted in causing violent trouble, who were often "notorious in [their] skill in fencing," and whom frequently engaged in duels or *rencontres*.[17] They were especially known to gather at Lucas's Coffee House, and later, after the closing of Lucas's, at Daly's Chocolate House. The Bucks' most well-known members included John "Buck" Lawless, Edmund "Buck" Sheehy, James "Buck" Farrell,[18] John "Jack the Buck" Geoghegan, Thomas "Buck" Whaley,[19] and Alexander "Buck" English. They were described thus:

A set of exclusives who called themselves "Bucks"...generally were, or had been, military men. These persons frequented all public places, and held it a point of honour to attack each other, wherever they met, with small-swords, like game cocks armed with steel spurs, and every coffee-house, theatre, square, or street, was a scene of their murderous encounters. It is a well-known fact, that they have ordered at a tavern pistols for two and breakfast for one, and the survivor coolly returned to take his meal, leaving his companion weltering in his blood at the back of the house. Had this even been confined to themselves, the community could well tolerate the mutual destruction of such a pestilent race; but

*"These powdered fops, of new commissions vain,*
*Who slept on thorns till they had killed their man,"*

delighted in insulting and murdering the peaceable and well-disposed. They literally "provoked a brawl, and stabbed you for a jest."...Instances of the above kind are in the recollection of thousands now living; while people still shudder at the names of "Buck English," "Buck Whaley," Buck Sheehan," &c..[20]

In 1818, John Warburton offered a similar recollection:

These young men were generally distinguished by the name of "Bucks," which was frequently prefixed to their surname, as an agnomen to distinguish the most eminent. In this way the names of several "Bucks" in Ireland have descended to posterity. It was their practice to walk up and down through Lucas's Coffee-house, with a train to their morning gown, sweeping the floor, and challenge any man to fight who by accident trod upon it.[21]

Another account in the *Dublin University Magazine* confirms the Bucks' obsession with cultivating luxuriously coiffed appearances—a deficiency in which, according to one source, sometimes resulted in death:

Barbers at that time were essential persons to "Bucks" going to parties, as no man could then appear without his hair elaborately dressed and powdered. When any unfortunate disappointed, he was the particular object of their rage; and more than one was, it is said, put to death by the long points, as a just punishment for their delinquency.[22]

Thomas "Buck" Whaley (1766-1800) of Dublin. From a painting reproduced in *Buck Whaley's Memoirs*.

It appears that, despite their apparent lack of organization, the Bucks occasionally acted in concert. Warburton describes a major fracas initiated by a group of Bucks in one of Dublin's best-loved theaters:

The incident which occurred in the theatre would be hardly credited in a civilized country. On the 19th of January, 1746, a young man of the name of Kelly, went to the pit much intoxicated, and climbing over the spikes, got upon the stage, and proceeded to the green-room, where he insulted some of the females in the most gross and indecent manner. As the play could not proceed, he was taken away and civilly conducted back to the pit; here he seized a basket of oranges, and amused himself by pelting the performers, particularly Mr. Sheridan, whom he publicly abused in the grossest manner. A few nights after he returned with 50 of his associates, who, climbing over the spikes of the stage, proceeded to the dressing rooms, in search of Mr. Sheridan, with drawn swords, which they thrust into the chests and presses of clothes to feel, as they faceliously observed, if he was there, and not finding him, they proceeded to his house in Dorset-street, with the same murderous intention.[23]

Jonah Barrington was present at similar riots that occurred in the theater—which were not infrequent, as he recounted in his memoirs:

> The young gentlemen as generally proceeded to beat or turn out the residue of the audience, and to break everything that came within their reach. These exploits were by no means uncommon; and the number and rank of the young culprits were so great, that the college would have been nearly depopulated, and many of the great families in Ireland enraged beyond measure, had the students been expelled or even rusticated.[24]

## THE PINKING DINDIES

By far the most notorious gang in eighteenth century Dublin—in terms of ferocity, sheer malice, and the amount of widespread damage that they managed to cause—was undoubtedly the group known as the "Pinking Dindies." In her memoirs of late eighteenth century Dublin, Margaret Leeson—better known by her alias "Peg Plunkett"—introduced them by stating

> At that time, Dublin was infested with a set of beings, who, however they might be deemed gentlemen by their birth, or connexions, yet, by their actions, deserved no other appellation than that of RUFFIANS. They were then called Pinking-dindies, and deriving boldness from their numbers, committed irregularities, abhorrent to humanity; and gave affronts when together, which singly they would not have had courage even to attempt. They ran drunk through the streets, knocking down whoever they met; attacked, beat, and cut the watch; and with great valour, broke open the habitations of unfortunate girls, demolished the furniture of their rooms, and treated the unhappy sufferers with a barbarity and savageness, at which, a gang of drunken coal porters would have blushed.[25]

In his own recollections, J.D. Herbert set down a more comprehensive account of the gang's appearance and activities, noting that its membership included college students and the sons of well-to-do families:

> They were of imposing appearance, being handsome and well made in general; so that, individually, you could not suspect them: it was by their acts only you could convict them, and they commonly pursued their schemes in parties, and by night; and they were so well prepared for battle that the "ancient and quiet watchmen," the only protectors of the citizens of Dublin at that period, were worsted in almost every attempt made to subdue them; so that they were permitted to assail passengers in the streets, to levy contributions, or, perhaps, take a lady from her protector; and many females were destroyed by that lawless banditti. Another vile plan they had of providing supplies, by exacting from unfortunate girls, at houses of ill-fame, their share of what

they deemed booty; and for this boon each had his wife, as he called her, and, if necessary, would assist her as bully, to awe, or compel, a flat to come down handsomely. Another source of gain they sought at a low gambling house, in Essex Street; and when unsuccessful, they sallied forth, enraged at their losses, and repaired them, by robbing the first eligible subject they met in the streets.

These descriptions are more or less accurate. This small-sword-wielding group of banditti seems to have first appeared in Ireland during the 1760s, when they were referred to as "Sweaters." The group was nearly exterminated soon after this point due to the efforts of the duelist Captain David "Tyger" Roche, who formed a corps of men to combat the gang:

> There was a set of beings at that time who infested the city of Dublin, who were called Sweaters. They were young men of some distinction, who used to amuse themselves (as they called it) after they left the tavern, with breaking off the bottom of their scabbards, and leaving out about half an inch of the point of their swords, with which they slightly wounded almost every one that was so unlucky as to fall into their hands. A set of these wretches had late one evening attacked an old Gentleman, his son and daughter, on Ormond [Quay]; Roche, accidentally hearing the cries of a woman, ran to her assistance, and rescued her, after desperately wounding the ringleader and two others of that abominable gang.
>
> The credit he got by this exploit was increased by his collecting together a number of Officers, who entered into an agreement to rid the public of those despicable disturbers of the city; which they spiritedly executed, and in a few weeks their depredations were no longer complained of.[26]

Although Roche may have indeed earned "credit" for his efforts, during the next decade, the group rose to prominence yet again. One of the earliest known accounts specifically mentioning the gang's distinctive new name pertains to a member named Patrick Reilly, who, in 1778, was arrested with his associates and charged with

> wounding two watchmen, and fracturing the skull of a third, whose life is despaired of. — The offender appears to be one of those riotous miscreants, called PINK-IN-DINDIES, that at present infest this metropolis.[27]

The above passage suggests that by this point, the Dindies were already well-established. That the gang's activities had seriously impacted the city, and its residents, is evinced by another report in the *Hibernian Journal*, published by the "Inhabitants of Dublin" thanking the church wardens and directors of several parishes for

> the new Regulation they have made in their Contracts for lighting the Streets, Lanes and Alleys of the Metropolis, by which the Contractors are only bound to supply the Lamps with just Oil suffi-

cient to last until Twelve o'Clock at Night; from which Time the City being involved in total Darkness, honest Folks are induced to keep good Hours, to preserve their Limbs from the Dangers of broken Pavements, their pockets from the Depredations of Footpads, and their Lives from the riotous Assaults of drunken Bucks and Pinking-dindies.[28]

According to the *Evening Post*, the Dindies were "directed by eight or ten desperadoes, who intice[d] apprentice boys, and lads of decent families, to join them in their infamous proceedings." During the next two subsequent years, a number of Irish newspapers reported on the depradations caused by the so-called "gang of infernal rioters," whose members—frequently described as "well dressed ruffians,"—committed acts of violence, then fled while "huzzaing for the pink-in-dindies" or crying out "Hie! For the Pink-in-Dindies!"[29] The group would go on to commit, according to one source, "as many outrages on the public as ever disgraced a community."[30]

The Dindies were noted for their near-universal use of the small-sword. A report from 1784 noted that the gang's colorful name originated "from the manner of stabbing and pinking with small swords."[31] Grose's *Classical Dictionary of the Vulgar Tongue*, published a year later in 1785, confirms this etymology[*]:

> To PINK. To stab or wound with a small sword: probably derived from the holes formerly cut in both men and women's clothes, called pinking. Pink of the fashion; the top of the mode. To pink and wink; frequently winking the eyes through a weakness in them.
> PINKING DINDEE. A sweater or mohawk. *Irish.*

Among his recollections, J. D. Herbert recalled the Dindies' peculiar manner of using of their small swords:

No gentleman was seen without a sword: if in undress, a *cuteau de chasse*; if full dressed, a small sword;—and the use of the sword was well understood. The pinking dindies made a rule to be well-dressed, and, to a man, they were skilful swordsmen. Their plan of attack was thus:—Two of them, walking arm-in-arm, jostled the victim they meant for prey; then, with their swords in their scabbards, chapeless, so that the point just protruded, they pricked him in various parts, and if he did not throw down his watch and money, two others came and took it by force; whilst two more in reserve were on the watch to give alarm if any persons approached. In that case they

---

[*]  In March, 1793, *Walker's Hibernian Magazine* referred to "'an affair of honour,' alias duelling, alias *pinking* a man." The verb "pink" derives from the Middle English *pinken*: "to pierce, or stab." The word "dindie" may be an invented eighteenth century term, or it may be derived from the phonetically-similar Irish word *duine* ("person") or *daoine* ("people"); in the latter case, Pinking Dindies would literally denote "stabbing people."

disappeared, and had their hiding-places adjacent, doors open; so, that if the punctured man was willing to pursue, he knew not where to go, but was glad to get away, bleeding and terrified.

It appears incredible that such a practice should be endured for years without any effort to check it effectually, and Dublin had all her nobles, gentry, citizens, mayor, aldermen, sheriffs, peers, and a garrison of soldiers—no small number. The only way I can account for it, is that the Pinks never attacked swordsmen, nor any but single men and citizens, who neither wore fine clothes nor swords; so that gentlemen never felt the pointed evil, as it did not point at them.[32]

A similar description of the gang's use of small-swords was published in the *Dublin University Magazine*:

It was their practice to cut off a small portion of the scabbards of the swords which every one then wore, and prick or "pink" the persons with whom they quarrelled with the naked points, which were sufficiently protruded to inflict considerable pain, but not sufficient to cause death. When this was intended, a greater length of the blade was uncovered.[33]

The Dindies' leader was none other than Richard Crosbie, a native of County Wicklow who had served as Jonah Barrington's second in the latter's duel with Richard Daly. Barrington described Crosbie thus:

Crosby was of immense stature; being above six feet three inches high; he had a comely-looking, fat, ruddy face, and was, beyond all comparison, the most ingenious mechanic I ever knew. He had a smattering of all sciences, and there was scarcely an art or a trade of which he had not some practical knowledge...He was very good-tempered, exceedingly strong, and as brave as a lion, but as dogged as a mule. Nothing could change a resolution of his when once made, and nothing could check or resist his perseverance to carry it into execution.[34]

On one special occasion, in 1785, Crosbie's extravagant manner of dress was described as consisting of "a robe of oiled silk, lined with white fur, his waistcoat and breeches in one, of white satin quilted, and morocco boots, and a montero cap of leopard skin."[35]

A terrifying firsthand encounter with the Pinking Dindies was recounted by Margaret Leeson, who, during the period, ran a brothel and was in a romantic relationship with John "Buck" Lawless. The incident—which is illustrative of how ill-prepared law enforcement was to deal with the gang—began one evening when a large group of Dindies appeared at Leeson's home on Drogheda Street and demanded admission:

On my refusal they smashed all my windows, broke the hall-door, and entered through the shattered pannels. They then demolished all the furniture of the parlours; and with drawn weapons, searched the house to find Mr. Lawless, whose head they swore they would cut off, and carry

RICHARD CROSBIE Esq.<sup>r</sup>

Richard Crosbie (1755-1800), leader of the Pinking Dindies, shown wearing a long, fur-lined coat, and holding his famous leopard skin hat. *Image copyright and courtesy of the National Library of Ireland*, EP CROS-RI (1) I.

away in triumph on the point of their swords; though he had not given offence to either of the party. Luckily he was absent. This shock, with the ill-treatment I received from these self called gentlemen, at a time when my being so very big with child, would have moved compassion in the hearts of wild Indians, threw me into a fit. I lay as dead, when some of my neighbours took me out lifeless, and carried me in that state to one of their houses. Still these ruffians continued their outrage, till the watch came. They then turned and gave battle, and many cuts and hurts were received on both sides. At length, the riot continuing, to the terror of the whole street, the then Sheriffs, (two of the best and most vigilant that Dublin ever boasted,) Messrs. Moncriesse and Worthington, arrived with a party of the military, at whose approach the rioters dispersed...[36]

Leeson brought charges against Crosbie, who, after threatening Leeson again, stood trial. Crosbie was sent to jail for his role in the attack on Leeson, but was later released, allowing him to become the first man in Ireland to successfully ascend in a hot-air balloon. The notoriety gained by Crosbie for this feat prompted Leeson to bitterly recount that he had "since made his name famous for contriving to *mount nearer to Heaven* than he had any reason for expecting ever to arrive."[37]

The rest of the gang briefly dispersed, but eventually reformed. By 1784, the Dindies had resurfaced in Dublin:

A desperate gang of villains have again made their appearance in this city, formerly known by the name Pinkindindies, and so called from the manner of stabbing and pinking with small swords unfortunate females, and then robbing them of their clothes and property...It may be remembered that such a gang, about five or six years since, committed similar acts of barbarity and depredation, but by the perseverance and activity of Alderman Rose, Alexander, Sankey, James, &c. (former Sheriffs) that banditti of nocturnal villains were effectually extirpated from the metropolis.[38]

This new crime wave continued through 1785, when Saunders's News-Letter again publicly complained about the pathetic state of the city's law enforcement:

The many alarming acts of street robbery and house breaking, which are almost every night committed in this city and suburbs, call loudly on the Police to form some immediate plan for the people. Much was expected from the new rules, but fatal experience convinces us, that neither detached small bodies of feeble Watchmen, or twenty Peace-officers, how brave, honsest or diligent soever, can be a match for some hundreds of desperadoes, who lie like foxes in their dens all day, and issue on the public at dark, and midnight hours.[39]

The Dindies continued to harass the city's residents until at least 1786, when the Dublin Police Act was passed, thus creating the "first modern police force in the British Isles." Virtually overnight, in September of that year, a new force of armed police began patrolling the streets, consisting of forty petty constables mounted on horses, and four hundred policemen armed with musket-bayonets. The new police "arrested hundreds of criminals in their first weekend, seeking to establish their superiority over the old, discredited watch."[40] According to J. D. Herbert, it was this act which finally led to the demise of the Pinking Dindies. He explained,

> The party of pinking dindies were never finally extirpated until the police was established. That useful institution, though decried by many, was more salutary, and timely to the city of Dublin, than any plan that has been since devised, coercive or otherwise; yet so capricious and unthinking are many, they condemn an establishment without proving its inefficacy; and though they suffered by the want of civil protection, and have been since, and are at present, in a state of tranquillity and security, many are insensible of the acquisition they possess in a well-regulated police establishment.[41]

Although the Dindies were finally defeated, their notoriety would be usurped by a new group—even more outwardly genteel and secretive—in less than decade.

## THE CHEROKEE CLUB

In the spring of 1792, an extraordinary article appeared in *Walker's Hibernian Magazine*. This journalistic piece, notable for its combination of detail, sense of astonishment, and undisguised paranoia, purported to expose the existence of "the Cherokee Club"—an elite, secret society of seasoned duelists, who would regularly set forth on armed sorties into various parts of Dublin to test their fighting skills, leaving a trail of violence in their wake. The article commenced by announcing,

> To the surprize and terror of civil society, the disgrace of common sense, and in the defiance of common and statute law, a set of young men, *fashionables* of fortune, in Dublin have lately formed themselves into a kind of hostile corps, which they call the CHEROKEE Squadron, the uniform is scarlet lined with yellow, and edged with black: they meet once a week at a noted tavern to a sumptuous dinner, and each member having loaded himself with four bottles of Claret, and primed with a large bumper of cherry Brandy, they proceed to the business of the institution.

The article proceeded to provide a list of the notorious accomplishments required for admittance into the Cherokee club. It included the following, some of which pertained to swordsmanship:

He [a prospective member] should have fought three duels; in one of which, at least, he must either have wounded, or have been wounded, by his antagonist...

It is absolutely requisite that the member should have killed, at least, one man in a duel...

Each candidate must be so good a marksman, as to split a bullet discharged from an ordinary pistol on the edge of a case knife, three times in five, at the distance of nine feet...

Each candidate must be an expert fencer.

The article also noted,

The CHEROKEES, and the *Police Men*, have had several close and desperate battles; but the latter are always defeated. No lives, however, have yet been lost, though several on both sides have been badly wounded. Such is the general dread of this new military corps, that the citizens actually go armed after dusk, and the whole town appears like a garrison in fear of an assault from a foreign power...[42]

Although the article's description of the group, and its by-laws, was so fantastic as to defy credulity, the following month, a second report of the club's activities appeared:

LONDON, *May* I, 1792.

THE Cherokee Club in Dublin, a society of young men, who agree to drink six bottles each after dinner, and to appear in public places in an uniform of red and blue, have committed such excesses in the Rotunda, which has been open for the benefit of a charitable institution, that it is now shut up. One of the rules of this society is, that if any member is seen sober after dinner, he shall be fined 30 l. for the first offence, 50 l. for the second, and for the third shall be expelled.

Notably, this same article also announced the creation of another club, formed in opposition to the Cherokees:

A club is forming in Dublin by a number of young gentlemen, who though not of the first fashion, are high in blood, and affluent in circumstances. They are to be called Mohawks; and without any thought of determined hostility, a resolute alienation from the practices of the Cherokee, forms a fundamental principle of their association.[43]

Evidently the Cherokees themselves were not pleased with the new publicity. The original article in *Walker's* was accompanied by a full-page engraving of an "Irish Cherokee"—splendidly dressed in a frock coat and wig, and brandishing a club. On May 12th, the *Dublin Evening Post* reported that

Alleged members of the Cherokee Club: on the left, John Willoughby Cole, 2nd Earl of Enniskellen (*image courtesy of Florence Court, The Enniskillen Collection, National Trust*); on the right, Major General Montague Matthews, pictured in Sir Jonah Barrington's *Historic memoirs of Ireland* (1835).

Among the singular occurrences of the day, the anger of the NOBLE CHEROKEE at seeing his person exhibited in WALKER'S MAGAZINE—is not the least *laughable!*—This YOUNG SPRIG of the PEERAGE whose *feats* in the CYPRIAN NUNNERIES have sometimes turned out *defeats* of a most *whimsical* kind, has sworn to commence a suit immediately against the *Printer, Publisher, Painter and Engraver of the Print*—Quere—If he proves the *likeness*—will not the *drunken* SIMILARILY excuse the prosecuted group in the breast of any *upright* Jury?[44]

Although no further period journalistic accounts of the Cherokee Club could be found, its existence (as well as its members' proclivity for imbibing copious amounts of alcohol) seems confirmed by a brief reference in the *Evening Post*, which mentioned that

30 cars, loaded with the produce of various vintages, were dispatched from the vaults of an eminent wine-merchant in Abbey-street, for the country villa of a noble member of the Cherokee club. Such a procession of wine carriages has not often been seen in this city.[45]

In subsequent decades, the violent and flamboyant members of the Cherokee Club would be remembered by former United Irishman Andrew O'Reilly in his book, *Reminiscences of an*

*Emigrant Milesian.* O'Reilly described the group as follows:

The Cherokees were the Dandies of their period, without the affected impertinence of the latter club, suggested by their extraordinary and inordinately foppish chief, Brummel. They were, for it was the fashion of their day, more riotous and more duellist, but possibly not more courageous or manly, than the Dandies. Foppery is not unfrequently accompanied by intrepidity...They were, generally speaking, young men of rank, and were remarkable for the personal appearance of the majority of their body, among whom were many of the handsomest and finest men in Europe. Of these several became afterwards well known in London, viz. the Mathews (Lord Llandaff and his brother, General Montague Mathew), the Butlers (Walter and James, first and second Marquesses of Ormond), Lord Cole (the late Earl of Enniskillen), Sir Henry Parnell, Sir Wheeler Cuffe, &c.

O'Reilly also provided the most detailed account of the Cherokees' costume and peculiar hair-style. Although the details provided by O'Reilly differ somewhat from earlier accounts, all are unanimous in describing the Cherokees' appearance as striking and highly immaculate:

The handsome dashing Cherokees rivalled in fact in personal appearance the distinguished descendants of Irishmen on the Continent, and who flourished at the same period...The costume of the Cherokees was not exactly that of the tribe whose name they assumed. It was on the contrary rich and recherche, as became men whose pretensions were ultra-aristocratic. In my day, in Ireland, the Cherokee Club dress-coat of William Palmer[*] (son of the beauty Lady Palmer[†], and father of the present baronet) was still preserved. It was of dark brown cloth, lined with pink satin...

The dress of the Mathews was, and remained nearly to the day of their deaths, as striking and singular as their personal qualities. It...[consisted] of a blue or green coat, made full, with large folding collar, double-breasted white waistcoat, and nankeen shorts or tights, with silk stockings... their linen trimmed, including a copious *jabot*, or frill. Their hair was powdered, flowing over their shoulders, but confined carelessly, as it were, near the ends with ribbon.

---

[*]  *Sir William Henry Palmer*, "the third Baronet, of Castle Lackin, co. Mayo. He was the younger son of Sir Roger Palmer, who was created a Baronet of Ireland in 1777. He succeeded to the title on the death of his elder brother Sir John Roger Palmer; and married Miss Alice Franklin." *Gentleman's Magazine*, October, 1840.

[†]  *Lady Eleanor Palmer*: "A celebrated beauty of the Viceregal court during the administration of the Earl of Chesterfield (1745-47). She was a Catholic heiress, of very ancient descent, allied to the best families in Ireland, gifted with exquisite beauty, and possessed of considerable mental acquirements...His lordship used to say that she was 'the most dangerous rebel in Ireland.' In 1752 she married Roger Palmer, M.P. for Mayo (ancestor of the present Sir Roger Palmer of Mayo); and by his elevation to a baronetcy in 1777, became Lady Palmer. She is said to have lived to the age of one hundred years, retaining to the last a vehement hatred of the wrongs under which her Catholic fellow-countrymen laboured. Although rich, she spent the latter years of her life in seclusion in a small lodging in Henry-street, Dublin." *Dictionary of National Biography, 1885-1900, Volume 43* (London: Smith, Elder & Co.).

Although the Cherokees became well-known for their fine dress and foppish appearance, O'Reilly noted, "Should this sketch convey an idea that the Mathews (or indeed the Cherokees generally) were effeminate, it would be a vast error." He recorded their disappearance from history as follows:

> The Cherokees are extinct. There is little good to record respecting them, I believe; but the worst with which their memory can be reproached, are exclusiveness, foppery, dissipation, and fast living. The subject is rather barren. Its only claim to be remembered is, that it was a feature of the closing part of the last century, or rather of the closing part of my reminiscences of it, terminating about 1792. It may not be uninteresting to observe the effect of the progress which the Cherokee Club exhibited, in comparison with its predecessor in notoriety and, it may be said, in profligacy in Ireland, the Hellfire Club. The improvement was immense.[46]

1   Richard Twiss, *A tour in Ireland in 1775* (London: Printed for the Author, 1776).

2   J. Cosgrave, *A genuine history of the lives and actions of the most notorious Irish highwaymen, Tories and Rapparees, from Redmond O'Hanlon, the famous gentleman-robber, to Cahier na Gappul, the great horse-catcher, who was executed at Maryborough, in August, 1735: To which is added, The gold-finder: or, The history of Manus Mac Oneil, who under the appearance of a stupid, ignorant country fellow, (on the bog of Allen, by the help of his man Andrew) played the most notorious cheats, and remarkable tricks on the people of Ireland, that ever was known. : Also, the remarkable life of Gilder Roy, a murderer, ravisher, incendiary and highwayman, with several others, not in any former edition* (Dublin: R. Cross, 1779).

3   *A Short History of the Watch Police*, Garda Síochána Museum/Archives, 2000.

4   *Freeman's Journal*, December 20, 1763.

5   *Saunders's News-Letter*, August 14, 1795.

6   Patrick Fagan, "The Population of Dublin in the Eighteenth Century" in *Eighteenth-Century Ireland / Iris an dá chultúr*, Vol. 6 (1991), 121-156.

7   Margaret Leeson, *Memoirs of Mrs. Margaret Leeson, written by herself; in which are given anecdotes, sketches of the lives and bon mots of some of the most celebrated characters in Great-Britain and Ireland, Volume II* (Dublin: Printed and sold by the principal Booksellers, 1797), 126-128.

8   *Hibernian Journal; or, Chronicle of Liberty*, August 5, 1776.

9   *Hibernian Journal; or, Chronicle of Liberty*, November 29, 1780.

10  *Dublin Journal*, September 23, 1775.

11  Barrington, *Personal Sketches, Vol. II*, 198-199.

12  *Hibernian Journal; or, Chronicle of Liberty*, January 23, 1784.

13  *Dublin University Magazine*, v. 21, June 1843, 728-733.

14  J. D. Herbert, *Irish varieties, for the last fifty years: written from recollections* (London: William Joy, 1836) 77-88.

15  *Walker's Hibernian Magazine*, August, 1773.

16  William Edward Hartpole Lecky, *A history of Ireland in the eighteenth century, volume VI* (London: Longmans, Green & Col, 1913), 393.

17  *Dublin University Magazine*, v. 21, June 1843, 728-733.

18  *Dublin Courier*, May 9, 1766.

19  Thomas Whaley, *Buck Whaley's Memoirs: Including His Journey to Jerusalem* (London: A. Moring, Limited, 1906).

20  The British Magazine, Volume I (London: Frederick Westley and A. H. Davis, 1830) 364-365.

21  John Warburton, *History of the City of Dublin: From the Earliest Accounts to the Present Time; Containing Its Annals, Antiquities, Ecclesiastical History, and Charters; Its Present Extent, Public Buildings, Schools, Institutions, &c., to which are Added, Biographical Notices of Eminent Men, and Copious Appendices of Its Population, Revenue, Commerce and Literature, Volume 2* (Dublin: T. Cadell and W. Davies, 1818), 1115.

22  *Dublin University Magazine*, v. 21, June 1843. 728-733.

23  Warburton, 1115.

24  Barrington, *Personal Sketches, Vol. II*, 199.

25  Margaret Leeson, *Memoirs of Mrs. Margaret Leeson, written by herself; in which are given anecdotes, sketches of the lives and bon mots of some of the most celebrated characters in Great-Britain and Ireland, Volume I* (Dublin: Printed and sold by the principal Booksellers, 1797), 255.

26  *The Universal Magazine*, March, 1774.

27  *Dublin Evening Post*, September 19, 1778.

28  *Hibernian Journal; or, Chronicle of Liberty*, November 2, 1778.

29  *Dublin Evening Post*, March 23, 1779. *The Gentleman's and London magazine*; July 1779, 437-438. *Saunders's News-Letter*, January 5, 1780.

30  *Dublin Evening Post*, December 30, 1780.

31  *Saunders's News-Letter*, December 17, 1784.

32  J. D. Herbert, *Irish varieties, for the last fifty years: written from recollections* (London: William Joy, 1836) 77-88.

33  *Dublin University Magazine, Vol. 21*, June 1843.

34  Barrington, *Personal Sketches, Vol. II*, 24.

35  Samuel A Ossory Fitzpatrick, *Dublin, a historical and topographical account of the city* (London: Methuen & Co., 1907), 189.

36  Leeson, *Memoirs, Volume I*, 256-257.

37  Leeson, *Memoirs, Volume I*, 255.

38  *Saunders's News-Letter*, December 17, 1784.

39  *Saunders's News-Letter*, September 1, 1785.

40  Brian Henry, "The First Modern Police in the British Isles: Dublin, 1786-1795" in *Police Studies*, vol. 1, no. 4, 1993, pp. 167—78.

41  J. D. Herbert, *Irish varieties, for the last fifty years: written from recollections* (London: William Joy, 1836) 77-88.

42  *Walker's Hibernian Magazine*, April, 1792.

43  *Walker's Hibernian Magazine*, May, 1792.

44  *Dublin Evening Post*, May 12, 1792.

45  *Dublin Evening Post*, March 24, 1792.

46  Andrew O'Reilly, *The Irish Abroad and at Home; at the Court and in the Camp. With Souvenirs of "The Brigade." Reminiscences of an Emigrant Milesian* (New York: D. Appleton and Co., 1856), 343-348.

Frontispiece from *Pranceriana* (Dublin: 1775), depicting a fencer in front of the gates of Trinity College, Dublin. Behind him, in the distance, duelists exchange pistols shots.

# V

## FENCING SCHOOLS *and* MASTERS *in* EIGHTEENTH CENTURY IRELAND

*"A perfect knowledge of that noble Science, which has been deemed in the present enlightened age, the master-piece of art..."*

During the eighteenth century, Ireland's "national propensity" for dueling, according to one contemporary, "gave rise to an assiduous cultivation of the arts of combat."[1] Stated simply, a duelist could not expect to preserve his own life unless he had acquired proficiency in the art of swordsmanship. To those ends, "professors" of the "noble science of defence" flourished in Ireland, and fencing schools sprang up in all four corners of the country—from Dublin, to Cork, to Limerick, to Belfast.[2] That the country did, in point of fact, produce some of the most feared swordsmen in eighteenth century Europe, is attested to by a number of journalistic reports and firsthand accounts. We find, for instance, that the most widely-renowned European fencers of the period—including James Figg, Timothy Buck (Figg's master), Edward "Ned" Sutton, James Miller, Donald McBane, and the Chevalier de Saint-Georges—were all stymied or completely defeated at some point in their careers by swordsmen from Ireland. An account of a duel which took place in 1734, between the celebrated French fencing-master Dubois (immortalized by both Hogarth and Captain John Godfrey)[3] and an Irish fencing master with the same surname, declared the latter to be the victor:

On Friday last between Two and Three O'Clock in the Afternoon, a Duel was fought...between Mr. Dubois a Frenchman and Mr. Dubois an Irishman; both Fencing-Masters, the former of whom was run thro' the Body; but walk'd a considerable Way from the Place, till proper Assistance could be had, and is under the Hands of an able Surgeon, who has great Hopes of his Recovery.[4]

Likewise, Donald McBane, a Scottish swordsman regarded as one of the most prolific duelists of all time (having fought close to one hundred combats), only admitted to having met his match once later in life—when he fought, to a draw, a fencing-master from the west of Ireland:

He came to me, and told he knew my Errand, and that he would give me Satisfaction; he and I took a Bottle of white Wine...we took a Snuff and a Dram, then we took a Turn...I could make nothing of him, so we took Breath a little, and fell to it again and Closed one another, and secured one anothers Swords, but none of us could get Advantage of another; we had Five such Turns, but could make nothing of it, we were Four or Five Times through [each] others Shirts, but could not draw Blood; then I told him I would agree with him...This Quarter-Master was an Old Fencing-Master in the West of *Ireland*.[5]

Other witnesses to Irish prowess during this period include Henry Blackwell, who, in his 1702 fencing treatise, *The Gentleman's Tutor for the Small Sword*, made reference to the "Irish" in his bold statement that "I am certain that we have as good masters in England, of English, Scots, French, Irish and Germans, as any in the Christendom..."[6] Again, in 1732, an anonymous citizen of London, who had "liv'd twenty Years in Ireland," wrote,

The Gentlemen in Ireland are of a Nature generous and hospitable, as well as brave in single Combat with the small Sword, and Sword and Pistol, and in the Field; which Courage recommends them into foreign Service...[7]

In 1771, the *Public Register* reported that Capt. Redmond Kelly, who served as second to Lord Poulett in a duel, was "said to be reckoned the best Swordsman in Europe, being capable of making the longest Longe of any Man living."[8]

Yet, despite their obvious formidability, Irish fencers and fencing masters have found little mention in histories of swordsmanship. Their relative obscurity can be attributed to a variety of factors—including lack of self-promotion, the extremely limited state of the eighteenth century Irish publishing industry, and the fact that so very few original Irish fencing treatises—a potential source of information on Irish masters—were published in Ireland during the era.[9]

The Irish gladiators known as the "Masters of the Science of Defence," who are described as having contested with sharp weapons for prize money in the Bear Garden during the early eighteenth century, do not seem to have left any extant records—that is, in the form of adver-tisements, references, or firsthand accounts—of their own schools or services in Ireland. This may be due to the fact that these individuals were not professional fencing masters at all, but rather—as noted in many English accounts—smiths, tailors, cooks, farmers, butchers, tobac-conists, woolcombers, felt-makers, and printers.[10] Moreover, evidence suggests that members of the professional class of fencing masters in the British Isles looked down upon the practices of the so-called "Masters of Defence"—regardless of whether they were English or Irish.[11] One anonymous fencing author, writing in 1714, noted,

> There is a Cunning and Subtilty, as well as Dexterity, which belongs to the true Art of the Sword, and which but few, professing the Art, are Masters of; Thrusts and Blows being to be avoided several other Ways, by a judicious and agile Artist, than by always meeting with, and obstinately opposing the Adversary's Sword; a Thing not known in the *Bear-Gardens*, where, at first engaging they come commonly close up to one another, and there with Fury discharge repeated Blows, whereby ensue *Contretemps* and grievous Wounds; which does indeed please the ignorant Mob, but ought to be abominate by all good Artists and Men of Judgment, seeing it is a most scandalous Disparagement to all true Art; which ought to be perform'd, not only with Calmness, but with a cautious Vigour and Judgment, otherwise such foolhardy Persons run headlong to their own Destruction, which, by a true Art is design'd to be prevented; Fencing being at first invented and design'd chiefly for Defending, and not for Offending; that falling in only by the Way, and mostly (except upon Necessity) to be made use of as a Means to effectuate the other main End, which is a Man's Defence and Preservation of his Life, when in good Earnest atack'd.[12]

In contrast to these aforementioned gladiators, the professional class of fencing masters that lived and taught in Ireland during the eighteenth century primarily offered instruction in the small-sword, broadsword, backsword, and spadroon, and catered to members of the nobility, military, and upper class. These individuals, for the most part, taught fencing for the expressed purposes of self-defense, for the cultivation of health, and for the sake of mental, physical, and moral development. The Dublin-based fencing professor Andrew Mahon summed up his views on the benefits of fencing as follows:

> Of all Arms, the Sword is probably the most ancient: It is honourable and useful, and upon Occa-sion, causes a greater Acquisition of Glory than any other... It is the most useful, having the Advantage of Fire Arms, in that it is as well defensive as offensive, whereas they carry no Defence with them; and it is far preferable to Pikes and other long Weapons, not only because it is more wieldy and easy of Carriage, but also by reason of the Perfection to which Art has brought the Use of the Small Sword; there being no Exercise that conduces so much as Fencing, to strengthen and supple the Parts, and to give the Body an easy and graceful Appearance.[13]

Likewise, the Belfast master Mr. Gallway (or Galwey), who specialized in teaching the small-sword, enthused over the "perfect knowledge of that noble Science [of fencing], which has been deemed in the present enlightened age, the master-piece of art..."[14] The practice of small-sword fencing in Ireland was at this time also intimately connected to the custom of the duel, as masters of the period often regarded fencing as preparation for "affairs of honor." Moreover, disputes over fencing contests, etiquette, and techniques—particularly in Ireland—frequently led to duels. The following incident, which took place in Dublin in 1784, is but one of many examples:

> A duel was fought last Friday between a Gentleman and a fencing-master; they met, accompanied by their seconds; and after the usual ceremonies practised among swordsmen, they began the assault, which lasted about a quarter of an hour. The former Gentleman was disarmed in the attempt of a particular thrust, but his sword being returned to him by the latter, they continued the attack for a few minutes longer, when the former Gentleman being wounded over the arm, and the seconds interfering in the matter, it was amicably settled. It seems that the challenge was given by the first-mentioned Gentleman, through a dispute at a fencing match a few days ago.[15]

Evidence suggests that at least some native Irish masters (such as the renowned Cornelius Kelly) were fluent in both English and Irish.[16] Although no fencing treatises written in the Irish language have yet been found, a handful of Irish fencing terms can be gleaned from various texts of the period. In eighteenth century Irish, to "fence" was sometimes referred to as *cloidh*, although this was more in the sense of "swordplay" or swordsmanship—termed *iom-chlóidhmheadh*, just as the word *iom-chlóidhmheóir* was used to denote a swordsman. All three words are directly related to the Irish term *cloidheamh*, which meant "sword" (the corresponding term in Scottish Gaelic, *claidheamh*, gave rise to the well-known Anglicization, "claymore"—literally, "large sword"). Another fencing-related term of the period was *colg*. In Middle-Irish, this term originally referred to a variety of pointed, thrusting weapons, as well as to a "sting or prickle." Later, the word *colg* came to refer to the rapier and small-sword, and the corresponding verb *colgthroidhim* referred to the act of fencing with such weapons. By the seventeenth century, the Irish term *pionnsóireacht*—used to describe "skillfullness" or "artfulness"—also came to be used to refer to the art of fencing. The root of this last term, *pionnsa* (fence), was connected to the act of "guarding" or defending—as can be seen in the fencing commands, *Ar do phionnsa!* ("On guard!"), and *Bí ar do phionnsa!* ("Be on your guard!"). Just as in English etymology, the Irish concept of fencing was fundamentally connected to the principle of defense. Other Irish fencing-related terms of the period included *maighistir pionnsa* (fencing master), *pionnsóir* (fencer), *bata pionnsa* (single stick), *cána* (cane or cudgel), *cloidheamh cúil* (backsword), *sáitéan* (foil), *d'imirt ar sháitéin* (to engage in an assault—literally, "to

A back sword. *Clojöeam crĺ.*
A back-sword-man. *feap clojöjm crĺ.*
A fencing fchool. *Sʒojl pjoñʏa.*
A fencing mafter. *Majʒjʏcjp pjoñʏa.*

Irish fencing terms of the period, from Conchobhar O Beaglaoich's *English Irish Dictionary*, or *An Focloir Bearla Gaoioheilge* (Paris: Seamus Geurin, 1732).

play on foils"), and *sgoil pionnsa* or *sgoil pionnsóireachta* (fencing school). An actual duel, fought in earnest, was referred to as *cómhrac aoinfhir** (literally, "combat of single man"), while "to fight a duel" was expressed as *do chómhrac fear le fear* ("to combat man with man").[17] Despite the existence of fencing masters fluent in such terms, Irish fencing masters of the eighteenth century elected to publish their treatises in languages more widely known throughout Europe, such as English, German, and French.

## FENCING IN DUBLIN

Although schools of arms could be found in all provinces of eighteenth century Ireland, in no place were they as numerous as in Dublin. From the very beginning to the very end of the century, this veritable fencing epicenter was home to a large variety of academies, run by native Irish masters, as well as foreign instructors hailing from France, England, and Scotland.[18] Many of their names have been preserved through numerous newspaper advertisements of the period, such as the following, from 1784:

F. O'CONNOR, Fencing Master,
WILL open School on Monday the 18th instant, at No. 5, Anglesea-street, and hopes his unremitted Exertions to forward his Pupils, may entitle him to their Notice, School Hours will be from twelve to three on Mondays, Wednesdays, and Fridays. Said O'Connor returns his sincere Thanks to the Noblemen and Gentlemen he had the Honour of instructing these twenty Years past, and who were pleased to allow him a sufficient Share of Merit in his Profession, particularly the Gentlemen of the second Regiment of Horse, whose Protection and undoubted Generosity to him shall at all Times be foremost in his most grateful Acknowledgments.[19]

---

* Also spelled *comhrag aoinfhir*.

This individual was no doubt the same "Francis O'Connor, Fencing-Master" who had previously run a fencing school in Limerick, outside of which could be seen a sign depicting two swords crossed.[20] References to Dublin-based fencing masters can also be found in memoirs and essays of the period. For instance, an anonymous Dublin-based fencing-master of French origin is mentioned in the 1755 tract, *A Vindication of the Irish Earl of Bath*, in which the author relates training in fencing to military strategy:

> You may remember, for I see you have been in the Hands of a *Fencing-master*; a *Frenchman*, who taught the small Sword in *Taylor's-Hall*, and gave Lessons of Prudence, as well as Science, to his Scholars. Here you shall attack, and here be on Guard; so far advance, and then stand firm with all the Variety to be known of defensive and offensive Knowledge. A Gentleman, one of the most finished in the School, wanted, he conceived, to learn but one Thing more to render him absolute in the Art of War, which was, how to advance on a flying Enemy? "Advance!" said the *Frenchman*, "For what? by gar let him "go." If ever you learn't, you have now forgot the *Rule* and when the Enemy has been parried, wounded, and forced on a Retreat, you would, in your Foolhardiness, make him rally again, and, like an infinite Number of Generals on Record, perhaps lose the Honour of the Day you had won...Were you less a *Man at Arms*, and had any Sort of Wit to take Place in your Anger, you would content yourself, and think you had done abundantly enough, when you had not only *put by your Adversary's Thrust*, but put him also to Flight; enough for Honour, and sufficient for Safety. The weakest Enemy may be dangerous when driven to Despair; and to pursue him to a *strong Hold* may testify Courage, but is no Symptom of Sense.[21]

Local Dublin instructors often gathered to cross blades before audiences in crowded theaters, and public fencing events became a popular feature of eighteenth century Dublin life. The following announcement, from 1762, refers to an upcoming contest between two anonymous but "eminent" combatants:

> This Day, at twelve o'Clock, there will be a great Fencing Match, at the Musick Hall, in Fishamble-street, between two Gentlemen, eminent in that Profession.[22]

Other obscure Dublin fencing masters of the period included James Fontaine, mentioned in the city as early as 1710,[23] and Christopher Plunket, an "expert" master who kept his school from 1749 to 1758 "over the old Exchange."[24] After Plunket was falsely reported to be deceased due to an illness, a local journal enthused that "So skill'd is Plunket in the Fencing Art, Ev'n Death can't touch him with his keenest Dart."[25] Other masters included Thomas Ceson, who opened a school at Mr. Lyon's in Harry street near Grafton in 1771,[26] and a large host of anonymous masters, whose names are now lost to history.[27] In contrast to such lesser-known individuals, a number of Irish masters did obtain considerable fame during their own lifetimes.

Established in 1706, Taylor's Hall, the oldest surviving guild hall in Dublin, was the site of the fencing school of William and Dominick Kelly, as well as that of an unnamed French fencing master. Image courtesy of *An Taisce*.

Of these, a few of the most celebrated are mentioned in the memoirs of John O'Keeffe, a writer and playwright who recalled the fencing climate in Dublin during the 1760s:

My companions and myself were active in learning to fence. The fencing-master of first note in Dublin, was Cornelius Kelly, a tall old gentlemanly man, highly respected: next to him was Dwyer. I and other youths learned of a Frenchman of the name of Gittarre, with whom we met to practice at one of the corporation halls. As I took peculiar delight in the art, I fenced well. The sword by the side, in those times, when in the street, was as much an appendage as the hat on the head: this was a very good fashion for the haberdasher's and milliner's shops, as the fashion of the sword-knot was as quick in succession as that of the shoe-buckle. Many of our sword-hilts were of the finest cut polished steel, and very expensive. [28]

What follows, then, is an examination of the most acclaimed individuals mentioned by O'Keeffe—including Kelly, Dwyer, and Gittarre—as well as some of the other masters of note who taught and practiced their art in eighteenth century Dublin.

## CAPTAIN BUTLER

One of the earliest extant accounts of an eighteenth century Irish fencing school can be found in the memoirs of the Jacobite duelist Peter Drake. In the year 1700, after acquiring a purse of twenty guineas. Drake left his home in County Meath and traveled to Dublin, where he sought out instruction in the use of the sword. Drake recounted,

> The first considerable Breach I made in my Treasure, was to gain a Qualification that I thought both useful and necessary for the Life I intended to lead, *viz.* to learn to handle the small Sword. Accordingly, I went to one Captain *Butler* who kept a School of that kind in *Cook-street*, who was then reputed the best Master of the Science in the City. I gave him a Guinea Entrance, and promised to pay him monthly, according to our Agreement. I went constantly twice a-day for three Months, and may justly say, I did not prove the worst of his Scholars for that Time. The Captain himself having freely owned, that he got Credit by me, there being several Gentlemen of much longer standing, who had not made half the Proficiency. The three Months being expired, and I thinking myself an able Swordsman, and the Money being above three Parts gone, I began to think of another Journey to the Country...

Drake soon left the city, but eventually returned to Dublin, where he remarked that

> While I staid in *Dublin* I used to go often to Captain *Butler*'s to take a Breathing with some of his Scholars, and sometimes with his Usher, having the Captain's Leave to do so; by which Means I retained what I had learnt, and made a farther Improvement.[29]

Drake's training would serve him well on the continent, where he engaged in a large number of duels, always emerging victorious—if not completely unscathed.

## DONALD MCBANE

Another early eighteenth century account of a Dublin fencing school comes from the pen of Donald McBane, a Scottish swordsman and duelist who served extensively in the British military. In his autobiography, published in 1728, McBane recounts coming to Carrickfergus with his regiment, and from thence to Belfast, and then, finally, to Dublin. There, McBane almost immediately began seeking out fencing instruction from local masters. He recounted,

> At that time I went to a *French* Master to Learn to Push[††], I tarried with him a Month; my Fellow Scholar and I fell out, he said I was not able to do with the *Sword*, what he could do with the Foil; we went to *Oxmentoun-Green* and drew on each other, I Wounded him in three places, then we went and took a Pot, and was good Friends, and I stayed at that School a Month longer.[30]

After his sojourn in Dublin, McBane traveled with his regiment to Limerick in the west of Ireland. According to a number of accounts, the western province of Connaught was the area of the country most renowned for the presence of skilled swordsman. Jonah Barrington claimed that of all of Ireland's counties, "Galway was most scientific at the sword" and one of the "ablest schools of the dueling science." It was Galway, notably, from which two of eighteenth century Ireland's most celebrated duelists—Richard Daly and Risteárd Buidhe Kirwan—hailed. Barrington also mentioned nearby County Mayo as being home to some of the best swordsmen in Ireland.[31] In his autobiography, McBane notes that the city of Limerick played host to several fencing schools—and eventually, to McBane's own:

> We remained in *Limrick* about Eighteen month, I continued still at the School and had several Turns with my Fellow Scholars, and continued still the formost Scholar in my Master's School: There was several other Schools in the City, with whom my Master's Scholars had several Conflicts; at last one of the *Masters* and I fell out about a Sister of his whom I Intended to Marry, all the Tocher[*] I got, was a Duel with her Brother: After which I set up for a Master my self, and keept a School while our Regiment lay there.[32]

Unfortunately, McBane neglects to records the names of these other Limerick masters. During the later part of the eighteenth century, the city would host at least two additional fencing masters, Francis O'Connor and John Russell.[33]

In 1728, after serving throughout much of Europe, participating in countless duels, and taking part in dozens of stage-fights, McBane published his fencing treatise, *The Expert Sword-Man's Companion: Or the True Art of Self-Defence.* Although McBane failed to provide details about specific Irish fencing practices in his book, he did, tellingly, use the technical term "light" to describe an opening in one's defense. This fencing term also appeared, several years later, in Andrew Mahon's *The Art of Fencing* (an English language translation of a French fencing treatise), published in Dublin in 1734. The term "light" is a translation of the French

---

[††] *Push*: In fencing, a thrusting attack executed on a lunge or a pass.

[*] *Tocher*: A marriage portion, esp. a bride's dowry. From the Scots Gaelic *tochradh*.

*jour*—meaning "daylight"—which was used by Labat to denote an opening. Aside from the treatises of Mahon and McBane, this term can only be found in one other English-language fencing text: *A Few Mathematical and Critical Remarks on the Sword,* published in Dublin in 1781. The fact that McBane's text is the only non-Irish, English-language fencing treatise to use this term suggests the possibility that McBane may have learned it during his time spent in Irish fencing schools.

## ANDREW MAHON

Of Andrew Mahon, a "Professor of the Small Sword in Dublin," little can be said aside from what may be gleaned from his 1734 book, *The Art of Fencing, or, the Use of the Small Sword.* Previously, Mahon had come from England, where, he tells us,

> I had my Instructions from the late Mr. *Hillary Tully* of *London,* who was (and I think with great Reason) esteemed a most eminent Master in his Time...

This same Tully was also mentioned by Monsieur Valdin (a London fencing master of French extraction), who described him as an "able" master and "for whom I have a very great value."[34] The fencing historian J.D. Aylward refers to Mahon as "an English master," although he does not cite any references to support this, and is likely alluding to Mahon's declaration that he was "a Stranger in this city [Dublin], being then lately come from England." However, it is interesting to note that both "Mahon" and "Tully" are old Gaelic names. The surname Mahon (which first appears in County Clare) is derived from the Irish word *mathghamha,* which, in English, translates to "bear," while Tully (originating in Connaught) is derived from the Irish *tuile,* meaning "flood." Whether Mahon was an Irishman who had previously ventured into England for training, or was an Englishman of Irish descent is, of course, a matter of speculation.

After arriving in Dublin, Mahon began teaching others to fence, and acquired a pupil in Lord George Sackville, son of the Duke of Dorset, then Lord Lieutenant of Ireland. Mahon dedicated his *Art of Fencing* to Lord George, although the latter was, at the time, a mere boy of eighteen who had just taken his degree at Trinity College.[35]

At some point in his travels, Mahon came across a copy of Labat's *L'Art en Fait d'Armes,* a French text treating of the use of the small-sword, published in 1696. Of this book, Mahon enthused:

Plates from Andrew Mahon's book, *The Art of Fencing, or, the Use of the Small Sword* (Dublin: 1734).

I thought it very suitable to my Business, when I met with so good an Author as Monsieur *L'Abbat*, on the Art of Fencing, to publish his Rules, which in general, will I believe be very useful, not only as they may contribute to the Satisfaction of such Gentlemen as are already Proficients in the Art, and to the better Discipline of those who intend to become so, but also in regard that the Nicety and Exactness of his Rules, for the most Part, and their great Consistency with Reason, may, and will in all Probability, lay a regular and good Foundation for future Masters, who tho' accustom'd to any particular Method formerly practised, may rather chuse to proceed upon the Authority of an excellent Master, than upon a vain and mistaken Confidence of their own Perfection, or upon an obstinate Refusal to submit to Rules founded on, and demonstrated by Reason.

Mahon thus determined to translate Labat's text into English. He began collaborating with a local Dubliner, "Mr. Campbell," who, according to Mahon, was "a better Master of the French

Tongue than I am." Mahon's edition of the book would be published by subscription in Dublin, and printed in 1734 by James Hoey "at the Sign of Mercury in Skinner-Row." Although the vast portion of this text is, as already noted, a translation of Labat's *L'Art en Fait d'Armes*, Mahon's preface is of his own composition, and thus represents the earliest detailed window into the mind of an eighteenth century Irish master of arms.

Mahon begins his preface by introducing himself, and praising the virtues of Labat's text. After a very brief discussion of fencing history, Mahon proceeds to outline some of his own views on the basic aspects of the art:

As the Art of Fencing consists in attacking and defending with the Sword, it is necessary that every Motion and Situation tend to these two principal Points, *viz*. In offending to be defended, and in defending to be in an immediate Condition to offend.

There is no Guard but has it's Thrust, and no Thrust without it's Parade, no Parade without it's Feint, no Feint without it's opposite Time or Motion, no opposite Time or Motion but has it's Counter, and there is even a Counter to that Counter.

Some injudicious Persons have objected to Mr. *L'abbat*'s Manner of Fencing, that it is too beautiful and nice, without observing that if it be beautiful, it cannot be dangerous, Beauty consisting in Rule, and Rule in the Safety of attacking and defending.

In Fencing, there are five Figures of the Wrist, viz. *Prime, Seconde, Tierce, Quart,* and *Quinte.* The first is of very little Use, and the last of none at all.

PRIME is the Figure that the Wrist is in, in drawing the Sword. *Seconde* and *Tierce* require one and the same Figure of the Wrist, with this Difference only, that in *Seconde*, the Wrist must be raised higher, in order to oppose the Adversary's Sword; but in both these Thrusts the Thumb Nail must be turned directly down, and the Edges of the Blade of the Foil of an equal Height.

QUART is the handsomest Figure in Fencing, the Thumb Nail and the Flat of the Foil being directly up, and the Wrist supported so as to cover the Body below as well as above. In *Quinte*, the Wrist is more turned and raised that in *Quart*, which uncovers the Body, and weakens the Point, and therefore is not used by the skilful.

Some Masters divide the Blade into three Parts, *viz*. the Fort, the Feeble, and the Middle. Others divide it into Four, *viz*. the Fort, the Half Fort, the Feeble, and the Half Feeble; but to avoid Perplexity, I divide it only into Fort and Feeble; tho' it may be divided into as many Parts as there are Degrees of Fort and Feeble to be found on the Blade.

In his preface, Mahon also mentions one point on which he particularly agrees with Labat:

Volting, Passing, and Lowering the Body, are three things which Mr. *L'Abbat* disapproves of, in which Opinion I join; because the Sword being the Instrument of Defence, there can be no Safety when the proper Opposition of the Blade is wanting, as it is in volting and lowering the Body, and in passing, by reason of the Weakness of the Situation, which cannot produce a vigorous Action.

Notwithstanding which, there is a modern Master, who as soon as he had seen this Book, and the Attitudes representing volting, passing and lowering the Body, began and still continues teaching them to his Scholars, without considering how unsafe and dangerous they are, for want of the proper Opposition of the Sword when within Measure.

While extolling the virtues of "Mr. L'Abbat's Rules," Mahon states that, nevertheless, he does not approve of everything stated by the Frenchman. Mahon notes, for instance, that

Monsieur *L'Abbat* recommends the turning on the Edge of the Left-foot in a Lunge, as may be seen by the Attitudes. This Method indeed was formerly practised by all Masters, and would be very good, if their Scholars had not naturally run into an Error, by turning the Foot so much as to bring the Ancle to the Ground, whereby the Foot became so weak as to make the Recovery difficult, for want of a sufficient Support from the Left-foot, which, in recovering, bears the whole Weight of the Body: Therefore I would not advise the turning on the Edge of the Foot to any but such as, by long Practice on the Flat, are able to judge of the Strength of their Situation, and consequently, will not turn the Foot more than is consistent therewith.

It may sometimes be necessary to turn on the Edge, on such Ground whereon the Flat would slip, and the Edge would not, if it were properly turned; but even in this Case, by turning it too much it would have no Hold of the Terrace, and therefore would be as dangerous as keeping it on the Flat.

The chief Reason for turning on the Edge, is that the Length of the Lunge is greater by about three Inches, which a Man who is a Judge of Measure need never have recourse to, because he will not push but when he knows he is within Reach.

Mahon claimed that his translation was well-received by other Dublin "masters," noting,

Lest I should meet with such Opposition as might perhaps have frustrated my Design of publishing this book, I thought proper to conceal my being concerned in it, 'till Mr. *Campbell* had shown the Translation to all the principal Masters in Town, and gained their Approbation much in Favour of it.[36]

Mahon's publication would be influential in a number of ways. The following year, in 1735, Richard Wellington printed a second edition of the text in London. During the same period, Mahon's translation would be quoted extensively in a fencing treatise authored by an "otherwise unrecorded master" named W. Bathurst, who, in his manuscript, offered advice to his pupil, Master Webster.[37] Decades later, towards the end of the century, Mahon would again be plagiarized, this time in James Underwood's *Art of Fencing*, published twice in Dublin, in 1787 and 1798.[38]

## DOMINICK AND WILLIAM KELLY

Dominick Kelly was another early fencing master whose name has barely survived in the historical literature. According to a Dublin advertisement published in 1746, Kelly—then deceased—was "one of the most famous Masters in the Art of Fencing that ever this Kingdom could boast of." However, no other accounts of this fencing master have been found. The same year, his brother, William, and nephew—also named Dominick—announced the opening of their own school, and provided the only extant account of the late, elder Dominick:

THE Name and Character of the late Dominick Kelly of Fishamble-street, in the City of Dublin, deceased; one of the most famous Masters in the Art of Fencing that ever this Kingdom could boast of, both for his Ability in performing, and for his Method and Diligence in teaching are so well known, that we judge it altogether needless to say one Word on that Head to the Publick; and shall therefore only give this Notice.—

That William Kelly, Brother and sole Coadjutor in said Business, to the said Dominick Kelly during his Life, a Master equally known and esteemed by all the Gentlemen who both said Brothers had the Honour to instruct, intends, in Conjunction with his Son Dominick Kelly, to open School at the Cock in Warbugh-street, in said City, on Monday the 10th Day of November next, where constant Attendance shall be given, and all possible Care taken to instruct Gentlemen as will be pleased to come to said School.[39]

The following year, William and the younger Dominick announced the removal of their fencing school to Taylor's Hall, a vast brick structure which, still today, remains the oldest surviving guild hall in Dublin:

WILLIAM and DOMINICK KELLY, who kept their Fencing School at the Cock in Warbugh-street, take this Opportunity to inform the Publick, that they have removed to the Taylor's-Hall in Back-lane, Dublin; and teach as usual on Monday's, Wednesday's, and Friday's, from Eleven O'Clock in the Morning until Two in the Afternoon. Where all young Gentlemen who favour them with their Company, may depend upon being properly instructed and taken Care of.[40]

Of William, nothing more is known. The younger Dominick would become a present, though obscure, figure in the Irish fencing world, and—as shall be seen—appeared in print sporadically throughout the remainder of the century.

## CORNELIUS KELLY

Although many celebrated, accomplished fencing masters of note existed in Ireland during the eighteenth century, the most outstanding figure among them all—by far—was Cornelius Kelly. Although little is known about Kelly's early years, towards the end of the century, his contemporaries would speak of him with unanimous veneration. In his memoirs, Tate Wilkinson refers to him as "the worthy Cornelius Kelly," "honest old Cornelius Kelly," and "the well known, ancient Cornelius Kelly."[41] In the *History of the City of Dublin*, John Thomas Gilbert declares that Kelly "was reputed the best swordsman of his day."[42] Likewise, in his own memoirs, John O'Keeffe refers to Kelly as "the fencing master of first note in Dublin," describing him as "a tall, old, gentlemanly man, highly respected."[43] More impressively, an early nineteenth century historical journal recounts that

> Kelly visited London in 1748 where, in a public match before a large number of nobility and gentry, he signally defeated the best fencing master in England, and was universally admitted to be the most expert swordsman then known.[44]

More than eighty years after this victory, Kelly's reputation was still strong enough to earn a reference in the classic memoirs of fencing-master Henry Angelo, who referred to him as "the late Kelly, whose abilities to this day are well-known in Dublin."[45]

Although few period accounts of the early part of Kelly's career exist, at least one source declares that, during his early years, he was "instructor to the celebrated Marquis of Granby," while another identifies him as the teacher of Ralph Howard, the future Lord Wicklow.[46] One of the oldest known extant advertisements for Kelly's services was published in 1747, and indicates that he had already been teaching in Dublin since at least 1731:

> The said Cornelius Kelly has opened his Fencing School in the Stationer's-Hall on Cork-Hill, and will teach Monday's, Wednesday's, and Friday's, in said Hall; where he hath kept it 16 Years.[47]

Given his surname, one wonders if Cornelius was related to the "famous" aforementioned fencing master Dominick Kelly, who had passed away prior to 1746. However, given that Dominick's brother, William, and nephew (also named Dominick) had been advertising their own school at the same time as Cornelius—and were thus competing for business in the same city—this possibility, barring a major family feud, seems unlikely.[48] Whatever the case, a public contest of arms between Cornelius and Dominick—described in 1750 in *Freeman's Daily Journal*—leaves little doubt as to which Kelly was the superior:

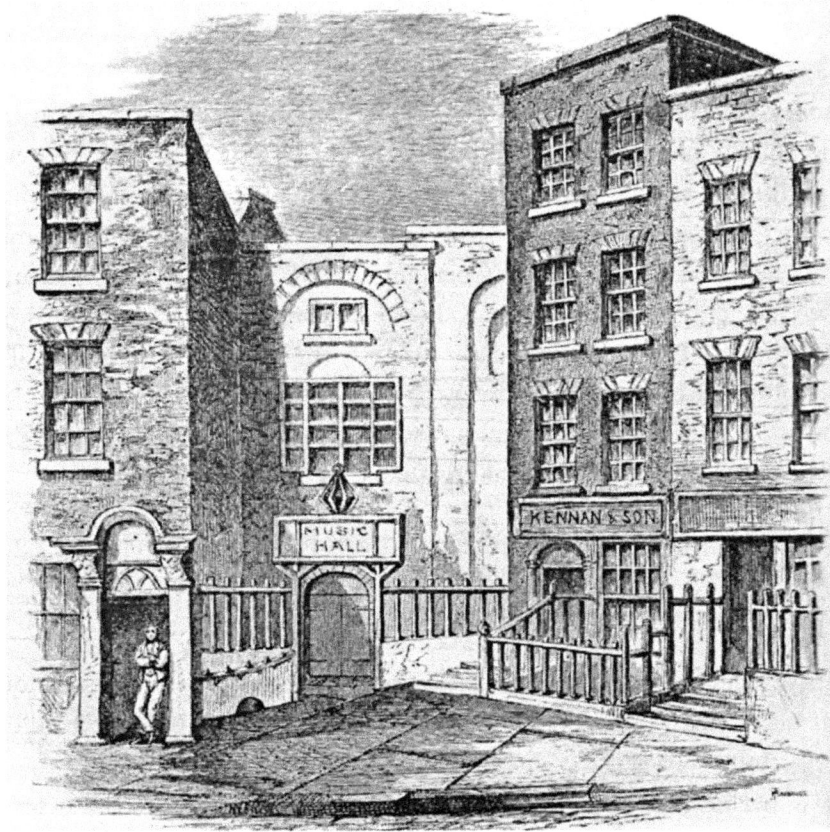

The Fishamble-street Music Hall, the site of Cornelius Kelly's fencing school in 1769.

On Thursday last Messieurs Cornelius and Dominick Kelly met at the Music Hall in Crow Street on a trial of skill at foils. They played several bouts in all of which Mr. Cornelius Kelly had manifestly the advantage, having disarmed his antagonist and hit him several times without receiving one thrust from him.

The match was for twenty guineas, which sum was immediately ordered by the judges appointed to be given to Mr. Cornelius Kelly, who very generously had deposited the same in the hands of the printer hereof to be equally divided to the four following charities viz. the society for the relief of prisoners, the hospital of incurables, the infirmary on the Inn's Quay and the Mercer's Hospital.[49]

In addition to the charities mentioned above, a portion of Cornelius's winnings were also donated to "the Charitable Musical Society."[50] After this time, Dominick is not recorded as operating his own school again, although, after 1781, he was teaching fencing at Patrick Prendergast's school in Loughrea, County Galway.[51]

Interior of the Music Hall on Fishamble-street, where Cornelius Kelly kept his fencing school after 1769.

Throughout the following decades, and for most of his long career, Cornelius continued to run a fencing academy in Stationer's Hall—a large building located across the street from Lucas's Coffee-house, the famous haunt of duelists—holding classes on Mondays, Wednesdays, and Fridays.[52] In addition to his work as a fencing master, Cornelius was also the well-known producer of a "shrub," or fruit liqueur, which was famous enough to inspire several unscrupulous imitators in both Galway and Roscommon.[53] In 1757, it was announced that "Mr. Cornelius Kelly, Fencing-master" had been appointed to teach at Dublin Castle.[54] And again, in 1769, Kelly opened a new school in the large "Musick-hall on Fishamble-street."[55]

Evidence suggests that despite his reputed prowess, Cornelius was a modest individual. He evinced a disdain for personal publicity, advertised infrequently, and—in later years—would become known more for the achievements of his students than for his own merits. Henry Angelo noted that Kelly's disciple, Anthony Gordon (with whom Angelo was personally acquainted), possessed a "perfect knowledge of fencing" and was "considered the best fencer in Ireland."[56] Even more impressive was the achievement of Cornelius's nephew, James Kelly, who, in 1770, traveled to Paris to face the best fencers that he could find. A contemporary letter described James's considerable exploits, which culminated in a spectacular contest with Joseph Bologne, the Chevalier de Saint-Georges, a man widely revered as one of the greatest European fencers:

> Extract of a letter from Paris to a gentleman in this city, dated Sept. 9, 1770.
>
> "A countryman of yours, Mr. James Kelly (nephew to Mr. Cornelius Kelly) has just gained the greatest honour and applause here, by his extraordinary skill and performance in the science of fencing; this brought on him the envy of all the capital French performers, particularly the so much talked of M. St. George, with whom he had a meeting and trial of skill the 7th inst. Mr. Kelly was attended by all the British and Irish nobility and gentlemen in Paris, and M. St. George by all the fencing masters of that city, and at least 600 of the French peers and gentlemen; before which great company the brave young Irishman gained a compleat victory over his antagonist, (who was esteemed the greatest swordsman seen in Paris for many years) and exhibited such a superiority in the noble science of defence, not only over M. St. George, but all the ushers and top fencers in France, as made it unsafe for him, from their envy and threats, to stay any longer in Paris, from whence he intends to set off immediately for London, crowned with laurels, from whence, I make no doubt, he will visit his native country. I assure you his gallant behaviour has done Ireland great honour, and is highly applauded by all the English, Irish, and Scotch nobility residing here, by whom he is very much caressed."[57]

Another account of the same event, published two weeks after the first, was slightly less glowing in its enthusiasm for Kelly, but no less adamant regarding the decisiveness of his victory:

> You have by this Time, without Doubt, heard of the great Trial of Skill between the celebrated Mons. St. George, supposed to be the ablest Fencer in Europe, and young Kelly. The Contest was sharp, and for some Time doubtful; (and however some People may choose to sacrifice Truth at the Altar of Flattery or Falsehood, the superior Skill of our Countryman was not so glaringly visible, as to strike the Mind with an instantaneous Conviction;) but after a full and repeated Exertion of their respective Merits, wherein the whole Theory and Practice of the noble Science seemed to be exhausted, the Company acknowledged his Superiority, and Envy itself was forced to give a reluctant Plaudit. But, however honourable a Victor over the reputed first Fencer in Europe may be deemed, his candid Behaviour and modest Deportment after it, were still more honourable, and entitle him to a Regard which mere Abilities must in vain expect.[58]

By 1774, James Kelly had returned to Ireland, where he taught fencing (alongside instructors of other arts and sciences) at the Dublin Academy on Abbey Street.[59] That fall, he seems to have emerged as the appointed successor to Cornelius, as he assumed the duties of running his uncle's fencing school "at the Great Music-hall, Fishamble-street."[60] Then, two years later, in

Painted by Mather Brown                                             Engraved by W. Ward.

MONSIEUR DE ST. GEORGE.

From an Original Picture at Mr. H. Angelo's Academy

James Kelly's celebrated antagonist, Joseph Bologne, the Chevalier de Saint-Georges (1745-1799).
From a portrait reproduced in Henry Angelo's *Reminiscences*.

1776, James's promising career was cut short, when the *Londonderry Journal* noted the untimely passing of "James Kelly, fencing-master."[61] In 1779, his uncle published a somber notice in the *Dublin Journal* which stated, "Cornelius Kelly, Fencing-Master, is in Town, at No. 71, Capel-street. He has no Nephew that teaches to Fence."[62]

As for Cornelius, he continued to appear as a "Fencing-Master" among the pages of *Wilson's Dublin Directory* throughout the 1770s. In the 1780 directory, his name is conspicuously absent, suggesting that by this time he may have retired or become semi-retired.[63]

Then, in 1781, Cornelius was in the press again—this time to respond to the repeated screeds of William Dwyer, another Dublin fencing master who had publicly disparaged the merits of other local Irish instructors, insisting that none of Dublin's professors could "merit" the title of fencing master unless they had traveled beyond Ireland (as had Dwyer) to receive foreign instruction. Answering Dwyer's charges in the pages of the *Evening Post*, Kelly noted that he had personally challenged Dwyer to a contest of arms, but that Dwyer had "evaded coming to the *point*"—and that, as a consequence, Kelly would disdain "any further paper controversy with such a character." Kelly's answer likely proved embarrassing for Dwyer, as the latter ceased publishing his critiques, and indeed, any fencing advertisements whatsoever, for the remainder of the year.[64]

In 1784, "having been desired by several of the Nobility and Gentry to commence teaching again" Kelly re-opened his school at Mr. Hewett's, No. 18 College green. He also hired another fencing master named "Mr. W. Gittar"—in actuality, William Guitar, who had opened his own fencing school in Dublin in 1766.[65] Guitar, who had previously served as "Usher to Mr. Cornelius Kelly for upwards of eighteen Years," was now to assist the more senior Kelly in teaching.[66]

During the next decade, in his 1790 memoirs, Tate Wilkinson recalled "the worthy Cornelius Kelly" who lived on Capel-street, and "who was then beloved and known by every body, and I believe is yet living, and must be a surprising age."[67] Kelly, during this period, lived at "No. 71 Capel-street, between Loftus and Bolton."[68] In addition to his continued work as a fencing master, Kelly evidently served as an adviser to younger men who found themselves embroiled in "affairs of honor." In one particularly interesting anecdote, Wilkinson recounted how he was late for dinner at Cornelius Kelly's house, on account of having been challenged to a duel by a rival actor and swordsman named Henry Mossop, who had vowed to "run him through the body" and "kill" Wilkinson on the morrow.[69] After responding to his challenger with firmness and presence of mind—though not by backing out of the duel—Wilkinson seemed to frighten Mossop away, and recounted:

I very swiftly posted and wished for wings to arrive at [Cornelius Kelly's on] Capel-street, where I was in good English and Irish well lectured, without any opportunity for a long time of making any defence; but when breathing-time allowe'd a possibility for me, the culprit, to make any vindication, and requesting a fair trial and a benevolent jury, and relying on the laws of the country for an honourable and just examination, though at that time under severe condemnation; yet trusting I might be indulged with a candid hearing in my own justification, I was not only listened to, but most honourably acquitted, and with great approbation; for Mossop's pride was so well known that they enjoyed his mortification; and, blessed be God, my veracity was so well believed, that though the dinner was spoiled, (a material circumstance against me, and to the feelings of each craving stomach) we had a most remarkable cheerful day.

Wilkinson also provided some details about Kelly's family, noting that Mrs. Kelly was sister to the wife of the Reverend Thomas Wilson, a senior fellow at Trinity College and "Professor of Natural Philosophy." Wilkinson also recalled that "Alderman Forbes and his Lady—the well known, ancient Cornelius Kelly and his wife—and many others made up a convivial Irish party at our cheerful board."[70]

Though Kelly may, as Wilkinson's account suggests, have taken a stern stance on the custom of dueling, the fencing master was also not without a sense of humor. When a young playwright named Oliver Goldsmith encountered Kelly in the town of Ardagh, the latter mischievously determined to play a prank on the former—misdirecting him to a "house of entertainment" that was actually the private residence of a distinguished friend. Goldsmith would later use the experience as a basis for part of the plot of his famous 1773 comedy, *The Mistakes of Night*, later re-titled *She Stoops to Conquer*.[71]

In 1794, Kelly was still running a "Fencing Academy" in the "great room, No. 32, Castle-street, next to Sir William Gleadowe's Bank," and offering instruction three days per week. His last known advertisement, addressed to the "nobility and gentry," was published in September, 1795. At this point, Kelly had been teaching in Dublin for at least sixty-four years, and must have been, at the very least, in his mid-eighties or nineties.[72]

# WILLIAM DWYER

According to the memoirs of John O'Keeffe, William Dwyer was the second most noted fencing master in Dublin. Dwyer himself claimed to have "lived in Paris fourteen years," where he had "made FENCING his chief study and practice during that time," and gave "the most convincing Proofs of his superior Abilities to the best Fencing Masters in Paris and

London."[73] Notably, in his first extant fencing advertisement, Dwyer claimed to have beaten a certain "famous" London fencing master, supposedly the best in that city:

Mr. DWYER, FENCING-MASTER,

   WHO beat the famous Mr. Redeau, first Fencing-Master in London, takes this Opportunity of acquainting the Nobility and Gentlemen that he is now determined to keep a regular Academie des Armes...There will be a public and general Assault held there this Day. Mr. Dwyer will give private Tuition to any Nobleman or Gentleman at their own Houses.
   March 18th, 1776.[74]

This same "Redeau"—in actuality, Monsieur Claude Reda, sometimes referred to as "Rheda" or "Redas"—first appeared in London during the 1760s, and his contest with Dwyer is worth recounting.[75] Henry Angelo described Reda as "a famous fencing-master," who "taught at the Opera House, previous to my teaching there," and whose *salle d'armes* was frequented by the famous Irish duelist, George Robert Fitzgerald.[76] Reda was known to appear in enterprising fencing contests at his own academy, where paying spectators were free to bet on the outcomes of the assaults. In 1764, it was reported that Reda had thrice defeated "the famous Neapolitan fencing Master, Mr. Celestini," and that the latter would now face "one of Mr. Reda's Scholars for a Wager of Ten Guineas."[77] Reda's advertisements continued to declare that

   Any Gentleman, Native, or Foreigner, having a mind to make a public assault with Mr. Reda, at his Fencing-Academy, is requested to signify his intention by a line addressed as above.[78]

In the spring of 1770, a fencing match was arranged between Reda and William Dwyer, the latter being described as "an Irish Gentleman" who had come from Dublin "on purpose to decide this feat of arms." Their public assault was held at Domenico Angelo's riding house, where, according to one source, "wagers to the amount of 3,000 l. were laid."[79] The first account of the contest's outcome was published in the *Independent Chronicle*, and reads as follows:

   Yesterday a very considerable fencing match was fought at Signior Angelo's riding house; between Monsieur Rheda, a fencing master, and Mr. Dweir, a gentleman who had formerly taught the noble science of defence in Dublin, but had lately retired from business.—The bets were considerable.—The combatants were to fight eighteen bouts; he that gave eight hits to be the winner.—The gentlemen gave very eminent proofs of their skill.—Mr. Dweir had the advantage of three out of five.—It was then proposed by that gentleman the bets should be drawn, and the affair resumed some other time.[80]

A little more than a week later, Reda himself published a very different account of the event, insisting that the outcome had actually been the reverse of what had been first reported:

MR. REDA, as well as every man of honour who has the least knowledge of the Art of Fencing, could not help being surprised at a false paragraph inserted in the Morning Chronicle of Tuesday, the 13th instant, which mentions, that Mr. DWYER had the advantage of three hits out of five, over Mr. Reda; when, to the knowledge of the first masters in London then present, the Sieur Reda had himself that very superiority over Mr. Dweir; who, through an incontestable proof of his inferiority, refused to go on with the assault, though a great number of bets were depending; and his friends (to Mr. Reda's great surprize) going about the room to hunt for suffrages against the Sieur Reda, not recollecting that it is quite contrary to reason and justice, that they should be both judge and party, in the same cause. In order, therefore, to bring truth to light, and to do justice to those interested in this fencing-match, Mr. Reda offers to begin another assault with the said Mr. Dweir, provided the best masters in that art be constituted the judges, and with them the nobility and gentry, most of whom are connoisseurs.[81]

The day before Reda published his response, another witness to the contest penned a lengthy letter to Dublin, where it was printed the following month. In this account, the author gave the clear advantage to Dwyer, and provided the most detailed description of the event:

Extract of a private letter from London, dated 20th March, 1770.

The famous fencing match between Mr. Dwyer, a native of your island, and the celebrated Mons. Reda of this city, and on, which so much money was depending, came on, on Monday the 12th, at the Riding-house of Mons. Angelo in Oxford road. The company was extremely numerous, and composed of the best people in this metropolis, who all seemed to be strongly prepossessed in favour of Reda. On Mr. Dwyer's entering the circle, he addressed the audience in a very laconick and gentleman-like manner; informed them, that he undertook to fence with Mr. Reda, by the invitation of some gentlemen who honoured him with their opinion that he was equal to that gentleman, then generally esteemed the first master of the foil in Europe; on the company composing themselves, after setting their different wagers on this combat, generally two to one in favour of Reda, a universal silence was called for, and here they threw themselves into their first attitudes: it is impossible to give you an idea of the beauty of the two figures dressed for the purpose, and standing with the utmost exactness. I do not remember ever to have felt a more agitated moment than when the points of their foils met, and each watching his opportunity. Mr. Dwyer found it was to no purpose to wait for the assault from his antagonist, and with the utmost coolness advanced upon Reda, and gave him the completest hit I ever saw. The manner in which your countryman behaved on this occasion so altered the sentiments of the audience, bets took a very different turn: Dwyer really from his appearance, after the first hit, seemed to think it a matter of course, and treated the matter so very cavalierly, that on the second onset he dropped his foil with a smile, and left Reda a fair open; this he repeated, but to no purpose, as Reda acted entirely on the defensive; on Dwyer's advance, Reda made a pass at him, and this hit was adjudged to the latter; the two next were allowed to Mr. Dwyer, and the last to Mr. Reda; and here it ended, three to two in favour of Mr. Dwyer. These five rencounters took a deal of time, as there were two hits a long time in dispute, and which were by the spectators universally given to Mr. Dwyer; however the judges, to avoid altercation, and by the particular request of Mr. Dwyer were declared dead hits. Upon the whole, there never was seen in this kingdom, nor perhaps in any other, a greater trial of skill in the accomplishment of fencing than on this occasion. I hear Dwyer has made several efforts to bring Reda to conclude this mater, as it was determined by the most hits out of fifteen, but Reda has declined it; so that your countryman stands now in the opinion of this metropolis, the first fencer at present known in Europe. If there should be any more of this matter, depend on it you shall hear from your old friend and servant.[82]

Reports of Dwyer's victory quickly spread throughout the British press, making their way to cities as far-flung as Williamsburg, Virginia, where it was noted that "on Saturday morning [Dwyer] set out for France, in order to encounter another French fencing master at Paris. Great bets are depending on the event of this combat, the odds now being three to one in favour of the Irish combatant."[83]

By 1776, Dwyer had returned to Dublin, where he determined to keep a "regular Academie des Armes."[84] In 1779 he was teaching at Trinity College, and announced, in a notice dated New Year's Day, that he would "open School, at his House, No. 19, Clarendon-street," instructing "any young Gentlemen...in the Greek and Latin Languages...His Terms are one Guinea per Quarter, and the same Entrance."[85]

During the early 1780s, Dwyer repeatedly published a screed in the Dublin press, in which he touted his own training in France and disparaged the skill of local Irish fencing masters—insisting that such individuals were not fencing masters at all on account of their having never left Ireland:

> Mr. Dwyer assures the Gentlemen of this Kingdom, that any man who stiles himself a Fencing Master, that teaches in this city, and that never was out of this country, and therefore could not have the opportunity of knowing what elegant or good Fencing is, can have no title to merit in the line of Fencing...[86]

In the following days, Dwyer's harangue would be publicly answered and rebutted by Cornelius Kelly, the reputed "fencing-master of first note" in Dublin.[87] In 1781, Dwyer was teaching "at the Music-Hall, Fishamble-street, on Mondays, Wednesdays, and Fridays." Within a year, he ceased appearing in the extant public records. His fate after this time is unknown.[88]

## JAMES PARDON

Another of Dublin's most prominent masters was James Pardon, an Irishman who had previously taught fencing in France, where he served in the Irish Brigades as one of the famed "Wild Geese." Pardon's first Dublin advertisement provided additional information about his past:

### FENCING.

MR. PARDON, from London, very respectfully begs Leave to inform the Nobility and Gentry of this Kingdom, that he is arrived in Dublin, and will open an Academy at the new Ball-room in Cope-street, near College-green, from the Hour of twelve to three, on Mondays, Wednesdays, and Fridays, for such Noblemen and Gentlemen as may wish to be properly instructed in that honourable Science. Mr. Pardon is a Native of Ireland, has lived many years in France, where he taught with Success, and for twelve Years that he has lived in London, taught at the Royal Academy, and instructed the Scholars of that well-known and established College, Westminster, jointly with Mr. Redmond, his Majesty's principal Teacher. Mr. Pardon is induced not only from these Motives, to solicit the Patronage of a generous Public, but from a flattering Confidence he has of giving every Gentleman who may be pleased to employ him the utmost Satisfaction.

Mr. Pardon teaches also the Use of the Back Sword and Spadon*, (Accomplishments very useful to Gentleman of the Army and Navy)...

By particular Desire Mr. Pardon will keep an Evening School, at the same Room, from six till nine, on the opposite Days. Feb. 12, 1785.[89]

As noted above, during his years in London, Pardon had assisted one John Redman—the Irish fencing master to King George II and III. The two were teaching together as early as 1776, when Pardon was described as a "Master" teaching "the use of the Broad Sword" at the Anchor and Baptist Head Tavern in Chancery-lane.[90] In March of 1778, Pardon was in attendance at a highly-publicized fencing contest between two Frenchmen, held before "numerous and genteel company" in Claude Reda's rooms in Haymarket. It was noted that "After this *assault* was over, another commenced between Mons. Granard and Mr. Pardon, both fencing-masters, and was decided in the first gentleman's favour, who gave his opponent eight thrusts to three."[91] Despite Pardon's reported loss, a rematch was soon arranged between the two, as stated in the following announcement:

---

\*   *Spadon*: Later notices by Pardon identify this weapon as a "Spadroon." *Dublin Evening Post*, February 26, 1785.

## FENCING ACADEMY
### Opera House, Hay-Market

It having been observed by several gentlemen spectators of the assault which followed that of Messrs. La Pierce and Abadie, on Wednesday the 18th of March, that the great disturbance which prevailed on the occasion, had evidently prevented the fencers from a fair and full exertion of their abilities; it has been therefore agreed by the said fencers, Messrs. Pardon and La Grenade, as well for the satisfaction of the above gentlemen, as of their respective scholars, who desire it particularly, to determine the matter by a second assault, which will take place This Day, the 8th instant, in order to defray the expences of the room, and of the accommodations requisite on the occasion.

Tickets at Five Shillings each, will be delivered at Mr. Pardon's, No. 126, Chancery-lane; at Mr. Reda's fencing school, Hay-Market, and at Mr. Abadie's, No. 9, Rupert-street.

N.B. To begin at Two o'clock precisely.[92]

The outcome of this contest was reported two days later by the London press:

### FENCING INTELLIGENCE.

On Wednesday was finally determined at Reda's Academy in the Haymarket, the contested match between Messrs. Pardon and La Grenade, the former hitting his antagonist eight thrusts to three, with an elegance and address that set his superiority in the most striking light.—While we congratulate Mr. Pardon on this successful display of his abilities, we cannot forbear recommending to him a prudent controul of that confidence and impetuosity, the too common vices of gentlemen of his country, and which, by inspiring him with a contempt for his opponent, were evidently the sole cause of the seeming advantage gained over him on a former occasion.[93]

In February, 1780, Pardon dissolved the partnership between himself and Redman.[94] The next year, he commenced teaching at Mr. Wall Du Val's Dancing and Fencing Academy, located in the Exeter Exchange on the Strand. Pardon noted,

Mr. Pardon having the honour to be Fencing Master to the Royal Academy, Westminster School, &c. for upwards of Seven years, hopes will intitle him to the patronage of those Noblemen and Gentlemen, whose situation requires the use of the sword, particularly the Broad Sword and Spadroon, accomplishments extremely requisite for the Gentleman of the Army and Navy. All Gentlemen who wish to be Compleated in the Science of Fencing, will be instructed on the most reasonable terms.[95]

About this time, prior to leaving London, Pardon became acquainted with Henry Angelo—then a business competitor—and the two eventually engaged in a heated fencing bout at Pardon's school. In his memoirs, Angelo derisively describes Pardon as a liar who told "incredible stories" about the many men he had "wounded and killed in duels," while nevertheless conceding that the Irishman was a tough adversary who was "one of the best fencers in the [Irish] brigade." During the course of their bout, Angelo found Pardon to be quite skilled in the use of the blade, and was eventually forced to resort to disarming techniques, which he admitted would not have impressed an audience "well acquainted with the science." Although Angelo managed to disarm Pardon several times, the "athletic" Irishman fenced so vigorously that the "exertion" and "exercise" gave Angelo a nosebleed:

Occasionally attending the boarding houses on those who took private lessons, in the next room to one of my scholars...was another master, named Pardone, an Irishman, who had served abroad in the Irish Brigades. The boys, desirous to see us contend together, contrived, after he had finished teaching, which was previous to my attendance (three o'clock), to keep him in the room in which I was expected, and, favourite as he was, I considered him the only one that stood in my way—possessed of that inducement, which I was not competent to, of amusing the scholars with lies; how many he had wounded and killed in duels. I could only have told them, "I eat all that I ever killed." However, it was good fun for them to laugh at his bouncing. It was then, "learn of Pardone, he's a queer fellow, he'll tell you such damned lies." Besides, he had got a strong footing there before me. At three o'clock, I made my appearance there, and having previously fenced together, our meeting was nothing new. Here I found the room full of boys, when the question was soon put, "Mr. Angelo, won't you fence with Mr. Pardone?" and the same to him; of course, neither refused. Here our separate abilities were at stake, to amuse school-boys. However, to please them, we stripped, and engaged. As I had but lately made my debut there, I exerted myself the more, to secure a good footing; but I had not an easy customer (pugilistic) to deal with; for some time it was what the fencers call *partie égale*[†]. Nevertheless, though each may have shown their skill, the spectators were not sufficient judges; merely silent: when the foil falling from my adversary's hand, a general applause and laughter ensued. At the time, seizing their moment of being pleased, neither my attack or defence occupying my attention, I took every opportunity to disarm him, which pleased them the more. This could not have continued long, and, from his athletic appearance surpassing mine, finding he was enraged at the notice bestowed on me, though I had turned up a trump in an encounter, the game might have taken a different turn. Having already won, I was glad to ground my arms; fortunately, my nose was bleeding at the time, from the heat of the room, and the exercise; it was a finale to the exertions imposed upon us. Had I engaged before those well acquainted with the science, the foil falling would have been of no consequence, nor attended to: it is the quickness of the point, that depends more on a light hand, than grasping the foil too strong. Indeed, many have a loop to their glove, to prevent it falling; and what is a sword-knot? but to fasten it to the wrist. Here fortune stood my friend, for my antagonist had his "capabilities," having been one of the best fencers in the brigade. When we left

---

†   *Partie égale*: without odds.

the place together, in our way he would have quarrelled with me; but asking him to dine with me, soon cooled his courage, he was perfectly agreeable to it; and what with the effects of the wine, assenting to his incredible stories, and praising his abilities, though a would-be lion before dinner, after, pleased with his reception, *en ami*, no longer opposed, he went away a lamb. A short time after, it was proposed by one of his former scholars, who resided in Dublin, to establish him there, at the same time that he had procured several to begin. To see his kingdom again, was such a temptation he could not refuse, and he resigned to me what scholars he had left.[96]

Back in Dublin, Pardon opened an enormous *salle d'armes* at No. 9 Cope-street, near College Green, where gentlemen were "properly instructed in the honourable science of the Sword." In one advertisement, Pardon also took a shot at his local competition, stating:

Mr. Pardon, in the most candid manner to evince his professional abilities, informs the Public, that his Academy will be open to all gentlemen amateurs of the science; this he hopes (for him) will obviate any charge of an imposition practised at present in this metropolis by pretenders to this science, and at the same time pretenders to other arts and sciences, who by teaching privately, shrink from public inspection through fear of a detection of their inability and ignorance.[97]

In May of 1788, a highly publicized fencing tournament took place at Pardon's academy on Cope-street, in which fencers contested for a "prize sword." During one of the assaults, a foil was broken—nearly resulting in a fatal accident—and another assault lasted nearly one hour. Throughout the event, contestants' hits were required to land within a "mark" in order to be counted; such a rule had also been used in earlier contests for "prize swords" held by the Knights of Tara (a celebrated Dublin fencing society), during which fencers' jackets were "marked a small circle, by blue lines, within which the hits must take place, or pass for nought."[98] Following is a full account of the tournament at Pardon's:

## FENCING
—

Yesterday a prize-sword was contested for at Pardon's fencing academy, in Cope-street. The candidates were four—Mr. Perceval—Mr. Lett—Mr. Hamilton—and Mr. Mequignon. Lots were drawn for the parties that were to be opposed to each other—and it fell to the chance of Mr. Mequignon and Mr. Perceval.—Eight hits were the number upon which the victory depended. Mr. Perceval made two or three at the beginning of the contest, without receiving one—but his antagonist regained his lost ground—and the contest continued equal for some time. The button was broken off Mr. Mequignon by Mr. P's foil parrying a thrust—and had it not been observed by the judges, fatal consequences might have ensued. The contest at length came to a crisis—each gentleman had made seven hits, and the eighth was decisive. After much caution, judgment and action on both sides, victory declared in favour of Mr. Perceval.

Mr. Hamilton and Mr. Lett, after a little pause, proceeded to action. This was a very disproportionate match. Mr. Hamilton is a youth of about 14 or 15 years of age; Mr. Lett is rather tall, and had a monstrous advantage in the length of his arm and foil. Notwithstanding these advantages Mr. Hamilton maintained the contest with spirit for a considerable time; it was difficult for him to reach his opponent, who continued on the defensive with much circumspection—beside from the advance he was obliged to make in each lounge, he nearly ran upon his adversary's foil. Almost all Mr. Hamilton's hits were made in *carte*, Mr. Lett's for the reasons above stated, in *tierce*. Mr. Hamilton lost the victory by one; but we must observe that he made a vast number of hits more than his opponent; but not being within the mark, were not counted.

The two successful gentlemen, Mr. Perceval and Mr. Lett, between whom the prize lay, encountered each other with much spirit for more than an hour—when the contest ended in favour of Mr. Lett, by *one* hit—and the numbers stood upon the

FIRST TRIAL,

| Mr. PERCEVAL | 8 | Mr. MEQUIGNON | 7 |
|---|---|---|---|

SECOND TRIAL,

| Mr. LETT | 8 | Mr. HAMILTON | 7 |
|---|---|---|---|

THIRD TRIAL,

| Mr. LETT | 8 | Mr. PERCEVAL | 7 |
|---|---|---|---|

The prize sword was decreed to Mr. Lett, amidst the plaudits of the spectators.

Mr. Dillon and Mr. J. T. Ashenhurst, acted as judges on the occasion.

A band belonging to one of the regiments in garrison attended, and amused the assembly, which was very polite and fashionable, during the pauses, with favourite airs. The whole was conducted with infinite propriety, and reflects much credit on the gentlemen who conducted the business.[99]

Four years later, on December 16, 1792, Pardon's school became the meeting-place of more than one hundred armed members of the United Irishmen, a revolutionary organization that would eventually take part in the Irish rebellion of 1798. During the trial of one of the group's leaders, Archibald Hamilton Rowan, several witnesses provided details of this meeting, and included descriptions of Pardon's *salle d'armes*:

The Volunteers were summoned to meet at the house of one Pardon a fencing master in Cope-street, on the 16th of December. In consequence, several corps did go to the fencing school upon that day; the defendants [Rowan] headed one, another very celebrated name was at the head of another, J. N. TANDY; who commanded the others. I am not able to inform you, but this I can say, that they were in all about one hundred assembled in arms.

In this fencing school there is a gallery, and into that gallery, (to such excess did they carry their designs) many auditors and spectators were admitted, so that what passed below, passed almost in the face of the world; and if any part of my statement be not true, multitudes may be found to disprove it. A table stood in the middle of the room, a vast bundle of printed papers was brought in and placed upon it. The different corps entered into resolutions, and taking into their wise considerations the propriety of the proclamation, resolved their several sentiments of disapproba-tion...The windows were opened, and several of the papers thrown into the street to the mob whom curiosity led to the door.[100]

Pardon would continue to teach through the mid-1790s, at which time he became connected with one of the most famous figures in the history of fencing, who happened to visit Dublin.

During the summer of 1794, the duelist and theater owner Richard Daly made a sensation when he engaged the famous transvestite fencer, popularly known as the Chevalier D'Eon, and his companion, the actress Mrs. Batemen, to enliven the performances at Daly's Cork Theatre. In November, the couple arrived in Dublin, where Daly engaged them for a series of perfor-mances at the Theatre Royal on Crow Street. *The Hibernian Journal,* announcing his arrival, described D'Eon as "the transvestite soldier now in her sixty-eighth year." Earlier that year, D'Eon had greatly impressed audiences in England with a series of fencing demonstrations, at least one of which was performed while "dressed in armour, with a helmet and feathers."[101] D'Eon's Dublin debut was set for Tuesday, November 11, but was deferred due to a "sudden indisposition." One week later, it was announced that "the Chevalier D'Eon will, for the first time on this stage, fence with a gentleman, when, at the particular request of several Ladies and Gentlemen, she will appear in the uniform she wore when Captain of Dragoons in the Army." The Chevalier's perfor-mances in Dublin continued on a weekly basis through January, 1795, when Pardon eventually participated in the event with D'Eon. On January 20th, after the play *Three Weeks After Marriage*, it was announced that D'Eon would give an exhibi-tion of fencing, after which,

Mademoiselle la Chevalière
D'EON de BEAUMONT.
Published July 12, 1787, by B.B. Evans in the Poultry. LONDON.

The Chevalier D'Eon. From Angelo's memoirs.

an address, written by Mrs. Bateman, will be delivered by her for the occasion; as it is the desire of her friends, that she should give a specimen of her skill in fencing, she will, on that evening, fence *quarte* and *tierce* and take a lesson (*a la Meuette*) of Mr. Pardon, fencing-master.[102]

Pardon passed away sometime prior to 1797, when his student, Massel Rabastin, advertised himself in Dublin as the "successor to the late Mr. Pardon." Rabastin taught fencing at the dancing academy of "Messrs. Duval," Senior and Junior, at the "Shakespeare Gallery" on Exchequer Street, near Grafton. Here, both Rabastin and Duval provided instruction in the "Broad and Small Sword, from twelve to three o'clock, on Mondays, Wednesdays, and Fridays, on the usual terms of the town."[103]

# THE PRACTICE OF ANCIENT WEAPONS

Aside from the the small-sword, broadsword, backsword, and spadroon—the predominant weapons of choice in the Irish *salles des armes*—other, more antiquated weapons such as the quarterstaff, sword and dagger, sword and shield, and falchion were also taught and practiced, although their use is not specifically documented within the context of Irish fencing schools. Instead, the available evidence suggests that knowledge in the use of such weapons was passed down between family members, and through private instruction. In 1827, Jonah Barrington recounted that his grandfather

> had bespoken a little quarter-staff to perfect me in that favourite exercise of his youth, by which he had been enabled to knock a gentleman's brains out for a wager, on the ridge of Maryborough, in company with the grandfather of the present Judge Arthur Moore, of the Common Pleas of Ireland. It is a whimsical gratification to me to think that I do not at this moment forget much of the said instruction which I received either from Michael Lodge the Matross, or from Colonel Jonah Barrington—though after a lapse of nearly sixty years![104]

Likewise, the Irish "Masters of Defence" who contested with sharps in English stage-fights were typically well-versed in the use of a variety of older weapons. In 1743, we are told that Irish champion Francis Sherlock and English champion Edward Sutton had fought a contest in Dublin

> for the Sum of Fifty Guineas, at the following Weapons, viz. single Sword, Sword and Dagger, Sword and Buckler, single Falchion, and Case of Falchions, of each three Bouts, no Wounds to be dress'd till the Battle is over...[105]

Clearly, instruction in such weapons was available in Ireland, even if not openly advertised as being taught in its respectable fencing academies.

Antiquated weapons also saw use in grand theatrical combats held in Dublin before vast audiences. In 1794, Astley's Aphitheatre Royal on Peter Street played host to a "new, superb, and military spectacle" which would be held for the "second time in this kingdom," entitled, "The Temple of Mars." An advertisement included a list of weapons that would be used during the contest:

THE TEMPLE OF MARS
TILTS and TOURNAMENTS, &c.
Knights of the Spear, Battle-axe, Small Sword, Broad Sword, Club, Gladiators, &c.[106]

It is not clear, from the little information available about this event, if its combats were contested in earnest, or were merely forms of staged, theatrical re-enactment. Whatever the case, Dublin audiences were impressed:

Yesterday evening in a great measure tended to convince us we were right in the opinion formed of the TEMPLE OF MARS—the Peter-street Theatre exhibited a scene of beauty, fashion, and numbers, and this unequalled and most splendid military spectacle was honoured, as it deserved, with universal approbation.[107]

Although the "Temple of Mars" is not recorded as having performed in Dublin again after 1794, it would not be the last such event held in the city. More than two decades later, in 1818, a similar "Tournament" was announced, which also included an exhibition demonstrating the use of both ancient and modern weapons:

A GRAND TOURNAMENT;
Or, Wage of Battle.
Consisting of various modes of Attack and Defence, with Small Sword, Broad Sword, Shields, Battleaxe, and Daggers!!
I. Combat, Small Sword—II. The Scotch Broad Sword—III. Roman Dagger Fight—IV. Old English Battle-axe and shields—V. Sword Combat of Four.

These combats were accompanied by a musical overture from the "Opera of Lodoiska," and concluded "with a Grand Combat of Eight, under the superintendance of Mr. Cordozo."[108]

## IRISH FENCERS ABROAD

In addition to masters James Kelly, William Dwyer, and James Pardon, a number of other Irish fencers are recorded as having contested and instructed abroad—in countries such as England, France, and Germany. In some cases—just as Kelly and Dywer had done—these Irish fencers crossed blades with some of the most celebrated swordsmen in Europe. An account of one such individual was provided by Henry Angelo:

> Above forty years ago, my fencing-room at the Opera House, Haymarket, was open to all those foreigners whose abilities as fencers gave them their entrie. Among those who frequented it was an Irish gentleman, Mr. McD—t, since a counsellor in Dublin, and who had practised at Paris under Monsieur de la Bossiere, and was often the antagonist of Monsieur St. George. On his return to England, he complimented me by preferring mine to the other fencing schools.[109]

While some Irish instructors—such as Alexander Doyle and Daniel O'Sullivan—managed to achieve significant success abroad, others were not so lucky. In America, in 1779, while the country's revolution was underway, the *Virginia Gazette* mentioned the death of an Irish fencing master named Claudius Peter Cary, a well-known character in Williamsburg, who was "endeavouring to get out of the enemies way, [and] died with fatigue in the Dismal Swamp."[110]

Probably the greatest repository for Irish fencing masters outside of Ireland itself was in England. There, during the eighteenth century, numerous Irish instructors advertised their services; in a prominent London and Westminster directory published for the year 1763, three out of seven professional fencing masters listed—almost half—were Irish.[111] Masters teaching in England included Mr. Fitzgerald, William O'Brien (both father and son), Mr. Fitzpatrick, James Cannon, and Francis Sherlock.[112] It was an Irishman named John Redman, however, who secured the most lucrative position of any—the role of personal fencing master to King George II, and to his son, the future King George III.

## JOHN REDMAN

John Redman was described by Henry Angelo as a "tall, athletic Hibernian." He first came to prominence in 1753, when Bartholomeo Balthazar, "Master of the small Sword" and "Fencing-Master to their Royal Highnesses the Prince of Wales and Prince Edward," suddenly passed away. The *Derby Mercury* soon noted that "great Interest is making to succeed [Balthazar] in his Employment."[113] Several weeks later, it was announced that "Mr. Redman is appointed

Fencing-Master to their Royal Highnesses the Prince of Wales and Prince Edward," the new master being described as "very eminent in that Science." The notice of Redman's appointment was published as far away as the American colonies.[114] For several decades, Redman fared well in London, running a school in Harley Street, Cavendish Square, and residing on Smith Street.[115] In 1770, he jointly ran a school with another master named Mollard, teaching six days per week at multiple locations:

> MESS. REDMAN and MOLLARD, Fencing Masters to the ROYAL ACADEMY, give Notice to the Nobility and Gentry, that they are removed from Vine Street to their Great Room in Picadilly, facing Darby's Court, near St. James's Church, where they teach Tuesdays, Thursdays, and Saturdays, from Ten O'Clock in the Forenoon till Two, and at the Horn Tavern in Fleet-street on Mondays, Wednesdays, and Fridays, from Ten till Two.[116]

Redman's apparent good fortune would be marred by a severe quarrel with Domenico Angelo, the renowned Italian fencing master who had come to London to teach the French school of small-sword fencing. When Angelo managed to displace Redman by securing the royal position for himself, the Irishman virtually declared war. Domenico's son, Henry, recounted:

> Soon after my father had been appointed fencing-master to their Royal Highnesses the Prince of Wales and the Duke of York, a man named Redman, a tall athletic Hibernian, who had instructed our late Sovereign, was so incensed at my father having displaced him, that he was continually abusing him as a foreigner coming to this country to take away his bread. My father meeting him in the Haymarket, at the corner of James-street, accosted him, at the same time inquiring, how he dared to speak disrespectfully of his coming to this country. Redman directly lifted up a thick stick, when my father, in his defence, raised his cane, and avoided a blow aimed at him. The result was, Redman had his head broke, and his wig left in the kennel. My father, the next day, sent his friend Mr. Frederick, son of the reputed King of Corsica, to Redman, to mention to him the disgrace attending two fencing-masters fighting with sticks in the streets, and if he would walk out any distance from town, and appoint the place, my father would meet him. His answer was, "He should put my father in the Crown-office," which was the case. A trial ensued in the Court of King's Bench, for an assault, and though this was in the middle of the Haymarket, Redman procured a shoeblack to swear (although his stand for years had been at the corner of Pall-mall) that my father gave him the first blow. Redman laid his damages at a thousand pounds, asserting that he had received violent bruises, his head being dangerously broken, his wig left in the kennel, and that he lost a diamond ring, valued at forty pounds; that the fracture on his head had ever since prevented him instructing his scholars, to the great loss of business, being only able to teach for a few minutes, when he was suddenly seized with a swimming in the head, which (nearly fainting) obliged him to be seated; and that, after the application of salts, he recovered slowly, and

was prevented that day from attending his scholars. My father had to pay one hundred pounds damages, and ninety pounds costs.[117]

Yet this was not the end of Redman, who continued to teach at Westminster School. Eventually, he came to quarrel with the Angelo family once again. Henry recounted,

Young as I was then, opposed to so many foils, no *foil* to my *nouvelle* situation. The repeated stories of the boys, to me, of the superiority the other masters had vauntingly boasted how *they* could instruct, all professing their abilities. The mere chatter of boys made no impression on me, except the vituperous tongue of one of the five, a tall Irishman, named Redman, whom I have spoken of in my second volume of *Reminiscences*, wherein I mentioned my father's paying one hundred pounds for caning him. Being told that *he* had boasted beating my father, and both of us having fencing rooms in Dean's Yard (the other masters only attending at the boarding houses), out of patience with the continual falsehoods related to me of his abuse, with my scholars and other students, I went to him. Exposing his base assertions, provoked as I was, I told him, his age (then above seventy) spared him that resentment he deserved. On refuting his saying he had beat my father, I called on him to take off his wig, and show the scars where he had received the blows on his head, that he laid his damages at a thousand pounds, at times they produced such a giddiness, that it often prevented him from following his business. Here he refused, telling me, "You lie like a dog." Convinced he was only laying a trap for me, to take the law, I could have spit in his face; or, at the moment, resented such a reply. It was only law, and his advanced years, prevented me. The boys satisfied, and Redman's assertions refuted, the more rapidly I established my new situation; and, from a circumstance which turned out in my favour, no longer had I to contend against five.[118]

Despite Angelo's extremely unflattering portrayal of Redman, the Irish fencing master was still valued—or at least fondly remembered—by the king. In 1787, when Redman became imprisoned for debt, the monarch directly intervened upon his former instructor's behalf. Redman was released from prison, and his installment as a "poor Knight" was hailed in the London press:

The ceremony of the installation of a poor Knight was performed on Sunday last at Windsor, in Saint George's church, during divine service in the afternoon; he was introduced in the usual manner, between two of the junior knights; and being conducted to his Stall, his patent of creation was delivered to him.

The name of this gentleman is Redman, by profession a fencing master, and who taught his Majesty's father, as well as the present King, to fence. The manner in which this poor old gentleman (for he is in the 85th year of his age) was brought to his present comfortable situation, ought not to be kept from public notice; his Majesty, who some years back, had settled upon him

100 l. per annum, heard by accident he had been compelled to sell the annuity, and was a Prisoner for debt in the King's Bench prison; directions were therefore given from the King to liberate him from his confinement; and his Majesty, out of his own privy purse, having paid his creditors, gave him the place of poor Knight, which will enable him to end the remaining few days of his life in peace and comfort.[119]

Even towards the end of his days, Redman, it seems, was not without benefactors.

## WILLIAM O'BRIEN

William O'Brien belonged to a "very ancient" dynasty, lineally descended from (and named for) Brian Boru, the last High King of Ireland—and many of whose members were, during the early eighteenth century, "enthusiastic duellists."[120] According to *Colburn's Magazine*,

From attachment to their monarch and their religion, [the O'Brien family] abandoned their country and property after the capitulation of Limerick. On the defeat of the friends of James II, they followed the fortunes of this monarch into France, where under the auspices of the head of their family, [Daniel] O'Brien, Viscount Clare, they became officers in the Irish Brigade.[121]

Whatever the Jacobite leanings of his disinherited and outlawed forebears, by the mid-eighteenth century, William O'Brien had resigned himself to living and teaching in England. His earliest known fencing notice appeared in 1750 among the pages of the *General Advertiser*:

We heard, that Mr. Obrien, Fencing-Master, has open'd a School at the Rose Tavern, Temple-bar; and teaches also at the Pope's-head Tavern opposite the Royal-Exchange; and at his House in Devereux Court, Temple-bar.[122]

Later, in 1757, he was also teaching fencing at the Swan and Hoop Tavern in Lombard Street, Cornhill.[123] In a more extensive advertisement, published in 1760, O'Brien called out one of his apparent detractors, and lamented the fact that he was prohibited from challenging his declared enemy to a duel:

In Ball-Alley, George-Yard, Lombard-Street,
    A FENCING SCHOOL is kept by WILLIAM O'BRIEN, Where Gentlemen are in a short Time, and on reasonable Terms, made complete Masters of the Use of the Small Sword: And on Saturdays, in the Afternoon, Strangers are admitted to fence with his Scholars. And whereas a certain Gentleman of the same Profession, has on sundry Occasions made very free with the Character of the said William Obrien, and in particular has represented him to various Acquain-

W. O'Brien Esq.

William O'Brien the younger, born in County Clare. Portrait by Francis Cotes.

tances as unqualified to set up for a Fencing Master; this is to inform the envious Slanderer, that Mr. Wm. O'Brien thinks him unworthy of any further Notice and Correction than what is here bestowed upon him, because the malicious Detractor is lame; otherwise there would be more than one Method of getting Satisfaction from him.[124]

Three years later, in 1763, O'Brien is listed as teaching at Devereux-court, near Temple-bar.[125]

O'Brien's son, also named William, initially followed in his father's profession. According to various sources, the younger William had been born in County Clare, about the year 1736 or 1738.[126] For a time, according to Henry Angelo, the younger O'Brien worked as a fencing master in Ireland, before deciding to pursue a career of a different kind:

> Previous to going on the stage, O'Brien was a fencing-master, in Dublin. However, he *pushed* himself into the good opinions of his scholars. His manners and deportment very much contributed to that general notice to which he was entitled. Quitting the foil, he made a *point* to try the stage. Here it was remarked at the time, from his ease and *manière dégagée*, that he was superior to all his contemporaries, as the first gentleman actor. Even our late favourite, Lewis, of Covent Garden, was said to be far inferior to him.[127]

Portrait of William O'Brien the younger, painted by Sir Joshua Reynolds (1723-1792).

Another contemporary concurred with Angelo's description, stating that O'Brien "had a good and gentlemanly bearing, easy manners, grace and elegance, and in the conduct of his sword (as befitted the son of a fencing master) was unapproachable."[128]

The younger O'Brien made his theatrical debut in 1758. Taken under the wing of the famous actor and theatrical manager, David Garrick, O'Brien would become a noted actor and playwright. O'Brien's fencing skills evidently served him well on the stage, for his "intimate friend," Tate Wilkinson, recounted that the Irishman

> had more ease than any young or old actor I ever remember, and in drawing his sword he threw all other performers at a wonderful distance by his swiftness, ease, grace, and superior elegance; to him, was Mr. Garrick afterwards much indebted for the applause he received in Hamlet in the fencing scene with Laertes, as he performed that character, and there 'twas visible Mr. Garrick's pupil was the master.[129]

After continuing on the stage for six years, O'Brien married Lady Susan Sarah Louisa Strangeways, eldest daughter of Stephen Fox, the first Earl of Ilchester. Many contemporary British reports speak disparagingly of this union (which was virulently opposed by Fox) due to O'Brien's Catholicism, and of Lady Susan's so-called act of "marrying beneath her"—but, by all accounts, the marriage proved a happy one. After abiding in exile for a time in America, the couple returned to Britain, where O'Brien wrote and published a number of plays, including *The Duel*, based on the French *Le Philosophe Sans le Savoir* by Michel-Jean Sedaine.[130] O'Brien's English language adaptation, which featured the addition of Irish characters, played for one night only. According to *Colburn's*, "This piece deserved more success than it met with."

The younger O'Brien died at Stritford House, near Dorchester, in 1815, and was survived by his wife for more than a decade. A portrait of O'Brien by Sir Joshua Reynolds, and another oval painting by Francis Cotes (also reproduced in mezzotint by J. Watson), currently represent the only known surviving likenesses of an eighteenth century Dublin fencing master.[131]

# DR. KEYS

In his *Reminiscences*, Angelo makes note of yet another Irish swordsman named "Dr. Keys." Although supposedly "reputed the most expert fencer in Ireland," no other accounts of Keys's prowess have been found, either in Britain or in Ireland. Given Angelo's unflattering description of Keys's abilities, the reputation imparted to him seems undeserved. Nonetheless, Angelo's account of Keys, and of the Irishman's "public trial of skill" with Henry's famous father Domenico, is both colorful and highly detailed, and worth reprinting:

> On his return to London with his patron and friend, the Earl of Pembroke, [Domenico Angelo] received a card, inviting him to a public trial of skill with Dr. Keys, reputed the most expert fencer in Ireland. The challenge being accepted, the Thatched House tavern was appointed for the scene of action, where my father attended at the time prescribed, two o'clock, though he had been riding the whole morning at Lord Pembroke's. His lordship, with his accustomed condescension, walked into the apartment arm in arm with his friend and *protégé*. My father was not prepared, however, for such an assemblage, many ladies of rank and fashion, as well as noblemen and gentlemen, being present, and he, expecting only to meet with gentlemen, was in his riding dress, and in boots.
>
> My father, who had never seen his antagonist until this moment, was rather surprised at the doctor's appearance, he being a tall, athletic figure, wearing a huge wig, without his coat and waistcoat, his shirt sleeves tucked up, exposing a pair of brawny arms, sufficient to cope in the ring with Broughton or Slack; and thus equipped, with foil in hand, he was pacing the apartment.

The spectators being all assembled, after the first salutation from the doctor, which was sufficiently open and frank, previous to the *assault* he took a bumper of *Cogniac*, and offered another to my father, which he politely refused, not being accustomed to so ardent a provocative.

The doctor having thus spirited himself for the attack, began with that violence and determined method, which soon discovered to those who were skilled in the science, that, in the true sense of the term used by the French, he was no better than a *tirailleur*[*], *jeu de soldat*—Anglicised, a poker.

My father, to indulge him in his mode of assault, for some time, solely defended himself against his repeated attacks without receiving one hit; for, as the brandy operated, a *coup d'hasard*[†] in the doctor's favour would have only encouraged him the more. Hence, allowing his opponent to exhaust himself, and my father having sufficiently manifested his superior skill in the science, by thus acting on the defensive, with all the elegance and grace of attitude for which he was renowned, after having planted a dozen palpable hits on the breast of his enraged antagonist, he made his bow to the ladies, and retired amidst the plaudits of the spectators.

When two accomplished fencers exhibit their skill with the foil, the spectators, even who have no knowledge of the science, may easily discover the superior adroitness in the defence than in the attack. Place the foil in the hand of the rudest fellow, having no pointed sword opposed to him to check his rashness, he will run on his adversary, and after reiterated efforts may succeed and plant his thrust. It is one thing to play with foils, guarded with a button, and another to stand opposed to a naked weapon...

I have ever found from the experience...of others, and from my own, that the best fencers could rarely shine with bad ones, who are invariably overbearing and rash. My father's coolness and address, on this and other public occasions, may be instanced, as the most memorable exceptions upon record. It was soon after this public display of his superior science, that the elder Angelo, urged by his friends, first commenced teacher of the science of fencing.[132]

Of Dr. Keys, nothing more is known.

## TREATISES BY IRISH FENCING MASTERS

At least two Irish fencing masters who taught abroad are known primarily from their writings on the art of fencing: Alexander Doyle and Daniel O'Sullivan.[133] Doyle, according to his writings, was an Irishman who served as fencing master to the court of Elector Lothar Franz von Schönborn in Mainz, as well as in Nuremberg, Bavaria, during the early eighteenth

---

[*]  *Tirailleur*: "This word originally meant a bad shot. It now signifies a soldier who fires as he pleases. TIRAILLER, *Fr.* To pester, to annoy. Hence the word *Tirailleur.*" Charles James, *A New and Enlarged Military Dictionary* (London: T. Egerton, 1802).

[†]  *Coup de hasard*: A French idiom meaning "a hit by mere chance."

Plates from Alexander Doyle's German-language treatise, *Neu Alamodische Ritterliche Fecht- und Schirm-Kunst.*

century. Doyle's German-language treatise about the "New Fashionable Knightly Fencing," or *Neu Alamodische Ritterliche Fecht- und Schirm-Kunst*, was first published in 1715, then again in 1716, and again, in a third edition, in 1729. Copiously illustrated with more than sixty figures, the text treats exclusively of the use of the small-sword, which Doyle claimed to have "now perfected in both the French and Italian manner."[134] Despite Doyle's mention of Italian influence, the fencing method presented in his treatise is overwhelmingly French in terms of technique. An additional volume, also authored by Doyle, illustrates various methods of vaulting and gymnastics.[135]

As to the origins of Daniel O'Sullivan, some information can be gleaned from the record of his arrest, which occurred in 1742, when the French authorities mistook him to be of Spanish or Portuguese extraction. O'Sullivan was, however—as his surname resoundingly proclaims— quite Irish. He was born about 1710, and had previously served as a *prévôt* in the *salle d'armes* of the French fencing master Ledroit. In 1751, O'Sullivan arrived in the town of Angers, where he presented a diploma—personally signed by King Louis XV—which stipulated that O'Sullivan was the only person permitted to open a *salle d'armes* in the entire village. O'Sullivan later traveled to Paris, and on July 16, 1765, was received as a fencing master—or, more specifically, as a *maître en fait d'armes des académies du Roi*. That same year, he also published his fencing treatise, entitled, *l'Escrime pratique, principes de la science des armes*.[136]

According to Egerton Castle, O'Sullivan was a "most orthodox master," whose treatise "calls for no especial notice beyond the fact that he is the first author to give the modern names of 'demi-cercle' and octave to the two parries in low lines with the hand in supination."[137] Castle may have been correct about O'Sullivan's use of *octave*, but was incorrect regarding his use of the *demi-cercle*, which is mentioned in earlier French treatises.[138] Additionally, O'Sullivan's text is notable for its dismissal of the *volt* (which the author declares, "is only occasionally used as a dirty trick") and for its brief discussion of "secret thrusts" (*bottes secrètes*), which O'Sullivan soundly ridicules, explaining, "The greater part of those Masters who write about the Science of Arms only boast about these pretend secret thrusts and they speak with great praise of them which degrades the judgment of those who hold these opinions." Nevertheless, despite this view, O'Sullivan includes a description of the "night attack" (*botte de nuit*), which, when used, "the result...will be that he who is attacking will throw himself on his Adversary's sword through his head, the point of which will come through about one foot."[139] O'Sullivan concludes his treatise by stating his intentions as well as his future hopes for his students, explaining:

> I wish all the amateurs for whom I write give me the benefit of thinking that I seek less to dazzle than to instruct. My intention is to prove the possibility of creating a Student inside a year in a

state where he can not only defend his life but also have the same intent of an Art which is not only easy to practice but can also be thought of highly.[140]

The fencing texts of both Doyle and O'Sullivan treat of purely foreign methods of fence, written by men who had trained in those foreign methods. Similarly, as already discussed, Andrew Mahon's *Art of Fencing* is largely a translation of a foreign work—its only original component being Mahon's short, introductory preface. As interesting and educational as these treatises are, none of them offer much insight into the fencing practices that existed in eighteenth century Ireland.

It was not until 1781 that an original and more distinctly *Irish* treatise on the art and science of fencing would appear on the shelves of Dublin's booksellers. Most importantly, the publication of this particular text would give rise to the most celebrated Irish fencing society of the eighteenth century, and perhaps of all time—a subject worthy of its own chapter.

---

1   Jonah Barrington, *Personal Sketches, Volume II*, 7-8.

2   Examples of Belfast masters not mentioned elsewhere in this chapter include "Mr. King" and "Mr. Galwey." The former is described in Belfast's *Northern Star* of January 14, 1796 as teaching the "genteel and manly science" at the "Market-House." As for the latter, Mr. Galwey (or Gallway), offered "sword instruction," also at the Market House, according to issues of the *Belfast News-Letter* published on May 4, 1781, and December 18, 1789. As for Cork masters, the *Cork Mercantile Chronicle*, of April 18, 1803, informs us that Mr. Mullins "teaches the ART of FENCING, the USE of the SMALLSWORD, &c.— He has had the honour of instructing some of the first Characters, both in ENGLAND and IRELAND, for the space of twenty-seven Years. It is supposed, that young Gentlemen who intend wearing Swords, should know the Use of the Weapons they wear. N.B.—MULLINS is to be met with at his House in William-street."

3   The French Dubois was portrayed by Hogarth in the second picture of *The Rake's Progress* series, now in the Soane Museum, Lincoln's Inn Fields. Godfrey described Dubois as "one of the most charming Figures on the Floor I ever beheld," and recalled a match between Dubois and a colleague as "one of the finest Matches I ever saw." J. D. Aylward, *The English master of arms from the twelfth to the twentieth century* (London, Routledge & Paul [1956]), 190.

4   *Ipswich Journal*, May 11, 1734. The French master Dubois did not, unfortunately, survive this encounter.

5   Donald McBane, *The Expert Sword-Man's Companion: Or the True Art of Self-Defence. With an Account of the Authors Life, and his Transactions during the Wars with France. To which is Annexed, the Art of Gunnerie* (Glasgow: J. Duncan, 1728) 128-129.

6   Henry Blackwell, *The Gentleman's Tutor for the Small Sword: Or, The Compleat English Fencing Master* (London: Printed for J. and T.W., 1730), 49.

7   A Citizen of London, *A Description of the City of Dublin in Ireland* (London: Printed, and sold by the author, 1732), 16-17.

8   *Public Register or the Freeman's Journal*, February 16, 1771. This duel is described in many histories of dueling and period accounts, such as *The Gentleman's Magazine, and Historical Chronicle*, January, 1771. Captain Kelly is identified as "Captain Redmond Kelly" in Henry Walrond's *Historical Records of the 1st Devon Militia* (New

York: Longmans, Green and Company, 1897), 68.

9  "Commercial publishing was in a poor way in Ireland [during the seventeenth century] just then. In a letter to Sir Charles Wogan (in 1732) Jonathan Swift observed 'They [books] cannot be printed here with the least profit to the author's friends in distress. Dublin booksellers have not the least notion of paying for a copy. Sometimes things are printed here by subscription; but they go on so heavily that few or none make it turn to account.'" Paul Jordan-Smith, foreword to *Amiable Renegade: The Memoirs of Captain Peter Drake, 1671-1753* (Stanford University Press, 1960), xi.

10  The sole exception being Francis Sherlock, who taught at "Charing-Cross Coffee-house." *General Advertiser*, February 8, 1750.

11  In 1692, the Scottish fencing master William Hope noted, "Mr. *Machrie*, at present Judge and Arbitrator in all Tryalls of Skill...is not only a great Master of the Small, but also understandeth the Art of the Broad or Back-Sword to perfection: so that I have seen several *English & Irish* who pretended to be publick Gladiators so baffled by him, when out of civility he presented them in his School with a Cudgel, that any Artist would have judged them to have been but the Scholars, and him the Master, as he indeed was but too much, considering the advantage his just and smart play had over theirs..." William Hope, *The Fencing-master's Advice to His Scholar: Or, A Few Directions for the More Regular Assaulting in Schools* (Edinburgh: John Reid, 1692), 30-31.

12  *A Few Observations Upon the Fighting for Prizes in the Bear Gardens, By a Lover and Well-wisher, not only to the True and Useful Art of the SWORD, but also to the Safety and Security of the Persons of those Brave, Courageous, and Bold Performers in these publick Places, for Trial of Skill in this Gentlemanly Art* (London: 1715), 6.

13  Andrew Mahon, *The Art of Fencing, or, the Use of the Small Sword. Translated from the French of of the late celebrated Monsieur L'Abbat; Master of that Art at the Academy of Toulouse* (Dublin: Printed by James Hoey, at the Sign of Mercury in Skinner-Row, 1734), iv.

14  *Belfast News-Letter*, December 18, 1789. A fuller transcription reads: "GALLWAY, *Fencing-Master*, RETURNS his sincere thanks to the Gentlemen of Belfast, for the repeated Instances of encouragement he has met with since his commencement as Fencing-Master in this town—that having from a series of years practice, acquired a perfect knowledge of that noble Science, which has been deemed in the present enlightened age, the master-piece of art—and having had the honour of teaching Gentlemen of the first consequence in the country, who can vouch for his abilities, still solicits for a continuance of their favour...Any Gentlemen residing within a few miles of Belfast, who would wish to be taught Fencing, GALLWAY shall be very punctual in his attendance on them."

15  *Saunders's News-Letter*, July 6, 1784.

16  For instance, see Tate Wilkinson's account of Cornelius Kelly, quoted later in this chapter.

17  The earliest use of the term *pionnsa* that we have been able to find appears in the seventeenth century poem, "Aiste Dhaíbhí Cúndún," reprinted in Cecile O'Rahilly, *Five seventeenth-century political poems* (Baile Átha Cliath: Institiúid Árd-Léinn Bhaile Átha Cliath, 1952), 47. For the use of this term and other fencing-related words in eighteenth century Irish, see Edward Lhuyd, *Focloir Gaoidheilge-Shagsonach: an Irish-English Dictionary* (Oxford: 1707); Hugh Mac Curtin, *The Elements of the Irish Language: Grammatically Explained in English* (Lovain: M. van Overbeke, 1728); Conchobhar O Beaglaoich, *The English Irish Dictionary. An focloir bearla gaoioheilge ar na chur a neagur le Conchobhar O Beaglaoich mar aon le congnamh Aodh bhuidhe Mac Cuirtin* (A bPairis: Seamus Geurin, 1732); John O'Brien, *Focalóir gaoidhilge-sax-bhéarla, or An Irish-English dictionary* (Paris: Printed by N. F. Valleyre, for the author, 1768); Thaddeus Connellan, *An English-Irish Dictionary intended to be used in schools with over eight thousand definitions* (Dublin: Graisberry and Campbell, 1814); Edward O'Reilly, *Sanas Gaoidhilge-Sagsbhearla: An Irish-English dictionary* (Dublin: J. Barlow, 1817); *Dictionary of the Irish language: based mainly on old and middle Irish materials. Published by the Royal Irish Academy, under the editorship of Carl J.S. Marstrander* (Dublin: Royal Irish Academy, 1913); Niall Ó Dónaill, *Foclóir Gaeilge-Béarla* (Baile Átha Cliath: Oifig An tSoláthair, 1977).

18 Fencing masters from Italy would not teach in Ireland until just after the turn of the nineteenth century; the first such recorded example appears to be "L. Albani, a native of Verona, educated at Rome and Sienna," who began teaching "Fencing, Counter-point, and Small Sword" in Dublin in 1804. *Saunders's News-Letter*, April 27, 1804.

19 *Saunders's News-Letter*, November 3, 1784.

20 *Limerick Reporter and Tipperary Vindicator*, March 24, 1882.

21 *A vindication of the Irish Earl of Bath: on occasion of the groundless imputations, malevolent insinuations, and unmannerly expostulations of a pretended Quaker: an answer to said Quaker's letters, etc.* (Dublin: 1755), 8-9.

22 *Dublin Courier*, November 1, 1762.

23 *Dublin Intelligence*, December 5, 1710.

24 John Thomas Gilbert, *A history of the city of Dublin* (Dublin: J. McGlashan, 1854), 11.

25 *Dublin Journal*, March 18, 1758, April 11, 1758.

26 *Hoey's Dublin Mercury*, September 24, 1771.

27 Examples of these "lost" anonymous masters include those referred to by Donald McBane and James Pardon, who are quoted elsewhere in this chapter.

28 John O'Keeffe, *Recollections of the life of John O'Keeffe*, Volume 2 (New York: B. Blom, 1826), 137-138.

29 Peter Drake, *The Memoirs of Capt. Peter Drake: Containing, an Account of Many Strange and Surprising Events, which Happened to Him Through a Series of Sixty Years, and Upwards; and Several Material Anecdotes, Regarding King William and Queen Anne's Wars with Lewis XIV of France* (Dublin: S. Powell, 1755), 29-31.

30 Donald McBane, *The Expert Sword-Man's Companion: Or the True Art of Self-Defence. With an Account of the Authors Life, and his Transactions during the Wars with France. To which is Annexed, the Art of Gunnerie* (Glasgow: J. Duncan, 1728), 92.

31 Barrington, *Personal Sketches, Vol. II*, 8.

32 McBane, 93-94.

33 "Just arrived from Paris, Mr John Russell who will teach the French and use of the small sword—at Mr Edward Russell's at 'The Bear' near the Market House." *Limerick Chronicle*, December 16, 1771. During the late eighteenth century, "Francis O'Connor, Fencing-Master," hung a memorable sign outside his Limerick business, depicting swords crossed. *Limerick Reporter and Tipperary Vindicator*, March 24, 1882.

34 Monsieur Valdin, *The Art of Fencing, as Practised by Monsieur Valdin* (London: J. Parker in Pall-Mall, 1729), 15.

35 J. D. Aylward, *The English master of arms from the twelfth to the twentieth century* (London, Routledge & Paul [1956]), 186-187.

36 Andrew Mahon, *The Art of Fencing, or, the Use of the Small Sword. Translated from the French of of the late celebrated Monsieur L'Abbat; Master of that Art at the Academy of Toulouse* (Dublin: Printed by James Hoey, at the Sign of Mercury in Skinner-Row, 1734).

37 Aylward, 224.

38 James Underwood, *Draw Not Your Sword But to Serve the King, Preserve Your Honour, or Defend your Life: The Art of Fencing; or the Use of the Small Sword* (Dublin: Printed by T. Byrne, Parliament-street, 1787); James Underwood, *Draw Not Your Sword But to Serve the King, Preserve Your Honour, or Defend your Life: The Art of Fencing; or the Use of the Small Sword* (Dublin: Printed by William Porter, 69 Grafton Street, 1798).

39 *Dublin Journal*, October 25 to 28, 1746.

40 *Dublin Journal*, November 7 to 10, 1747.

41 Tate Wilkinson, *Memoirs of His Own Life* (York: Printed for the Author, 1790), Volume 3, 177, Volume 1, 8-14.

42  John Thomas Gilbert, *A History of the City of Dublin, Volume 1* (Dublin: Hodges and Smith, 1854), 90.

43  John O'Keeffe, *Recollections of the Life of John O'Keeffe: In Two Volumes, Volume 1* (London: Henry Colburn, 1826), 137.

44  William B. Kelly, T*he Irish Quarterly Review, First Series in Three Volumes, Volume 2* (Dublin: William B. Kelly, 8, Grafton Street, 1852), 326.

45  Henry Angelo, *Reminiscences with Memoirs of His Late Father and Friends, Including Numerous Original Anecdotes and Curious Traits of the Most Celebrated Characters that Have Flourished During the Last Eighty Years, Volume 2* (London: Henry Colburn and Richard Bentley, 1830), 300.

46  *The Gentleman's Magazine*, Volume LXXXVIII, Part II, (London: John Nicholas & Son, 1818), 21. Account book of Ralph Howard, Baron Clonmore, Viscount Wicklow, 1748-9, NLI, Wicklow Papers, MS 1725.

47  *Dublin Journal*, January 31 to February 3, 1747.

48  At least one nineteenth century source declares that William Kelly (the same who was teaching in 1746) was the *son* of Cornelius; however, given the obvious issues of the men's respective ages, this seems impossible. See Kelly, 52.

49  *Freeman's Daily Journal*, December 11-15, 1750.

50  *Dublin Journal*, December 18, 1750.

51  *Dublin Evening Post*, December 11, 1781. "LOUGHREA SCHOOL. Pat. Prendergast begs leave to inform the Public, that his young Gentlemen are now regularly attended by Mr. Dominic Kelly in Fencing..." *Dublin Evening Post*, January 7, 1783.

52  *Pue's Occurences*, October 11, 1757.

53  "CORNELIUS KELLY, being informed by several Gentlemen, that many retailers of Liquors in the Country, particularly the Counties of Galway and Roscommon report, that the Shrub which they sell, is made by him. This Notice he therefore gives, lest Gentlemen should be further imposed upon, that he will...send every retailer, to whom he shall sell Shrub, a Certificate signed by himself on the Back of the Permit, from the Land-Permit Office, Dublin; and as the Quantity and Time of sending it are specified in the Permit, Gentlemen will be able to judge whether the Shrub be really his own. The said Cornelius Kelly has opened his Fencing School in the Stationer's-hall on Cork hill, and will teach on Mondays, Wednesdays, and Fridays, in said Hall." *Dublin Journal*, October 14, 1746.

54  *Lloyd's Evening Post and British Chronicle*, November 7 to 9, 1757.

55  *Dublin Mercury*, October 21 to 24, 1769.

56  Henry Angelo, *Reminiscences with Memoirs of His Late Father and Friends, Including Numerous Original Anecdotes and Curious Traits of the Most Celebrated Characters that Have Flourished During the Last Eighty Years, Volume 2* (London: Henry Colburn and Richard Bentley, 1830), 299-301.

57  *Hoey's Dublin Mercury*, September 22 to 25, 1770.

58  *Public Register or the Freeman's Journal*, October 4 to 6, 1770.

59  *Saunders's News Letter*, January 10, 1774.

60  *Dublin Journal*, November 19, 1774.

61  Donald M. Schlegel, *Irish Genealogical Abstracts from the "Londonderry Journal," 1772-1784* (Baltimore: Genealogical Publishing Co., 2009), 59.

62  *Dublin Journal*, November 16, 1779.

63  *Wilson's Dublin Directory* (Dublin: Printed for William Wilson), for the years 1774, 1776, 1777, 1780 and 1783.

64  For a full account of the controversy between Dwyer and Kelly, see Part II of this book, "Introduction: On the Authorship of *A Few Mathematical and Critical Remarks on the Sword*."

65  *Belfast News-Letter*, January 10, 1766.

66  *Saunders's News Letter*, February 7, 1784; *Hibernian Journal*, September 27, 1776.

67  Tate Wilkinson, *Memoirs of His Own Life* (York: Printed for the Author, 1790), Volume 2, 290.

68  *Saunders's News-Letter*, June 3, 1783.

69  This same Henry Mossop had, in 1769, fought an actual duel on the stage of his own Dublin theatre, with an audience member who "would not accede to his request." Peter Kavanagh, *The Irish theatre: being a history of the drama in Ireland from the earliest period up to the present day* (Tralee: The Kerryman limited, 1946), 290.

70  Tate Wilkinson, *Memoirs of His Own Life* (York: Printed for the Author, 1790), Volume 2, 289-95, Volume 3, 177, Volume 1, 8-14. Further information about the Reverend Thomas Wilson (1726-1799) can be found in *Alumni dublinenses: a register of the students, graduates, professors and provosts of Trinity college in the University of Dublin,1593-1860* (Dublin: A. Thom & co., ltd., 1935), 888.

71  *The Gentleman's Magazine*, Volume LXXXVIII, Part II, (London: John Nicholas & Son, 1818), 21.

72  *Saunders's News-Letter*, October 7, 1794, September 22, 1795, September 28, 1795.

73  *Dublin Evening Post*, January 6, 1781.

74  *Hibernian Journal; or, Chronicle of Liberty*, March 18, 1776.

75  *Reading Mercury and Oxford Gazette*, September 16, 1771.

76  Angelo, *Reminiscences, Volume 2*, 92.

77  *Public Advertiser*, May 29, 1764.

78  *Morning Post and Daily Advertiser*, December 4, 1777.

79  *Gazetteer and New Daily Advertiser*, March 20, 1770.

80  *Independent Chronicle*, March 12, 1770.

81  *Gazetteer and New Daily Advertiser*, March 21, 1770.

82  *Dublin Mercury*, April 14 to 17, 1770.

83  *Virginia Gazette*, May 24, 1770.

84  *Hibernian Journal; or, Chronicle of Liberty*, March 18, 1776.

85  *Saunders's News-Letter*, January 2, 1779.

86  *Dublin Evening Post*, January 6, 1781.

87  For a full account of the controversy between Dwyer and Kelly, see Part II of this book, "Introduction: On the Authorship of *A Few Mathematical and Critical Remarks on the Sword*."

88  *Dublin Evening Post*, January 6, 1781.

89  *Saunders's News-Letter*, February 17, 1785.

90  *Gazetteer and New Daily Advertiser*, December 7, 1776.

91  *Morning Chronicle and London Advertiser*, March 19, 1778.

92  *Morning Post and Daily Advertiser*, April 8, 1778.

93  *Morning Post and Daily Advertiser*, April 10, 1778.

94  "Notice is hereby given, that the Partnership between us, the under-named John Redman and James Pardon, late of Chancery-lane, Fencing-masters, was dissolved on the 2d Day of this instant February. All Persons indebted to the said John Redman and James Pardon are desired to pay their respective Debts to Mr. Robert Harper, at his Academy, Harley-street, Cavendish-square, who only is authorized to receive and adjust the same. Witness our Hands, *John Redman. James Pardon.*" *London Gazette*, February 12, 1780.

95  *Morning Chronicle and London Advertiser*, December 3, 1781.

96 Henry Angelo, *Angelo's pic nic, or, Table talk: including numerous recollections of public characters, who have figured in some part or another of the stage of life for the last fifty years: forming an endless variety of talent, amusement, and interest, calculated to please every person fond of biographical sketches and anecdotes* (London: J. Ebers, 1834), 360-363.

97 *Dublin Evening Post*, October 22, 1785.

98 *Dublin Evening Post*, April 29, 1783. For a full account of the Knights of Tara, see Chapter VI.

99 *Belfast News-Letter*, May 16, 1788.

100 *A full report of the trial at bar, in the court of King's bench, in which the Right Hon. Arthur Wolfe, His Majesty's attorney general, prosecuted, and A. H. Rowan, esq. was defendant, on an information filed ex officio against the defendant for having published a seditious libel. January 29, 1794.* (Perth: R. Morison and Son, 1794), 19-20.

101 *The World*, September 9, 1793.

102 John C. Greene, *Theatre in Dublin, 1745–1820: A Calendar of Performances* (Bethlehem: Lehigh University Press, 2011 ), 2851-2877.

103 *Saunders's News-Letter*, January 27, 1797.

104 Barrington, *Personal Sketches, Vol. I*, 57.

105 *Daily Advertiser*, October 10, 1743.

106 *Dublin Evening Post*, February 11, 1794.

107 *Dublin Evening Post*, February 13, 1794.

108 *Saunders's News-Letter*, May 2, 1818.

109 Angelo, *Reminiscences, Vol. 2*, 298-299.

110 *Virginia Gazette*, May 22, 1779, and Fairfax Harrison, *The Virginia Carys, An Essay in Genealogy* (New York: The De Vinne Press, 1919), 158.

111 Irish fencing masters listed for this year include William O'Brien, Francis Sherlock, and John Redman. See Thomas Mortimer, *The universal director; or, the nobleman and gentleman's true guide to the masters and professors of the liberal and polite arts and sciences* (London: Printed for J. Coote, in Pater-noster-row, MDCCLXIII), 3, 16, 18, 20, 24, 25, 27.

112 *Public Advertiser*, January 25, 1764; *Caledonian Mercury*, August 16, 1755; *General Advertiser*, February 8, 1750; Angelo, Volume 2, 224.

113 *Derby Mercury*, January 26, 1753.

114 *Caledonian Mercury*, February 27, 1743; *Boston News-Letter*, May 10, 1753; Mortimer, 32.

115 Aylward, 199. See also the 1774 voting record for "John Redman, Fencing Master" in Westminster Pollbooks: Votes in Westminster Elections, 1749-1820 1st January 1774 - 31st December 1774, *London Lives, 1690-1800*, pollbook_148-14835 (www.londonlives.org, version 1.1, 17 June 2012), Westminster Archives Centre.

116 *Public Advertiser*, March 31, 1770.

117 Angelo, *Reminiscences, Volume 2*, 265-266.

118 Angelo, *Angelo's pic nic*, 358-360.

119 *The European Magazine: And London Review*, April, 1787.

120 James Kelly, *That Damn'd Thing Called Honour* (Cork: Cork University Press, 1995), 48.

121 *Colburn's New Monthly Magazine*, October 1, 1815.

122 *General Advertiser*, March 4, 1750.

123 *Public Advertiser*, December 16, 1757.

124 *Public Ledger or Daily Register of Commerce and Intelligence*, January 22, 1760.

125 Mortimer, 28.

126 *The Dublin University Magazine*, May, 1855. See also Robert Herbert, *The Worthies of Thomond*, II (Limerick: 1944).

127 Angelo, *Reminiscences, Volume 2*, 270.

128 Robert Herbert, *The Worthies of Thomond*, II (Limerick: 1944).

129 Tate Wilkinson, *Memoirs of His Own Life, Volume 2* (York: Printed for the Author, 1790), 5, 9-10.

130 William O'Brien, *The duel: A play, as performed at the Theatre-Royal in Drury-Lane* (London, 1772). *A Biographical Dictionary of the Living Authors of Great Britain and Ireland* (London: Printed for Henry Colburn, 1816), 443.

131 *Deuxième Catalogue De La Galerie Charles Brunner, 11 Rue Royale, Paris* (Paris: Moreau, 1910). *Colburn's New Monthly Magazine*, October 1, 1815.

132 Henry Angelo, *Reminiscences with Memoirs of His Late Father and Friends, Including Numerous Original Anecdotes and Curious Traits of the Most Celebrated Characters that Have Flourished During the Last Eighty Years, Volume I* (London: Henry Colburn and Richard Bentley, 1830), 100-103.

133 Some writers have speculated than Andrew Lonnergan, author of *The Fencer's Guide* (London: W. Griffin, 1771), was also Irish—and indeed, "Lonergan" is an Anglicized old Gaelic name prevalent in County Tipperary. However, to date, no evidence has yet been found (or presented) to indicate that Andrew Lonnergan, the fencing author and instructor, was ever in Ireland.

134 English translation by Elani Koogle. See Alexander Doyle, *Neu Alamodische Ritterliche Fecht- und Schirm-Kunst: Das ist: Wahre und nach neuester Frantzösischer Manier eingerichtete Unterweisung Wie man sich in Fechten und Schirmen perfectioniren und verhalten solle; Denen respective Herren Liebhaberen zu besserer Erleuterung mit 60 hierzu dienlichen Figuren herausgegeben* (Nürnberg: P. Lochner, 1715).

135 Alexander Doyle, *Kurtze und deutliche Auslegung Der Voltagier-Kunst Sowol Denen Meistern als Scholaren nützlich, Indeme Es nicht nur allein die vortheilhafftigsten Handgriffe, sondern auch die schönsten darzu dienlichen Maniren und Stellungen deutlich lehret und zeiget, daß einer dardurch in kurtzer Zeit capabel seyn kan, solche zu practiciren; Und also füglich der andere Theil, der auch unlängst heraus gegebenen Fecht- und Schirm-Kunst, kan genennet werden* (Nürnberg: P. Lochner, 1720).

136 Lionel Lauvernay, *L'Escrime Pratique & Daniel O'Sullivan* (Ensiludium, 2009).

137 Egerton Castle, *Schools and masters of fence, from the Middle Ages to the eighteenth century* (London: G. Bell & Sons, 1885), 160.

138 For instance, the *demi-cercle* is mentioned by Gérard Gordine in his *Principes et quintessence des armes* (Liége: S. Bourguignon, 1754).

139 Daniel O'Sullivan, *The Practice of Fencing, Or the principles of the science of arms*, trans. Phillip T. Crawley (Raleigh: Lulu Press, 2012), 16-17. Original French from Daniel O'Sullivan, *L'Escrime Pratique, ou Principes de la Science des Armes. Par Daniel O'Sullivan, Maître en Fait d'Armes des Académies du Roi* (Paris: Chez Sébastien Jorry, imprimeur-libraire, rue, et vis-a-vis de la Comédie Francaise, au Grand Monarque, 1765).

140 Ibid.

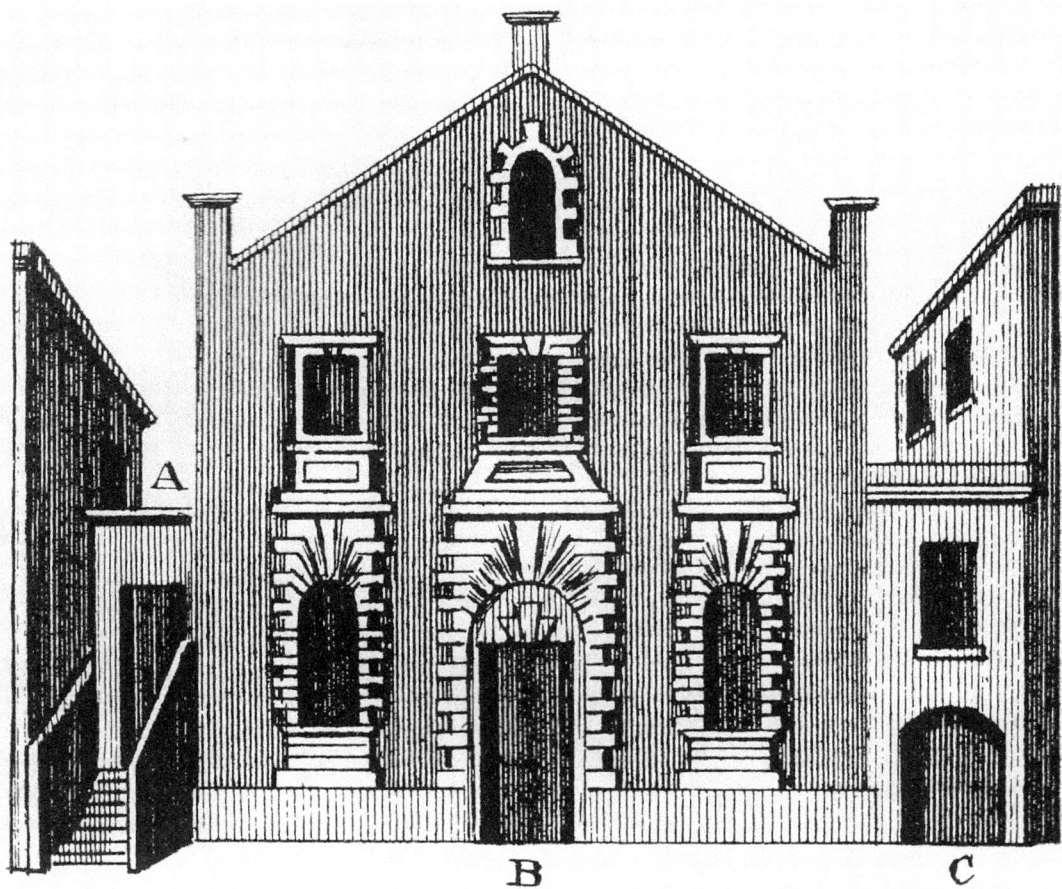

The Theatre Royale in Smock Alley, Dublin, as it appeared during the eighteenth century. Also known as the Smock Alley Theatre, this edifice was the setting for fencing exhibitions held by the Knights of Tara.

# VI

## THE KNIGHTS *of* TARA

*"We bind ourselves by all the sacred Ties of Honour..."*

In 1781, a mysterious book appeared in Dublin, published under the modest title, *A Few Mathematical and Critical Remarks on the Sword.*[1] Among its one-hundred and fourteen pages, the author, who deigned to remain anonymous, treated extensively of the art and science of fencing—and, toward his conclusion, called for the formation of a "society of gentlemen" to be specifically instituted "for the encouragement of this art"—that is, for the encouragement of fencing.

Approximately two years later, in the spring of 1783, the the call was heeded, and thus was born the most celebrated fencing society that Ireland has ever known—the Knights of Tara. This distinguished group would bring together some of Ireland's highest-ranking nobility with its greatest amateur fencers, and would include its most feared duelist. Although the association was relatively short-lived, the Knights were the culmination of an official alliance between fencing experts and authorities on dueling that was without parallel in eighteenth century Ireland and Britain. Most importantly, one of its members would go on to have an indelible impact on the history of fencing in the British Isles.

\* \* \*

When they first appeared in March, 1783, the Knights of Tara announced that they had been reconstituted from another order—the Knights of Saint Patrick, formed only a few months prior in 1782. An announcement by the Knights of Tara, published in the *Dublin Evening Post*, explained how the change in name came about:

> WHEREAS it appears from the Proceedings of this Society, that on the 10th of December, 1782, several gentlemen of this Kingdom, not only distinguished for their public Spirit, personal Intrepidity and Dexterity in the Use of Arms, but actuated by the most laudable Motives of employing those Endowments to noble Purposes, formed an Association under the Title of KNIGHTS OF St. PATRICK. This Title they bore until the 17th of March 1783, when, from a Principle of the most profound Deference to his Majesty, the Fountain of Honour, who had been pleased to dignify, with the aforesaid Title, several of the full Nobility of Ireland, this Society relinquished their original Name and assumed that of THE KNIGHTS OF TARA.[2]

The above statement seems to imply that, with the King's creation of the new Knights of St. Patrick in 1783, two groups were at that time simultaneously operating under this same name. The second Knights of St. Patrick were described as an "Order of Chivalry" consisting of only sixteen members, which restricted its membership to men who were both knights and gentlemen—the latter being defined as having three generations of "noblesse" on both their father's and mother's side.[3] In contrast to the original knights formed the year prior, this second group does not seem to have had any expressed connection to fencing or dueling. Thus, in order to avoid confusion between the two groups, and in "deference" to the King's newest creation, the earlier group chose to relinquish their name.

The new name taken by the original group, the "Knights of Tara," was inspired by the Hill of Tara (in Irish, *Cnoc na Teamhrach*, or *Teamhair na Rí*), an ancient Neolithic archaeological complex more than five thousand years old—located near the River Boyne in County Meath, and deeply connected with Irish myth and legend. According to tradition, Tara was the original seat of the High Kings of Ireland, as well as the site of coronations, parliamentary gatherings, and religious rites. Even more importantly, it was a place where the ancient knights (or chivalric orders) were created, trained, and made to receive their honors and rewards. The Knights founded in 1782 may well have taken inspiration from Sylvester O'Halloran's *A General History of Ireland*, which had been published only a few years prior in 1778, and which provided many details extracted from legend regarding the various ancient orders:

> There were five equestrian orders in Ireland—the first was the Niagh-Nase, or knights of the Golden Collar; and this order was peculiar to the blood royal, as without it, no prince could presume to become candidate for the monarchy...Of the other orders of chivalry, the Curaithe na

Craobh-ruadh, or knights of Ulster, for number, prowess, and discipline, seem to rank foremost in our history. Why they have been always distinguished by the name of Craobh-ruadh, or of the Red Branch, is not said...The Clana-Deagha, or Munster knights, were a most intrepid order of men...The Leinster knights were called Clana-Baoisgne, from Baoisgne, an ancestor of the celebrated Fion, who reformed and gave new laws to them. Their ensign was the same of the same province, i. e. "Jupiter, an harp, Sol, "stringed Luna." The knights of Conaught, in these early days, were of the Danaan race, and yielded not the palm, in point of courage and discipline, to any heroes in Europe.[4]

According to O'Halloran's history, ancient military academies were formed at Tara, into which the knights entered for instruction in various combative arts:

The utmost care [was] taken of [the knights'] education, and of their military rules. Academies, at the national expence, were founded for them (like the royal military military school of Paris) at Tara, Emania, Cashell, Cruachan, Naas, &c. The candidate was entered at seven years old, when a slender launce was put in his hand, and a sword by his side...At the use of the sword and target they were uncommonly skilful; and they fought on foot, on horseback, or in chariots, according to their situation and circumstances.

   At eighteen they took their last vows; and from the accounts of this order of men, still pretty well preserved, we are surprised how elevated their sentiments were, and their ideas of honour and heroism. To swear by their knighthood, was the most sacred oath, as it at once reminded them of all their vows.[5]

In perusing such passages, it seems clear that by changing the second part of their name to *Tara*, the group of knights formed in 1782 were attempting to draw a connection between themselves and the most romantic elements of Irish mythology, legend, and martial history.[6] As a poem published in Ireland during the early 1780s proclaimed,

> *GLORIOUS Tara! Ireland's pride!*
>    *Seat of antient heroes hail!*
>    *Still may thy auspicious side*
>    *Swell the lisping children's tale!*[7]

The expressed object of the new Knights of Tara was twofold. By their own proclamation, they were a "society instituted for the encouragement of the Science of Defence with the Sword," as outlined in their first set of published resolutions:

That a more general cultivation of the Science of Defence...should therefore be looked on as an additional fort towards securing the advantages already obtained.

That abstracting however from these considerations, the Sword should be worn for defence, as well as ornament, so as that no Irish Gentleman may be in the predicament of the man covered with the ostentatious dust of books, and yet found ignorant of the alphabet.

And whereas other kinds of military and manly exercises have been studiously cultivated here, whilst the most martial, spirited, salutary, and certainly momentous to the individuals whose existences may be at stake, viz. That the Sword has been heretofore, in our judgment, unaccountably neglected.

For the furtherance of these motives, the Knights of Tara thus resolved, "for the encouragement of this science," to offer three annual prize swords "to the three ablest and best fencers," noting that "foreign noblemen and gentlemen, although not members, may be candidates for the prizes."[8] The Knights were, therefore, not an insular organization, but—in the interests of education and propagation—one which invited outsiders into their midst. In addition to awarding prize swords, the amount of admission money was to be "laid out on silver cups, and given to the best fencers as prizes, at quarterly exhibitions of pupils and amateurs."[9]

## THE REFORMATION OF DUELING

The Knights of Tara had another motive, however, that was deemed just as important as—if not more so than—its encouragement of fencing: that is, the regulation of the duel. Jonah Barrington summarized how this plan came about:

At length, so many quarrels arose without sufficiently dignified provocation, and so many things were considered quarrels of course, which were not quarrels at all, that the principal fire-eaters of the south saw clearly disrepute was likely to be thrown on both the science and its professors, and thought it full time to interfere and arrange matters upon a proper, steady, rational, and moderate footing; and to regulate the time, place, and other circumstances of dueling, so as to govern all Ireland on one principle—thus establishing a uniform, national code of the *lex pugnandi*—proving, as Hugo Grotius did, that it was for the benefit of all belligerents to adopt the same code and regulations.

In furtherance of this object, a branch society had been formed in Dublin, termed the "Knights of Tara," which met once a month at the theatre, Chapel Street, gave premiums for fencing, and proceeded in the most laudably systematic manner.[10]

In their second list of resolutions, published in 1784, the Knights of Tara explicated their unified stance on dueling:

> [The Knights of Tara] resolved their Exertions should be particularly made for the furtherance in general of the Blessings of Society; for which End, they conceived, that to moderate the Excess— to restrain, if possible, the Practice of Duelling, and the consequent wanton effusion of Blood, would add much to the Happiness, Dignity, Lustre, and Elevation of the national Character, whose Skill, Spirit, and Fortitude ought not to be idly, and in many Instances, barbarously exhausted in little private Feuds and Quarrels, but directed to their proper Objects, the Enemies of the Land, and the common Enemies of Mankind. Wherefore this Society cultivated the Science of Defence with the Sword, and other martial Weapons, not as a primary, but as a secondary Measure, subservient to the aforesaid national Purposes. — The Members, rendered critically conversant in the Use, can be the more effectually interpose their Skill, Spirit, and Authority in suppressing the Abuse of Arms.[11]

The Knights thus proposed to reform dueling by establishing a special committee to arbitrate all affairs of honor, and any disputes that might lead to an armed combat—and, if possible, to resolve them peacefully. Their resolutions of 1784 included the following:

> RESOLVED UNANIMOUSLY, "That we bind ourselves by all the sacred Ties of Honour, to refer and submit our Disputes, &c. touching Points of Honour, to a Committee composed of Members of this Order, and invited by them with juridicial Authority competent to decide thereon. Any refractory contumacious Member or Members appealing from the Decision of said Committee, (except to the Body at large, to whose controul all its Committees are necessarily subject) shall be expelled with every possible Stigma of Ignominy, their Names published, and prosecuted also at Law, by this Order, if fatal Consequences shall have resulted from their Pertinacity."
>
> RESOLVED, "That we will hold in the highest Estimation, all such Noblemen and Gentlemen (not Members of this Order) who may have Disputes, in Points of Honour, either with each other, or with any Member or Members of this Order, who shall refer and submit the Adjudication of the same to our Tribunal. We pledge ourselves that these Points shall undergo similar impartial Discussion and Judgment, as in the Cases of Members; and we flatter ourselves that they shall receive a more adequate mental Satisfaction—a more consummate honourable Triumph than they could otherwise possibly have enjoyed from the Immolation of Thousands of human Victims, in Gratification of those insatiable Idols, Pride and Resentment."[12]

Although the Knights described such efforts as a "most arduous Reformation," according to Jonah Barrington, the Knights did not actually advocate—or even desire—the complete extirpation of dueling. Barrington explained,

The Knights of Tara... held a select committee to decide on all actual questions of honour referred to them: to reconcile differences, if possible; if not, to adjust the terms and continuance of single combat. Doubtful points were solved generally on the peaceable side, provided women were not insulted or defamed; but when that was the case, the knights were obdurate and blood must be seen. They were constituted by ballot, something in the manner of the Jockey Club, but without the possibility of being dishonourable...[13]

The large-scale purpose, then, of the Knights of Tara—as they expressed it themselves—was to mitigate the excesses of dueling, to "restrain" the practice, and its "consequent wanton effusion of Blood." They aimed to accomplish this through regulation, supervision, and mediation—rather than by the complete elimination of the custom. Dueling had spiraled out of control; the Knights aimed to moderate it. In a sense, their formation was a logical follow-up to the creation of the Clonmel dueling code, which had been drafted only six years earlier.

Although such objectives might appear ambitious, to help bring them about, the Knights included in their membership some of the great luminaries of the Anglo-Irish nobility. Among these were Arthur Gore, 2nd Earl of Arran, Edward Stratford, 2nd Earl of Aldborough, Henry de Burgh, 1st Marquess of Clanricarde, General Henry Luttrell, 2nd Earl of Carhampton, Captain John Cradock (later 1st Baron Howden), John FitzGibbon, 1st Earl of Clare, John Butler, 17th Earl of Ormonde, and George Frederick Nugent, 7th Earl of Westmeath (also known as Lord Delvin). In addition to General Luttrell and Captain Cradock, the ranks of the Knights also comprised a number of distinguished military officers, such as Lieutenant General Richard Wilson, Lieutenant Colonel St. George and Captain Cradock (both "Aids du Camps" to "his Grace the Duke of Rutland"), Colonel John Butler of Kilkenny, Major John Kelly of Castle Kelly, Major Wemys of Kilkenny, Captain Cole of Dublin, Captain Holmes of the 66th regiment, Joseph Deane of the 67th regiment, and a young lieutenant named Anthony Gordon, of the Dublin Barracks.[14]

Another important member was James Keogh, one of the original signatories (and probable co-author) of the influential Clonmel dueling code. In addition to serving as an authority and consultant on matters pertaining to dueling, Keogh also served as a judge for the Knights' fencing tournaments. Jonah Barrington described him thus:

I knew Jemmy Keogh extremely well. He was considered in the main a peacemaker, for he did not like to see anybody fight but himself; and it was universally admitted that he never killed any man who did not well deserve it. He was a plausible, although black-looking fellow, with remarkably thick, long eyebrows, closing with a tuft over his nose... He was a land-agent to Bourke of Glinsk, to whom he always officiated as second.[15]

Barrington also claimed that Keogh was among a select "few" individuals who were "supposed to understand the points of honour better than any men in Ireland, and were constantly referred to."[16]

Undoubtedly the Knights' most astonishing and unexpected member, however, was George Robert Fitzgerald, Ireland's most feared duelist, who is mentioned in the group's 1784 resolutions. That a such a ferocious and inveterate duelist such as Fitzgerald—a man who, in all respects, embodied the worst excesses of the custom—decided to join a society whose self-appointed task was to restrict and regulate dueling, almost defies common sense. In trying to reconcile the fact of his membership, it may be wondered, perhaps, that Fitzgerald was not the monster he has been made out to be—although this seems unlikely, given the volume of evidence against him. A more plausible scenario is that, considering the Knights' status as the ultimate group of swordsmen in Ireland—and, with their lavish fencing tournaments and romantic masquerade balls—the society of the Knights of Tara was simply the most desirable place to be, at least for a swordsman who was anyone of note in eighteenth century Dublin.

The Knights continued to meet and dine regularly together, "according to custom," at Ryan's Tavern on Fownes's Street, and to hold various fencing events in local Dublin theaters.[17] These activities were greeted with considerable fanfare in the Dublin press. In the fall of 1783, *Saunders's News-Letter* declared:

As a court of honour...as promoters of the science of defence, and a military body at one time, [the Knights'] purpose to secure such a national character as it is expected will at once raise the people of this kingdom in the estimation of foreigners, and at the same time operate to the general peace, improvement, and benefit of society.[18]

The Knights' efforts to regulate dueling, having evidently been somewhat successful, were similarly lauded:

Our Countrymen have long and justly censured for their Duels! All Europe beheld our false Honour with Horror. To the Credit of the Knights of Tara be it remembered, they were the first to discountenance this inhuman Practice, by making it an established Proof that a Man may be as brave by submitting a Dispute to the Decision of a Committee, as the Sword or Pistol. —

We sincerely wish that every Country and Neighborhood in the Kingdom would adopt these generous and charitable Mode of settling Quarrels. — This Utility is evident.[19]

## FENCING CONTESTS AND EXHIBITIONS

Whereas the Knights of Tara secretly deliberated on matters of honor and dueling behind closed doors, they held their fencing tournaments before the Irish public—and it was for these grand and lavish events that the society would be best remembered. Decades later, Henry Angelo recounted that

> At that time [during the 1780s] there was an annual meeting of amateurs of the *première force*, called the Knights of Tara. There were three classes, and prizes given to each. To the first an elegant steel diamond-cut sword, which [Major Anthony Gordon] won, and has shewn me. This exhibition of the science was always honoured with the presence of the lord-lieutenant and ladies, and concluded with a ball in the evening.[20]

A more vivid, detailed, and highly romantic description of the Knights' tournaments was provided by Jonah Barrington:

> The theatre of the Knights of Tara, on these occasions, was always overflowing. The combatants were dressed in close cambric jackets, garnished with ribbons, each wearing the favourite colour of his fair one; bunches of ribbons also dangled at their knees, and roses adorned their morocco slippers, which had buff soles to prevent noise in their lunges. No masks or visors were used as in these more timorous times; on the contrary, every feature was uncovered, and its inflections all visible.
>
> The ladies appeared in full morning dresses, each handing his foil to her champion for the day, and their presence animated the singular exhibition. From the stage-boxes the prizes were likewise handed to the conquerors by the fair ones, accompanied each with a wreath of laurel, and a smile then more valued than a hundred victories!
>
> The tips of the foils were blackened, and therefore instantly betrayed the hits on the cambric jacket, and proclaimed without doubt the successful combatant. All was decorum, gallantry, spirit, and good temper.[21]

The Knights held their tournaments in a number of prominent Dublin theaters, including the Theatre Royale in Smock Alley, and the Little Theatre on Capel-street. The latter had been leased in 1770 by William Dawson, and was physically described by John O'Keeffe, who had attended puppet-shows there as a child:

> Within those very walls I afterwards saw plays acted with more precision and neatness than I had ever seen in any other theatre in England or Ireland (I never was in Scotland) and filled by a most

select, elegant, and fashionable audience. The house was hired jointly by Dawson and Robert Mahon; the stage was deep, and it had pit, boxes, and lattices, and two galleries...[22]

The Theatre Royale in Smock Alley, on the other hand, was a much older edifice, having opened its doors in 1662, when its "velvet drapes, glittering chandeliers and beautiful hand painted sceneries" dazzled Dublin audiences. It is related that, as of 1770, the House was adorned with new "Paintings and Decorations," and was "fitted up in a most elegant Manner."[23] In 1780, the Theatre was acquired by Richard Daly,[24] the actor and well-known duelist—making it the perfect location for the Knights' activities:

Mr. Richard Daly was an extremely high spirited young Irishman, who, like Sheridan and Mossop before him, had been educated at Trinity College. He was tall, and well-built, and except for a cast in his eye, most agreeable to look at. His handsomeness, combined with a propensity for duelling, frequently accorded to him the role of the gallant chevalier, and being more inclined for mischief than for study, he left Trinity without benefit of a degree. There are many amusing accounts of Daly's sky larkings around Dublin and his coup d'etat in acquiring Smock-alley was only mildly in character.[25]

The veracity of Barrington's romantic characterization of the Knights' fencing tournaments can be verified by contemporary accounts published in the Dublin press. As these accounts are, quite possibly, some of the richest descriptions of fencing events to appear in the literature of the eighteenth century, they shall be reprinted here in full. The first appeared at the end of April, 1783—soon after the group's formation—and reads as follows:

Yesterday exhibited a spectacle novel and highly pleasing. A number of gentlemen of the first consequence in Ireland having lately formed a society, distinguished by the title of *Knights of Tara*, for the express purpose of promoting the science of defence, gratified the curiosity of the town by a public exhibition of that manly and graceful accomplishment. To accommodate their friends and the public, the Knights engaged the little Theatre in Capel-street, which was most happily adapted for the purpose. The stage was reserved for the gentlemen of the society who contended for the prizes, and the judges. The pit was allotted for the Knights, who each appeared decorated with a narrow ribbon of garter blue, on which was introduced a small star, with the motto *presidium & decus.*[*] The boxes and lattices were crowded with ladies of the first fashion. Admittance to other parts of the house was obtained by Knight-tickets, of which each member had two. His Excellency and Lady Temple were invited and expected, but sent a most polite apology addressed to Sir Wm. Fortick, President of the Knights of Tara. At 12 o'clock scarce a seat could be obtained in any part of the house. About one, the stage was cleared, lighted from above by some large

---

[*]  *Presidium & decus:* Latin for "Protection and Honor."

windows. The gentlemen who contended for the prize in the first class, took their station on the stage, dressed in a most becoming manner, in super-fine white casimir jackets, and the cuffs and collars of garter blue silk: on the right breast of the jacket, was marked a small circle, by blue lines, within which the hits must take place, or pass for nought. Each gentleman also, wore red Morocco slippers, and had a small bunch of blue ribbons tied at his knees. The judges were chosen, General Luttrell, Lord Delvin, and Colonel Eustace, who, with the President and Secretary, were seated upon the stage: only four gentlemen, Mr. Parvisol, Mr. Underwood, Lt. Gordon, and young Mr. Dillon, of Jervis-street, appeared for the first prize, which was a highly ornamented sword, value 25 guineas. After the names were called over, and numbered 1, 2, 3, and 4, they were drawn by the President, who should engage. The first lot fell to Mr. Underwood and Mr. Parvisol, and second lot to Lieutenant Gordon and Mr. Dillon. — Mr. Underwood and Mr. Parvisol took their ground, and exhibited much coolness, elegance, and judgment. After a contest that continued for a considerable time, the Judges declared out of seven hits, Mr. U. had four, and Mr. P. three. The foils were blacked at the points each bout, which told in a conspicuous manner in the white circle. — Lieutenant Gordon and Mr. Dillon next took ground; Mr. G. gave Mr. Dillon four, and received none. Mr. G. and Mr. P. then took ground, which terminated in favour of Mr. G. The trial of skill then remained between Mr. U. and Mr. G. which ended also in favour of the latter, to whom the prize sword was delivered, by the unanimous voice of the judges and society. There were six candidates for the second prize, who were dressed in the same manner of the first. The etiquette was strictly observed as in the arrangement for the first prize. The sword was won by Mr. L'Estrange.

| | No. 2. Underwood | No. 3 Dillon | No. 4 Gordon |
|---|---|---|---|
| No. 1. Parvisol gave | III | IV | I |
| Parvisol received | IV | III | IV |
| | *Parvisol* | | *Gordon* |
| No. 2. Underwood gave | IV | | none |
| Underwood recd | III | | IV |
| | *Parvisol* | | *Gordon* |
| No. 3. Dillon gave | III | | none |
| Dillon received | IV | | IV |
| | *Parvisol* | *Dillon* | *Underwood* |
| No. 4. Gordon gave | IV | IV | IV |
| Gordon recd | I | none | none |

Mr. Dillon and Mr. Underwood declined fencing together.

The exhibition closed about five o'clock, highly to the satisfaction of the society and spectators. The Knights afterwards dined together. Everything was conducted with the greatest good humour, which was still heightened by the harmony of the gentlemen who contested the prizes, who shook hands and congratulated the victors after each bout.[26]

Word of the Knights and their fencing tournaments soon reached Scotland, where the *Caledonian Mercury* reported that

...the elegance of their appearance, and the respectability of its Members, will far exceed any thing which has hitherto appeared in that line in this kingdom; their uniform to be light blue, richly embroidered with silver, and ornamented with spangles, a pair of epaulets equally splendid, and silver laced hats.[27]

Oftentimes, the Knights' fencing exhibition would be followed by a "fancy ball" or masquerade. The *Hibernian Journal; or, Chronicle of Liberty*, on January 23, 1784, included an "Account of some of the Characters who intend to figure at the superb Masquerade to be given by the Knights of Tara, at the Rotunda, on the 19th of February next, as follows" and listed the following characters: "Lovegold the Miser, Moses the Jew, A Bear Leaden, An Harlequin, Wrestlers, Sapskull in the Honest Yorkshiremen, Proteus and a Posturemaster, Goliath of Gath, An Alembic, A Cat, A Bull-dog, A Shuttlecock, Nobody, Somebody." A public account of the "principal Female Characters" was not permitted, possibly due to privacy concerns.[28]

In May, 1784, the Knights announced the arrangement of another fencing exhibition at the Theatre Royal, in Smock Alley, "for the Benefit of the distressed Manufacturers in this City," and solicited the Duke and Duchess of Rutland to nominate a day for the event.[29] The event was soon set for May 20th, when it was to "commence at the Hour of One o'Clock." Ticket sales for the tournament, it was noted, would benefit the underprivileged classes of Dublin, endeavoring "to relieve the long and severe Distresses of the Poor of this Metropolis"—a plan submitted by Anthony Gordon, and possibly inspired by the previous actions of Dublin's veteran fencing master, Cornelius Kelly.[30] Tickets were to be sold, among other places, at "the Bar of Daly's Chocolate-house." It was also announced that "there will be a general Meeting of the Order on Tuesday evening next. The Knights, according to Custom, dine on Thursday at Ryan's in Fownes's-street, after the Exhibition; Noblemen and Gentlemen are requested not to absent themselves, and to send their Names to the Bar on or before Wednesday next."[31]

A full account of this tournament appeared in the following month's issue of the *Hibernian Magazine*:

The Smock Alley Theatre today. Photograph courtesy of Patrick Sutton, director, Smock Alley Theatre.

The Knights of Tara celebrated their annual exhibition in the noble science of defence. The prizes were two elegant swords; one of the value of twenty guineas, the other of ten. The company were exceeding brilliant, and their Graces the Duke and Duchess of Rutland honoured the Theatre with their presence on this very pleasing occasion. The Knights appeared on the stage decorated with the ribband and star peculiar to the order, and the judges who were the Earl of Arran and Aldborough, Lord Delvin, Mr. J. Keogh, Captain Gordon, &c. being seated, Messrs. O'Berne and Parvisol entered as candidates. The most perfect skill and graceful dexterity in that useful and difficult science marked the honourable contest, but at length the victory was decreed in favour of Mr. Parvisol, who won four out of seven hits for the first prize sword. The two next who entered the lists for the same prize, were Mr. Michael Dillon and Mr. Underwood, whose remarkable skill and agility gave universal satisfaction. The contest was nice, and some time dubious, but the judges declared for Mr. Dillon, who won four hits out of seven. The second class sword being now the object of emulation; Mr. Anthony Dillon and Lieutenant Cunningham appeared as candidates, and after a most elegant contest of fifteen minutes, in which also the young gentlemen exerted great judgment and dexterity, the sword was decreed to Mr. Dillon. After this the grand prize sword remained to be contended for by the two successful candidates in the two first trials, viz. Mr. Parvisol, who had defeated Mr. O'Berne, and Mr. Michael Dillon, who had won from Mr. Underwood. — And now began a contest which evinced the most eminent degree of perfection, and delighted every spectator; Mr. Michael Dillon having given four out of seven hits to his antagonist was crowned victor, and adjudged the first grand prize. The remarkable success which attended these two young gentlemen, who are brothers, is perhaps the only instance of the kind, and cannot be paralleled in ancient or modern story, and reflects the highest honour on their skill in one of the most difficult manual exercises that can be performed.[32]

The article in the *Hibernian Magazine* then concluded with the following notice:

The Delegates from all the Volunteer corps of the city and county of Dublin, unanimously resolved, That the training to the use of arms every honest and industrious Irishman, however moderate his property, or depressed his situation, was a measure of the utmost utility to his kingdom, and would produce a valuable acquisition to the Volunteer arms and interest.[33]

It seems that, at least to some degree, the Knights' mission to cultivate and popularize knowledge in the use of arms had met with success.

## THE END OF THE KNIGHTS

After the winter of 1784, The Knights ceased advertising their meetings and events. A few scattered references indicate that some former Knights of Tara continued to participate in the events held by the Knights of St. Patrick. This included both Anthony Gordon and one of the Dillon brothers—who, at a 1785 masquerade ball held by the latter group, appeared as a "Fencing Master."[34] However, the Knights of Saint Patrick, as far as we know, never involved themselves in matters of fencing and dueling. This order would continue to last until 1921, when most of Ireland became independent as the Irish Free State.

The exact reason for the disbanding of the Knights of Tara remains unclear. Decades later, Henry Angelo—who evidently received his information from Anthony Gordon—mentioned that "I have been told, that the knights disagreeing among themselves, these annual meetings have long been discontinued."[35] Jonah Barrington seems to confirm the existence of discord within the Knights, relating in his memoirs,

This most agreeable and useful association did not last above two or three years. I cannot tell why it broke up: I rather think, however, the original fire-eaters thought it frivolous, or did not like their own ascendency to be rivalled. It was said that they threatened direct hostilities against the knights...[36]

Whatever the reason behind the group's disbandment, their reputation continued to spread throughout the British Isles. Three years later, in 1788, the following appeared in an English newspaper:

The Prince of Wales has hinted an Intention to patronize a select Fraternity on the Plan of the Knights of Tara in Ireland, which consists of a certain Number of Noblemen and Gentlemen proficients in the Art of Fencing.[37]

A month later, this new English "Fraternity" was constituted under the supervision of Monsieur James Goddard, a well-known London-based fencing master who would soon cross swords in an assault with the famous Chevalier de Saint-Georges and the Chevalier d'Eon.[38] The latter also attended the first gathering of the new London society:

On Saturday the long expected contest for the Prize Sword, given by the Society of Fencers, under the direction of Mr. Goddard, was decided by the amateurs of that noble science, after a well-disputed and long contest, in which all parties displayed great scientific knowledge; the Judges decided it in favour of Mr. Lynch. La Chevalier d'Eon then presented him the Sword, complimenting him on his success in a short and elegant speech suitable to the occasion. Amongst the Company, which was both numerous and brilliant, were many of the Nobility, Foreign Ambassadors, and Ladies of distinction. The Society then with many other Gentlemen adjourned to the Thatched House, and ended the day with great mirth and conviviality.[39]

Despite this glowing account, a notice appearing in the next day's *London Times* indicated that the new society paled in comparison to the original that it was attempting to imitate:

Goddard's prize sword falls very short of the institution from which he has taken his idea. We allude to the Knights of Tara in Ireland, a company of Noblemen and Gentlemen who fence annually on the stage of a small theatre, in the presence of their friends, for honorary rewards. In this society, it is supposed, are the best private fencers in Europe.[40]

A few months later, in May of 1788, another fencing tournament, in which fencers contested for a "prize sword," was held in Dublin at Mr. Pardon's Academy; this event was also likely inspired by the former activities of the Knights of Tara. Among the judges of this event was one "Mr. Dillon"—possibly one of the two Dillon brothers who had contested in the Knights' assaults.[41] Goddard himself continued to instruct in London throughout the 1790s. Although it is not clear how long his London fencing society endured, it is recorded as having still been in force in 1792.[42]

Several decades later, the Knights of Tara were once again remembered in the obituary of its former member, Michael Dillon—who had been killed by rebels in County Wexford, wielding his sword until the very end:

> In the *Packet* of Tuesday the 6th instant, there was some mention made of the county of Dublin militia having been engaged with the rebels at New Ross, county of Wexford, and which *corps* had *acted very gallantly*, (and which all *Irish* corps have acted so, and will continue to do the same...) but no notice whatever was made of Captain Michael Dillon, who was killed on the same day also, and who, previous to being overpowered by the rebels, dispatched three of that body with his own sword. Captain Michael Dillon was one of the first swordsmen of his day, and much so, that he won the prize sword for three successive years, which entitled him to keep it ever after, *he being a member of the Knights of Tara*, a club then in being in Ireland of that day.
>
> Captain Dillon was also one of the principal aides-de-camp to the late Earl of Charlemont, when the Earl *commanded the far-famed Volunteers of Ireland in the year* 1782, and who left as only son, the present Earl of Roscommon.

Additional information regarding the disbandment of the Knights of Tara remains elusive. According to Jonah Barrington, the Knights had been the embodiment of all that made fencing noble, illustrious and admirable—the last martial representation of "decorum, gallantry, spirit, and good temper" in Ireland. Writing in 1827, he completed the group's epitaph with the following observation:

> Fencing with the small-sword is certainly a most beautiful and noble exercise; its acquirement confers a fine, bold, and manly carriage, a dignified mien, a firm step, and graceful motion. But, alas! its practicers are now supplanted by contemptible groups of smirking quadrillers with unweaponed belts, stuffed breasts, and strangled loins—a set of squeaking dandies, whose sex may be readily mistaken, or, I should say, is of no consequence.[43]

## TREATISES BY THE KNIGHTS

Among the legacies bequeathed by the Knights of Tara are a number of fencing treatises, published by its members (or former members) at various points during the 1780s. The first such text, published at the height of the Knights' activities, was a revised, bilingual edition of

Parry of *prime* and disarm by seizure, after Angelo's treatise. From Alfred Hutton's *Sword and the Centuries.*

Domenico Angelo's classic and influential text, *The School of Fencing*. One of the first announcements of this publication, which was by subscription, appeared in 1784:

New engraving, and printing by Subscription,

The SCHOOL OF FENCING

With a general Explanation of the principal ATTITUDES and POSITIONS peculiar to the ART By Mr. ANGELO. In ENGLISH and FRENCH. Enlarged, revised, and improved, by JAMES UNDERWOOD, Esq.; a Knight of TARA, and others.

CONDITIONS

I. THIS Work will form an elegant QUARTO Volume, containing about fifty large Copperplates, engraved in a capital Manner, and two hundred Pages of Letter Press, on a superfine Paper.

II. It will be published in twenty-five Numbers; each Number to contain two of the Copperplates, and eight Pages of Letter-Press.

III. The Price to Subscribers to be One Shilling and Seven-pence Half-penny per Number; Half a Crown, British, to be deposited, and allowed in the two last Numbers. Non-subscribers to pay two Shillings and Two-pence each Number.[44]

Although widely advertised, no copy of this Dublin edition has yet been found.

A few years after the announcement of the revised Angelo edition, in 1787, the Knights' former secretary, James Underwood, published another fencing treatise under the lengthy title of

*Draw Not Your Sword But to Serve the King, Preserve Your Honour, or Defend your Life: The Art of Fencing; or the Use of the Small Sword. Collected, revised, and enlarged, by James Underwood, Esq.*[45]

Beneath Underwood's name, notably, appeared the words *"Præsidium et decus,"* the motto of the Knights of Tara. In the preface of this book, Underwood writes,

I have long regretted the want of a treatise, containing such instructions only as are absolutely necessary to inculcate a thorough knowledge of the Sword. But a diffidence in my abilities to arrange my thoughts, prevented for years my engaging in such a talk; however, that universal passion, from which scarcely any human breast is exempt, added to repeated intreaties, has at length prevailed over my natural timidity.

From my having been honoured with distinguished testimonies of approbation, by characters too exalted to abuse the humility of my station by flattery, and also having the satisfaction of the Public often manifested in my favour, I hope I shall not be accused of vanity when I say, I think I may lay a just claim to some considerable knowledge of the theory and practice of the art.

Underwood's text would be reprinted again, more than a decade later, in 1798.[46] Considering the contemporary descriptions of the fencing contests in which he took part, Underwood's claim to "some considerable knowledge of the theory and practice of the art" may well have been merited. His book, however, is merely an edited version of Mahon's *Art of Fencing*. The English historian J. D. Aylward refers to Underwood's edition as an "astonishing" act of plagiarism—identifying passages extracted verbatim from the treatises of Domenico Angelo, John Godfrey, William Hope, and Donald McBane. In examining the contents of Underwood's text, Aylward's description seems justified.[47] However, it is important to note that fencing texts in late eighteenth century Dublin—even Mahon's edition of Labat—were extremely scarce, and, at the very least, Underwood was making classic literary material on the art of fencing available to others. Although Underwood claimed to have "Collected, Revised, and Enlarged" the text, his edits to Labat's treatise seem to consist mainly of the occasional excision, and includes very little new material.

To find purely original works, then, authored by a Knight of Tara, one must look to the society's most accomplished fencer—who shall be treated of in our next chapter.

1   This treatise is reprinted in full in Part II of this book.

2   *Hibernian Journal; or, Chronicle of Liberty*, April 23, 1784.

3   Nicholas H. Nicolas, *History of the orders of knighthood of the British empire, Vol IV* (London: John Hunter, 1842), 9.

4   Sylvester O'Halloran, *A general history of Ireland: from the earliest accounts to the close of the twelfth century, collected from the most authentic records. In which new and interesting lights are thrown on the remote histories of other nations as well as of both Britains, Volume I* (London: Printed for the author, by A. Hamilton, 1778), 190-193.

5   Ibid., 193-194.

6   According to historian Iain McBride, "Pre-Norman Ireland had possessed all the social and cultural attributes (kingship, a hierarchical society, clerical learning) of those societies which England acknowledged as civilised; and this would facilitate the increasing identification of [eighteenth century] Protestant intellectuals with Gaelic antiquity, a process culminating in the establishment of the Royal Irish Academy (1785). The spokesmen of the Protestant Ascendancy sometimes behaved as if they had roots deep in the Irish past." See introduction of McBride's *Eighteenth Century Ireland: The Isle of Slaves* (Dublin : Gill & Macmillan, 2009).

7   "Tara. A Poem," in *The Hibernian Magazine, Or, Compendium of Entertaining Knowledge*, December, 1784.

8   *Dublin Evening Post*, April 5, 1783.

9   Barrington, *Personal Sketches, Volume II*, 10-11.

10  Ibid.

11  *Hibernian Journal; or, Chronicle of Liberty*, April 23, 1784.

12  *Hibernian Journal; or, Chronicle of Liberty*, April 23, 1784.

13  Barrington, *Personal Sketches, Volume II*, 13.

14  For a complete list of the Knights of Tara, see Appendix V.

15  Barrington, *Personal Sketches, Volume II*, 10.

16  Ibid., 8-9.

17  *Saunders's News-Letter*, May 17, 1784.

18  *Saunders's News-Letter*, September 17, 1783.

19  *Hibernian Journal; or, Chronicle of Liberty*, April 12, 1784.

20  Henry Angelo, *Reminiscences with Memoirs of His Late Father and Friends, Including Numerous Original Anecdotes and Curious Traits of the Most Celebrated Characters that Have Flourished During the Last Eighty Years, Volume II* (London: Henry Colburn and Richard Bentley, 1830), 300.

21  Barrington, *Personal Sketches, Volume II*, 12-13.

22  La Tourette Stockwell, *Dublin Theatres and Theatre Customs, 1637-1820*, (Kingsport, Tenn.: Kingsport Press, 1938.), 136.

23  Stockwell, 137.

24  For a full account of Daly's duel with Jonah Barrington, see Chapter I.

25  Stockwell, 148-149.

26  *Dublin Evening Post*, April 29, 1783.

27  *Caledonian Mercury*, Sept. 15, 1783.

28  *Hibernian Journal; or, Chronicle of Liberty*, January 23, 1784

29  *Hibernian Journal; or, Chronicle of Liberty*, May 5, 1784.

30 By the Knights' own admission, this "liberal plan, submitted...to this Society, for the relief of the poor," was the work of Anthony Gordon, fencing disciple of Cornelius Kelly. *Hibernian Journal; or, Chronicle of Liberty*, April 23, 1784. In 1750, upon winning a public fencing contest in Dublin, Cornelius Kelly "very generously had deposited the [complete winnings of twenty guineas] in the hands of the printer hereof to be equally divided to the four following charities viz. the society for the relief of prisoners, the hospital of incurables, the infirmary on the Inn's Quay and the Mercer's Hospital." *Freeman's Daily Journal*, December 11-15, 1750. "The twenty Guineas, which Mr. Cornelius Kelly won from Mr. Dominick Kelly, as mentioned in our last, was given to the Printer hereof, and disposed of in the following manner, as directed, to wit, five Guineas to the Charitable Musical Society; five to the Charitable Infirmary on the Inn's-Key; five to Mercer's Hospital; and the other five to the Hospital for Incurables." *Dublin Journal*, December 18, 1750.

31 *Saunders's News-Letter*, May 17, 1784, and June 19, 1784.

32 *The Hibernian Magazine, Or, Compendium of Entertaining Knowledge*, May, 1784.

33 Ibid.

34 *The Gentleman's and London magazine; or monthly chronologer*, April, 1785.

35 Angelo, *Volume II*, 300.

36 Barrington, *Personal Sketches, Volume II*, 13.

37 *Manchester Mercury*, February 5, 1788.

38 *Oxford Journal*, June 5, 1790.

39 *London Times*, March 3, 1788.

40 *London Times*, March 4, 1788.

41 *Belfast News-Letter*, May 16, 1788.

42 *London Times*, January 9, 1792.

43 Barrington, *Personal Sketches, Volume II*, 12.

44 *Hibernian Journal; or, Chronicle of Liberty*, September 15, 1784.

45 James Underwood, *Draw Not Your Sword But to Serve the King, Preserve Your Honour, or Defend your Life: The Art of Fencing; or the Use of the Small Sword* (Dublin: Printed by T. Byrne, Parliament-street, 1787).

46 James Underwood, *Draw Not Your Sword But to Serve the King, Preserve Your Honour, or Defend your Life: The Art of Fencing; or the Use of the Small Sword* (Dublin: Printed by William Porter, 69 Grafton Street, 1798).

47 J. D. Aylward, *The English master of arms from the twelfth to the twentieth century* (London, Routledge & Paul [1956]), 221.

*Plate 13th*

*A front view of the Tierce planted home, by the Fort against the Foible*

*The Point Volant in Tierce*

*The Guard of the Point Volant in Quarte, a front View.*

Illustrated page from Anthony Gordon's 1804 manuscript, *An Idea of Defence: a Treatise on Swordsmanship*. Courtesy of the Council of the National Army Museum, London. NAM 1968-07-67.

# VII

## ANTHONY GORDON,
## *the* LAST KNIGHT *of* TARA

*"An inexhaustable source of power, a mystery too sacred to be divulged."*

When the Knights of Tara published their second list of resolutions in 1784, its last paragraph included the following tribute:

> Resolved unanimously, That the thanks of this Society be given to Anthony Gordon, Esq; Lieutenant of the 67th regiment, for his indefatigable attention, not only to the institution of the order of the Knights of Tara, and to the support of its honour and dignity, but also for the foregoing resolutions, and very liberal plan, submitted by him to this Society, for the relief of the poor.[1]

Decades later, this same Anthony Gordon would be remembered by none other than Henry Angelo, whose *salle d'armes* he frequently visited, and whom Angelo referred to in his memoirs as "Major Gordon, an Irish gentleman." The son of Domenico described Gordon as being "tall," "handsome," about six-foot two inches in height, and remarked that Gordon had a "perfect knowledge of fencing" and was "considered the best fencer in Ireland." Angelo recounted being shown "an elegant steel diamond-cut sword"—which Gordon had won in a tournament held by the Knights of Tara. Angelo also related the following anecdote about "Major Gordon," which gives an idea of the Irishman's colorful personality:

> As foreigners of different countries, who frequented my academy, not only added to the amusement, but information (particularly the Italians) of the various methods of attack and defence peculiar to themselves, they were welcome visitors. One of the major's antagonists, Monsieur Tranard, piqued himself on his superiority. Being told of the Frenchman's boasting, the next time they engaged, Monsieur was beaten, using a fencing term, a *plate couture.** When denying repeated thrusts he had received, the major being irritated, lifted up his arm, and called out aloud, "I'll throw you out of the window." Though the action, if not the words, must have convinced him of what was intended, yet he affected not to understand, and to prevent any further dissatisfaction, I thought it better for them to change partners.[2]

Gordon's threat was memorably reminiscent of the antics supposedly perpetrated at Daly's Chocolate-house in Dublin, where "it was not uncommon to see a gambler, suspected of cheating, flung out of one of the upper windows."[3] Regarding Gordon's feud with the Frenchman, Angelo noted that despite their mutual animosity, the two "afterwards became better friends," humorously recounting, "The major was an excellent classical scholar, but spoke very little French; and the other pretended to know less English, so that during these assaults they afterwards conversed in Latin, very much to the amusement of the scholars."[4]

In scrutinizing the various reports of the Knights of Tara, it seems clear that in many respects, Anthony Gordon was the heart and soul of the group's efforts to popularize fencing. Unlike many other Knights whose names appear and disappear from the record, Gordon is mentioned in nearly every notice published by the society. He is credited with composing their resolutions. He took part, as a fencer or judge, in every known fencing tournament held by the Knights. During his tenure with the group, he also began writing out his thoughts and ideas on the science of fencing—an effort he would continue to pursue for the rest of his life, and which would have considerable impact on the history of fencing in the British Isles.

Anthony Gordon was born in County Donegal in 1746, the son of Nathaniel Gordon, a farmer, and Agricola Gordon. The Gordon family had, evidently, enough means to send the young Anthony to college, but not enough to pay for his military commissions—a fact which suggests that they were middle-class freehold farmers. On November 1, 1770, at age 24, the young Anthony entered Trinity College, Dublin, as a pensioner, and later as a "Scholar of the House or Master."[5] At some point around this time, according to Angelo, Gordon also became

---

* *à plate couture:* an old French expression meaning "entirely, utterly, without question."

a "scholar of the late Kelly, whose abilities are well-known today in Dublin"—a clear reference to the renowned Dublin-based fencing master, Cornelius Kelly.[6] On April 30, 1781—the same year that he earned a "Master of Arts" degree at Trinity—Gordon joined the 77th Regiment of Foot as an ensign.[7] Already a seasoned fencer, and now a member of the military, Gordon was shocked to find that his fellow soldiers apparently received no training in any particular self-defense method for close-quarters combat with the bayonet. Gordon explained:

> On joining the regiment, [I] was astonished to find no Exercise for close action; no notions of making thrusts, cuts, and parades; no system of defence or offence; for the established Exercises are adapted only to the missile weapon, and to the movements in Line, Column, Square, and Echellon, &c.

Although elite units of the British military may have received more advanced training in the use of the bayonet[8], with respect to rank and file troops, the historical record indicates that Gordon's experience seems to have been the norm. Nearly two centuries later, the truth of his observation would be confirmed by John Alan Houlding in his dissertation on British Army training. According to Houlding,

> Bayonet drill was, curiously, rather neglected in the eighteenth century. Buried away in the manual exercise, it was performed in a most unrealistic fashion; and the command in use—'Push your Bayonets!'—betrays both its origin and underdevelopment. Not until 1805...was the subject treated in depth by anyone. Many writers lamented this lapse, recognizing the efficacy of the weapon against both horse and foot: Bennett Cuthbertson, for example, writing in 1768 (op. cit., 210) thought it an 'essential matter, for Soldiers to be perfectly well acquainted with their use', and deplored the fact that British troops in training were seldom even 'permitted to fix them, but on certain occasions'. From Marlborough's campaigns onwards it was the touchstone of British tactical thinking that heavy fire was all-important; and so it was doctrine, perhaps, as much as indifference, which dictated the army's approach. As Campbell Dalrymple wrote (op. cit., 56), 'human nature will always shrink [in the face of heavy fire], and never dare to approach within push of bayonet'.[9]

In 1771, a treatise on military tactics by "Sieur B," published in London, lamented the bayonet position "almost general through Europe," which was "of pernicious consequence, as it is an evident obstacle to the action of a soldier." This common position did not guard the soldier at all, but was a direct descendant of the old "firelock" stance which had replaced that of the pike. In the common exercise, attacks with the bayonet were made by first "charging" the weapon—that is, withdrawing the rear arm so that "the soldier has the butt-end behind him, and the left elbow advanced toward the middle of the barrel"—and then "pushing" the bayonet forward

*Charge y Bayonet Breast High*
IV.ᵗʰ Motion.

*Push your Bayonet.*
I.ˢᵗ Motion.

The old bayonet exercise. From Benjamin Cole's *The Soldier's Pocket Companion* (London: 1746).

using the arms alone, and sometimes with a slight lean of the body. The 1771 text advocated an altered stance that placed more distance between the soldier's feet, and a placement of the weapon which better guarded the soldier and threatened his adversary. Beyond this, however, Sieur B's text did not further treat of the weapon's use in close-quarters combat; nor do its prescriptions seem to have been adopted.[10]

Determined to correct what he viewed to be an immense deficiency in army training, Gordon quickly became obsessed with developing a new method of defense—that is, of applying the fencing principles he had learned with the foil and small-sword to the bayonet.

John Scott (1739-1798), 1st Earl of Clonmel, by Gilbert Stuart.

Late in life, Gordon claimed that the idea originated not with himself, but with John Scott, the Earl of Clonmel, who was at that time Ireland's Attorney-General. Gordon recounted:

It was and is to my dearest friend and Protector, the late Earl of Clonmel, of the King's bench in Ireland, I owe everything...[and including] to his goodness I owe the idea of the Bayonet Exercise; This invention while living he ascribed to me. I had been about Ten years in Trinity Coll., Dublin, either as Scholar of the House or Master, etc. My noble friend was critically conversant in the first application of the powers of the Lever. He taught me the mode of applying the musket, so as to obtain the advantage of 100 [to] 1 ! against a man not similarly instructed. He attended all the exhibitions of it before the Lord Lt., the Duke of Rutland and the Comm.-in-Chief. It was proved and admitted that the 30 men I had could easily defeat in close action the whole garrison in equal numbers at the same time.[11]

Although, according to the dictates of society, Scott was Gordon's superior in terms of birth and class, the two evidently became close friends, and Scott reportedly did everything he could to help Gordon's career. On September 1, 1781, Gordon "removed...into 67th [Regiment of Foot], by the benevolence of Lord Clonmel [John Scott];" two and a half years later, on February 21, 1784, Scott "purchased a [Lieutenancy]" for Gordon.[12] As a lieutenant, Gordon would retain his station at the Dublin Barracks—likely no small task, as the Barracks were "the largest peacetime concentration of regular regiments of horse and marching foot in the British Isles," and the third largest in the entire British Empire.[13] During the same year, Gordon received the gratitude of the Dublin press for his efforts in suppressing a "dangerous" riot—which, as the account seems to suggest, was resolved with little or no bloodshed:

> When the qualities of the citizen and soldier are happily blended in an individual, how amiable, how respectable is the character? This city is peculiarly indebted to lieutenant Gordon, of the 67th regiment, for his attention to its police, and his deference to the civil power. He has already obtained the merited thanks of a very respectable parish; also of the lord lieutenant and commander in chief. His judicious and spirited conduct on Saturday, when he suppressed a dangerous riot between a body of the military and some townsmen, must endear him to every friend of humanity.[14]

In tandem with Gordon's military activities, he and Scott continued to share their knowledge and thoughts about fencing. Although Scott's diaries, published during the next century, do not mention his fencing activities, they do contain the following advice, under the heading *"Intercourse With the World"*:

> Always contrive to have as many things to ask from others as they have from you, and try to have somewhat to do with all those who have anything to do with you. Be a fencer throughout, and hit as often as you can.[15]

In order to further develop the system that he and Scott had created, Gordon engaged in extensive research (primarily studying ancient Greek and Roman literature) and travel, hoping to find some method of bayonet fencing elsewhere in Britain, or abroad. He recounted, speaking of himself in the third person,

> Unable to account for this defect, he [Gordon] made much research, first in this country, and afterwards on the Continent, to no purpose. The system every where established was the same, and differed only in some trifling minutiæ. Being thus unexpectedly disappointed, he was obliged to trace the Exercises to their origin. At length, he was gratified with the sight of the Exercises in question, which still remains dormant in the magazines of antiquity; in those magazines which are

stored with gold and diamonds, from which great kings, philosophers, orators, poets, and historians, have illumined themselves and their countries....Under these circumstances, and the conviction of his own mind, he solicited the attention of the late General Burgoyne, then commanding the Forces in Ireland, to the project of introducing some kind of Exercise for close action.[16]

In the subsequent decades, Gordon would author a number of treatises on the use of the bayonet. Nearly a century later, the fencing author and antiquarian Alfred Hutton would laud Gordon's 1805 book as "the earliest known work giving any idea of attack and defence with the bayonet."[17] Hutton, however, seems to have been unaware of three earlier treatises that Gordon had authored on the subject, the first of which was written in the spring of 1783 when the Knights of Tara were at their height. This was a twenty-eight page tract, entitled

> A letter on the bayonet exercise, submitted to the Right Hon. General Burgoyne, Commander in Chief of His Majesty's forces in Ireland, &c. &c. &c.

Only three copies of this extremely rare text, reportedly published around 1787, are known to have survived. Of these, one copy—somewhat incredibly—made its way into the hands of the American revolutionary general and president, George Washington. This book, which remained in Washington's library at Mount Vernon after the President's death in 1799, was eventually acquired by the Boston Athenæum, where it resides today.[18]

## A LETTER ON THE BAYONET EXERCISE (1783)

In this short treatise, Gordon outlines in writing, for the first time, his method and ideas for fencing with the bayonet. Gordon begins the text by noting,

> I do not enter into the merits of the military exercises common to Europe, which regard precision in the essentials of the distant action: as they advance not into the business of close action, I propose to fill up the void, with an exercise beginning its operation precisely at the termination of the present.

Gordon devotes a sizable portion of his text to criticizing the bayonet exercises currently in use. He lambasts the standard "position prescribed by [the common] exercise,"—that of "the Soldier on parade"—as "the weakest and most contrary to exertion," thus rendering the soldier "unpractised in the use and application of the amazing powers of the instrument, the fort or the feeble." Gordon proceeds to prescribe a new method of forming and arranging ranks, with each soldier adopting a guard position "with their feet at right angles, thirty-six inches asunder." He explains its advantage:

> In each exertion they are to extend their bodies, limbs, and arms to the utmost, covering their persons, by the extent and interposition of arms in the line opposed, thus giving to every exertion, efficacy, and safety.

Gordon thus lays out a step-by-step plan of exercise designed to unfold over a several month period, in which the soldiers of the regiment are to practice their new positions. He acknowledges that the "first step"—and perhaps the most difficult one—was to overcome the attachment to old practices, and prejudices against ideas which deviated from the established exercises:

> THE first step is difficult—It is the exertion of wisdom reflecting on herself. This reflection will burst open the temple of power, unfold the mystery, give both hands liberty, and dissolve in pieces the prejudicial chain of inveteracy, rather of inadvertency, which restrains the right from defending the left.

As shall be seen, Gordon's observation respecting the difficulty of this step would prove to be a prescient one.

Regarding the use of the weapon itself, Gordon notes that the rifle-bayonet "unites the properties" of both the "missile weapon" (the firelock) and the "Hand-weapon" (the bayonet blade). He claims that nothing can *justify a perseverence in concealing an inexhaustable source of power, a mystery too sacred to be divulged,"* and outlines his theory for applying principles of leverage to the bayonet—explaining how a practical understanding of the mechanical advantage of the fort (according to Gordon, "the part of the weapon held by the hand") applied to the feeble (the weaker portion of the weapon, closest to the point) gives a soldier so instructed an immense advantage on the field of battle:

> DEMONSTRATION of the faculty of invigorating his Majesty's Soldiers individually, with tenfold power and dexterity from the powers of the lever.
>
> THE Firelock, and the hands containing it, are a compound lever of the third kind. Resolve the compound into its simple parts, the simple being determined, give and determine all the minute parts of the compound.
>
> THUS the power at the elbow (or of the muscles there, contiguous on each side of it) is that of the fingers, in the ratio of ten to one, as proved by the experiment, that ten pounds appended to the elbow, and one pound in the hand extended parallel to the horizon are equal: Wherefore as the power at the elbow is to that of the fingers (ten to one) so is the Fort of the Firelock, held by

the finger, to one cubit's length of it, in the same ratio, ten to one. The Fort is to double, triple, and quadruple, &c. that distance, as twenty to one, thirty to one, and as forty to one, respectively.

CONSEQUENTLY, the power of the Fort of the Firelock, the Bayonet affixed, is more than forty fold the power of the Feeble, and therefore much more than ten fold, ten being but a part of forty.

I HAVE, therefore, demonstrated the facility of invigorating each individual Soldier, with ten fold powers, he actually having much greater, from dexterity in their application, with the instrument in hand.

SUCH are the powers that a man has from this practice, against another not practiced. These powers accumulate in proportion to the magnitude of the engine, whose operative parts are doubled, and in the habit of exerting them, sixty times in one minute.

He thus extols the benefits of this new method:

First, it places and practises the men in the positions the most formidable and commodious for exertion, whereby the number of those actually engaged, whatever it was before, becomes now doubled in the crisis of action. Secondly, it invigorates them individually with tenfold power, by the judicious application of all the powers of the Lever, the instrument in their hands. And Thirdly, it gives such precision in the use of these powers; that their daily exercise consists in being committed, one battalion against the other, making all manner of exertions with the Bayonet, without molesting each other.

Gordon promises that although the rank and file soldiers may wonder at the wisdom of this new exercise, they will come to see its efficacy after several months of practice, asserting, "Two or three hundred experiments made daily on every minute part of the instrument, demonstrate what seemed incredible; namely, that the power of the fort is forty times greater than at the feeble." Gordon devotes much of the remainder of his text to arguing for the merits of his system, to countering objections previously made to it, and to urging its adoption by the British military. He concludes,

Right liberal and honourable men will...see that the laws of motion and reason are not objections; but demonstrations for this exercise. May I the parent, but very feeble advocate, supplicate investigation, as that, I am persuaded, would shew this to be the most important subject ever agitated in these kingdoms; whereas, without a liberal trial, it perishes a mere nullity, unable to vindicate itself. My wish is, that the combination of ideas may not perish at the moment of their first existence; or rather that the Engine representing the combination, may not be dissolved before the facts are tried, the operations examined.[19]

General John Burgoyne (1722–1792). Courtesy of the Library of Congress.

Despite this last plea, upon the completion of his treatise, opposition to Gordon's method began almost immediately. The first draft, according to Gordon, was submitted in the form of a "paper" to superiors within the British military, but was eventually "returned, and [Gordon's] prayer refused." Not one to be deterred, Gordon edited and resubmitted a copy of his manuscript to General John Burgoyne, a noted veteran of the Seven Years' War and the American War of Independence. In 1777, Burgoyne had returned to Britain after surrendering his army to American rebels at Saratoga, New York. In 1782, he was made commander-in-chief of British forces in Ireland, a position he continued to hold until 1784. Gordon described Burgoyne's reception as follows:

The project (in the opinion of the General) was of great magnitude, and required mature delibera-tion; wherefore, after three months consideration, he thought it incredible that any science could enable one man to defend himself against twenty grenadiers in immediate succession; nor would he believe it, until he had seen the experiment exhibited, and proved by repetition. The General being thus convinced, had no hesitation in ordering a detachment to be trained in the Bayonet Exercise. Unfortunately for this Science, its Protector resigned his situation; but he took care to recommend the prosecution of the subject to the succeeding Commander-in-Chief [of Ireland], Sir William Pitt, who gave it similar encouragement.[20]

In a letter appended to the 1787 publication of Gordon's treatise, Burgoyne himself described Gordon's method in glowing terms:

> In regard to his exercise, it is admitted by the very few who have seen and understood it, that it gives uncommon vigor, dexterity, and confidence to the men conversant in it; that it actually doubles the number of the forces in the crisis of action, by his ingenious mode of introducing the centre rank into the front, and by placing them in the strongest attitude to act together in offence and defence. This is a wonderful addition of strength, and not attended with any addition of expence; it requires only labour and attention.[21]

In addition to John Scott, Gordon now had another benefactor—and one directly connected to the highest members of the British military establishment.


# MEETING WITH KING GEORGE III

In 1785, Gordon departed Ireland for England. That November, the *Belfast Mercury* reported: "Lieut. Gordon of the 67th regt. the inventor of the new bayonet charge, has introduced it at Chatham Barrack in England.—The English call it a wonderful kind of *Irish fencing* with the gun and bayonet."[22] Early the next year, in 1786, the *London Times* further noted:

> The new mode of exercise with the firelock, (which, with the bayonet fixed, is used as the sword in fencing) was reviewed at Chatham barracks, on Wednesday last, in the square before the Marine barracks, by Generals Faucitt, Townshend, and Colonel Williamson, (the Deputy Adjutant General) who expressed the greatest satisfaction at the *novelty* and *effect* which the manœuvres seemed to promise. Lieutenant Gordon, the inventor of this new mode of attack and defence, was recommended to persevere in his attention to this part of Tactics.[23]

Word of Gordon's new bayonet exercise reached as far as Maryland, in the United States, and was lauded back in Dublin, where one newspaper enthused that it "received the approbation of several great military characters; so that it is expected this new mode of attack will be universally adopted."[24]

It was about this time that Gordon's new exercise came to the attention of King George III. Many decades letter, *Fraser's Magazine* would publish the following incredible story, detailing how the first meeting between Gordon and the King supposedly came about:

As far back as 1785, Captain-Lieutenant Gordon, of the 67th regiment, brought forward his method of using the bayonet; and his scheme fell to the ground, partly through an odd circumstance, which we shall relate.

Gordon, then quartered at Chatham, having drilled the squads of the different regiments in the garrison handed over to him for the purpose, was directed to parade his men on a certain day at the Queen's Riding-house, in London; and, full of anticipated success, he appeared at the appointed hour—drew up his men outside—entered the building by himself—and found only one person in the interior, whom he took for one of the attendants belonging to the establishment. This individual was a homely-looking, elderly fellow, in a bob-wig and cut-velvet coat, rather worn; a broom was in his hand, and, as he walked up and down, he whisked off any impediment that happened to lie in his way with the broom. Gordon, to while away the time till the authorities should appear, entered into conversation with him. The attendant happening to ask Gordon if he had ever been in Ireland, led to a discussion on Irish politics, in which they both waxed warm; and Gordon thought the individual in the seedy cut-velvet coat was inclined to be disputatious beyond what his appearance warranted. Presently the latter, reverting to Gordon's business at the riding-house, observed that he had understood every assistance had been given him, at Chatham, in the prosecution of his object. Nettled at the old boy's obstinacy about Irish affairs, Gordon flatly replied that the fact was quite the reverse; and, on the contrary, every obstacle had been thrown in his way by old General Fox, old Marsh, and others, who were jealous of any one's doing any thing but themselves. He of the cut-velvet then pointed out a part of the ridinghouse which, he conceived, would be most favourable for the performance of the bayonet exercise; but Gordon, determined to contradict him in every thing, abruptly answered that it was just the very worst spot in the whole place. At this moment, in came Sir William Fawcett, adjutant-general to the forces; who, taking no notice of Gordon, approached his companion hat in hand, and apologised to "his majesty" for having detained him so long. Gordon was paralysed: the bob-wig and cut-velvet coat belonged to none other than King George III. The captain-lieutenant had been as rude as he could be to his sovereign. Abashed, confounded, incapable of putting the men through the exercise with his usual precision and energy, he bungled, stammered, failed; and eventually returned to Chatham, cowed and crest-fallen, never more to teach the proper use of the bayonet.[25]

Although there indeed seem to have been multiple meetings between Gordon and the king, the substance of the above story—though amusing—appears to be without foundation. The article in which it appears is overwhelmingly dismissive of the utility of the bayonet, and highly biased against Gordon's idea—as well as against any attempt whatsoever to develop a system of close-quarters combat. Regarding the king, in 1828, Gordon himself stated,

It was, under the illustrious sanction of the Duke and Sir William Pitt, offered to His Majesty's notice, notwithstanding the hostility of Sir David Dundas. His Majesty ordered 100 recruits to be drilled in Chatham; they were honoured with His Majesty's inspection, and approbation, Feb. 1, 1796, in Pimlico; and on the Friday after at his Royal Levee, His Majesty extended his Royal hand to my lips, using the expression "Col. Gordon".[26]

In the introduction to one of his treatises, Gordon also recounted,

After repeated experiments [by Gordon] exhibited before [General William Pitt] and the late Duke of Rutland, who was then the Lord Lieutenant of Ireland, the project was offered, under that illustrious sanction, to His Majesty's notice. His Majesty was pleased to order one hundred recruits to be prepared in the New Exercise: these men were honored by the Royal Inspection, and by His Majesty's high approbation, which was most graciously and directly signified by His Majesty, and after that, also by a royal message delivered by the late Sir William Fawcett, then the Adjutant-General.[27]

As shall be seen, Gordon's good relationship with the king seems borne out by a number of other reports. In a letter dated November 20th, 1787, General Burgoyne recounted:

[Gordon] has testimonies of far greater consequence in his favour, viz. [General Pitt's] commendation and very honorable protection; the same from the Duke of Rutland, marked in the strongest manner by word of mouth, and by recommendation to the King; and lastly, a message from His Majesty, after he had seen the experiment, by the Adjutant General, expressing his Royal and high Approbation.[28]

And yet, despite the support of the king, Gordon continued to encounter resistance and hostility from other leading members of the British military establishment. In May, 1786, it was announced, "At the review on Wednesday many were disappointed. It was expected that Lieutenant Gordon's late improvement of the bayonet would have been adopted; but we understand it has been rejected."[29] General Burgoyne further explained,

Lieut. Gordon has had the misfortune to remain unnoticed from the time he was approved. I would be very sorry that his feelings, which are very acute, should urge him to quit the Service; I sincerely think he would be a great loss to it.

The prejudice of party, of attachment to old practices, and preconceived contempt of innovation, but above all, the want of a Commander in Chief, render it impossible at present to revive the matter on this side the water...His misfortune is, that Officers have formed judgments upon hearsay or cursory thoughts.

Burgoyne's solution was to advise Gordon to write yet another treatise, more detailed and extensive than the first, which could then be circulated and promoted to high-ranking members of the military.[30]

## GORDON'S SECOND TREATISE

According to the *Gentleman's Magazine*, sometime prior to 1801, Gordon published yet another fencing treatise, entitled, *Method of Performing the Bayonet Exercise, Invented by Lieutenant Gordon, of the 67th Regiment, to which is added, a Plan for reforming the Army.* The title of this treatise appears among a list of works published by one John Williamson—a native of Northern Ireland, a former officer in the American war, and a writer on various military matters. Since no other references to such a book by Gordon have been found, it is possible that this title is a mistake, and is merely a reference to Gordon's earlier 1783 letter. However, the other titles of Williamson's books (that is, listed in the same issue of the *Gentleman's Magazine*) appear to be without error, and it seems equally likely—if not more so—that this second text by Gordon was, just like his first, exceedingly rare, and has simply not survived.[31] In his 1787 letter, General Burgoyne extolled the virtues of Gordon's first treatise on the bayonet, and added,

> I have advised Mr. Gordon to make a new and more concise statement of his system, and convinced as I am of the solid principles upon which it is built, I shall very readily annex the remarks which occurred to me when I first espoused it.

It may be that Burgoyne's call for a "new and more concise statement" of Gordon's system, cited above, resulted in the now lost *Method of Performing the Bayonet Exercise*. Gordon would not complete another such text until 1804.

Throughout the following decade, Gordon continued to pursue a military career, and ascended to various ranks. In 1793, he was promoted to Captain-Lieutenant, in 1794 to Captain, and in 1797, to Major of Invalids in Alderney, the most northerly of the Channel Islands.[32] At this time, he was instrumental in the capture of the French privateer *Epervier*, which had boldly attempted to board an English ship off the coast of Alderney. In a public account of the incident, Secretary of War Henry Dundas lauded Gordon's role in the capture, stating, "I cannot too much praise the readiness and alacrity shewn by Major Gordon..."[33] During the late 1790s, Gordon's efforts were hampered by the onset of serious health issues, including a "nervous disorder" which "terminated in a species of palsy." Gordon recounted,

I could not articulate words, and could not support myself in an erect posture without crutches. A general tremor seized me whenever I attempted to move or rise from my seat, and the tone of my nerves seemed entirely gone...I had tried the waters of Bath and Buxton, and a long course of electricity, but all to no purpose.

Though Gordon labored "long" under this condition, he was eventually cured by the noted doctor Henry St. John Neale, to whom he happily wrote in April, 1799, from Alderney:

DEAR SIR,

It is with heart-felt pleasure I take up my pen to give you the pleasing information, that I continue to enjoy very good health, and a perfect freedom from a return of the paralytic symptoms, with which I had been so severely afflicted for upwards of two years...I shall avail myself of every opportunity to demonstrate my gratitude for the advantages derived to me, through your skill in the restoration of my health.[34]

# THE NINETEENTH CENTURY

In the years following his recovery, Gordon organized a number of high-profile events demonstrating the superiority of his exercise. The following account, published in 1803, was the first of a flurry of articles celebrating Gordon's "new" method:

Yesterday morning on St. George's Parade, Wood's Mews, was exhibited a novel spectacle. A detachment of 60 of Lord HOBART'S regiment (the QUEEN'S Volunteers) under the command of Capt. MERRY, had the honour of being critically inspected by His Royal Highness the Commander in Chief, who expressed his satisfaction at the dexterity they displayed in exhibiting the new bayonet exercise. The Adjutant-General and other Officers of distinction, expressed their astonishment at seeing the Gentlemen of the War office so correct in marching and performing a difficult exercise. We understand that Captain MERRY has trained his company to the bayonet exercise, under the direction of Major GORDON, who some years ago offered it to HIS MAJESTY's notice, when it was honoured with royal approbation. It was on the present occasion submitted to His Royal Highness, under the auspices of Lord HOBART and the Adjutant General, from their conviction of its utility after a fair trial.[35]

And again, only a few days later, another account was published. This one was, in all likelihood, the first to ever mention the use of specialized training bayonets:

Major GORDON has submitted a mode of bayonet exercise, we understand, to the Duke of YORK, which is highly approved. One hundred of the Guards well skilled in the exercise are

*"The new method of charging the bayonet."* Courtesy of the Anne S.K. Brown Military Collection, Brown University Library. In the summer of 1803, the Loyal North Britons, "a corps entirely composed of Highland gentlemen," commanded by Lord Eric Reay, adopted Gordon's bayonet exercise. See also *Monthly Magazine*, August 1, 1803.

immediately to be appointed to instruct the Volunteers. The Pimlico Corps have made great progress in the art, which gives a surprising superiority over those who are unacquainted with such a mode of defence. The advantage is equal to that which a skilful fencer has over a person who was never taught the use of the small sword. The instrument with which the men are instructed, is made of wood, and the bayonet resembles a tragedy dagger, which *marks the hit* of the assailant without injuring the person hit.[36]

One of the many Volunteer units instructed in Gordon's method: *"Dedicated to the officers and privates of the St. James Westminster Loyal Volunteer Regiment: This plate represents their uniform in the position of the new charge bayonet"* (1804). Courtesy of the Anne S.K. Brown Military Collection, Brown University Library.

The best news for Gordon came just two days later, on New Year's Eve, when the following announcement appeared in the *Ipswich Journal*:

The new bayonet exercise is immediately to be adopted. Lieut. Col. Robinson and Capt. Gordon are to train 100 of the Guards, who are to disseminate these new manœuvres through the different regiments and corps.[37]

One month later, after having commenced the training of his one hundred new Guards, Gordon received additional public praise in the form of the following review:

Major Gordon's improvement of the use of the bayonet, is one of the most expert and efficient ever adopted in the art of war. It is founded on equally just and certain principles as those of the lever, or any part of military tactics. Were two battalions to meet in conflict, it is evident that the one skilled in the Major's scientific invention would lay their antagonists prostrate, before the latter, by the usual mode of charging with the bayonet, could reach a single opponent. It is, in short, a system of attack that is not to be parried by the unskilful, and gives full as great an advantage as the most expert fencer possesses over him who is utterly ignorant of science. Several military characters of high rank, we hear, have distinguished the improvement with their warm approbation.[38]

This favorable review was reprinted one month later in Ireland, among the pages of *Walker's Hibernian Magazine*.[39] In March, the Duke of York inspected Gordon's trainees, and the King himself "expressed the highest approbation." The new system was, reportedly, "to be adopted by all the Troops of the Line, Militia, Volunteers, &c."[40] In April, the *Times* further reported:

> Yesterday morning General WHITELOCK, Governor of Portsmouth, accompanied by Major-General CALVERT, Adjutant-General, and several other Officers, attended at the Tilt-yard, to inspect a party of the Light Infantry of the First Regiment of Foot Guards, in the performance of the bayonet-exercise. The General expressed himself highly pleased with the activity and precision of the men.[41]

Back in Dublin, a popular journal declared Gordon to be "a gentleman well known in Ireland," and optimistically enthused that his method was "to be introduced also in Ireland, and will render our troops invincible against the attack of the enemy."[42] Later that year, Gordon again took up his pen to compose yet another fencing treatise in manuscript. Although never published in its pure original form, this text would, quite importantly, give rise to Gordon's most comprehensive work—which would be released one year later, and which was destined to become a classic.

## AN IDEA OF DEFENCE (1804)

This one hundred and thirty-six page illustrated manuscript was written London, dated September 29, 1804, and was "humbly" dedicated in flowing script to "Major General Harry Calvert the Adjutant General of the Forces" by "Anthony Gordon, A. M. Trinity College Dublin."[43] It was later acquired by the library of the Royal United Service Institute in London, where it remained for nearly two centuries until the 1960s, when the Institute closed its doors and dispersed much of its former collection. In 1968, the manuscript found its way into the archives of the National Army Museum, London, where it resides today.

"Plate the 16th", never published, from Gordon's 1804 manuscript, *An Idea of Defence*, showing the "weakness of [Roworth's] Hanging Guard..." Courtesy of the Council of the National Army Museum, London.

This text is essentially an early draft of, or preparation for, Gordon's most comprehensive work, *A Treatise on the Science of Defence: For the Sword, Bayonet, and Pike in Close Action*—which would be published one year later. The 1804 manuscript differs, however, from Gordon's published work in numerous aspects. It contains, for instance, much unique textual material which did not make it into the published book. Several of the illustrations contained in *An Idea of Defence* differ from what appears in the 1805 *Treatise*—in fact, five plates from the manuscript are not to be found in the published work at all, or appear in radically altered forms.[44] Although the bulk of Gordon's manuscript covers topics and ideas that are treated of in the published work, many of them are worded, expressed, and structured in considerably different ways. Gordon's *Idea of Defence* is thus unique, important, and worthy of close examination and study.

In the opening dedication of the manuscript, Gordon acknowledges his obedience to Sir Harry Calvert's commands "to turn in my thoughts [to] the subject of the science of Defence generally," rather than focusing on his "own notions." This likely explains Gordon's decision to expand his work beyond the confines of the bayonet exercise, and to treat of fencing on a wider scale—that is, to expound upon its fundamental theory, history, and practical application to other types of swords and staff weapons. In the next few pages, Gordon provides the following outline for the general structure of his work:

> I propose to treat of this subject in the following order. First, I shall inquire into its origin, extent, & effect, now particularly upon the Romans, so renowned for this preeminence in the use of the Sword; The abuse and extinction of this, in common with other Sciences; The attempt of the French to revive it upon erroneous principles.[†]
>
> Secondly, will be submitted a sketch of the solid principles indispensable as a foundation to defend against assaults generally.
>
> The third part respects the mode of receiving, & frustrating the Cuts of Cavalry, and of causing them to end in the fall of the Cavalry Man.
>
> To which will be subjoined an appendice containing a sketch of the Disposition of the bones and muscles of the arm; and also of the powers of the Lever: These being the Principles, & not those of the French, upon which the Science of Defence should be founded, in the opinion of the Writer.[45]

Another notable difference between the manuscript and the published version concerns the treatment of the pike. While the title of Gordon's 1805 published *Treatise* implies that the use

---

† Gordon later alludes that this faulty "attempt of the French" was the publication of Henry de Sainct Didier's 1573 treatise, *Les secrets du premier livre sur l'espée seule*. See *An Idea of Defence*, 13.

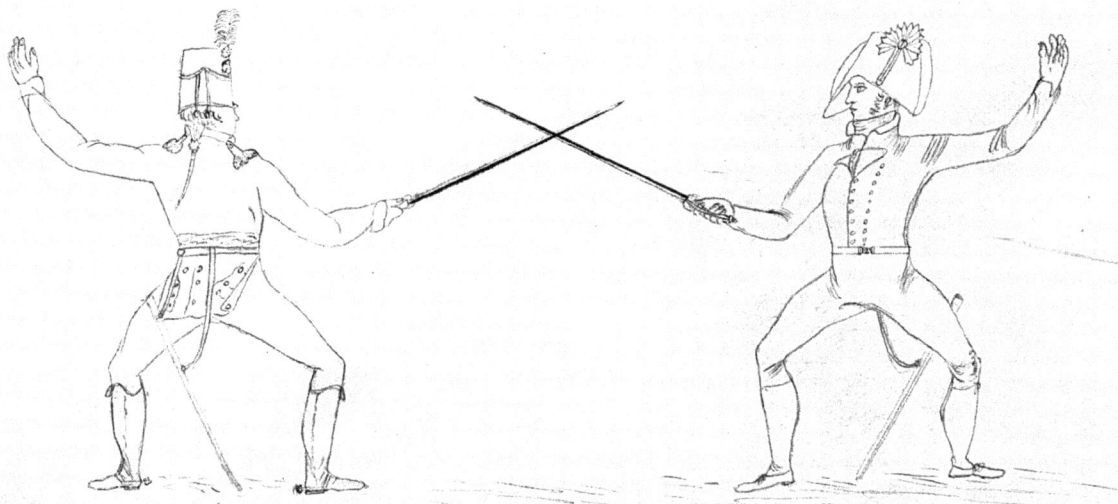

*The mode of guarding any cut or Thrust in Quarte.*

*An Idea of Defence*: Plate 6th (on top) shows two fencers "On Guard joined in Quarte"; Plate 10th (on bottom) shows defense against an adversary wielding a saber. Courtesy of the Council of the National Army Museum, London.

of the pike is treated of therein, mention of the weapon is glaringly absent from its pages, except for a few historical references. In *An Idea of Defence*, however, Gordon notes: "The Sword is the Instrument mentioned. But the Firelock or Pike may be substituted. The Principles being equally applicable to all hand-weapons."[46] Later in the manuscript, Gordon elaborates:

> The Practice of the sword, which with all deference is offered to your serious consideration, is (as I take it) general and applicable to all kinds of Hand weapons, whatsoever. Every syllable of instruction for the use of the sword is peculiarly adapted to the Bayonet which is nothing but the best sword that perhaps ever was invented and to the firelock affixed.[47]

Many additional passages pertaining to aspects of fencing and swordsmanship, which did not make it to publication, can be found in this manuscript. In his introduction, for instance, Gordon explains, "Man is a rational, & by his very frame 'a Political Animal'...naturally impelled to enter into, and enjoy the Blessings of Society. The first Law impressed upon him, and upon all Animals is that of Self-Defence..." He continues:

> Notwithstanding the Bounty of Divine Providence, in supplying talents, passions to stimulate, and hands to execute, yet men in general are not born artists. The Ideas of music, painting, sculpture &cc. are not stamped on the soul, on its formation; & perhaps some instruction might be found necessary for the use of the hands even in Boxing; taking this for granted, notwithstanding the opinion of respectable men, that "all particular instruction for close action is superfluous", the Science of Defence however congenial to nature, yet, results not entirely from it, but rather from the union of the power of Nature, and of Art combined. It consists in <u>clear perception</u>, and in the just & practical <u>application</u> of all our energies and powers directed according to the <u>Laws</u> of <u>Nature</u>, and of <u>Motion</u>, to frustrate the attack of the aggressor, and to direct it to terminate in his Submission or Destruction.[48]

Gordon also emphasizes the importance of instilling morality in prospective swordsmen, a notion that is barely touched upon (in less than one sentence) in his published work. In his manuscript, Gordon writes,

> As Cicero defines an orator, *"Vir bonus, dicendi peritus"*, thus placing Virtue in her station superior to Science. So virtue, and honor are the primary qualities of a proper Swordsman. Being first disciplined in these, he will be more formidable to the Enemy, than he could, by mere dexterity in the Sword—by having command of <u>Body</u> &c., 2$^d$ of the Line, & thirdly by the judicious <u>opposition</u> of the <u>Fort</u> which are the secondary qualities. Such a man will be always on Guard, always feeling, but never pressing the adverse blade, except in the act of striking <u>home vertically</u> with a <u>cut</u> or thrust applying the Fort, & with it forcing the adversary out of the Line.[49]

**Above:** "Plate 2nd." Gordon's large, annotated "Mathematical Standard." The upper right reads: "A Mathematical Standard calculated to ascertain the precise force, deriving from Gravity, of all Cuts &c. whatsoever made from any point above the horizon, either vertically, or obliquely, from the zenith to the Horizon." The lower left reads: "Scale shewing the precise Disadvantages of all cuts made upward, from different points below the Horizon from the Horizon to the Nadir a space of 90 degrees." Courtesy of the Council of the National Army Museum, London.

As compared to his published treatise, Gordon's elucidations on fencing theory using mathematics are, if anything, even more elaborate and extensive in *An Idea of Defence*. His novel application of plane trigonometry, in the form of the *sine* function (perhaps a first in the history of fencing), is utilized no less than seventeen times, largely in the context of an annotated geometrical diagram, which Gordon uses to prove the superiority of descending cuts:

These Laws [of Nature] furnish a <u>Standard</u> for the purpose of measuring and ascertaining the precise difference, and <u>exact merits</u> of all cuts, and thrusts whatever, from the first and last, through all the intermediate points, which are really indefinite…Having thus a Mathematical Standard measuring the force of gravity of one cut, you have the precise measure of the advantages, and disadvantages of all Cuts &c. whatsoever.[50]

311

Gordon's "Mathematical Standard" would appear in a simplified form, without his original annotations, in the published *Treatise on the Science of Defence*.

In terms of practical application and technique, Gordon includes instructions regarding the salute, and the gripping of the weapon, which do not appear in his published work. He writes,

> The Sword being gracefully drawn, after the usual salute, is to be held fast by all the fingers and the thumb clenched about the grip, to prevent disarms, which might be inevitable were it held by the forefinger and thumb only; and altho a sword-knot is useful, yet the recovery of the weapon by it, is impracticable in time sufficient to prevent destruction from a Swordsman. Do not depend on the two fingers if you can use the five.[51]

In another similar example, Gordon provides more information on defending against low-line cuts than he does in the published *Treatise*:

> Low cuts at the advanced leg are eluded, by withdrawing it, with celerity from the 2$^d$ or 3$^d$ position, to the first; or more properly, by timing the adversary, who absurdly exposes himself by his attempt to cut.
>
> If you wish to spare him, you parry all low cuts and thrusts whatsoever, by the round parade of quarte and half circle combined, with due celerity, or by a rapid rotation of your hand in the half circle as long as such revolution may be necessary.
>
> The perfect Command of the Body, the power and flexibility of the Limbs enables the man, to elude many Cuts, and thrusts, without using any parades.[52]

Gordon continues to describe numerous other techniques, most of which would be included in his 1805 publication, including the use of the bayonet against mounted cavalrymen. Missing from his manuscript is the treatment of the use of the bayonet against other soldiers wielding the bayonet, and methods of group combat. Both would be included in the published version. In closing his text, Gordon encourages the testing of his method, and notes,

> To demonstrate by practical proof, the Truth of this System, has been the great object of my heart at all times. This object induced me to relinquish my situation as a Master in Trinity College Dublin, & to enter into His Majesty's Service. Since that, I have persevered upon all occasions; nor have I lost, but on the contrary sought every occasion of offering, if not of obtruding this subject during these twenty four years past.

Gordon finishes by stating, "I feel my inferiority & that the subject is worthy of Talents more commensurate to its importance—such a Genius as could illustrate and adorn the most harsh, rigid and intractable materials to which I am unequal."[53]

## A TREATISE ON THE SCIENCE OF DEFENCE
## FOR THE SWORD, BAYONET, AND PIKE IN CLOSE ACTION (1805)

Gordon's final fencing text treats of both the sword and the bayonet, and is, in many respects, his magnum opus. The first edition of the book, published in 1805 by B. McMillan, "Printer to His Royal Highness the Prince of Wales," and dedicated "with all humility and respect" to "The Duke of York, Commander in Chief of the Forces," is sixty-five pages long, and includes nineteen illustrations redrawn by the well-known artist and Royal Academy member Robert Smirke.[54] Although the book was published several years following the turn of the nineteenth century, the methods described therein are highly influenced by eighteenth century fencing theory, and represent the culmination of several decades of Gordon's thinking on the art and science of fencing, as well as on group combat.

Gordon begins the first section of his treatise with an eloquent paragraph about the fundamental aspects of self-defense:

SELF-DEFENCE is the first law of Nature implanted in all animals; hence men have been impelled to associate, and to frame laws securing the blessings of society. Although men are admirably supplied with passions to excite them to action, with reason to direct their efforts, and with hands to execute; yet they are not furnished with innate ideas, or science, which points out the best mode of using and applying their strength and their hands to any work. If the arts of writing, painting, and the mechanical arts, require skill and dexterity, which result only from time and instruction, the science of Defence, which consists in a just perception of our powers, and in the proper application of our natural strength against the weakest point of the adversary, cannot be the result of inspiration. Our knowledge of this, or any science, is in proportion to our ideas of the principles.[55]

Gordon proceeds to outline the history of swordsmanship, beginning with the eras of ancient Greece and Rome. He then discusses the origin of the various guards and parry positions used with the sword. It is to the genius of the classical authors that Gordon attributes the understanding of the "powers of the lever," which he divides into three kinds. He notes that the human arm itself is a kind of lever, explaining,

On account of the beauty and symmetry of the parts, the Almighty, in his infinite wisdom, was graciously pleased to form the legs and arms of animals levers of the third, rather than of the first or second kind. Now, as the legs and arms are thus divinely composed, and as all instruments, such as swords, firelocks, pikes, sticks, &c. &c. are levers of this kind...you may consider an attempt to collect, concentrate, and mechanically to apply, if not the whole, yet certainly a considerable portion of these powers in a favourable light.[56]

In an appendix, which includes an in-depth discussion of anatomy, physiology, and a list of "the bones and muscles of the arm," Gordon demonstrates how the same principles applied to the sword or bayonet can be demonstrated with one's own arm, empty-handed. He reminds the reader that all of the muscles—and hence the weapon itself—are ultimately directed by one's own consciousness:

> The voluntary motions result from the commands of the mind, wonderfully but unaccountably impressed on the muscles by the nerves, who are the ministers for the purpose of thus communicating orders from within, outwards, or for carrying intelligence from without, inwards, for the information of the mind.[57]

In his elucidation of body mechanics, Gordon also assails the "present doctrine" of British swordsmanship, which stipulates "that all cuts, thrusts, and guards are made by the action of the wrist and shoulder alone." This last comment was undoubtedly a reference to Major-General John Gaspard Le Marchant's influential *Rules and Regulations for the Sword Exercise of the Cavalry*, which had been published in 1796, and which was widely reprinted throughout the British Isles and United States.[58] In an annotated edition of his own book, Gordon wrote in the margins that "You must see the absurdity of the positions of Col Le Marchant who pretended that he had used some lessons from Gordon, and got the [illegible] Duke to form an Institution for himself."[59]

In the treatise's section on the "Origins and Effects of this Science," and the "Sketch of the Roman Practice," Gordon frequently quotes from the original Greek and Latin sources, which he also translates. In the same section, Gordon's unusual, erudite application of mathematical and geometrical principles, as well as basic Newtonian physics, to fencing can be seen in the following passage, in what is possibly the first instance of an author utilizing the language of trigonometry (in the form of the *sine* function) in a published treatise on fencing:

> The laws of Nature, which measure and determine the moment or force of bodies descending along inclined planes, and compare it with the whole force of gravity with which they fall perpendicularly, are a standard for measuring the force of all cuts whatsoever derived from the laws of gravity.
>
> Gravity is the most obvious phenomenon in all bodies; it pervades the universe. It is that uniform tendency of bodies exerted in a vertical direction to the centre of the earth; it uniformly accelerates all motions, or cuts, vertically downwards, and retards uniformly all bodies projected

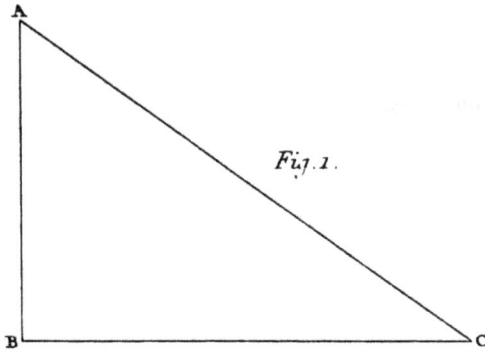

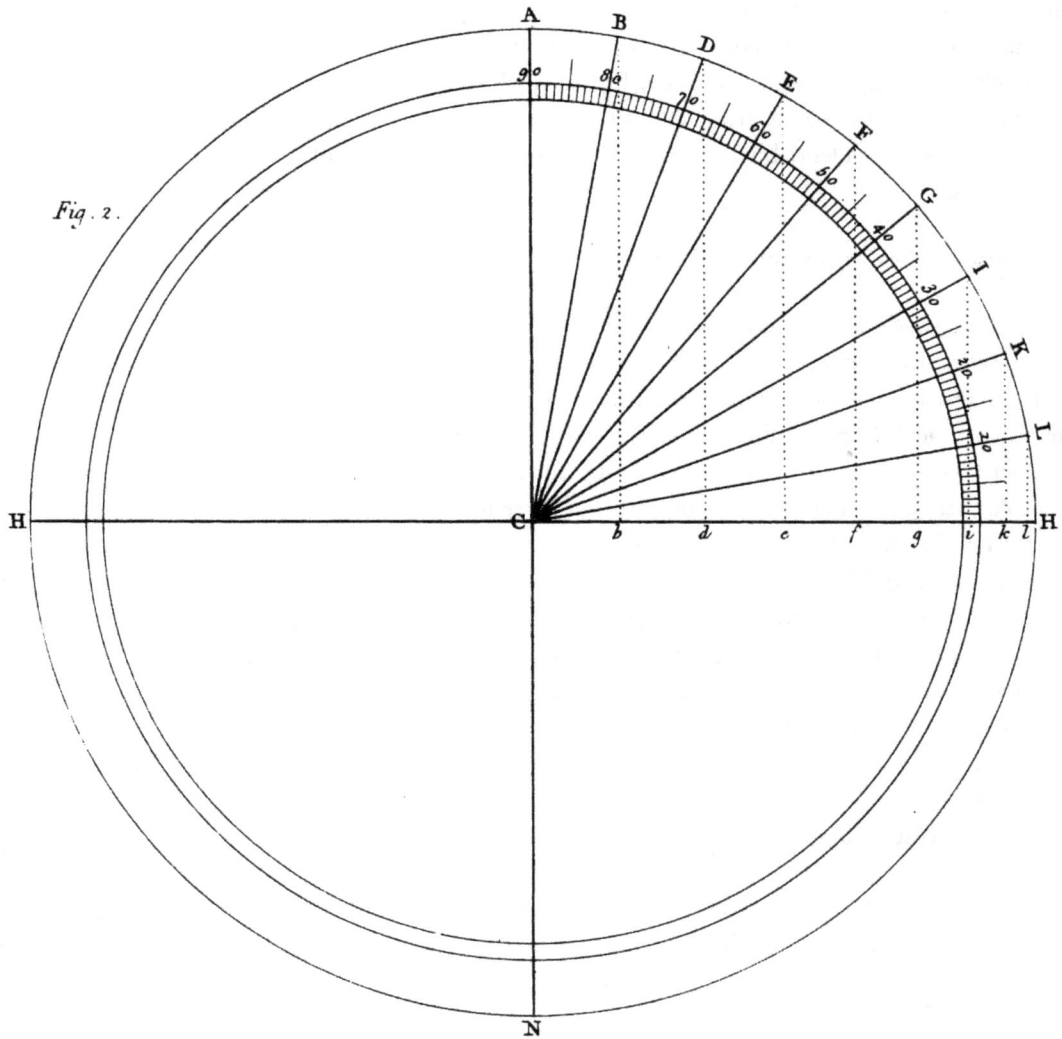

Plate II from Gordon's *Treatise on the Science of Defence*, showing his simplified Mathematical Standard.

perpendicularly upwards. The force of any cut from gravity is determined by the following proposition, viz. "The force of gravity by which a body descends along an inclined plane, is to the whole force of its gravity with which it falls perpendicularly, as the height of the plane to its length; or as the sine of the angle of elevation to radius."

Plate 2d, Fig. 1st, AG is the plane or cut; BC its base, parallel to the horizon, and AB its perpendicular height, or sine of the angle of elevation. The force of the cut AC is to the force of the cut AB as AB :: AC; that is, as the height to the length of the plane.

The force of gravity of any one cut being thus determined, the force of all are determined by the same rule; for example, fig. 2d, plate 2d, AHN is a circle; ACH is a quadrant containing ten cuts, viz. AC, BC, DC, EC, FC, GC, IC, KC, LC, HC; and there might be ten millions of cuts in the same space, differing in their force from gravity, no two being alike. Their perpendicular altitudes, viz. the dotted lines Bb, Dd, Ee, Ff, Gg, Ii, Kk, Ll, determine their respective forces. For example, what is the force, from gravity, of the horizontal cut HC? Nothing: the horizontal motion is not coincident, but at right angles, with the tendency of gravity, which is vertically downwards.

Or, likewise, in Gordon's approach to feints in Section III, he explains:

Feints are either single or double, but rarely triple. The single feint is the least complex of all compound thrusts; it menaces an attack on one point to cover the real impulse intended upon another. The French mode (which is erroneous) is as follows: Plate 3d, No. 4, the point describes the arc, or line AB, in the direction of the arrow; 2d, it retrogrades in the same line, say BC, that is, describing the base, or rather the whole triangle, twice; 3d, the point is projected from the point A; that is, the single feint is composed of three motions equal to the three sides of a triangle; but by Euclid, 20th Prop, lib. 1, any two sides of a triangle are greater than the third, and the three are much greater; and the times being as the space described, the velocities being equal, the time of the single feint is to that of the simple thrust 3 :: 1; therefore the celerity and advantage of the simple thrust are in that proportion, Q. E. D. Any further illustration of the advantage of the simple thrust over cuts and thrusts still more complex than the feint, seems to be superfluous. The right mode of executing the feint is this: after disengaging from A to B, from the point B push straight home, without returning to A, raising and opposing your hand, so as to force his blade out of the line; recover quickly, using the round parade of quarte; yet even so, the advantage of the simple thrust would be two to one.

Though his application of trigonometry and physics may seem extremely over-complicated or obtuse to the layman, Gordon insists that it is not necessary for the soldier to fully understand such principles in order to utilize his method. He explains,

*Round Parade in Quarte.*

1

*Round Parade in Tierce.*

2

*2.ᵈ position, Parade of the Demicircle.*

*1.ˢᵗ position of Quarte.*

3

*Single Feint.*

4

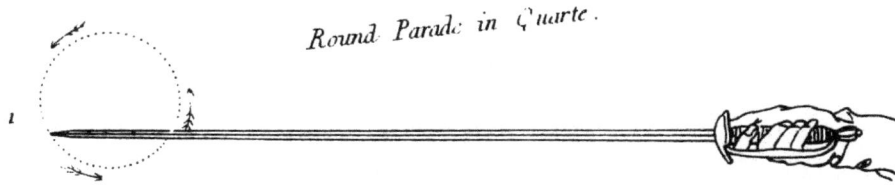

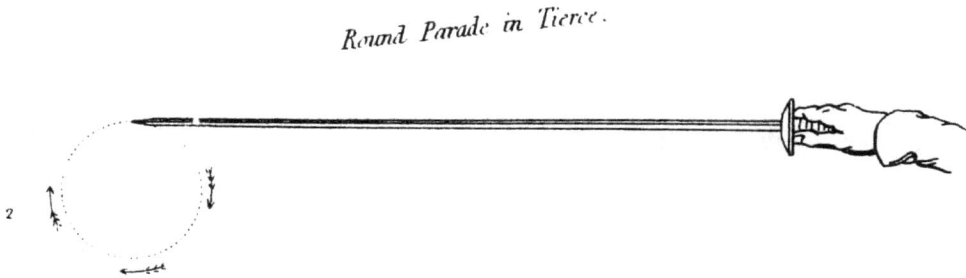

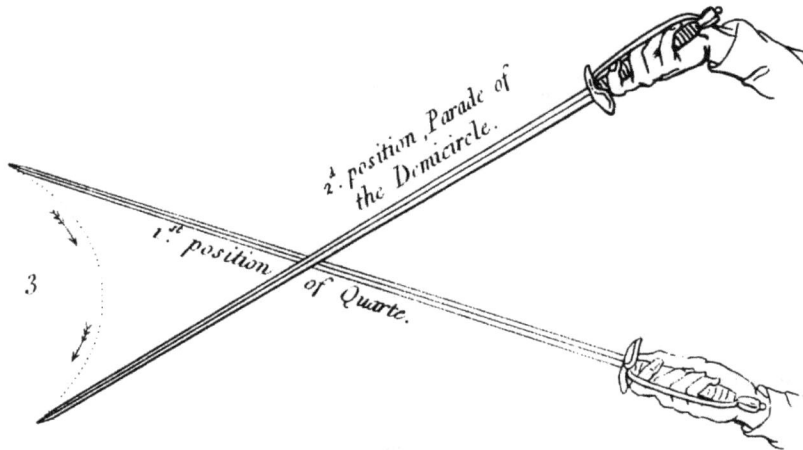

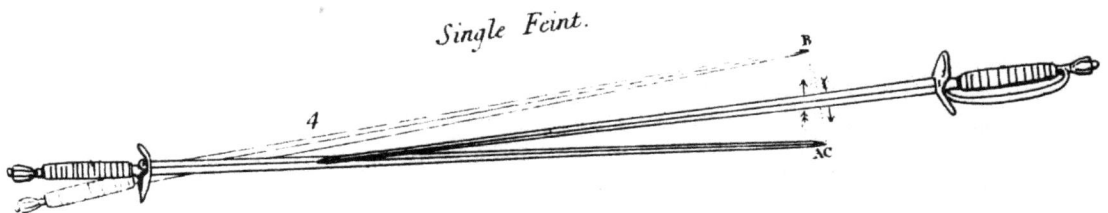

Plate III from Gordon's *Treatise*, illustrating the feints and parades.

As to the theory of mechanics, it cannot be necessary to the soldier. The man who conducts the wagon, regards not the theory of the wheel and axle. Thus soldiers might be instructed to apply the fort to the foible, and to demonstrate the truth by their practice, although strangers to the mathematical principles.[60]

After his treatment of the theoretical, Gordon proceeds to the practical. Many of Gordon's physical descriptions of various fencing techniques are remarkably precise. He describes the lunge, for instance, in the following terms:

The exertion of these powers will place you in the third position, with your feet about 36 inches asunder at right angles. This attitude is termed the allonge.

The allonge is to be made with all possible rapidity; this will be better accomplished by engraving the ideas of it upon the mind one after another. Thus, first form your extension: Plate 5th, No. 2; elevate your right hand in quarte, as high as the direction of your left eye-brow; lower your point in a line of the cavity under the arm of the adversary; extend your left hand and left knee; then project the thrust, rolling your hand still more in quarte, or supination; throw forward your right foot at the same instant, 15 or 16 inches, so that your feet may be at least 36 inches asunder. Plate 6th, Fig. 2d. The foot should resound in striking the ground. Repeat this practice until you can execute it in one rapid motion. Examine your attitude in this third position, and practise unremittingly in the air, until you acquire a graceful precision in the execution...Your own feelings and judgment will best determine the length of your allonge: it should be such as would enable you to recover to your second position with the utmost ease and celerity in real action.

With similar precision, Gordon describes an attack in *quarte* as follows:

When you are engaged on guard in the second position, the blades are to touch in a point, about ten inches distant from their extremities. The quarte is to be thus delivered:

Form the extension by a rotatory motion of the arm and wrist raised and extended, &c. (Plate 5th, Fig. 2); project the sword or firelock in and along the identical point of contact, as in a nick; oppose your fort thus upwards against his feeble, as it were in the nick. Direct your thrust, or cut, in the line, in such a manner as to infix your point into the cavity under his arm. See Plate 7th.

All this is to be executed in one motion, and with such celerity as to hit your adversary an instant before your foot strikes the ground. Recover quickly, using your round parade of quarte on this and all occasions.[61]

Notably, as demonstrated in the above passage, Gordon frequently relates his technique to both the sword and bayonet in the same passage, rather than treating of the weapons separately.

*The thrust and Cut in Quarte.*

*Allonge in Tierce.*     *Guard of Tierce by the Fort.*

Plates VII and IX from Gordon's *Treatise*, illustrating the "Thrust and cut in Quarte," the "Allonge in Tierce," and the "Guard of Tierce by the Fort."

Regarding the attack in *tierce*, Gordon explains the importance of precision and point control:

Feel your adversary's blade constantly, but do not press it, as you will be exposed to his time thrust by your relinquishing the point of contact; therefore, in disengaging from quarte to tierce, move your point closely, within a hair's breadth of his blade; so quickly, that your change shall be imperceptible, your hand being in supination, as it was before: for if you roll your hand into pronation as you change your point, your motion will be wide. Roll your hand into pronation as you project the thrust along his blade, in the point indented in it, as it were in a nick, to direct your course. Oppose your hand high, and over his blade, to your right. Direct your point into the cavity under his arm. His effort to parry this thrust (if you have seized his foible), by his parade in tierce, will materially serve you, as it will be a fulcrum assisting your thrust, unless your sword whips or bends. Plate 8th, No.1, gives an idea of planting the tierce.[62]

Gordon also instructs the reader in various aspects of training. He advises the student, for instance, to be extremely well-practiced in all the footwork, parries, extensions, and cuts before attempting to learn the lunge:

You cannot be too much practised in advancing, retiring, and parrying, simple thrusts and cuts in this attitude. Having fully obtained the command of your person by this practice, and not before, you are to spring from it into your third position, which is that of the allonge.[63]

Gordon also instructs the reader to perfect their form and technique by practicing before a mirror:

Examine and adjust your attitudes before a glass. The practice of allonging first in the open air, and after that against a post, will contribute to invigorate your limbs, and to grace your person. You had better avoid the diversion of running at a post, to take the ring on the point of your sword; such ludicrous practice tends only to ruin your opposition, and consequently to expose your person.

Gordon's method, though largely based on the French small-sword fencing of the eighteenth century, includes some modifications, or preferences, of his own.[64] For instance, Gordon generally rejects the use of the parries of *prime*, *seconde*, and *quinte*, which he states are "weak," and should be resorted to only in special cases. Regarding the various parries and hand positions applied to the broadsword and saber, Gordon also rejects, as "dangerous to the persons using them," the three hanging guards and "side protects," as well as "all cuts, save only two." Gordon explains the inclusion of cuts in his system as follows:

There are only two good cuts, and these have not been noticed by the French, nor by their disciples: the first is the cut *made vertically downwards* in *quarte*, the second is hurled vertically *downwards* in *tierce*.

Make the vertical cut in quarte thus: "Raise your point vertically, and oppose your *identical fort* (that is, that point of your sword which is in contact with the shell) to the very extremity of his sword; contract your arm; and having thus secured his *foible*, strike in this vertical cut on the quarte, or inside of your adversary; terminate this cut in a thrust, and recover, using your round parade of quarte with all celerity." Plate 7th.

In cutting, the hand is to be in the most natural position, between supination and pronation; but it is to be turned into complete supination when you end your cut in a thrust. The best mode of parrying this cut is by the *pointe volante;* that is, by contracting the arm, and opposing the fort of the weapon, which must be raised perpendicularly to extricate the foible. By this parade he opposes his fort to your feeble. Plate 8th, Nos. 2 and 3...

The guard, cut, and thrust of tierce, are formed by turning the forearm, wrist, and the hand, into pronation. As in the guard of quarte, the hand is to be less in supination than when it finishes the thrust, so in the guard of tierce it is to be less in pronation than when it delivers the thrust.

Besides this motion of pronation, the hand is to describe an arc of about eight inches, from the guard of quarte to that of tierce, from the left to the right.

The delivery of the thrust and cut in tierce, is similar in principle to that of quarte, in justly applying your fort. The formation of the extension and the allonge are the same in all thrusts; but your opposition in tierce, and in quarte over the arm, is to your right.

Gordon also places strong emphasis on the round parades, or circular parries, which he applies to the use of both the sword and bayonet. He explains,

The complex guards, termed the round parades of *quarte*, of *tierce*, and of the half circle, cannot be sufficiently practised. These guards counteract and confound the projects of the adversary. The round parade of quarte circled twice round with celerity, and combined with the half circle annexed; or the rapid rotation twice, or thrice, of the half circle, with the round parade immediately annexed, or any combination of the round parade of quarte with the round parade of tierce, terminated by simple quarte and tierce, form a *shield* sufficient to guard off all cuts and thrusts whatsoever...Dexterity, in the combination of these parades, will enable you, although blindfolded, to parry all superior cuts and thrusts...[and] the dextrous combination of the round parades will enable you to frequently disarm your adversary.[65]

Gordon concludes this chapter of the text with sections on both disarming and timing—this last concept, as noted by the author, being "the summit and very last stage of the science of Defence," which is "not to be attempted, except by the ablest swordsman." After describing four kinds of time-thrusts, Gordon proceeds to a "cursory View of the Origin and Defect of the established Exercises," which consists of a historical overview of the ancient phalanx, and an elaborate criticism of the exercises in currently use in the United Kingdom. Gordon lambasts the low regard with which officers in the service have for the intelligence of the average foot soldier, observing that "this art [of defence] is withheld, as if it were a secret of *Bona Dea*, or of the Eleusinian mysteries, too sacred to be revealed to his Majesty's subjects and soldiers."

Following the chapter's conclusion is a new section treating of the use of the bayonet in group actions. Gordon begins it thus:

> *The application of the Science of Defence to the Bayonet.*
> Will it not be difficult to instruct a battalion in the art of defending itself in close action? All arts appear to be either difficult or easy, in proportion to our ignorance or knowledge of them. If you are practised in the three positions already described, and in the thrusts and guards, all difficulty is surmounted; the same gamut which enabled you to play on the violin, will serve you in learning to play on the violincello.

In this section, Gordon gives instructions for forming two ranks, the front and center, which "may be consolidated into one close action, and after that moment, resolved again into two ranks." In minute detail, he describes the basic guard position and footwork used when forming such ranks. He explains how to attack and defend as part of a unit, by utilizing the advantages of the fort and foible:

> In the present established position of the charge, the left side is presented as in No. 1, plate 12th. If you charge with the right in front, you will have a most decisive advantage, as appears from No. 2 of the same plate; for your firelock will be placed in the inside of his left arm, your fort applied to his foible, you stand upon a broad, while he stands upon a narrow base; you seize and bind down his foible by your right hand, your left holds the extremity of the butt of the piece, your right holds that part which is intermediate between the lock and the lowest pipe, your point is raised thirty-five degrees above the horizon, his point is parallel to the horizon, and if it be not, depress it with your fort; by these means he must fall on your point, without any effort made on your part, as he is exposed from head to foot. Any effort of his to parry your point would be useless to him, and serve only as a fulcrum to your firelock. This is so evident, that had he the strength of fifty men in addition to his own, it would be impossible for him, in this situation, to guard himself; therefore the dexterity of your right hand applied in this manner, will answer all the purposes of a shield, perhaps as effectually as that of Achilles. As you have from this position, such facility to destroy your enemy, you may suppose, and with great justice, that any additional aid must be superfluous. Very true, you have one hundred to one in your favor.[66]

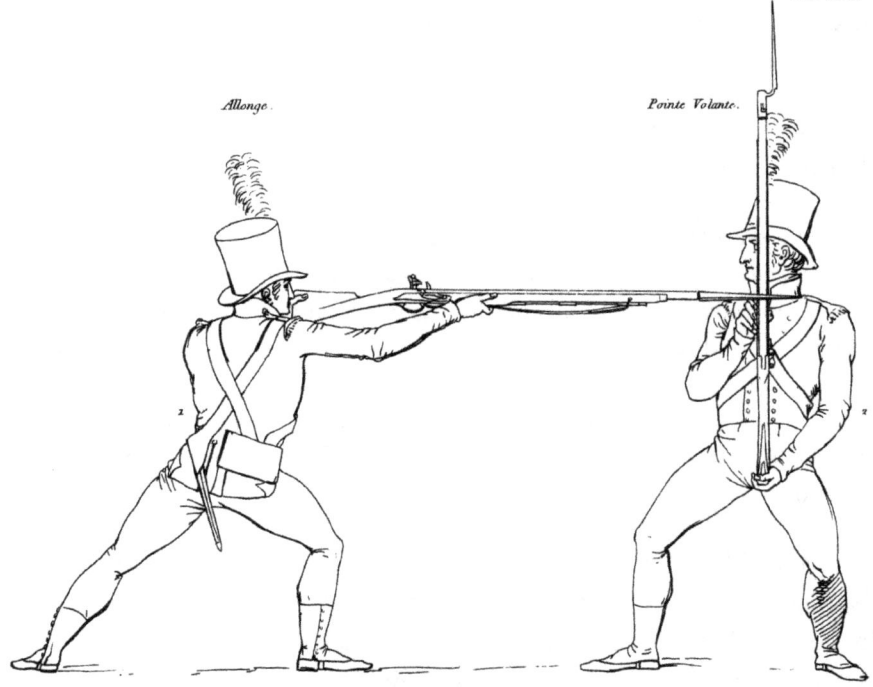

Plates XII (restored) and XIII, illustrating methods of attack and defense with the bayonet.

Gordon also explains the spatial (and hence mechanical) advantages inherent in this particular method of organizing and combining the front and center ranks:

> At the instant the front rank comes on guard, the centre rank springs into the vacant intervals; thus, the two ranks are consolidated as in plate 12th, No. 2. In this situation the centre rank man has nothing to guard against, not even the foible of the enemy to oppose: he has only to destroy the enemy without any opposition. If this is the necessary result of your second position, what would the consequence be to the enemy, were you and your companion to make an exertion of your powers, that is, to allonge out in the third position? You see that this practice gives two to one in the same space in the front, and that consequently it gives the same advantage in the flanks and rear, and that, in all times and places it must prove the inevitable destruction of the enemy.

Gordon concludes this chapter with several pages on pedagogy, detailing various words of command for the exercise. He touches upon methods of training, and describes the manner in which the soldier should both practice the lunge and accustom his arm to the weight of the firelock:

> Suffer them not to move or drag the hinder leg, which they would be apt to do, from their eagerness in the allonge. The firelock which appeared heavy to beginners, will, in the course of four weeks become so light, that they will readily hold it out with the one hand only, on the allonge. Observe, first to exercise them in the positions without arms; secondly, with the firelocks simply; and thirdly, you are to use the bayonet.

Gordon finishes by including a number of lessons and drills for the bayonet, of which the following is but one example:

> 1. Prepare to charge. 1. On guard. 3. Allonge in quarte. 4. Recover and parry quarte over with the round parade of quarte. 5. Circle twice, and push quarte over. 6. Recover with the point volante in tierce. 7. Cut vertically in tierce, and end this cut in a thrust. 8. Recover with the round parade twice made in tierce, and dart home in tierce. 9. Recover, using the round parade of tierce once, and come to the point volante in quarte. 10. Dart in a vertical cut in quarte, end it in thrust. 11. If he feigns or raises his point, time him on his first movement. 12. If he parries your quarte over, or tierce, as you recover, throw in the octave. 13. Retire, and if he advances in tierce, time him in quarte. 14. If he deceive your half circle, dart in the octave...[67]

The final chapter of Gordon's treatise consists of a detailed discussion, copiously illustrated, of how the bayonet should be used when opposed to the cavalry officer wielding a saber on horseback. In this combat scenario, the author unhesitatingly gives the advantage to the foot soldier trained in the use of the bayonet. He explains:

*Plate XIV.*

*Plate XV.*

*The Head guarded against any Cut.*

Plates XIV and XV, illustrating methods of defense against cavalry.

The cavalry man thinks that from his elevated situation, and his knowledge of the mode he has been taught of flourishing his sword, that he has an indubitable advantage. On the contrary, the infantry man who has been really instructed in the use of the sword, is convinced that the horseman does not, in truth, know how to make one single thrust or parade. An elevated situation is an advantage, if it can be used with effect...The movements of the rider depend much on the situation and movements of his horse. He cannot with due celerity and quickness make the minute movements of one step, and of a step and a half, or of less than half a step, so as to be instantly within and without the proper distance at the same instant. The minute motions of the horse, are too slow and inaccurate for this purpose. The horse moves as he may be commanded; his ear and reason are centered in his mouth, which is governed by the bit; this by the reins, and these are directed by the rider. On the contrary, the infantry man, although inferior in situation, stands ready, collected, and independent upon a broad base, upon terrâ firmâ; he knows and takes his distance at a glance; he is trained in the method of anticipating his enemy; he *nicks* the critical moment, and delivers the *time thrust*, to which the horseman is a stranger. In delivering this thrust, he knows and applies the fort of his firelock, which is a formidable weapon, to the *foible* of the sword, which is a trifling, insignificant weapon, in comparison with the bayonet.

After detailing several additional techniques, Gordon modestly concludes his treatise by noting,

The Writer hastens to the conclusion. If he has failed in the explanation of the principles of his System of Defence, and of its decisive advantages against either infantry or cavalry: if he has not fully obeyed the orders of His R. H. the Commander in Chief, that failure will be imputed to the true cause—to the want of strength and perspicuity in the Writer, and not to any weakness in the principles of the Science, which are eternal and immutable. His gratitude and feelings for the honor conferred upon this occasion, can be more easily conceived than expressed...With the most profound respect, therefore, he lays this mite of assistance, for the public service, at the feet of His Royal Highness, and the Public.

ANTHONY GORDON[68]

In perusing his treatise, it is apparent that that Gordon was a man of great humility. While always expressing great confidence in the efficacy of his system, Gordon never attributes it to that of his own devising, but, instead, to classical authors such as Homer, Polybius, and Vegetius. Later in life, he would bestow the honor of inventing his method upon his old friend and benefactor, John Scott, the Earl of Clonmel. And yet, a thorough reading of the period literature leaves no doubt that the development of bayonet fencing in the British Isles during this period was due to the tireless, passionate, and lifelong efforts of Gordon himself.

## RECEPTION TO GORDON'S TREATISE

Just as in the case of his earlier *Letter on the Bayonet Exercise*, Gordon's 1805 treatise was greeted with considerable controversy and debate. There were still a number of writers, including those within the British military establishment, who were not receptive to his ideas —particularly to the notion that a knowledge of fencing could offer an advantage in combat. The *Critical Review* sarcastically ridiculed "Gordon's magical powers," musing,

> [Captain Gordon] assures, us, in his introduction, that from different experiments, 'this science, as laid down in the present volume, doubles the number of forces in all times and places of close action, and that it invigorates each man with an addition of power twenty times greater than his natural force, as is demonstrated in the appendix, from the powers of the lever.' It thus appears, that, like Milton's celestial combatants, 'in strength each armed hand' may become 'a legion;' and the collective force of an army is increased forty-fold...We cannot help wishing that this gentleman had been General Mack's adjutant during the late campaign; that commander, we think, would have found his forces so much strengthened by Captain Gordon's magical powers, that he would not have thought it necessary to surrender Ulm so easily.[69]

The same year, an even more scathing review appeared among the pages of *The Annual Review*, in which an anonymous author, claiming to be a military officer, assailed the very notion that fencing principles—or any technical skill whatsoever—could have a role in determining the outcome of combats between large numbers of soldiers:

> [Gordon] wishes that our troops should be instructed in a regular and scientific use of that weapon [the bayonet]. As far as relates to single combat this is all very feasible, but to suppose that a charge of bayonets can be rendered more irresistible by a knowledge of the rules of fencing, betrays a considerable portion of credulity. In the tremendous shock of two contending armies, the skill of the swordsman can avail nothing; muscular strength must determine the contest...

Championing the old, conventional bayonet drill, the reviewer continued to argue that, instead of utilizing skill and scientific principles, "common experience will teach every man to make his thrust in the most powerful and effective way." The only value in Gordon's system, the reviewer claimed, might be in its application to encounters between "small bodies" of men, in which "individual skill and personal activity will go far towards deciding the contest." The reviewer finishes by stating, "Captain Gordon has adopted a new theory, and like all other men in a similar case, he cannot be content with praising it as it deserves, but he must attempt to prove that it will perform impossibilities."[70]

In contrast to such negative screeds, several glowing reviews also made their way into print. An analysis in *The Anti-Jacobin Review and Magazine* was particularly favorable:

[The treatise] proves beyond dispute that Captain Gordon is thoroughly acquainted with the powers and use of the sword, and discovers on his part much ingenuity, with no small share of erudition. He studiously avoids egotism, and modestly declines taking to himself the credit ascribed to him by many, of being the projector of a new exercise, fancying he has found it in the magazines of antiquity, or writings of the ancients, and that it was practised more than two thousand years ago...We are inclined, however, to think that the merit of inventing this exercise is wholly and exclusively his own.

Although the reviewer disagreed with some of Gordon's classical literary translations—such as those of Vegetius—he ultimately extolled the virtues of the new exercise, concluding,

It must be allowed that [Gordon's] method of defence in close action with this compound weapon appears to be by far the best that has as yet been discovered or proposed, and proves the inventor to be a man of information and sound reflection. If this country be attacked or invaded, close combat may often become necessary. And should it not be thought adviseable to introduce his bayonet-exercise among our infantry, in general, it is to be hoped that a considerable body of them will be carefully instructed in it...Captain Gordon writes with much modesty, and at the same time, with becoming confidence in the justness of the principles on which he grounds his exercise. And we cannot help thinking that instead of barely furnishing his mite, he has contributed very bountifully towards improving the science of defence.[71]

Although the *Anti-Jacobin*'s review of the book was highly approving, it was the *Universal Magazine* which offered the most enthusiastic—as well as lengthy—assessment:

We have with due attention perused this new and extraordinary Treatise; and from our conviction of its utility, we have no hesitation in recommending it as a most instructive and interesting production, illustrating a great military subject, as important in its consequences to the present and future generations, as any ever agitated in this country.

Whatever our favourable opinion of this work may be, we confess that we are not so much surprised with its intrinsic merits and its present appearance, as we are to find that a military subject of such immense magnitude and importance should have remained so long neglected, and as it were concealed from the wisdom and sagacious penetration of so many ages.

The *Universal Magazine* printed its review in segments across four separate issues—amounting to twenty-nine pages in total—in which it quoted from Gordon's treatise extensively, and praised its many virtues. In the critique's second installment—and in a passage which could only have made Gordon smile—the reviewer compared the struggles of the book's author to those of Galileo: "We are concerned to find, that all the sciences were first received with similar coldness and slight; in many places the professors were persecuted. Galileo was imprisoned." Later, the reviewer enthused,

[Gordon] is unquestionably the first who has given just rules for extending this science to battalions. He seems to think, as we do, that the most arduous part of the business consists in the preparing and grounding the individuals in the elementary parts, and that the general instructions of the battalions becomes easy, when the component parts are thus previously prepared.

In the critique's final installment, the reviewer countered many of the points put forth by the treatise's detractors—even pointing out fallacies in the *Anti-Jacobin Review*'s criticism of Gordon's translations of Greek and Latin—while nevertheless stating,

We agree, however, in the opinion, that Major Gordon is the inventor of the bayonet exercise, which is taken (as we think) from the sword exercise, as improved by himself, and not by Vegetius, to whom he ascribes the merit of it.

The reviewer in *Universal Magazine* concluded, somewhat momentously:

Although this treatise is not free from blemishes, yet we have no hesitation in announcing it to be by far the best we have seen, and perhaps the best ever written upon the subject of the science of defence...The idea of the bayonet exercise is original, immense, and of the utmost national interest. But, like the Principia of Newton, it will require time and attention to be understood.[72]

## GORDON'S METHOD TESTED

Gordon's *A Treatise on the Science of Defence* must have met with some success, for in 1806, a second edition was published. At the same time, Gordon continued to press members of the government and military to adopt his method. In addition to Generals Burgoyne and Pitt, other supporters of Gordon's method eventually included George Nugent-Temple-Grenville (Lord Lieutenant of Ireland), General William Fawcett, Sir Adam Williamson, Robert Hobart (Earl of Buckinghamshire), Colonel Philip Robinson, and Major-General Sir Harry Calvert. Additionally, Gordon makes note of another mysterious benefactor, insistent on anonymity:

There are many other illustrious characters, and one in particular, whose friendship and protection have been an ornament to Gordon for these last twenty years. He adorns the list of Major

Generals; his greatest delight consists in doing good, and in concealing the glory of it. To this singular character Gordon owes every thing that he possesses, and yet he is not at liberty to gratify himself by naming him.[73]

In 1807, encouraged by his "friend" Francis Rawdon-Hastings, the Earl of Moira, Gordon wrote to William Windham, the Secretary for War, from Pimlico in London:

My object in repeatedly soliciting the honour of seeing you was to lay before you the means of completing a measure of the greatest national magnitude. I do not know what force you can raise and bring into activity; But, whatever your force may be, my object was and is (if permitted) to show you, not by words or theory, but by facts and experiments submitted to your senses, that you can by labour and attention actually double the number of your forces in all circumstances of close action with the enemy with firelocks; And that, if you should use any men with pikes you can in all points of attack have against the Enemy 4 to 1.

Should you gratify me, it will be necessary to indulge me with 4 of your servants or permit me to bring 4 boys or persons before you to convince you. Or you can commend any number of soldiers who have not been instructed by me; by which you will see the truth and the utility and imposition of the exercises for close action cultivated by the Commander-in-Chief and Sir David Dundas, and the whole army. *Unde Lachrymae Nostrae.*

My Lord Vincent has been and is cultivating this exercise. Enclosed is a letter containing the opinion of Lt.-General Barclay on this subject.

I have the honour to be, with all respect, Sir, your most obedient and very dutiful serv[an]t.

ANTHONY GORDON.[74]

It is uncertain if, in the ensuing years, Windham took any action regarding Gordon's method. During the subsequent decade, Gordon seems to have settled into retirement, and left the management and teaching of his method to his nephew, Lieutenant James Faden, a member of the Royal Marines who had reportedly acted with "gallantry" during the capture of Dwarka.[75] According to *Frazier's Magazine*,

Some years afterwards, Gordon's nephew, a Lieutenant Faden, reintroduced the same exercise; and so far succeeded as to convert a sort of shamfight at Portsmouth, between two regiments that had been instructed in this art, into a real one.[76]

Faden had begun training members of the Royal Marines in Gordon's system as early as the spring of 1806, when Admiral John Jervis wrote the following to Viscount Howick:

Being a very meritorious officer, and well acquainted with the bayonet exercise, in which the flank companies in the French army so much excel all other troops, I, at [Lieut. Faden's] request, got him embarked on board this ship, and he has brought the marines forward in the use of that powerful weapon in a very extraordinary manner. His uncle, Major [Gordon], now resident at Pimlico, has written a treatise upon the subject, and I hope is known to Mr. Wyndham and Gen. Fitzpatrick; considering, as I do, that expertness in this exercise may some day or other decide the fate of the country, I beg leave to recommend this officer as a candidate for an adjutancy in the Royal Marines.[77]

That same year, Faden authored a treatise of his own on Gordon's method, which he entitled,

*Proposals for a New Regulation of the Bayonet Exercise, with Testimonials.*

This book, which only existed as a single manuscript, was bound in Morocco leather, contained gilt leaves, and was sold at a Sotheby's auction on May 14, 1827, along with the rest of the collection of the Duke of York. Since then, no extant copy has been located.[78]

While continuing to teach Gordon's exercise, Faden was assisted by Major Torrens, brother of Sir Henry Torrens. Their "experiments" were officially authorized in 1815, and continued throughout the next several years.[79] As early as the summer of 1815, a reporter enthused of their activities: "The bayonet has lately proved to be so decisive a weapon, that a new bayonet-exercise has been established; and a select body of soldiers are daily trained at Chelsea, with a view to instructing the whole British infantry hereafter."[80] That fall, a more detailed—and spectacular—account of their demonstrations was published:

On Thursday about two o'clock, a new Bayonet Exercise was honoured by the inspection of his Royal Highness the Commander-in-Chief in the Queen's Riding-house, at Pimlico. The soldiers present were about 200, one half of whom were practised in the new, and the other half in the usual mode of charging. They were commanded to move one body against the other in double-quick time, charging, &c. when it seemed evident that all the men charging in the established mode were hit (with the exception of two men only), by the opposite party, that is, by the men charging in the new mode with their right in front.— The second part of the exercise consisted in shewing the facility of introducing the rear rank into the front in all movements in line or column, the knapsacks being laid aside. This part seemed to attract the attention and the approbation of his Royal Highness, as he said "very well—very well drilled and executed." A young Officer, Lieutenant Faden, proposed, that if his Royal Highness entertained a doubt of the superiority of the exercise in close action, he was ready then to demonstrate the truth, by suffering all the Officers and men of the Guards to charge him one after the other, in the presence of the Commander-in-Chief.— There were many Officers and others present.[81]

In 1818, Faden supervised another bayonet demonstration "in order to evince the superiority of the new exercise." This large "experiment" took place on Mount Wise, Plymouth Dock, and included the participation of the 90th and 64th regiments, who had been "for some time practising" the new exercise.[82] The event was attended by Major-General Brown, a number of military officers, and a "numerous assemblage of spectactors." The results were triumphantly recounted in the pages of the *Hereford Journal*:

> The utmost caution was used to prevent accidents, and the points of the bayonets were enveloped in a ball or foil, which being sprinkled with white powder, would shew the number of thrusts received by either party. It soon, however, became necessary to separate the combatants, as the lunges of the 90th, who practised the new exercise, enabled them to over-reach the 64th, their supposed opponents; and the latter, not being inclined to recede, received the thrusts with no great complacency. After some deliberation the men were marched into George's square, and the gates were closed to all but the officers. Several charges were given and received, in bodies and in individual attacks; but the superiority of the new exercise was such as to render it evident, that combatants on the old plan, receiving its attacks, would be destroyed on the first moment of onset.[83]

More than three decades after its inception, Gordon's system was finally vindicated. Reflecting on the latest demonstrations, Brigadier-General Sir Charles Shaw wrote,

> This bayonet exercise is really most admirable; as one man drilled properly to it is a match for any two undrilled, and more than a match for any single horseman. To light troops I consider it indispensable, as it gives a confidence to the soldier which nothing else can give. Fortified by this drill, the soldier, in skirmishing, knowing his advantage, advances steadily, and never allows himself to be impeded by an opponent; in short, a spirit, a desire to come to personal combat is instilled into him, and thus he becomes brave and confident.[84]

When a reporter mistakenly attributed the creation of the new method to Faden, rather than Gordon, the former was quick to set the record straight, writing to the editors of the *Post*:

### THE NEW BAYONET EXERCISE.

MR. EDITOR—Perceiving in your Paper of Wednesday a paragraph quoted from the *West Briton* on the subject of an experiment which took place in presence of General Brown respecting the advantages possessed by the Bayonet Exercise, I request you will insert the following correction:—The Bayonet Exercise, the superior powers of which were so decisively exemplified in late trial between detachments of the 64th Regiment and 90th Light Infantry, were not invented by Captain FADEN, but by Major ANTHONY GORDON. Mr. FADEN, accompanied by Major TORRENS, went to Plymouth for the purpose of executively introducing the New System; but to Major GORDON belongs the undivided honour of inventing this decisive improvement in the military art.—I have the honour to be, Sir, your very humble servant, JAMES FADEN.[85]

Additional laurels continued to follow. In May, the 90th Light Infantry was assigned to the entire Eastern District Command (comprising the counties of Essex, Suffolk, Norfolk, Cambridgeshire, Huntingdonshire, and Hertfordshire), "for the purpose of teaching other regiments the new bayonet exercise."[86] And in July, the Royal Marines, now also thoroughly trained in Gordon's system, were reviewed at Woolwich by the Grand Duke Michael of Russia, who "highly approved of the evolutions formed by them."[87]

Ultimately, despite the existence of hundreds—and likely thousands—of soldiers who were now well-instructed in Gordon's system, the method never seems to have been universally adopted by the military for the purpose of training its rank and file troops. Sir Charles Shaw explained how Gordon's method came to be praised, and yet ignored, following the demonstrations of 1818:

> After some time, His Royal Highness the Duke of York and Lord Lynedoch (who was then Colonel of the 90th) came to inspect the regiment; and at the same time to decide, whether this exercise was to become the drill of the British army. As with many other improvements, the inventor, by his indiscreet zeal in proclaiming it as the first in the world, caused this most useful exercise to be thrown aside. He had all the old prejudices to master; he had all the Peninsular officers against it, because they had never seen it in that glorious war; but who is the man in this age of wonder, will dare to say that a thing is useless because he himself has not seen its utility?[88]

Like that of many other forward-thinking men throughout history, Gordon's genius was not made full use of by the authorities of his era, or by the larger society in which he lived, during his own lifetime. Gordon, however, would have had no regrets. He wrote,

> Tedious as the disquisition of [my ideas] has been, yet the hours dedicated have been the happiest. That person cannot regret his occupation who thinks or even dreams of contributing his Mite even by his pen to the Public Service.[89]

Notwithstanding the government's actions, Gordon's impact on the history of fencing in the British Isles remains indisputable, and his final text would continue to influence others through the next several decades. In 1834, Donald Walker's *British Manly Exercises* would utilize Gordon's treatise as the basis for its small-sword method; this popular book would be reprinted in numerous editions throughout the 1830s, 1840s, and 1850s.[90] In 1845, the *Sportsman's Magazine* would also reprint Gordon's small-sword fencing chapters as a running series.[91]

Regarding Gordon's bayonet techniques, subsequently published military texts continued to praise those contained in his *Treatise on the Science of Defence* and urge the adoption of his bayonet exercise.[92] The account of Sir Charles Shaw, written in the present tense in 1837, suggests that some military officers continued to be trained and well-versed in Gordon's method.[93] The 1830s also saw the publication of a number of foreign bayonet fencing treatises (an occasion which Gordon had warned about) in France, Prussia, Switzerland, and Sweden—some of which, it seems clear, would also impact the progress of British bayonet fencing.[94] In more than one of these, Gordon's illustration of the "the Head guarded" by the bayonet against cavalry can be seen replicated, indicating that his influence had reached beyond the British Isles.[95] In subsequent decades, during the 1850s and 1860s, bayonet fencing contests would become regular features of British Grand Assaults-of-Arms and military fêtes—no doubt at least partly inspired and enacted by soldiers who had been trained by Gordon himself, or by students of Gordon's method.[96] This renewed practice of bayonet fencing would continue well throughout the end of the nineteenth century, and into the early twentieth. In the end, it is of some irony that the man who was justly regarded as the "modern father" of bayonet fencing in Great Britain was a relatively humble farmer's son from County Donegal.[97]

## LATER YEARS

About 1823, Gordon's wife passed away. Despite this "unhappy" setback, Gordon also saw his first son, Anthony, enter Trinity College, Cambridge, and become a curate at Westminster. His second son, Francis, was educated at Bristol, and also entered Trinity College. In 1828, Gordon was living at 118 Paul Street in Kingsdown, Bristol, Gloucestershire.[98] Soon after this time, he was paid a visit by his old friend Henry Angelo, who described him thus:

Major Gordon, an Irish gentleman, late of the 67th regiment. When I last waited upon him at Bristol, where he resided about a year, he was then ninety-five, a tall stout handsome man, with a florid complexion, and in height six feet two, or more. According to his information, he was once fellow of the college at Dublin, and at one time tutor to General Hutchinson (my old schoolfellow at Eton), now Lord Donoughmore. When about forty, his *éleve* offered him a commission in the army, which he accepted; and having, from his perfect knowledge of fencing, made some improvements on the use of the bayonet, he instructed a number of soldiers, who, under his inspection, exhibited the new exercise before his late Majesty, at the Riding-house, Pimlico. Though the system was approved of, the result did not answer his expectation; however, it procured that preferment which led to his appointment to a situation in the island of Stark, near Guernsey; I think, lieutenant-governor.[99]

In 1828, Gordon wrote in his return of service that he was "in good health considering the infirmities of [my] age, through the infinite Goodness of the Almighty." Even late in life, he had still not given up on the adoption and popularization of his bayonet exercise. In a letter penned the same year, he urged the following to the Minister of War:

> Were I honoured with your permission, I should at my leisure prepare, and wait upon you, with a statement of particulars such as might induce you to rescue a momentous subject [fencing with the bayonet] from destruction. If you will grant me an opportunity, I promise by facts to make this subject clear and as true as one of the Corollaries of Euclid.
>
>     With great respect, I have the honour to be, Sir
>
>         your most Obedient
>
>         & dutiful servant
>
>         Anthony Gordon
>
>         Capt on the retired List[100]

On April 8, 1831, Gordon—evidently sensing that the end was near—made out his last will and testament, bequeathing property to his nephew and steadfast disciple, Lieutenant James Faden, as well as to his surgeon and two sons. On May 9, 1831, Major Anthony Gordon, Knight of Tara, was buried at Holy Trinity Church in Westbury-on-Trym, Gloucestershire.[101] The golden age of Irish fencing was over.

---

1   *Hibernian Journal; or, Chronicle of Liberty*, April 23, 1784.

2   Henry Angelo, *Reminiscences, Volume 2* (London: Henry Colburn and Richard Bentley, 1830), 299-301.

3   See Chapter I.

4   Angelo, 299-301.

5   Constance Oliver Skelton and John Malcolm Bulloch, *Gordons under arms; a biographical muster roll of officers named Gordon in the navies and armies of Britain, Europe, America and in the Jacobite risings* (Aberdeen: The New Spalding Club, 1912), 49-50. *Alumni Dublinenses: a register of the students, graduates, professors and provosts of Trinity college in the University of Dublin, 1593-1860* (Dublin: A. Thom & Co., Ltd., 1935), 333.

6   Angelo, 300.

7   Skelton and Bulloch, 49-50. *Alumni Dublinenses*, 333.

8   In 1787, Lieutenant Colonel John Graves Simcoe (1752-1806), commander of the Queens Rangers, recounted, "above all, attention was paid to inculcate the use of the bayonet, and a total reliance on that weapon...It was the object, to instill into the men, that their superiority lay in close fight, and in the use of the bayonet, in which the individual courage, and personal activity that characterise the British soldier can best display themselves." John Graves Simcoe, *A journal of the operations of the Queen's Rangers: from the end of the year 1777, to the conclusion of the late American war* (Exeter: Printed for the Author, [1787]), 4-9.

9   John Alan Houlding, "The Training of the British Army, 1715-1795" (PhD Dissertation, King's College, University of London, 1978), 159.

10  Le Roy de Bosroger, *The elementary principles of tactics, with new observations on the military art, originally in French by Sieur B, and translated by an officer of the British Army* (London: S. Hooper, 1771), 13-20. See also Benjamin Cole, *The Soldier's Pocket Companion, or the Manual Exercise of Our British Foot* (London: Sold by the proprietor B. Cole, 1746), 71-75; and *The New Manual and Platoon Exercises, as practised by His Majesty's Army*.

(London: Bowles and Carver, 1795).

11  National Archives, Return of Officer's Services, Reference No. WO 25/759/162.

12  Skelton and Bulloch, 49-50.

13  Houlding, 41. The author also notes that the Dublin Barrack was "rivalled [in size] only by the Gibraltar and Minorca garrisons in the Empire as a whole."

14  *Saunders's News-Letter*, March 5, 1784.

15  William J. Fitzpatrick, *Ireland before the Union: with extracts from the unpublished diary of John Scott, earl of Clonmell, Chief Justice of the King's Bench, 1774-1798* (Dublin: W. B. Kelly, 1867), 26.

16  Anthony Gordon, *A Treatise on the Science of Defence for the Sword, Bayonet, and Pike, in Close Action* (London: B. McMillan, 1805), 2-3.

17  Alfred Hutton, *Fixed bayonets: a complete system of fence for the British magazine rifle, explaining the use of point, edges, and butt, both in offence and defence* (London: William Clowes, 1890), 166.

18  Appleton P. C. Griffin, *A Catalogue of the Washington Collection in the Boston Athenæum, Parts 1-4* (University Press: John Wilson and Son, 1897), 86. A second copy of Gordon's 1783 *Letter* resides in the National Library of Ireland in Dublin. It is to Gerald Gaidmore, Director of Special Collections at the Swem Library, College of William and Mary, that we are indebted for the third inscribed copy of Gordon's text quoted from herein.

19  Anthony Gordon, *A letter on the bayonet exercise: submitted to the Right Hon. General Burgoyne, Commander in Chief of His Majesty's forces in Ireland, &c. &c. &c.: dated, Dublin Barracks, 20th March, 1783.* [Dublin: 1787], 6-16.

20  Gordon, *A Treatise on the Science of Defence*, 3-4.

21  Gordon, *A letter on the bayonet exercise*, 25-27.

22  *Belfast Mercury or Freeman's Chronicle*, November 19, 1785.

23  *London Times*, January 24, 1786.

24  *Maryland Journal*, April 16, 1786; *Saunder's News-Letter*, January 30, 1786.

25  *Fraser's Magazine for Town and Country*, Volume XVII, No. CI (London: James Frazier, 1838), 607.

26  Skelton and Bulloch, 49-50.

27  Gordon, *A Treatise on the Science of Defence*, 4.

28  Gordon, *A letter on the bayonet exercise*, 25-26.

29  *Times*, May 29, 1786.

30  Gordon, *A letter on the bayonet exercise*, 25-27.

31  *The Gentleman's Magazine*, Volume 90 (London: Nichols and Son, 1801), 957.

32  Skelton and Bulloch, 49-50.

33  *The European Magazine, and London Review*, January, 1798.

34  Henry St. John Neale, *Practical essays and remarks on that species of consumption incident to youth, and the different stages of life, commonly called tabes dorsalis* (London: J. Crowder, 1800), 198-199.

35  *Morning Post*, December 15, 1803.

36  *Morning Post*, December 29, 1803.

37  *Ipswich Journal*, December 31, 1803.

38  *Staffordshire Advertiser*, January 28, 1804.

39  *Walker's Hibernian Magazine, Or, Compendium of Entertaining Knowledge*, February, 1804.

40  *Morning Post*, March 5, 1804.

41  *Times*, April 7, 1804.

42  *Walker's Hibernian Magazine*, July, 1804.

43  Anthony Gordon, *An Idea of Defence: a Treatise on Swordsmanship*, 1804. Manuscript. National Army Museum. NAM 1968-07-67. 1.

44  These include plates 2, 10, 11, 15, and 16 of Gordon's *Idea of Defence*.

45  Gordon, *An Idea of Defence*, 2-4.

46  Ibid, 20.

47  Ibid, 72.

48  Ibid, 5.

49  Ibid, 47.

50  Ibid, 26-28.

51  Ibid, 35.

52  Ibid, 44-45.

53  Ibid, 84-86.

54  *The Universal Magazine*, Vol IV, July to December 1805, 342.

55  Gordon, *A Treatise on the Science of Defence*, 5.

56  Ibid, 61.

57  Ibid, 67.

58  Le Marchant writes, "To make a Cut with effect, and at the same time without exposing the person, there are two points which principally demand attention. The first is to acquire a facility in giving motion to the arm by means of the wrist and shoulder, without bending the elbow: for in bending the elbow, the sword-arm is exposed..." John Gaspard Le Marchant, *Sword Exercise, and Movements, for Cavalry* ([London]: 1797), 2.

59  From a second edition of Gordon's text, annotated by Gordon himself, and sold by Skinner Auction House in Boston on May 31, 2014 (Books & Manuscripts – 2730B, Lot 162).

60  Gordon, *A Treatise on the Science of Defence*, 65.

61  Ibid, 17-18.

62  Ibid, 19-20.

63  Ibid, 18.

64  Despite "throwing out these strictures upon the errors of the French System," Gordon concedes that "our knowledge of the subject [of fencing], whatever it is, derives from them." *An Idea of Defence*, 14.

65  Gordon, *A Treatise on the Science of Defence*, 23-25.

66  Ibid, 40-43.

67  Ibid, 47-48.

68  Ibid, 49-52.

69  *The Critical Review, Or, Annals of Literature, Series the Third, Vol. VI* (London: J. Mawman, 1806), 447-448.

70  *The Annual review, and history of literature, for 1805, Vol. IV* (London: Longman, Hurst, Rees, and Orme, 1806), 754-756.

71  *The Anti-Jacobin Review and Magazine, Vol. XXI* (London: J. Hales, 1805), 371-380.

72  *The Universal Magazine*, Vol IV, July to December 1805, 46-50, 140-144, 234-240, 331-342.

73  Gordon, *A Treatise on the Science of Defence*, 66.

74 *Aberdeen Journal, Notes and Queries, Vol. VI* (Aberdeen: Aberdeen Daily Journal Office, 1913), 114-115.

75 *The Asiatic Journal*, June 1, 1821, 591.

76 *Fraser's Magazine for Town and Country, Volume XVII, No. CI* (London: James Frazier, 1838), 607.

77 Edward Pelham Brenton, *Life and Correspondence of John, Earl of St. Vincent, Volume II* (London: H. Colburn, 1838), 255-256.

78 *Catalogue of the Extensive and Valuable Library of His Royal Highness the Duke of York* (London: Compton & Ritchie, Printers, 1827), 65.

79 Keith John Bartlett, "The Development of the British Army During the Wars with France, 1793-1815" (PhD Dissertation, Hatfield College, University of Durham, 1997), 183.

80 *Chester Chronicle and Cheshire and North Wales General Advertiser*, August 4, 1815.

81 *Salisbury and Winchester Journal*, October 16, 1815.

82 *Edinburgh Magazine*, January, 1818.

83 *Hereford Journal*, January 4, 1818.

84 Sir Charles Shaw, *Personal memoirs and correspondence of Colonel Charles Shaw. Volume 1.* (London: Henry Colburn, 1837), 103-104.

85 *Morning Post*, January 12, 1818.

86 *Royal Cornwall Gazette, Falmouth Packet & Plymouth Journal*, May 9, 1818.

87 *Times*, July 13, 1818.

88 Shaw, 103-104.

89 Gordon, *An Idea of Defence*, 86.

90 Donald Walker, *British Manly Exercises* (London: Hurst, 1834).

91 *Sportsman's Magazine of Life in London and the Country, Volume the First* (London: E. Dipple, 1845), 400-451.

92 See, for instance, *Strictures on the Army: Interspersed with Interesting Anecdotes and Illustrative Facts. By a Field Officer* (Dublin: Published for the author by W. Figgis, 1809), 82.

93 Shaw, 103-104.

94 Gordon wrote in 1805, "If that moment should unhappily arrive (which may God avert!) when the enemy would also apply the science of Defence to the use of the bayonet..." Gordon, *A Treatise on the Science of Defence*, 21. Foreign bayonet treatises published during the 1830s include those by Joseph Pinette (1832), E. Von Selmnitz (1832), A. Muller (1828), Sinner (1835), and Perh Henrik Ling (1838). See Hutton, *Fixed Bayonets*.

95 See *Infantry and uhlans engaged in bayonet exercise* [Bavaria: 1830] in the Anne S.K. Brown Military Collection, Brown University; and Alexandre Muller, *Maniement de la baïonnette* (Paris: Chez Ancelin, 1835), 7-8.

96 Examples of such Assaults-of-Arms can be found in the *Era*, May 21, 1854, and *Wells Journal*, July 12, 1862.

97 "The Modern Father of Bayonet Exercise" in *Aberdeen Journal, Notes and Queries, Vol. VI* (Aberdeen: Aberdeen Daily Journal Office, 1913), 174-176.

98 Skelton and Bulloch, 50.

99 Angelo, 299-301.

100 National Archives, Return of Officer's Services, Reference No. WO 25/759/162.

101 "England, Bristol Parish Registers, 1538-1900", database, FamilySearch (https://familysearch.org/ark:/61903/1:1:XT9W-7XP : 12 December 2014), Major Anthony Gordon, 1831.

# PART TWO

# INTRODUCTION:

## on the AUTHORSHIP of

## "A FEW MATHEMATICAL and CRITICAL REMARKS on the SWORD"

*A Few Mathematical and Critical Remarks on the Sword*, a treatise on the art of fencing, was published anonymously in Dublin in March of 1781. For more than two hundred years, it has remained an obscure enigma. Despite the wave of interest in historical fencing methods that swept Britain during the late nineteenth century, the book escaped the notice of fencing scholar Egerton Castle, as well as his fellow author and antiquarian Alfred Hutton. Nor is it mentioned anywhere in the 1891 or revised 1896 editions of Carl Thimm's massive, landmark bibliography, *A Complete Bibliography of Fencing and Duelling*. No authors, historians, or antiquarians have ever discovered or exposed the identity of the book's author—or indeed, seem to have had any interest in doing so. In fact, among all the literature of the nineteenth century, there appears to be only a single reference to this fencing treatise. It is mentioned in William White's *Notes and Queries*, in a very small article which is solely concerned with the treatise's opening dedication—which it mistakenly attributes to John Scott, the 1st Earl of Eldon, instead of the book's actual dedicatee, the fencer, duelist, and Attorney-General John Scott, who, in 1793, became the 1st Earl of Clonmel.[1] Throughout the twentieth and twenty-first centuries, the book has continued to evade the notice of scholars and authors on fencing; only in James Kelly's modern history of dueling, *That Damn'd Thing Called Honour*, is the very existence of this fencing treatise even briefly mentioned.[2]

Considering all of the above, one might be tempted to despair of ever discovering anything regarding the book's authorship. However, a convergence of historical clues provided by other eighteenth century sources, as well as from within the text itself, point to a likely—and, in fact, most illustrious—author.

The first clue regarding the author's identity can be found in the treatise's opening pages, which contain a dedication to "The Right Honourable John Scot, His Majesty's Attorney General, &c. &c." This individual, as previously noted, was the prominent Dublin lawyer and duelist John Scott, who would later become the 1st Earl of Clonmel. Of especial note is Scott's known connection to Lieutenant Anthony Gordon, who credited Scott with first giving him the idea to apply fencing principles to the use of the bayonet. Scott was also Gordon's benefactor; the latter recounted that in 1781, he "removed...into 67th [Regiment of Foot], by the benevolence of Lord Clonmel, who purchased a [Lieutenancy] for him."[3] Gordon would go on to author at least three fencing treatises himself, culminating in his classic 1805 work, *A Treatise on the Science of Defence: For the Sword, Bayonet, and Pike in Close Action*. Given Gordon's close connection with Scott, as well as his passion and predilection for writing on the subject of fencing, he seems—at least at first glance—to be a likely candidate for authorship of the 1781 treatise. However, several facts somewhat refute this possibility. First, in comparing Gordon's known writings to those found in *A Few Mathematical and Critical Remarks on the Sword*, it is glaringly apparent that the latter text was composed by a completely different personality. Gordon's published writing style, and method of expressing himself, is absolutely nothing like that found in the 1781 book. Second, as Henry Angelo noted, and as evinced by the Lieutenant's writings, Gordon was deeply steeped in classical history and literature, which he constantly refers to in all of his known works on fencing. By contrast, the author of *A Few Mathematical and Critical Remarks on the Sword* is more fond of quoting Shakespeare and eighteenth century philosophers such as Burke, Addison, and Rousseau (though he does, in a few places, cite anecdotes from the works of Homer, Horace, and Rollin's *History of Rome*). And lastly, another aspect of the 1781 treatise which makes Gordon's authorship unlikely is its anonymous nature. If Gordon had no qualms about publishing two highly controversial fencing treatises under his own name—one of which was written and submitted in Dublin only two years following the appearance of *A Few Mathematical and Critical Remarks on the Sword*— why would he have had such qualms in 1781?

For exactly the same reason, James Underwood—secretary of the Knights of Tara, who published two other fencing treatises in Dublin during the 1780s—is also an unlikely candidate for authorship. Underwood had no problem placing his name on an English translation of Domenico Angelo's *School of Fencing*, nor in intimating that his revised version of Labat's *The Art of Fencing* was his own original work—a virtual act of plagiarism. Underwood, it certainly seems, was the last sort of person who would hesitate to place his name on a published fencing treatise.

Who, then, could have authored the 1781 book?

Despite Anthony Gordon's unlikely candidacy, the mutual connection with John Scott, Earl of Clonmel, does suggest that the author of *A Few Mathematical and Critical Remarks on the Sword* was someone who moved in the same fencing circles as Gordon. Additionally, the

1781 text repeatedly emphasizes the application of "Mathematics" and the "nature of the lever" to fencing—something Gordon would specifically (and extensively) expound upon in his own writings. Notably, Gordon was a member of the celebrated fencing society, the Knights of Tara (though John Scott was not), and was also a student of Ireland's great veteran fencing master, Cornelius Kelly.

As it turns out, a tantalizing clue pertaining to the author's identity was published in the *Hibernian Journal; or, Chronicle of Liberty* on May 9th, 1783—a time soon after the founding of the Knights of Tara—in which the following letter appeared:

*To the* KNIGHTS *of* TARA.

GENTLEMEN,

Having been present at your Exhibition on Monday last, I was not only highly entertained but surprized, at the Performance. The vast Coolness, Elegance, and Judgment exhibited by Mr. Underwood, and Mr. Parvisol, excited my Admiration: Mr. Dillon, no Way inferior in Elegance of Attitude, Mr. Gordon, amazingly quick in his Thrusts; upon the whole, there was every Thing which constitutes the Science; but as your Society is at the present in its infant State, though likely to become the first in Europe, I shall beg Leave to remark, that at the grand Exhibition at Toulouse, there is no second Class permitted. The Gentleman who gives the Majority of Hits, receives the Prize, and a distinguished Mark of Honour is conferred on him who is adjudged to have shewed most Skill and Knowledge in the Science. I shall submit to you whether that would not be a proper Mode for you to adopt.

I am, Gentlemen,

Your most humble Servant,

*May,* 2, 1783          *An Old Soldier.*

The anonymous nature of the above letter, its style and choice of words, and, most tellingly, its unusual reference to fencing exhibitions in Toulouse (also mentioned in Remark 93 of *A Few Mathematical and Critical Remarks on the Sword*) leave one in little doubt that this letter-writer is none other than the mysterious author of the 1781 fencing treatise. The letter-writer's signature, *"An Old Soldier,"* is, of course, suggestive of an individual with age and experience.[4]

At first glance, this would seem to greatly contradict the self-description provided by the author of *A Few Mathematical and Critical Remarks on the Sword*. In its opening pages, the author claims to be one who "knows very little of the practice" of fencing, who modestly declares that he is not even a "tolerable proficient," and confesses that he "never read one line on the subject [of fencing]." And yet, despite these humble assertions, the author goes on to lecture the reader on almost every aspect of the art and science of fencing. He gives extensive training advice, lists the requisite qualities for attaining "excellence" in the art, describes mistakes that "even fine Swordsmen fall into," notes specific errors that "all the fencers I have ever seen (two only excepted)" are guilty of, describes the qualities and tactics of "great swordsmen," makes suggestions to (and criticisms of) "masters," and even includes elaborate drills for fencing students! In short, despite the several highly modest and self-deprecating assertions found throughout the treatise, its author speaks with uninhibited authority on the subject of fencing, and positions himself as a judge of all other fencers. Contradictory, indeed.[5]

Perhaps the greatest clue, however, to the identity of the author of *A Few Mathematical and Critical Remarks on the Sword* can be found in the curious timing of its publication, which happened to coincide with a public fencing controversy that erupted in the pages of the *Dublin Evening Post,* and concerned one William Dwyer.

As far as the records show, Dwyer had begun teaching in Dublin a few years prior, in 1777. His school frequently changed locations, and at one point he was instructing at Trinity College. Just after the New Year, in 1781, Dwyer unleashed a broadside when he published the following advertisement, disparaging the skill of local fencing masters—and indeed, of all fencing masters in Ireland:

> MR. DWYER, who has lived in Paris fourteen years, and has made FENCING his chief study and practice during that time, and has given the most convincing Proofs of his superior Abilities to the best Fencing Masters in Paris and London, teaches to FENCE at the Music-Hall, Fishamble-street, on Mondays, Wednesdays, and Fridays...Mr. Dwyer assures the Gentlemen of this Kingdom, that any man who stiles himself a Fencing Master, that teaches in this city, and that never was out of this country, and therefore could not have the opportunity of knowing what elegant or good Fencing is, can have no title to merit in the line of Fencing, which Mr. Dwyer is ready to demonstrate by a public trial of skill, if called upon.[6]

The gauntlet had been thrown down. Three days later, it was taken up by Cornelius Kelly, Ireland's most renowned fencing master, who had been teaching in Dublin for more than fifty years—though, since the 1750s, he had rarely advertised.[7] In the pages of the *Evening Post*, Kelly responded thus:

> MR. KELLY, with every sense of gratitude for the favours conferred on him by the Gentlemen of Ireland, since he commenced Fencing-Master, takes this opportunity of acknowledging (whatever his merits may be) that their liberality and attachment to him have hitherto prevented him from having the mortification of exhibiting himself in *ridiculous, vapouring, Newspaper Addresses.*
>
> However fortunate for Mr. Dwyer, and the science of defence, that emerging from this menial situation, he now must be considered the first Fencing-Master in Ireland (vide his advertisement)

yet Mr. Kelly would be defective in truth and candour, if he did not declare, that there are many persons, who, like him, never left this kingdom, superior to him in the art of Fencing. Mr. Kelly then acknowledging himself inferior to many private Gentlemen here, would never have taken up the pen, could he by any possible arguments, have forced this mighty champion to use the proper instrument, and appoint time and place for that purpose.

N. B.   A Friend of Mr. Kelly's called on Mr. Dwyer the day before he published his Advertisement, and delivered him, in his public School, a message from Mr. Kelly, yet he evaded coming to *the point;* therefore, Mr. Kelly, however willing to degrade himself on this occasion, for the purpose of gratifying his private feelings, disdains any further paper controversy with such a character.[8]

Kelly's acknowledgment that he had "never left this kingdom" suggests that he was indeed the specific target, or one of the targets, of Dwyer's attack. In reading Kelly's response, one is also struck by his incredibly modest dismissal of "his [own] merits," and his assertion that he was "himself inferior to many private Gentlemen here." This, coming from the man who was reputed to be "the best swordsman of his day," who, in 1748, "defeated the best fencing master in England," and who, according to Henry Angelo, trained a student who became "the best fencer in Ireland" and possessed a "perfect knowledge of fencing," was humility itself.[9]

Only two months following the Dwyer-Kelly exchange, on March 8th, 1781, a one-hundred and fourteen-page fencing treatise was published, under the modest title, *A Few Mathematical and Critical Remarks on the Sword*.[10] It was the first fencing treatise to be published in Ireland in almost fifty years. In perusing its pages, it is clear that the book required very little preparation for publication, aside from the most basic printing logistics. The book contains no illustrations or engravings of any kind—nor an index, or even a table of contents. Its text is not arranged in any organized fashion. It is literally what it professes to be—a compilation of notes, "thrown aside among waste paper for above ten years," and written "merely as a relaxation of my mind from severer studies"—that is, the thoughts, insights, and experiences of a man poured out onto the page.

And, yet, despite its haphazard organization, and contents supposedly worthy of being "thrown aside among waste paper," the author tells us that he only "consented" to make his writings public "at the solicitation of a few friends." Likewise, in the earliest advertisements announcing the book's availability for purchase, we are told:

The Editors acquaint the Public, that this little Performance, handed to them in Manuscript, has the warm Approbation of some of the best Judges of Fencing, and therefore they hope it may be acceptable to all Gentlemen, more particularly to those of the Army, and the Volunteer Associations of this Kingdom.[11]

That the book was taken extremely seriously, and was greatly valued, by the highest members of Irish society (and its fencers) can be discerned by the public reaction to the book's call to arms, the original of which can be found in Remark 93:

> I think some institutions similar to those established by the French legislature, for the encouragement of this art [fencing], would in some measure mark the spirit and liberality of the present period...I have not a doubt, if a society of gentlemen were instituted on a proper plan, the legislature would confer on the gentlemen, publicly excelling in this art, some honourable mark of their approbation.
>
> I must confess, I think it a shameful reflection, that my countrymen should rest contented, while any nation on earth is universally allowed to excel them in any exercise, that Irishmen think worthy their attention; but how much more so, in an accomplishment so distinguishing to, and characteristic of, the man of spirit and the gentleman.

The anonymous author thus called for the formation of a "body for the encouragement of this art." More than a year later, in late 1782, the call was heeded, and the Knights of Saint Patrick (soon to be renamed "The Knights of Tara") were officially formed, explicitly instituted "for the encouragement of the Science of Defence with the Sword." A notice published in the *Evening Post* in May, 1783, confirms that the 1781 fencing treatise itself was the impetus for the formation of the Knights:

> This final original tract, which was published a short time ago, and received the warmest approbation of some of the best judges of the Art of Fencing in this kingdom, concludes with some thoughts on Dueling, Honour, and Exercise...The idea thrown out in these remarks for forming an institution for the improvement of the Art of Defence, has since been adopted by a number of the most respectable characters in this kingdom.[12]

The final clue to the author's identity comes, once again, from within the treatise itself, in a footnote to its "call to arms" in Remark 93. It reads as follows:

> * Gentlemen who like the idea, and would desire to constitute a body for the encouragement of this art [of fencing], may intimate their approbation to Mr. HUGH KELLY, fencing-master, Dublin.

A noted Irish dramatist named Hugh Kelly had lived in Dublin, but had died in 1777, four years prior to the treatise's publication. An exhaustive search of the newspapers, archives, and literature of the period has turned up no record of a fencing master named Hugh Kelly.[13] However, Cornelius Kelly was often known to fence and work with members of his own family, such as Thomas Kelly and James Kelly, although neither of these individuals—aside from Cornelius himself—are recorded as having operated their own school.[14] At the time of the treatise's publication, during the early 1780s, it appears that Cornelius was in retirement or semi-retirement, for in February, 1784, roughly one year after the initial founding and success of the Knights of Tara, the following notice appeared in *Saunder's News Letter:*

### FENCING.

CORNELIUS KELLY, Fencing-master, having been desired by several of the Nobility and Gentry to commence teaching again, has for that Purpose engaged a capital Assistant, Mr. W. Gittar, and taken a commodious Room at Mr. Hewett's, No. 18, in College green, where he will attend on Mondays, Wednesdays, and Fridays, from the Hour of eleven o'Clock until four on the above Days. — Capel-street, No. 71, February 3, 1784.[15]

According to the above advertisement, Kelly's school was located only a few doors away from the printing office of D. Chamberlaine, the publisher of *A Few Mathematical and Critical Remarks on the Sword.*[16] In another notable coincidence, the book's anonymous author also endorsed the services of local small-sword cutler John Marsh, whose shop was located on Capel-street—the same street on which Cornelius Kelly's private residence happened to be situated.[17]

Is it possible that the most celebrated fencing society Ireland has ever known—composed of some of its greatest fencing luminaries, including its most feared duelist, and comprising numerous noblemen as well as its top military brass—could it be that such a society was formed at the heed of an obscure, amateur fencer? It is certainly possible—but highly improbable.

A much more likely scenario is that the Knights of Tara heeded the call of someone they greatly respected—an individual who was long experienced, well-favored by members of the nobility, and highly skilled in the art of fencing.

The confluence of available evidence—the author's age, the respect he commanded, his excessive (almost ridiculous) sense of modesty, his disdain for personal fame and publicity, his love and sincere concern for Irish fencers, his connection with John Scott (and hence Anthony Gordon), his referral to a "Kelly" as a point of contact in forming a new institutional body of fencers, the locations of his publisher and favorite sword-cutler, and the timing of the public controversy involving Dwyer—all strongly suggest that the author of *A Few Mathematical and*

*Critical Remarks on the Sword* is none other than Ireland's most legendary and renowned fencing master, Cornelius Kelly.

If Kelly is, indeed, the author of the 1781 treatise, his public feud with William Dwyer throws into sharp relief the final paragraph of the book's introduction, which contains the Latin phrase *in propria persona,* an old legal term used to denote a person who is acting as his or her own attorney in a lawsuit. Within this new context, the following passage from the book's introduction can be interpreted as exhibiting coy sarcasm, rather than modesty:

> I have enjoyed myself, not a little, in having a demonstration, in propria persona, how much may be said on an A R T , by one who knows very little of the practice.

Clearly anticipating his critics (or critic), the author also addresses "any persons [who] are pleased to censure the manner in which I have amused myself on this subject" by quoting two lines of poetry:

> Damn with faint praise, assent with civil leer,
> And, without sneering, teach the rest to sneer—

The poem from which these lines are extracted—*A Portrait of Addison* by Alexander Pope— was, according to its author, a "bill of complaint" directed at an ungenerous critic, and a fuller quotation of the pertinent passage may provide further insight into the motives of the author of *A Few Mathematical and Critical Remarks on the Sword*:

> PEACE to all such! but were there one whose fires
> True genius kindles, and fair fame inspires;
> Blest with each talent and each art to please,
> And born to write, converse, and live with ease;
> Should such a man, too fond to rule alone,
> Bear, like the Turk, no brother near the throne,
> View him with scornful, yet with jealous eyes,
> And hate for arts that caused himself to rise;
> Damn with faint praise, assent with civil leer,
> And, without sneering, teach the rest to sneer;
> Willing to wound, and yet afraid to strike,
> Just hint a fault, and hesitate dislike...[18]

In the years following, no public criticisms of the 1781 fencing treatise, or its contents, evidently surfaced—nor is William Dwyer recorded as having ever taken up his pen again to disparage the skill of Irish fencing masters.

\* \* \*

In conclusion, it must be acknowledged that the numerous aforementioned instances of converging, suggestive evidence may be no more than a series of extraordinary coincidences, and that the author of the 1781 treatise could be another lesser-known fencer—perhaps another member of the Kelly family, or one of Kelly's students, partisans, or associates. In subsequent years, the book's author never publicly identified himself—nor did any of his acquaintances, as far as we know, ever expose him. In the end, it is difficult to make any conclusions regarding this topic with certainty, and the identity of the author of *A Few Mathematical and Critical Remarks on the Sword* may forever remain a mystery.

But then, what is life without a good mystery?

------

1    William White, *Notes and Queries, 2nd Series, IX, Feb. 18, No. 216* (London: Bell & Daldy, 1860), 121.

2    James Kelly, *That Damn'd Thing Called Honour* (Cork: Cork University Press, 1995), 164.

3    See Chapter VII for more information on Anthony Gordon, and his connection to John Scott.

4    Interestingly, more than twenty years later, Anthony Gordon would use the same appellation (an "Old Soldier") to refer to himself in his 1805 treatise on the bayonet. However—all issues of age aside—Gordon could not be the author of the anonymous 1783 letter, as he himself is one of the tournament participants described therein. See Anthony Gordon, *A Treatise on the Science of Defence for the Sword, Bayonet, and Pike, in Close Action* (London: B. McMillan, 1805), 2. It is also worth noting that the anonymous letter-writer, in his remark on fencing tournaments in Toulouse, somewhat contradicts, or qualifies, what is written in *A Few Mathematical and Critical Remarks on the Sword*, in regards to what constitutes a "first" or "second" fencer in Toulouse. Although it is unclear whether the letter-writer's comment is an outright contradiction, or merely a qualification, it gives rise to the possibility—improbable, but one that cannot be denied—that the letter-writer was another Dublin fencer with specific knowledge of the proceedings of fencing tournaments in Toulouse. If this is the case, it may be wondered if this letter-writer is the same "ingenious and respectable friend" who is noted as having provided information about French fencers in Remark 95 of *A Few Mathematical and Critical Remarks on the Sword*. A list of rules pertaining to the Toulouse fencing tournaments are given in Andrew Mahon's *Art of Fencing*, but do not contain the above-quoted stipulations. Andrew Mahon, *The Art of Fencing, or, the Use of the Small Sword. Translated from the French of of the late celebrated Monsieur L'Abbat; Master of that Art at the Academy of Toulouse* (Dublin: Printed by James Hoey, at the Sign of Mercury in Skinner-Row, 1734).

5    Another contradiction in the 1781 treatise is its polemic against the custom of dueling (see Remark 61). These comments are highly ironic, considering the praise heaped by the author upon the book's dedicatee, John Scott, who was both a legal defender of dueling, and a four-time duelist himself.

6    *Dublin Evening Post*, January 6, 1781.

7    For more information on the life, career, and accomplishments of Cornelius Kelly, see Chapter V: Fencing Schools and Masters in Eighteenth Century Ireland.

8   *Dublin Evening Post*, January 9, 1781.

9   For these references to incidents in the career of Cornelius Kelly, see Chapter V: Fencing Schools and Masters in Eighteenth Century Ireland.

10  *Saunders's News Letter*, March 8, 1781.

11  *Dublin Evening Post*, March 10, 1781.

12  *Dublin Evening Post*, May 13, 1781.

13  This includes the *Dublin Evening Post, Dublin Courier, Dublin Journal, Hoey's Dublin Mercury, Saunder's News Letter, Hibernian Journal; or, Chronicle of Liberty, Pue's Occurrences, Walker's Hibernian Magazine, Freeman's Daily Journal*; also, *Wilson's Dublin Directory* for the years 1774, 1776, 1777, 1780 and 1783.

14  *Pue's Occurrences*, February 26, 1757, *Saunders's News Letter*, January 10, 1774, *Freeman's Daily Journal*, December 11-15, 1750.

15  *Saunders's News Letter*, February 7, 1784.

16  As per the title page of *A Few Mathematical and Critical Remarks on the Sword*, as well as numerous advertisements, the office of D. Chamberlaine was located at No. 5 College-Green.

17  See footnote to Remark 75 of *A Few Mathematical and Critical Remarks on the Sword*.

18  Alexander Pope, *The Complete Poetical Works, ed. by Henry W. Boynton* (Boston and New York: Houghton, Mifflin & Co., 1903).

# TOPICAL GUIDE

to

*A Few Mathematical and Critical Remarks on the Sword.*

| Topic | Remark |
|---|---|
| Virtues of the Science of Defense | 1 – 2 |
| Requisites for Excellence in the Art | 3 |
| Line of Direction | 4 |
| Position of the Arm | 5 |
| Parrying | 6 – 8 |
| Recovering | 9 |
| The Pass | 10 – 11 |
| Leverage | 12 |
| Direct and Round *Parades* | 13 |
| Executing the Pass | 14 |
| Springing Back | 15 |
| Tending to the Center | 16 |
| Exceptions to Rules | 17 |
| Applying One's Knowledge | 18 |
| Determining the Manner of Attack | 19 – 20 |
| Disordering the Adversary | 21 |
| Dependence upon Superior Attributes | 22 |
| Retiring | 23 |
| True Source of Apparent Superior Strength | 24 |
| Violent Fencers | 25 |
| Distance | 26 |

Deceiving the *Parade*                                                27

Throwing Yourself on Guard                                            28

Landing the Foot                                                      29

Force of the *Parade*                                                 30 – 32

Feints                                                                33 – 34

Practising the Attack                                                 35

Guard Position                                                        36

Bad Habits of Fencers, and Principles to be
   Observed in Loose Play                              37

Qualities of a Good Swordsman                                         38

Use of the Fort and Feeble                                            39

Flanking                                                              40 – 41

Timing                                                                42 – 44

Directing the Point                                                   45

Additional Remarks on the Position of the Arm                        46

Parrying with a Pass                                                  47

Additional Remarks on Timing                                          48

Angle of the Thrust                                                   49

Battering                                                             50

Equilibrium of the Body                                               51

Parrying Wide                                                         52

Theoretical versus Executive Knowledge                               53

Mathematics and Philosophy                                           54

Palming                                                               55

The Pass and Return                                                   56

Changing with Exactness                                              57

Breaking Measure                                                      58

Parrying at the Wall                                                  59

Fear and Timidity                                                     60

The Custom of Duelling                                                61 – 62

Advancement and Progression of Scholars                              63

Training Devices                                                      64 – 65

| | |
|---|---|
| Differences in Terrain | 66 |
| Erroneous Opinions on Training | 67 |
| Attacking with a Feint | 68 |
| Attainment of Dexterity | 69 |
| Additional Use of the Unarmed Hand | 70 |
| Dirty Tricks | 71 |
| Position of the Feet When on Guard | 72 |
| Center of Gravity | 73 |
| Tactics to Be Used When Backed Against a Wall | 74 |
| Qualities of a Good Foil | 75 |
| Multiple Adversaries and Assassins | 76 |
| Preserving the Line | 77 |
| Parts of the Sword | 78 |
| Importance of Theory | 79 |
| Use of *Tierce* and *Quart* | 80 |
| Fencing Terms in General Use | 81 – 82 |
| A Series of Fencing Lessons | 83 |
| Position of the Left Hand | 84 |
| Utility of Knowledge of the Sword | 85 |
| Cutting Over the Point | 86 |
| Beginners | 87 |
| Disarming | 88 |
| True versus Mistaken Notions of Honour | 89 – 90 |
| True Greatness and Solid Glory | 91 |
| Heroism and Bravery of the Irish | 92 |
| Establishing an Irish Institution for the Encouragement of Fencing | 93 |
| Customs and Etiquette in the Fencing School | 94 |
| *Parades,* and French and Spanish Fencers | 95 |
| Cultivation of the Use of Arms | 96 |
| Health and Vigour of Mind and Body | 97 |

# NOTE *to the* READER

The anonymous author of *A Few Mathematical and Critical Remarks on the Sword* uses a wide range of technical terms found in various early and late eighteenth century fencing treatises published in the British Isles. As the author does not define many of these terms, but assumes a great deal of technical knowledge on the part of the reader, definitions for these terms have been included both in numbered footnotes (on the pages where such terms first appear) and in an appended glossary. The text's original author—who was evidently quite well-read—also frequently quotes eighteenth century works of philosophy and poetry (some well-known, others obscure), Shakespearean plays, and works of ancient history, often without citing his original sources. He occasionally utilizes Latin phraseology, refers to Biblical figures and places, and uses period Hiberno-English. These terms have also been defined, cited, or explained with the inclusion of modern footnotes. We hope that these notes, both to sources and to parallel works, will help make this unique treatise more accessible to all readers.

Aside from the addition of these footnotes, the text of *A Few Mathematical and Critical Remarks on the Sword* remains unchanged, and its original grammar, antiquated spelling, italics, and capitalization have been preserved. To distinguish the author's original footnotes (typically denoted by asterisks) which appeared in the 1781 text from those numerical footnotes which have been newly added by the current editor, the former have been included within the body of the text (directly following the remarks which they pertain to), whilst the latter have been placed beneath the main text, at the bottom of the page.

A FEW

MATHEMATICAL AND CRITICAL

REMARKS

ON THE

SWORD.

*"Nihil honestum esse potest,*
*"Quod justitia vacat."*

DUBLIN:

PRINTED BY D. CHAMBERLAINE, NO. 5,
COLLEGE-GREEN.

M DCC LXXXI.

# THE RIGHT HONOURABLE

# JOHN SCOT,

His Majesty's Attorney General, &c. &c.

S I R,

Being unknown to the Great, is attended with this pleasing circumstance, that the humble tribute of honest admiration and genuine applause, cannot be ascribed to the overflowing gratitude, nor, to the meanness of adulation: conscious of my own integrity, I ingenuously declare, if I knew but one man in the kingdom, to have a sounder judgment and a finer imagination, a more humane and expanded heart, and a more spirited and judicious arm, I should have been still more presumtuous than I am, in prefixing YOUR NAME to so trifling a production.

I am,

S I R,

With the greatest respect,

Your most humble, and

Most obedient Servant,

THE AUTHOR.

# INTRODUCTION.

At the solicitation of a few friends, I have consented to let these Remarks be made public, after their having been thrown aside among waste paper for above ten years. Let me now declare, I wrote them merely as a relaxation of my mind from severer studies: I also candidly confess, I never read one line on the subject. And though this acknowledgment may at once prejudice these lines in the opinion of many, yet I am aware there are some men, who would willingly fill up the parenthesis of a leisure half hour, in reading O R I G I N A L T H O U G H T S in almost any Art or Science, especially at this period, when hundreds of volumes are published annually, without containing one new or original idea.

As business has prevented me from copying these lines (and consequently from either correcting, diminishing or augmenting the original) the hints are penned just as they arose to my mind at different times, which is the reason they have frequently no immediate connexion with each other.

I have, indeed, by this little effort, the satisfaction of proving, that there is scarce any art in nature but may receive some lights from the Mathematics. If any persons are pleased to censure the manner in which I have amused myself on this subject, or, as the first of English poets expresses himself,

> Damn with faint praise, assent with civil leer,
> And, without sneering, teach the rest to sneer—

they have my hearty concurrence; for I can assure them, it will by no means offend me, if that was of consequence; as I have enjoyed myself, not a little, in having a demonstration, in propria persona, how much may be said on an A R T , by one who knows very little of the practice.

# A FEW

## MATHEMATICAL AND CRITICAL

# REMARKS

## ON THE

# SWORD.

## REMARK I.

On reflecting that our lives are given us, as sacred bequests from the Almighty, which it is our duty to defend: can it be either whimsical or irreligious to assert, that endeavouring to arrive at dexterity and knowledge in the Science of Defence, must be equally virtuous, as it is polite and spirited?

2. If a nation does not acquire the use of arms, in the same proportion of its celebrity for fertility, trade, manufactures, and riches, it must one day become the prey of some warlike people. Hence may we not conclude, that individuals acquiring the knowledge of Arms, must be, tho' perhaps in a remote degree, of public utility?

Therefore, on the first law of nature, Self-preservation, and in some degree on the love of our country and the good of society, we may ground the Art of Fencing; to defend, being its grand object. And as no man ought to draw his Sword, but in a case of necessity (what I think such I shall mention hereafter); so even the offensive part, or what, in the language of our art, is called Attacking and Returning[1], may be said to arise from the first principle, Defence; for,

---

1  *Returning:* "RETURN, [In French *riposté*] Is when you deliver a thrust instantly after parrying one made by your adversary.—If your parade has been well formed, your return must be well delivered.  There are various sorts of returns, either by the complete longe, the complete extension, the extension of the arm only, or a return of the wrist.  Straight returns, or those that touch your adversary at the moment of parrying before he can recover to guard are by far the best." McArthur, 158.

to defend properly in action, a man must make vigorous and spirited Passes.[2] I shall not here mention the necessity of acquiring a knowledge of the Sword, either as an essential to a liberal education, and of which no gentleman with any property can plead ignorance; as an exercise, more immediately recommended to those who lead a sedentary life; nor as a polite and spirited relaxation, most powerfully preventing and overcoming obstructions, which physicians acknowledge to be the primary cause of almost all disorders. I must confess, that I look on the exercise of Fencing in such a light, that I esteem professors of the Sword as the most respectable physicians; for the same reason that I would deem a man more my friend, who would prevent my wants, than he who would relieve them. *

* See Remark 90.

3. As excellence is scarce attainable in any art, so it is no less difficult in this, and requires a very rare and happy union, viz. A tolerable degree of strength, agility, and spirit: strength, not to be overcome by the most vigorous passes; agility, to advance[3], retire[4], or return, as occasion may require, almost instantaneously; and spirit, to attack with a glow and ardour, a confidence and intrepidity, that may damp and dismay. But no less requisite are coolness, deception, and quickness of apprehension; for that warmth of attack that is praise-worthy, must ever flow from thought, and be the result of design: (for attacking violently, often proceeds from cowardice, despair, or ignorance): like a prudent general, you must ever have in view the possibility of your failure, and by all means endeavour to acquire a steadiness of mind and body, that may prevent you from being thrown into confusion, should your pass miss the center. Deception, manœuvre, or feints[5], are also essential to the art; to wit, making the passes in

---

2   *Passes*: Although other fencing authors of the period give more specific definitions for the term "pass," this author seems to use it as a general term for footwork (including that used on an attack). He also uses the term when describing the lunge or discussing an attack. "Suppose on the advance, or after passes have been made, I see full light on the tierce, I throw with the utmost vigour a full tierce..." (See Remark 19) "...there are no passes preferable to the straight allonges." (See Remark 23) "A simple pass is expressed by one, (or ha); a feint and pass, one, two, (or ha, ha); of a double feint and pass, one, two, three, (or ha, ha, ha.)" (See Remark 33) "The left knee and right arm bent, gives the power of darting in, with an elastic spring, on your pass..." (See Remark 36) "I by all means recommend parrying with a pass..." (Remark 47)

3   *Advance*: "ADVANCE, In Fencing, The act of stepping forward toward your adversary, while on guard; the left foot instantly following the right so as that your primative posture is still preserved." McArthur, 151.

4   *Retiring*: "Retiring is, when you have a Mind to give Ground to your Adversary when he approaches you." Henry Blackwell, 4. "To RETIRE, to step back with the left foot, when your adversary is too near, making the right follow, without altering the distance that was between the heels before retiring." Fergusson, 17.

5   *Feints*: "FEINT, Is a false attempt of making a thrust towards a particular part of your adversary's body, with a view to induce him to form a parade to guard that part, that you may with greater facility execute your

attacks or returns, which you may apprehend to be unexpected, and least dangerous to your-self, or where you see an opening; but in this case, you must beware that it is not a design to take you on: and in general, be cautious lest you should be worsted by a deception of your own. Quickness of thought is requisite, to determine in the heat of action, the passes most likely to deceive, or quickest of return. I shall here observe, what indeed is universally known, that any pass which is not expected must deceive; so frequently the most simple passes become central. To these qualifications may be added, those necessary to acquire excellence in any art; attention in the observance of directions and rules, indefatigable practice, and a certain taste and grace in execution, which characterises the performer in every exhibition.

4. If we conceive a right line drawn on the ground, in the direction of your adversary, it is evidence, the more your body, legs, thighs and arms are in that direction, the less liable you are to be hit; and the closer your parades[6] are, that is, the less they deviate from that line the better; also, the lower you lie the safer: for it is manifest, the less the surface presented to your antagonist the better, provided you always stand, or throw yourself in such an attitude, that you can parade and pass with the utmost ease and vigour; for you diminish the surface in breadth, the more accurately you preserve your line; and in length, the lower you lie, as any person may experience, by throwing himself in a regular, and then into an irregular position.

5. To hollow the hand may be attended with the worst consequence, (what I mean by hollowing the hand, is not keeping the elbow in the line with the shoulder and the wrist) as by so doing you leave an opening for your antagonist, and of which an able and quick-sighted one will certainly avail himself. Again, supposing you hit when your arm is hollowed with a certain force; the same hit with the same exertion, if your hand and arm made a right angle with his body, that is, if you were in right position, would meet your adversary with greater force. The reason of this, and also the proportion of the loss, is immediately deducible from this well known demonstrated theorem, That the force wherewith a body impinges on a given surface, in a rectangular direction, is to its percussion in an oblique one, as radius is to the fine

---

intended thrust against the unguarded part.—There are various kinds of feints and they are divided into simple and compound, high and low." McArthur, 154-155.

6  *Parade*: "PARADE, PARRY or PARRYING, Is the act of defending yourself against a particular thrust of an adversary, by the turn of your wrist and the forte of your blade in opposition.—There are properly six simple parades or parries, each having its compound, termed a round parade. It is a most essential branch in fencing to form just and powerful parades, as thereby you make good returned thrusts upon an adversary. The parades are divided into upper and lower, inward and outward. Carte and tierce, with their compounds are called upper; semi-circle and octave, prime and seconde, with their respective compounds are termed lower parades. Each parade has a thrust of the like denomination." McArthur, 157.

of the angle of incidence. — And to extend this consideration, the force which in passing might be of no effect when your arm is hollowed, will often become home, central and satisfactory, if in proper position.

6. In the round parades,[7] (or counter in tierce and quart) the Sword should describe in its proper movement, either the whole or part of a conical superfices, the base being nearly parallel to the breast of your adversary, and the apex or vertex, being the center of the shell[8], or rather indeed the wrist; for the motion should arise and continue from the wrist, and not from the arm; the reason for which I apprehend to be, that the motion can be made with more expedition from the wrist (leaving the arm in the line for opposition); yet were we to allow the arm could be moved with equal velocity, the motion from the wrist would be preferable; for in the former case, the line describing the conical superficies would be lengthened. And here it may not improperly be considered as a mechanical lever, and consequently less force at the feeble (or foible)[9] would be requisite to put the Sword from the line.

7. If it is asked me, to determine the diameter of the circle, which is the base of the conical fluent (if I may be allowed the expression)? I answer, that this must be principally, if not wholly, determined by the superficial content of what this parade is to guard. A man who singles his body finely, and lies low, may make his parades much closer, than he whose position is false and irregular.[10]

---

7   *Round Parades, or Counter*: "ROUND PARADES, Are compound movements, and performed with circles of like magnitudes. There are six in number, named after the simple parades. As the diameters of the circles are demonstrated to be equal to the distance of the wrist from one opposite parade to another, that is six inches, so is the periphery of these circles equal to about nineteen inches." McArthur, 158.

8   *Shell*: "SHELL, of a sword or foil is that part of the hilt or handle next the blade, serving both for an ornament and guard." McArthur, 159.

9   *Foible*: "FOIBLE, or FEEBLE, Is the weak part and third division of a blade, and is that part at the farther extremity next the point." McArthur, 155.

10  *Irregular*: Contrary to the established principals of swordsmanship. William Hope notes that "*Artists* are generally not so *foreward* and *irregular* in their Pursutes as *Ignorants*, but more *cautious* and *slow*, and consequently more *certain* and *safe*. Is it not therefore (from what I have been saying) far more commendable, to be *dexterous* and *regular* in our *Offensive* and *Defensive* motions, then *irregular*, and as it were out of all Hope, and in Despair, that if we overcome, we may be said to have done it by *Art* and *Judgement*, and not at *randome*, and by *chance*, more beseeming an *irrational* than a *rational* Creature." William Hope, *The Sword-Man's Vade Mecum* (Edinburgh: John Reid, 1691), 6-7.

8. When you parry, or are parried, be careful to come to your line as accurately and as quick as possible, and not, through a flutter of spirits, allonge[11] before you come thereto; and be equally careful not to pass or cross your line, as in one case you leave an open on the tierce, and in the other upon quart, and in both cases are abandoned, in a more or less degree, proportionable to your deviation.

9. In not having a fine recovery[12] to your line, I apprehend you lose the opportunity of feinting in action, and, in general, there is scarce any thing more decisive: for example, in the most simple case, suppose a quart[13] thrown, which I ought to parry neatly and at once from the wrist; but on the contrary, if I follow and bear[14], my adversary if expeditious may slip[15] and pass again, or if in recovery I pass the line to the tierce, I must leave an opening; therefore it would be the greatest folly to attempt to feint in such a circumstance.

10. A straight arm is of such utility, in preventing the approach of your adversary, that I apprehend it could never have been recommended to bend it, but for the sake of expedition; for without this reserve is made with the greatest accuracy, there will be light[16] or an opening

---

11  *Allonge*: "LONGE, [From the French verb *alonger*, to extend or stretch out] Is the act of extending yourself on the line of direction the full distance of your stride, in order to make your approaches to an adversary's body in delivering a thrust... All longes are performed from guard position, by first forming the position of extension... then instantaneously moving the right foot forward on the same line, with the knee bent and perpendicular, while your left foot remains firmly planted and the left leg and thigh are to be extended along.—The extent of a longe is proportional to your stature.—The extent in general is supposed to be about four feet, or equal to twice the distance or measure of the two heels from each other, when on guard posture.  A person of tall stature makes a more extensive longe than one of a short stature; but he cannot recover with that degree of ease and agility unless he is of a very active frame." McArthur, 156.

12  *Recovery*: "RECOVERING, Is the act of resuming your guard posture after having made a longe at your adversary.  A quick and easy recovery to guard, forming the most natural parade is an essential branch to your safety." McArthur, 158.

13  *Quart, thrust in*: "CARTE THRUST inside, Is the natural thrust corresponding to the parade of carte.  It is an upper thrust, and the opposition to your adversary's blade is inwards, so as to be covered on the longe by seeing the point over your arm." McArthur, 152.

14  *Bear*: "BEARING is to bear heavy upon the blade, without wrenching it any way." Lonnergan, 51.

15  *Slip*: "Slipping, is to slip quickly away from this Bearing [see prior footnote] into a thrust at the other side of the blade." Lonnergan, 51.

16  *Light*: Defined here as synonymous with "opening," this unusual fencing term was used extensively—but never defined—by Andrew Mahon in his translation of Labat's *Art of Fencing*: "In order to take Advantage of the Time and Light which you get by your Feint, you must take care to avoid an Inconveniency into which many People fall, by uncovering themselves in endeavouring to uncover the Adversary." (Mahon, 45). The original French term used by Labat is *jour*, in the sense of "daylight." See Jean de Labat, *L'Art en Fait* [continued]

given (light and an opening are synonymous terms) when the arm is angulated: now as the body cannot be moved with the desired and necessary expedition, a flexure in the arm encreases the velocity of the pass; for the Sword is moved by the combined forces of the forward motion of the body and the elastic extension of the arm; and if the arm has the proper bent, and the allonge properly made, these two forces act in the same direction; consequently, the pass is sent home with a vast encrease of velocity.

11. The arm at every pass should be raised, and the head somewhat inclined, that it may be covered by the hand; I say, the arm should be raised instantaneously on making the pass*, the body spring from the left knee, the right foot in the line, and right leg perpendicular; and in recovery, as before mentioned, be cautious not to deviate from the line, or let your arm fall.

* Particularly the wrist, so that the point of the Foil should be directed to the breast; by this the thrust appears more graceful, and shews fine opposition: on hitting, the Foil gets a proper bent, and is not liable to be snapped. Beginners, by not observing this, run the risk of hitting each other in the face, and are constantly breaking the Foils.

12. Suppose two men nearly of equal judgment engage, but one superior in strength, I conceive, if the weaker parries a few inches nearer his antagonist's feeble than usual, and a few inches nearer his own shell, he will render the superiority of his adversary's strength of little service; the reason is evident from the nature of the lever.

13. All direct parades I take to be quicker than the round parades, pretty nearly in the proportion of the diameter of a circle, to its semi-circumference, and sometimes to the whole circumference: hence it seems to follow, that we should always make use of the direct parades; and indeed it would be certainly best so to do, if we could be sure of the pass that would be made; but from the variety of feints and deceptions, this is almost impossible; therefore, those parades that parry all the thrusts are, I think, those we should bestow our particular attention on: but certainly, great practice is required to arrive at a sufficient degree of expedition in their performance.

14. In making a good pass, the left knee must spring, the body be thrown forward, and the right arm straightened in one and the same instant; for if one of these are performed a moment after the other, it degrades the pass.

---

[cont'd] *d'Armes ou de l'Epée seule* (Toulouse: J.Boude, 1696). In 1728, Donald McBane also directs: "Let your Side be only in [the adversary's] View, for the less Mark you give, the better, this is call'd *Light*." McBane, 3.

15. To spring back[17], I apprehend, is necessary, when in some measure you have lost your line or position, and are apprehensive of an attack thus unprepared; for in this spring you are to throw yourself in guard[18], and be ready for an attack. When you hit, I think it is best to spring back with a bate[19], a batter[20], or the round parade, until you find the touch satisfactory to your adversary; but, continuing in guard, be prepared to give him one if he advances, that may be decisive; for, tho' mercy is the constant attribute of the Christian and the Gentleman, yet it would be, in this case, a kind of suicide to hesitate a moment from giving, if possible, the terminating passes.

" Let's leave the hermit pity with our mothers ;
" And when we have our armour buckled on,
" The venom'd vengeance ride upon our swords. "[21]

16. Whenever you make a pass send it with the utmost spirit, and be sure to plant the center, let the pass be what it may; for, as rays passing through convex glasses have their partic-ular focii, or points of coincidence, so all allonges must tend to once center, namely, the breast of your antagonist; after which, it is your business to recover with all imaginable agility, and this, in a great degree, is accomplished by what is termed Breaking Measure[22], which consists

---

17  *Spring Back,* or *Spring Off*: "To Spring Off. Is a quick Retreat out of the Reach of your Adversary, by leaping backward." Thomas Page, 11.

18  *In Guard*: "On Guard, signifies being placed on your feet, and well covered with your weapon." Lonnergan, 261. *Guard*: "GUARDS, particular postures, adapted either for defending yourself from the attempts of an adversary, or from whence you may with facility execute any offensive movements against him.—By modern practice, only two guards are used in small sword play, viz. the guard of carte, and the guard of tierce. The one covers your body from a straight inside thrust, by crossing the blades on that side, and the other covers you from a straight outside thrust by opposing the blade outwards." McArthur, 155-156.

19  *Bate*: Possibly an Irish variation of the English term "beat," or the French *battement*. This author seems to use this term interchangeably with "batter," but it is unclear if he regards the terms as synonymous, or not. Hary Fergusson notes: "To BEAT, to put your antagonist's sword off the line, in order to procure an open, by moving only your wrist, and giving a smart jerk or dry blow with the fort of your blade on his foible." Fergusson, 3. See also *Batter*.

20  *Batter*: "To BATTER, to beat with the foible of your blade on that of your adversary, when you are going to make an attack." Fergusson, 3. "Battering is thus practised; if you are in Quarte, and would batter on the Tierce-side, strike with your Forte in a slanting and strong manner upon my Foible, near the point; and sustain your stroke, by sliding your Foil along mine, still hard and smartly towards my shell; this will make my Foil spring out of my hand, or make way for your thrust to hit me as before." Lonnergan, 86.

21  Shakespeare, *Troilus and Cressida*, Act V, Scene 3.

22  *Breaking Measure*: "Breaking Measure is to advance or retire from your due measure, also to sway your body back from a thrust, without moving your feet." Lonnergan, 257. "MEASURE, Is the distance or [continued]

not only in moving your whole body at once backward, but having a motion from the small of the back; this almost lessens by one half the time of your recovery, by doubling your velocity, and gives an uncommon grace at the foils when finely executed.

17. The general rule for direct passes, apparently admits of a judicious exception, from considering the equality of the angle of incidence and reflection: for, I conceive it may sometimes happen, the center when covered in a direct direction, may be hit by an allonge reflected from your adversary's Sword. This I mention rather as a matter of speculation: thus we find gunners, when they cannot see the place intended to be hit in a rectilineal direction, plant themselves so that the incident angle shall reflect the ball to, or on, the place desired. I am aware that in so doing you must injure your line, and consequently give light; but it ought to be only great swordsmen that, like Shakspeare in poetry, "Snatch a grace beyond the rules of art."[23] But this graceful negligence, and heroic soaring above rules, should never be attempted but when there is a guard for the failure; and perhaps, as already hinted, it is too daring in the case of life and death.

18. In the knowledge of the Sword, as in some of the greatest of the sciences, there are many things in which you must be perfect, and expeditious in the performance of, before you can attempt their general application: thus in the Analysis we learn the arithmetical rules and geometrical axioms; but when these rules had best be used, or these axioms applied in any particular investigation, depends entirely on the judgment of the artist; so in like manner we learn a variety of advances, passes and feints, when taking what is called the Breast Lessons[24] from a master; but when we face an antagonist in loose play[25], the manner of attack must depend upon our own taste, judgment and execution. But ever design, before you attempt to

---

[cont'd] space between two adversaries, when they have joined blades for an assault.— Out of Measure, is when you are so far from your adversary that is not possible for the extent of your longe to touch him; in that situation it is necessary to advance, in order to gain your measure previous to longeing." McArthur, 157.

23 Alexander Pope, *An Essay on Criticism* (London: Printed for W. Lewis, 1713): "Great Wits sometimes may *gloriously offend*, And *rise* to Faults true Criticks *dare not* mend; From vulgar Bounds with *brave Disorder* part, And *snatch* a *Grace* beyond the Reach of Art, Which, without passing thro' the *Judgment*, gains The *Heart*, and all its End at *once* attains."

24 *Breast Lessons from a master*: "PLASTROON, [in French *plastron*] Is, in a literal meaning, the breastpiece of an armour, or a leather cover for the stomach.—But the term in fencing is applied to scholars, while under the academical rules and lessons of a master previous to the practical application of them in assaults; the master's breast being covered with a leather cushion, for the purpose of the scholar's exercising his various thrusts thereat." McArthur, 158.

25 *Loose Play*: "LOOSE-PLAY, synonymous with assault;—where you practice with foils all the variations of small-sword play, offensive or defensive." McArthur, 157.

execute; and let this be an universal maxim, or as Shakspeare expresses it, "Be one of those that with the fineness of their souls, by reason guide their execution."[26] Thus Homer describes Achilles, when on the point of encountering Hector, approaching with circumspection and meditating the wound. *

* Shakspeare describes Achilles in much the same manner in Troilus and Cressida, as Homer has done in the 22d book of the Iliad.

> Tell me, ye heavens, in which part of his body
> Shall I destroy him; whether there or there?
> That I may give the local wound a name,
> And make distinct the very breach, whereout
> Hector's great spirit flew. Answer me, heavens![27]

19. It is impossible to determine the best manner of attack, as has been already observed; for that depends in a great measure on the sight of your adversary, on your own excellence in certain passes and parades; but still there may some advice be given on this head. You must be ever cautious (if with any tolerable swordsman, for a person very ignorant will not know he gives the opportunity) at too warmly or incautiously taking the light that may be given you; but notwithstanding, by great dexterity, you may make a pass become central, in consequence of the great open given, which you were designed to be hit or timed upon[28]; that is, when you see an open, though you apprehend it be designedly given: I am not absolutely for declining to attempt sending a pass in, but you are undone if you do not guard against the return or parading pass your antagonist may make. As I think this is of the greatest importance, I shall endeavour to illustrate more fully my meaning by an example. Suppose on the advance, or after passes have been made, I see full light on the tierce, I throw[29] with the utmost vigour a full tierce[30] or quart over[31]; this is what is expected, and your adversary takes you thereon: if you are not mindful of this you are certainly hit, but if you parry and return, it is greatly in your favour; for his mind being engrossed by his first design, and you passing where he

---

26  Shakespeare, *Troilus and Cressida*, Act I, Scene 3.

27  Shakespeare, *Troilus and Cressida*, Act IV, Scene 5.

28  *Timed upon*: See Remark 42.

29  *Throw*: To "throw in a thrust." Angelo, 35, 54, 56, 79; Lonnergan, 184-209.

30  *Tierce*: "TIERCE THRUST...in performing it the nails are turned downwards as in seconde, and in this manner delivered towards the breast, opposing your adversary's blade on the outside." McArthur, 160.

31  *Quart over*: "CARTE THRUST over the arm, Is the natural thrust corresponding to the parade of tierce: it is the opposite thrust to carte inside; for the opposition to your adversary's blade is outwards." McArthur, 152.

expected, perhaps he may, nay he certainly will, imagine you to be deceived, and will therefore be unprepared for being thrown off and returned on.

20. If possible, make those passes which if you fail leave you the least exposed and have the best returns, and beware of approaching too near; for there are men who seem to be insensible, that while they advance, their adversary may be considered to approach, though he continue his former situation and position.

21. A vigorous attack will sometimes disorder your antagonist, which must be of service to you, either by giving you a better opportunity of passing, or by his passing in a hurry, leave you an easy return: but an attack seldom makes any considerable impression on a good swordsman.

22. A man ought not to depend or lay too much stress, either on his activity, strength, intrepidity, prudence, or his knowledge of the art; for, on an engagement, it is impossible to determine or foresee from which of these he is to hope for superiority: they ought to be as life-guards, always ready to be called to your assistance in any imminent contingency.

23. I think it may be no bad device to retire once or twice, particularly with one you are stranger to, which perhaps will give a confidence to your antagonist, and render him incautious, of which you may avail yourself. Or you must have the opportunity of seeing if he advance perfectly in the line; and if he deviate on making his next advance, he may be finely timed by a spirited pass, which had better be a plain quart, or quart over; for after all, there are no passes preferable to the straight allonges.

24. The superior strength that many seem to have, proceeds from a greater degree of quickness, for the force of any body, striking or meeting another, is as the product of the quantity of matter and celerity; therefore, the greater degree of quickness, the greater the absolute force; or, as philosophers term it, the greater the momentum.

25. With a violent fencer, or one who advances without adhering to rules, and depends on the violence of his attack and strength of arm, your best way is to wait temperately, or retire, with a fine line and opposition, as before, until the moment he comes within distance; shew him then, by the vigour and spirit of your pass, that you only waited for the proper period to evince him, that your coolness was the result of intrepidity, rectified by judgment.

26. You should never let the point of your Sword pass the shell of your adversary's, except on an allonge; for it is certain he need not let you approach so near if he pleases, and has judgment; therefore, do not accustom yourself to advance so close, even with those who may suffer you, for if you get such a habit, you will certainly be hit when you face a tolerable proficient.

27. When you find your adversary has one particular parade which he constantly uses, then it is your business to deceive him on this his favourite parade; thus if he uses the round parade, you may deceive him by circling; if the half circle, by coming round and throwing; if he forces[32] or batters, slip and pass; if he flanks[33], throw a full quart, &c. &c. Hence it follows, that if you find your adversary parries with the simple parades, you have no reason to expect success from, or to attempt doubling or circling him.[34]

28. The reason I make use of the expression, Throwing yourself in Guard, is in order to convey an idea of the necessity of taking the proper attitude in a moment, without settling or fixing by a number of motions. The utility of being in an instant ready to defend or attack with propriety, is abundantly manifest. But to consider this in another light: Surprize is one cause of the sublime, which is ever attended with a more or less degree of terror; it follows then, the more instantaneous your transition from a common to a fencing attitude, the more the mind of your adversary is unsettled, and the spectators opinion of you raised if at the foils. Mr. Burke's remark, in his treatise on the Sublime,[35] perfectly agrees with this observation: "Whatever either in sights or sounds makes the transition from one extreme to the other easy, causes no terror, and consequently can be no cause of greatness. In everything sudden and unexpected we are apt to start." And in this surprize which may be raised in the breast of your opponent, it is not impossible you may disarm or worst him immediately.

---

32 *Forces*: "FORCE is the act of advancing within measure, and delivering your thrust forcibly, so as your adversary may not have sufficient power to throw it off with a natural parade.—It is also applied to the act of leaning or pressing hard upon your adversary's blade at any time." McArthur, 155.

33 *Flanking*, or *Flankonade*: "FLANCONADE, Is a particular thrust made towards your adversary's flank, by crossing and binding the feeble of his blade with your forte, and dropping the point so as to form a good opposition in octave thrust.—This thrust is seldom practised except on favourable occasions, when your adversary holds his wrist low on guard." McArthur, 155.

34 *Doubling*: "When your adversary follows the blade with the counter, you double, forming well your extension and managing your body in such a manner that you may judge what parade he will use...When you are engaged in tierce, the wrist in carte, if you imagine your adversary will parry with half-circle or the counter-in-tierce, then double, stretching the arm proportionally as the thrust approaches the body. If he parries twice with the circle, you must double...All these thrusts require a great deal of judgement, as also flexibility in the arm, as they must only come from the hand." Olivier, 87-89

35 *A Philosophical Enquiry into the Origin of Our Ideas of the Sublime and Beautiful*, by Edmund Burke, 1757.

29. The right foot should not report on an allonge till after the thrust is lodged: the reason I have heard assigned for this direction was, that the report before the thrust, would be a warning for your adversary to be on his guard; but this reason is by no means sufficient. I conceive the following to be the true one: if the right foot comes not down until the instant after the thrust has been lodged, the pass has the additional force of your body, which is thrown with violence forward; therefore, whatever obstacle it meets first, subducts from the absolute momentum a quantity of force sufficient to resist it, which in a thrust rightly made is the breast of your adversary.

Sometimes on changing you should stamp the right foot, (this we usually term an Attack, the French Appel[36]) in order to deceive your adversary, by calling his attention that way, and then make the single or double feint. To put your antagonist on his guard by rousing his atten-tion, and then instantly to overcome him, is an honourable Coup de Main at the Sword.[37]

30. In the round parades, there is an addition of force to the feeble, arising from a cause perhaps never properly considered: every part of the Sword in these parades, may be conceived as a body revolving about a center; now as every part of the Sword makes a revolution in the same time, the velocity of the extreme of the feeble is the greatest, from the conical nature of its motion; and as the momenta of bodies are as the quantities of matter multiplied into their respective celerities, and as the quantity of matter in this case, are not considered or supposed to be equal, the momenta will be as the different celerities, therefore the force of the feeble is the greatest; I say greatest, abstracting the nature of the power communicating the motion and the resistance of the medium.

31. If I chose to estimate the real force on every inch of the Sword to parry a thrust when in the round parade, I would consider the Sword as a lever, supported at one end by a fulcrum, and then make allowance for the different celerities of the parts; but as this would be trouble-some, and must be built upon hypotheses that from the nature of things could not be universal, I imagine it would, indeed, be too refined a speculation. I would not be apprehended as if it were my opinion, that this little addition of force, arising from the different celerities of

---

36 *Appel*: "APPEL, [From the French *appel*, a call] Is applied to a sudden beat with your right foot, by raising and letting it fall on the same spot, previous to, or at the instant of, making a feint against an adversary; thereby star-tling him and obtaining some opening to deliver your intended thrust." McArthur, 151.

37 *Coup de Main*: "UN COUP DE MAIN, signifies a *bold action*; and un homme de main, *a man fit for a bold and hazardous enterprise*. Des coups de main, *handy blows*." In the context of military operations, a surprise attack with overt force. Louis Chambaud, *A grammar of the French tongue* (London: C. Bathurst, 1775), 375.

the parts of the Sword, by any means counterbalances the different forces of the feeble and fort[38] arising from the nature of the lever.

32. When you parry, the force wherewith you strike your adversary's Sword, must in some measure quicken your return; for the reaction on your Sword, must ever be equal to the action on your opponent's, and this reaction brings you to, or towards the line; and therefore it appears to me, the person who parries, if he is equally as good a Swordsman as his antagonist, ought to hit on the return.

33. A simple pass is expressed by one, (or ha); a feint and pass, one, two, (or ha, ha); of a double feint and pass, one, two, three, (or ha, ha, ha.) When one, two, three are mentioned, they have no reference to any space or divination of time, (like the notes of a bar in music) as might be at first imagined; but what I conceive by it is, that a simple pass should be made by one uniform motion in the line; that a feint should have one motion only in the feint, and one more in bringing it to the like and passing, that is, feint and pass, in one, two: a double feint in like manner, one motion in each feint, and one for the allonge, that is, one, two, three: it is generally thought they cannot be too expeditious, provided the directions already given are closely adhered to.

34. I say, it is my opinion that the feints cannot be too expeditious, provided they are answered[39] by your antagonist; but if otherwise, I see no particular reason why you should continue your first design; therefore, in order to make your adversary answer them, perhaps they should be marked more deliberately than is usual, and let your exertion be shewn in the quickness of your pass.

35. I would not have a learner be very anxious if his passes are not as quick as he could wish, for it is better he should at first give his attention to the manner of throwing, for prac-tice alone will beget celerity; but an accurate and just method of throwing, can be acquired only from consideration, and attention to rules; for if once a bad habit is acquired, which often arises from endeavouring to be expeditious, the difficulty, or rather impossibility, attending the cure, is very notorious.

---

38 *Fort*: The author defines the "fort" as the middle part of the blade (see Remark 78), whereas most other fencing authors of the period define the fort as the portion of the blade closest to the shell or guard: "FORTE of a blade, Is the first division of a blade of a sword or foil, and is sometimes called the shoulder, or strength, as it comes from the shell to the middle division." McArthur, 155.

39 *Answer*: When "your adversary goes to parry where you feint, which gives you a right to proceed with your design…" See Remark 83.

36. If we make a strict observation on the Guard, we shall find the human frame could not possibly be put in any attitude so well calculated for the different intentions of the art, namely, Offence and Defence. I have already proved the utility of preserving the line and lying low; I shall now consider the rest of the attitude. Lying in quart, you are perfectly covered, that is, there is no open, therefore your Sword must be disordered before you can be well hit. Of all positions the quart is the strongest the arm can be kept in; the joints being as it were supporters, to prevent the arm from falling. The left knee and right arm bent, gives the power of darting in, with an elastic spring, on your pass; your belly kept in, makes you more perpendicular, and consequently firmer on the ground, having your body as a pillar upon the center of its pedestal: a full chest is also necessary, to preserve the perpendicular, and gives a greater power to the arm: the left arm extended, or rather forming a gentle curve, preserves the equilibrium, and serves to give the body that play which is desirable; and letting it fall, or rather forcing it down on the side and thigh at the time of the pass, is an addition thereto. The legs extended at what is called the Distance, gives the power of lying low, and your body finely poised in the middle, as already mentioned, makes the line of direction, as philosophers term it, pass through the center, and consequently you are in the position which admits of the least danger of falling, being in that case as firm as possible. I have not here said any thing on the elegance of the guard; for if any one position were taken merely for being graceful, without being calculated for some use, I would adopt the most inelegant in its place, if the utility of such an attitude were evident or demonstrable; but it is not a little pleasing, that the attitudes most spirited and graceful, are those which have been experienced to answer best the grand objects of the Sword.

37. In throwing quart and tierce, a man cannot indeed be too perfect, as scarce any thing is more improving at first, or shews the taste, elegance and politeness of the Sword; but in this, as often in loose play, there are many things practiced which had much better be omitted; such as dropping the point of your Foil, standing carelessly out of guard, parrying in a manner impossible to be put in execution in real action, &c. which sometimes even fine Swordsmen fall into, from a wanton exuberance of taste; and through really wrong, and absolutely contrary to the first principles of the Sword, yet as original in them, they become, abstracted from a rigorous judgment, no unpleasing peculiarity: but how ridiculous is it to see every puny whipster, playing off at second-hand the faults of persons, whom they are incapable of copying in any of their excellencies. There is a maxim I think that ought to be universal, That every position, parade and pass, be calculated either to preserve yourself, or annoy your antagonist, I say in loose play particularly; for if taste and elegance are to be looked for in throwing quart and tierce, execution is the object of loose play. I would therefore recommend, whenever you fence

loose, to suppose yourself at the Sword facing an antagonist, and playing that great game where life is the stake; consequently you will give yourself no airs, or what are falsely called elegancies, that may subject you to be hit or disarmed[40], as every such circumstance must be extremely dangerous at the Sword, which those who are accustomed to, cannot, in action, wholly divest themselves of. Besides, a man being inured to reflect on any circumstance which must, or may probably happen, will doubtless be the better prepared to meet that action or crisis, however dreadful, with determined coolness and dauntless intrepidity. Therefore, I think it but a fair and rational deduction, that one who has been accustomed to the supposition of defending in the case of life and death, will not be so liable to be intimidated, or thrown into confusion, whenever this unfortunate circumstance may really happen, as the man, who never considered in loose play more than mere taste and exercise *.

* I hope no person will do me the injustice to conceive, that I could wish any Gentleman should divest himself for a moment of any action or motion elegantly useful. If Virgil is applauded for breaking even his clods with the air of a gentleman, and happily engrafting, as it were, a kind of rural dignity on the more laborious exercises of agriculture, how absolutely essential must it be to adhere with exactness, to all the etiquette which politeness and custom have wisely established, in so liberal, yet so warm and animated an exercise as that of Fencing. Men of sense and education, more particularly while Fencing, will never deviate from that manly and elevated good breeding, which indeed no man ever knew in theory without the practice, and is the happy mean between the frippery of the dancing-school and the blunt rusticity of the sod.

38. To be a good Swordsman, it seems to me necessary, to have a certain philosophic consistency, an elevated steadiness of mind, which, in all human occurrences, is the undoubted characteristic of the truly great. A man ought to have so much diffidence, as will prevent him from forming any contemptible opinion of the abilities of his adversary, arising from an ideal comparison; and consequently, this happy distrust will render him circumspect and wary; for the best Swordsman, plumbing himself on his knowledge, may fatally be convinced of his error by a mere bungler. On the other hand, a certain degree of confidence is requisite to prevent him from a mean timidity, which may at least be equally prejudicial. In a word, be cautious and spirited.

---

40 *Disarm*: "DISARMING, The act of depriving your adversary of his sword or foil." McArthur, 154. "To DISARM, to secure your enemy's sword by the handle, when he is either thrusting, has his point off the line, or when he neglects to rispost:—To beat the sword out of one's hand with a parry." Fergusson, 6.

39. Whenever you pass, endeavour to come with your fort on your adversary's feeble; this, when the pass is nearly instantaneous, as all allonges should be, binds your adversary's Sword, by weakening his force and encreasing your own, and may make that pass become central, which otherwise might be parried.

40. I would recommend Flanking principally when your adversary's Sword is in play, and his motion favours your binding[41]; for by taking him thus, you make his own force conspire against him, and consequently less force of yours necessary.

41. When you flank, be sure endeavour to secure or bind your adversary's Sword well; but attempt this in such a manner, that supposing you miss, you may not fly from the line. To acquire this method, I think a very good device is for a master, when giving a flanking lesson, now and then, when he thinks it is least expected, to slip his foil away; this will more effectually brings a learner to perform it in the manner to be desired, than any direction whatever, even from a master, as the manner is not easily defined; but there is scarce any person but will perceive his defect, after a few disappointments.

42. The time of a pass being one; of a change[42] and pass, or feint and pass, being one, two; it follows, in my mind, that while your adversary is changing, or feinting, you have time to send in a thrust: this is usually called Timing[43], and when finely executed, is the perfection of the art; but should not be attempted for a considerable time, or until you become a very tolerable proficient, for with beginners it is nothing but a scene of confusion and precipitancy.

---

41 *Binding*: "BINDING the Sword, Is the act of crossing your adversary's blade, with pressing the fort of yours on the feeble of his, and by a sudden jerk of the wrist securing or binding his blade, so as to be covered either from a time thrust or an interchanged thrust. It is generally performed from the guard or engagement of carte, when your adversary holds his wrist low on guard. A thrust thus delivered on the act of binding, is termed the thrust of *flanconnade*." McArthur, 152.

42 *Change*: "Changing is performed by a conical motion, the vertex being at the wrist, as already mentioned, therefore the smallest motion at the shell is sufficient to make a change at the point..." (See Remark 57).

43 *Timing*: "TIME THRUST, [in French *coup de tem*] Is the act of delivering a thrust to your adversary in the momentary duration of time employed by him in executing any feint or design against you.—They are esteemed the most delicate thrusts in fencing; and may with facility be executed against an adversary that makes wide feints and erroneous movements.—The nicety required in executing the time-thrust depends more upon the susceptibility of your hand and wrist than upon eye-sight.—A good fencer is so sensible of the contact of blades, that he feels the least disengagement." McArthur, 160.

43. At the same time let me remark, that it is equally wrong in tolerable Swordsmen to exclude timing, as it is in beginners to attempt it; resolving not to practice it until you can perform it well, would be equally judicious with resolving never to mount a horse, until you were perfect in the manage; or of bathing, until you knew how to swim.

44. Therefore, whenever you change before you pass, or feint before you allonge, be sure to remember you may be timed, which, without you are prepared, will be very dangerous.

45. In every parade, keep your point as near to the breast of your adversary as possible, for the convenience of an immediate return; and (as the congress of your point, with the breast of your opponent, is the sole object of your contention) on every advance and retreat, let the point be kept in this, its proper direction, as much as possible; even a bad Swordsman adhering to this direction, will in a great measure disconcert a good one.

46. When you bend your arm, be sure have the bent, or elbow, in the line; this, I think, is by no means sufficiently attended to, and therefore repeat the hint; for the flexure of the arm is not what gives light, but the deviation from the line.

47. I by all means recommend parrying with a pass; for this is really expedition itself, and therefore it may be sometimes adviseable to give light, when you are thus prepared to receive your opponent.

48. Timing, as I have just mentioned, is the perfection of the art, when finely executed; for you must be all eye and attention when you face a regular timer, for he will certainly throw, if you make but one motion beside the pass. But it is also necessary to manifest, what appears to me to be yet a safer and finer manner of timing: when two men throw themselves in guard, they seldom or ever are within the sphere of action, or within allonging reach of each other; therefore, one must advance, before either can possibly throw to effect; the one who does not advance, has it in his power to wait for the other, with a precision and watchfulness indeed very hard to arrive at, until the instant he comes within reach, when a pass may be sent in spiritedly, before the person who is advancing with a design of throwing, has time to send in his. For, to allonge when out of distance, would be equally absurd, as for a gunner to fire at an object out of reach; therefore you must, by a Geometrical Glance, if I may be allowed the expression, measure your distance before you throw: and if you are accustomed to estimate distances by your eye, which is a matter of more utility than may at first be imagined (and

therefore justly inculcated by Rousseau to his Emilius[44]) you will scarce ever be mistaken. This is termed Timing on the Advance. Hence it follows, from this and what has already been said, that after you have thrown yourself in guard, you must be cautious of either advancing, changing or feinting, as you may be in general be timed in any one of them. But again, let me repeat it, for I think it cannot be inculcated too often, do not by any means let this lead you to a watchfulness that may degenerate into timidity; for, on the whole, I think the intrepidity of a Cæsar, to the full as requisite as the circumspection of a Fabius. It seems to follow, that you had better, as much as possible, keep at one side of your adversary's Sword, for every change admits of a time, if you are within distance.

49. I am highly pleased to have discovered, that raising the hand on making the pass, sends the thrust into your adversary's breast, in a rectangular direction, which justifies the desiring that position to be constantly preserved, in the most philosophical sense; for when you throw, your adversary is on the parade breaking measure; therefore, the surface of his breast makes an acute angle with its former perpendicular, being changed from its vertical direction; and this angle will be found, I believe, to be nearly equal to the angle which the Sword makes on the pass with the level or horizontal line; and if so, the thrust is sent in an angle of ninety degrees to the breast. So this, which has ever been considered only as a security to the person passing, I have here proved to be that direction which is of the most force, as well as security; at one and the same time defending, or covering yourself, in the best manner possible, and sending the thrust in with the greatest force, proportionate to the power.

50. To force a man's Sword from the line by a batter, I think dangerous; for when a man advances with a batter, with intent to disorder, he may be finely timed thereon. This method I believe to be seldom used by a good Swordsman; for while he is making the batter, you may throw either before he comes to the line, or after he has passed it; for your adversary in order to add force, finds it necessary to raise his Sword; this will manifestly encrease the impetus, but gives the double opportunity of timing, as above mentioned.

51. To preserve the equilibrium of the body is of the greatest consequence; for when that is injured, a man is no longer in possession of himself: whenever you find your opponent thus, attack with a double ardour, and aim at ending the day with an eclat, which may redound as much to your humanity as your courage. What would be dangerous to attempt before, may

---

44 See Jean-Jacques Rousseau, *Emilius and Sophia: Or, a New System of Education. Translated from the French of J.J. Rousseau, Citizen of Geneva. by the Translator of Eloisa.* (London: Printed for R. Griffiths, T. Becket and P.A. de Hondt, in the Strand, 1762).

now, perhaps, be accomplished; for he may be disarmed, thrown, or overcome in some manner, without taking his life. Telemachus, when engaging the Rhodian in the island of Crete, is made to owe his victory to putting this advice in practice: "Stepping back he writhed his body, to avoid the stroke; by this motion the equilibrium was destroyed, and I easily threw him to the ground."[45]

52. An error attending all the fencers I have ever seen (two only excepted) is parrying wider than there is occasion, particularly in loose play; hence it must appear, that the greatest difficulty attends acquiring accuracy in this point; for, by right, the Sword of your adversary should not be followed an hair's breadth beyond what is absolutely necessary to throw it completely off from the body, as your return can be quicker. It may be said, the farther you have to go, the farther he has to come to parry. This proves too much, therefore proves nothing. But I would recommend a determined force, such as I have endeavoured to describe in the remark on flanking.

53. I am aware that beginners will think it impossible from written instructions, their minds and bodies being all confusion when engaged; but custom will soon habituate them to arrange and associate their ideas in such a manner, that the moment an opportunity offers for a pass, the proper one will arise in the mind, and present itself for execution. But it is not to be expected that the most accurate description, or the best advice and explanation, can make a man fence well, without indefatigable industry; yet this is most certain, that it is with this art as with every other, a theoretic knowledge must ever lead to the perfection of the executive. I desire no cavilling at my mentioning the theory of the art; I am aware (as well as any man who will criticise, for the querulous are generally of weak parts) of the usual distinction between a Science and an Art; I use the expression in its common, and perhaps equally just acceptation, for every thing as it demonstrates, becomes speculative or theoretic; and executive, as it reduces to practice. But, on second thought, I shall give any one leave (though doubtless he will not wait for my permission) to be as elaborately dull, or critically insignificant, with any of these lines as he pleases.

54. Perhaps it may be objected, though it is in fact done away by the title page, that I have used too many physical terms; but this I believe has neither weight nor force; for almost every Gentleman who applies himself to the Sword, has had a liberal education, and consequently will be pleased at an attempt at grafting this art upon the most elevated of the sciences, i.e. the

---

45  François Fénelon, *The Adventures of Telemachus* (London: Alex Hogg, 1775), Book V.

mathematical; and perhaps it may be something novel, to have proved this art, in many instances, to be so closely connected with the common precepts of philosophy.

55. Palming[46], or throwing passes aside with the left hand or arm, is entirely condemned by most masters. I shall here consider it unprejudiced; and though I am not even a tolerable proficient in the executive part of the Sword, yet as any thing contrary to reason must be repugnant to science, it follows, that almost every cool and dispassionate reasoner may judge of general principles. The grand objection, I take to be, that those who palm, in order to have the full play with their left hand, stand in a false position, encreasing the breadth presented to their antagonist: this is allowed to be wrong, by the advocates for palming, and it is unfair in gentleman of the contrary opinion to argue from the abuse of it; for they must allow the practice, or not: if they do, there is no argument; if they do not, it certainly ought not to be for some persons performing it irregularly and injudiciously. Again, I have heard it said, that indeed it may do very well in real action, but at the foils it is mere bungling, and no fencing. This reason is so very futile, that it is scarce worth answering: for, to what purpose do young men practise, if not to defend themselves in the best manner possible; and if it be allowed proper in action, how are we to attain a facility or expedition in performance without practice? Or how are we to practise but with foils? If we are to look on Fencing only in the light of an exercise, the left hand used as an auxiliary renders still a more general one to the human frame. Again, it is well known that two of the best Swordsmen existing, mistaking each other's design, through an intemperate warmth, or some undefinable accident, may both parts pass at the same time: I ask any Gentleman, on this occasion, or any other that may be supposed, if palming would be of service. If it be allowed, and I believe it cannot be denied, I then must conclude, it is improper to exclude palming entirely from a place in the art. If I may be allowed here, in some measure to digress, and indulge in speculation, I shall draw an argument from unimproved nature. I am persuaded no man unintroduced but would use his left hand, and perhaps would deem it ridiculous and absurd, that when nature gave two arms to protect and defend, art should exclude one from the most grateful of all offices. I speak this from experience, having made warm passes with a foil against many almost ignorant of the art, to prove the hypothesis, and have found them all endeavour to palm; in general would do so, and of consequence that it is natural, and therefore, when directed and improved by reason,

---

46 *Palming:* "Another way of Parrying, I call Palming, thus demonstrated, Stand your direct Line as before said, and lie with your Weapon full [tierce], hold your left Hand in manner of a half Moon against your Chin, or Clap the back of it upon your right Pap; then if your Opponent Pushes at you, instead of Parrying with your Sword, Palm with your left Hand, and quicker than I can speak, perform your Pass in Cart." Wylde, 10-11. For more information on *palming,* see the Glossary.

may be serviceable: for to bring any art to perfection, we must ever have in view the grand original, Nature, who, notwithstanding her outlines may be coarse, yet they are ever just; Providence leaving imperfect things within the reach of human abilities, to impel us to the exertion of our faculties. But when we go opposite to Nature, we fly from the useful and beautiful; it is our business to fill up the voids, and our judgment is shewn by continuing in the direction where Nature seemed to quit us, until we trace out her footsteps, and discover her happy vestiges once more; for on the Doric base of Nature, the Corinthian superstructure of the sciences must be ever erected: Art may indeed give polish, but Nature alone can give the substance.[47]

That palming was the custom of former ages, we have many instances to prove; I shall mention but one, from that inimitable copier of Nature, Shakspeare, "Tybalt here slain, whom Romeo's hands did slay: Romeo that spoke him fair, bid him bethink how nice the quarrel was; all this uttered with gentle breath, calm look, knees humbly bowed, could not take truce with the unruly spleen of Tybalt, deaf to peace, but that he tilts with piercing steel at bold Mercutio's breast, who all as hot, turns deadly point to point, and with a martial scorn, *with one hand beats cold death aside*, and with the other sends it back to Tybalt."[48] This one instance demonstrates, that this manner of defending has some degree of antiquity on its side, and has been used by men whose bravery and judgment were never controverted; for I have heard it mentioned as a want of either or both, to use palming. At this period, it was absolutely necessary for men to be expert at the Sword, as personal combats were then not only considered as a redress for grievances (or rather imaginary evils) not cognizable by law, but were used as a judicial process, even to the greatest enthusiasm of folly, as all historians of those times agree. I say, by their making personal engagements a mode of decision in cases of honour, (for there have been certain ideas of honour in all countries and ages) as well as of life and property: and as a test of truth, justice and fidelity, it is more than probable that in those days of chivalry and knight-errantry, when, I suppose, all hand weapons were used with more dexterity than at present (the use of the pistol being unknown), that if it were prejudicial or unnecessary to use palming occasionally, its inutility would have been much sooner discovered. If you engage with one, in other respects of superior judgment and execution, palming puts you on a level; if

---

47 *On the Doric base of Nature, the Corinthian superstructure of the sciences must be ever erected*: The author alludes to the relationship between the Classical architectural orders. The Doric, being simple, fundamental, sturdy, and unadorned, was, according to Vetruvius, "of the greatest antiquity," giving rise to the subsequent Ionic and Corinthian orders. The Corinthian, by contrast, was the final development of the ancient Greek canonical orders, and was considered to be the most ornate, elegant, and graceful. See Vitruvius, *De Architectura*.

48 Shakespeare, *Romeo and Juliet*, Act III, Scene 1.

with one of equal skill, it makes you his superior; but in that case, which is not the least dangerous, namely, engaging with a desperate bungler, it is perhaps of all things most definitive; for he, not aware of his danger, or in a desperate phrenzy, giving his own life as lost, and resolved on taking yours, throws continually in a most irregular and violent manner; there is no way, therefore, more terminating than to palm and pass at the same instant. But notwithstanding, I am not for making a constant practice of palming, (for this would be running into the contrary extreme) at least until you are master of some good parades; apprehensive that if you depend upon the left hand too much, perchance you may neglect in some measure your parades. If this indeed was or could be fairly proved a necessary consequence of palming, which I am of opinion it never can, I would then agree to its exclusion from the art of fencing.

56. Every good pass and return should be like the shot of two pistols, fired after each other instantly; for the moment your antagonist's foot is heard, your foot should report your return, and execution should be done before the sound can reach the ear.

57. A great perfection in fencing is changing with exactness: we should remember, that changing is performed by a conical motion, the vertex being at the wrist, as already mentioned, therefore the smallest motion at the shell is sufficient to make a change at the point; also let your parades be elastic, that is, without waiting an instant, or resting on your adversary's Sword. These directions will hold good for all hand weapons. Shakspeare, that rigorous adherer to nature, has the following description in Hamlet:

> His antique Sword, rebellious to his arm
> *Lies where it falls,*
> Repugnant to command unequal match'd.
> Pyrrhus at Priam derives, in haste *strikes wide,*
> But with the whiff and wind of his fell sword
> Th' unnerv'd father falls.[49]

58. Notwithstanding that many censure the motion at the small of the back, or breaking measure, I must recommend it to be constantly used in loose play, by reason, the pass that might otherwise become central, may only have that direction: for instance, you miss the parade; if you do not break measure you are unavoidably hit, but if you do, there is not only a possibility, but a probability of your not being hit; at the worst, it cannot be altogether so dangerous, provided you do not let your opponent approach too near, which entirely depends

---

49 Shakespeare, *Hamlet*, Act II, Scene 2.

on yourself. Again, in many cases it saves retiring, or advancing; when the first, your return must be quicker; when the second, it must also be quicker, without the hazard of your being timed on the advance. A man indeed in this case, as well as in every other, must be careful not to run to an extreme, nor with Hudibrastic[50] agility give such an unmerciful swing, as to leave himself aground on the opposite side, or abandon himself in the least; he must strike at the medium; let him be neither as inflexible as the oak, nor as pliable as the willow.

59. The objection to this, is in some degree the same as to palming, namely, that it prevents a man's acquiring a good parade. But to obviate this apparent bad consequence, I would have a person accustom himself to stand against a wall and parry feints; this will make his wrist or parade good: but in loose play, I must confess, I am (as before) for Defence and Execution; nor shall I ever be persuaded, whatever opinion may predominate, to exclude from the art, or not to adopt, any one motion or position, that can have a proper tendency to either.

60. Never engage but when your honour is indeed really concerned,—for your country or your king, your friend, your life, or your property: no matter if your antagonist had overcome thousands, actuated by such a glorious or honest impulse, believe me, you will not find him invulnerable.

> "What stronger breast-plate than an heart untainted;
> Thrice is he arm'd that has his quarrel just;
> And he but naked (though lock'd up in steel)
> Whose conscience with injustice is corrupted."[51]

He deserves to lose his life, who holds it in estimation when his conscience sanctifies the engagement; he attacks the equity of Providence by fearing the catastrophe. If once a dread takes place, all is lost. Homer wisely makes Hector's timidity a forerunner of his defeat. Had Hector never heard of the prowess of Achilles, he would have met him without fear. Impressions therefore of this nature, are of very bad consequence, in respect to men whose character for courage and abilities is very great. Dangers (says the great Fenelon, in his instructions to

---

50 *Hudibrastic*: The hero of the satirical poem, *Hudibras* (1663), is thus vanquished by Trulla, a peasant woman: "The Knight [Hudibras] with one dead-doing blow / Resolving to decide the fight, / And she, with quick and cunning slight, / Avoiding it, the force and weight / He charged upon it was so great, / As almost sway'd him to the ground. / No sooner she th' advantage found, / But in she flew; and seconding / With home-made thrust the heavy swing, / She laid him flat upon his side…" Samuel Butler, *Hudibras* (Dublin: S. Powell, 1732), 115.

51 Shakespeare, *Henry VI, Part II*, Act III, Scene 2.

Telemachus[52]) should ever be carefully avoided, nay, feared at a distance; but when they are unavoidable and present, they certainly should be despised.* The Love of life, if carried beyond a certain degree, leads to destruction instead of security; for courage and resolution protect, whilst cowardice and timidity deprive men of the power of defending.

> "Cowards die many times before their deaths,
> The valiant never taste of death but once:
> Of all the wonders that I yet have heard,
> It seems to me most strange that men should fear,
> Seeing that death, a necessary end,
> Will come, when it will come."[53]

Timidity, indeed, is a base-born passion, which, by a wretched misnomer, is frequently termed Prudence or Humanity, and thus, like other vices, endeavours to hide its deformity in the golden sanctuary of some acknowledged virtue: but he must have a weak head, or a bad heart, who can take vice for virtue, or virtue for its contrary. There can be no mistaking a veteran coolness, for "a pale cold cowardice," or a despicable pusillanimity. In a word, stand always on the broad bottom of Virtue, and then be in action, as the amiable Rollin describes Virgil in his writings, "Cool even in enthusiasm."[54]

* We find the same sentiment inculcated by Shakspeare; and Tully[55] has pretty much the same idea in the 24th chapter of his Offices.[56]

61. While I despise that wretched timidity of some men's disposition which renders it almost impossible for them to be either a valuable friend, a worthy member of society at large, or even a good neighbour, or safe acquaintance; let no man conceive I am an advocate for, or that I by any means countenance or approve of the Gothic and Cowardly act of duelling. I glory in being one of those who look on such actions with an equal degree of pity and contempt; and action directly contrary to reason and religion, can never be rendered virtually

---

52 The author refers to *Les aventures de Télémaque* by Fénelon, Archbishop of Cambrai. This French novel, first published in 1699, pretends a completion of Homer's *Odyssey*, and recounts the education of Telemachus by his tutor, "Mentor," who is revealed at the story's conclusion to be the goddess of wisdom in disguise.

53 Shakespeare, *The Tragedy of Julius Caesar*, Act II, Scene 2.

54 A misquote of Rollin: "Or as Virgil, who is sober even in his enthusiasm." Charles Rollin, *The Method of Teaching and Studying the Belles Lettres, Vol. 3.* (London: Printed for A. Bettes-worth and C. Hitch, 1734), 61.

55 *Tully*: An eighteenth-century name for the Roman orator and statesman, Marcus Tullius Cicero (106–43 BC).

56 *Offices*: *De Officiis*, Cicero's essay on duty.

praise-worthy by the wretched predominancy, or the unhappy tyranny of custom. Custom indeed may, and does give weight and strength, nay, almost sanctifies those things that were originally just or inoffensive, but can never change the absolute nature of any action, by converting wrong into right, or vice into virtue.

Men give up some of their natural rights, and consequently feelings, to enjoy the blessings of society: now he who recurs to this mode of redress, which perhaps would be allowable in the state of nature, breaks his actual or implied contract with society, and as much as in his power lies, turns the face of nature to an Aceldema[57], a scene of butchery and horror. No gentleman would willingly seek redress by personal engagement with a mean and illiberal man, or a villain of public notoriety; now he who wantonly injures any worthy man, is no better, whatever character he might have formerly supported; for, by a flagrant act of injustice, a man debases himself, and consequently does not deserve to be considered any longer in the light of a gentleman. Again, it is a dogma among Civilians and Lawyers, that there is no real evil without a legal remedy; if this be so, and as the causes of all duels, must be real or imaginary, it follows, that if a real, the law provide satisfaction or retribution, and if ideal, it is petulance or weakness to seek revenge for what has really no existence. Again, duelling does not answer the end proposed, namely, satisfaction. What satisfaction does the duellist receive for a real or imaginary evil,* perhaps a mere bagatelle?[58] why truly, to be run through the body, or shot through the head.

Duelling is an act of downright cowardice. One of the greatest of the antients demonstrates in his Ethics[59], that it is no action of courage in a soldier to fight, if a river runs at his back, into which he must be precipitated if he retreats, or, when the serjeant of the band is ready to transfix the veins of his back with an halberd if he swerves from his ranks: and universally, any action that arises from worldly fear of any nature, is truly pusillanimous. Now I believe it cannot be controverted, that the real cause of almost all duels, arises from the fear of the reproaches of mankind; it is this fear, this cowardice, that stimulates men to actions they would otherwise reprobate and abhor. For perhaps there is not in Europe, a man of common understanding and humanity, that would run the chance of murdering, or being murdered, for

---

57 *Aceldema*, more usually *Aceldama:* 1. The place near Jerusalem purchased with the bribe Judas took for betraying Jesus (*Acts* I:18-19): "And it was known unto all the dwellers at Jerusalem; insomuch as that field is called in their proper tongue, Aceldama, that is to say, The field of blood." 2. Any place of slaughter and bloodshed.

58 *Bagatelle:* French, from Italian *bagattella*. Something of little value or importance; a trifle.

59 The author likely refers to Aristotle's *Nicomachean Ethics*, Book III, Chapter 8.

some trifle scarce worth mentioning, if the fear of a sneering world did not urge him to such a cowardly phrenzy. It was this false idea of honour (as Tully mentions in his Offices) that actuated Callicratidas the Lacedæmonian, in the Peloponnesian war, to continue at Arginusæ, by which he was overcome by the Athenians[60]: and the same false principle, the fear of an idle report, made Cleombrotus, another of their generals, rashly engage with Epaminondas, by which the power of the Lacedæmonians at once fell to the ground.[61] Every man is acquainted with the behaviour of Augustus Cæsar, when challenged to a single combat by Mark Antony: compare the characters of these men, the former is equally revered for his courage, his wisdom, and his clemency, the latter runs away to the arms of his concubine, and meanly abdicates the empire of the world; yet it is Antony that dares Cæsar to the meeting, and it is Cæsar that declines it.

* What a mere trifle (the precedency in a Temporary Council) occasioned the dispute between two gallant brothers-in-law, the dukes of Beaufort and Nemours, in which the latter was killed; as also their two noble friends, the Counts Herecourt and Ris.[62] A thousand instances of a like nature might be given.

I perceive the youth as he reads, laughs at this doctrine. What, suffer a man's self to be despised, abused, nay, kicked out of company, by every hectoring fellow he meets with. No, no, sir, this is going farther than I intended;—draw your sword, and prevent any man, however great or exalted, from committing such insult and outrage. The laws of God and man

---

60  For this anecdote in full, see Charles Rollin, *The Ancient History of the Egyptians: Carthaginians, Assyrians, Babylonians, Medes and Persians, Macedonians, and Grecians* (London: J. Rivington, 1768), 273-277.

61  For the story of Cleombrotus's battle with Epaminondas, see Oliver Goldsmith, *The Grecian History: From the Earliest State to the Death of Alexander the Great, Volume II* (London: J. Rivington, 1774), 17-21.

62  This quintuple duel, fought in Paris in 1658, is recounted at length in Coustard de Massi's *The History of Duelling: In Two Parts* (London: E. and C. Dilly, J. Walter and J. Robson, 1770), 89-90:

"They fought in the Horse-market, five against five. The seconds of the duke de Nemours were the marquis de Villars, le chevalier de la Chaise, D'Uzerches, and Compan; those of the duke de Beaufort were, D'Henricourt, De Ris, Buri, and Brillet. The duke de Nemours brought pistols along with him, which he had charged himself.

"The duke de Beaufort said, as they were standing in presence of each other, 'Ah! my dear brother, what a shameful proceeding is this we are going upon? Let us forget what is past, and be henceforward friends, I conjure you.' To this mild entreaty the duke de Nemours brutally replied, 'No, rascal, I must. either kill you, or you kill me.' These words were scarce spoken, when he fired his pistol. He missed the duke of Beaufort; then immediately drew his sword to charge him; but Beaufort fired three balls into his adversary's stomach, who dropped down dead in a moment.

"The marquis de Villars killed D'Henricourt; and D'Uzerches slew De Ris. The others were only slightly wounded. The duke de Nemours was brother-in-law to the duke of Beaufort."

are on your side, and the dignity of human nature requires you should not suffer it to be degraded. But he sends you a message, inviting you to kill him, (or he will kill you) in Cold Blood, the day or two following. This is indeed the point I would willingly settle. I deny from the reasons here adduced (as well as the common arguments urged against it), the possibility of any man, as a Christian, a man of sense and morality, and consequently, as a Gentleman, to accept of such an invitation;—then what is to be done? it is indelicate to point out the line to be pursued. No man of the elevation of soul I am speaking of, that is unwarped by the opinion of a mistaken majority, will think it necessary. But suppose the purport of your answer should be, that you could not consistent with Your ideas of a man, a christian, and a member of society, go to a meeting, where there was no alternative, but to commit Murder or Suicide. Yet notwithstanding, you will always convince the man who attacks your person, that you are both able, and willing to defend it. Go then as usual, neither striving to shun, nor endeavouring to meet this man of blood, to all places you were accustomed to frequent: conscious that you act on the most just and elevated principles, enter all places with your head erect, and if this man of Gath[63] seeks and attacks you, draw then your honest weapon,—your conscience approves of it, and the catastrophe cannot be, in respect to you, justly called fatal.

You have acted thus;—the dread moment is passed;—the point is decided;—what consolation to you? Providence, suppose, has permitted for ends unknown to us, that though just, you fall. How happy your last tho' awful moments must be!—clear in the eyes of the world, to yourself, and above all, justifiable in the sight of the Almighty. But on the contrary, your adversary has unhappily precipitated himself into the grave,—his intemperate warmth has forced you to punish his injustice and temerity; and while you shed a tear of pity for the fate of the individual, you have the consolation to reflect, that you have rid the world of a man, whose mistaken, whose wretchedly perverted notions of honour, rendered him a curse, instead of a blessing to society.

> "Who noble ends by noble means obtains,
> Or failing, smiles in exile, or in chains,
> Like good Aurelius let him reign; or bleed
> Like Socrates; that man is great indeed."[64]

---

63 *Gath*: One of five Philistine city-states frequently mentioned in the Old Testament. The men of Gath were described as the warlike descendants of the legendary Anakim, a race of giants, and were the supposed remnants of the early Canaanites. The giant Goliath, famously defeated by David, was said to have hailed from Gath.

64 Alexander Pope's "Essay on Man," *Works of Alexander Pope, Esq., Vol. III* (London: J. & P. Napton, 1751), 135.

I am aware this is a harsh doctrine; to fight an hundred duels (even considering duelling as a spirited act) would require less fortitude and true courage, less passive valour, as the great Blackstone[65] well expresses it; or less of the real "Altitudo Animi,"[66] than to decline one, on these manly, rational, and elevated principles: for, to go down with the current, requires scarce any exertion; but uncommon strength and resolution are required, to swim against the stream, to rise superior to the errors and weaknesses of mankind.

62. If a prescription is admitted as a sufficient plea to demonstrate the impossibility of avoiding an improper act, all vices as well as duelling, may be defended upon the same principle. Persecution can produce kingdoms, not only those which are blinded by ignorance but even the most enlightened by science, her powerful advocates. Licentousness of all kinds has nine-tenths at least of mankind on her side; yet are persecution, lust, gluttony, and sloth, not to be despised. Pride, avarice, and dissimulation, are so powerfully and universally predominant in the heart of man, that were we, with invidious inquisitiveness, to turn over the historic page, we should find even the very Clergy to have heretofore fallen into these vices; nay, Dignified Prelates, have been known (*I say some ages ago*) to be haughty, avaricious, and voluptuous. The lust of inordinate power rages like a fever in the breast of mankind: what else should urge many worthy citizens (*of a neighboring kingdom*) with such keenness and avidity, to hunger and thirst after mural dignities; nay, after being inebriated by an acquisition of honours, they are scarce ever to be satisfied, but are still eager to quaff larger libations at the shrine of Civic power and pre-eminence. Idleness and folly are so general, that I have known a teacher of Mathematics, deviate so far from the propriety of his character, as to write on the very subject of these remarks, yet could any thing more powerfully demonstrate his weakness? —what would mankind conclude of the divine, that should write on the military art, or the soldier that would harangue on religion and morality? What folly! what insanity! for a man, thus neglecting the refined pleasures of philosophy, to leave himself open, not only to the poignant sarcasms of the ingenious, but even to the broad grins and loud laughter of vociferous dullness!

---

65 Sir William Blackstone (1723-1780), an English judge and politician, wrote, "Yet it requires such a degree of passive valour to combat the dread of even undeserved contempt, arising from the false notions of honour too generally received in Europe, that the strongest prohibitions and penalties of the law will never be entirely effectual to eradicate this unhappy custom [of dueling]; till a method be found out of compelling the original aggressor to make some other satisfaction to the affronted party, which the world shall esteem equally reputable, as that which is now given at the hazard of the life and fortune, as well of the person insulted, as of him who hath given the insult." *Commentaries on the Laws of England*, Volume 4 (Oxford: Clarendon Press, 1769), 199.

66 *Altitudo Animi:* Magnanimity, nobility of soul, elevation of spirit. A phrase used by Cicero in his *De Officiis.*

Honesty and integrity are such strangers to the world, that men most capable of distinguishing that fine line, that celestial meering[67], which upon all occasions divides right from wrong, have been known, alas! more than once, to depress the former, and espouse the latter. I have been told, it is common for (French) lawyers and advocates, notwithstanding they are conscious of being in the wrong, and are depriving the fabled widow of a scanty subsistence, or the unhappy orphan of his untimely and mutilated inheritance, for a paltry emolument, to debase language, degrade eloquence, make reason blush and justice tremble, in order that wealthy and plethoric oppression, should triumph over the wretched inanition of impoverished and appal'd innocence. Yet will any man maintain that pride, avarice, ambition, idleness and dishonesty are no crimes, because mankind in general are prone to, and give into these vices? For shame! away with such reasoning.

63. The eagerness most young men have to arrive at loose play, I take in a great measure to be the cause we have of so few good Swordsmen; for they in a manner force their teachers to advance them, tho' against their judgment, before they are grounded in what is, in my opinion, the most material, and what so few ever attain to, namely, advancing and retiring perfectly in the line, and throwing regularly and with a fine opposition. Let any person (for any one who has the rules imprinted on his mind is capable) watch attentively even those who have acquired the name of good Swordsmen, and he will find few adhere, with the desired accuracy, to the rules prescribed for a proper advance, allonge, and retreat. For tho' some very illiberally charge their masters with retarding them, I believe for one who is injured by that means, (if ever any one was) five hundred are prejudiced by an intemperate zeal in the teacher to advance his scholars, and make them distinguished. The major part of mankind are not real judges of any art or science, therefore frequently give applause for the superficial, more than for a solid knowledge; being qualified in some measure to taste the one, but having neither feeling nor discernment to relish the other. Masters through interest, being approved by a majority, either to captivate the public, or through a want of judgment, or rather of resolution, are often content to fall into the prevailing error; sometimes, particularly in the more abstract studies, they may indeed be justifiable. Some understandings have not tine enough to sound any of the sciences; there is a certain force necessary to break through the resisting medium by which they are surrounded; and, without apology for the expression, those who arrive at their happy mansions, if their genius and application are not equal, they must be inversely proportional. Masters, as well as writers in general, do not seem to be aware of the

---

67 *Meering*: A Hiberno-English word denoting a well-marked boundary, such as a ditch or fence, between farms, fields, or bogs.

difficulty a youth labours under, to conceive distinctly what they see with noon-day clearness, therefore often pass the tiro[68] to something new before he is grounded in the old, and by that means renders his ideas of all imperfect and confused.

64. Now in order to expedite the learner with the wished for rapidity, and at the same time to ground him thoroughly in Allonging, Advancing and Retreating, I submit the following device. Let a right line be marked out on the floor, and two sticks placed perpendicularly thereon, a few feet or yards asunder; then throw yourself in guard upon this line, your eye being in that direction when the perpendicular next you covers the remote one; advance on this line, and if you deviate therefrom, you can easily correct yourself without any help whatever, then allonge out, and see whether you cover the two perpendiculars as formerly; perhaps it might also be convenient to mark on the nearest upright, the height you should raise your wrist when you allonge or advance; but there is a difficulty in determining this by any object, except one very remote, for you will see the tops of the sticks under a greater angle, the nearer you approach; but if the object be very remote, as before, your advancing the length of the room, will not to sense alter the visual angle; but it would not be ten minutes trouble, to mark out in presence of a teacher, or a judicious friend, on the nearest perpendicular, the different elevations the wrist should be on a level with, at each allonge. It is with this art as with several others; a master always at hand, frequently prevents a youth from studying and meditating. I would by no means be understood, that I did not maintain, constant lessons from a master absolutely essential; but I would have him inured to think for himself upon all occasions, and only be accustomed to apply to superior judgment, when after speculating, he could not assign a reason for, or discover the cause of such a direction, or such an effect: for, where a man applies a force without knowing the reason of his exertion, I can look on him, in regard to that action, as no better than a mere mechanical power*.

* See Remark 90.

65. To accustom yourself to keep the left foot steady, you may when pushing[69] against a wall (on which a small cushion might be placed at the proper height) tie a piece of string to the ankle, or to the foot, (or have a cord with a loop) and the other end to a weight of one or two pounds; by this you will discover the moment you slip or move the foot, by the check: this is better than fixing your foot over a determined spot, as you must lose your attitude to discover if you have moved from that point; it is also better than fixing it to an immoveable object, for

---

68  *Tiro*: The same as *tyro*, i.e., a beginner or novice.

69  *Push*: A thrusting attack executed on a lunge or a pass.

the check might be too great for the ankle to receive without hurt, or the apprehension thereof might prevent a person from throwing with a sufficient spirit.† A device which I take to be a good one, for those whose professions may engage them in the day, is to practice at night; which may be very easily effectuated by placing all the lights in the room at the back, (then advance, retire, or push against a wall) and you will have your attitude accurately represented by your shadow on the opposite surface. These hints, I think are sufficient, as several improvements may be made according to circumstances: it is enough for me to shew the possibility of improving when alone, or in absence of your teacher.

† Wearing Sandals[70], perhaps, might preclude the necessity of this remark; which, as well as the former, is intended only for those who are resolved to become good Swordsmen.

66. That fine method of retiring with a slide, which is both expeditious and graceful, and should always be practised when you fence on a plain surface, I think would be dangerous on an irregular one; but let the left foot be lifted off the ground and laid down at once, this will prevent you from stumbling or falling, which on any rise in the ground might otherwise be the case, were you to slide as usual; as one who has been always accustomed to fence on a level will certainly do. Therefore, I would advise young gentlemen accustom themselves to fence on flags[71], as well as the sod; and if sometimes on pavement, it would by no means be improper: for besides it being necessary to acquire the method of advancing I recommend to be practised on a rugged surface, it will prove to them, that no dependence must be laid on the stamps wherewith some people are confused on boards. I have known those who have succeeded in perplexing unsteady fencers, by a thundering stamp, an Indian warhoop[72], and an ha* on their attack: such exclamations may sometimes be of service, if used with discretion and occasionally; but there is an equal share of weakness in being moved at, as in depending on, such adventitious auxiliaries. Mr. Rollin's description of young Manlius, previous to his engaging the Gaul, a remarkable instance in Roman history, is not unapplicable to our present remark. "The Roman was of a reasonable size, and such as one would desire in a soldier; his arms were rather adapted to use, than intended for beauty; he was not heard to raise any cries, or make

70  *Sandals*: "SANDAL, a light pump wanting the heel, made fast on the foot with leather thongs, used when fencing." Fergusson, 19.

71  *Flags*: Flagstones.

72  *Indian warhoop*: The Cherokees, a notorious Dublin dueling society, reportedly would, prior to combat, discuss "whether the attack shall commence with CAT CALLS, which they call the WAR-HOOP, or with whistlings, which is termed the WOOD-HOOP; or whether by direct assault or surprize; and this question being also disposed of, they all examine their sword canes, and sally forth for action." (See Appendix VI)

any violent motions in advancing; but full of intrepid courage and tacit indignation, he reserved all his efforts for the combat."[73]

* Good Swordsmen, in France, use a small exclamation, which has a fine effect, and is very proper, as it frequently deceives: thus for instance, when two great Swordsmen are fencing, perhaps a pause ensues; this engaging the attention of the spectators, one of them suddenly cries Un! on changing; and if he in the least disorders his antagonist, he instantly makes the single feint, saying, Un, deux, la! Sometimes he says, Un, deux! and makes a feint, Un, deux, trois la!

67. There is no popular opinion more erroneous, than that when men are so unhappy as to be under a necessity of defending themselves in reality, all they have been taught and accustomed to at the foils is neglected; for, on the contrary, the attitude will precede even thought; and one skilled in fencing, will throw himself mechanically into that position he has been habituated to; unless anger or fear are entirely predominant, and this cannot be in a moral and spirited man; and all men should be considered as such, until they prove the contrary.

68. As in the time of a feint, a pass may be sent in; it seems to me, therefore, necessary that you should disorder your adversary's sword, that is, put his point from the line, before you feint; as it will be very dangerous to depend upon his coming to a parade: for you will almost certainly be hit if your adversary passes while you feint; it is not impossible you may hit him; but besides it being much in his favour this by no means answers the intention of the art, which is at least, equally concerned in preserving yourself, as in annoying your adversary.

69. There are many, who may think that the passes and parades, as well as all motions and exertions in this art, are, or ought to be, so very expeditious, that it is scarce possible to attain so great a dexterity in their performance, as many of these remarks may seem to require; but let such call to mind, with what accuracy and rapidity the fingers, wrists, and arms, are moved by those who arrive to any degree of excellence on the violin, &c. By this and many other instances which might be given, they will be convinced, that care and perseverance, are capable of uniting the greatest velocity, with the most perfect precision.

70. When a forced thrust is parried with the prime, which occasionally will answer very well; I have heard it acknowledged, even by those who would exclude palming in general, that it is allowable to put the adversary's sword from the breast with the left hand; and I am

---

73 Charles Rollin and Jean B. L. Crevier, *The Roman History from the Foundation of Rome to the Battle of Actium: That Is, to the End of the Commonwealth. Translated from the French. in Ten Volumes* (London: Printed for J. Rivington, R. Baldwin, Hawes Clarke and Collins, R. Horsefield, W. Johnston and 7 others, 1768), 298.

informed the politest fencers, when throwing a flankonade, guard the breast in like manner; at least, if it is not allowed, it would be very dangerous, if not absolutely wrong, ever to make use of the prime; and perhaps the same may be said of the flankonade, except on a return.

71. If you are so unhappily circumstanced, as to be under a necessity of engaging a man, whom you have reason to think would take any advantage; be on your guard, lest he should instantly on your joining blades, throw with his left hand his hat, glove, &c. with violence in your face and pass at the same instant; for by such an artful and mean device, the poorest swordsman, might hit the best fencer in Europe. If any thing of this nature should ever happen, instead of swerving for a moment, allonge with the greatest vigour, and perfectly in the line: I believe without this, there is not a possibility of your escaping; but by instantly darting forward, you may be time enough to preserve yourself, and perhaps your pass take place also.

72. As the right foot should always be exactly on the line; I think the left toe should not be much turned out, but rather cross the line at right angles nearly; by this you will be more steady, your base encreasing in breadth; for if you conceive a line drawn from your left toe (when in guard) to your right toe, and then to your left heel, the triangle formed by your left foot and these two lines, should be nearly isosceles; as it is evident the nearer it approaches to an equality of sides, provided you preserve the line, you must be proportionally the firmer on the ground.

73. The center of gravity of a man being the middle point between the hips; it follows, the more central nearly he keeps this point (on the line), or rather the more central he keeps the line of direction, that is, the line which may be conceived to connect the center of gravity and the center of the earth, the more general command he must have of his body, and the more ability to advance, &c. with strength and spirit.

74. If your adversary advances spiritedly, or rather warmly, you may retire once or twice, &c. and on his advancing again, which it is probable he will with confidence, change the line instantly upon him; that is, let the line you now have taken, cross the former at right angles, by which you flank your antagonist, and perhaps may hit him; but this, in general, had better not be attempted, unless you find yourself distressed by coming too near a wall, or perceive you have the worst of it if you proceed perfectly regular.

75. I think foils should, in the handle and blade, nearly resemble the shape of the swords in fashion, and if possible, they should be the same weight: perhaps by changing the shape of the

blade, they will be more liable to break on advancing too near, or hurt somewhat more on your hitting, or being hit, than the foils now used. But these circumstances, as they must have a tendency to make men more cautious, I believe will be rather serviceable in general, than disadvantageous.*

* The grip of a small sword, I think, should be longer than that of a Cutteau de Chace[74], or Hanger[75], as it is held in a different position; this is not sufficiently attended to.—I have seen some Swords properly formed in this respect, at Marsh's, Sword Cutler near Essex-Bridge.[76]

76. If ever you are set upon by a number of assassins, (for if more than one person attacks an honest and inoffensive man, they deserve that epithet) I think you cannot be advised better for your manner of defence, than by recurring to the well known Roman story, of the surviving Horatius, when left to engage the three Albans, the Curiatti[77]: for, by the laudable

---

74  *Couteau de chasse:* "a short, small, edged-sword, usually worn in undress." Angelo, *Reminiscences, Vol. II,* 213-14.

75  *Hanger:* "a short broad sword." Thomas Sheridan, *A Complete Dictionary of the English Language* (London: Charles Dilly, 1790).

76  "JOHN MARSH, Knife and Sword-Cutler, in Caple-street, three Doors down from the Bridge, is lately returned from LONDON, and has laid in a large and elegant Assortment of studded Steel Sword Hilts, ditto inlaid with Gold, and Silver Hilts, all of the newest Patterns: He is determined to carry on that Business in the most extensive Manner, by being well assorted with the best and newest Patterns from London: He hopes for the Countenance of the Nobility, Gentry, and others." *Hibernian Journal,* Dec. 1, 1773. "MARSH, No. 3, Capel street, Has landed this Day from Paris, London, and Woodstock, a large and elegant Assortment of Steel and Good Swords, very fine studded ditto, superior to any in this Kingdom." *Saunders's News-Letter,* Jan. 15, 1779. "MARSH, CUTLER, No. 3, Capel-street, Has just landed from London and Woodstock, a large and elegant Assortment of Steel Swords, Cutteaus, &c. &c. also a large Variety of Pistols, Carbines, and Blunderbusses, all of which he will engage." *Saunders's News-Letter,* Feb. 1, 1782.

77  This combat arose from a treaty established between the ancient Roman and Alban nations, which decreed that three champions from each side would "decide the fate of their country in combat, assuring them, that the sovereignty over both nations was to be determined by the victory." Two Romans were the first to fall. The historian Livy related that: "the Roman legions, though they had lost all hopes of victory, were yet under great concern for their surviving champion, whom the three three Curiatii had surrounded. As good luck would have it, he had received no wound, and though no match against all the three, was yet able enough for them singly. Wherefore, in order to separate them, he betakes himself to flight, judging they would pursue him faster or slower as their wounds would permit. He had already run a good way from the place they had fought in, when, looking back, he perceives them following him at large intervals; and one of them not far from him: on him he turns short with great fury. And while the Alban army called out to the Curiatii to assist their brother, the victorious Horatius, having killed the first, was running to encounter the second. Then the Romans, with such shouts, as are commonly made on success after despairing of victory, encourage their champion, and he made all possible haste to finish the combat: therefore, before the third, who was not far off, could come up, he dispatches the second; And now there remained but one champion on each side to decide the quarrel; but their strength and hopes were very unequal. A body free from wounds, and a double victory, gave Horatius vigorous

artifice of retiring, it is morally certain you will separate them for a moment (as some one will be more sanguine and precipitate than the rest), and instant being sufficient for extirpating them singly, if you are determined and expeditious.

77. Above all let your judgment and resolution be apparent in preserving your line, with the most rigorous precision, as a moment's deviation may not only be dangerous, but irreparable. It would be almost better to make no parade, than by parrying, to lose your line and opposition; and were we to view it merely as a point of honour, we indeed must pronounce it most shameful, as it generally proceeds from timidity, and the pass received in such an attitude, wounds your honour thro' your person. Shakspeare makes old Siward on hearing of the death of his son, ask with heroic ardour, "Had he his hurts before."[78] And Priam, in his pathetic speech to Hector, before he engages Achilles, consoles himself for the loss of his sons formerly slain, by reflecting that their wounds were all honourably received on the breast[79]: and Pyrrhus, after defeating the Romans near Hereclia, finding all their wounds received before, cries out, in an apostrophe, no less indeed favourable to himself, than a just tribute to the bravery of the slain: "How easy could the world be conquered by Romans, were they commanded by Pyrrhus."[80]

78. The blade of a sword has three parts, the feeble, which is one extreme; the fort, the middle; and the shoulder, the other extreme: the handle has likewise three parts; the shell, which is next the shoulder; the grip, the middle of the handle or part covered by the hand; and the pommel, the other extreme.

---

to a third encounter; the other, dragging after him a body weakened with loss of blood, and fatigued with running, dispirited likewise with the slaughter of his two brothers before his eyes, is presented to his victorious enemy. It could not be called a fight. The Roman exulting, 'Two,' says he, 'I have already given to the manes of my brothers; the third I will sacrifice to the cause of this war, that the people of Rome may obtain the sovereignty over the people of Alba.' And as he tottered under the weight of his arms, Horatius struck him on the throat, and stript him as he lay dead. The triumphing Romans receive Horatius with hearty gratulations, and with the greater joy, as they had been nearer despair." *Titus Livius's Roman History from the Building of the City* (Edinburgh: A. Donaldson and J. Reid, 1761), 50-54.

78 Shakespeare, *Macbeth*, Act V, Scene 8.

79 Homer, *Iliad*, Book XXII.

80 "The next day, as [Pyrrhus] walked to view the field of battle, he could not help regarding with admiration, the bodies of the Romans which were slain: upon seeing them all with their wounds before; their countenances, even in death, marked with noble resolution, and a sternness that awed him into respect; he was heard to cry out, in the true spirit of a military adventurer, 'O with what ease could I conquer the world, had I the Romans for soldiers, or had they me for their king!'" Oliver Goldsmith, *The Roman History: From the Foundation of the City of Rome, to the Destruction of the Western Empire, Volume I* (London: S. Baker and G. Leigh, 1770), 217.

79. I must again repeat, that I am aware of censure for considering the sword in a specula-tive light, and treating an art that has been considered to arise wholly from indefatigable prac-tice, in the light of a science. But I must confess I should be better pleased to be able to reason thereon, than I would be to have the greatest execution devoid of the theory; for by the one, numbers might benefit, while the former kind of knowledge is centered in self. I am strength-ened in this opinion, as I find the greatest genius of the antients, both as to speculative and practical knowledge, value himself more on one discovery and demonstration in speculative geometry, than for innumerable of the greatest performances ever completed by man: this, by the way, evinces that when speculative men descend to the executive, they have the greatest advantages over those who are ignorant of theory, and unaccustomed to reason from first prin-ciples.

80. Do not lie full in quart or tierce, but between both; and on making the thrust, then turn to the full pass, and on recovery let your hand come to the same position it was in before you made the allonge: for instance, you lie in tierce and push tierce, let your wrist be turned more to the tierce on the pass than when you lay in tierce (and the same in quart), for you will find yourself very much distressed, if you keep your wrist to the full tierce on recovery, therefore let the hand move towards the quart.

81. Though I first intended these remarks should principally consist of original hints; on reflection I imagined it might be acceptable to mention and define a few terms, and insert some lessons that may be useful to gentlemen who have not always at hand a master for their instruction.

82. The terms generally used are,—In guard, advance, retire, allonge, a pass or thrust, parry, parry quart, throw quart, parry tierce, throw tierce, parry low quart, parry segoon; flankonade, quart over, half circle, round parade on the quart and on the tierce, or the counter in quart or tierce, octave, feinting, changing, slipping, attacking, breaking measure, binding, disordering, opposition, heel parade, singling, the line, palming, answering, abandoned, prime, a bate, a batter, light or an open, half allonge, recovering, closing, a hit, &c.[81]

83. Answering, is when you feint and your adversary goes to parry where you feint, which gives you a right to proceed with your design; but if you are not answered, you may use some other kind of attack, or wait for his coming on: for instance, if my intention is to feint tierce and throw quart, if when I feint, my adversary goes to the tierce parade, then I may proceed

---

81 See the appended Glossary for more information on these terms.

and throw a full quart; but if he does not, that is, if he does not answer me and I throw quart, he is fully prepared to parry, therefore, I can have no great expectation of that pass becoming central. In all feints be cautious to deviate as little from the line as possible, for by so doing you lessen the danger of being timed, and your pass can be sent in with greater expedition. By opposition, you are to understand such an attitude, that a pass in the line can scarce become central, that is, in every allonge; if the sword arm is not extended exactly in the line, there is said to be no opposition. The heel parade or low quart, is parrying with a bate from the shoulder; this parade I think dangerous in general, (except when a segoon is well thrown, and then it will be found much more expeditious and effectual than the half circle) yet it will not be so dangerous if the advice I have given for flanking be put in practice, to wit, applying the force in such a manner as will not, should you miss the parade, make you cross the line.

I shall mention a few lessons without giving them perhaps, as they should follow one another with a beginner: In guard, advance, advance, advance, ditto, retire, retire, retire, ditto, allonge, recover, allonge in quart, recover, allonger in tierce, recover, allonge, recover, parry quart, throw quart, parry tierce, throw tierce, parry low quart, parry segoon, parry quart, parry tierce, ditto, ditto, ditto.

Advance in quart, and throw quart, advance in tierce, and throw tierce, ditto.

Advance in tierce, change and throw quart; advance in quart, slip and throw tierce; feint tierce and throw quart, feint quart, and throw quart over, ditto, ditto, ditto.

Cut quart over the point, cut tierce over the point; retire in tierce, and throw tierce; retire in quart, and throw quart; retire, parry quart and throw quart over; ditto.

Retire, and parry the counter in tierce, and throw tierce; retire, and parry the counter in quart and throw quart; retire and parry the counter in tierce, and drop a segoon; but let the point have the proper, that is, a central direction, before you begin to move your body on the allonge; the same repeated again.

If you are bore on the quart, slip and throw tierce or quart over; if bore on the quart, feint tierce and throw quart; if bore on the tierce, feint quart and throw quart over; or in any of the above make a double feint if you please: ditto, ditto.

Returns from the round parade, first, when you parry in quart throw a full quart, if with the tierce throw tierce; second, change and throw; third, feint and pass; fourth, double on your adversary's sword and throw: when you parry in quart, let the hand and wrist be turned up in quart as much as possible, this keeps your sword in the line, and throws your adversary's off.

Advance with a feint in order to try the abilities of your antagonist, if he is a cool swordsman, he will pay no regard thereto, but if he does, you may hit him at once.

Advance and flank; a quart thrown, parry with a flankonade; advance in segoon, feint tierce and throw segoon. Your adversary cuts quart over the point, wait till he has come round to the line and flank him with spirit.

I lie in quart out of distance, my adversary advances in tierce, I time him by throwing quart; he advances in quart, time him by throwing tierce or quart over; he advances in tierce, perhaps expecting to be timed with a quart, then feint quart and throw quart over.

Suppose you are both lying in quart; a quart thrown, do you come under and parry with the tierce edge, your hand not altered from the quart position, and throw a fine quart over; this is an excellent thrust, provided you are quick at the parade. Advance spiritedly, bearing strong upon quart, and leaving a great open; your opponent, it is ten to one, throws tierce or quart over, this is what you want, and instantly send tierce along the blade, you will in this case almost hit to a certainty; I have scarce ever known it to fail with any man who was unacquainted with your design; but the danger lies in your adversary's feinting, yet if you are accustomed to palm, you guard against this: I repeat it, if you acquire dexterity in this pass, and facing a good fencer, I know of nothing that seems to bid fairer for certainty.

84. If you do not intend to palm, let your left hand on every pass fall to the side, with the back to the left thigh; some strike the palm to the left thigh, but the former is better (as a motion in the scapula, and the articulation of the shoulder is prevented), for according to the universal maxim that I would wish to have established, every motion must have an oblique, if not a direct tendency to offence or defence, and as this has no reference to either, it is superfluous, and therefore ought to be rejected.

85. I look on the knowledge of the sword, to be of more utility than at first presents itself: I imagine it must be of service in every sudden exigence, as a person who is a good swordsman, is accustomed to determine in a moment what is best to be done, and this will certainly have a remote effect in general emergencies.

86. Cutting over the point[82] is often very successful; for, I apprehend the elastic extension of the flexure of the arm, is by far the quickest motion of an allonge. But as cutting is performed by two motions, one on raising the wrist to get clear of your adversary's sword, and the other on the pass; therefore, it seems to me to be possible, at your adversary's first motion, for you to send in a spirited plain quart. If he performs his part with great accuracy, by covering his breast, you perhaps will hit him in the sword arm, which I think as desirable a circumstance as can happen. If you are too near to allonge out when your adversary cuts, suppose you were to make use of what may be called a reverse allonge; that is, leave the right foot where it is, throw the left leg and body instantly back, and dart forward your arm perfectly in the line; it is more than probable he will run on your point, which will answer as well as if you sent your point into him.

87. The disagreeable sensations young men must feel on beginning to fence, should be one reason to induce them to an early application: and fencing, I think, much fitter for youth than is usually imagined; for, the exercises of boys should always mark their sex, they should be in some degree manly and spirited. Rousseau, in his treatise on education, says, I have sometimes asked the reason why children were not made to learn games of skill and address; such as tennis, fives, the bow, billiards, foot-ball, &c. The answer given me was, that some of those games were above their strength, and that neither their limbs nor organs were sufficiently formed for the rest; and that games less fatiguing and dangerous would be preferable; but for this very reason, Rousseau approves those games; for, continues he, can we, who are formed for vigour and activity, imagine they are to be attained without trouble; and what defence shall we be capable of making, if we are never attacked. People seldom play with any spirit when they can be faulty without risk; and he therefore prefers tennis, &c. for boys, to shuttle-cock, &c. for if a shuttle-cock falls it hurts nobody; but nothing makes the arm so pliant, as to be obliged to cover the head with it; nothing renders the eye so nice and exact as to be under a necessity of guarding it from harm: to spring from one end of the hall to the other, to judge of the rebound of a ball while in the air, to return it with a sure and steady arm; such diversions as these, are less proper for men, than to give them strength and vigour while young. I believe nothing can be more applicable to fencing than these observations.

---

82 *Cutting over the point*: "CUT over your adversary's point, Is performed with a simple movement of the wrist upwards, by which your point is raised nearly perpendicular, and thereby disengaged from one side to the other.—The arm is not to deviate from the line of direction.—The cuts over the point answer the purposes of disengagements, when your adversary has his point too much elevated on guard." McArthur, 153.

88. As disarming* is attended with the most decisive and momentous consequences, I shall adduce two or three instances, wherein there may be a reasonable probability of success; e. g. Suppose your adversary throws a spirited tierce or quart over, do you instantly take his feeble with a nervous tierce parade, never deviating from your line, but darting the reserve out of your arm and allonging spiritedly; it is probable your adversary will be either hit or disarmed. Should he, aware of your intention, make a single feint, instead of the quart over, you may come forcibly to the half circle, which perhaps will accomplish your purpose. But should your adversary multiply his motions, which must at all times be dangerous to him, your instantaneous return from the half circle will counteract his deception of it; for cæteris paribus[83], they must mutually destroy each the other's effect: and lastly, by coming forcibly to the round parade, either in quart or tierce, you will have another fair chance of disarming your antagonist. Were I desired to give a short general rule for disarming, I would recommend the bearing, or rather parrying spiritedly with your own fort, on your adversary's feeble, endeavouring to throw the sword toward that side, his hand must open of itself; this is co-operating with nature.

* The antients branded with an indelible stigma, the man who had been deprived of, or had derelinquished his weapon of defence. Horace briefly and elegantly censures it in these words, "Relicta non bene parmula."[84]—In Sparta the very women, when they embraced their sons and their husbands, previous to an engagement with an enemy, conjured them *to return armed as they were, or never to return:* For their great lawgiver, Lycurgus, (whose institutions, in general, are revered to this day) had ordered in the first table of his laws, that the very statues of their Deities, even to Venus herself, should be represented armed and in military array; and this was in order to impress on the minds of the people at large the most favourable and honourable ideas of the use of arms.

Having disarmed your antagonist,* and thus vindicated the first law of nature, you must be vigilant lest you should violate any of her noble and sacred principles, by the farther prosecution of an enemy now solely at your mercy. Humanity revolts at such an idea: nor does human nature admit of a more noble triumph, a more glorious revenge, than to possess the power to punish an enemy;—yet, to have the will and resolution to forgive him.

* Whenever you disarm, secure your adversary's weapon; in real action the utility is evident; and if fencing, your politely presenting your antagonist with his foil, will do away the unpleasing sensation

---

83 *Cæteris paribus*: Latin, "all other things being equal."
84 *Relicta non bene parmula*: Latin, "having dishonorably left my shield behind." Horace, *Odes*, Section II.

which in some degree is ever attendant on this circumstance, for nothing demonstrates superiority more than an instantaneous and fine disarm.—I think indeed, beginners should by no means ever attempt disarming.

89. In writing on this subject, as it is almost confined, at least in these kingdoms, to Gentlemen, and Men of Honour, I shall, without apology, make and adopt some extracts, which it is impossible that any one man of genius or true courage can be displeased with; to strengthen those who have a true, and rectify those who have a false idea of those terms.

"Every principle that is a motive to good actions ought to be encouraged, since men are of so different a make, that the same principle does not work equally upon all minds; what some men are prompted to by conscience, duty, or religion, which are only different names for the same thing, others are prompted to by honour.

"The sense of honour is of so fine and delicate a nature, that it is only to be met with in minds which are naturally noble, or in such as have been cultivated by great examples or a refined education. This, therefore, is chiefly designed for those who by means of any of these advantages are, or ought to be actuated by this glorious principle.

"But as nothing is more pernicious than a principle of action when it is misunderstood, I shall consider honour with respect to three sorts of men: First of all, with regard to those who have a right notion of it; secondly, with regard to those who have a mistaken notion of it; and thirdly, with regard to those who treat it as chimerical and turn it into ridicule.

"In the first place, true honour, though it be a different principle from religion, is that which produces the same effects. The lines of action, though drawn from different parts, terminate in the same point. Religion embraces virtue as it is enjoined by the laws of God; honour, as it is graceful and ornamental to human nature. The religious man fears, the man of honour scorns, to do an ill action. The latter considers vice as something that is beneath him, the other, as something offensive to the Divine Being. The one as what is unbecoming, the other as what is forbidden. Thus Seneca speaks in the natural and genuine language of a man of honour, when he declares, that were there no God to see or punish vice he would not commit it, because it is of so mean, so base, and so vile a nature.[85] I shall conclude this head with the description of honour in the part of young Juba.

---

85 Lucius Annaeus Seneca (ca. 4 BC–65 AD), a Roman Stoic philosopher, wrote extensively on the subjects of God, morality, and the spirit.

Honour's a sacred tye, the law of kings.
The noble minds distinguishing perfection,
That aids and strengthens virtue where it meets her,
And imitates her actions where she is not.
It ought not to be sported with.

CATO.[86]

"In the second place, we are to consider those who have mistaken notions of honour, and these are such as establish any thing to themselves for a point of honour, which is contrary either to the laws of God or of their country, who think it more honourable to revenge, than to forgive an injury, who make no scruple of telling a lie, but would put any man to death that accuses them of it, who are more careful to guard their reputation by their courage, than by their virtue. True fortitude is indeed so becoming in human nature, that he who wants it, scarce deserves the name of a man; but we find several who so much abuse this notion, that they place the whole idea of honour in a kind of brutal courage, by which means we have had many among us who have called themselves men of honour, that would have been a disgrace to a gibbet. In a word, the man who sacrifices any duty of a reasonable creature to a prevailing mode or fashion, who looks upon anything as honourable that is displeasing to his Maker, or destructive to society, who thinks himself obliged by this principle to the practice of some virtues and not of others, is by no means to be reckoned among true men of honour.

"Timogenes was a lively instance of one actuated by false honour: Timogenes would smile at a man's jest who ridiculed his Maker, and at the same time run a man through the body that spoke ill of his Friend. Timogenes would have scorned to have betrayed a secret that was entrusted with him, tho' the fate of his country depended upon the discovery of it. Timogenes took away the life of a young fellow in a duel for having spoken ill of Belinda, a lady whom he himself had seduced in her youth, and betrayed into want and ignominy. To close his character; Timogenes, after having ruined several poor tradesmens' families, who had trusted him, sold his estate to satisfy his creditors; but, like a man of honour, disposed of all the money he could make of it, in paying off his play-debts, or to speak in his own language, his debts of honour.

---

86 Joseph Addison, *Cato, a Tragedy*, Act II, Scene V. Regarded as Addison's most famous fictional work, this play, written in 1712, dramatizes the last days of the Stoic Roman statesman, Marcus Porcius Cato Uticensis (95–46 BC). It deals with themes of liberty and Republicanism, and explores correct and incorrect notions of honor.

"In the third place, we are to consider those persons who treat this principle as chimerical, and turn it into ridicule. Men who are professedly of no honour, are of a more profligate and abandoned nature than even those who are actuated by false notions of it, as there is more hopes of a Heretic than an Atheist. These sons of infamy consider honour with old Syphax, in the play before mentioned, as a fine imaginary notion that leads astray young unexperienced men, and draws them into real mischiefs, while they are engaged in the pursuits of a shadow.[87] These are generally persons who, in Shakspeare's phrase, are worn and hackneyed in the ways of men, whose imaginations are grown callous, and have lost all those delicate sentiments which are natural to minds that are innocent and undepraved; such old battered miscreants ridicule every thing as romantic that comes in competition with their present interest, and treat those persons as visionaries, who dare stand up in a corrupt age for what has not its immediate reward joined to it. The talents, interest, or experience of such men, make them very often useful in all parties, and at all times. But whatever wealth and dignities they may arrive at, they ought to consider, that every one stands as a blot in the annals of his country, who arrives at the temple of honour by any other way than through that of virtue."[88]

90. "The inhabitants of the earth may properly be ranged under the two general heads, Gentlemen and Mechanics. This distinction arises from the different occupations wherein they exert themselves. The former of these species is universally acknowledged to be more honourable than the other, who are looked upon as a base and inferior order of men. But if the world is in the right in this natural judgment, it is not generally so, in the distribution of particular persons, under their respective denominations. It is a clear settled point, that the gentleman should be preferred to the mechanic. But who is the gentleman and who is the mechanic, wants to be explained.

"The philosophers distinguish two parts in human nature; the rational and the animal. Now if we attend to the reason of the thing, we shall find it difficult to assign a more just and adequate idea of these distinct species, than by defining the gentleman to be him, whose occupation lies in the exertion of his rational faculties; and the mechanic him, who is employed in the use of his animal parts, or the organic part of his body.

---

87 *Syphax:* A character from Addison's *Cato*, who speaks the following lines: "Honour's a fine imaginary notion, That draws in raw and unexperienc'd men To real mischiefs, while they hunt a shadow." Act II, Scene V.

88 Joseph Addison, *The Works of the Right Honourable Joseph Addison, Esq., in Four Volumes. Volume IV* (London: Printed for Jacob Tonson, 1721), 269-271.

"The concurring assent of the world in preferring gentlemen to mechanics, seems founded in that preference which the rational part of our nature is intitled to above the animal: When we consider it in itself, as it is the seat of wisdom and understanding, as it is pure and immortal, and as it is that which, of all the known works of the creation, bears the brightest impress of the Deity.

"It claims the same dignity and preeminence, if we consider it with respect to its object. Mechanical motives or operations are confined to a narrow circle of low and little things: Whereas reason inquires concerning the nature of intellectual beings, the great Author of our of our Existence, its end and the proper methods of attaining it: or, in case that noble faculty submits itself to nearer objects, it is not, like the organic powers, confined to a slow and painful manner of action, but shifts the scenes, and applies itself to the most distant objects with incredible ease and dispatch; neither are the operations of the mind like those of the hands, limited to one individual object, but at once extended to a whole species.

"And as we have shewn the intellectual powers to be nobler than those of motion, both in their own nature, and in regard to their object, the same will still hold, if we consider their office. It is the Province of the former, to preside and direct; of the latter, to execute and obey. Those who apply their hands to the materials, appear the immediate builders of an edifice; but the beauty and proportion of it is owing to the architect, who designed the plan in his closet. And in like manner, whatever there is, either in art or science, of use or regularity, will be found to proceed from the superior principle of reason and understanding. These reflections, however obvious, do nevertheless seem not sufficiently attended to by those, who, being at great pains to improve the figure and motions of the body, neglect the cultivation of the mind.

"From the premises it follows, that a man may descend from an antient family, wear fine cloaths, and be master of what is commonly called good breeding, and yet not merit the name of Gentleman. All those whose principal accomplishment consists in the exertion of the mechanic powers, whether the organ made use of be the eye, the muscles of the face, the fingers, feet, or any other part, are in the eye of reason to be esteemed Mechanics."[89]

91. The epithets Gentleman, and Man of Honour or real greatness, convey pretty much one and the same idea; yet, as there are degrees in vice, so there are in virtue; and I think men of true greatness and solid glory, are no other than men who possess, in a more eminent degree, the most refined and genuine ideas of this noble and elevated principle, honour. How many

---

89 *The Guardian*, August 10, 1713.

pretenders have we, that endeavour to pass on the world as men who have true notions of honour and solid glory; who, indeed, may seem great in the execution of the little occurrences of life, but on any exigence, when the great soul could have an opportunity for its exertion, how little do they appear. In short, the endeavouring to seem or possess more true Courage and real Magnanimity than we have ever nurtured in our breast, is an involuntary tribute mankind in general pay these virtues.

True Greatness, and solid Glory, can only be shewn in the eminent exertion of some uncommon virtue (for virtues of such a nature, that the want of them is attended with ignominy, can have no great degree of honour annexed to their possession); but more particularly, in a contempt of riches and pleasure, a love of country, and what surpasses all others in the catalogue of virtues, *the forgiving of injuries, and despising of revenge.* Souls capable of exerting this God-like attribute, are indeed, truly great, heroic, and uncommon; it is a virtue of such magnitude, and weight, that vulgar souls cannot contain, nor weak minds support it. So true is it what Mr. Addison says in some of his papers, (which tho' they are more admired than any tracts of a like nature, yet they can never be sufficiently so) "A Coward has often fought, a Coward has often conquered, but *a Coward never forgave.* The power of doing that flows from a strength of soul conscious of its own force, whence it draws a certain safety, which its enemy is not of consideration enough to interrupt; for it is peculiar in the make of a brave man, to have his friend seem much above him, his enemies much below him."[90] Beautiful as these lines are, they must fall short of exciting the idea one would wish to raise of such a character; but I am apt to imagine, as some things are too volatile to bear the chains of a definition, as Mr. Burke elegantly expresses it[91], there are others too great to admit one, and perhaps what solid Glory and real Greatness are, may best be conveyed by example: for to the honour of human nature, such are not wanting, to which every man must pay the just tribute of his applause; and tho' few have strength enough to imitate such actions, yet all mankind are sufficiently ingenuous to admire and revere them.

92. The love of country, and heroic intrepidity, are seldom mentioned without the tribute of admiration being offered to the manes of Regulus, a Curtius, a Scævola, or a Decius[92]: but

---

90  *The Guardian*, April 3, 1713.

91  In the introduction to his *Philosophical Enquiry into the Origin of Our Ideas of the Sublime and Beautiful*, Edmund Burke states that "there is not the same obvious concurrence in any uniform or settled principles which relate to taste. It is even commonly supposed that this delicate and aerial faculty, which seems too volatile to endure even the chains of a definition, cannot be properly tried by any test, nor regulated by any standard."

92  *Regulus, Curtius, Scævola, Decius*: Roman rulers and generals.

why should moderns, and more especially Irishmen, recur to the antique volumes of Roman records for instances of heroism and patriotic valour; their own history, both of remote and latter times, furnishing innumerable instances of heroic magnanimity, that cannot be exceeded either in Roman or Grecian story. To mention but one of antient times; (for the united voice of nations, for near ages past, proclaim the bravery of the emigrated, poor, but not dishonoured, Irish) that of the Fiangauls when engaging the Danes by sea, was as desperate and heroic as any ever executed.[93]

---

93 *Fiangauls...engaging the Danes by sea*: It is uncertain to which battle the author refers. The Fiangauls may represent the *Finnghoill* or *Finngaill*, the Norwegian invaders of Dublin. Although this group fought a sea-battle with rival Danes in 852 (mentioned very briefly in the *Annals of the Four Masters* and the *Annals of Ulster*), the *Finngaill* lost this battle—and considering this, as well as the fact that all known participants were foreign invaders of Ireland, the incident hardly seems a good example of "Irish heroism."

The author more likely refers to (or may be identifying the Fiangauls with) the men who fought valiantly under Fingall against the Danes in 941. This sea-battle was reportedly waged in an attempt to rescue Cellachán Caisil, King of Munster, who had been taken prisoner aboard a Danish ship: "The Irish fleet...made its way up to the Danes, and prepared immediately for battle. A fight so unexpected as this threw Sitric [Danish Lord of Dublin] and his men into great confusion; however, perceiving there was no way to escape, they began a desperate engagement, in which both their superior numbers and superior skill more than once gave them a prospect of victory; for the Irish were but new to the practice of sea battles, whereas the Danes, being old pirates, were experienced navigators. Nevertheless, what the former wanted in numbers and judgment, they made up in valour and resolution. In this hard contest, the Irish admiral sought out the vessel of the Danish general, which he boarded in spite of all opposition: there he saw Ceallachan bound to the mast. Hastening to his assistance, he quickly cut the cords and prevailed on the king, whom he had thus unexpectedly rescued, to quit the Danish and repair immediately on board the Irish vessel.—This generous advice, however, which saved the king, proved fatal to the gallant admiral; for not being supported by a sufficient number of his countrymen, he was at last overpowered, and slain by the Danish guards, who by Sitric's order, severed his head from his body, and exposed it to the Irish, in order thereby to dishearten them. But this sight only served the more to inflame their courage.—Fingall...again boarded the Danish ship, with a determined resolution to revenge the death of Failbhe.—This brave officer soon found his men so far out-numbered by the enemy, that conquest seemed out of their reach: But as he valued not his own life, he found means to get that of his foe into his power, for, forcing his way through all the fighting crowd to Sitric, he singled him out, grasped him in his arms, and threw himself with him into the sea, where both were drowned together. Two other of the Irish chiefs following the example, seized on Sitric's brothers in the like manner, and thus at once put an end to their existence, while they perished with them. The Danes were astonished and confounded when they saw the Irish thus at the expence of their own lives making sure of the destruction of their enemies, bold as they were, and accustomed to scenes of blood and slaughter, yet they were struck with dread and horror at this new method of fighting. Besides, as they now saw their general and his brothers destroyed, the royal prisoners released; and almost every thing they contended for entirely lost, they began to slacken their opposition, while the fury of the Irish still continued; and after some vain attempts to turn the fortunes of the day, fell into disorder, whilst the Irish, improving their advantage, renewed their attacks with fresh vigour, till at length the Danes were put

I shall also, for brevity sake, wave repeating the often, tho' not too much celebrated actions of a Fabricius, a Cincinnatus, a Quintus, and a Scipio[94], in the despising riches and sensual enjoyments, in order to mention an instance of the highest degree of honour, and greatness of soul, in the exertion of that first of all virtues, *the forgiving,* or rather, *nobly revenging of injuries.* The following is mentioned by one of the best and most amiable of authors. "When the great Conde[95] commanded the Spanish army in Flanders, and laid siege to one of our towns, a soldier being ill-treated by a general officer for some disrespectful words he had let fall, answered very coolly, that he should soon make him repent of it. Fifteen days after, the same general officer ordered the colonel of the trenches to find out a bold and intrepid fellow in his regiment, for a notable piece of work he wanted to be done, for which he promises a reward of an hundred pistoles. The soldier we are speaking of, who passed for the bravest in the regiment, offered his service, and taking with him thirty of his comrades, of whom the choice was left to himself, he discharged his commission, which was a very hazardous one, with incredible courage and success. Upon his return, the general officer highly commended him, and gave him the hundred pistoles he had promised. The soldier presently distributed them among his comrades, saying he did not serve for pay, and demanded only, that if his late action seemed to deserve any recompence, they would make him an officer. *And now, Sir,* adds he to the general officer, who did not know him, *I am the soldier you abused so much fifteen days ago, and I told you I would make you repent it.* The general officer, in great admiration, and melting into tears, threw his arms around his neck, begged his pardon, and gave him a commission that very day." Mr. Rollin further adds, that, "The great Conde took a pleasure in telling this story, as the bravest action in a soldier he had ever heard of."[96]

93. Public institutions ever mark the policy, taste, and judgment of the times; for though power and riches lead to the refinement of society; yet, that very refinement often creates an enervating luxury, which is the parent of poverty and imbecility. For this reason, institutions that have a tendency to enfeeble the body, or to weaken the mind, no man who really loves his country, would ever wish to see established: human nature, already too prone to ease, embraces with avidity relaxations that indulge this tendency, more especially when they have

---

to flight and destruction." John Huddlestone Wynne, *General History of Ireland* (Dublin: D. Chamberlaine, 1773), 163-165.

94 *Fabricius, Cincinnatus, Quintus, Scipio*: Examples of Roman generals, commanders, and statesmen.

95 Louis de Bourbon, Prince of Condé (1621–1686) was a French general who, during the Thirty Years' War, commanded armies in France, Germany, and Flanders. For his successes, he became known as *Le Grand Condé.*

96 Charles Rollin, *The Method of Teaching and Studying the Belles Lettres, Vol. 3* (London: Printed for A. Bettesworth and C. Hitch, 1734), 89-90.

the sanction of public approbation. On the other hand, exercises that injure the heart, by inuring it to scenes of cruelty and horror, are ever degrading to the character of those nations and individuals in which they are customary, and to whom they are pleasing. Hence it seems no very easy matter to steer clear of those extremes; for what polishes, often debilitates; and what animates, frequently renders us ferocious. That refinement of manners, or that corporal strength and activity, obtained but in the same proportion as the mind is injured, are, indeed, too highly purchased acquisitions. Therefore, I think some institutions similar to those established by the French legislature,* for the encouragement of this art, would in some measure mark the spirit and liberality of the present period; for I think this exercise an happy mean between the two extremes hinted at; as fencing is spirited, without ferocity, refined without effeminacy, and warlike, without cruelty. And I have not a doubt, if a society of gentlemen were instituted on a proper plan, the legislature would confer on the gentlemen, publicly excelling in this art, some honourable mark of their approbation.

* In Toulouse, two Swords are given annually by the magistrates, to the two best Fencers; the first gets a gold hilted one, the other a silver; on each are engraven the arms of that ancient and respectable city. This trial lasts three days, on a kind of stage erected for that purpose. Any person is admitted a candidate that is not a professor, and has received a few months instructions from a master teaching in the city. The privileges enjoyed by the successful persons are, the freedom of the theatre that year, and during said time to wear the Sword in the Hotel de Ville, or Town House: an honourable distinction no other persons enjoy.

I must confess, I think it a shameful reflection, that my countrymen should rest contented, while any nation on earth is universally allowed to excel them in any exercise, that Irishmen think worthy their attention; but how much more so, in an accomplishment so distinguishing to, and characteristic of, the man of spirit and the gentleman.

I beg leave to remind gentlemen, that the Greeks, (the most refined of nations) to hand down to posterity their opinion of manly exercises, made the Olympic Games the great Æra of their reckoning of time. The Romans copied the Greeks in the exercises of the Circus, as well as in the honour paid to the victors; and in this they agreed with all the institutions of the greatest lawgivers of the antients, as well as with some of the most celebrated of the moderns.*

* Gentlemen who like the idea, and would desire to constitute a body for the encouragement of this art, may intimate their approbation to Mr. HUGH KELLY, fencing-master, Dublin.

94. It may not be improper also to remind gentlemen of the French custom of always throwing quart and tierce, previous to loose play, or the *assaut*. — On a stranger's entering a fencing-school in France, a case of foils is presented to him, the handles cross-ways, and in salute, (which ought ever to precede the action) they measure their distance within an inch or two of their antagonist's breast.* This shews an equal degree of politeness and command of body, and is performed by good fencers with the greatest ease and elegance of motion. As their design in throwing quart and tierce is only to shew the beauty of the attitude, and quickness and accuracy in passing, they never attempt hitting each other; and by parrying, as they always do in a lively manner, as it is expressive of attention, they pay an elegant, tho' silent, compliment to the abilities of their antagonist. By first throwing quart and tierce, they become in some degree acquainted with the abilities of their antagonist, which must excite confidence or circumspection; and, indeed, the easier motions of quart and tierce, seem a very proper prelude to the more vigorous exertions necessary on the *assaut*.

* I think no one should touch his adversary on taking his distance, nor put the button of his foil to the floor; a proper place might be assigned for giving the foil that bent which is sometimes necessary to make it agreeable to the hand. There are many circumstances that masters might enforce the observance in their schools, by small fines, to which no gentleman could have an objection, as they must be productive of regularity and politeness.

95. There are eight parades, viz. prime, second, (or segoon) tierce, quart, counter in tierce, ditto in quart, (or round parade in quart and tierce) half circle, and octave. Perhaps fencing was formerly taught somewhat differently from the present method; it is certain, the swords were considerably longer, (and of course the foils) being girted higher up, and sometimes held under the arm by the shell down along the body. The Spaniards, (who retain their old customs longer than any other nation) at least those among them who do not copy the French, to this day carry very long swords; and their fencing masters, I am informed, make their scholars extend the arm in tierce when in guard. It cannot be doubted, from the etymology of the terms, that antiently the principal parade was the prime; 2d, segoon; 3d, tierce; 4th, quart, &c. but modern teachers make quart and tierce their 1st and 2d parades, tho' they have retained the old names, signifying third and fourth. We still parry prime on certain close engagements. An ingenious and respectable friend of mine (to whom I am indebted for this remark) informs me, he knew a swordsman in France, who made the prime his constant parade; and by the elastic extension of his arm, scarce ever missed even the best fencer on the return. The segoon, as a parade, is not now used; the half circle being found safer, and to take up more thrusts, and with greater advantage. The heel parade, called by the French, *bas quarte*, or low quart, is, I

think, very properly not considered as a distinct parade; for, strictly speaking, it is a bate, or a batter, rather than a parade.—It is but justice to declare, I received the hint for another of the foregoing remarks, from a gentleman, whose perfect knowledge of the sword in theory and practice, is among the least of his accomplishments.

96. I think it would be just policy in any great nation to cultivate the general use of all kinds of arms. I grant, if but one part of the inhabitants acquire this knowledge, it may be productive of the worst consequences, as power creates ambition, and cruelty is frequently the offspring: for those in arms, having power to oppress, may become actually oppressive; but when an happy equipoise is supported by every reputable individual, being in this respect equal, they will only unite against, and consequently become formidable to a common enemy. Nor will any just power, by any means, be endangered; for no people ever unanimously, with heart and with hand, opposed their governors on moot points; nor until the executive power had first notoriously violated, by a series of oppression, the laws of Nature and of God; which laws are, no doubt, superior to, and the test of, all human institutions.[97]

97. The following extract from a late treatise on Chronic diseases, I shall take the liberty of inserting, in order to rouse men of a sedentary life, to some degree of action, if they hold their own lives, and the good of society, in any degree of estimation. "It is upon the minutest and almost invisible parts of the body, our best health, strength, and spirits depend: these fine parts, commonly called capillaries, are little pipes or tubes, the extended continuations of the

---

97 *Until the executive power had first notoriously violated...the Laws of Nature and of God*: This passage strongly recalls the American Declaration of Independence issued on July 4, 1776 (and reprinted throughout the British Isles), which refers to the "Laws of Nature and of Nature's God." During the late 1770s, pro-American toasts were a feature of Dublin society dinners, with one reading: "May every mercenary be obliged to pile his arms and march to the tune of Yankee Doodle." During the 1780s, the rhetoric of Irish reformers was "full of appeals to American precedent." The ideals of the Irish Patriot Party, for instance, led by Henry Grattan and Henry Flood, bore many similarities to those of the American colonists—including free trade, less taxation, and greater self-governance. In 1778, to fill the vacancy of soldiers in Ireland (many of whom had been deployed to suppress the American rebellion), local armed militias known as the Irish Volunteers were raised, ostensibly to guard against invasion and to preserve law and order. Jonah Barrington, who participated in one such regiment, recalled the "military ardour which seized all Ireland, when the whole country had entered into resolutions to free itself for ever from English domination. The entire kingdom took up arms, regiments were formed in every quarter, the highest, the lowest, and the middle orders, all entered the ranks of freedom, and every corporation, whether civil or military, pledged life and fortune to attain and establish Irish independence." Such units would eventually take part in the 1798 rebellion. See Stuart Andrews, *Irish Rebellion: Protestant Polemic 1798-1900* (New York: Palgrave Macmillan, 1988), 3-7; Jonah Barrington, *Personal Sketches of His Own Times, Vol. I* (London: Henry Colburn and Richard Bentley, 1830), 89.

larger blood-vessels, through which the finest parts of the blood must constantly pass, not only to keep these very small channels always free and open, but also that the particles of the blood may in their passage be attenuated, broken, and rubbed into globules perfectly smooth and round, and easily divisible into still less and less, till they escape the sight assisted even by the microscope, which gives ocular demonstration of this most amazingly minute circulation. I have observed myself, and any curious patient man may see with a good microscope, in the pellucid membrane of any living animal, this surprizing minuteness; he may select and observe one single vessel, the smallest of those that convey red blood, many of which would not equal the smallest hair in size, through which the blood may be seen passing, not like a fluid, but a number of little red solid balls pushing one another on till they come to the extremity or ramification of the vessel where it divides into two still less. There the first globule stopping a little, and recoiling, is pushed on again till it divides into two, and, losing its red colour, passes on in the smaller pipes fitted only to receive the serum, which undergoes the same circulation till it be refined into lymph, and thus into still finer fluids, which, being thus prepared, escape into a subtilty beyond all possible observation. Now the strength of the heart and arteries alone, in a sedentary course of life, is by no means sufficient to keep up and perpetuate this motion through these capillaries, but requires the assistance and joint force of all the muscles of the body to act by intervals, compress the veins, propel and accelerate the circulation of the whole mass of blood, in order to force and clear these pipes, and to triturate, cribrate, and purify the fluid passing through, forming every particle of it into a perfect globule, which is the form all the atoms of matter must take from much agitation. Without this extraordinary occasional aid, the little vessels would, by their natural elasticity, close up into fibres, or be obstructed by rough angular particles sticking in them, and stopping all passage. Numberless evils of the chronic kind, especially all nervous diseases, owe their origin to this cause alone.

"Accordingly, we see most of those who have lived for any time in a state of indolence, grow emaciated and pale by the drying up of these fine vessels, or if they happen to be of a lax habit, having a good appetite, and little to vex them, they may be loaded with fat, but they grow pale withal, many of those fine pipes being nevertheless closed up, so that they appear bloated and their fat unwholesome, having much less blood in their veins than thinner people. Hence we may learn why these languid pale persons, upon the least motion become faint and breathless, the blood hurrying through the larger vessels yet free, and like a crowd obstructing its own passage, causing a dangerous suffocation; or if they have not been long in this state, nor the capillaries quite closed, they glow with a momentary red, the fine vessels being for that time expanded. This inactivity first forms obstructions in these exquisitely fine parts, upon which the health and vigor both of Body and Mind entirely depend, and lays the foundation of many diseases to come, which other concomitant circumstances, such as a violent cold, excess of any kind, infection from without, or a particular disposition of the body within, make often fatal to many in this habit of life, and *which those who use exercise never feel.*

"Now I would ask any reasonable person capable of considering this operation of nature with the least glimmering of philosophy, or even the attention of common sense, and most assuredly it concerns every man to consider it well, whether he can conceive it possible to substitute any medicine to be swallowed that shall act upon the blood and vessels like the joint force of all the muscles of the body, acting and re-acting occasionally in a regular course of moderate daily labor or exercise."[98] To this let me add the following admirable sentence: "As I am a compound of soul and body, I consider myself obliged to a double scheme of duties; and I think I have not fulfilled the business of the day when I do not thus employ the one in labour and exercise, as well as the other in study and contemplation."[99]

I shall conclude these remarks with observing, that I know of no exercise so spirited and liberal, that can be taken at all seasons, at any hour, either in town or in country, within doors or without, and at so small an expence of time as that of Fencing.

The writer does not presume to maintain the absolute justness of all the preceding remarks; on the contrary, he acknowledges to have thrown some of them out problematically, in order that their propriety may be evinced, or their inutility demonstrated, by the opinion of the Candid and Judicious. However, if truth forces them to impeach his understanding, he will still rest satisfied, if his heart escapes censure.


# F I N I S.


---

98  William Cadogan, *A dissertation on the gout: and all chronic diseases, jointly considered, as proceeding from the same causes; what those causes are; and a rational and natural method of cure proposed. Addressed to all invalids.* (London: Printed for J. Dodsley, 1771), 30-34. The author of *A Few Mathematical and Critical Remarks on the Sword* has altered the last line of the second paragraph of this quotation to include the term "*exercise*"; the original passage had concluded: "and *which the industrious and active never feel.*"

99  Joseph Addison, *Spectactor*, July 12, 1711.

# GLOSSARY

Below is a list of terms which appear in *A Few Mathematical and Critical Remarks on the Sword*. It should be noted that the author does not define all of his terms, but assumes much knowledge on the part of the reader. Therefore, some definitions in this glossary have been taken from other British and Irish fencing texts of the eighteenth century. They include:

Zachary Wylde, *The English Master of Defence* (York: John White, 1711).

Donald McBane, *The Expert Sword-Man's Companion* (Glasgow: J. Duncan, 1728).

Henry Blackwell, *The Gentleman's Tutor for the Small Sword: Or, The Compleat English Fencing Master* (London: Printed for J. and T.W., 1730).

Edward Blackwell, *A Compleat System of Fencing: or, The Art of Defence, in the Use of the Small-Sword* (Williamsburg: William Parks, 1734).

Andrew Mahon, *The Art of Fencing: or, the Use of the Small Sword* (London: Printed for Richard Wellington at the Dolphin and Crown, 1735).

Hary Fergusson, *A Dictionary, Explaining the Terms, Guards, and Positions, Used in the Art of the Small Sword* ([Edinburgh]: 1767).

Andrew Lonnergan, *The Fencer's Guide* (London: Printed for the Author, 1771).

Olivier, J. *Fencing Familiarized; or, a New Treatise on the Art of Sword Play* (London: Printed for John Bell; And C. Etherington, at York, [1771]).

John McArthur, *The Army and Navy Gentleman's Companion* (London: J. Murray, 1784).

Domenico Angelo, *The School of Fencing* (London: 1787).

\* \* \*

**Abandoned**—From the French fencing term *l'abandonnement*. This is a word that has been used in different ways throughout the period. As the author of *A Few Mathematical and Critical Remarks on the Sword* neglects to define this term, it is difficult to know in what precise sense he means it. Domenico Angelo refers to those "who abandon their bodies after they thrust, and who do not recover with that quickness and care which is necessary." (Angelo, 79) Labat refers to when "your Body is too much abandoned forward to recover itself easily..." (Mahon, 55).

**Advance**—"ADVANCE, In Fencing, The act of stepping forward toward your adversary, while on guard; the left foot instantly following the right so as that your primitive posture is still preserved." (McArthur, 151)

**Allonge**—"LONGE, [From the French verb *alonger*, to extend or stretch out] Is the act of extending yourself on the line of direction the full distance of your stride, in order to make your approaches to an adversary's body in delivering a thrust... All longes are performed from guard position, by first forming the position of extension... then instantaneously moving the right foot forward on the same line, with the knee bent and perpendicular, while your left foot remains firmly planted and the left leg and thigh are to be extended along.—The extent of a longe is proportional to your stature.—The extent in general is supposed to be about four feet, or equal to twice the distance or measure of the two heels from each other, when on guard posture. A person of tall stature makes a more extensive longe than one of a short stature; but he cannot recover with that degree of ease and agility unless he is of a very active frame." (McArthur, 156)

**Answer**—When "your adversary goes to parry where you feint, which gives you a right to proceed with your design..." (*A Few Mathematical and Critical Remarks on the Sword*, Remark 83)

**Appel**—"APPEL, [From the French *appel*, a call] Is applied to a sudden beat with your right foot, by raising and letting it fall on the same spot, previous to, or at the instant of, making a feint against an adversary; thereby startling him and obtaining some opening to deliver your intended thrust." (McArthur, 151)

**Attack**—"Simple, Is the offensive attempts against your adversary, when engaged in an assault, by simple movements. Compound, The Offensive attempts against an adversary, by deceiving with feints, counter disengagements, glizades, &c. and repelling every feint and thrust he may attempt against you." (McArthur, 151)

**Attitude**—"ATTITUDE, the posture or position in fencing." (Fergusson, 2)

**Bate**—Possibly an Irish variation of the English term "beat," or the French *battement*. The author of *A Few Mathematical and Critical Remarks on the Sword* seems to use this term interchangeably with "batter," but it is unclear if he regards the terms as synonymous, or not. Hary Fergusson notes: "To BEAT, to put your antagonist's sword off the line, in order to procure an open, by moving only your wrist, and giving a smart jerk or dry blow with the fort of your blade on his foible." (Fergusson, 3) See also *Batter*.

**Batter**—"To BATTER, to beat with the foible of your blade on that of your adversary, when you are going to make an attack." (Fergusson, 3) "Battering is thus practised; if you are in Quarte, and would batter on the Tierce-side, strike with your Forte in a slanting and strong manner upon my Foible, near the point; and sustain your stroke, by sliding your Foil along mine, still hard and smartly towards my shell; this will make my Foil spring out of my hand, or make way for your thrust to hit me as before." (Lonnergan, 256)

**Bear, to**—"BEARING is to bear heavy upon the blade, without wrenching it any way." (Lonnergan, 51)

**Binding**—"BINDING the Sword, Is the act of crossing your adversary's blade, with pressing the fort of yours on the feeble of his, and by a sudden jerk of the wrist securing or binding his blade, so as to be covered either from a time thrust or an interchanged thrust. It is generally performed from the guard or engagement of carte, when your adversary holds his wrist low on guard. A thrust thus delivered on the act of binding, is termed the thrust of *flanconnade*." (McArthur, 152)

**Blade**—"The blade of a sword has three parts, the feeble, which is one extreme; the fort, the middle; and the shoulder, the other extreme." (*A Few Mathematical and Critical Remarks on the Sword*, Remark 78)

**Breaking Measure**—"Breaking Measure is to advance or retire from your due measure, also to sway your body back from a thrust, without moving your feet." (Lonnergan, 257)

**Breast Lessons**—"PLASTROON, [in French *plastron*] Is, in a literal meaning, the breastpiece of an armour, or a leather cover for the stomach.—But the term in fencing is applied to scholars, while under the academical rules and lessons of a master previous to the practical application of them in assaults; the master's breast being covered with a leather cushion, for the purpose of the scholar's exercising his various thrusts thereat." (McArthur, 158)

**Changing**—"Changing is performed by a conical motion, the vertex being at the wrist, as already mentioned, therefore the smallest motion at the shell is sufficient to make a change at the point..." (*A Few Mathematical and Critical Remarks on the Sword*, Remark 57)

**Closing**—"To ENCLOSE, to come too near one's antagonist, by securing his blade, or other-wise. The being enclosed, hinders one from making a risposte..." (Fergusson, 8) "A Close at Small-Sword is performed thus, Make a full Thrust in Cart, and at the same juncture, as your Opponent Parries, step in with your left Foot, with all Expedition, and with your left Hand seize his Weapon, hold it fast, and withdraw yours so far back that the Point thereof reach but the Center of your Body, then use your most merciful Discretion. You may perform the like by thrusting full in Ters, and perform as aforesaid." (Wylde, 21)

**Counter**—See *Parade, Round.*

**Couteau de Chasse**—"a short, small, edged-sword, usually worn in undress." (Angelo, *Reminiscences, Vol. II*, 213-14).

**Cutting Over**—"CUT over your adversary's point, Is performed with a simple movement of the wrist upwards, by which your point is raised nearly perpendicular, and thereby disengaged from one side to the other.—The arm is not to deviate from the line of direction.—The cuts over the point answer the purposes of disengagements, when your adversary has his point too much elevated on guard." (McArthur, 153)

**Disarm**—"DISARMING, The act of depriving your adversary of his sword or foil." (McArthur, 154) "To DISARM, to secure your enemy's sword by the handle, when he is either thrusting, has his point off the line, or when he neglects to rispost:—To beat the sword out of one's hand with a parry." (Fergusson, 6)

**Disordering**—The act of disturbing the adversary's sword, guard position, or mind: "A vigorous attack will sometimes disorder your antagonist, which must be of service to you, either by giving you a better opportunity of passing, or by his passing in a hurry, leave you an easy return..." (*A Few Mathematical and Critical Remarks on the Sword,* Remark 21) "...your Sword must be disordered before you can be well hit." (Remark 36) "...you should disorder your adversary's sword, that is, put his point from the line before you feint..." (Remark 68)

**Double, or Doubling**—"When your adversary follows the blade with the counter, you double, forming well your extension and managing your body in such a manner that you may judge what parade he will use...When you are engaged in tierce, the wrist in carte, if you imagine your adversary will parry with half-circle or the counter-in-tierce, then double, stretching the arm proportionally as the thrust approaches the body. If he parries twice with the circle, you must double...All these thrusts require a great deal of judgement, as also flexibility in the arm, as they must only come from the hand." (Olivier, 87-89)

**Feeble, or Foible**—"FOIBLE, or FEEBLE, Is the weak part and third division of a blade, and is that part at the farther extremity next the point." (McArthur, 155)

**Feint**—"FEINT, Is a false attempt of making a thrust towards a particular part of your adversary's body, with a view to induce him to form a parade to guard that part, that you may with greater facility execute your intended thrust against the unguarded part.—There are various kinds of feints and they are divided into simple and compound, high and low." (McArthur, 154-155)

**Flank, to**—See *Flankonade.*

**Flankonade**—"FLANCONADE, Is a particular thrust made towards your adversary's flank, by crossing and binding the feeble of his blade with your forte, and dropping the point so as to form a good opposition in octave thrust.—This thrust is seldom practised except on favourable occasions, when your adversary holds his wrist low on guard." (McArthur, 155)

**Foible**—see *Feeble*.

**Foil**—"FOIL, a blunt sword, (having a button at the end of the blade) generally about 38 or 40 inches in length inclusive of the mounting, used for learners to practise with." (Fergusson, 9)

**Force, to**—"FORCE is the act of advancing within measure, and delivering your thrust forcibly, so as your adversary may not have sufficient power to throw it off with a natural parade.—It is also applied to the act of leaning or pressing hard upon your adversary's blade at any time." (McArthur, 155)

**Fort**—Defined by the author of *A Few Mathematical and Critical Remarks on the Sword* as the middle part of the blade (see Remark 78), whereas most other fencing authors of the period designate the fort as the portion of the blade closest to the shell or guard: "FORTE of a blade, Is the first division of a blade of a sword or foil, and is sometimes called the shoulder, or strength, as it comes from the shell to the middle division." (McArthur, 155)

**Guard**—"GUARDS, particular postures, adapted either for defending yourself from the attempts of an adversary, or from whence you may with facility execute any offensive movements against him.—By modern practice, only two guards are used in small sword play, viz. the guard of carte, and the guard of tierce. The one covers your body from a straight inside thrust, by crossing the blades on that side, and the other covers you from a straight outside thrust by opposing the blade outwards." (McArthur, 155-156)

**Half-Circle, parry of**—"OF THE HALF-CIRCLE PARADE. This parade, which is the chief defensive parade of the sword, parries not only all the thrusts, but also obstructs all the feints that can be made; and, to execute it well, you should straiten your arm, keep your wrist in a line with your shoulder, your nails upward, and, by a close and quick motion of the wrist, the point should form a circle from the right to the left, large enough to be under cover from the head to the knee; in this manner, by doubling your circle till you have found the adversary's blade, your parade will be formed." (Angelo, 42)

**Handle, or Hilt**—"The handle has likewise three parts; the shell, which is next the shoulder; the grip, the middle of the handle or part covered by the hand; and the pommel, the other extreme." (*A Few Mathematical and Critical Remarks on the Sword*, Remark 78)

**Hanger**—"a short broad sword." Thomas Sheridan, *A Complete Dictionary of the English Language* (London: Charles Dilly, 1790).

**Heel Parade**—"The heel parade or low quart, is parrying with a bate from the shoulder..." (*A Few Mathematical and Critical Remarks on the Sword*, Remark 83) "The heel parade, called by the French, *bas quarte*, or low quart, is, I think, very properly not considered as a distinct parade; for, strictly speaking, it is a bate, or a batter, rather than a parade." (Remark 95)

**In Guard**—"On Guard, signifies being placed on your feet, and well covered with your weapon." (Lonnergan, 261)

**Irregular**—Contrary to the established principles of fencing. William Hope notes that "*Artists are generally not so foreward and irregular in their Pursutes as Ignorants, but more cautious and slow, and consequently more certain and safe. Is it not therefore (from what I have been saying) far more commendable, to be dexterous and regular in our Offensive and Defensive motions, then irregular, and as it were out of all Hope, and in Despair, that if we overcome, we may be said to have done it by Art and Judgement, and not at randome, and by chance, more beseeming an irrational than a rational Creature.*" William Hope, *The Sword-Man's Vade Mecum* (Edinburgh: John Reid, 1691), 6-7.

**Light**—Defined by the author of *A Few Mathematical and Critical Remarks on the Sword* as synonymous with "opening" (see Remark 10), this unusual fencing term was used extensively —but never defined—by Andrew Mahon in his translation of Labat's *Art of Fencing*: "In order to take Advantage of the Time and Light which you get by your Feint, you must take care to avoid an Inconveniency into which many People fall, by uncovering themselves in endeavouring to uncover the Adversary." (Mahon, 45). The original French term used by Labat is *jour*, in the sense of "daylight." See Jean de Labat, *L'Art en Fait d'Armes ou de l'Epée seule* (Toulouse: J.Boude, 1696). In 1728, Donald McBane also directs: "Let your Side be only in [the adversary's] View, for the less Mark you give, the better, this is call'd *Light*." (McBane, 3)

**Line of Direction**—"If we conceive a right line drawn on the ground, in the direction of your adversary, it is evidence, the more your body, legs, thighs and arms are in that direction, the less liable you are to be hit; and the closer your parades are, that is, the less they deviate from that line the better..." (*A Few Mathematical and Critical Remarks on the Sword*, Remark 4) Later, the author also describes the "line of direction" as "the line which may be conceived to connect the center of gravity and the center of the earth..." (Remark 75)

**Longe**—See *Allonge.*

**Loose Play**—"LOOSE-PLAY, synonymous with assault;—where you practice with foils all the variations of small-sword play, offensive or defensive." (McArthur, 157) "ASSAULT, Is where you engage an adversary with foils, as in single combat with swords, using such efforts and academical rules, either offensive or defensive, as your judgment may direct, for the purpose of succeeding in the execution of your designs, or in baffling those of your adversary." (McArthur, 151)

**Measure**—"MEASURE, Is the distance or space between two adversaries, when they have joined blades for an assault.—Out of Measure, is when you are so far from your adversary that is not possible for the extent of your longe to touch him; in that situation it is necessary to advance, in order to gain your measure previous to longeing." (McArthur, 157)

**Octave, parry of**—"OCTAVE PARADE, Is a lower parade and the opposite to semicircle.—The point in its tract in performing the parades of semicircle and octave alternately, forms the figure of eight; from thence derives its name.—Octave is one of the most useful lower parades, being the most favourable for making straight returned thrusts therefrom." (McArthur, 157)

**Octave, thrust in**—"OCTAVE THRUST, Is the natural thrust corresponding to the parade of that name. Some masters term it low tierce—It is a lower thrust, and your adversary's blade is opposed outwards." (McArthur, 157)

**Open**—"OPEN, any part of your antagonist, or yourself that is not guarded; Opens are procured by Feints, Beats, Appells, and by Binding the Sword." (Fergusson, 13) See also *Light.*

**Opposition**—"By opposition, you are to understand such an attitude, that a pass in the line can scarce become central, that is, in every allonge; if the sword arm is not extended exactly in the line, there is said to be no opposition." (*A Few Mathematical and Critical Remarks on the Sword,* Remark 83) McArthur claims this term is synonymous with "Resistance": "Is the act of opposing your adversary's blade either inwards or outwards according to the thrust you may make, by which you are covered on the longe. *See Opposition, and Covering.*" (McArthur, 158)

**Palming**—"To PALM, to put off or defend any thrust with the palm of the hand, by turning the points of the fingers downward, and the back of the hand to the right." (Fergusson, 13) "Another way of Parrying, I call Palming, thus demonstrated, Stand your direct Line as before said, and lie with your Weapon full [tierce], hold your left Hand in manner of a half Moon against your Chin, or Clap the back of it upon your right Pap; then if your Opponent Pushes at you, instead of Parrying with your Sword, Palm with your left Hand, and quicker than I can speak, perform your Pass in Cart." (Wylde, 10-11)

"Of the Parade of the Hand. There are, in Fencing, three Parades with the Left-hand: The first, like the Opposition that is from the Top to the Bottom; the second, with the Palm of the Hand without, towards the Right Shoulder, and the third, from the Bottom to the Top, with the Outside of the Hand: Of these three Parades, the first is the easiest, the most used, and the least dangerous: They are condemned by able Men, as weakening those of the Sword; wherefore it is wrong in a Master to shew them to a Scholar, before he has practised those of the Blade a good while, which being longer, can return to all feints, which the Left-hand cannot, it being impossible to parry with it except you be near, which is very dangerous, as well by reason of the Difficulty of meeting properly with the Sword, as of the Facility of deceiving the Hand, which in this Case has not Time to come to the Parade, because of it's small Distance; and besides the Facility of deceiving it, you need only push at the Arm, Sword in Hand, in order to make it useless.

"Of the Opposition of the Hand. Many People make no Distinction between the Parade and Opposition of the Hand, tho' there is a very great Difference, the Parade being made only against the Adversary's Thrust, and the Opposition to prevent a following Thrust after having parryed with the Sword, which is very necessary in most Thrusts, especially in the Risposts which may be made to your Thrust in Seconde. Besides the Opposition of the Hand, after having parryed with the Sword, you may oppose with it, taking the Time, that is to say, when the Enemy pushes from above to below, as the motion of his sword is greater than your's, having only a strait line to push Quarte on, whereas his from above to below, is crooked, so that pushing upon his time, he cannot avoid the thrust, and you may easily oppose his with the Left-hand, which is very different from the parade with the Hand, to which you do not push 'till after you have parryed." (Mahon, 88-90)

**Parade**—A French term for "parry." See *Parry*.

**Parade, Direct**—The author of *A Few Mathematical and Critical Remarks on the Sword* uses this term to refer to a simple parry. See *Parry*.

**Parade, Round; or Counter**—"ROUND PARADES, Are compound movements, and performed with circles of like magnitudes. There are six in number, named after the simple parades. As the diameters of the circles are demonstrated to be equal to the distance of the wrist from one opposite parade to another, that is six inces, so is the periphery of these circles equal to about nineteen inches." (McArthur, 158)

**Parry**—"PARADE, PARRY or PARRYING, Is the act of defending yourself against a particular thrust of an adversary, by the turn of your wrist and the forte of your blade in opposition.—There are properly six simple parades or parries, each having its compound, termed a round parade. It is a most essential branch in fencing to form just and powerful parades, as thereby you make good returned thrusts upon an adversary. The parades are divided into upper and lower, inward and outward. Carte and tierce, with their compounds are called upper; semi-circle and octave, prime and seconde, with their respective compounds are termed lower parades. Each parade has a thrust of the like denomination." (McArthur, 157)

**Pass**—Although other fencing authors of the period give more specific definitions for the term "pass," the author of *A Few Mathematical and Critical Remarks on the Sword* seems to use it as a general term for footwork (including that used on an attack). He also uses the term when describing the lunge or discussing an attack: "Suppose on the advance, or after passes have been made, I see full light on the tierce, I throw with the utmost vigour a full tierce or quart over with the utmost vigour..." (See Remark 19) "...there are no passes preferable to the straight allonges." (Remark 23) "A simple pass is expressed by one, (or ha); a feint and pass, one, two, (or ha, ha); of a double feint and pass, one, two, three, (or ha, ha, ha.)" (Remark 33) "The left knee and right arm bent, gives the power of darting in, with an elastic spring, on your pass..." (Remark 36) "I by all means recommend parrying with a pass..." (Remark 47)

**Pommel**—"Is the round knob or ball fixed as a counterpoise at the farthest extremity of the hilt or handle of a sword or foil." (McArthur, 158)

**Prime, parry of**—"PRIME PARADE, Is one of the lower parades, seldom practised, except on emergencies, when an adversary presses vigorously upon you, and endeavours to force in within his measure—It is then a very essential parade." (McArthur, 158)

**Push**—A thrusting attack executed on a lunge or a pass.

**Quart, Guard of**—"CARTE GUARD, [*In French quarté*] Anciently the fourth, is now one of the principal guard-postures.—The other is called Tierce Guard.—The greatest elevation of the point on guard should be nearly fifteen degrees; if the point is elevated more, it will make too great a cross in the juncture of the blades. The greater the cross of the blades, the more easily are thrusts parried, as the curves formed by the point in parrying will be greater; but it will at the same time impede the approach towards the body.—Hence the smaller the cross of the blades, when in contact or guard, the more dextrous should the movements be, to render thrusts effectual." (McArthur, 152)

**Quart, parry of**—"CARTE PARADE, [*In French quarte*] Anciently the fourth, is now the first of the upper parades. It throws off all simple thrusts made inwards to the upper part of the body. It is performed from the medium guard, by a gradual turn of the wrist ascending inwards—the point receding to its original direction." (McArthur, 152)

**Quart, thrust in**—"CARTE THRUST *inside*, Is the natural thrust corresponding to the parade of carte. It is an upper thrust, and the opposition to your adversary's blade is inwards, so as to be covered on the longe by seeing the point over your arm." (McArthur, 152)

**Quart over, or Quart over-the-arm**—"CARTE THRUST over the arm, Is the natural thrust corresponding to the parade of tierce: it is the opposite thrust to carte inside; for the opposition to your adversary's blade is outwards.—This thrust is a good substitute for tierce thrust, it being rather aukward in execution, and a such is seldom or never practiced." (McArthur, 152)

**Recover**—"RECOVERING, Is the act of resuming your guard posture after having made a longe at your adversary. A quick and easy recovery to guard, forming the most natural parade is an essential branch to your safety." (McArthur, 158)

**Retire**—"Retiring is, when you have a Mind to give Ground to your Adversary when he approaches you." (Henry Blackwell, 4) "To RETIRE, to step back with the left foot, when your adversary is too near, making the right follow, without altering the distance that was between the heels before retiring." (Fergusson, 17)

**Return**—"RETURN, [In French *riposté*] Is when you deliver a thrust instantly after parrying one made by your adversary.—If your parade has been well formed, your return must be well delivered. There are various sorts of returns, either by the complete longe, the complete extension, the extension of the arm only, or a return of the wrist. Straight returns, or those that touch your adversary at the moment of parrying before he can recover to guard are by far the best." (McArthur, 158)

**Reverse Allonge**—"Leave the right foot where it is, throw the left leg and body instantly back, and dart forward your arm perfectly in the line..." (*A Few Mathematical and Critical Remarks on the Sword*, Remark 86)

**Round Parade**—See *Parade, Round; or Counter.*

**Sandal**—"SANDAL, a light pump wanting the heel, made fast on the foot with leather thongs, used when fencing." (Fergusson, 19)

**Segoon, parry of**—An early eighteenth century British term for *seconde*: "Sagoone is parried dropping the Point down the same way as you thrust Sagoone; but your Foile and your Arm must be straighter than when you make the thrust, your Body and Feet in the same Order as when you were on your Guard." (Henry Blackwell, 12) "SECONDE PARADE, Is a lower outward parade, the nails being reversed, as in tierce; and it forms the same angle with guard point as semicircle, and has for its opposite the inward parade of prime." (McArthur, 159)

**Segoon, thrust in**—An early eighteenth century British term for *seconde*: "Sagoon must be given with the Nailes downwards from Tierce side, dropping the point, hitting your Adversary in the Belly near to his Ribs, your Head must be quarter'd under your right Arm, rising your Wrist, and looking under it in the Face..." (Henry Blackwell, 10) "SECONDE THRUST, Is the natural and corresponding thrust to the parade of seconde; but it is often delivered after parrying your adversary's thrust with tierce—The nails are turned downwards when you thrust seconde, in the same manner as when you form that parade, and your adversary's blade is opposed outwards." (McArthur, 159)

**Shell**—"SHELL, of a sword or foil is that part of the hilt or handle next the blade, serving both for an ornament and guard." (McArthur, 159)

**Shoulder**—The part of the blade lying closest to the shell or guard. (*A Few Mathematical and Critical Remarks on the Sword*, Remark 78)

**Singling**—Although the author of *A Few Mathematical and Critical Remarks on the Sword* cites this as one of the "terms generally used" in fencing, he merely notes, "A man who singles his body finely, and lies low, may make his parades much closer, than he whose position is false and irregular." (Remark 7) This term, as used in this manner, is not explicitly defined else-where in the known fencing literature of the eighteenth century.

**Slip**—"Slipping, is to slip quickly away from this Bearing [see *Bear*] into a thrust at the other side of the blade." (Lonnergan, 51) "The Slips are good against the *Bindings*, *Beats*, and *Batters*, as I have given you a small Instance in my last Lesson; and when you have, by the Rule taught there, discover'd your Adversary's Play to be dependent upon the *Bindings*, *&c.* as aforemen-tioned, your safest Defence will be then to *Slip* him: And to do it, you must dip down your Point close under his Sword as he attempts to touch yours, and raise it on his contrary to your Guard, in Readiness to receive his next Attack, or to attack him, which may seem to suit with your Conveniency best..." (Edward Blackwell, 63)

**Spring Back, or Spring Off**—"To Spring Off. Is a quick Retreat out of the Reach of your Adversary, by leaping backward." Thomas Page, *The Use of the Broad Sword* (Norwich: Printed by M. Chase, 1746), 11. The author of *A Few Mathematical and Critical Remarks on the Sword* also notes, "in this spring you are to throw yourself in guard, and be ready for an attack." (Remark 15)

**Throw**—To "throw in a thrust." (Angelo, 35, 54, 56, 79; Lonnergan, 184-209)

**Thrust**—"THRUSTS in general, Are offensive attacks upon an adversary; and are chiefly executed with the longe. On every thrust it is necessary to be covered or secured from an inter-changed one, by gently forming a gradual opposition against your adversary's blade, either inwards or outwards according to the thrust you may intend to deliver. *See...Opposition, and Resistance.*—Thrusts are divided in the same manner as the parades, simple and compound, upper and lower.—Simple may be performed without disengaging straight home, or they may be performed with a single disengagement.— Compound are such thrusts as follow counter disengagements or compound movements.—Besides, there are a few miscellaneous thrusts, such as carte over the arm, thrust of extension, time thrust, thrust of the wrist, &c." (McArthur, 160)

**Tierce, guard of**—"TIERCE GUARD, Is the outside guard, the blades being crossed on that side.—It is the usual guard taken by skilful fencers, as from it may be executed a variety or favourite movements; and is synonymous with tierce engagements." (McArthur, 159)

**Tierce, parry of**—"TIERCE PARADE, Is the upper outward parade, and the opposite to carte; and it was anciently the third parade in fencing.—This is a favorite parade for disarming your adversary by crossing the sword...Tierce is performed by the gradual descent of the wrist outwards, the nails reversed downwards, the point always receding to its identical direction." (McArthur, 159-160)

**Tierce, thrust in**—"TIERCE THRUST...in performing it the nails are turned downwards as in seconde, and in this manner delivered towards the breast, opposing your adversary's blade on the outside." (McArthur, 160)

**Time, to**—see *Timing*.

**Timing**—"TIME THRUST, [in French *coup de tem*] Is the act of delivering a thrust to your adversary in the momentary duration of time employed by him in executing any feint or design against you.—They are esteemed the most delicate thrusts in fencing; and may with facility be executed against an adversary that makes wide feints and erroneous movements.—The nicety required in executing the time-thrust depends more upon the susceptibility of your hand and wrist than upon eye-sight.—A good fencer is so sensible of the contact of blades, that he feels the least disengagement. TIME THRUST on the extension, Is the act of delivering your thrust to an adversary, when he has made a full longe towards you, by yielding forward on the extension before he can possibly recover to guard, or form any parade to oppose it.—This is parrying and thrusting at the same moment." (McArthur, 160)

# APPENDICES

# APPENDIX I

## THE IRISH DUELING CODE *of* 1777

This influential dueling code was first published in 1827 the memoirs of Jonah Barrington. It was originally written and compiled in Clonmel, County Tipperary, at the summer assizes of 1777, and circulated in manuscript form. The following transcription of the code, from an early edition of Barrington's text, faithfully preserves the original layout, spelling, and italicizations.

* * *

The practice of duelling and points of honour settled at Clonmell Summer Assizes, 1777, by the gentlemen delegates of Tipperary, Galway, Mayo, Sligo, and Roscommon, and prescribed for general adoption throughout Ireland.

## RULES.

1.—The first offence requires the first apology, though the retort may have been more offensive than the insult. Example,—A. tells B. he is impertinent, &c., B. retorts that he lies; yet A. must make the first apology, because he gave the first offence, and then, after one fire, B. may explain away the result by subsequent apology.

2.—But if the parties would rather fight on, then, after two shots each, but in no case before, B. may explain first, and A. apologise afterwards.

N. B.—The above rules apply to all cases of offences in retort not of a stronger class than the example.

3.—If a doubt exists who gave the first offence, the decision rests with the seconds; if they *won't* decide or *can't* agree, the matter must proceed to two shots, or to a hit, if the challenger require it.

4.—When the *lie direct* is the *first offence*, the aggressor must either beg pardon in express terms, exchange two shots previous to apology, or three shots followed up by explanation, or fire on till a severe hit be received by one party or the other.

5.—As a blow is strictly prohibited under any circumstances amongst gentlemen, no verbal apology can be received for such an insult: the alternatives therefore are, the offender handing a cane to the injured party, to be used on his own back, at the same time begging pardon; firing on until one or both is disabled, or exchanging three shots, and then asking pardon, *without* the proffer of the *cane*.

If swords are used, the parties engage till one is well blooded, disabled, or disarmed; or until, after receiving a wound, and blood being drawn, the aggressor begs pardon.

N. B.—A *disarm* is considered the same as a *disable*: the disarmer may strictly break his adversary's sword; but if it be the challenger who is disarmed, it is considered as ungenerous to do so.

In case the challenged be disarmed and refuses to ask pardon or atone, he must not be *killed* as formerly; but the challenger may lay his own sword on the aggressor's shoulder, then break the aggressor's sword, and say, "I spare your life!" The challenged can never revive that quarrel—the challenger may.

6.—If A. gives B. the lie, and B. retorts by a blow, being the two greatest offences, no reconciliation *can* take place till after two discharges each, or a severe hit; *after* which B. may beg A.'s pardon humbly for the blow, and then A. may explain simply for the lie; because a blow is *never* allowable, and the offence of the lie therefore merges in it. (See preceding rule.)

N.B.—Challenges for undivulged causes may be reconciled on the ground, after one shot. An explanation or the slightest hit should be sufficient in such cases, because no personal offence transpired.

7.—But no apology can be received in any case after the parties have actually taken their ground, without exchange of fires.

8.—In the above case no challenger is obliged to divulge his cause of challenge, if private, unless required by the challenged so to do *before* their meeting.

9.—All imputations of cheating at play, races, &c., to be considered equivalent to a blow; but may be reconciled after one shot, on admitting their falsehood, and begging pardon publicly.

10.—Any insult to a lady under a gentleman's care or protection, to be considered as, by one degree, a greater offence than if given to the gentleman personally, and to be regulated accordingly.

11.—Offences originating or accruing from the support of ladies' reputation, to be considered as less unjustifiable than any others of the same class, and as admitting of slighter apologies by the aggressor—this to be determined by the circumstances of the case, but *always* favourable to the lady.

12.—In simple unpremeditated *rencontres* with the small sword, or *couteau-de-chasse*, the rule is—first draw, first sheathe; unless blood be drawn, then both sheathe, and proceed to investigation.

13.—No dumb-shooting or firing in the air admissible *in any case*. The challenger ought not to have challenged without receiving offence; and the challenged ought, if he gave offence, to have made an apology before he came on the ground; therefore, *children's play* must be dishonourable on one side or the other, and is accordingly prohibited.

14.—Seconds to be of equal rank in society with the principals they attend, inasmuch as a second may either choose or chance to become a principal, and equality is indispensable.

15.—Challenges are never to be delivered at night, unless the party to be challenged intend leaving the place of offence before morning; for it is desirable to avoid all hot-headed proceedings.

16.—The challenged has the right to choose his own weapon, unless the challenger gives his honour he is no swordsman; after which, however, he cannot decline any *second* species of weapon proposed by the challenged.

17.—The challenged chooses his ground; the challenger chooses his distance; the seconds fix the time and terms of firing.

18.—The seconds load in presence of each other, unless they give their mutual honours they have charged smooth and single, which should be held sufficient.

19.—Firing may be regulated—first, by signal; secondly, by word of command; or thirdly, at pleasure, as may be agreeable to the parties. In the latter case, the parties may fire at their reasonable leisure, but *second presents* and *rests* are strictly prohibited.

20.—In all cases a miss-fire is equivalent to a shot, and a *snap* or a *non-cock* is to be considered as a miss-fire.

21.—Seconds are bound to attempt a reconciliation *before* the meeting takes place, or *after* sufficient firing or hits, as specified.

22.—Any wound sufficient to agitate the nerves and necessarily make the hand shake, must end the business for *that day*.

23.—If the cause of meeting be of such a nature that no apology or explanation can or will be received, the challenged takes his ground, and calls on the challenger to proceed as he chooses: in such cases firing at pleasure is the usual practice, but may be varied by agreement.

24.—In slight cases the second hands his principal but one pistol, but in gross cases two, holding another case ready-charged in reserve.

25.—Where seconds disagree, and resolve to exchange shots themselves, it must be at the same time and at right angles with their principals, thus:—

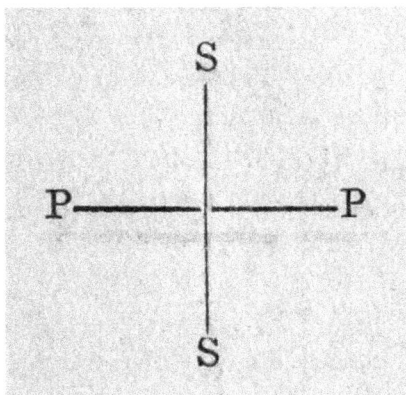

If with swords, side by side with five paces interval.

N. B.—All matters and doubts not herein mentioned will be explained and cleared up by application to the committee, who meet alternately at Clonmell and Galway, at the quarter-sessions for that purpose.

CROW RYAN, President.

JAMES KEOGH,

AMBY BODKIN, Secretaries.

## ADDITIONAL GALWAY ARTICLES:

1.—No party can be allowed to bend his knee or cover his side with his left hand; but may present at any level from the hip to the eye.

2.—None can either advance or retreat if the ground be measured. If no ground be measured, either party may advance at his pleasure, even to touch muzzle; but neither can advance on his adversary after the fire, unless the adversary steps forward on him.

N. B.—The seconds on both sides stand responsible for this last rule being *strictly* observed, bad cases having accrued from neglecting of it.

# APPENDIX II

# WORKS *on* FENCING, DUELING *and* SWORDSMANSHIP

## Written by, or Attributed to, Irish Authors or Editors

*Organized chronologically, by date of publication.*

Alexander Doyle, *Neu Alamodische Ritterliche Fecht- und Schirm-Kunst: Das ist: Wahre und nach neuester Frantzösischer Manier eingerichtete Unterweisung Wie man sich in Fechten und Schirmen perfectioniren und verhalten solle; Denen respective Herren Liebhaberen zu besserer Erleuterung mit 60 hierzu dienlichen Figuren herausgegeben* (Nürnberg: P. Lochner, 1715).

—, *Neu alamodische ritterliche Fecht- und Schirm-Kunst. Das ist: Wahre und nach neuester Französischer Manier eingerichtete Unterweisung wie man sich in Fechten und Schirmen perfectioniren und verhalten solle; denen respective Herren Liebhaberen zu besserer Erleuterung mit 60. hierzu dienlichen Figuren herausgegeben von Alexander Doyle aus Irrland gebürtig* (Nürnberg and Franckfurt: P. Lochner, 1716).

—, *Neu Alamodische Ritterliche Fecht- und Schirm-Kunst: Das ist: Wahre und nach neuester Frantzösischer Manier eingerichtete Unterweisung Wie man sich in Fechten und Schirmen perfectioniren und verhalten solle; Denen respective Herren Liebhaberen zu besserer Erleuterung mit 60 hierzu dienlichen Figuren herausgegeben* (Nürnberg: P. Lochner, 1729).

Andrew Mahon, *The Art of Fencing, or, the Use of the Small Sword. Translated from the French of of the late celebrated Monsieur L'Abbat; Master of that Art at the Academy of Toulouse* (Dublin: Printed by James Hoey, at the Sign of Mercury in Skinner-Row, 1734).

—, *The Art of Fencing, or, the Use of the Small Sword. Translated from the French of of the late celebrated Monsieur L'Abbat; Master of that Art at the Academy of Toulouse* (London: Printed for Richard Wellington at the Dolphin and Crown, 1735).

Daniel O'Sullivan, *L'Escrime Pratique, ou Principes de la Science des Armes. Par Daniel O'Sullivan, Maître en Fait d'Armes des Académies du Roi* (Paris: Chez Sébastien Jorry, imprimeur-libraire, rue, et vis-a-vis de la Comédie Francaise, au Grand Monarque, 1765).

*A Few Mathematical and Critical Remarks on the Sword* (Dublin: D. Chamberlaine, No. 5 College-Green, 1781).

Domenico Angelo, *The School of Fencing: With a general Explanation of the principal Attitudes and Positions peculiar to the Art By Mr. Angelo. In English and French. Enlarged, revised, and improved, by James Underwood, Esq.; a Knight of Tara, and others* ([Dublin: 1784]).

Anthony Gordon, *A letter on the bayonet exercise: submitted to the Right Hon. General Burgoyne, Commander in Chief of His Majesty's forces in Ireland, &c. &c. &c.: dated, Dublin Barracks, 20th March, 1783* ([Dublin: 1787]).

James Underwood, *Draw Not Your Sword But to Serve the King, Preserve Your Honour, or Defend your Life: The Art of Fencing; or the Use of the Small Sword* (Dublin: Printed by T. Byrne, Parliament-street, 1787).

—, *Draw Not Your Sword But to Serve the King, Preserve Your Honour, or Defend your Life: The Art of Fencing; or the Use of the Small Sword* (Dublin: Printed by William Porter, 69 Grafton Street, 1798).

John Williamson, *Method of Performing the Bayonet Exercise, Invented by Lieutenant Gordon, of the 67$^{th}$ Regiment, to which is added, a Plan for reforming the Army* ([before 1801]).

*Observations on duelling with a plan to prevent the frequency of single combat. By an Irish barrister. Dedicated to the Earl of Moira* (London: J. H. Hart, 1803).

Anthony Gordon, *An Idea of Defence: a Treatise on Swordsmanship*, 1804. Manuscript. National Army Museum. NAM 1968-07-67.

—, *A Treatise on the Science of Defence for the Sword, Bayonet, and Pike, in Close Action* (London: B. McMillan, 1805).

—, *A Treatise on the Science of Defence for the Sword, Bayonet, and Pike, in Close Action* (London: B. McMillan, 1806).

James Faden, *Proposals for a New Regulation of the Bayonet Exercise, with Testimonials* (1806).

*Strictures on the Army: Interspersed with Interesting Anecdotes and Illustrative Facts. By a Field Officer* (Dublin: Published for the author by W. Figgis, 1809).

William Butler Odell, *Essay on duelling, in which the subject is morally and historically considered; and the practice deduced from the earliest times* (Cork: Odell and Laurent, 1814).

*A complete treatise on the infantry sword exercise, as established for the British Army, and instructed at Dublin, October, 1816* (Dublin: Printed and Published by J. Findlay, 1816).

Abraham Bosquett, *The Young Man of Honour's Vade-Mecum, Being a Salutary Treatise on Duelling. Together with the Annals of Chivalry, the Ordeal Trial, and Judicial Combat, from the Earliest Times* (London: C. Chapple, 1817).

Joseph Hamilton, *Some Short and Useful Reflections Upon Duelling, which Should be in the Hands of Every Person who is Liable to Receive a Challenge, Or an Offence. By a Christian Patriot.* (Dublin: Printed by the Author, by C. Bentham, 1823).

—, *The Code of Honor for the regulation of duels* (Dublin: 1824).

—, *The Royal Code of Honor for the regulation of duelling* (Dublin: 1825).

—, *The court of honor, for the adjustment of disputes; and the Royal Code, as it was submitted to the European Sovereigns: with anecdotes, cases and documents, interesting to Christian moralists who decline the combat; to experienced duellists, and to benevolent legislators* (London: Printed for the author, 1829).

—, *The Only Approved Guide through all the Stages of a Quarrel: Containing the Royal Code of Honor; reflections upon duelling; and the Outline of a court for the adjustment of disputes; with anecdotes, documents and cases, interesting to Christian Moralists who decline the combat; to experienced duellists, and to benevolent legislators. By Joseph Hamilton. Author of "The School for Patriots," and other popular works* (London: Hatchard & Sons; Bentham & Co. Liverpool; and Millikin, Dublin, 1829).

Major R. I. Dunn, *A military pocket manual, for militia officers, condensed, and agreeable to the system laid down of the United States army: with a short treatise on the cavalry and infantry swords: also, by-laws for volunteer companies, &c., &c., &c.* (Cincinnati: Published for Joseph Medary, 1831).

[Simon Ansley O'Ferrall], *On the Duel* (London: Houlston & Stoneman, 1838).

Major R. I. Dunn, *A Condensed Military Pocket Manual: For Volunteer and Militia Officers, Non-commissioned Officers and Privates. Agreeable to the System Laid Down for the United States Army* (Lexington, KY: J. Cunningham, printer, 1841).

Oliver Byrne, *Freedom to Ireland: The Art and Science of War for the People. The Pike Exercise, Foot Lancers, Light Infantry, and Rifle Drill. To which is Added a Short Practical Treatise on Small Arms, and Ammunition, Street and House Fighting, and Field Fortification* (Boston: Patrick Donahoe, 1853).

Lucius O'Trigger, *History of Duelling in all Countries; Translated from the French of M. Coustard de Massi, with Introduction and Concluding Chapter by Sir Lucius O'Trigger* (London: Newman & Co., 1880).

Captain David Fallon, *How to Learn and Instruct in Bayonet Fighting: with General Rules and Directions* (Sydney: Angus & Robertson, 1915).

*The Manual of the Sword*, [ca. 1923-1925]. Manuscript. Papers of Col. Padraig O'Connor.

[Irish Free State, Department of Defence], *Defence Force Regulations: Bayonet Training (Provisional)* (Dublin: Published by the Stationery Office, 1928).

—, *Defence Force Regulations: The Manual of the Sword. Training Regulations No. 24* (Dublin: Printed for and Published by the Stationery Office, 1940).

# APPENDIX III

# FIRST RESOLUTIONS *of the* KNIGHTS *of* TARA.

## Knights of Tara.

AT a full Meeting of the Knights of Tara, a Society instituted for the encouragement of the Science of Defence with the Sword, the following Resolutions were unanimously agreed to:

That the inestimable benefits of commerce, constitution, and a liberality of sentiment have, in a great measure, resulted from that patriotic, military ardour which has so distinguished and immortalized the nations.

That measures tending to cherish and invigorate such ardour should be considered as objects of national importance.

That a more general cultivation of the Science of Defence has that tendency, and should therefore be looked on as an additional fort towards securing the advantages already obtained.

That abstracting however from these considerations, the Sword should be worn for defence, as well as ornament, so as that no Irish Gentleman may be in the predicament of the man covered with the ostentatious dust of books, and yet found ignorant of the alphabet.

And whereas other kinds of military and manly exercises have been studiously cultivated here, whilst the most martial, spirited, salutary, and certainly momentous to the individuals whose existences may be at stake, viz. That the Sword has been heretofore, in our judgment, unaccountably neglected.

Resolved, therefore, for the encouragement of this science, that henceforward three annual prizes, Swords, one of 20, one of 10, and the third of 5 guineas value, shall be adjudged to the three ablest and best fencers, in the three classes (the candidates so previously arranged) in conformity to the laws of the Science, which will be read immediately before the exhibition.

That the first exhibition ball shall be on Monday the 28th instant, in the Theatre in Capel-street.

Foreign noblemen and gentlemen, although not members, may be candidates for the prizes.

Noblemen and gentlemen, desirous of becoming members, will apply to some of the under-written gentlemen, who as present constitute the Committee appointed for the purpose of proposing candidates to the considerations of the Society, viz.

The Hon. John Butler, Castle Kilkenny
Col. Butler, Kilkenny
General Luttrell
Major Wemys, Kilkenny
Major John Kelly, Castle Kelly
William Holt, Esq; Stephen's-green
Thomas Roach, Esq; Dublin
Sir William Fortick, Belmont
Hugh Trevor, Esq; Dublin
Captain Cole, Dublin
Pat. Bellew, Esq; Mt. Kelly, co. Galway
Captain Holmes, 66th regt.
Joseph Deane, Esq; 67th regt.
Anthony Gordon, Esq; 67th regt.
James Farrell, Esq; Black-pits

It is expected that the company, which will be admitted by Tickets from the Members, will be seated by twelve, as the exhibition will commence precisely at one o'clock.

Sir WILLIAM FORTICK, President.

- *Dublin Evening Post.*
Saturday, April 5, 1783.

# APPENDIX IV

---

## SECOND RESOLUTIONS *of the* KNIGHTS *of* TARA.

# KNIGHTS of TARA.

I n Order that the Purposes of this Institution may be more clearly and generally under-stood, it was resolved at a full Meeting of the Members, that the following Extracts should be published from their Journals:

WHEREAS it appears from the Proceedings of this Society, that on the 20th of December, 1782, several gentlemen of this Kingdom, not only distinguished for their public Spirit, personal Intrepidity and Dexterity in the Use of Arms, but actuated by the most laud-able Motives of employing those Endowments to noble Purposes, formed an Association under the Title of KNIGHTS OF St. PATRICK. This Title they bore until the 17th of March 1783, when, from a Principle of the most profound Deference to his Majesty, the Foun-tain of Honour, who had been pleased to dignify, with the aforesaid Title, several of the full Nobility of Ireland, this Society relinquished their original Name and assumed that of THE KNIGHTS OF TARA.

AND WHEREAS it appears, among a Variety of Objects of national Moment, pointed out by their Laws and Regulations, that they resolved their Exertions should be particularly made for the furtherance in general of the Blessings of Society; for which End, they conceived, that to moderate the Excess—to restrain, if possible, the Practice of Duelling, and the conse-quent wanton effusion of Blood, would add much to the Happiness, Dignity, Lustre, and Elevation of the national Character, whose Skill, Spirit, and Fortitude ought not to be idly, and in many Instances, barbarously exhausted in little private Feuds and Quarrels, but directed to their proper Objects, the Enemies of the Land, and the common Enemies of Mankind. Wherefore this Society cultivated the Science of Defence with the Sword, and other martial Weapons, not as a primary, but as a secondary Measure, subservient to the aforesaid national

Purposes. — The Members, rendered critically conversant in the Use, can be the more effectually interpose their Skill, Spirit, and Authority in suppressing the Abuse of Arms.

And whereas it may be of public Utility, that such Institutions should have extensive Operation, the following Resolutions, extracted from the Laws of the Society, are with Deference submitted to the Noblemen and Gentlemen of Ireland, who are hereby most respectfully invited to co-operate with them in this laudable, though most arduous Reformation;

RESOLVED UNANIMOUSLY, "That we bind ourselves by all the sacred Ties of Honour, to refer and submit our Disputes, &c. touching Points of Honour, to a Committee composed of Members of this Order, and invited by them with juridicial Authority competent to decide thereon. Any refractory contumacious Member or Members appealing from the Decision of said Committee, (except to the Body at large, to whose controul all its Committees are necessarily subject) shall be expelled with every possible Stigma of Ignominy, their Names published, and prosecuted also at Law, by this Order, if fatal Consequences shall have resulted from their Pertinacity."

RESOLVED, "That we will hold in the highest Estimation, all such Noblemen and Gentlemen (not Members of this Order) who may have Disputes, in Points of Honour, either with each other, or with any Member or Members of this Order, who shall refer and submit the Adjudication of the same to our Tribunal. We pledge ourselves that these Points shall undergo similar impartial Discussion and Judgment, as in the Cases of Members; and we flatter ourselves that they shall receive a more adequate mental Satisfaction—a more consummate honourable Triumph than they could otherwise possibly have enjoyed from the Immolation of Thousands of human Victims, in Gratification of those insatiable Idols, Pride and Resentment."

RESOLVED, That our next Exhibition shall be on the 10th of May next, in the Theatre, Crow-street, where our three annual Prize Swords, the 1st of 20, the 2d of 10, and the 3rd of 5 Guineas Value, shall be adjudged to the best and most meritorious Performers, in Conformity to the Laws of the Science, as at our first Exhibition, Any Noblemen or Gentleman whatever may be Competitors for the first Prize.

RESOLVED, That this Society, wishing to pursue the Example of several great and humane Characters, who have endeavoured to relieve the long and severe Distresses of the Poor of this Metropolis, propose to deliver out Tickets to such Gentlemen and Ladies who chuse to honour their Exhibition with their Presence at the following Prices:— For the Boxes, Gentlemen's Ticket 11s. 4½d. Ladies Ditto 5s. 5d. — Pit Ticket 5s. 5d. — First Gallery Tickets 4s. 4d. Upper Gallery Dittor 2s. 2d.

RESOLVED, That the Right. Hon. The Earl of Clanricarde, Lord Delvin, Right. Hon. Henry Flood, General Luttrell, the Right. Hon. John Fitzgibbon, his Majesty's Attorney General, Joseph Deane, Esq; John Lees, Esq; Alexander Montgomery, Esq; George Robert Fitzgerald, Esq; Sir Robert Scott, Anth. Gordon, Esq; Dublin Barracks, the Rev. Mr. Dwyer, Chaplain to the order, the Rev. Doctor Butler, Dublin Castle, the Rev. Dr. Law, Alderman Nathaniel Warren, John White, Esq; Stephen's-Green, Francis Higgins, Esq; Ross-Lane, M. Dowling, Esq; Aungier-Street, Wm. Burke, Esq; Ross-Lane, James Underwood, Esq; Lieutenant Colonel St. George, and Captain Cradock, Aids du Camps to his Grace the Duke of Rutland, be and are appointed to deliver Tickets and superintend the collection and distribution of the money arising from such exhibition to the most indigent and proper objects, according to the direction of the Governors of the House of Industry.

Signed by order,
    JAMES UNDERWOOD, Sec.

RESOLVED UNANIMOUSLY, That the thanks of this Society be given to ANTHONY GORDON, Esq; Lieutenant of the 67th regiment, for his indefatigable attention, not only to the institution of the order of the KNIGHTS OF TARA, and to the support of its honour and dignity, but also for the foregoing resolutions, and very liberal plan, submitted by him to this Society, for the relief of the poor.

Signed by order,
    JAMES UNDERWOOD, Sec.

- *Hibernian Journal; or, Chronicle of Liberty.*
April 23, 1784.

# APPENDIX V

## LIST *of the* KNIGHTS OF TARA.

Arthur Gore, 2nd Earl of Arran.

Edward Stratford, 2nd Earl of Aldborough.

Henry de Burgh, 1st Marquess of Clanricarde.

"Lord Delvin." George Frederick Nugent, 7th Earl of Westmeath.

General Henry Luttrell, 2nd Earl of Carhampton.

Captain John Cradock, 1st Baron Howden.

John FitzGibbon, 1st Earl of Clare.

Hon. John Butler of Kilkenny, 17th Earl of Ormonde and 10th Earl of Ossory.

Sir James Stratford Tynte, Bart.

Sir Robert Scott.

Right. Hon. Henry Flood.

Honourable John Stratford.

Major Wemys of Kilkenny.

Lieutenant-General Richard Wilson.

Col. Butler, Kilkenny.

Col. Crosbie.

Col. Harris.

Major John Kelly, Castle Kelly.

Counsellor Anthony King, Major.

Joseph Deane, Esq.

Thomas Roach, Esq; Dublin.

George Robert Fitzgerald, Esq.

John Lees, Esq.

Alexander Montgomery, Esq.

James Underwood, Esq.

The Rev. Doctor Butler, Dublin Castle.

The Rev. Dr. Law.

Anthony Gordon, Esq; Dublin Barracks.

Alderman Nathaniel Warren.

John White, Esq; Stephen's-Green.

Francis Higgins, Esq; Ross-Lane.

M. Dowling, Esq; Aungier-Street.

William Burke, Esq; Ross-Lane.

Lieutenant Colonel St. George, Aid du Camp to his Grace the Duke of Rutland.

Richard Wilson, Dawson-street.

Henry Hatton, Esq. Great Denmark-street.

Sir John Freke, Bart. In Sackville-street.

William Holt, Esq; Stephen's-green.

Hugh Trevor, Esq; Dublin.

Captain Cole, Dublin.

Patrick Bellew, Esq; Mt. Kelly, co. Galway.

Captain Holmes, 66th regt.

Joseph Deane, Esq; 67th regt.

James Farrell, Esq; Black-pits.

*Fencing Contestants:*
James Underwood
Anthony Gordon
Mr. Parvisol
Captain Michael Dillon
Anthony Dillon
Mr. L'Estrange
Lieutenant Cunningham
Mr. O'Berne

*Fencing Judges:*
Arthur Gore, 2nd Earl of Arran
Edward Stratford, 2nd Earl of Aldborough
"Lord Delvin" (George Frederick Nugent)
General Henry Luttrell
Colonel Eustace
James Keogh
Captain Anthony Gordon

*Chaplain to the Order:*
The Rev. Mr. Dwyer

*Treasurer to the Order:*
Francis Higgins, Esq., Ross-Lane

*President:*
Sir William Fortick, Belmont

*Secretary:*
James Underwood, Esq.

SOURCES:
*Dublin Evening Post,* April 5, 1783; April 29, 1783. *Saunders's News-letter*, October 18, 1783; November 11, 1783; May 17, 1784. *Hibernian Journal; or, Chronicle of Liberty*, April 23, 1784; May 5, 1784. *Caledonian Mercury,* September 15, 1783. *Hibernian Magazine, Or, Compendium of Entertaining Knowledge,* May, 1784.

# APPENDIX VI

---

## RULES *of the* CHEROKEE CLUB.

WHEN institutions of very extraordinary and eccentric natures rise up before an astonished and affrighted people, it is perhaps of little consequence whether the origin be imputable to Great Britain, or the sister kingdom: besides, at that variegated duty of human vice and folly, commonly called fashion, flies swiftly even from one corner of the world to the other, there is little reason to doubt but the principles of the society or club, of which we now treat, will find their sudden adoption in this country.

To the surprize and terror of civil society, the disgrace of common sense, and in the defiance of common and statute law, a set of young men, *fashionables* of fortune, in Dublin have lately formed themselves into a kind of hostile corps, which they call the CHEROKEE Squadron, the uniform is scarlet lined with yellow, and edged with black: they meet once a week at a noted tavern to a sumptuous dinner, and each member having loaded himself with four bottles of Claret, and primed with a large bumper of cherry Brandy, they proceed to the business of the institution. But before we enter into the detail of its several purposes, it is necessary to state the qualifications which are indisputable to admission; and in this we pledge ourselves, notwithstanding the incredulity which we suspect will attend our British reader, to be perfectly authentic, and to set down nought in malice.

To become a member of the CHEROKEE CLUB of Dublin; it is first necessary that the candidate should have carried off and debauched a MAID, a WIFE, and a WIDOW or an indefinite number of each.

Secondly, that he should have fought three duels; in one of which, at least, he must either have wounded, or have been wounded, by his antagonist.

Thirdly, he must at some one time of his life, have drank six bottles of Claret after dinner, in half pint bumpers, and given a new Cyprian toast with each bumper.

Fourthly, to arrive at the honour of the President's chair, it is absolutely requisite that the member should have killed, at least, one man in a duel, or a waiter in a violent passion.

Fifthly, that no religious distinctions should disturb the tranquillity of the several meetings, it is absolutely necessary that the members in general should disavow every theological knowledge.

Sixthly, each candidate must be so good a marksman, as to split a bullet discharged from an ordinary pistol on the edge of a case knife, three times in five, at the distance of nine feet.

Seventhly, each candidate must be an expert fencer.

Eighthly, each candidate must have either won or lost the firm of one thousand pounds, at one sitting, at the game of hazard.

Ninthly, each candidate must be proposed by a brother in a full meeting, and proper evidence given of his qualifications. And,

Tenthly, he must take an oath before admission, to support the interests of the society by every possible means, and at risk of life and fortune.

Although we may not be perfectly regular in the above arrangement, we yet pledge ourselves, that the different articles of qualification, as there mentioned, are indispensable to the honour of being a member of the CHEROKEE CLUB.

Having each man drank his quantum, as before mentioned, the first question proposed is, what places of public amusement are open for the evening, and that being determined, the question of ANNOYANCE is proposed, whether the attack shall commence with CAT CALLS, which they call the WAR-HOOP, or with whistlings, which is termed the WOOD-HOOP; or whether by direct assault or surprize; and this question being also disposed of, they all examine their sword canes, and sally forth for action. Although there is much *bravery* in their attacks, they cannot boast of much *gallantry*; for they charge indiscriminately, both men and women, who are unlucky enough to fall in their way, and from the *parts* assaulted one would be apt to suspect them of cowardice, as their wounds are all *a posteriori*; but this we find is done as a mark of contempt to the enemy.

When they enter the play-house, or the rotunda, and set up the War Hoop, the women in general respond through terror, and nothing is heard or seen but screams and faintings; the candles are all knocked out, and darkness follows, to be pinched and pricked in the most indecent manner.

Several actions have been already commenced in the courts of justice, against individuals of this new institution; but as they are sworn to have but one *purse* upon such occasions, there is but little hope of retribution: besides, the several prosecutrixes will, in the issue, be loth to undergo the witty consequences of *cross examination*.

The CHEROKEES, and the *Police Men,* have had several close and desperate battles; but the latter are always defeated.

No lives, however, have yet been lost, though several on both sides have been badly wounded.

Such is the general dread of this new military corps, that the citizens actually go armed after dusk, and the whole town appears like a garrison in fear of an assault from a foreign power. Should, as we have before said, and is not at all improbable, the spirit of the Cherokee Club pass into this kingdom, the CAIRA DEMOGOGUES will no doubt be the first to associate.

- *Walker's Hibernian Magazine,* April, 1792.

# APPENDIX VII

―――――――⎯⎯⎯⎯◆◆◆⎯⎯⎯⎯―――――――

# THE IRISH PIKE EXERCISE.

In 1853, a treatise on guerrilla warfare appeared in Boston, entitled, *Freedom to Ireland: the Art and Science of War for the People*.[1] The author, Oliver Byrne, was an Irishman well-known for his numerous works on engineering, mechanics, navigation, arithmetic, trigonometry, as well as for his arguments against the pseudoscience of phrenology. He was also an enterprising inventor, having discovered a process for smelting a new type of metal alloy, and having created the "Byrnegraph"—an instrument for "multiplying, dividing, and comparing lines, angles, surfaces, and solids."[2]

Unbeknownst to many, Byrne was also an ardent Irish republican. After emigrating from Ireland to New York City, Byrne helped establish the Fenian Movement, and became associated with a number of militant Irish exile organizations, including the Irish Republican Brotherhood (also known as the Fenian Brotherhood), the Phoenix Brigade, the Wolfe Tone Guards, and the ultra-secretive Emmet Monument Association.[3] He also served as captain of Company E of the First Irish Regiment, and captain of Company F of the Second Irish Regiment—Irish republican militias which would eventually give rise to the famed "Fighting 69th" Irish Regiment of New York.[4] As Chair of the Irish Military Library, Byrne also personally authored two military books, entitled *The first fifty lessons on military art and science*, and *Lectures on the Art and Science of War*.[5] At a meeting of New York's Irish revolutionaries, Byrne delivered a rousing speech, later recounted as follows:

"To round shot and the pike it must come at last." (Loud cheers.) [Byrne] was now fifty years old, and during twenty-five years of that time he had been impressing that doctrine on the minds of Irishmen, and urging them to procure arms and learn how to use them. Unless they had the proper tools they would never be either feared or respected. He was glad that they had at length set about their work in the right way, and were preparing to imitate the example and follow in the foot-steps of the brave men of '98.[6]

Another contemporary source noted that "Oliver Byrne, of New York, the distinguished engineer and mathematician, has done more than any other man to infuse into his emigrant countrymen a military spirit."[7]

In 1853, Byrne published his third martial treatise, *Freedom to Ireland: the Art and Science of War for the People,* which advocated armed rebellion against British rule in Ireland. The book included extensive tactics and techniques for "irregular" warfare—for use in both urban and rural environments—as well as methods for using the rifle or firelock. Especially notable was the book's inclusion of pike exercises, which appear to have been greatly inspired by the prolific use of the pike made by the United Irishmen during their famous rebellion of 1798. Byrne's *Freedom to Ireland* opens with the following dedication:

> To the memory of WILLIAM BYRNE, Esq., of Ballymanus, County Wicklow, Ireland, who was executed for fidelity and loyalty to his country in 1798, this work is dedicated. Byrne was a man of large fortune and estates, of rare courage, and great military skill, and of much personal strength and beauty; he did not lose his life and estates, or betray his country, by making long speeches to teach the enemy. He was not one of the beggarly briefless spouting political trickster humbugs; no, but one who in conjunction with his brother Garret Byrne and cousin Michael Dwyer, led on his countrymen, and by the dextrous use of the PIKE, destroyed 2000 of his country's enemy; and out of 27 engagements in the open field, won twenty one.

During the 1850s, Oliver Byrne claimed direct genealogical descent from "the men of '98," although it is unclear if he was related to the famous Byrnes mentioned in his dedication.[8] What is known is that Oliver had been born around 1810 in Avoca, County Wicklow, to Lawrence Oliver Byrne and his wife Mary.[9] The elder Lawrence was described as having hailed from "the Vale of Avoca, co. Wicklow."[10] Avoca happened to lie adjacent to Ballymanus, where several of the famous rebel Byrnes—including William and Garret—originated.[11] Oliver's obituary claimed that his immediate family had lived "in exile after the 1798 Irish Rebellion," which suggests that his family had suffered some sort of consequences for participation in the conflict.[12] Oliver's father, Lawrence, may possibly be the same individual mentioned in a genealogical study of the Byrnes which notes:

> A Lawrence Byrne of Ballymanus does appear on the listing of United Irishmen in Wicklow for 1797 as do James and William Byrne of Ballymanus, presumably two of Lawrence's three brothers.

Another account relates that Lawrence Byrne of Ballymanus, a United Irishman, hid in a cave at Lugnaquilla after the failure of the rebellion, and was later arrested. Sentenced to be hanged,

**Top:** Henry Munro, chief of the Irish rebels. 1798, Hand-colored aquatint after Thomas Rowlandson. *Courtesy of the Anne S.K. Brown Military Collection, Brown University Library*.
**Bottom:** Pike warfare at the Battle of New Ross, Wexford, 1798, by George Cruikshank (1845).

Byrne was later granted a reprieve. After serving time in both Newgate and Dublin Castle, he was released from prison through the intercession of a family member, and returned to Bally-manus, where he lived to be eighty-seven years old.[13] Although it is impossible to identify this man as Oliver's father with absolute certainty, considering all of the aforementioned facts, there seems little reason to doubt that Oliver's family was somehow involved in the rebellion of 1798.

It is thus tantalizing to wonder how much impact or influence the old Irish pike exercises—such as those mentioned by the rebel general Joseph Holt—may have had on Oliver Byrne's method.[14] In the initial chapter of *Freedom to Ireland*, Byrne claimed inspiration from Colonel Francis Maceroni's *Defensive Instructions for the People*[15], as well as from "American" military exercises. A perusal of earlier American treatises on the use of the pike, spear, and lance reveals Byrne's writings on pike technique to have been influenced by American lance exercises first published a decade earlier, in 1841.[16] In the epilogue of his book, Byrne quotes both Maceroni and a paper by Lord Edward Fitzgerald—a leader of the United Irishmen who was killed in 1798. Notably, Byrne's own published method specifically utilizes a type of hinged pike which had previously been created by rebel leader Robert Emmet during the Irish uprising of 1803, and which could be folded in half and concealed beneath the bearer's coat or cloak.

Whatever the actual origins of Byrne's pike exercise, history records that it was put to prac-tical use. In 1853, Byrne's lessons were being utilized as the basis for the training of the "Meagher Rifles," a regiment commanded by Thomas Francis Meagher—a former leader of the failed 1848 Irish Rebellion who had escaped to New York City.[17] Later, in 1860, the exercises were used to train a New York regiment commanded by Byrne himself:

> The Irishmen in this city are organizing corps of pikemen. The 2d regiment, Phoenix brigade, is commanded by Col. Oliver Byrne. "Those who are anxious to join the regiment, and get drilled and become dextrous in the use of our national arm—the queen of weapons—to which the alle-giance of brave hearts and stout arms was freely rendered by our ancestors of '98, will call at No. 6 Centre street and have their names enrolled on the regimental books."[18]

Nor was this the last time that the pike was to be wielded by Irish rebels, as the weapon would go on to see limited use during the risings of 1867, 1916, and the Irish War of Independence.[19]

In the end, any direct connections between Byrne's method and late eighteenth century Irish pike exercises are speculative at best. However, as nineteenth century treatises on staff technique (especially Irish ones) are exceedingly scarce, Byrne's lessons on the pike are presented here as a rare curiosity.

## MANUAL EXERCISE OF THE PIKE.

The exercise is best taught to four or five men at a time, placed in one rank, fifteen feet from each other. The lancers being at the position, ATTENTION, with both firelock and pike slung. The feet should form with each other an angle a little less than a right angle; the knees straight but not stiff; the body perpendicular on the haunches, and inclined a little forward; the shoulders falling equally; the arms hanging naturally, with the elbows a little turned out, the back of the hand turned a little to the front; the thumb and fore finger of the right hand in contact with the firelock; and the thumb and forefinger of the left in contact with the pike. The face to the front, the chin drawn in, but without restraint; the eyes cast on the ground in front fifteen paces off. There are two sorts of commands—namely, one to *caution,* and the other to EXECUTE. Every motion is performed by these two commands, or rather every command is divided into two parts: the first used to caution, and the second as a signal to execute; this is the first thing to be impressed on the recruit's memory. The words to *caution* ought to be pronounced distinctly in a full voice; to designate them from those of execution we shall print them in italics. The commands of EXECUTION will be printed in small capitals, and should be pronounced in a firm quick manner. The instructor should always execute what he commands to exemplify the principle he is explaining. The length of the ordinary step is twenty-eight inches, reckoning from heel to heel; in point of time, ninety of these paces or steps should be taken in a minute. The quick step is twenty-eight inches also, but one hundred and twenty of them are taken in a minute.

The motions of the head to the right and left are taught by the commands—1. *Eyes*—RIGHT.—2. FRONT.—3. *Eyes*—LEFT. At the command REST, the soldier is to rest, and then he needs not maintain either his position or steadiness, only his *left heel is not to quit its place.*

### Atten—TION.

The soldier will fix his attention on the caution *Atten——*, and resume the required position when the last of the command ——TION is given. It is not usual for a soldier to go through his facings at first, when he is fully accoutred, but it is best for him to do so, for he cannot act with that steadiness and gravity that becomes a soldier so well until he feels himself in possession of a pike or a gun. In going through the facings, when halted, the left heel should not be lifted from the ground.

1. *Right*—FACE. 2. *Left*—FACE. At the word FACE, the soldier will turn on his left heel, *right* or *left* as the caution is given. This command is executed in one motion, as the soldier

turns on the left heel he carries the right to the side of it, and places it on the same line, which line must be at right angles with the line occupied by the heels before the command was given.

*About*—FACE, is the command given when the soldier has to make a full face to the rear; at the word *about*, make a half face to the right, then slip the right foot to the rear, so that its hollow will be three inches from the heel of the left, keeping the firelock and the pike steady by a slight touch of the hands. At the word FACE, turn on both heels, raising the toes a little; bring the right heel to the side of the left. *Left-about*—FACE is a useless motion, as the same front can always be gained by the right. FRONT. At this command, after the commands *Right*—FACE or *Left*—FACE, the soldier is to face back to the proper front, by the left, if he had last faced to the right; and by the right, if he had last faced to the left.—The command,

*About*— FACE is given, to come from a full face to the rear to the proper front.

## *Carry*—PIKES.

At the last part of the command, which is PIKES, slip the thumb of the left hand, (see plate 4,) under the sling or belt, and pass it along till it raises the pike over the shoulder-horn, and bring it in front between the feet, the butt an inch or two outside the line of the toes, seizing it quickly with the right hand, and placing it perpendicularly; the firelock being slung, the right hand is at liberty to move the point off the guard, while the left hand holds the lower staff firmly upright. (See plate 2.) The pike is then straightened by the right hand, which also moves the slipper over the middle joint, which, when secured and perfectly straight, drop the right arm by the side, and raise the left along the staff as high as the neck. In open ranks, the blade of the pike, in extending or opening the weapon, may be moved in an arc perpendicular to the line upon which the men are standing. But it may be opened in closed ranks by turning the blade at an angle to the right or left. (See plate 2.)

## *Charge*—PIKES.

At the first part of the command, which is *Charge*, half face to the left, turning on the left heel, at the same time bring the heel of the right foot against that of the left; feet perfectly at right angles to each other. At the last part of the command, which is PIKES, slip down the left hand along the staff, seize it with the right, raise the pike perpendicularly until the left hand arrives at a proper distance from the butt, which is about the length of the fore-arm, lower the point to the front, advance the right foot about one and a half its length, in a line directly at right angles to the left, plant it firmly on the ground; both knees slightly bent, the left the most, as that leg should principally sustain the weight of the body; body erect and resting well

Plate I.

upon the legs; chest thrown out, head up, and turned in the direction of the right foot; muscles of the neck supple and free from constraint.— The lance horizontal; well supported by the left hand to the left hip; the right hand on the staff, fingers closed, and about eighteen inches from

NOTE:—A hand is said to be in quarte, (pronounced cart) when the nails are up. The hand is said to be in tierce, when the nails of the fingers are down.

### Front—POINT.

At the first part of the command, which is *Front*, carry the left arm to the rear to its full length; with the left hand near the extremity of the staff, partly in *tierce;* the right hand partly in *quarte;* in throwing round the left shoulder the head and right shoulder should be kept steady, and the point of the pike as high as the right breast.

At the last part of the command, which is POINT, straighten the left knee strongly: this throws the body forward upon the right leg. Carry forward the body, advance the right foot close along the ground, raising the toe slightly, and plant the right foot about two feet six inches from the left; at the same time throw forward the pike with force, bringing the left arm to the front, the wrist passing near and a little below the left breast, extend the arms to their full length, both hands in quarte, the point dipping a little, and directed at the height of a man's breast; make a slight pause, and resume the position of *Charge*—PIKES. The length of the *longe* may be increased or diminished, according to circumstances. In advancing the right foot the heel should not slide along the ground, and on the other hand, the opposite error of lifting the foot too high, so as to describe with it an arc, must also be avoided. By the first, the movement is retarded; by the last, the equilibrium of the body is destroyed.

### Right—POINT.

This command is executed the same as *Front*—POINT, except that the soldier points his right foot in the direction the point is to be delivered, turning the left foot on the heel so as to be perpendicular to this direction, so that before delivering the point, the soldier is in position of *charge*—PIKES, faced a little to the right. The right hand always moves within the range of the sling, which is kept under the staff.

### Left—POINT.

This command is executed in the same manner as *Front*—POINT, except that the soldier points his right foot in the direction in which the point is to be delivered; turning the left foot

Plate II.

on the heel to be perpendicular to that direction; so that the soldier is in the position of *charge* —PIKES, faced a little to the left; the sling, as before, hangs under the staff. The instructor should, with his own hand, gently correct any deviations from the directions given. In executing the commands,

*Front*—POINT; *Right*—POINT; *Left*—POINT; the change required in the positions of the feet is scarcely perceptible. The recovery from the *development* or *longe*, is always to the position *Charge*—PIKES, it should be easy and graceful, and free from violent exertion.

## ADVANCE.

Standing in the position *charge*—PIKES, move the right foot forward with ease, about half a pace, or fourteen inches, bring up the left instantly the same.

## RETREAT.

Standing in the position *charge*—PIKES, move the left foot to the rear half a pace or fourteen inches, bringing back the right foot instantly the same distance, and planting it firmly on the ground with an *appel*. A sudden beat of the foot, by raising and letting it fall on the same spot, previous to taking up a position by the foot, or before or at the instant of rendering the point, is termed an *Appel*. Much steadiness and regularity are necessary in advancing or retreating; for it is supposed that the pikeman is engaged with an enemy. The body should be kept firmly and steadily in the position *charge*—PIKES. The instructor should pay much attention here, and observe between each step, whether the distances be correctly taken or not, and the right position of the guard maintained.

### *Left Parry*—RIGHT POINT.

At the first part of the command, *left parry*, raise the point of the pike towards the right, the soldier being in the position *charge*—PIKES, not more than six inches higher than the head; lower the pike with force from right to left, and extending the arms to the left, so as to strike forcibly the weapon or body of a man, then bring the pike quickly back to the position *charge pikes*. At the second part of the command, RIGHT POINT, the command *right*—POINT is executed in the manner before described.

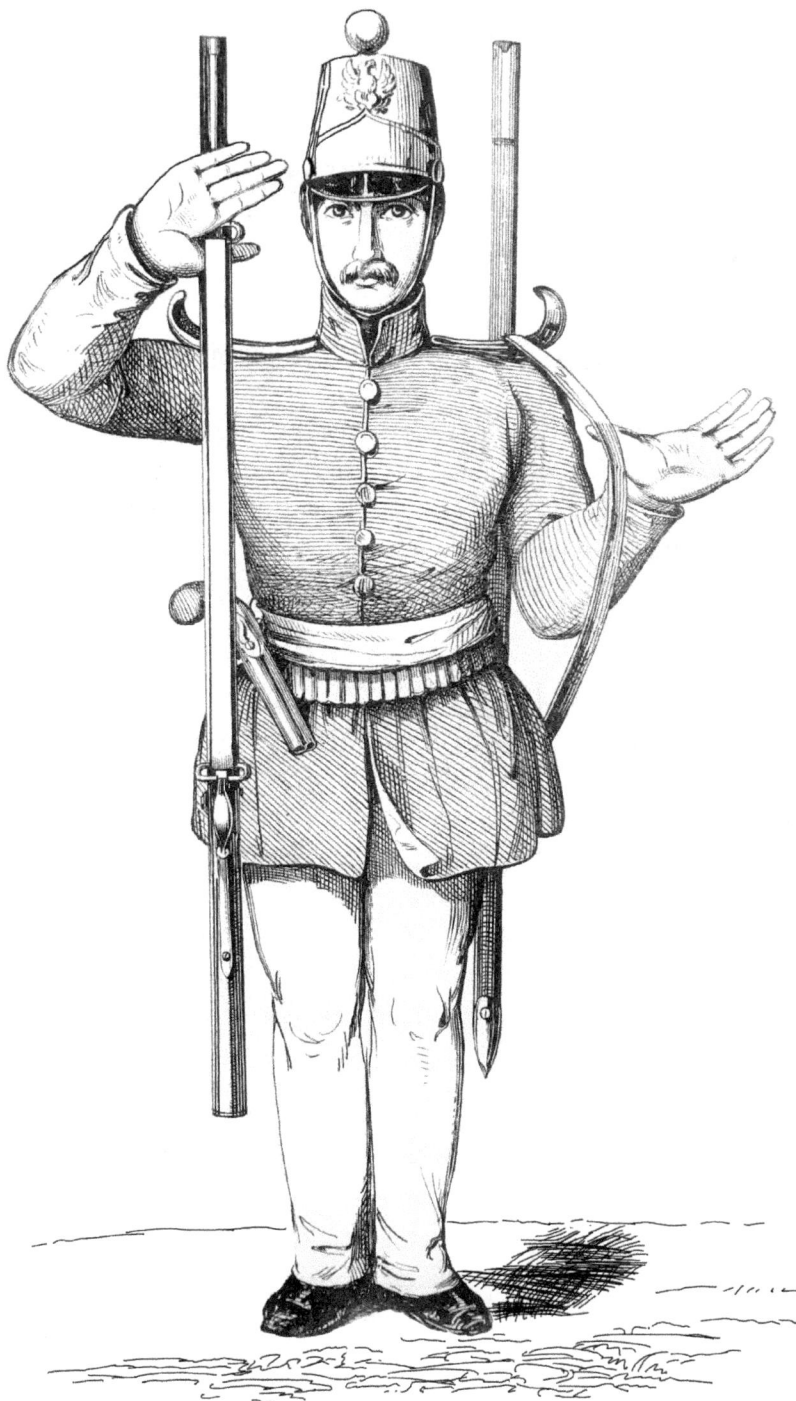

Plate IV.

### *Right Parry*—LEFT POINT.

At the first part of the command, *Right Parry*, raise the point of the pike towards the left, not more than six inches higher than the head, and as much lower as the case may require, the soldier being in the position of *charge pikes;* lower the pike with force from left to right, extending the arms to the right, so as to strike forcibly the weapon or body of a man, then bring the pike quickly back to the position from which it started. At the second part of the command which is LEFT POINT, the command *left* POINT is executed as before described.

### *Left and Right Parry*—FRONT POINT.

As in the former cases the soldier is in the position of *charge*—PIKES. At the first of the command, which is *left* and *right parry*, raise the point of the pike towards the right, not more than six inches higher than the head, lower the pike with force from right to left; describe an arc of a circle in elevating the point on the left, then lower the point with force from left to right, to turn aside the adversary's weapon, and return to the position, *charge*—PIKES.

At the last part of the command, which is FRONT POINT, the command *right*—POINT, is executed in the manner before described.

### *Right and Left Parry*—FRONT POINT.

At the first command, which is, *Right and Left Parry*, raise the point of the pike towards the left not more than six inches over the head; lower the pike with force from left to right; describe an arc of a circle in elevating the point on the right, then lower the point with force from right to left, so as in the quickest possible manner to turn aside the adversary's weapon. Then at the last part of the command, FRONT POINT, assume the position *charge*—PIKES, and deliver the point to the front, in the manner before directed.

### *Around*—PARRY.

At the first part of the command, *Around*, carry the point of the pike towards the right, as high as the eyes; then at the last part of the command, which is, PARRY, move the lance with force from right to left, and from left to right, keeping up a quick and steady motion, by a motion of the hands, the right in *quarte*, the left in *tierce*, until the command *Front*—POINT; *Left*—POINT; or *Right*—POINT, is given, which execute and return to the position *charge*—PIKES.

Plate VI.

## Carry—PIKES.

At the word PIKES, face to the front, bring up the point and drop the butt before the feet, the staff perpendicular, seize it as high as the neck by the left hand; drop the right quickly by the side. The butt of the staff must be an inch or two outside the line of the toes.

## Rest—PIKES.

At the first part of the command, *Rest*, place the staff against the left shoulder without removing the butt; and at the word PIKES, lower the left hand along the staff nearly to the full extent of the arm; then the soldier may talk, turn, in any position so that he does not remove the butt of the staff or his left heel. Mind, talk here does not mean spouting. I have a great horror of those animals called spouters.

*Shoulder*—PIKES.

At the first part of the command, *shoulder*, come to the position *carry*—PIKES; *which is the position the soldier generally assumes before the execution of any other command.* At the second part of the command, which is PIKES, raise the pike against the left shoulder with the right hand, the butt twelve inches from the ground, let fall the left hand to nearly its full extent, seize the staff, with the fore finger and thumb pointing down along it, and the remaining three fingers clinched in round it; then let the right hand fall smartly to the side, in the usual position.

*Sling*—PIKES.

At the first part of the command, *Sling*, bring the pike to the position *carry*—PIKE, seize the lower joint of the staff firmly with the left hand, and remove the slipper of the hinge with the right, (see plate 2.) Then at the second part of the command, which is PIKES, close up the weapon securely and raise it with the left hand under the sling over the left shoulder horn, take it at the same time with the right hand to guide it over the horn, then let go both hands and assume the position, *Attention.*

EXAMPLE.

Let a Regiment of Six Companies, be deployed,—two skirmishing, two in support, and two in reserve; and let form square be sounded without the alarm, which is generally the case when a sudden rush of Cavalry is expected, what is to be done.

The left skirmishers will rally on the officer, who will take up his position on the line on which they were extended, clear off the left support. The commander of the right skirmishers will run at least twenty paces to rear, placing himself clear of the supports, under cover, against a wall or a tree, if possible and his men will rally on him. The right support will receive the word, *On the first section form square and resist cavalry.* The left support will receive the word, *Double march,* and when advanced about twenty-five or thirty paces, the word, *On the first section form square and resist cavalry,* will be given. The reserve will form four deep, close to centre, and the rear division will be faced about. In these five squares, plate 6, represents the men of the front rank, the position of *charge*—PIKES is assumed by the second rank; Plate 1, represents the men of the third and fourth ranks, only that those of the third rank have the right foot square behind the left heel, heels together half faced to the right. Plate 1, represents a fourth rank man about to take aim. The left heels of the fore men, are in the same line perpendicular to the side of the square whether the ranks are operating obliquely or to the front. To resist cavalry by one rank, Plate 6, gives the best position of the soldier, when the cavalry is near. When there are two ranks only, Plate 1, gives the best position for the second rank, and Plate 6, the position of the first. When the formation is three deep, see Plate 6, for the first rank, *charge*—PIKES for the second, and Plate 1, for the third rank, when attacked by cavalry. But the emergency of the case must always decide the nature of the formation.

\* \* \*

"However well exercised standing armies are supposed to be, by frequent reviews, and sham battles, they are never prepared for broken roads, or inclosed fields in a country like Ireland, covered with innumerable and continued intersections of ditches and hedges, every one of which is of advantage to an irregular body, and may, with advantage, be disputed against an army, as so many fortifications and entrenchments. The people in large cities would have an advantage by being armed with pikes or such weapons. The first attack, if possible, should be made by men whose pikes were nine or ten feet long; by that means they could act in ranks deeper than the soldiery, whose arms are much shorter; then the deep files of the pikemen, by being weightier, must break the thin order of the army. The charge of the pikemen should be made in a smart trot. On the flank, or extremity of every rank, there should be intrepid men placed, to keep the fronts even, that, at closing, every point should tell together. They should have at the same time two or three like bodies, at convenient distances, in the rear, who would be brought up, if wanting to support the front, which would give confidence to their brothers in action, as it would tend to discourage the enemy. At the same time there should be, in the rear of each division, some men of spirit to keep the ranks as close as possible.

"The apparent strength of the army should not intimidate, as closing makes its powder and ball useless; all its superiority is in fighting at a distance; and all its skill ceases, and all its action must be suspended when once within reach of the pike."[20]

With the pike Cavalry may be beaten off, and should always be faced, charged, and beaten back. To fly from cavalry, or to fly at all, before any troops, is miserable work.—When within gun shot, it is better to face it; and attended with less danger and loss of life, to fight it out desperately. Pieces of artillery should be stormed and taken at all hazards. A body of determined men armed with pikes, must undoubtedly overthrow their opponents, whether infantry, cavalry, or artillery, of the present arming, if they have the opportunity and courage to close on them with alacrity. I have limited the length of the pike to ten feet; because, if it were longer it would not, when doubled up, hang steady on the shoulder. But the length of a common unjointed pike may be advantageously extended to eighteen or twenty feet, by which means, the pikemen being formed six deep, the weapons of the hindermost rank, will, in a charge project beyond the breasts of the front rank at least eight feet; that is to say, nearly twice as far as the front rank of the adversary's bayonets. In the construction of long pikes, care should be had that they be not top heavy, in order that advantage may be taken of their length without fatigue, and that the point may be moved about with alacrity. To obtain this the head should be smaller than that of the folding pike, and the shaft must gradually increase in thickness towards the butt. A ten or twelve foot ash pike, properly constructed, can be held out its whole length.

The shaft must be only three quarters of an inch in diameter at the point, regularly increasing to an inch and a quarter at the butt. The head should not weigh more than three or four ounces. In order to facilitate the construction of pikes on an emergency, several experiments have been made, in the view of ascertaining whether such woods as are most generally at hand, easily and expeditiously worked, and cheap to boot, may not be substituted for *ash* or *beech;* the former of which, particularly, has hitherto been considered, in Ireland, as almost the only material proper for pike shafts, and consequently the English have rendered this article very scarce in Ireland. Are they afraid of the pike, aye, or no? A kind of deal, called in Ireland and England American pine, is to be had at most of the timber yards. It is very straight grained and free from knots. Some of this was sawed into eighteen feet lengths, two inches square; planed down round, to one and a half inch diameter at the butt, gradually diminishing to three-fourths of an inch at the point, on which was fixed a sharp and sufficiently strong head, weighing four ounces. This eighteen foot pike, weighs only eight pounds, though exceedingly stiff and strong. It was tried in vain to break it by driving and bending it with all the strength of a man against a wall. Another great advantage is, it costs only a dollar complete. American *birch*, Irish *willow*, and *larch*, will also answer the purpose we are speaking of Infantry and artillery must be charged so as to render their fire comparatively useless, by preventing its being repeated. *Be prompt and you will destroy them; hesitate, and you will be destroyed!* As to cavalry, it will hardly ever be necessary for you to form into squares to resist them; for, armed with pikes, you may defy them, and even charge them in line, without receiving a scratch. But you must take care that they do not out flank you, and get into your rear; in which case you must form into a square or a circle as speedily as possible. It must be borne in mind, that when pikes are used alone they should be six deep, which will give them an irresistible impetus; and should any be floored, by the first fire of the enemy, you will still be more than strong enough to knock him head over heel before he can have time to repeat it. Should any man be unable to provide himself with any other weapon than a sword; in the first place, let him take care it be kept very sharp. When he shall have occasion to use it, let him bind a blanket, which he should always have with him, or a great coat, around his left arm, like a muff, or a large book tied up in a pocket handkerchief. This will serve as an excellent shield, with which he may either entangle or parry the point of a lance or bayonet, or the cut of a sabre. His grand object must always be, to step in and make his thrust, or stroke, *at the very moment*, of receiving that of the enemy, who will thus be unable to parry. A piece of wood, might be made into a good shield for a swordsman. If covered with sheet iron, it might turn a slanting musket shot. But I shall be told, that a man capable of getting such a shield will be equally capable of getting a pike. This may be; but a body of men armed with a properly constructed shield and sword would, say at close quarters, beat an equal number of either pikes or bayonets. This not only stands to reason, but has been proved in innumerable instances, both in ancient and modern times. Such an armament, however, cannot stand against cavalry; for which reason, and for several others, the jointed or common pikes are to be preferred to the sword as arms for the people. The jointed lance is evidently the best, because it can be borne and used conjointly with a fowling piece, a musket, rifle, or a carbine, and a pistol. What I have said therefore, in favor of the common long pike, must be understood, to apply to those who cannot furnish themselves with a jointed one, or are incapable of using a musket. Any how, those men who will bear the long pikes should endeavour to provide themselves with a large pistol, to wear in the belt.[21]

Can Americans forget their struggles for liberty, the scalping-knife, and the blood-hound, and think of an alliance with her most deadly enemy and unceasing vilifier?—no, true Americans would die first. The butchered Caffers and the bamboozled Canadians do not forget how England patronised them. Desolated India, her people over-taxed, starved, and murdered, her Chiefs robbed and poisoned cannot forget. China can remember too.—Can NAPOLEON III, and the French people, forget the brutal treatment of NAPOLEON THE GREAT, the glory and destiny of France, Ireland's only hope, poisoned on a barren rock? But God has ordained that Irish American soldiers are to give the *coup de grace* to the scarlet whore of Babylon, the infernal English government. Irishmen, swear by the sufferings of your millions starved to death by design and buried without a coffin, swear by the blood and grief of your murdered and banished patriots, by the religion given as by God himself, now degraded by our enemies in the basest manner, that you will in this great and glorious republic acquire the use of arms, and study the art of war, and be ready for a day not far distant. *Avengers*—FALL IN.

---

1   Oliver Byrne, *Freedom to Ireland: The Art and Science of War for the People. the Pike Exercise, Foot Lancers, Light Infantry, and Rifle Drill. to Which Is Added a Short Practical Treatise on Small Arms, and Ammunition, Street and House Fighting, and Field Fortification* (Boston: P. Donahoe, 1853).

2   "Important Metallic Discovery," *The Weekly Arizonian*, October 20, 1859. Oliver Byrne, *Description and Use of*

the *Byrnegraph: An Instrument for Multiplying, Dividing, and Comparing Lines, Angles, Surfaces, and Solids* (London: C. and J. Adlard, 1846).

3   Joseph Denieffe, *A personal narrative of the Irish revolutionary brotherhood, giving a faithful report of the principal events from 1885 to 1867, written, at the request of friends, by Joseph Denieffe, to which is added, in corroboration, an appendix containing important letters ad papers written by James Stephens, John O'Mahony, John Mitchel, Thomas J. Kelly, and other leaders of the movement* (New York: The Gael Publishing Co., 1906), 17-18. John Devoy, *Recollections of an Irish rebel: the Fenian movement. Its origin and progress* (New York: Chase D. Young Co., 1929), 16-18. *The Phoenix*, March 24, 1860.

4   *Irish American Weekly*, February 1, 1851, March 22, 1851.

5   *Irish American Weekly*, November 25, 1854. Oliver Byrne, *The first fifty lessons on military art and science* (New York: D. &. J. Sadlier, 1850); *Lectures on the Art and Science of War: addressed to Irish American citizen soldiers* (Boston: Patrick Donahoe, 1853).

6   *The Phoenix*, March 24, 1860.

7   Thomas D'Arcy McGee, *A History of the Irish Settlers in North America: From the Earliest Period to the Census of 1850* (Boston: Patrick Donahoe, 1852), 192.

8   *The Phoenix*, March 24, 1860.

9   Susan M. Hawes and Sid Kolpas, "Oliver Byrne: The Matisse of Mathematics," *Convergence 12* (August 2015).

10  *The Gentleman's Magazine and Historical Review*, August, 1853, 213.

11  Miles Byrne, *Memoirs of Miles Byrne* (Dublin: Maunsel & Co., Ltd., 1907), 11, 93, 227, 241.

12  "The Late Mr. Oliver Byrne," *Kent Messenger and Maidstone Telegraph*, December 18, 1880.

13  Daniel Byrne-Rothwell, *The Byrnes and the O'Byrnes, Volume 2* (Great Britain: House of Lochar, 2010), 60-61.

14  Joseph Holt, *Memoirs of Joseph Holt, general of the Irish rebels in 1798* (London: Colburn, 1838), 43, 48, 98, 156.

15  Francis Maceroni, *Defensive Instructions for the People: Containing the New and Improved Combination of Arms, Called Foot Lancers: Miscellaneous Instructions on the Subject of Small Arms and Ammunition: Street and House Fighting, and Field Fortification* (London: Printed and published by J. Smith, 1832).

16  See *Cavalry Tactics* (Washington: J. and G.S. Gideon, 1841). For early American pike or spear treatises, see: John Roulstone, *Sword and Pike Exercise for Artillery: As Taught by Capt. John Roulstone, and Practised by the Boston Sea Fencibles* (Boston: Munroe & Francis, 1818); Artemas Dryden, *The Sword Exercise: Comprising the Sword Manual of Officers, the Attack and Defence, and the Defence against Combined Numbers of the Artillery Exercise, Together with Exercises for the Pike or Spear* (Worcester, Mass.: Published by Artemas Dryden, Jr, 1829).

17  *Boston Daily Bee*, April 25, 1853.

18  *New York Daily Tribune*, March 17, 1860.

19  "The Pike in 1916: The Failed Assault on Dublin Castle" in *History Ireland*, December/November 2012; James J. Comerford, *My Kilkenny I.R.A. Days: 1916-22* (Kilkenny: Dinan Pub. Co.: 1980), 100-104, 187, 215, 772-775.

20  Extracted from a paper by rebel leader Edward Fitzgerald, printed in *The History of the Irish Rebellion, in the Year 1798, &c.,: Containing an Impartial Narrative of the Proceedings of the Irish Revolutionists, from the Year 1782 Till the Total Suppression of the Insurrection: with a Review of the History of Ireland, from Its First Invasion by the English, Till the Commencement of the Rebellion. In Two Volumes* (Alston, Cumberland: John Harrop, 1809), 280-281.

21  The preceding section quotes extensively from Maceroni, 49-51.

# BIBLIOGRAPHY

## BOOKS, PAMPHLETS, and MANUSCRIPTS.

*A Biographical Dictionary of the Living Authors of Great Britain and Ireland* (London: Printed for Henry Colburn, 1816), 443.

A Citizen of London, *A Description of the City of Dublin in Ireland.* London: Printed, and sold by the author, 1732.

*A complete treatise on the infantry sword exercise, as established for the British Army, and instructed at Dublin, October, 1816.* Dublin: Printed and Published by J. Findlay, 1816.

*A Few Mathematical and Critical Remarks on the Sword.* Dublin: D. Chamberlaine, No. 5 College-Green, 1781.

*A Few Observations Upon the Fighting for Prizes in the Bear Gardens, By a Lover and Well-wisher, not only to the True and Useful Art of the SWORD, but also to the Safety and Security of the Persons of those Brave, Courageous, and Bold Performers in these publick Places, for Trial of Skill in this Gentlemanly Art.* London: 1715.

*A full report of the trial at bar, in the court of King's bench, in which the Right Hon. Arthur Wolfe, His Majesty's attorney general, prosecuted, and A. H. Rowan, esq. was defendant, on an information filed ex officio against the defendant for having published a seditious libel. January 29, 1794.* Perth: R. Morison and Son, 1794.

*A Gentleman of that city [Dublin], Modern honour: or, the barber duellist: a comic opera in two acts; as it is now performing at the Theatre-Royal in Smock-Alley.* Dublin: Printed for the author by R. Stewart, Abbey-Street, 1775.

A Traveller. *The Art of Duelling.* London: Joseph Thomas, 1836.

*A vindication of the Irish Earl of Bath: on occasion of the groundless imputations, malevolent insinuations, and unmannerly expostulations of a pretended Quaker: an answer to said Quaker's letters, etc.* Dublin: 1755.

*Account book of Ralph Howard, Baron Clonmore, Viscount Wicklow,* 1748-9, National Library of Ireland, Wicklow Papers, MS 1725.

Addison, Joseph. *The Works of the Right Honourable Joseph Addison, Esq., in Four Volumes. Volume IV.* London: Printed for Jacob Tonson, 1721.

*Alumni Dublinenses: a register of the students, graduates, professors and provosts of Trinity college in the University of Dublin, 1593-1860.* Dublin: A. Thom & Co., Ltd., 1935.

*An Account of a battle fought between Mr. Smith, an attorney in Smithfield, and Mr. Lee, son to Captain Lee in the county of Westmeath viz.* [Dublin]: Printed in the year MDCCXIX.

*An Account of a Desperate Duel, Fought at Talla-Green, in the County of Catharlow, between Lieutenant Barkley, a Lt. of Horse, and Mr. Edvv. Culling, Steward to the Late Lord Chief Justice Doyn's Eldest Son, Viz.* Dublin: Printed by Thomas Toulmin, 1719.

An English Gentleman, *The United States and Canada During the Years 1822-1823.* London: Baldwin, Cradock, and Joy, 1824.

Andrews, Stuart. *Irish Rebellion: Protestant Polemic 1798-1900.* New York: Palgrave Macmillan, 1988.

Angelo, Domenico. *The School of Fencing.* London: 1787.

Angelo, Henry. *Angelo's Pic Nic, or, Table talk: including numerous recollections of public characters, who have figured in some part or another of the stage of life for the last fifty years: forming an endless variety of talent, amusement, and interest, calculated to please every person fond of biographical sketches and anecdotes.* London: J. Ebers, 1834.

—. *Reminiscences with Memoirs of His Late Father and Friends, Including Numerous Original Anecdotes and Curious Traits of the Most Celebrated Characters that Have Flourished During the Last Eighty Years, Volume I.* London: Henry Colburn and Richard Bentley, 1830.

—. *Reminiscences with Memoirs of His Late Father and Friends, Including Numerous Original Anecdotes and Curious Traits of the Most Celebrated Characters that Have Flourished During the Last Eighty Years, Volume II.* London: Henry Colburn and Richard Bentley, 1830.

*At his Majesty's Bear-Garden. In Hockly-in-the-Hole, this present Wednesday, being the 14th of May, 1735. Will be performed a tryal of skill by the following great masters in that noble art, call'd defence.* London: Printed by G. Buckeridge in Baldwin's-Garden, 1735.

*Authentic Memoirs of George Robert Fitzgerald, Esq; with a Full Account of His Trial and Execution, for the Murder of Patrick Randell Mcdonnell, Esq.* London: Printed for the Editor; sold by E. Dodd, 1786.

Aylward, J. D.. *The English master of arms from the twelfth to the twentieth century.* London, Routledge & Paul [1956].

Barrington, Sir Jonah. *Historic memoirs of Ireland; comprising secret records of the national convention, the rebellion, and the union; with delineations of the principal characters connected with these transactions, Vol. I.* London: Published for H. Colburn by R. Bentley, 1835.

—. *Personal Sketches of His Own Times, Vol. I.* London: Henry Colburn and Richard Bentley, 1830.

—. *Personal Sketches of His Own Times, Vol. II.* Philadephia: Carey, Lea, & Carey, 1827.

—. *Personal Sketches of His Own Times, Vol. II.* London: Lynch Conway Gent., 1871.

—. *Personal Sketches of His Own Times, Vol. III.* London: Colburn and Bentley, 1832.

—. *Rise and Fall of the Irish Nation.* New York: D. & J. Sadlier, 1848.

Barritt, Thomas. *Ancient Armour and Weapons in the possession of Thomas Barritt.* [1793-1811]. From Manchester Libraries, Information and Archives, Manchester City Council. Ref # BR MS f 399 B13.

Barry, Michael. *An Affair of Honour.* Fermoy, Ireland: Éigse Books, 1981.

Beaumont, Francis, and John Fletcher. *Bonduca, a Tragedy.* London: Printed for J.T., 1718.

Blackstone, William. *Commentaries on the Laws of England, Volume 4.* Oxford: Clarendon Press, 1769.

Blackwell, Edward. *A Compleat System of Fencing: or, The Art of Defence, in the Use of the Small-Sword.*

Williamsburg: William Parks, 1734.

Blackwell, Henry. *The Gentleman's Tutor for the Small Sword: Or, The Compleat English Fencing Master.* London: Printed for J. and T.W., 1730.

Bosquet, Abraham. *Howth, a Descriptive Poem: By Abraham Bosquet, Esq. Late Commissary of Musters.* Dublin: Printed by P. Byrne, No. 108, Grafton-Street, 1787.

Bosquett, Abraham. *The Young Man of Honour's Vade-Mecum, Being a Salutary Treatise on Duelling. Together with the Annals of Chivalry, the Ordeal Trial, and Judicial Combat, from the Earliest Times.* London: C. Chapple, 1817.

Boswell, James. *The Life of Samuel Johnson, LL.D., Volume II.* London: Henry Baldwin, 1791.

Bowden, Charles Topham. *A Tour Through Ireland.* Dublin: W. Corbet, 1791.

Brenton, Edward Pelham. *Life and Correspondence of John, Earl of St. Vincent, Volume II.* London: H. Colburn, 1838.

Burke, Bernard. *A Visitation of the Seats and Arms of the Noblemen and Gentlemen of Great Britain and Ireland.* London: Hurst and Blackett, 1855.

Burke, James Peller. *Burke's genealogical and heraldic history of the landed gentry, Volume I.* London: H. Colburn, 1847.

Burke, John-Bernard. *A Genealogical and Heraldic Dictionary of the Peerages of England, Ireland.* London: Henry Colburn, 1846.

Burke, Oliver J.. *Anecdotes of the Connaught Circuit: From Its Foundation in 1604 to Close Upon the Present Time.* Dublin: Hodges, Figgis, 1885.

Burke, Sir Bernard. *A genealogical and heraldic history of the landed gentry of Ireland.* London: Harrison & Sons, 1912.

Burke, William P.. *History of Clonmel.* Waterford: Printed by N. Harvey & co. for the Clonmel Library Committee, 1907.

Burton, Lady Isabel. *The Life of Captain Sir Richard F. Burton, Volume I.* London: Chapman & Hall, 1893.

Burton, Richard F.. *A Complete System of Bayonet Exercise.* London: William Clowes & Sons, 1853.

—. *A New System of Sword Exercise for Infantry.* London: W. Clowes and Sons, 1876.

—. *Ogham-Runes and El-Mushajjar: a Study.* London: Harrison & Sons, 1882.

—. *The Book of the Sword.* London: Chatto and Windus, 1884.

—. *The Sentiment of the Sword. A Country-House Dialogue.* London: Horace Cox, 1911.

Butler, Richard. *A Treatice of Ireland, by John Dymmok. Now first published from a MS. preserved in the British Museum, with Notes, by the Rev. Richard Butler, A. B., M. R. I. A. in Tracts relating to Ireland. Volume 2.* Dublin, University Press, Graisberry and Gill, 1843.

*By the Lords-Justices of Ireland: A Proclamation against Duelling. Charles Porter, Tho: Coningesby. His Majesty Being Informed That Heretofore Quarrels and Duels Have Frequently Happen'd between the Officers and Soldiers of the Army in This Kingdom.* Dublin: Printed by Andrew Crook assignee of

Benjamin Took, printer to the King and Queens most excellent Majesties on Ormonde-Key, 1691.

Byrne-Rothwell, Daniel. *The Byrnes and the O'Byrnes, Volume 2*. Great Britain: House of Lochar, 2010.

Byrne, Miles. *Memoirs of Miles Byrne*. Dublin: Maunsel & Co., Ltd., 1907.

Byrne, Oliver. *Description and Use of the Byrnegraph: An Instrument for Multiplying, Dividing, and Comparing Lines, Angles, Surfaces, and Solids*. London: C. and J. Adlard, 1846.

—. *Freedom to Ireland: The Art and Science of War for the People. The Pike Exercise, Foot Lancers, Light Infantry, and Rifle Drill. To which is Added a Short Practical Treatise on Small Arms, and Ammunition, Street and House Fighting, and Field Fortification*. Boston: Patrick Donahoe, 1853.

—. *The first fifty lessons on military art and science*. New York: D. &. J. Sadlier, 1850.

—. *Lectures on the Art and Science of War: addressed to Irish American citizen soldiers*. Boston: Patrick Donahoe, 1853.

Cadogan, William. *A dissertation on the gout: and all chronic diseases, jointly considered, as proceeding from the same causes; what those causes are; and a rational and natural method of cure proposed. Addressed to all invalids*. London: Printed for J. Dodsley, 1771.

*Calendar of the Patent Rolls of the Chancery of Ireland*. Dublin: 1800.

Campbell, James. *Memoirs of Sir James Campbell, of Ardkinglas, written by himself, Vol. 2*. London: H. Colburn and R. Bentley, 1832.

Campbell, Thomas. *A Philosophical Survey of the South of Ireland, in a series of letters to John Watkinson*. Dublin: Printed for W. Whitestone, 1778.

Carr, Sir John. *Stranger in Ireland; or, A tour in the southern and western parts of that country in the year 1805*. Philadelphia: F. Bradford, 1806.

Casanova, Giacomo. *The Duel*. London: Hesperus Press Ltd., 2003.

Castle, Egerton. *Schools and Masters of Fence, from the Middle Ages to the eighteenth century*. London: G. Bell & Sons, 1885.

*Catalogue of the Extensive and Valuable Library of His Royal Highness the Duke of York*. London: Compton & Ritchie, Printers, 1827.

*Catalogue of the Library of the Royal United Service Institution, to January 1st, 1908, Part I*. London: 1908.

*Catalogue of the Manuscripts in the Library of Trinity College, Dublin, to which is Added a List of the Fagel Collection of Maps in the Same Library*. Dublin: Hodges, Figgis, & Company, Limited, 1900.

Chambaud, Louis. *A grammar of the French tongue*. London: C. Bathurst, 1775.

Cole, Benjamin. *The Soldier's Pocket Companion, or the Manual Exercise of Our British Foot, As Now Practis'd by His Majesty's Special Command: With Previous Directions to Officers, in Regard to Their Proper Salutes to the King, or Any of the Royal Family, &c.: to Which Is Added a Short View of the Use of the Small Sword*. London: Sold by the proprietor B. Cole, 1746.

Connellan, Thaddeus. *An English-Irish Dictionary intended to be used in schools with over eight thousand definitions*. Dublin: Graisberry and Campbell, 1814.

*The Correspondence of Horace Walpole, Volume 32*. New Haven: Yale University Press, 1965.

Cosgrave, J. *A genuine history of the lives and actions of the most notorious Irish highwaymen, Tories and Rapparees, from Redmond O'Hanlon, the famous gentleman-robber, to Cahier na Gappul, the great horse-catcher, who was executed at Maryborough, in August, 1735.* Dublin: R. Cross, 1779.

Coustard de Massi, Anne-Pierre. *The History of Duelling: In Two Parts.* London: E. and C. Dilly, J. Walter and J. Robson, 1770.

Croker, Thomas Crofton. *Researches in the South of Ireland.* London: Murray, 1824.

Darrell, William. *The gentleman instructed, in the conduct of a virtuous and happy life. Written for the Instruction of a Young Nobleman.* London: Printed for E. Evets at the Green Dragon in St. Paul's Church-Yard, 1704.

De Bosroger, Le Roy. *The elementary principles of tactics, with new observations on the military art, originally in French by Sieur B, and translated by an officer of the British Army.* London: S. Hooper, 1771.

*Dedicated to the officers and privates of the St. James Westminster Loyal Volunteer Regiment: This plate represents their uniform in the position of the new charge bayonet.* London: I. Mease, Sergeant of the Seventh Company, No. 2 Queens Street Soho Square, 1804.

Denieffe, Joseph. *A personal narrative of the Irish revolutionary brotherhood, giving a faithful report of the principal events from 1885 to 1867, written, at the request of friends, by Joseph Denieffe, to which is added, in corroboration, an appendix containing important letters ad papers written by James Stephens, John O'Mahony, John Mitchel, Thomas J. Kelly, and other leaders of the movement.* New York: The Gael Publishing Co., 1906.

*Deuxième Catalogue De La Galerie Charles Brunner, 11 Rue Royale, Paris.* Paris: Moreau, 1910.

Devoy, John. *Recollections of an Irish rebel: the Fenian movement. Its origin and progress.* New York: Chase D. Young Co., 1929.

*Dictionary of National Biography, 1885-1900, Volume 43.* London: Smith, Elder & Co..

*Dictionary of the Irish language: based mainly on old and middle Irish materials. Published by the Royal Irish Academy, under the editorship of Carl J.S. Marstrander.* Dublin: Royal Irish Academy, 1913.

*Dispatches, Correspondence and Memoranda of Field Marshal Arthur Duke of Wellington, K.G.: May 1827 to August 1828, Volume 12.* London: John Murray, 1865.

Doyle, Alexander. *Kurtze und deutliche Auslegung Der Voltagier-Kunst Sowol Denen Meistern als Scholaren nützlich, Indeme Es nicht nur allein die vortheilhafftigsten Handgriffe, sondern auch die schönsten darzu dienlichen Maniren und Stellungen deutlich lehret und zeiget, daß einer dardurch in kurtzer Zeit capabel seyn kan, solche zu practiciren; Und also füglich der andere Theil, der auch unlängst heraus gegebenen Fecht- und Schirm-Kunst, kan genennet werden.* Nürnberg: P. Lochner, 1720.

—. *Neu Alamodische Ritterliche Fecht- und Schirm-Kunst: Das ist: Wahre und nach neuester Frantzösischer Manier eingerichtete Unterweisung Wie man sich in Fechten und Schirmen perfectioniren und verhalten solle; Denen respective Herren Liebhaberen zu besserer Erleuterung mit 60 hierzu dienlichen Figuren herausgegeben.* Nürnberg: P. Lochner, 1715.

—. *Neu alamodische ritterliche Fecht- und Schirm-Kunst. Das ist: Wahre und nach neuester Französischer Manier eingerichtete Unterweisung wie man sich in Fechten und Schirmen perfectioniren und verhalten solle; denen respective Herren Liebhaberen zu besserer Erleuterung mit 60. hierzu dienlichen Figuren *herausgegeben von Alexander Doyle aus Irrland gebürtig*. Nürnberg and Franckfurt: P. Lochnern, 1716.

—. *Neu Alamodische Ritterliche Fecht- und Schirm-Kunst: Das ist: Wahre und nach neuester Frantzösischer Manier eingerichtete Unterweisung Wie man sich in Fechten und Schirmen perfectioniren und verhalten solle; Denen respective Herren Liebhaberen zu besserer Erleuterung mit 60 hierzu dienlichen Figuren herausgegeben*. Nürnberg: P. Lochner, 1729.

Drake, Peter. *The Memoirs of Capt. Peter Drake: Containing an Account of Many Strange and Surpising Events, Which Happened to Him Through a Series of Sixty Years, and Upwards; and Several Material Anecdotes, Regarding King William and Queen Anne's Wars with Lewis Xiv. of France*. [in two volumes]. Dublin: Printed and sold by S. Powell in Crane-Lane, for the author.

*The Dramatic Works of Wycherley, Congreve, Vanbrugh, and Farquhar*. London: George Routledge and Sons, 1871.

Dryden, Artemas. *The Sword Exercise: Comprising the Sword Manual of Officers, the Attack and Defence, and the Defence against Combined Numbers of the Artillery Exercise, Together with Exercises for the Pike or Spear*. Worcester, Mass.: Published by Artemas Dryden, Jr, 1829.

Duffy, Charles Gavan. *The Ballad Poetry of Ireland*. Dublin: J. Duffy, 1845.

Dunn, Major R. I.. *A Condensed Military Pocket Manual: For Volunteer and Militia Officers, Non-commissioned Officers and Privates. Agreeable to the System Laid Down for the United States Army*. Lexington, Ky.: J. Cunningham, printer, 1841.

—. *A military pocket manual, for militia officers, condensed, and agreeable to the system laid down of the United States army: with a short treatise on the cavalry and infantry swords: also, by-laws for volunteer companies, &c., &c., &c.*. Cincinnati: Published for Joseph Medary, 1831.

Edgeworth, Richard Lovell. *Essays on professional education*. London: Printed for J. Johnson, 1809.

Fénelon, François. *The Adventures of Telemachus*. London: Alex Hogg, 1775.

Fergusson, Hary. *A Dictionary, Explaining the Terms, Guards, and Positions, Used in the Art of the Small Sword* ([Edinburgh]: 1767).

Figueredo, Danilo H.. *Revolvers and Pistolas, Vaqueros and Caballeros: Debunking the Old West*. Santa Barbara: Praeger, 2015.

Fitzgerald, George Robert. *An appeal to the Jockey Club, or, A true narrative of the late affair, between Mr. Fitz-Gerald and Mr. Walker*. London: Parker; J. Ridley; and T. Evans, 1775.

—. *An Appeal to the Public*. Dublin: 1782.

—. *The Reply to Thomas Walker, Esq. Ci-devant Cornet in Burgoyne's Light Dragoons*. London: Parker; J. Ridley; and T. Evans, 1775.

—. *The Riddle. By G----- R----- F---------, Esq*. Dublin: 1782.

—. *The Riddle. By the Late Unhappy George-Robert Fitzgerald, Esq. With Notes, by W. Bingley*. London: Printed for the editor, and sold by R. Jameson, 1787.

Fitzpatrick, Samuel A. Ossory. *Dublin, a historical and topographical account of the city*. London: Methuen & Co., 1907.

Fitzpatrick, William J.. *Ireland before the Union: with extracts from the unpublished diary of John Scott, earl of Clonmell, Chief Justice of the King's Bench, 1774-1798*. Dublin: W. B. Kelly, 1867.

Gibbon, Edward. *The miscellaneous works of Edward Gibbon, Esq.: with memoirs of his life and writings. Composed by himself: illustrated from his letters, with occasional notes and narrative, by the right honourable John, Lord Sheffield.* London : Printed for John Murray, 1814.

Gilbert, John Thomas. *A History of the City of Dublin.* Dublin: J. McGlashan, 1854.

—. *A History of the City of Dublin, Volume 1.* Dublin: Hodges and Smith, 1854.

Godfrey, Capt. John. *A Treatise Upon the Useful Science of Defence, Connecting the Small and Back-Sword, And showing the Affinity between them.* London: T. Gardner, 1747.

Goldsmith, Oliver. *The Roman History: From the Foundation of the City of Rome, to the Destruction of the Western Empire, Volume I.* London: S. Baker and G. Leigh, 1770.

Gordine, Gérard. *Principes et quintessence des armes.* Liége: S. Bourguignon, 1754.

Gordon, Anthony. *A letter on the bayonet exercise: submitted to the Right Hon. General Burgoyne, Commander in Chief of His Majesty's forces in Ireland, &c. &c. &c.: dated, Dublin Barracks, 20th March, 1783.* [Dublin: 1787].

—. *An Idea of Defence: a Treatise on Swordsmanship,* 1804. Manuscript. National Army Museum. NAM 1968-07-67.

—. *A Treatise on the Science of Defence for the Sword, Bayonet, and Pike, in Close Action.* London: B. McMillan, 1805.

—. *A Treatise on the Science of Defence for the Sword, Bayonet, and Pike, in Close Action.* London: B. McMillan, 1806.

Greene, John C.. *Theatre in Dublin, 1745–1820: A Calendar of Performances.* Bethlehem: Lehigh University Press, 2011.

Gregory, Lady. *Sir William Gregory, K. C. M. G., Formerly Member of Parliament and Sometime Governor of Ceylon: An Autobiography.* London: J. Murray, 1894.

Griffin, Appleton P. C.. *A Catalogue of the Washington Collection in the Boston Athenæum, Parts 1-4.* University Press: John Wilson and Son, 1897.

Hall, Samuel Carter. *Retrospect of a Long Life: From 1815 to 1883, Volume 1.* London: Richard Bentley & Son, 1883.

Hamilton, Joseph. *Some Short and Useful Reflections Upon Duelling, which Should be in the Hands of Every Person who is Liable to Receive a Challenge, Or an Offence. By a Christian Patriot.* Dublin: Printed by the Author, by C. Bentham, 1823.

—. *The Code of Honor for the regulation of duels.* Dublin: 1824.

—. *The court of honor, for the adjustment of disputes; and the Royal Code, as it was submitted to the European Sovereigns: with anecdotes, cases and documents, interesting to Christian moralists who decline the combat; to experienced duellists, and to benevolent legislators.* London: Printed for the author, 1829.

—. *The Only Approved Guide through all the Stages of a Quarrel: Containing the Royal Code of Honor; reflections upon duelling; and the Outline of a court for the adjustment of disputes; with anecdotes, documents and cases, interesting to Christian Moralists who decline the combat; to experienced duellists, and to benevolent legislators. By Joseph Hamilton. Author of "The School for Patriots," and other popular works.* London: Hatchard & Sons; Bentham & Co. Liverpool; and Millikin, Dublin, 1829.

—. *The Royal Code of Honor for the regulation of duelling*. Dublin: 1825.

Hardiman, James. *The history of the town and country of the town of Galway: from the earliest period to the present time*. Dublin: Printed by W. Folds, 1820.

Harland, John. *Collectanea Relating to Manchester and Its Neighborhood, at Various Periods, Vol. II*. Printed for the Chetham Society, 1847.

Harrison, Fairfax. *The Virginia Carys, An Essay in Genealogy*. New York: The De Vinne Press, 1919.

Herbert, J. D.. *Irish varieties, for the last fifty years: written from recollections*. London: William Joy, 1836.

Herbert, Robert. *The Worthies of Thomond, II*. Limerick: 1944.

*Hibernia curiosa. A letter from a gentleman in Dublin, to his friend at Dover in Kent. Giving a general view of the manners, customs, dispositions, &c. of the inhabitants of Ireland. With occasional observations on the state of trade and agriculture in that kingdom. Collected in a tour through the kingdom in the year 1764*. London: Printed for W. Flexney, 1769.

*History of Duelling in all Countries; Translated from the French of M. Coustard de Massi, with Introduction and Concluding Chapter by Sir Lucius O'Trigger*. London: Newman & Co., 1880.

*The History of the Irish Rebellion, in the Year 1798, &c.,: Containing an Impartial Narrative of the Proceedings of the Irish Revolutionists, from the Year 1782 Till the Total Suppression of the Insurrection: with a Review of the History of Ireland, from Its First Invasion by the English, Till the Commencement of the Rebellion. In Two Volumes*. Alston, Cumberland: John Harrop, 1809.

*Holinshed's Chronicles of England, Scotland and Ireland. In Six Volumes. Vol. VI. Ireland*. London: Printed for J. Johnson, F. C. and J. Rivington, 1808.

Hope, William. *The Sword-Man's Vade Mecum*. Edinburgh: John Reid, 1691.

—. *The Fencing-master's Advice to His Scholar: Or, A Few Directions for the More Regular Assaulting in Schools*. Edinburgh: John Reid, 1692.

Huish, Robert. *Memoirs of George the Fourth, descriptive of the most interesting scenes of his private and public life, and the important events of his memorable reign; with characteristic sketches of all the celebrated men who were his friends and companions as a prince, and his ministers and counsellors as a monarch. Compiled from authentic sources, and documents in the king's library in the British museum, Vol. 1*. London: Printed for T. Kelly, 1830.

Hurley, John W.. *Shillelagh: The Irish Fighting Stick*. Pipersville, PA: Caravat Press, 2007.

Hutton, Alfred. *Fixed Bayonets: A Complete System of Fence for the British Magazine Rifle*. London: William Clowes and Sons, 1890.

—. *The Sword Through the Centuries*. Mineola, N.Y.: Dover Publications, 2002.

*Instruction of a Young Nobleman*. London: Printed for E. Evets at the Green Dragon in St. Paul's Church-Yard, 1704.

Jordan-Smith, Paul. *Amiable Renegade: The Memoirs of Captain Peter Drake, 1671-1753*. Stanford University Press, 1960.

Joyce, Patrick Weston. *A Social History of Ancient Ireland, Volume 1*. New York: Longmans, Green, and Co., 1903.

Kavanagh, Peter. *The Irish theatre: being a history of the drama in Ireland from the earliest period up to the present day.* Tralee: The Kerryman limited, 1946.

*The Keepsake.* London: Hurst, Chance and Co, 1851.

Kelly, James. *That Damn'd Thing Called Honour.* Cork: Cork University Press, 1995.

Kenrick, William. *The Duellist, a comedy in five acts and in prose.* Dublin: Printed for Messrs. Williams, Wilson, Husband, Colles, Walker, and Jenkins, 1774.

Labat, Jean de. *L'Art en Fait d'Armes ou de l'Epée seule.* Toulouse: J.Boude, 1696.

Lauvernay, Lionel. *L'Escrime Pratique & Daniel O'Sullivan.* Ensiludium, 2009.

Lecky, William Edward Hartpole. *History of Ireland in the Eighteenth Century, Volume I.* London: Longmans, Green, 1913.

—. *History of Ireland in the Eighteenth Century, Volume VI.* London: Longmans, Green & Col, 1913.

Leeson, Margaret. *Memoirs of Mrs. Margaret Leeson, written by herself; in which are given anecdotes, sketches of the lives and bon mots of some of the most celebrated characters in Great-Britain and Ireland* [in three volumes]. Dublin: Printed and sold by the principal Booksellers, 1797.

Lhuyd, Edward. *Focloir Gaoidheilge-Shagsonach: an Irish-English Dictionary.* Oxford: 1707.

*The Life of George Robert Fitzgerald, Esq. Containing Every Interesting Circumstance Which Happened to That Unfortunate Man: Including Several Anecdotes of His Family; to Which Is Added a Number of Facts, Relative to His Trial and Execution.* London: J. Ridgway, 1786.

*Lives of the Late George Robert Fitzgerald, and P.R. McDonnel, Esqrs.* [Place of publication not identified, 1786].

Longueville, Thomas. *Pryings among private papers, chiefly of the seventeenth and eighteenth centuries.* London: Longmans, Green, 1905.

Lonnergan, Andrew. *The Fencer's Guide.* London: Printed for the Author, 1771.

Mac Curtin, Hugh. *The Elements of the Irish Language: Grammatically Explained in English.* Lovain: M. van Overbeke, 1728.

MacDonagh, Michael. *Irish Life and Character.* London: Hodder & Stoughton, 1898.

Maceroni, Francis. *Defensive Instructions for the People: Containing the New and Improved Combination of Arms, Called Foot Lancers: Miscellaneous Instructions on the Subject of Small Arms and Ammunition: Street and House Fighting, and Field Fortification.* London: Printed and published by J. Smith, 1832.

Mackay, Charles. *An Antiquarian Ramble in the Streets of London: With Anecdotes of Their More Celebrated Residents, Volume I.* London: Bentley, 1846.

Macnamara, Nottidge Charles. *The story of an Irish sept: their character & struggle to maintain their lands in Clare.* London: J.M. Dent, 1896.

Mahaffy, Robert Pentland. *Calendar of the state papers relating to Ireland preserved in the Public Record Office. September 1669–December 1670.* London: Printed for H. M. Stationery Off., by Eyre and Spottiswoode.

Mahon, Andrew. *The Art of Fencing, or, the Use of the Small Sword. Translated from the French of of the late celebrated Monsieur L'Abbat; Master of that Art at the Academy of Toulouse.* Dublin: Printed by James Hoey, at the Sign of Mercury in Skinner-Row, 1734.

—. *The Art of Fencing, or, the Use of the Small Sword. Translated from the French of of the late celebrated Monsieur L'Abbat; Master of that Art at the Academy of Toulouse.* London: Printed for Richard Wellington at the Dolphin and Crown, 1735.

Malcolm, James Peller. *Anecdotes of the Manners and Customs of London during the eighteenth century.* London: Longman, Hurst, Rees, and Orme, Paternoster Row, 1808.

Marchant, John Gaspard le. *Sword Exercise, and Movements, for Cavalry.* [London]: 1797.

Marsh, Charles. *The Clubs of London: with anecdotes of their members, sketches of character, and conversations, Vol. 1.* Philadelphia: Carey, Lea & Carey, 1828.

Maynard, Josias, and William Swinnow. *A Tryall [of] Skill, Betwen Josias Maynard Citizen, and Cutler of London, and Master of the Noble Science of Defence ... of the House of White Friers, and William Swinow, Alias Scot, Citizen and Cooke of London, and Master of the Noble Science of Defence, of the House of Tower Royall.* 1652.

McArthur, John. *The Army and Navy Gentleman's Companion.* London: J. Murray, 1784.

McBane, Donald. *The Expert Sword-Man's Companion: Or the True Art of Self-Defence. With an Account of the Authors Life, and his Transactions during the Wars with France. To which is Annexed, the Art of Gunnerie.* Glasgow: J. Duncan, 1728.

McBride, Iain. *Eighteenth Century Ireland: The Isle of Slaves.* Dublin : Gill & Macmillan, 2009.

McCullough, David Willis. *Wars of the Irish Kings.* New York: Three Rivers Press, 2002.

McGee, Colonel James E.. *Sketches of Irish Soldiers in Every Land.* New York: J. A. McGee, 1873.

McGee, Thomas D'Arcy. *A History of the Irish Settlers in North America: From the Earliest Period to the Census of 1850.* Boston: Patrick Donahoe, 1852.

*Memoirs of the Life of the Late George R. Fitzgerald and P. R. McDonnel, Esqrs.* Dublin: James Moore, 1786.

*The Metrical Dindshenchas.* Dublin: Dublin Institute for Advanced Studies, 1991.

Miller, Captain James. *A Treatise on backsword, sword, buckler, sword and dagger, sword and great gauntlet, falchon, quarterstaff.* London: [1738].

Moore, Thomas. *Memoirs of the life of the Right Honourable Richard Brinsley Sheridan, Volume I.* London: Longman, 1826.

Mortimer, Thomas. *The universal director; or, the nobleman and gentleman's true guide to the masters and professors of the liberal and polite arts and sciences.* London: Printed for J. Coote, in Pater-noster-row, MDCCLXIII.

Nary, Cornelius. *The Case of the Roman Catholicks of Ireland humbly represented to both houses of Parliament.* Dublin: 1724.

Neale, Henry St. John. *Practical essays and remarks on that species of consumption incident to youth, and the different stages of life, commonly called tabes dorsalis: with an account of the nature, causes, and cure* of that distemper, and the diseases arising therefrom, especially the nrevous atrophia, and the phthisis, or consumption in general : to which are added, extracts from the works of the most distinguished practitioners of the present and former ages, coinciding with the author's own practice and experience, demonstrating the baneful effects of unnatural venery on the finest functions in the animal oeconomy. London: printed for the author by J. Crowder, 1800.

Nichols, John, and George Steevens. *The genuine works of William Hogarth; illustrated with biographical anecdotes, a chronological catalogue, and commentary.* London: Longman, Hurst, Rees, and Orme, 1808-17.

Nicolas, Nicholas H.. *History of the orders of knighthood of the British empire, Vol IV.* London: John Hunter, 1842.

O Beaglaoich, Conchobhar. *The English Irish Dictionary. An focloir bearla gaoioheilge ar na chur a neagur le Conchobhar O Beaglaoicch mar aon le congnamh Aodh bhuidhe Mac Cuirtin.* A bPairis: Seamus Geurin, 1732.

O'Brien, John. *Focalóir gaoidhilge-sax-bhéarla, or An Irish-English dictionary.* Paris: Printed by N. F. Valleyre, for the author, 1768.

O'Brien, William. *The duel: A play, as performed at the Theatre-Royal in Drury-Lane.* London, 1772.

O'Callaghan, John Cornelius. *History of the Irish Brigades in the Service of France, from the Revolution in Great Britain and Ireland Under James II, to the Revolution in France Under Louis XVI.* Glasgow: Cameron and Ferguson, 1883.

Ó Dónaill, Niall. *Foclóir Gaeilge-Béarla.* Baile Átha Cliath: Oifig An tSoláthair, 1977.

O'Dowd, Peadar. *Old and new Galway.* Galway: Archaeological, Historical & Folklore Society, 1985.

O'Gorman, Chevalier Thomas. *The Genealogy of the very ancient and illustrious House of O'Reilly: formerly princes and dynasts of Brefny O'Reilly, now called the County of Cavan in the kingdom of Ireland.* Belfast: Published by Rademon House in partnership with Linen Hall Library, [2014].

O'Halloran, Sylvester. *A general history of Ireland: from the earliest accounts to the close of the twelfth century, collected from the most authentic records. In which new and interesting lights are thrown on the remote histories of other nations as well as of both Britains, Volume I.* London: Printed for the author, by A. Hamilton, 1778.

O'Keeffe, John. *Recollections of the life of John O'Keeffe, Volume 2.* New York: B. Blom, 1826.

—. *Recollections of the Life of John O'Keeffe: In Two Volumes, Volume 1.* London: Henry Colburn, 1826.

O'Rahilly, Cecile. *Five seventeenth-century political poems.* Baile Átha Cliath: Institiúid Árd-Léinn Bhaile Átha Cliath, 1952.

O'Reilly, Andrew. *The Irish Abroad and at Home; at the Court and in the Camp. With Souvenirs of "The Brigade." Reminiscences of an Emigrant Milesian.* New York: D. Appleton and Co., 1856.

—. *The Irish Abroad and at Home; at the Court and in the Camp. With Souvenirs of "The Brigade." Reminiscences of an Emigrant Milesian.* New York: P. M. Haverty, 1857.

—. *The Irish Abroad and at Home; at the Court and in the Camp. With Souvenirs of "The Brigade." Reminiscences of an Emigrant Milesian. Volume I.* London: Richard Bentley, 1853.

O'Reilly, Edward. *Sanas Gaoidhilge-Sagsbhearla: An Irish-English dictionary*. Dublin: J. Barlow, 1817.

O'Sullivan, Daniel. *L'Escrime Pratique, ou Principes de la Science des Armes. Par Daniel O'Sullivan, Maître en Fait d'Armes des Académies du Roi*. Paris: Chez Sébastien Jorry, imprimeur-libraire, rue, et vis-a-vis de la Comédie Francaise, au Grand Monarque, 1765.

—. *The Practice of Fencing, Or the principles of the science of arms*. Translated by Phillip T. Crawley. Raleigh: Lulu Press, 2012.

Olivier, J. *Fencing familiarized; or, a new treatise on the art of sword play. Illustrated by elegant engravings, representing all the different attitudes on which the principles and grace of the art depend; painted from life, and executed in a most elegant and masterly manner*. London: Printed for John Bell; And C. Etherington, at York, [1771].

Page, Thomas. *The Use of the Broad Sword*. Norwich: Printed by M. Chase, 1746.

Palmer, Samuel. *St. Pancras: being antiquarian, topographical, and biographical memoranda, relating to the extensive metropolitan parish of St. Pancras, Middlesex; with some account of the parish from its foundation*. London: S. Palmer, 1870.

Pasquin, Anthon. *An authentic History of the Professors of Painting, Sculpture and Architecture who have practised in Ireland, involving original letters from Sir J. Reynolds which prove him to have been illiterate, to which are added Memoirs of the Royal Academicians*. London: H. D. Symonds, 1796.

Pinks, William John. *The History of Clerkenwell*. London: Charles Herbert, Goswell Road, 1881.

Pope, Alexander. *An Essay on Criticism*. London: Printed for W. Lewis, 1713.

—. *The Complete Poetical Works, ed. by Henry W. Boynton*. Boston and New York: Houghton, Mifflin & Co., 1903.

—. *The Works of Alexander Pope, Esq., Vol. III*. London: J. and P. Napton, 1751.

*Pranceriana. A select collection of fugitive pieces, published since the appointment of the present Provost of the University of Dublin*. Dublin: 1775.

Prévost d'Exiles, Antoine François. *The Memoirs and Adventures of the Marquis de Bretagne and Duc d'Harcourt: The wonderful Vicissitudes of Fortune, exemplified in the Lives of those Noblemen, To which is added The history of the chevalier de Grieu and Moll Lescaut. Translated from the Original French by Mr. Erskine, Volume II*. London: T. Cooper, 1743.

*The Repertory of Arts and Manufactures, Volume IX*. London: G. & T. Wilkie., 1798.

Roche, David. *A plain and circumstantial account of the transactions between Capt. Roche and Lieut. Ferguson, from their first meeting to the death of Lieut. Ferguson. To which is added, the trial and depositions at the Cape of Good Hope, where Capt. Roche was acquitted: also his second apprehension ; and the judicial proceedings of the governor and Council of Bombay*. London: Sold by G. Allen, 1775.

Ronan, Gerard. *The Irish Zorro: The Extraordinary Adventures of William Lamport*. Dingle: Brandon, 2004.

Rollin, Charles. *The Method of Teaching and Studying the Belles Lettres, Vol. 3*. London: Printed for A. Bettesworth and C. Hitch, 1734.

Rollin, Charles and Jean B. L. Crevier, *The Roman History from the Foundation of Rome to the Battle of Actium: That Is, to the End of the Commonwealth* [in Ten Volumes]. London: Printed for J. Rivington, R. Baldwin, Hawes Clarke and Collins, R. Horsefield, W. Johnston and 7 others, 1768.

Roulstone, John. *Sword and Pike Exercise for Artillery: As Taught by Capt. John Roulstone, and Practised by the Boston Sea Fencibles.* Boston: Munroe & Francis, 1818.

Rousseau, Jean-Jacques. *Emilius and Sophia: Or, a New System of Education. Translated from the French of J.J. Rousseau, Citizen of Geneva. by the Translator of Eloisa.* London: Printed for R. Griffiths, T. Becket and P.A. de Hondt, in the Strand, 1762.

Rowan, Archibald Hamilton. *Autobiography of Archibald Hamilton Rowan, Esq: With Additions and Illustrations.* Dublin: T. Tegg and Company, 1840.

Ryan, John. *The History and Antiquities of the County of Carlow.* Dublin: Richard Moore, 1833.

Saussure, Cesar de. *A foreign view of England in the reigns of George I and George II: The letters of Monsieur Cesar de Saussure to his family.* London: John Murray, 1902.

Schlegel, Donald M.. *Irish Genealogical Abstracts from the "Londonderry Journal," 1772-1784.* Baltimore: Genealogical Publishing Co., 2009.

Scully, Denys. *A statement of the penal laws which aggrieve the Catholics of Ireland: with commentaries; in two parts.* Dublin: H. Fitzpatrick, 1812.

*Selections from The Irish quarterly review, First series. Vol II.* Dublin: William B. Kelly, 8 Grafton Street, 1857.

Shaw, Sir Charles. *Personal memoirs and correspondence of Colonel Charles Shaw: comprising a narrative of the war for constitutional liberty in Portugal and Spain, from its commencement in 1831 to the dissolution of the British legion in 1837. Volume 1.* London: Henry Colburn, 1837.

Sheridan, Richard Brinsley. *The Rivals, a comedy. As it is acted at the Theatre-Royal in Covent-Garden.* London: Printed for John Wilkie, 1775.

Simcoe, John Graves. *A journal of the operations of the Queen's Rangers: from the end of the year 1777, to the conclusion of the late American war.* Exeter: Printed for the Author, [1787].

Simson, Robert. *The Elements of Euclid.* Glasgow: A. Foulis, 1781.

Skelton, Constance Oliver, and John Malcolm Bulloch. *Gordons under arms; a biographical muster roll of officers named Gordon in the navies and armies of Britain, Europe, America and in the Jacobite risings.* Aberdeen: The New Spalding Club, 1912.

Smith, Charles. *The ancient and present state of the county and city of Cork: Containing a natural, civil, ecclesiastical, historical and topographical description thereof.* Cork: Printed by J. Connor, 1815.

*Stanzas on duelling: inscribed to Wogdon, the celebrated pistol-maker. By an Irish volunteer.* London: Printed for J. Kerby, 1782.

Steinmetz, Andrew. *The Romance of Duelling, Volume I.* England: Richmond Pub. Co, 1971.

Stockwell, La Tourette. *Dublin Theatres and Theatre Customs, 1637-1820.* Kingsport, Tenn.: Kingsport Press, 1938.

Swift, Jonathan. *The works of Jonathan Swift D. D., Dean of St. Patrick's, Dublin. Carefully selected: with a biography of the author, by D. Laing Purves; and original and authetic notes.* Edinburgh: William P. Nimmo & Co., 1880.

Thackeray, William Makepeace. *The Luck of Barry Lyndon: A Romance of the Last Century, Volume 1.* New York: D. Appleton & Co., 1853.

Thimm, Carl. *A Complete Bibliography of Fencing & Duelling: As Practised by All European Nations from the Middle Ages to the Present Day.* London and New York: John Lane, 1896).

Thornbury, Walter. *Old and New London, a Narrative of Its History, Its People, and Its Places.* London: Cassell, Petter, Galpin & Co., 1881.

*Titus Livius's Roman History from the Building of the City.* Edinburgh: A. Donaldson and J. Reid, 1761.

Todhunter, John. *Life of Patrick Sarsfield, Earl of Lucan: With a Short Narrative of the Principal Events of the Jacobite War in Ireland.* London: T. F. Unwin, 1895.

*To the Right Honorable Lord Reay, Lieutenant Colonel Commandant, the officers and gentlemen of the Loyal North Britons Association: This print representing a Private of that corps in the new method of charging the bayonet is most respectfully dedicated by their most ched. servant John Hollis, Jun.* London: John Wallis Junior, No. 16 Ludgate Street, 1804.

*The Triumphs of Brittania. A Poem.* London: Printed by the author, 1773.

Twiss, Richard. *A tour in Ireland in 1775.* London: Printed for the Author, 1776.

Underwood, James. *Draw Not Your Sword But to Serve the King, Preserve Your Honour, or Defend your Life: The Art of Fencing; or the Use of the Small Sword.* Dublin: Printed by T. Byrne, Parliament-street, 1787.

—. *Draw Not Your Sword But to Serve the King, Preserve Your Honour, or Defend your Life: The Art of Fencing; or the Use of the Small Sword.* Dublin: Printed by William Porter, 69 Grafton Street, 1798.

Valdin, Monsieur. *The Art of Fencing, as Practised by Monsieur Valdin.* London: J. Parker in Pall-Mall, 1729.

Victoria and Albert Museum. *A catalogue of the miniatures.* London: Printed for H.M. Stationery Off., by Wyman and Sons, 1908.

Walker, Donald. *British Manly Exercises.* London: Hurst, 1834.

Walker, Thomas. *An answer to Mr. Fitzgerald's Appeal to the gentlemen of the Jockey Club.* London: G. Kearsly, 1775.

Walrond, Henry. *Historical Records of the 1st Devon Militia.* New York: Longmans, Green and Company, 1897.

Walsh, John Edward. *Sketches of Ireland Sixty Years Ago.* Dublin: James McGlashan, 1847.

Warburton, John. *History of the City of Dublin: From the Earliest Accounts to the Present Time; Containing Its Annals, Antiquities, Ecclesiastical History, and Charters; Its Present Extent, Public Buildings, Schools, Institutions, &c., to which are Added, Biographical Notices of Eminent Men, and Copious Appendices of Its Population, Revenue, Commerce and Literature, Volume 2.* Dublin: T. Cadell and W. Davies, 1818.

Whaley, Thomas. *Buck Whaley's Memoirs: Including His Journey to Jerusalem*. London: A. Moring, Limited, 1906.

White, William. *Notes and Queries, 2nd Series, IX, Feb. 18, No. 216*. London: Bell & Daldy, 1860.

Wilkinson, Tate. *Memoirs of His Own Life* [in three volumes]. York: Printed for the Author, 1790.

Wilson, John Lyde. *The Code of Honor: Or, Rules for the Government of Principals and Seconds in Duelling*. Charleston, S.C.: J. Phinney, 1858.

*Wilson's Dublin Directory*. Dublin: Printed for William Wilson [1774, 1776, 1777, 1780 and 1783].

Wylde, Zachary. *The English Master of Defence*. York: Printed by John White, for the Author, 1711.

Wynne, John Huddlestone. *General History of Ireland*. Dublin: D. Chamberlaine, 1773.

Young, Arthur. *A Tour in Ireland. 1776–1779*. London, Paris, New York, Melbourne: Cassell & Co. Ltd., 1887.

# EIGHTEENTH CENTURY JOURNALS.

*Anthologia Hibernica: or, Monthly Collections.*
*The Argus.*
*Belfast Evening Post.*
*Belfast News-Letter.*
*Belfast Mercury or Freeman's Chronicle.*
*Boston News-Letter.*
*Caledonian Mercury.*
*Covent-Garden Journal.*
*Covent Garden Magazine Or the Amorous Repository.*
*Daily Advertiser.*
*Daily Courant.*
*Daily Journal.*
*Daily Post.*
*Derby Mercury.*
*Dublin Courier.*
*Dublin Evening Post.*
*Dublin Intelligence.*
*Dublin Journal.*
*Dublin Mercury.*
*European Magazine: And London Review.*
*Fortnight's Register, or, a Chronicle of Interesting and Remarkable Events, Foreign and Domestic.*
*Freeman's Daily Journal.*
*Gazetteer and New Daily Advertiser.*
*General Advertiser.*
*General Evening Post.*
*Gentleman's and London Magazine; or Monthly Chronologer.*
*Gentleman's Magazine, and Historical Chronicle.*
*The Guardian.*
*Guest's Journal.*
*Hibernian Journal; or, Chronicle of Liberty.*
*Hibernian Magazine, Or, Compendium of Entertaining Knowledge.*
*Hoey's Dublin Mercury.*
*Independent Chronicle.*
*Independent Ledger.*
*Ipswich Journal.*
*Kentish Gazette.*
*Limerick Chronicle.*
*Lloyd's Evening Post and British Chronicle.*
*London Chronicle.*
*London Evening Post.*

London Gazette.

London Gazetteer and New Daily Advertiser.

London Intelligencer.

London Star.

London Times.

Manchester Mercury.

Maryland Journal.

Middlesex Journal and Evening Advertiser.

The Mirror.

Monthly Review.

Morning Chronicle and London Advertiser.

Morning Herald and Daily Advertiser.

Morning Post and Daily Advertiser.

Newcastle Courant.

Oxford Journal.

Pennsylvania Gazette.

Penny London Post or Morning Advertiser.

Pocket Magazine.

Public Advertiser.

Public Ledger or Daily Register of Commerce and Intelligence.

Public Register or the Freeman's Journal.

Pue's Occurences.

Read's Weekly Journal.

Reading Mercury and Oxford Gazette.

Saunders's News Letter.

Scots Magazine.

The Spectator.

Sporting Magazine.

St. James's Chronicle, or the British Evening Post.

Stamford Mercury.

Town and country magazine, or, Universal repository of knowledge, instruction, and entertainment.

Trifler: a new periodical miscellany.

Universal Spectator and Weekly Journal.

Virginia Gazette.

Walker's Hibernian Magazine.

Weekly Journal or British Gazetteer.

Weekly Journal or Saturday Post.

Whitehall Evening Post.

The World.

# NINETEENTH CENTURY JOURNALS.

The Academy.

All the Year Round.

Annual review, and history of literature.

Anti-Jacobin Review and Magazine.

Asiatic Journal.

Bentley's Miscellany.

Boston Daily Bee.

British Magazine.

Chester Chronicle and Cheshire and North Wales General Advertiser.

Colburn's New Monthly Magazine.

Cork Mercantile Chronicle.

Critical Review, Or, Annals of Literature.

Dublin Penny Journal.

Dublin University Magazine.

The Era.

Fraser's Magazine for Town and Country.

Gentleman's Magazine.

Gentleman's Magazine and Historical Review.

Graphic: A Weekly Illustrated Newspaper.

Harper's New Monthly Magazine.

Hereford Journal.

Ipswich Journal.

Irish American Weekly.

*The Irish Quarterly Review.*
*Journal of the Cork Historical and Archaeological Society.*
*Kent Messenger and Maidstone Telegraph.*
*Limerick Reporter and Tipperary Vindicator.*
*Living Age.*
*London Literary Gazette and Journal of Belles Lettres, Arts, Sciences, Etc.*
*London Quarterly Review.*
*The Monthly Magazine, Or, British Register.*
*Morning Post.*
*New York Daily Tribune.*
*Palatine Note-Book.*

*The Phoenix.*
*Proceedings of the Royal Irish Academy.*
*Royal Cornwall Gazette, Falmouth Packet & Plymouth Journal.*
*Salisbury and Winchester Journal.*
*Sportsman's Magazine of Life in London and the Country.*
*Staffordshire Advertiser.*
*Tuam Herald.*
*Universal Magazine.*
*Weekly Arizonian.*
*W. R. Chambers's journal of popular literature, science and arts.*
*Walker's Hibernian Magazine.*

## TWENTIETH and TWENTY-FIRST CENTURY JOURNALS.

*Aberdeen Journal, Notes and Queries.*
*The Ancestor.*
*Convergence 12.*
*Eighteenth-Century Ireland / Iris an dá chultúr.*
*History Ireland.*
*Journal of the Cork Historical and Archaeological Society.*
*Martial Arts Studies 3.*
*Police Studies.*

## UNPUBLISHED MATERIALS.

Bartlett, Keith John. "The Development of the British Army During the Wars with France, 1793-1815." PhD Dissertation, Hatfield College, University of Durham, 1997.

Houlding, John Alan. "The Training of the British Army, 1715-1795." PhD Dissertation, King's College, University of London, 1978.

Partlon, Anne. "The Life and Times of Sir John Waters Kirwan (1866-1949)." PhD Dissertation, Murdoch University, 2011.

# INTERNET RESOURCES.

Association for Historical Fencing. The Association for Historical Fencing (AHF) is an organization created specifically to meet the needs of those who are engaged in the practice, teaching and research of classical and historical fencing. As an educational institution it provides factual information on the fencing arts and related martial systems as practiced in Europe from the Middle Ages through to the beginning of the 20th century. http://www.ahfi.org/ (last accessed February 1, 2017)

A Short History of the Watch Police, Garda Síochána Museum/Archives, 2000. http://www.policehistory.com/watch.html (last accessed October 10, 2016)

Dublin City Library & Archives. This online listing of early Dublin freemen is a Dublin City Council project, under the overall direction of Dublin City Librarian, Margaret Hayes, and Dublin City Archivist, Dr. Mary Clark. The project was researched and developed by genealogist John Grenham. http://databases.dublincity.ie (last accessed September 23, 2016)

"England, Bristol Parish Registers, 1538-1900", database, FamilySearch. (https://familysearch.org/ark:/61903/1:1:XT9W-7XP : 12 December 2014), Major Anthony Gordon, 1831.

London Lives, 1690-1800, pollbook_148-14835 (www.londonlives.org, version 1.1, 17 June 2012), Westminster Archives Centre. London Lives makes available, in a fully digitised and searchable form, a wide range of primary sources about eighteenth-century London, with a particular focus on plebeian Londoners. This resource includes over 240,000 manuscript and printed pages from eight London archives and is supplemented by fifteen datasets created by other projects.

Miller, Ben. "A History of Cane Self-Defense in America: 1798-1930," last modified August 16, 2016, https://martialartsnewyork.org/2016/08/16/a-history-of-cane-self-defense-in-america-1798-1930/ (last accessed February 1, 2017)

Myles, Franc. Early development of Smithfield & Stoneybatter, 2015. http://www.smithfieldstoneybatter.com/history.html (last accessed November 17, 2016)

National University of Ireland Galway's Connacht and Munster Landed Estates Database. The Landed Estates Database provides a comprehensive and integrated resource guide to landed estates and historic houses in Connacht and Munster, c. 1700-1914. It is maintained by the Moore Institute for Research in the Humanities and Social Studies, National University of Ireland, Galway. http://www.landedestates.ie/ (last accessed January 20, 2017)

The Schools' Collection. A project to digitize the National Folklore Collection of Ireland. The objectives of the National Folklore Collection (NFC) are to collect, preserve and disseminate the oral tradition of Ireland. http://www.duchas.ie/ (last accessed February 1, 2017)

# Index of Notable Persons and Texts

*A Few Mathematical and Critical Remarks on the Sword* ..........ix, 228, 269, 341-414, 415-422, 424, 425, 434

Angelo, Domenico...26, 130, 240-241, 252-253, 257, 284, 285, 342, 415, 434

Angelo, Henry...........................................26-28, 61, 113-114, 130-131, 133, 138, 233, 235, 240, 244-246, 251, 253, 256, 276, 281, 289, 334, 342, 345

*Art of Fencing, or, the Use of the Small Sword*....................228-231, 285, 433

Barker, Robert (gladiator)..........................................148, 160-162

Barret, Thomas "Old Chopping Block" (gladiator)............xi, 173, 184-187

Barrington, Sir Jonah (duelist)...................ix, 22-23, 26, 30, 32, 34, 36-38, 45-47, 55-59, 92, 109, 112, 199, 206, 209, 227, 249, 272-277, 281, 283, 429

Bennet, Rowland (gladiator)...............................149, 150, 163-167

Bodkin, Ambrose "Amby" (duelist)........................49, 55, 432

Bosquett, Abraham (duelist).........................17, 53-55, 61, 434

Buck, Timothy (gladiator)............................84, 164, 176, 219

Bucks (gang).........................25, 26, 125, 196, 200, 204-206, 208

Butler, Michael (gladiator)............................148, 173-176, 184

Byrne, Oliver................................................xi, 435, 447-450

Cherokee Club...............196, 200, 212-216, 393, 445-446

Clonmel dueling code of 1777....................55-59, 274, 429-432

Collins, James (gladiator)................................148, 149, 163

Crosbie, Richard (duelist, gang leader)....................58-59, 209-211

Cutting Weavers (gang)..................................196, 200-203

d'Eon, Chevalier..........................................131, 248, 282

Daly, Richard (duelist)....................58-59, 209, 227, 248, 277

Dillon, Anthony (fencer)..............................281-282, 444

Dillon, Michael (fencer).............................280-283, 444

Doyle, Alexander (fencing-master)..........10, 251, 258, 261, 433

Drake, Peter (duelist)..........4, 5, 10, 17, 29, 47, 75-85, 87, 88, 90, 147, 226

Dwyer, William (fencing-master). .225-226, 238-242, 251, 344, 345, 347-349

English, Alexander "Buck" (duelist)..........17, 43, 103, 122, 125-129, 204

*Escrime Pratique, Principes de la Science des Armes*..................260, 261, 433

*Expert Sword-Man's Companion*........................76, 227-228, 415

Faden, Lieut. James..........................330-332, 335, 434

Figg, James (gladiator). ........................................4, 84, 145, 147, 150-152, 154, 156, 159, 161-171, 173, 175-179, 181, 184, 219, 434

Finn (or Fenn), William (gladiator)...................148, 150, 152, 153

Fitzgerald, George Robert .......15, 17, 29, 40, 42, 43, 56, 109-124, 126, 127, 240, 275, 441, 443

Gill, William (gladiator)..........147, 158-159, 161-162, 165-166, 171, 176-177

Gittarre, William (fencing-master)....................225, 226, 238, 347

Gordon, Anthony..............................................ix, xii, 235, 274, 276, 278-281, 285, 289-338, 342, 343, 347, 434, 438, 441, 443, 444

Hamilton, Joseph (duelist)......................2, 36, 60-61, 109, 435

Holmes, William (gladiator)........................149, 150, 168, 170

*Idea of Defence*...........................................xi, 288, 306-312, 434

Kelly, Cornelius (fencing-master) x, 222, 225, 233-39, 242, 279, 291, 343-50

Kelly, Dominick (fencing-master)........................232-234

Kelly, Hugh (fencing-master)........................346, 347, 410

Kelly, James (fencing-master)..............xii, 235, 236, 238, 251, 347

Keogh, James "Jemmy" (duelist)..................55, 274-75, 280, 432, 444

Kirwan, Richard Buidhe (duelist)....................10, 20, 91-97, 227

Knights of Saint Patrick....................................270, 281, 346, 439

Knights of Tara...xi, 123, 246, 269-87, 289, 290, 295, 342-43, 346-47, 437-44

Labat, Monsieur (fencing-master)..............228-231, 285, 342, 415, 420, 433

*Letter on the Bayonet Exercise*........................ix, xii, 295-299, 327, 434

Liberty Boys (gang)..............................................196, 200-202

Mac Guire, Felix (gladiator) ....................148, 166-173, 184

Mac Guire, Lætitia (gladiator)..........................149, 173, 184

Mahon, Andrew..................221, 227-231, 261, 277, 285, 415, 420, 422, 433

McBane, Donald..................4, 76, 81, 84, 219, 220, 226-228, 285, 415, 420

Miller, James (gladiator, duelist)........................4, 84-87, 219

Mohawks (gang)..........................................196, 200, 213

*Neu Alamodische Ritterliche Fecht- und Schirm-Kunst*............x, 259-261, 433

O'Brian, Bonduca (gladiator)....................148, 156, 157, 160

O'Brien, William (fencing-master, the elder)................9, 10, 251, 254-255

O'Brien, William (fencing-master, the younger)........................9, 255-257

O'Connor, Francis (fencing-master)..........................224, 227

O'Keeffe, John....................178, 225, 226, 233, 239, 276

O'Sullivan, Daniel (fencing-master)..........10, 251, 258, 260, 261, 433

O'Trigger, Lucius....................................16, 130, 435

Ormonde Boys (gang)..................................196, 200-202

Pardon, James (fencing-master)..........10, 80, 87, 243-249, 251, 282

Parvisol, Mr. (fencer)....................278, 280, 281, 343, 444

Perkins, Christopher (gladiator)....................148, 153-159, 163

Pinking Dindies (gang)..................58, 103, 196, 200, 201, 206-209, 211, 212

Reda, Claude (fencing-master)....................113, 114, 240-244

Redman, John (fencing-master)....................243, 244, 251-254

Roche, David "Tyger" (duelist)..........xii, 17, 29, 99-108, 126, 127, 146, 207

Rowan, Archibald Hamilton....................................116-117, 247

Saint-Georges, Chevalier de........................xii, 219, 236, 251, 282

Sarsfield, Patrick, 1st Earl of Lucan....................7, 8, 9, 76

Scott, John, Attorney General and 1st Earl of Clonmel. .............32-33, 123, 291, 293, 294, 299, 326, 341-44, 347, 348

Sheridan, Richard Brinsley..................16, 130-138, 205, 277, 419

Sherlock, Francis (gladiator, fencing-master).....147, 149, 178-184, 249, 251

Sherlock, James (gladiator)........................................148, 176

Sherlock, William (gladiator)....................................149, 176, 177

Stokes, Elizabeth "Championess".......146, 148, 156, 157, 160-162, 168, 173

Sutton, Edward "Ned" (gladiator)..........................................xi, 147, 152-155, 158, 163, 164, 166, 167, 169-171, 173-177, 179, 181, 219, 249

Swift, Jonathan....................................................ix, 19, 48, 478

*Treatise on the Science of Defence*..................295, 308-329, 333, 342, 434, 471

Underwood, James. .231, 278, 280-281, 284-285, 342-343, 434, 441, 443-444

United Irishmen, Society of.............xi, 18, 60, 116, 188, 214, 247, 448, 450

Waller, Mary (gladiator)....................................149, 162

Washington, George..............................................295

Welsh (or Welch), Mary (gladiator) ........................148, 160-162

"Wild Geese"..........................................7-10, 14, 93, 243

# About the Author

BEN MILLER is an American filmmaker and author. He is a graduate of New York University's Tisch School of the Arts, was the winner of the Alfred P. Sloan Foundation Grant for screenwriting, and has worked for notable personages such as Martin Scorsese and Roger Corman. For the last twelve years, Miller has studied fencing at the Martinez Academy of Arms, one of the last places in the world still teaching an authentic living tradition of classical fencing. He has served as the Academy's *chef de salle*, and has authored articles for the Association of Historical Fencing, focusing on the fencing and dueling of the American colonial period. He is the editor of *Self-Defense for Gentlemen and Ladies: A Nineteenth-Century Treatise on Boxing, Kicking, Grappling, and Fencing with the Cane and Quarterstaff* (Berkeley: North Atlantic Books, 2015), containing the writings of the noted duelist and fencing master, Colonel Thomas Hoyer Monstery. He wrote the foreword to the republication of Donald McBane's classic martial arts treatise, *The Expert Sword-Man's Companion: Or the True Art of Self-Defence* (New York: Jared Kirby Rare Books, 2017). Miller's articles about fencing and martial history can be found on the websites *martialartsnewyork.org* and *outofthiscentury.wordpress.com*.

www.ingramcontent.com/pod-product-compliance
Lightning Source LLC
Chambersburg PA
CBHW062008090426
42811CB00005B/792